Using Symphony

David Paul Ewing
Geoffrey T. LeBlond

Que Corporation
Indianapolis

Library of Congress Catalog No.: LC 84-60645

ISBN 0-88022-124-0

89 88 87 86 85   8 7 6 5 4 3

Interpretation of the printing code: the rightmost double-digit number is the year of the book's printing; the rightmost single-digit number, the number of the book's printing. For example, a printing code of 83-4 shows that the fourth printing of the book occurred in 1983.

Editors

Virginia D. Noble, M.L.S.
Jeannine Freudenberger, M.A.

Technical Editor

Estel Hines

Technical Assistant

Thomas D. Perkins

Editorial Director

David F. Noble, Ph.D.

Managing Editor

Paul L. Mangin

Dedications

To Sheila

D. P. E.

To my grandfather

G. T. L.

Acknowledgments

The authors would like to thank the following people for their invaluable assistance in completing this book:

Thomas D. Perkins, Senior Analyst, Que Corporation, for producing and organizing the figures in this book and for his advice on many of the chapters. His support and assistance were invaluable throughout the writing, editing, and production stages for this book.

Ginny Noble, editor; David Noble, editorial director; Paul Mangin, managing editor; and Rick Sheehan, production assistant, all of Que Corporation, who gave much extra time, effort, and attention to the editing and design of this book

Sheila Ewing for her advice and work on the book's appendixes

Maury Cox, vice president of marketing, CompuServe Corporation

Tim Shelton, Lang Systems, Inc.

About the Authors

Geoffrey T. LeBlond, president of a new software company, received his B.A. degree from Brown University and his M.B.A. in finance from Indiana University's Graduate School of Business. Mr. LeBlond is coauthor of *Using 1-2-3* and a contributing author to *1-2-3 for Business*, both published by Que Corporation. Prior to his current position, Mr. LeBlond was also a technical editor at Que Corporation for the *IBM PC UPDATE* magazine and Editor-in-Chief of *Absolute Reference: The Journal for 1-2-3 and Symphony Users.*

David Paul Ewing is Training Products Director for Que Corporation and author of Que's *The Using 1-2-3 Workbook.* Mr. Ewing received his B.A. from Duquesne University and his M.A. from North Carolina State University. He is presently completing his Ph.D. at Purdue University. Prior to his position at Que, he was the Assistant Director of the Business Writing Program at Purdue University, where he developed course materials and trained instructors. For eight years, Mr. Ewing taught college-level writing and business communications courses. He has published articles in leading business communications books and journals and given numerous presentations at national conferences on writing and business communications.

Conventions Used in This Book

A number of conventions are used in *Using Symphony* to help you learn the program.

New with Symphony printed in the margin indicates that a paragraph, section, or complete chapter discusses commands, operations, or program applications that are not included in the Lotus 1-2-3 program.

Boldface letters indicate that the word is a Symphony command and that you can select the command by typing the boldface letter after you have retrieved the appropriate menu. For example, SERVICES **W**indow **C**reate indicates that you retrieve the SERVICES menu, type W, and then type C to select this command.

Words printed in all capital letters signify the following:

Function keys for retrieving Symphony menus: ACCESS SYSTEM, SERVICES, TYPE, and MENU. (When the book refers to specific menus for spreadsheet, word processing, graphics, data form, or communications environments, then SHEET, DOC, GRAPH, FORM, and COMM are used.) For example, SHEET **E**rase indicates that you retrieve the spreadsheet menu and select the **E**rase command.

Mode indicators that appear on the screen in all capital letters are printed in all capital letters.

Range names, including those used for macros, appear in all capital letters.

In general, words appearing in all capital letters within the Symphony control panel are printed in all capital letters.

Function key names are used in the text with function key numbers appearing often in parentheses after the name. GoTo (F5), for example, indicates to press the GoTo key, which is F5 on IBM and Compaq computers. Whenever the Symphony function key requires that you press the Alt key and the function key simultaneously, the function key name is given followed by the Alt and function key in parentheses—for example, Learn (Alt + F5).

Worksheet cell addresses are indicated as they are in the Symphony control panel, for example, A1..G5 or a range name—SALES.

Macro statements are printed as they appear on the screen. However, in cases where there is not enough room on a single typeset line to place all the characters that appear on the screen, carryover lines are indented.

The word "file" is used in some cases to refer to a previously created worksheet that the user has saved and retrieved afterwards for changing or adding new data.

Color graphs and charts referred to in Chapter 9 are presented in a section immediately preceding the appendixes and are referred to by name rather than figure number.

Trademark Acknowledgments

Introduction

Symphony is the exciting fully integrated software package from Lotus Development Corporation, creators of the best-selling integrated software 1-2-3. A totally integrated package, Symphony gives you not only the best of 1-2-3—popular electronic spreadsheet, business graphics, and personal data management—but also word processing, data form capability, and communications. Symphony's power and sophistication, plus the outstanding capability to integrate all applications, make it the hottest product in the microcomputer industry.

Although 1-2-3 users will find Symphony similar to 1-2-3 in many ways, Symphony is much more versatile and more powerfully integrated than its forerunner. First, Symphony's word processor gives you the features of many stand-alone word-processing programs. Second, Symphony's full data form capabilities go well beyond data management operations in 1-2-3. And third, Symphony's communications program gives you complete flexibility to connect to time-sharing services and send or receive data to and from other microcomputers.

Using Symphony

With the added capabilities of Symphony comes complexity. Although learning to use some of Symphony's individual applications may be easy, especially for the experienced 1-2-3 user, learning how to use Symphony's window feature, to integrate applications, and to take advantage of its special functions and Command Language can take months to master. Many users, therefore, may not be taking full advantage of the program.

Using Symphony helps both the experienced 1-2-3 user and the new user of Lotus products to learn all of Symphony's powerful features. The book explains Symphony's command menu system and special features in a clear, easy-to-understand style. You wili particularly appreciate the detailed discussions of Symphony's new elements: word processing, data form capability, communications, window capability, and Command Language. Your learning is made easy by numerous figures showing spreadsheets, word-processing text, and data bases, and by graphs—some in color—that illustrate command operations. Many examples of commands and functions will help you apply the program to your business problems.

Who Should Buy This Book?

If you own Symphony, you should own this book. *Using Symphony* picks up where the Symphony manual leaves off. The book explains both the basics and fine points of the program. Every chapter includes clear explanations and examples, and special care has been taken to cover in detail those topics that are not thoroughly explained in the Symphony manual. For example, many chapters give specific examples of how one of Symphony's features can be integrated with others. Chapter 11 demonstrates how you can use the full capabilities of Symphony's data management function with its new data form. And Chapter 13 covers Symphony's Command Language (macros) by providing sample macros you can create for each of Symphony's five applications.

If you do not own Symphony but are considering purchasing the program, this book is also for you. It will help you understand Symphony's unique features. Each chapter points out specifically in what ways Symphony differs from 1-2-3. If you are an experienced 1-2-3 user considering upgrading to Symphony, you will appreciate the special attention this book pays to those elements of the program that may be unfamiliar to you.

About this Book

Chapter 1, An Overview of Symphony, discusses Symphony in the context of 1-2-3. This chapter explains the basic concepts of Symphony as well as those new features that, when combined, make the program different from 1-2-3. To give you a comprehensive introduction to Symphony, Chapter 1 also includes a brief history of the microcomputer industry and of Lotus Development Corporation.

Chapter 2, Getting Started, covers the process of preparing Symphony disks for your computer, the Symphony menu system, features of the display screen and keyboard, and the program's special window capability. Chapter 2 also discusses the exceptional Symphony tutorial and the program's help-screen facility.

Chapter 3, The Symphony SHEET Window, introduces the foundation application of the program—the spreadsheet—and covers its size and memory capacity. If you are new to spreadsheet programs and to Lotus products, this chapter teaches you the fundamentals of entering data into the Symphony worksheet.

Chapter 4, SHEET Window Commands, discusses the basic Symphony spreadsheet commands, including **R**ange, **C**opy, **M**ove, **E**rase, and **F**ormat. In this chapter you will also learn which commands and operations are not included in 1-2-3 and which 1-2-3 commands have been renamed. If you have used 1-2-3 and want to learn quickly how Symphony's spreadsheet feature is different, this chapter will help you.

Chapter 5, Functions, explains all of Symphony's sophisticated functions, including those that are in 1-2-3 and those which are new to Symphony. Particular attention is paid to new functions, such as Symphony's string arithmetic functions, date and time functions, and other special functions that give you information about the contents and locations of cells (or ranges) in the worksheet.

Chapter 6, File Operations, covers the important commands for saving and retrieving files. And it also explains those commands you will use for file management and for consolidating and merging worksheets.

Chapter 7, Word Processing: Working in a DOC Window, introduces you to Symphony's new word-processing capabilities by explaining special features of the display screen, function keys for word processing, and keys used for cursor movement. The chapter also covers word-processing commands, showing how they are used for setting format and editing your text.

Chapter 8, Printing Reports, introduces you to Symphony's printing commands. They are for printing reports generated from Symphony's spreadsheets, and text created by Symphony's word-processing application. Through examples of printed reports and a list of the print commands used for each, Chapter 8 shows you how to take advantage of Symphony's special print capabilities.

Chapters 9 and 10, Creating and Displaying Graphs, and Printing Graphs, respectively, cover in detail Symphony's graphics capabilities. Chapter 9 not only provides examples of all the types of graphs that can be created, but also explains how Symphony's GRAPH window is integrated with the other features of the program. The special section of color graphs shows you the full capabilities of producing graphs and pie charts on a color monitor. Chapter 10 describes how to use the PrintGraph program to print graphs. Examples help you to use the program's special settings.

Chapter 11, Data Management, explains how you can use Symphony's full data management capabilities by integrating the data form features with the data management commands and data base statistical functions. This chapter particularly shows how Symphony's data management capability goes beyond 1-2-3's.

Chapter 12, Communications, provides the guidelines for connecting with many kinds of computers. The chapter also explains how to access a time-sharing service and how to communicate with another person's microcomputer. Chapter 12 gives you the background for making good use of Symphony's communications.

Chapter 13, Macros—The Symphony Command Language, goes beyond the Symphony manual by presenting examples of macros that you can use with each of Symphony's five applications—spreadsheets, word processing, graphics, data management, and communications. This chapter covers in depth the process for using

Symphony's Learn mode as well as the features of Symphony's special programming language—Command Language.

The final chapter, A Comprehensive Model, draws together into one comprehensive Symphony application all the concepts and operations presented in earlier chapters. This model includes accessing stock market data through Symphony's communications, creating a data base and graph for analyzing the information, and finally putting this information together in a written report. The comprehensive model will show you how the knowledge you have gained from *Using Symphony* can be applied to your needs.

This book has three appendixes. The first two (A and B) will help you prepare your Symphony disks to use with your equipment. The third appendix (C) compares 1-2-3 commands with Symphony commands. This appendix is particularly useful for 1-2-3 users who are considering upgrading to Symphony.

More Symphony Knowledge

Available through dealers carrying Que publications is the specially designed Symphony Command Menu Map. This map displays all the Symphony menus and identifies Symphony commands that are comparable to 1-2-3 commands. For home or office, this map is a valuable reference for learning and using Symphony.

Que publishes several additional titles that are excellent companions to *Using Symphony*. *Using Symphony's Command Language* and *Symphony: Advanced Topics* provide in-depth coverage of special program applications, such as creating macros, integrating windows, and using Symphony's communications capability. *Symphony for Business* shows you how to build practical Symphony applications for business management. *Symphony Tips, Tricks, and Traps* offers shortcuts, time-saving tips, and suggestions for avoiding problems, all designed to help you get the most from the powerful Symphony program.

For more on each of these titles, see the product information in the back of this book. If you own Symphony, you should own these books.

Assistant to the Managing Editor

Tim P. Russell

Production

Jonathan Mangin
Dennis R. Sheehan
Deborah L. Summe
Gerta Noble

Composed by Que Corporation

in Megaron

Printed and bound by

Banta Company

Design by

Paul L. Mangin

Cover designed by

Cargill Associates
Atlanta

Using Symphony

Table of Contents

Chapter 13   Macros—The Symphony

1

An Overview of Symphony

What Is Symphony?

Symphony is the long-awaited expansion of 1-2-3, the popular integrated spreadsheet from Lotus Development Corporation. To 1-2-3's three business applications programs—electronic spreadsheet, business graphics, and data management—Symphony adds word processing, and data form and communications capabilities. Symphony makes all these expanded applications available in one sophisticated program.

Symphony is an impressive integration of five microcomputer software applications: spreadsheet, word processing, graphics, data management, and communications. All five of these environments are available as soon as you access the program, and they are identified on the screen as the types of windows in which you can work.

Symphony's exciting new window feature enables you to create bordered areas on the screen and to perform different applications within them with a great deal of flexibility. (See fig. 1.1.) You can create a spreadsheet in one window, word-processing text in

1

another window, a data base in a third window, and a graph in a fourth window. At the same time in a fifth window, you can receive data from another computer or send data to that computer. You can make these different windows appear on the screen simultaneously. (Whether or not graphs will appear on the screen with other applications depends on your equipment, however.) Or you can use the full screen area to work on one application and then, by pressing one key, retrieve any other window you have created in the worksheet.

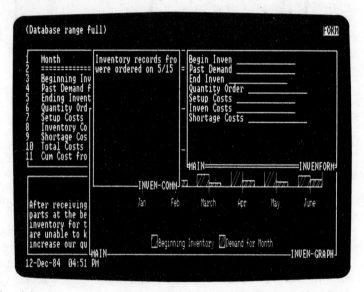

Fig. 1.1.

The five Symphony environments include the following features: (1) in the SHEET window, the ability to create numerous kinds of spreadsheets by using Symphony's incredibly large worksheet area (256 x 8,192 cells), sophisticated SHEET command MENU, and many functions; (2) in the DOC window, the ability to draft, revise, and edit documents through Symphony's word-processing capability; (3) in the GRAPH window, the ability to create and save graphs that can be displayed in color (with the right kind of equipment) and that can also be displayed on the screen along with other applications, such as spreadsheets, data bases, and word-processing text; (4) in the FORM window, the ability to create a data form, generate a data base, and perform sort and query operations; and (5) in the COMM window, the ability to send and receive data through telecommunications lines.

Each of the five Symphony environments, used singly, is an extremely powerful tool. Symphony's real power, however, is best illustrated by its ability to integrate applications. If you use Symphony to create a spreadsheet, retrieve the spreadsheet, create a new window, then create a graph on the screen while your spreadsheet still appears, you are using Symphony's integrative power. Whenever you create a data base and then use it on the screen to help you compose an important report, you are also using Symphony's integrative power. And if you use Symphony's communications environment to receive on-line data, transfer it into a spreadsheet, graph the information to help you analyze it, then use both the spreadsheet and the graph to prepare a report, you are taking further advantage of Symphony's ability to integrate.

The best way to introduce you to Symphony is to present a simple example showing how four of the environments (data management, spreadsheet, graphics, and word processing) can be used and then integrated. In this example, you will note some new features not included in 1-2-3. Later, in Chapter 14, another model illustrates how you can integrate Symphony's communications environment with the other environments.

Let's suppose you want to use Symphony at home to maintain a record of payments you have made on household bills. You can begin by creating a data form like the one in figure 1.2, which was made in Symphony's FORM environment. In this environment, you can create a data form and then enter records into it. From the information that you supply to make the form and from the records themselves, Symphony will create a data base similar to that in figure 1.3.

Now suppose you want to find out how much your gas bills increased during the fall and winter months of 1983-84 over the previous year's bills. Using Symphony's spreadsheet feature (referred to as SHEET in the top right corner of the screen), you can view a data base that includes only gas utility costs. (See fig. 1.4.) Such a data base, although originating from records entered in a

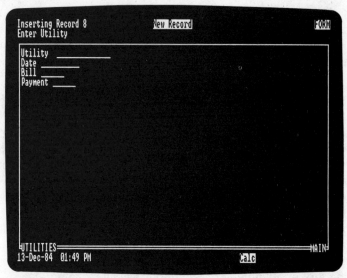

Fig. 1.2.

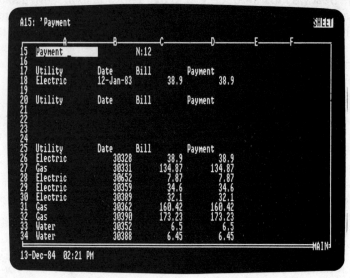

Fig. 1.3.

FORM environment, can be changed within a SHEET environment
by using Symphony's **Q**uery commands. The data base in figure 1.4

was created from the larger data base in figure 1.3, which contains not only gas but also electric, water, and telephone utility costs.

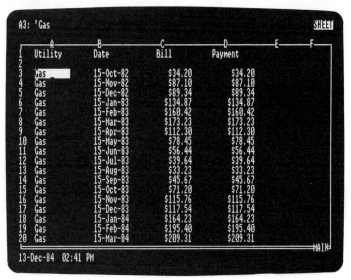

Fig. 1.4.

When you shift from Symphony's FORM environment to the SHEET environment, you can then perform data query and sort operations on the data base created in the FORM environment. You can also apply to the data base the same functions used to create spreadsheets. For example, Symphony's spreadsheet environment allows the formatting of columns in your data base and the adjusting of column width. Sorting the data base, extracting certain categories (or fields), changing the format of values, and changing column width are all operations provided by Symphony's spreadsheet function.

The data base of gas costs in figure 1.4 provides a much better idea of how your gas bills have increased than does the data base in figure 1.3. If, however, you want to see very quickly the relationship of gas costs for the fall and winter of 1982-83 to costs for the fall and winter of 1983-84, then Symphony's GRAPH environment enables you to view those relationships. Using the values in the "Gas Costs" data base, Symphony created the graph shown in figure 1.5. As the graph indicates, a steady and significant increase is occurring in your gas costs.

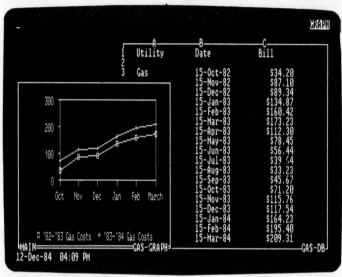

Fig. 1.5.

Now let's assume that your discovery of this steady increase prompts you to write a letter to your state's public service commission to voice your concern about rising utility rates. While leaving both your data base and graph on the screen, you can write your letter and even include with it a copy of the data base that emphasizes so dramatically how much gas costs have increased. (See figs. 1.6 and 1.7.) And to make your point really emphatic, you can attach to the letter a printing of the graph pictured in figure 1.8.

If this simple example above hasn't convinced you of Symphony's expanded power and capabilities, read on. The following sections, containing background to the program, a comparison of 1-2-3 and Symphony, and an introduction to Symphony's features, provide further evidence.

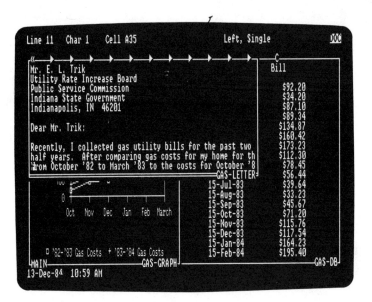

Fig. 1.6.

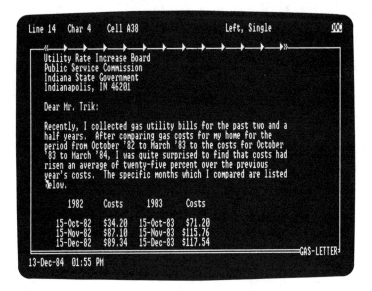

Fig. 1.7.

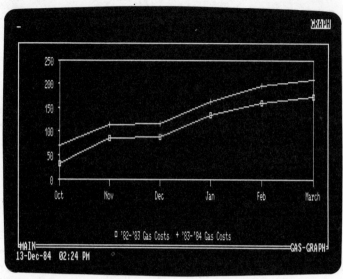

Fig. 1.8.

Symphony at a Glance

*New
with
Symphony*

From this brief introduction to Symphony's capabilities, you can see that the equipment requirements for Symphony are much different from those for 1-2-3. (See table 1.1.) First, Symphony requires more memory—320K, compared to 1-2-3's required 128K. To make full use of Symphony's capabilities, you will need equipment for displaying graphs in color, for displaying text and graphs on the screen at the same time, and for using Symphony's communications feature.

Table 1.1
Symphony at a Glance

Published by: Lotus Development Corporation
                       161 First St.
                       Cambridge, Massachusetts 02142

System requirements: IBM PC, IBM PC/XT, IBM Portable,
                     Compaq Portable, and Compaq Plus

Display: color or monochrome

Disk capacity: two 320K double-sided disk drives

Memory size: 320K

Operating system: PC DOS V2.0, V2.1

Optional hardware: color/graphics adapter, printer, plotter, modem or acoustic coupler, additional monitor, and add-on memory board

Price: $695

Update option: $200 update option for the 1-2-3 owner

Chapter 2 includes the procedure for installing your Symphony disks so that they can operate with your equipment. Before you begin this installation procedure, though, keep several points in mind. Symphony can only be used with DOS versions 2.0 and 2.1, not earlier versions. If you want to display graphs on the screen simultaneously with other environments—such as spreadsheets, data bases, and word-processing text—you need to check the equipment requirements listed within the Symphony Install program.

The History of Symphony

The history of Symphony begins with the history of computing. This discussion begins, therefore, with the origins of computers.

The Beginning

The first computers were developed during World War II. They were used exclusively for military applications, such as breaking coded messages and computing shell trajectories. During the 1950s, these large computers began to find their way into the nation's largest businesses. By the 1970s, virtually every large corporation had at least one large computer, and many small- and medium-sized firms had the smaller minicomputer. These machines were used primarily for accounting and payroll applications and for specialized functions like processing banking records—all jobs that required rapid processing of large volumes of data.

Because these computers required a carefully controlled and secure environment, they were sequestered in special computer rooms. Since the computers were expensive to purchase and operate, they were run 24 hours a day on tight schedules to achieve the highest possible return on investment. Work on these machines was usually scheduled to make the most efficient use of the computer, but not to meet the needs of the user. These two factors combined to make the computer inaccessible to the average manager. Special requests for programming time were frequently put off until time could be found to fit them into the schedule. "You want it when?" became a popular poster in data processing departments everywhere.

The First Microcomputers

In 1974 Intel Corporation developed the first microprocessor, the 8008. It condensed thousands of electronic circuits onto a single, tiny silicon chip. The processing power of the room-sized computers of a few years earlier could now fit onto a piece of silicon less than one inch square. Intel soon followed the 8008 with the 8080 microprocessor, which was selected by early computer hobbyists as *the* chip for many microcomputer kits.

About the same time, another integrated circuit manufacturer, MOS Technologies (later purchased by Commodore Business Machines), developed a more advanced processor, the 6502. This processor was selected for several early microcomputers, including the Commodore PET and the Apple II.

Soon, these microprocessors were integrated with other components to make the first commercial microcomputers, which were sold as kits. The most famous computer kit was the Altair MITS. Kit computers did not look much like the popular computers we know today. Instead of having the familiar video displays and keyboards, the front panels consisted of lights and programming switches. All programming was done in machine language. Printers and disk drives were not available for these early machines. Needless to say, the first micros were as inaccessible and impractical for the average businessperson as the mainframe computers. Not surprisingly, when microcomputers were first developed, they were used only by a few hardy individuals with advanced technical abilities.

The Appliance Computers

In 1977 Steve Wozniak and Steve Jobs introduced a microcomputer kit called the Apple I. About 500 units of this machine were eventually sold. Wozniak and Jobs soon offered the Apple II. Unlike all the computers that had gone before, the Apple II was sold preassembled. It also had a disk drive and a powerful disk operating system (both developed by Wozniak).

Near that time, Tandy/Radio Shack also developed a micro-computer, the TRS-80 Model I. This machine used an advanced derivative of the 8080 chip, the Z80, manufactured by Zilog.

These appliance microcomputers opened the doors of micro-computing to nontechnical users. Because the machines did not have to be assembled, no advanced technical knowledge was required. Both machines were shipped fully assembled and factory tested and were sold through a new kind of store, the computer store. It offered help in acquiring the computer as well as factory-authorized service. Both these computers had several expansion slots that could be used to attach devices like printers, disk drives, and telephone modems to the computer.

Chips inside the appliance microcomputers contained the BASIC programming language. (Occasionally, the language was provided on a floppy disk packaged with the computer.) Because BASIC is easier to learn and use than machine or assembly language, users of the computers found it practical to write their own programs in BASIC.

Although BASIC uses English-like words to develop relationships, programs designed to accomplish simple tasks, such as multiplying two numbers, can require eight to ten lines of code. Imagine the complexity of using BASIC to solve sophisticated problems. A program written in BASIC to produce a financial report for a large company would be quite large, containing hundreds, or even thousands, of lines of code.

In the early days of microcomputers, little canned software (pre-written for a specific purpose and sold by a software publisher) was available. This absence left users with three choices: become experts in programming, pay a programmer, or accomplish very little with the expensive microcomputers. Because most business people are too busy (or too intimidated) to learn BASIC, many of those who bought micros during this period found themselves "all dressed up with no place to go." Countless others simply avoided micro-computers altogether.

The First Generation of Integrated Software Packages

In 1983, software packages emerged that built on the spreadsheet-only programs, such as VisiCalc and SuperCalc. These new programs integrated business applications with spreadsheet appli-cations. The most popular of these integrated software programs includes Context Management Systems' Context MBA and Lotus' 1-2-3.

Many factors influenced the development of the first generation of integrated software programs. First, because enough people used VisiCalc and its imitators to become aware of the limitations of these programs, a "wish list" developed containing features and benefits to serve as the basis for the new programs. This wish list included the desire for more memory; the ability to link individual spread-sheets together into an integrated system of sheets; the need for more powerful arithmetic and formatting functions; and the desire for more fully integrated graphics, data base management, and word processing.

A second factor that influenced this new software was the availa-bility of more powerful microcomputers, led by the IBM Personal Computer. The memory capacity and processing power of these new 16-bit computers enabled the new generation of integrated packages to offer an extremely high level of power and sophistication.

Context MBA

Context MBA and 1-2-3 stand out in the history of spreadsheet software because they integrate graphics and data management with advanced spreadsheets. Context MBA also includes simple text processing and data communications and incorporates all of these applications in a single, extremely powerful package.

Context MBA was the first integrated program to be introduced, incorporating all five applications into one package. The MBA program was the result of a long study done by the Arthur D. Little Company on the needs and desires of business people for desktop management software. The program, however, has suffered from some unfavorable criticism about its speed and "jack of all trades" orientation. Context MBA is nevertheless an impressive program backed by a serious and professional organization.

Lotus 1-2-3

1-2-3 is a highly advanced spreadsheet that combines the features of an easy-to-use spreadsheet program with graphics and data management functions. Even Context MBA does not approach the power, speed, and sophistication of 1-2-3.

1-2-3 is the brainchild of Mitch Kapor, president of Lotus Development Corporation, and Jonathan Sachs, vice president of research and development at Lotus. Like many of the early leaders of the microcomputer industry, Kapor taught himself the art of programming. He learned well. Prior to founding Lotus, Kapor scored one of the largest successes in the young microcomputer software industry with VisiTrend/Plot, a graphics and statistical package that he sold to VisiCorp. After working for VisiCorp for a brief time following this sale, Kapor left and founded Lotus with the intention of producing the ultimate spreadsheet software program. Sachs had been involved in three spreadsheet development projects prior to joining Lotus.

Kapor's first step was to assemble an experienced team of financiers and business managers to help launch his new product. Ben Rosen, one of the most respected businessmen in the industry, was one of the first investors in Lotus and is a member of the board of directors of the company. (Rosen was one of the original VisiCorp investors and is the chairman of Compaq Computer Corporation.) Kapor also recruited Chris Morgan, previously editor-in-chief of *Byte* magazine and *Popular Computing* magazine, to be vice president of communications. Because every member of the Lotus team had prior experience in the microcomputer industry, Kapor calls Lotus a "second generation" software company.

Since 1-2-3 was introduced in 1983, it has become one of the most successful software programs ever produced. By the end of April, 1983, 1-2-3 was outselling VisiCalc. And by the end of 1983, Lotus 1-2-3 had become the leading software program sold for spreadsheet applications. At the end of 1983, Lotus reported $53 million in sales.

Symphony marks the second stage of Mitch Kapor's goal to create a sophisticated integrated software package. 1-2-3 proved that microcomputer users wanted a program that integrated spreadsheet, data management, and graphics applications. Symphony should likewise show the benefits of integration, this time with word processing, and communications and data form capabilities.

Symphony Compared to 1-2-3

From first appearances, you may think that Symphony shares little similarity with 1-2-3. But once you begin experimenting with Symphony, you will find that it does build on the 1-2-3 foundation. Throughout this book, similarities between Symphony and 1-2-3 will be specifically explained. The following discussion compares the two programs.

The ACCESS SYSTEM and Selecting Commands

The Symphony ACCESS SYSTEM, like 1-2-3's, contains the selections for accessing the PrintGraph program (located on a separate Symphony disk), which enables you to configure your graphics printer and then print graphs you have created in the

Symphony program. The ACCESS SYSTEM also enables you to transfer files to Symphony from such programs as dBASE II and VisiCalc. But probably the most important similarity between Symphony's ACCESS SYSTEM and 1-2-3's is that both systems access the main program.

In addition, the command menus in Symphony follow the same logic as the command menus in 1-2-3, and the process for using them is the same. Both menu systems are structured hierarchically, consisting of multiple levels of commands. To use either menu system, you retrieve the menu, move the cursor to the command or type the first letter of the command, and enter responses to complete certain commands.

Although Symphony has many more menus than 1-2-3 has, you will recognize a number of commands, particularly in the spreadsheet menu of the program. (See Chapter 2 on Getting Started.) For example, when you select the Format command in Symphony, you will find that it contains many of the same format options provided in 1-2-3. File commands, too, are similar to those in 1-2-3.

The Display Screen and Keyboard

Because of Symphony's added applications (word processing, data management, and communications), you can expect both the display screen and keyboard to be different from those of 1-2-3. Yet when you are working in Symphony's spreadsheet environment (SHEET), you will notice familiar territory. The border of Symphony's spreadsheet window, like the reverse-video border of 1-2-3, contains the letters and numbers marking columns and rows. In Symphony, however, letters and numbers appear within the border of a single narrow line, instead of in reverse video as in 1-2-3.

The Symphony screen displays mode, lock key, cell contents, and commands in the same locations as on the 1-2-3 screen. But the Symphony screen does contain additions to the screen display. (See Chapter 2 for more information on the display screen and keyboard.)

The Help and Tutorial Disk

The Help and Tutorial disk in Symphony provides the same kind of support as its counterpart disk in 1-2-3. In Symphony the on-screen help, for example, is much like that of 1-2-3 in the index, the organization of topics, and the procedure for selecting topics. Symphony's help screens, however, are context-sensitive. In other words, as soon as you change an application and then press the Help key (the F1 key on the IBM PC and compatibles), a help screen will appear for the specific application you are using. If you are working in the word-processing environment and you press the Help key, a word-processing help screen will be displayed.

Spreadsheet Capabilities

Symphony's spreadsheet component, like 1-2-3's, is the most powerful of its features. Because both programs emphasize the spreadsheet application, the following discussion briefly enumerates those features that Symphony shares with 1-2-3 as well as other spreadsheet programs.

Symphony's spreadsheet environment, like 1-2-3's, is an electronic replacement for the traditional financial modeling tools: the accountant's columnar pad, pencil, and calculator. In some ways spreadsheet programs are to these tools what word processors are to typewriters. Spreadsheets offer dramatic improvements in creating, editing, and using financial models.

The typical electronic spreadsheet configures the memory of a computer to resemble an accountant's columnar pad. Because this "pad" exists in the dynamic world of the computer's memory, the pad is different from paper pads in some important ways. For one thing, electronic spreadsheets are much larger than their paper counterparts. Symphony has 8,192 rows and 256 columns.

Each row in Symphony's spreadsheet environment is assigned a number, and each column is assigned a letter or a combination of letters. The intersections of the rows and columns are called cells, which are identified by their row-column coordinates. For example, the cell located at the intersection of column A and row 15 is called

A15. The cell at the intersection of column X and row 55 is called X55. These cells can be filled with three kinds of information: numbers; mathematical formulas, as well as special spreadsheet functions; and text (or labels).

A cursor allows you to write information into the cells in much the same way that a pencil lets you write on a piece of paper. In the Symphony spreadsheet environment, the cursor looks like a bright rectangle on the computer's screen. Typically, the cursor is one row high and one column high.

Because the Symphony grid is so large, the entire spreadsheet cannot be viewed on the screen at one time. The screen thus serves as a "window" onto the worksheet. As mentioned at the beginning of the chapter, in Symphony this window can contain other windows within it. To view other parts of the sheet, you can scroll the cursor across the worksheet with the cursor-movement keys; or if you have created multiple windows on the worksheet, you can retrieve another window to take you to that part of the worksheet. In Symphony, you can create different windows in the worksheet area, all containing different applications, such as word processing and data management.

As in 1-2-3, in Symphony the spreadsheet feature is the foundation of the program. For example, when you are working in a word-processing (DOC) window or data form (FORM) window, all data is entered and stored within the worksheet boundaries. Because of this setup, entries and changes in a DOC or FORM window can affect a spreadsheet entered on the same worksheet.

To understand this concept, you might imagine a large grid containing 256 columns across the top and 8,192 rows along the side—which is the size of the Symphony worksheet. Then imagine various work areas you have created on this worksheet. (See fig. 1.9.) In the upper left corner of the worksheet is a balance sheet. Directly to the right of the balance sheet is a data base (created either by you or by Symphony through its FORM capability). Then below the balance sheet are a few of your notes—important points relating to the information in the balance sheet or data base.

Furthermore, to prevent one range of data from affecting another, you can restrict each work area or window so that the cursor doesn't

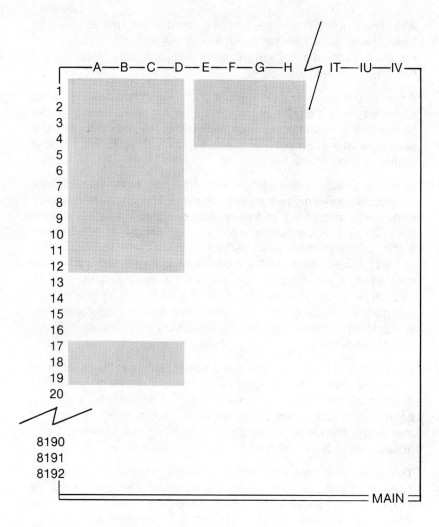

Fig. 1.9.

move outside of the window and so that some command operations affect data only within the restricted area.

New with Symphony

Symphony's window feature makes it possible for you to create a spreadsheet, a data base, and word-processing text on the same worksheet within the worksheet's 256 x 8,192 boundaries. How much of this worksheet area you can use and how far apart you can keep one application from another depend on your machine's memory. (Chapter 3 provides a discussion of Symphony's SHEET window.)

So far, you have seen that Symphony and 1-2-3 are most alike in spreadsheet applications. Moving about the Symphony worksheet, for example, is much like moving about in 1-2-3's worksheet although a difference in size is evident. 1-2-3's worksheet measures 256 columns by only 2,048 rows.

Symphony incorporates those functions and commands that make 1-2-3 a more powerful spreadsheet program than many spreadsheet-only programs. For instance, Symphony contains all the statistical and date functions of 1-2-3. You will see in Chapter 5, however, that Symphony has added many new functions, thus making possible more applications than are available in 1-2-3.

Symphony, like 1-2-3, offers a wide variety of formats for numeric entries. These formats also let you display or print numbers with embedded commas, dollar signs, parentheses, and percent signs. You can also specify an exact number of digits that will be displayed to the right of the decimal. For example, both Symphony and 1-2-3 can format the number 12345 to look like $12,345.00, 12,345, 1.23E3, or 12345. The number -12345 can be formatted to appear as ($12,345.00) or -12,345. And the number .45 can look like 45% or $.45.

Symphony, like 1-2-3, provides the full range of commands for entering and changing individual cells and ranges, for adjusting columns and rows, creating and using range names, and recalculating a worksheet. (See Chapters 3 and 4 and the 1-2-3/Symphony Cross-Reference Guide in Appendix C.)

Playing "What If . . . ?"

The act of building a model on a spreadsheet establishes all the mathematical relationships in the model. Until you decide to make changes, every sum, product, division, subtraction, average, and net present value will remain the same. Each time you enter data into the model, computations will be calculated at your command with no effort on your part. All these computations will be calculated correctly; spreadsheets don't make math errors. And next month, when you decide to use the same model again, the formulas will still be set, ready to calculate at your command.

Even more important, spreadsheet software allows you to play "What if . . . ?" with your model after it has been developed. This is particularly true when you use Symphony's command, function, and graphics capabilities. Once a set of mathematical relationships has been built into the sheet, it can be recalculated with amazing speed, using different sets of assumptions. If you use only paper, a pencil, and a calculator to build a model, every change to the model will require recalculating every relationship in it. If the model has 100 formulas and you change the first one, you must make 100 calculations by hand to flow the change through the entire model. If, on the other hand, you use a spreadsheet, the same change requires the press of only a few keys—the program does the rest. This capability permits extensive "what if" analysis.

Two specific parts of the Symphony program that allow you to perform easily "what if" analysis are its "what if" graphing capability and SHEET **R**ange **W**hat-If command. Symphony's graphics can be an integral part of "what if" analysis by enabling you to fine-tune projections, budgets, or projects. Symphony's GRAPH window will help you understand the impact of changes in your data on the results of your models. For example, you can create one window to display spreadsheet data and another window to display a related graph. You can then display both windows simultaneously on the screen. When you make a change in the data, the GRAPH window will immediately reflect the change.

Symphony's SHEET **R**ange **W**hat-If command, on the other hand, enables you to conduct extensive sensitivity analysis and to display the results in tabular form. The SHEET **R**ange **W**hat-If command lets you do the kind of thorough analysis that you might not do otherwise, given the time required to perform the analysis.

These are only two examples of how Symphony can help you with "what if" analysis. As you use the program, you will find numerous ways for conducting sophisticated "what if" analysis through the power of Symphony's functions and Command Language.

Data Management Capabilities

Even though Symphony provides data management capabilities that are more sophisticated than those of 1-2-3, many of the data management features and commands of the two programs are similar. The integration capability of Symphony, which was mentioned earlier, allows you to perform data base operations within the spreadsheet environment of the program. Some of the tasks you will want to perform on a Symphony data base can be accomplished with the Symphony SHEET commands. For instance, records can be added to a data base with the SHEET Insert Rows command. Fields can be added with the SHEET Insert Columns command. Editing the contents of a data base is like editing the contents of any other cell in the worksheet.

In Symphony, as in 1-2-3, data can also be sorted. But in Symphony you have three options for sorts instead of two: primary key, secondary key, or third-order key. As in 1-2-3, in Symphony you can conduct a sort in ascending or descending order by using alphabetical or numeric keys. In addition, various kinds of mathematical analyses can be performed on a field of data over a specified range of records. For example, you can count the number of items in a data base that match a set of criteria; compute a mean, variance, or standard deviation; and find the maximum or minimum value in the range.

Graphics Capabilities

Once you begin using Symphony, you will see that graph commands are contained in two parts of the program where graphs can be created. You will find graph commands in Symphony's spreadsheet menu and also in the GRAPH environment of the program. The location of graph commands in the spreadsheet menu makes Symphony much like 1-2-3 in graphics applications.

Like 1-2-3, Symphony is capable of creating bar, stacked bar, line, scatter, and pie graphs. Besides these, two new options for graphs are now included in Symphony: exploded pie and high-low-close-open charts. The exploded pie chart is like 1-2-3's standard pie chart except that one or more of the slices are separated from the pie for emphasis. High-low-close-open charts are useful for graphing the prices of stocks over time and for evaluating trends.

New
with
Symphony

Other new graphics features in Symphony include the ability to control scaling factors manually, new cross-hatchings, nonzero origins, and logarithmic graph scales.

If you have used 1-2-3, though, you won't find it difficult to use Symphony's graphics application. As with 1-2-3, with Symphony you can access all the graphing capabilities by using the **G**raph command within the SHEET environment.

The most important difference between the graphics capabilities of 1-2-3 and Symphony is Symphony's GRAPH window. When you create a graph by selecting the **G**raph command from Symphony's spreadsheet menu, Symphony, like 1-2-3, temporarily replaces the worksheet with the graph you have created. But Symphony's GRAPH window allows you to create a graph window, display the graph, and simultaneously display a spreadsheet window (SHEET).

New
with
Symphony

With the right equipment and the correct driver set, you can display on the screen both the graph and the spreadsheet at the same time. If your system cannot display the graph and spreadsheet simultaneously, you can shift back and forth between the spreadsheet and the graph by pressing one key repeatedly.

What Makes Symphony Different from 1-2-3?

New
with
Symphony

The primary differences between Symphony and 1-2-3 include the following Symphony features: (1) the new applications—word-processing, data form, and communications capabilities; (2) the window capability; (3) the command menu system; (4) the settings sheets; and (5) some special features, such as new spreadsheet functions, international formats and character set, a security system for protecting worksheets, and the Command Language.

New
with
Symphony

Symphony's Word-Processing Capabilities

When you use Symphony's DOC environment, you have the full range of commands and operations that are included in sophisticated stand-alone word-processing programs. And when you use Symphony's Command Language to create macros for simplifying word-processing operations, you will find that the word processor is not only easy to use but also very powerful.

Symphony's word processor provides a number of capabilities. You have the ability to move the cursor forward or backward character by character, word by word, or from the beginning to the end of a line, paragraph, or text (and vice versa). In addition, Symphony enables you to move the cursor to any character by pressing the End key and then pressing that character. Furthermore, a command for naming lines in your text allows you to use Symphony's GoTo key for moving quickly from any location in your text to the line you have named.

Besides being able to move the cursor in various ways, you can also regulate and change the format of your text. You can set and store configuration settings for margins, spacing, tabs, and paragraph justification. When you store these settings in Symphony's configuration file (see the section on Configuration in Chapter 2), the margins, spacing, tabs, and paragraph justification will automatically be set for your text every time you begin a new word-processing session.

If you want to change temporarily these configuration settings for a particular document, you can use Symphony's DOC Format Settings. And if you need to change format in the middle of a document, Symphony's format lines enable you to change margins, spacing, paragraph justification, and tabs for only one section, then return to the original settings for your document after you have finished formatting the section.

Symphony's word processor also includes complete editing and revising capabilities. With Symphony's **E**rase command or Erase key (a special-function key for initiating erase operations), you can erase any number of characters, from single characters to large blocks of text. Symphony makes possible the marking and erasing of large blocks of text with a couple of keystrokes. And when you create macros for erase operations, the number of keystrokes is reduced to one. (See Chapter 13 for more information on creating word-processing macros.)

In addition, Symphony's **S**earch and **R**eplace commands can help you edit text. When you use **S**earch, you have the options of searching either forward or backward and of easily exiting from the search at any time. Although Symphony doesn't perform a backward search-and-replace operation, the **R**eplace command is also easy to use and regulate.

For composing and revising, Symphony's **C**opy, **M**ove, **F**ile **X**tract, and **F**ile **C**ombine commands can be used for creating form letters, combining parts of one document with another, and reorganizing sections of text.

Symphony's DOC environment is an integral part of the program for many reasons. First, using Symphony's word-processing environment is similar to using the other program applications— spreadsheet, graphics, data management, and communications. Second, you can easily integrate a DOC window with other types of windows. Being able to display a SHEET or GRAPH window along with a DOC window can help you to draft certain kinds of reports. In addition, you can readily incorporate parts of spreadsheets and data bases into your text and have your text printed with tables or figures inserted right where you want them.

Symphony's Data Form Capabilities

*New
with
Symphony*

If you have used 1-2-3, you will find that many of its data management operations are duplicated in Symphony. Some of 1-2-3's data management commands, however, have different names and menu locations in Symphony. In 1-2-3 you do not have the full power of Symphony's data management capabilities. These capabilities are particularly evident when you make use of the data form environment (FORM window), the data management commands included in Symphony's spreadsheet menu, and the data base statistical functions.

With its data management capabilities, Symphony can handle many chores for you, such as setting up data base ranges, criterion ranges, and output ranges. When you work in a FORM window, much work is done for you by the program itself.

While you are in a FORM window, you rarely see the entire data base at one time. You view the records through a special data form that you build with Symphony's help. To create a data form, such as the one shown earlier in the chapter, you begin in a SHEET or DOC window and enter the field names you want in your form. After you enter the field names, you shift to a FORM window to have Symphony generate an actual data form and then to begin entering records into the form. (The specific procedures for creating and using a data form are covered in Chapter 11.)

After you enter records into your data form, you can use the data commands in the FORM menu to perform data sort operations. You can also sort records by using the SHEET environment. In fact, when you switch from a FORM window to a SHEET window, Symphony provides a number of data management operations that you can use on the data base you have created. In a spreadsheet environment, for example, you can have Symphony (1) find records that match the given criteria, (2) copy in a specified area of the worksheet all or some of the records in certain fields that match given criteria, and (3) delete records in a data base. In a SHEET environment, you can also change the column width of columns in the data base, change the format of values, and insert or delete columns or rows.

Symphony expands considerably the data management capabilities of 1-2-3. Once you begin using Symphony's data management operations, you will find how much more powerful they are.

Symphony's Communications Capabilities

*New
with
Symphony*

Symphony's communications capability (COMM environment/window) allows you to use your personal computer to receive data base information from a corporate mainframe computer or mini-computer. You can also connect to a time-sharing service to get current news, stocks, weather, and other information. Finally, Symphony's communications capability enables you to exchange information with another microcomputer. The communications capability of Symphony is really quite powerful, rivaling that of many stand-alone packages. You can even connect with many different kinds of computers.

Symphony supports asynchronous communications transmission and XMODEM protocol for file transfer. With asynchronous trans-mission, a clock in the computer is used to time the sampling of incoming data and the recording of the number of bits in each sample. You specify the transmission speed (the baud rate or bits per second) for the clock. Symphony uses the XMODEM protocol, a special system of rules established for exchanging information between computers. XMODEM protocol, developed by Ward Christensen, has become a standard in the microcomputer industry for communications protocols.

Like other Symphony environments, the communications environ-ment enables you to enter settings for a specific COMM window in the **S**ettings selection from the COMM menu. In the COMM **S**ettings sheet, for example, you enter such settings as the protocol parameters: baud rate, byte length, stop bits, and parity. Included in the COMM **S**ettings sheet are also selections for automatic dialing (if your modem has an auto-dial feature) and settings for matching the service or computer you are calling with the characteristics of the COMM window in which you are working.

The World of Lotus

Available through the time-sharing service CompuServe is a source of new information called The World of Lotus. When you access

CompuServe's Executive Information Service (EIS), you can receive messages from Lotus Development. These messages may contain, for example, information on Symphony product services, tips and techniques for Symphony users, a Symphony user newsletter, and a library of Command Language programs and worksheet models. In addition, you can send and receive messages to and from other Symphony users.

When you send in your Symphony registration card, you will receive a list of CompuServe's services and one hour of free connect time. This on-line time will give you an introduction to The World of Lotus. One other benefit is that the free on-line time will give you a chance to try out Symphony's COMM environment.

New
with
Symphony

·*Window Features*

The window capability is probably the one feature that most distinguishes Symphony from 1-2-3. As indicated at the beginning of this chapter, with Symphony's window capability you can move among any of the five applications (spreadsheet, word processing, data management, graphics, and communications) and view different parts of the same worksheet. In other words, you can create and work within multiple windows on a single screen.

Symphony keeps track of the windows you create by labeling each one with a name that either you assign or Symphony assigns automatically. And whenever you are working in a particular window, it is bordered at the bottom with a double line. The double line tells you that the window is the currently "active" window—the one in which you can perform command operations, enter data, and make changes.

The **W**indow command menu and special window function keys enable you to change the type of window, create new windows, change the size and shape of windows, and split a window horizontally and vertically. You can also restrict a window to a specific range in the worksheet so that data you enter and changes you make won't interfere with data entered in other windows on the worksheet.

As mentioned earlier, you can organize a single worksheet into different parts, or applications. To do this, you create multiple windows of different types. And if you store the worksheet by using the **F**ile **S**ave command, these different windows will be stored in one file.

Once you begin using Symphony's window features, you will discover unlimited possibilities for integrating various types of windows onto one screen. Creating windows will allow you, for example, to compare and analyze spreadsheet data from different areas of the worksheet. You can also write memos and short reports while you view spreadsheets and data bases. And you can see data displayed in graphs and change those graphs as you change data.

Command Menu System

Besides Symphony's window feature, the most noticeable difference between 1-2-3 and Symphony is the menu system. Yet 1-2-3 and Symphony are not different in their methods of retrieving and using command menus, but in the number of commands and their locations. Because of the added applications of word processing, data form capability, and communications, Symphony's menu system is more complex than 1-2-3's. Learning 1-2-3 involves learning two primary menus: the ACCESS SYSTEM menu, which includes **1**-2-3 (the main program), **F**ile-Manager, **D**isk-Manager, **P**rintGraph, and **T**ranslate; and the Worksheet menu. Learning Symphony, however, involves eight independent menus.

As in 1-2-3, in Symphony the first menu to appear is the ACCESS SYSTEM. This menu lacks the two 1-2-3 options of **F**ile-Manager and **D**isk-Manager. Symphony provides an alternative, however, through its **A**pplication add-in feature, described in detail in Chapter 2. **A**pplication add-in allows you to use DOS commands, the Symphony Help and Tutorial disk, and other special add-in programs without having to exit from the Symphony program. If, for example, you want to format a disk using your DOS FORMAT command, and you want to continue working in Symphony after formatting the disk, the **A**pplication add-in feature allows you to invoke DOS commands temporarily and to return to your worksheet without having to access Symphony again.

*New
with
Symphony*

Aside from the ACCESS SYSTEM, seven other command menus are available in Symphony. These menus include (1) a SERVICES menu for global operations such as File **S**ave, **R**etrieve, and **D**elete, (2) a TYPE menu for changing the type of window you are working in (SHEET, DOC, GRAPH, FORM, and COMM), (3) a SHEET menu for spreadsheet work, (4) a DOC menu for word processing, (5) a GRAPH menu for graphics, (6) a FORM menu for data form operations, and (7) a COMM menu for communications.

Although a number of 1-2-3 commands are retained in the Symphony command system, some 1-2-3 commands have different names and locations in Symphony. Some of 1-2-3's "hidden" commands, for example, are first-level commands in Symphony. The spreadsheet **E**rase command, which is located within the **R**ange command structure in 1-2-3, is equal to **R**ange in Symphony's SHEET menu.

Although some commands may be easier to find in Symphony than they are in 1-2-3, a few Symphony commands are harder to find than comparable 1-2-3 commands. Because of the locations, these Symphony commands require more keystrokes than they do in 1-2-3. For example, the command for specifying a range to print is the first option after selecting **P**rint in 1-2-3. The same command in Symphony requires that you move down three levels in the command structure.

New
with
Symphony

Settings Sheets

In the seven Symphony menus listed above, you will find settings sheets. Except for the DOC menu, all command menus contain settings sheets at the first level. These settings sheets enable you to enter settings for such operations as creating graphs, for printing reports and documents, or for using Symphony's communications capability.

Some 1-2-3 commands now operate within Symphony's settings sheets. If, for example, you want to set horizontal or vertical titles in a worksheet, you will find **T**itles located in the **S**ettings selection of the spreadsheet menu.

1-2-3 users will find that Symphony settings sheets provide two major advantages. Unlike 1-2-3, in which special settings can exist in various locations in the command menu, Symphony displays multiple settings on a single screen. This feature is helpful when you need to remember special print or graph settings. Another advantage of settings sheets is that you can create a catalog of some types of sheets and retrieve them when needed. To store a settings sheet, you must assign a name that Symphony will attach to the sheet. By naming a settings sheet, you can locate and use that sheet again.

Functions

New with Symphony

Symphony includes all the functions included in 1-2-3 but has added many functions to 1-2-3's selection. Like 1-2-3, Symphony has mathematical, statistical, financial, logical, and date functions. Symphony, however, extends its function capability to include new string functions and new date and time functions. In addition, a set of special functions is available that gives you detailed information about the contents of cells (or ranges) and their locations in a spreadsheet. In Chapter 5 you will find a detailed explanation of all the Symphony functions. Here, however, is a brief introduction to the new functions.

Symphony has a variety of new string functions that give you significantly more power to manipulate strings than do earlier integrated packages, including 1-2-3. In fact, 1-2-3 has very limited power to manipulate strings, and 1-2-3 offers no string functions whatsoever. The @FIND function, for example, allows you to locate the starting position of one string within another string. The @MID function lets you extract one string from another, whereas @LEFT and @RIGHT are used to extract one string of characters from another. These string functions, only a few of the many functions available in Symphony, can be used to increase the power of Symphony's data base and Command Language capability.

The new date and time functions in Symphony include @DATEVALUE, @NOW, @TIME, and @TIMEVALUE. @DATEVALUE, a variant of the @DATE function, accepts a date-string rather than a numeric argument, as does the @DATE function.

With @DATEVALUE, you can enter @DATEVALUE ("21-JUN-84"), and it will produce a serial number, just as @DATE does when you enter @DATE(84,6,21). The @TIME function is used to arrive at a serial number for a specified time of day that you enter in numeric arguments: @TIME(3,12,30). @TIMEVALUE, on the other hand, uses string arguments to produce a serial number from the information you provide for the hour, minute, and second: @TIMEVALUE ("12:30:59").

The special functions in Symphony are @CELL, @CELLPOINTER, @ROWS, @COLS, @TRUE, and @FALSE. All of these provide information about the contents of cells or ranges and their locations in a spreadsheet. For example, if you enter @CELL ("width", B12..B12), Symphony will return the width of column B as viewed in the current window. In addition to indicating width, the @CELL function can indicate the address of a cell, the type of value, the label prefix, and the format or the row and column number location. (See Chapter 5 for a listing of the capabilities of the special functions.)

When you combine Symphony's new functions with those initially available in 1-2-3, you have a very comprehensive set of built-in functions. And when you use these functions with Symphony's Command Language, you will have the ingredients of a sophisticated programming language.

International Formats and Character Set

New with Symphony

One other feature that sets Symphony apart from 1-2-3 is the availability of International formats and an international character set. First, through the configuration settings, you have the options of changing Currency, Date, and Time formats to International formats. The Currency option, for example, enables you to change the default dollar sign ($) to a foreign currency sign, such as the British pound (£), if you are going to use that format regularly throughout your worksheet. Second, the international character set, referred to as the Lotus International Character Set (LICS), provides characters from many languages. You can enter these characters at any keyboard. In Symphony's *How-To Manual*, you will find a complete list of international and special characters available in LICS.

Security System

*New
with
Symphony*

Like 1-2-3, Symphony provides the ability to protect cells in a worksheet so that changes cannot be made in cells containing, for example, important formulas. Symphony's range protection capability, however, also extends to protecting a section of word-processing text in a DOC window. In addition, you can use a special password security system to lock an entire worksheet or range of cells.

Whenever you protect an area of your worksheet, whether the area is part of a spreadsheet or part of word-processing text, you use two commands: Symphony's SERVICES **S**ettings **G**lobal-Protection command and SHEET **R**ange **P**rotect command. These two commands, which enable you to protect a range of cells, will prevent someone from erasing, moving, or changing the cells although the cell contents are displayed on the screen. If you want not only to protect cell contents from being changed but also to keep them from being displayed on the screen, you can use the two commands mentioned here along with the SHEET **F**ormat **O**ther **H**idden command. (See Chapter 4 for details on protecting a range in the worksheet.)

In addition to the range protection capability, Symphony enables you to "lock" an entire worksheet or range of cells. With Symphony's security system, you create a password for locking and unlocking the worksheet. Only by using the password can someone make changes or even see cell contents.

To use the security system, you must select a number of commands in a particular order. The commands and steps for locking a worksheet are provided in Table 1.2.

Table 1.2
Steps for Using the Security System

1. Turn on global protection (SERVICES **S**ettings **G**lobal-Protection **Y**es) and set SHEET **R**ange **P**rotect.

2. Hide cells from being displayed on the screen by selecting **F**ormat **O**ther **H**idden from the SHEET menu.

This command applies to cell entries that you made in a SHEET environment, so don't use **F**ormat **O**ther **H**idden with entries made in a DOC or FORM environment.

3. Once you go through the steps for locking a worksheet, you can unlock it only with the password you have created. You may therefore want to create a backup file of your worksheet at this point in case you forget the password. To create a backup, save your worksheet under a file name that is different from the one containing the security system.

4. Lock the worksheet by selecting the SERVICES **S**ettings **S**ecurity **L**ock command. Enter a password when the "Password" prompt appears. Before pressing RETURN, write down the password and check the spelling closely. To unlock a worksheet, you must enter the password exactly as you originally created it, including uppercase and lowercase letters.

After you have completed the four steps listed in table 1.2, they will have certain effects on your worksheet. A user won't be able to change the cell protection setting that you entered in SHEET **R**ange **P**rotect. The SERVICES **S**ettings **G**lobal-Protection setting cannot be changed. Finally, a user cannot have "hidden" cells redisplayed. With the security system, cell contents will not appear either in the worksheet or in the control panel.

Whenever you want to unlock a worksheet that you have locked, you retrieve the worksheet and select the SERVICES **S**ettings **S**ecurity **U**nlock command. At the "Password" prompt, you enter your password. As long as you have entered the password in the exact form in which it was created, you can now control any of the settings that were previously frozen.

Symphony's security system goes beyond the ability simply to protect ranges. With the security system, you can not only protect ranges from change, but also prevent users from viewing important data.

The Command Language and Macros

*New
with
Symphony*

In Symphony the Command Language is the programming language available to you for automating repetitive keyboard tasks. In 1-2-3 this capability is referred to as "keyboard macros." Symphony provides not only the same keyboard macro capability of 1-2-3, but also a sophisticated programming language.

The Symphony Command Language contains a programming language that is nearly full featured, including the ability to call subroutines, iterative looping, improved conditional logic, and error trapping. Through these tools, you can develop special applications programs to run on Symphony.

Another feature of Symphony's Command Language, a feature not included in 1-2-3, is Symphony's ability to store commands automatically. Using Symphony's Learn mode, you can easily create keyboard macros that you can use with little or no editing. When you use the Learn mode, Symphony converts the commands and keystrokes you enter into Command Language statements, and stores the statements in a special range that you set in the worksheet. Then through a name that you assign to this range of statements, you can invoke the macro to simplify an operation.

If you want to go beyond the Learn mode capability and build your own macros to perform many types of complex operations, Symphony's Command Language enables you to do so. These macros do not simply duplicate keystrokes, as do the macros created by the Learn mode. The Command Language actually allows you to program, which is much like using a programming language such as BASIC.

Symphony's Command Language has its own special grammar and set of keywords. For example, if you want to enter a command into your macro to cause it to stop processing temporarily so that you can enter a label, you use the following:

{GETLABEL "Enter label: ",FIRST FIELD}

GETLABEL is one of the Command Language's keywords. The items that come after it are examples of arguments that you include in Command Language statements. (For a detailed look at macros and Symphony's Command Language, see Chapter 13.)

New
with
Symphony

Naming in Symphony

Besides Symphony's window and integration features, another important feature for you to know before you jump into the program is *naming*. You will do a lot of naming when you use Symphony. Naming, in fact, is fundamental to the program. Naming files, of course, is one kind of naming but file naming is only the beginning to naming in Symphony.

If you have used 1-2-3, naming in Symphony won't be new to you. You already know that getting around the 1-2-3 worksheet quickly and entering ranges for commands can be done through range names. Symphony also has worksheet range names, and you will be naming other things as well. For example, when you are working in the word-processing environment, you can name lines in your document. They may include lines of text or special lines you insert in a document whenever you want to vary the format of the text. You can also name settings sheets for printing, for creating graphs and data bases, and for communications.

In some cases, Symphony will give you the option of providing names for all the windows you create on the screen for using different applications. And when you don't name the windows, Symphony will take the initiative and name them for you, using numbers.

Whenever you assign names, Symphony keeps track of them for you. By keeping track of named print settings, lines of text, format lines, and so on, Symphony helps you get more out of the program. If you want to use a name again and again, Symphony will save for you the name (and what's attached to it). Then, for example, when you want to print a letter with most, if not all, of the same print settings for a letter you previously printed from the same worksheet, you can call up those original settings—but only if you gave them a name. In addition, if you have named a line in your document, Symphony will help you find that line quickly. As you begin using Symphony, watch out for the special commands that refer to names. When you become accustomed to Symphony's naming feature, you will find that it is quite an advantage to use.

Conclusion

This chapter summarizes what Symphony is all about. The chapter gives you a comprehensive view of Symphony by introducing you to the program's features; by providing a history of Symphony, beginning with the early development of microcomputers; by discussing similarities between Symphony and its forerunner 1-2-3; and finally by pointing out the differences between Symphony and 1-2-3. As a first step in learning Symphony, you now have an overview of the features and concepts that make Symphony what it is—an outstanding integrated software package.

For a more specific idea of the power of Symphony's spreadsheet, word-processing, graphics, data management, and communications applications, turn to the following chapters. In the next chapter, you will learn how to get started, by preparing and installing your Symphony disks and by understanding the program's command system, special screen display features, and uses of the keyboard. You will also learn in later chapters how to use each of Symphony's five environments (SHEET, DOC, GRAPH, FORM, and COMM), how to print reports and graphs, how to use Symphony's Command Language, and how Symphony's five applications can be integrated.

2
Getting Started

Getting started in using your Symphony program requires two kinds of preparation. First, you need to complete the following "maintenance" operations: (1) copying your Symphony master disks, including adding DOS commands to two different disks; (2) installing the Symphony disks to run with your equipment; (3) configuring the printer and data disk; and (4) preparing data disks.

If you have a two-disk drive system, copying your master disks involves copying DOS commands to your master Symphony Program disk and to the backup copy of the Help and Tutorial disk. Second, you need a general understanding of the Symphony program, including its Help and Tutorial disk, its menu structure, special uses of the keyboard, general features of the Symphony display screen, and the functions and operations of Symphony's windows.

This chapter presents the required maintenance operations for getting started and an overview of the program. Furthermore, if you are a 1-2-3 user, the chapter will help you understand the differences between 1-2-3 and Symphony.

Preparing Symphony Disks

Six disks come with the Symphony package:

Symphony Program Disk
Help and Tutorial Disk
Tutorial Lessons Disk
PrintGraph Program Disk
Install Program Disk
Install Library Disk

The most important of these, the Symphony Program disk, contains all of Symphony's operations excluding one: the commands for printing graphs. Printing graphs requires using the separate Print-Graph Program disk. (See Chapter 10.) The Help and Tutorial disk provides access to the help screens and to the tutorial program, although the actual tutorial lessons are on the Tutorial Lessons disk. (See the sections below on the Help and Tutorial disks.) The last two disks—Install Program disk and Install Library disk—are the two disks necessary for creating and saving driver sets so that you can run Symphony with your equipment. (See the Installing Drivers section below.)

Lotus Development has protected its Symphony Program disk; it can be copied, but the copy cannot be used to boot and access the program. In order to boot and access the program, you must use the original master Symphony Program disk. Even though you can't use a backup copy of the program disk to boot and access Symphony program, it is, nonetheless, important for you to make a backup.

Having a backup copy of the Symphony Program disk is necessary if the master disk is lost or destroyed. If it is lost or destroyed, Lotus provides a method for recovering use of the program. (See the section on If Your Program Disk Is Lost or Destroyed later in the chapter.) The important thing to remember is that you must have a backup copy of the Symphony Program available before you begin the recovery procedure.

Preparing and using Symphony disks, therefore, require a few different operations from preparing and using other software programs, which enable you to use backup copies directly. Because the Symphony Program disk is protected, here is the general procedure for preparing and then using the six disks that come with your Symphony package:

1. Make backup copies of all six Symphony disks that come with your Symphony package.

2. Add DOS commands to the master Symphony Program disk and backup copy of the Help and Tutorial disk.

3. As is explained in the Installing Drivers section below, install the following four disks:

   Symphony Program Disk (the master disk)
   Help and Tutorial Disk (backup copy)
   PrintGraph Program Disk (backup copy)
   Install Program Disk (backup copy)

4. Use the master Symphony Program disk for booting and accessing the Symphony program; use the backup copies of your other disks.

5. If the master Symphony Program disk is lost or destroyed, follow the recovery procedure described below. Refer to the Customer Assurance Plan that comes with the disks for directions on how you can get a replacement of lost or destroyed disk(s).

Making Backup Copies

In addition to allowing you to recover use of the program if your master program disk is lost or destroyed, copying provides a safeguard in case the other five disks are lost or destroyed as well. Making backup copies is the preliminary step to using your Symphony program. If you follow the steps outlined below, you will be able to replace disks easily in case anything happens to the ones you are using.

The following two sections provide general directions for making backup copies of your Symphony disks and for adding DOS to the master Symphony Program disk and to the backup copy of the Help and Tutorial disk. Keep in mind that these are general directions. If you need more specific information on DOS commands, file directories, and hard disk systems, please consult *PC DOS User's Guide* or *MS-DOS User's Guide,* both by Chris DeVoney, Que Corporation, 1984.

Before making backup copies, you should become familiar with your computer's disk operating system. Refer to the books mentioned above or to your system's manual for specific explanations of formatting disks, copying files, and adding DOS. Also, remember that you can use Symphony with either DOS V2.00 or later versions, but not with versions prior to V2.00. Follow these steps for creating backup copies and adding DOS.

To copy disks with a system that has two disk drives:

1. Format five blank disks, following the directions in Appendix A.

2. Label these five disks with the following:

    Backup Copy: Symphony Program Disk
    Backup Copy: Tutorial Lessons Disk
    Backup Copy: PrintGraph Program Disk
    Backup Copy: Install Program Disk
    Backup Copy: Install Library Disk

3. Format one more blank disk, but this time add DOS commands to the disk when you format it. See Appendix B for directions on formatting blank disks with DOS commands added.

4. Label this last disk with the following:

    Backup Copy: Help and Tutorial Disk

5. Begin to copy each Symphony master disk onto the appropriate formatted blank disk.

6. With DOS operating, place the master Symphony Program disk in Drive A and the formatted blank disk in Drive B.

7. At the A> prompt, type COPY A:*.* B: and press RETURN. (Lotus Development suggests using COPY rather than DISKCOPY.)

8. Once all files have been copied from the master disk onto the formatted disk, remove the master disk from Drive A and the backup copy from Drive B.

9. Insert the next master disk in Drive A and the formatted blank disk in Drive B and repeat the COPY A:*.* B: command.

10. Repeat steps 6-9 until you have made backup copies of all six Symphony disks.

To copy disks with a hard disk drive system:

1. Start your computer with DOS.

2. Type C: and press RETURN if the hard disk is not the default.

3. Create a directory for your Symphony files, making it the current directory.

4. Insert the source disk (for example, the Symphony Program disk in drive A.)

5. Type Copy A:*.* and press RETURN.

6. When copying is completed, remove the disk (when the red light on the disk drive has gone off.

7. Repeat steps 3, 4, and 5 until you have copied all six Symphony disks.

After you have copied all six disks, check to make certain that the copies have been appropriately labeled and are placed in their protective sleeves. Finally, put all master Symphony disks (except the master Symphony Program disk) and the backup copy of the Symphony Program disk in a safe location.

Adding DOS to the Master Symphony Program Disk (For a System with Two Disk Drives)

As mentioned above, you should format the Help and Tutorial disk with DOS commands added to it. With DOS added to your backup copy of the Help and Tutorial disk, you will be able to use the disk when you need operating system commands. (See the section on

Application later in the chapter.) Adding DOS to the master Symphony Program disk will enable you to use the operating system commands and to access the program automatically.

To copy DOS to the Symphony Program disk, do the following:

1. With the A> on the screen, insert the DOS disk into Drive A.

2. Insert the Symphony Program disk into Drive B.

3. Type SYS B: and press RETURN.

4. When the red light on the disk drive goes off, type COPY COMMAND.COM B: and press RETURN.

5. When the red light goes off, indicating that copying is complete, remove the Symphony program disk from Drive B.

At this point, you are ready to prepare the Symphony disks so that they can be used with your equipment.

Installing Drivers

You will need to install driver programs to tailor Symphony for your particular computer system. The drivers are programs that reside in files on the Install Library disk. These files store information about your specific system—the display, printer, plotter, modem, and so on. You can create one or many driver files, depending on your needs. If, for example, you want to run Symphony on an IBM Personal Computer that is capable of displaying graphics in multicolor, and also run the program on a Compaq displaying graphics and text in one color, then two separate driver files will enable you to run Symphony on both computers whenever you like.

When you make your driver selection, review carefully the options. Whether or not your system can display graphs and text at the same time, and in color, depends on a number of factors—the type of monitor(s) you will be using, color cards, etc.

Some equipment selections enable you to view text and graphics only at different times on the screen—what Lotus calls toggle mode.

An IBM color monitor with a color card, for example, will display graphs and text in color, but not at the same time. Some dual monitor combinations, on the other hand, enable you to view color graphs on one screen and text on the other at the same time (dual mode). Finally, other equipment options permit you to view simultaneously both graphs in single color and text on the screen (shared mode).

You will notice many figures in this book displaying both graphs and text (spreadsheets, data base, and documents) on the same screen. These figures were shot from equipment capable of displaying both but only in single color—an example of shared mode. You will notice also a few figures displaying graphs in color. These graphs were shot from equipment capable of displaying graphs in color, but not displaying color graphs and text simultaneously—an example of toggle mode.

Before you begin to run the Install program, prepare a list of the kinds of equipment you will be using. First, Symphony has to know what kind of display hardware you have. For example, a color monitor uses graphics control characters that are different from those for a monochrome monitor equipped with a Hercules Graphics Card that displays regular black-and-white graphs. Second, Symphony needs to know what kind of printer you have. Third, Symphony will ask you to indicate the graphics printer or plotter you will be using, if any. And finally, Symphony needs information about your modem so that you can use the Symphony communications feature. A complete list of driver options is presented in figures 2.1A and 2.1B.

Although not affected by the kind of equipment you are using, one other piece of information for setting drivers should be supplied: the type of data sort order.

Two data sort options are available:

1. English-like language—numbers first

2. English-like language—numbers last

The data sort selection regulates whether Symphony sorts data base entries beginning with numbers before (selection 1) or after (selection 2) it sorts entries beginning with letters. For example, consider a data base containing inventory codes—some beginning

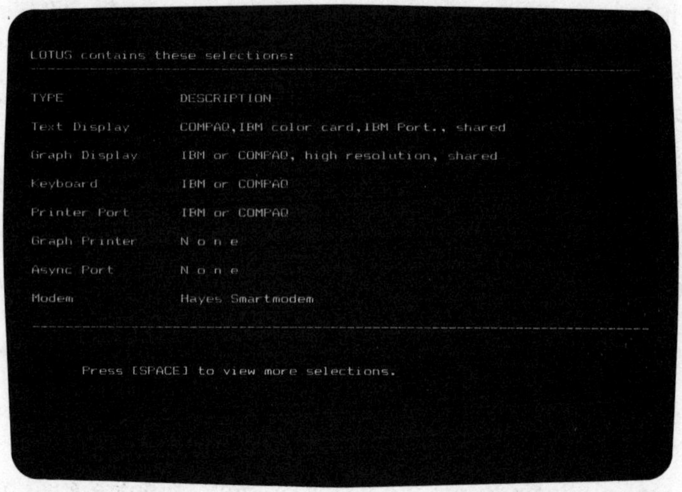

```
LOTUS contains these selections:
----------------------------------------------------------------
TYPE              DESCRIPTION

Text Display      COMPAQ,IBM color card,IBM Port., shared

Graph Display     IBM or COMPAQ, high resolution, shared

Keyboard          IBM or COMPAQ

Printer Port      IBM or COMPAQ

Graph Printer     N o n e

Async Port        N o n e

Modem             Hayes Smartmodem
----------------------------------------------------------------

     Press [SPACE] to view more selections.
```

Fig. 2.1A.

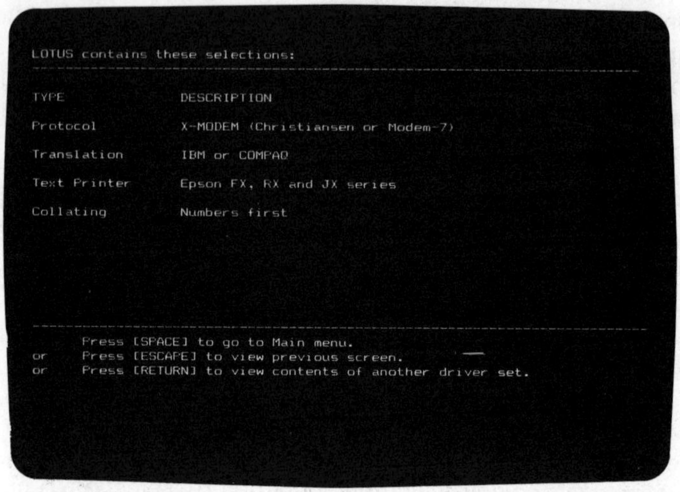

```
LOTUS contains these selections:
----------------------------------------------------------------
TYPE              DESCRIPTION

Protocol          X-MODEM (Christiansen or Modem-7)

Translation       IBM or COMPAQ

Text Printer      Epson FX, RX and JX series

Collating         Numbers first


----------------------------------------------------------------
       Press [SPACE] to go to Main menu.
or     Press [ESCAPE] to view previous screen.        —
or     Press [RETURN] to view contents of another driver set.
```

Fig. 2.1B.

with numbers, others beginning with letters. Symphony will sort those beginning with numbers first and then those with letters, if you have selected 1 for your driver set.

To set drivers, you will need to consider not only the kinds of equipment required to run Symphony, but also the optional equipment that can be used. As mentioned in Chapter 1, the required hardware for running Symphony is the following:

- The IBM Personal Computer, the IBM PC/XT, or the Compaq Personal Computer, with at least 320 kilobytes (320K) of RAM required for each

- One double-sided, double-density floppy disk drive and hard disk or two double-sided, double-density disk drives

- A monochrome monitor or a graphics monitor (single color or multicolor)

The following optional equipment will enable you to use all of Symphony's features:

- Printer (parallel or serial port)
- Modem or acoustic coupler
- Additional monitor
- Add-on memory board

New
with
Symphony

With Symphony's window capability a dual monitor system will enhance your ability to integrate Symphony's environments (spreadsheet, word processing, graphics, data management, and communications). An add-on memory board will enable you to use more of Symphony's worksheet area.

When installing drivers, you must provide information for all required equipment, but you can select only the sections for the optional equipment you will be using. If, for example, you are not going to use a plotter or modem, the Symphony Install program allows you to skip the steps for adding these pieces of equipment to the driver set. Following is the procedure for setting drivers to run Symphony with your equipment:

1. Load the Install Program disk. Then at the prompt, type *Install*. (A> is the prompt for systems with two disk

drives, and C> is the prompt for hard disk drive systems.)

2.   Begin the Install process. If you have a system with two disk drives, you must replace the Install Program disk with the Install Library disk when Symphony gives you the signal to do so. If you have a hard disk drive system, type 1 when the Install menu appears; 1 is the option for creating a driver. (You can also edit a driver that you have previously created or ask for a display of selections in a previously created driver.)

3.   Follow the step-by-step directions that appear on the screen for creating and naming the driver. If you are creating only one driver, you may use the default driver name "Lotus". If you are creating two or more drivers, you must name each driver.

4.   Follow the directions for placing the driver(s) on the master Symphony Program disk, the backup copy of the Help and Tutorial disk, and the backup copy of the PrintGraph disk. If you need to return at any time to the main Install menu, press Esc or Ctrl-C.

Once you have completed installing your Symphony disks, they should be ready to run with your equipment.

If Your Symphony Program Disk Is Lost or Destroyed

As mentioned above, Lotus provides a recovery procedure in case your master Symphony Program disk is lost or destroyed. If this does occur, then following the procedure outlined below will enable you to continue using the program.

If you have a hard disk drive system, then you can use your master Help and Tutorial disk to access the program.

If you have a system with two disk drives, then you should follow this procedure:

1. Begin your computer with DOS, and when the A> appears, remove your DOS disk.

2. Place the backup copy of the Symphony Program disk in drive A.

3. Place the master Help and Tutorial disk in drive B.

4. Type B:ERASE *.* and press RETURN.

5. When the system asks whether you want to proceed, type Y and press RETURN.

6. When the A> reappears, type COPY *.* B: and press RETURN.

7. Install driver sets on the Help and Tutorial disk by following the directions in the Installing Drivers section above.

The backup copy of the Symphony Program disk will now be added to the Help and Tutorial disk, making it possible for you to use it for accessing the program. For information on replacing your Symphony Program disk, refer to the Customer Assurance Plan that comes with the Symphony disks.

Configuring the Printer and the Data Disk

After drivers are installed, the configuration must be set for the printer and the default drive for disk storage. Symphony helps in this process by saving certain default settings from session to session. Lotus provides a default configuration for all settings, but you will want to change some of its choices.

The actual settings for the printer are accessed by entering the Configuration Printer command in the SERVICES menu, which is one of three types of Symphony menus. (Symphony menus and the Configuration command are discussed later in the chapter; printer settings are discussed in Chapter 8.) The setting for the default drive for disk storage is accessed by entering the Configuration File command in the SERVICES menu. The default drive for transferring data to and from disk storage is drive B. This drive assignment may have to be changed if you have a hard disk system.

Preparing Data Disks

The final step in getting started in Symphony is preparing data disks. For those who are unfamiliar with preparing blank disks, these disks must all be properly formatted before they can be used to store the data entered in worksheets. Symphony enables you to initialize a blank disk without having to exit from the program. After you have installed DOS on your Symphony Program and Help and Tutorial disks, you can then format a disk by using the Application add-in feature (discussed later in the chapter).

The Symphony Menus

New with Symphony

Possibly the best way to begin learning the Symphony program is by examining the menu system, understanding the various levels, and being aware of the location of certain commands and operations. Four main menus make up the Symphony menu system: the ACCESS SYSTEM menu, the SERVICES menu, the command MENU system, and the window TYPE menu. (See fig. 2.2 for locations of menu keys on the IBM PC and compatibles.)

Here's how you retrieve any of the four menus:

- To retrieve the ACCESS SYSTEM, you must type *ACCESS* (plus the name of the driver if you are not using the default drive "Lotus"). This operation is necessary only if you have not configured your Symphony Program disk to retrieve the ACCESS SYSTEM automatically.

- To retrieve the SERVICES menu, you press the SERVICES key (F9 on the IBM PC and compatibles).

- To retrieve the command MENU for each application (SHEET, DOC, FORM, GRAPH, and COMM), you press the MENU key (F10).

- To retrieve the window TYPE menu, you press the TYPE key (Alt + F10).

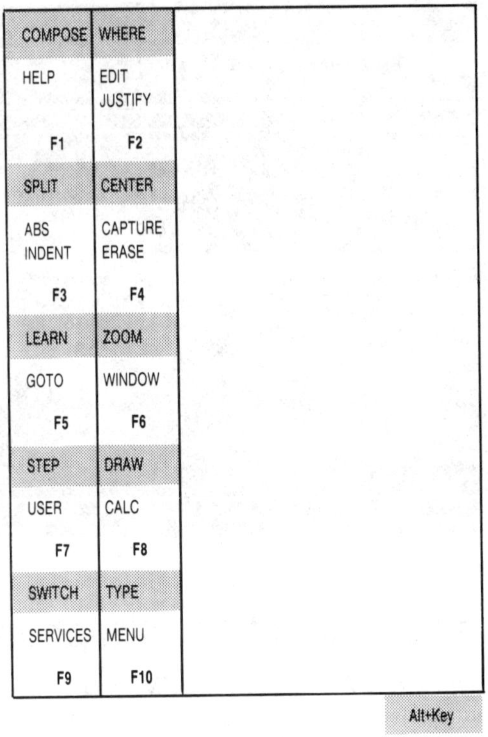

COMPOSE	WHERE
HELP	EDIT JUSTIFY
F1	F2
SPLIT	CENTER
ABS INDENT	CAPTURE ERASE
F3	F4
LEARN	ZOOM
GOTO	WINDOW
F5	F6
STEP	DRAW
USER	CALC
F7	F8
SWITCH	TYPE
SERVICES	MENU
F9	F10

Alt+Key

Fig. 2.2.

Throughout the book, whenever directions are provided for completing an operation, references are to the names of menus instead of the corresponding function keys. For example, "Press SERVICES" means to press the F9 key on the IBM PC and compatibles.

The Symphony ACCESS SYSTEM

Like 1-2-3, Symphony contains a main access menu that provides options for accessing programs on the separate Symphony disks. (See fig. 2.3.) With the ACCESS SYSTEM you can move back and forth between Symphony and the PrintGraph and Translate programs.

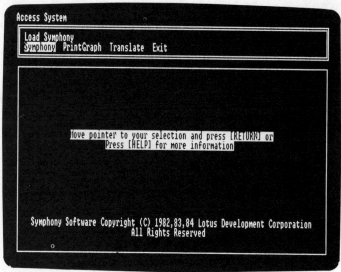

Fig. 2.3.

Entering and Exiting from Symphony

To enter the Symphony ACCESS SYSTEM, you must first load the System disk into drive A. If you are using a system with two disk drives, you should also load a blank formatted disk into drive B. Then at the A>, type *ACCESS* (or *ACCESS* and the name of the driver if you are not using the default driver name "Lotus"). You can also enter Symphony without going through the Symphony ACCESS SYSTEM if your disk contains the AUTOEXEC.BAT file supplied by Lotus. After a few seconds, the Symphony ACCESS SYSTEM command menu will appear. The following four functions are available in the command menu:

   Symphony PrintGraph Translate Exit

The first option in the Symphony ACCESS SYSTEM menu is to enter Symphony. To do this, either point to Symphony in the menu by using the cursor movement keys (→ ←) and hit RETURN, or type S. (All Symphony menus enable you to select commands either by moving the cursor and pressing RETURN or by typing the first letter of the command.) Several seconds will pass before the next screen appears. (See fig. 2.4.)

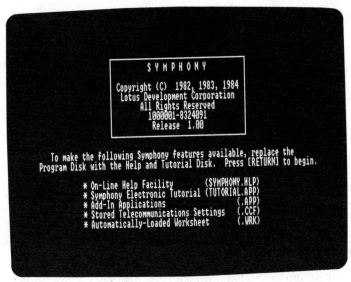

Fig. 2.4.

Whatever way you choose to enter Symphony, you should make sure that the date and time have been entered correctly with the DOS DATE command. Symphony's @NOW function takes the date and time from the entries you make in DOS. If this function is not entered correctly, it will not work properly.

If your system has an internal clock or you don't intend to use the @NOW function, you won't have to worry about entering the time and date. The AUTOEXEC.BAT file automatically prompts you for the date and time.

When the second screen appears, you have five options before continuing to access the main Symphony program. These options include the following:

> On-Line Help Facility
> Symphony Electronic Tutorial
> Add-in Applications
> Communications Settings
> Automatically Loaded Worksheets

To select any of these options, you must replace your Symphony Program disk with the Help and Tutorial disk. If you don't want to use any of these options, press RETURN, and a Symphony window will appear.

To exit the Symphony program, select **E**xit from the SERVICES menu. Afterward, Symphony will remind you to save your work if you haven't done so beforehand. If you entered Symphony from the ACCESS SYSTEM, **E**xit will return you to it. To exit from the ACCESS SYSTEM, you also select **E**xit from the command menu.

PrintGraph

The **P**rintGraph option in the ACCESS SYSTEM menu initiates the PrintGraph program for printing graph files. When you choose this option, the PrintGraph disk must be loaded before you can run the program. (See Chapter 10 for a detailed discussion of the PrintGraph program.)

As with other programs, you can go directly to the PrintGraph program without going through the Symphony ACCESS SYSTEM. Type *pgraph* at the operating system prompt. If the driver name is not "Lotus," you must enter the driver name after you enter *pgraph*.

Translate

The **T**ranslate option accesses the Translation utility. This utility provides a link between Symphony and outside programs, including VisiCalc and dBASE II. The Translation utility is located on the Install Program disk, and like the PrintGraph program, the Translation utility can be accessed directly from the operating system prompt. To access the program from the system prompt, type *Trans* and press RETURN. If the name of your driver is not "Lotus," you must type *Trans* and the driver name. (The Translation utility is discussed in detail in Chapter 6.)

SERVICES

Once you have selected the main Symphony program, three types of command menus are available for retrieving commands and performing operations: SERVICES, MENU, and TYPE. To select a command from any menu, you can either move the cursor to the

New
with
Symphony

selection and press RETURN, or you can type the first letter of the command. If you want to move out of a command menu completely, press Ctrl-Break. To move back to a prior command-menu level, press Esc.

If you have used 1-2-3 and become familiar with its menu structure, you will find the Symphony menu structure quite different. You should be aware of the following differences in the two menu structures. (See Appendix C for a comparison of 1-2-3 and Symphony commands.)

Whereas 1-2-3's ACCESS SYSTEM contains File-Manager and Disk-Manager, Symphony's file and disk operations are available through the Application add-in feature of the SERVICES menu. Remember that SERVICES is one of the three menus you can retrieve after you enter the Symphony program.

Because of Symphony's added features, its menu structure is, as expected, more complex than 1-2-3's. Once you access 1-2-3's main program, all spreadsheet, data management, and graphics operations are available in this main menu. In Symphony, however, a SERVICES menu contains the primary operations relating to all applications: spreadsheet, data management, graphics, word processing, and communications.

Then each application has its own command menu. You will also find that some 1-2-3 commands, which are subheadings under other commands, are first-level commands in Symphony. In 1-2-3, for example, the Erase command is located within the Range command menu. But in Symphony the Erase command is separate from Range and located at the same level as the Range command menu. (Again, see Appendix C for a listing of the differences between the commands in 1-2-3 and Symphony.)

Within the SERVICES and MENU menus you will find a number of settings sheets. (See fig. 2.5 and also the section on Settings Sheets.) Some 1-2-3 operations are located within Symphony's settings sheets system.

The SERVICES menu provides the major operations controlling the five Symphony environments. It also provides configuration, special settings, and add-in program options. This menu, which contains

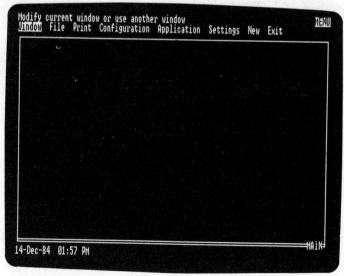

```
Database, Criterion, Output ranges                          MENU
Basic Form Underscores Sort-Keys Report One-Record Name Cancel Quit
Basic Ranges                        Report Ranges
  Database:                           Main:
  Criterion:                          Above:
  Output:                             Below:
Form Ranges                           Type        Single
  Entry:                                Entry list:
  Definition:                           Input cell:
Underscores:     Yes                  One-Record:   No
Sort-Keys
  1st-Key:              2nd-Key:              3rd-Key:
    Order:                 Order:                Order:
                                           Database Settings: MAIN

Query Settings
```

Fig. 2.5.

the major commands operating in all windows (fig. 2.6), can be
retrieved while you are working in any window.

```
Modify current window or use another window                MENU
Window File Print Configuration Application Settings New Exit





14-Dec-84  01:57 PM                                        MAIN
```

Fig. 2.6.

The first selection in the SERVICES menu is **W**indow. It enables you to retrieve a window already created; create and name new windows; delete windows; change window size, location, or shape; hide, isolate or expose windows; or split one window into two or four. The **F**ile selection contains commands for saving, retrieving, and deleting files, as well as commands for special file operations, such as copying files (or parts of files) into worksheets. (See Chapter 6 on File Operations.) The **P**rint selection provides the commands for printing all Symphony documents except graphs. **C**onfiguration allows you to change default settings.

Another selection, **A**pplication, lets you add-in programs and use them when needed. For example, adding DOS through **A**pplication will enable you to perform such operations as copying or formatting disks without having to exit from the Symphony program.

A **S**ettings selection displays and enables you to change operations for (1) creating and using macros, (2) locking a worksheet, (3) protecting cells in a worksheet, and (4) automatically loading a communications file. The final two commands in the SERVICES menu, **N**ew and **E**xit, let you create a new worksheet (after you have saved the current one) and exit from Symphony.

New
with
Symphony

Window

One of the most important selections in the SERVICES menu is **W**indow. As mentioned in Chapter 1, Symphony consists of five applications: spreadsheet, word processing, data management, graphics, and communications. Each of these operates through the window system. At any time you may shift from one type of window to another by pressing the TYPE key (Alt + F10), then selecting the type of window you want. For example, if you wish to shift from working in a spreadsheet window to working in a word-processing window, you select DOC; if you wish to work in the data forms window, you select FORM; and so on. (See the section on Function Keys Working in All Windows for a detailed explanation of specific **W**indow commands.)

If you are an experienced 1-2-3 user, you will notice that Symphony's window capability is probably the feature that most distinguishes Symphony from 1-2-3. With Symphony's window capa-

bility, you can move among any of the five components—spreadsheet, word processing, data management, graphics, and communications—and view different parts of the same worksheet. (See
fig. 2.7.)

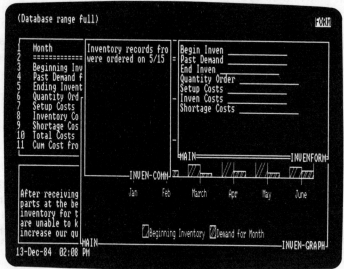

Fig. 2.7.

Through the SERVICES **W**indow command menu, you will be able to
change the type of window, create new windows, change the size
and shape of windows, split windows horizontally and vertically,
and easily change the number of windows on the screen at any one
time. Included also are capabilities for restricting a SHEET or DOC
window to a specific range in the worksheet, changing the type
of border around a window, and automatically redisplaying a
worksheet after changes. Both the function keys and the **W**indow
menu from the SERVICES menu make possible the many window
operations.

Windows and Files

Once you begin using Symphony's window feature, you will see that
it enables you to organize a single file into many different parts,

displaying information in different forms. With the Symphony window feature, you have the capability of creating multiple windows of different types or shifting easily from one type of window to another.

If, for example, your file contains a spreadsheet beginning at cell A1 and ending at cell M90, and a data base beginning at cell AA1 and ending at cell AT300, you can easily display sections of both the spreadsheet and the data base in two separate windows. If you wish to view a graph that analyzes the spreadsheet data, a third window can be added to your screen. Finally, if you want to use the information from your spreadsheet, data base, and graph to prepare a report, you can create a fourth window. (See fig. 2.7.)

All these windows are created and can be stored within the same file. Although you may be writing a report in a separate window, the text is entered into the same worksheet file in which you created your spreadsheet and data base. Changes that you make in one window can affect all other windows, unless you have set restrict ranges. (See the section on restricting ranges.) When you are working within a window, make sure that different spreadsheets, data bases, and texts are far enough away from each other so that one doesn't erase part of another or interfere with it. Remember also that when you initiate the **File S**ave command, windows will be saved within a file as they appear on the screen. Windows, like data, can be stored within individual files, unless you delete the windows by using the **W**indow **D**elete command.

You can also create two or more separate screens and view data from different files. If you want to view data from different files, use the **File C**ombine command to pull data from one file into another. (See Chapter 6.)

New
with
Symphony

Function Keys for Window Operations

Five function keys control special window operations, such as changing the type, rotating windows, moving the cursor from one window to another, zooming from a small-screen window to a full-screen window, and redrawing a window. (See pages 84-85.)

The *Window Menu*

*New
with
Symphony*

The **W**indow menu, like other primary menus from the SERVICES menu, contains numerous levels that require different types of responses. (See fig. 2.8.) And like other menus, the **W**indow menu contains a settings sheet, which indicates the current settings for the present window: the name, the type, the range for which pointer movement and data entry are restricted, the display of borders, and the redisplay of a window after spreadsheet changes are made. In addition to the **S**ettings command, other commands control creating, retrieving, and deleting windows; removing and redisplaying windows; changing the size and position of windows; and dividing a window into two or four parts.

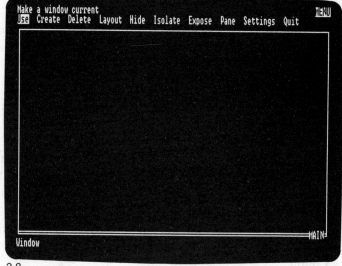

Fig. 2.8.

Creating, Using, and Deleting Windows

*New
with
Symphony*

Within the **C**onfiguration selection of the SERVICES menu, both window type and name are preset. When you first enter Symphony, you will find that an initial window type and name have been set: SHEET (type) and MAIN (name). You can change these settings if you wish, but an initial window type and name must be set at all times. If, for example, you find yourself using the FORM window more frequently than the SHEET window, you can change the **C**onfiguration setting to FORM. Then every time you enter Symphony, a FORM window will appear as the first one.

For creating new windows, Symphony provides two procedures. In the first procedure, you (1) select **C**reate from the **W**indow menu, (2) provide a name for the new window, (3) select the window type (SHEET, DOC, GRAPH, FORM, or COMM), (4) identify the size and shape of the new window, and (5) make changes in the **W**indow settings sheet.

The second procedure is to select **P**ane from the **W**indow menu and to indicate the type of split—vertical, horizontal, or both. Symphony will automatically name each window and create each one in the same size and shape. If you wish to change the type and / or name of a window, select **S**ettings; if you wish to change the size and shape of the window, select **L**ayout.

To use windows you have previously created, select the **U**se command from the **W**indow menu, then indicate which window you want displayed on screen. When you retrieve another window, the cursor moves from the current window to the window just retrieved. To return the cursor to the other window, press the Window key (F6). This function key will also retrieve previously created windows and display multiple windows on the screen at the same time. The Switch key (Alt + F9), on the other hand, will switch a current window type, such as DOC, to a previous window type, such as SHEET.

To delete windows, select the **W**indow **D**elete command. If you want to remove a window from the screen only temporarily, use the **W**indow **H**ide command.

Removing and Redisplaying Windows

*New
with
Symphony*

Sometimes you may want to create three or four windows and be able to use any of them when needed, but also have access at times to a full screen. Three commands—**H**ide, **I**solate, and **E**xpose—and a function key enable you to remove any or all windows from the screen and to expand a single window to full-screen size. Using **H**ide and **I**solate does not delete a window; you can at any time redisplay the window on screen. If you use the **H**ide and **I**solate

commands and then save your file, all previously created windows
remain when you retrieve the file later. As illustrated in figures 2.9A

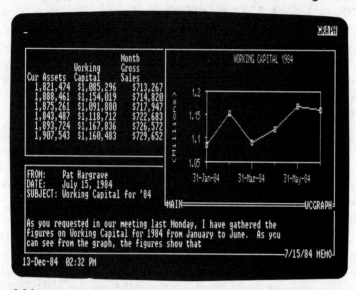

Fig. 2.9A.

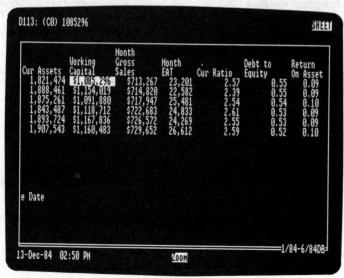

Fig. 2.9B.

and 2.9B, you can easily change from a screen containing three or four windows to a screen with one window expanded to full-screen size, then redisplay all windows again. If you remove all but your main window, use the Zoom key (Alt + F6) to expand the remaining window to full-screen size.

<table>
<tr><td>

*New
with
Symphony*
</td><td>

Changing Window Size, Shape, and Position

In addition to using the Zoom key (Alt + F6) to expand a window, you can use the **W**indow **L**ayout command to expand or decrease the size of any window, as well as regulate its shape and position on the screen. When you select **W**indow **L**ayout, you can position the window anywhere on the screen by anchoring the cursor at a spot that will become one of the four corners of the new window.

Position the cursor in any corner of the window by pressing either the period (.) or Tab key. (Pressing Home will move the cursor to the top left corner of the current window.) Next, highlight the size and shape of the screen you want, using the cursor-movement and PgUp and PgDn keys. (See fig. 2.10.) Then press RETURN. If you decide to change the position of a window but want to retain the
</td></tr>
</table>

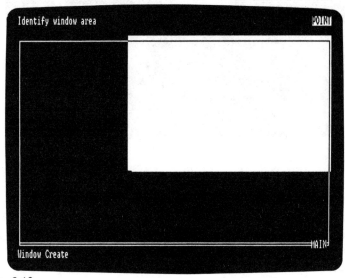

Fig. 2.10.

current size and shape, select **W**indow **L**ayout, press the Scroll Lock key, and move the cursor.

As mentioned earlier, one quick way to create multiple windows is by using the **W**indow **P**ane command. This command enables you to divide an existing window into two parts, horizontally or vertically, or into four windows. (See fig. 2.11.) After you have created two or four windows with the **W**indow **P**ane command, you can then change position, shape, and size of any of the windows. If window size or location causes one window to overlap another, the window you are currently working in will remain on top of the other one until you move to work in another window. That window will then cycle to the top of the stack.

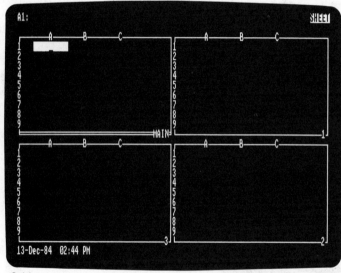

Fig. 2.11.

Restricting Ranges in Windows

Restricting your work area within a SHEET, DOC, FORM, or COMM window is an important step in creating windows for two reasons. First, restricting the area in which you can enter text in a DOC window or data in a SHEET window will prevent you from accidentally erasing or changing work in another part of the work-

New with Symphony

sheet. Second, restricting the work area can speed up the operation of certain commands. Restricting your work area is particularly important when you are working within a DOC window on a worksheet containing spreadsheet data, because changes in the DOC window can affect the spreadsheet.

To restrict a window area, you (1) press the SERVICES key; (2) select **W**indow, then **S**ettings; (3) select **R**estrict; (4) select **W**indow if you are going to use only the space in the current window, but select **R**ange if your work area will be larger than the current window; (5) select **Q**uit to enter the restrict range; and (6) then select **Q**uit once more to return to the DOC mode. Note that when you select **R**ange, you also must indicate the area either by typing the beginning and end points or by moving the cursor.

*New
with
Symphony*

Taking Advantage of Symphony's Window Feature

After you begin using Symphony's window feature, you will find the possibilities limitless for integrating various types of windows onto one screen. Creating windows will allow you to compare and analyze spreadsheet data from different areas of the worksheet. Windows will enable you to write memos and short reports, while at the same time viewing spreadsheets and data bases. And with windows, you will be able not only to see data displayed in graphs, but also to watch graphs change as you change data.

File

The **F**ile menu in Symphony is very much like 1-2-3's. As in 1-2-3, Symphony contains **F**ile **S**ave, **R**etrieve, **C**ombine, **X**tract, **E**rase, **L**ist, **I**mport, and **D**irectory selections. And Symphony includes two additional selections: **B**ytes and **T**able. **B**ytes indicates the available disk space on the current drive. (In 1-2-3 the **W**orksheet **S**tatus selection provides this information.) The **T**able selection creates in a specified range of the worksheet a table with information on files in the specified directory. This information includes file names and extensions, the date and time that each file was last changed, and the number of bytes for each file. (For more information on the Symphony **F**ile menu, see Chapter 6 on File Operations.)

Print

Except for printing graphs, the **P**rint menu is used to print all other documents—spreadsheets, data bases, and documents created in the word-processing environment. Although the print settings in 1-2-3 are included in Symphony, its **P**rint menu is easier to understand and use. The Symphony **P**rint menu contains a settings sheet (fig. 2.12) that displays print options and either default or changed settings. Because the settings sheet is displayed as soon as you retrieve the **P**rint menu, you can tell immediately what settings need to be changed before saving a print file or printing your report.

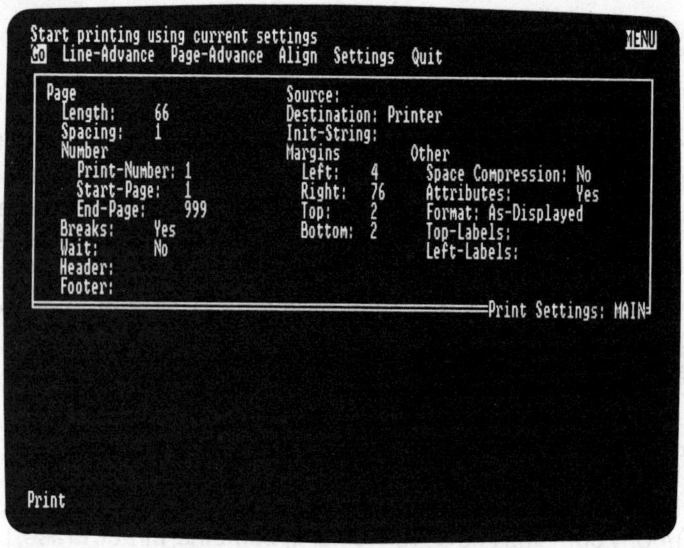

```
Start printing using current settings                              MENU
Go  Line-Advance  Page-Advance  Align  Settings  Quit

Page                        Source:
  Length:      66            Destination: Printer
  Spacing:      1            Init-String:
  Number                    Margins        Other
    Print-Number: 1           Left:    4    Space Compression: No
    Start-Page:   1           Right:  76    Attributes:       Yes
    End-Page:   999           Top:     2    Format: As-Displayed
  Breaks:      Yes            Bottom:  2    Top-Labels:
  Wait:         No                          Left-Labels:
  Header:
  Footer:
                                            ======Print Settings: MAIN




Print
```

Fig. 2.12.

Although the **P**rint settings sheet in Symphony is an improvement over the **P**rint command structure of 1-2-3, some print commands require more keystrokes than they do in 1-2-3. For example, the command for specifying a range to print is the first option in 1-2-3; the same command in Symphony requires that you first choose **S**ettings on the **P**rint command menu, then **S**ource, and then **R**ange.

The Symphony **P**rint command menu also differs from 1-2-3's because Symphony's **P**rint selections include settings for printing documents created in the word-processing environment. One other difference is that Symphony allows you to name and save settings sheets so that you won't have to reset a sheet every time you need to change margins, headings, and so on. (See Chapter 8, Printing Reports, for specific explanations of commands.)

*New
with
Symphony*

Configuration

Configuration, the fourth selection from the SERVICES menu, provides an easy way for viewing and changing default settings. (See fig. 2.13.) Configuration settings affect numerous operations, from changing the type of window that initially appears after you access Symphony to changing the size of margins for printing reports. When you display the configuration settings for the first time

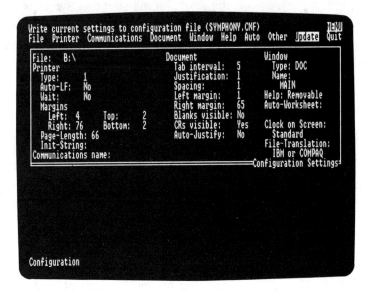

Fig. 2.13.

(press F9 and select **C**onfiguration), you will see the default settings provided by Lotus. You can easily change any setting by selecting the appropriate category in the menu, entering the change(s), and then selecting **U**pdate to store the new setting.

Symphony stores configuration settings in a configuration file named SYMPHONY.CNF. Whenever you make a change in these settings, you have the option of updating the configuration file. To update the file, you select **U**pdate from the **C**onfiguration menu after you have entered all the changes you want to make. Whenever you select **U**pdate, Symphony stores all current settings in the file. If you do not select **U**pdate, all newly entered settings will be in effect only until the end of your current work session, or until you exit from the Symphony program.

Throughout the remaining chapters of the book, various configuration settings are referred to. Following are the types of settings you can enter in **C**onfiguration:

File	Stores the disk drive and current directory for the start of a Symphony session. (See Chapter 6.)
Printer	Contains the configuration settings for the type of printer, paper advance, pause between printing pages, margins, page length, and initialization string. (See Chapter 8.)
Communications	Indicates which communications configuration file should be loaded at the beginning of a session; also used to cancel an existing file. (See Chapter 12.)
Document	Stores default format settings for Symphony's DOC (word-processing) environment. These default settings are for tabs, paragraph justification, spacing, margins, display of hard spaces and carriage returns, and automatic justification of paragraphs. (See Chapter 8.)

Window	Controls what window type and name are first displayed when you begin a Symphony session or create a new worksheet file by selecting SERVICES **N**ew. (See the section earlier in the chapter on Creating, Using, and Deleting Windows.)
Help	Controls whether the Symphony Help file remains open throughout a session (**I**nstant), or opens only when you press the Help key and closes once you return to Symphony (**R**emovable)
Auto	Enables you to load automatically a worksheet file as soon as you begin a Symphony session
Other	Contains the default settings for (1) **C**lock, which regulates the format for date and time, appearing in the bottom left corner of your screen; (2) **F**ile-Translation, which regulates character-code translation tables; (3) International, which regulates punctuation in values and arguments in functions; and in Currency, Date, and Time formats (see Chapter 4); and (4) **A**pplication, which regulates automatically loaded add-in programs
Update	Updates the Symphony configuration file (.CNF) to include any changes in settings

Although the SERVICES **C**onfiguration settings provide global default settings, you can override many of these settings within the specific type of window in which you are working. Settings sheets in the SHEET, DOC, GRAPH, FORM, and COMM environments enable you to override the default settings. (See the section on Settings Sheets.)

Application

*New
with
Symphony*

The **A**pplication selection in the SERVICES menu allows you to add-in outside programs and retrieve and use those programs without leaving Symphony. The **A**pplication selection enhances Symphony in two ways. First, the selection enables you to use operating system commands, as well as the tutorial, without having to leave Symphony. Second, the **A**pplication selection provides the flexibility for adding-in other programs, such as a spelling checker.

Four **A**pplication commands control the loading and unloading of add-in programs: **A**ttach, **D**etach, **I**nvoke, and **C**lear. The **A**pplication **A**ttach command loads an add-in program into main memory, except when you have entered add-in programs into the **C**onfiguration **O**ther **A**pplication setting of the SERVICES menu. In that case the add-in program(s) will automatically load when you select **A**pplication. Whenever you add-in a program, Symphony adds the file extension .APP when the program is attached.

After a program is loaded into main memory (either automatically or through **A**ttach), you select **I**nvoke. This command activates the program so that you can begin to use it. **D**etach and **C**lear are necessary when you need to free up the memory space being used by add-in programs. **D**etach unloads a single add-in program, and **C**lear unloads all add-in programs, completely freeing the memory space for add-ins.

The function of the **A**pplication selection is illustrated in a later section on Accessing the Tutorial. There the procedure is described for using Symphony's tutorial: the tutorial is accessed only when you enter the main Symphony program, select **A**pplication from the SERVICES menu, select **A**ttach to load the tutorial into memory, and then select **I**nvoke to begin the tutorial. If you are using a system with two disk drives, this procedure involves changing disks twice. However, the **A**pplication feature enables you to move back and forth between Symphony's Tutorial Lessons and the Symphony Program disks. This shifting is a great advantage if you want to complete a lesson in the tutorial and then return to the Symphony program to practice a few operations on your own. Other examples of using **A**pplication are provided in Chapter 6, File Operations.

Settings

The **S**ettings selection indicates the amount of memory available as you work within the Symphony program and permits you to enter special global settings. The following chapters present specific applications of the **S**ettings options. Provided here, however, is a brief description of each selection. The **S**ettings selection, for example, allows you to change and save special settings for creating and executing macros. (See Chapter 13 on keyboard macros.) To create keyboard macros automatically, you select **L**earn. To execute a macro automatically at the beginning of a worksheet, you select **A**uto-Execute.

Settings also enables you to secure a worksheet so that the only way to view and change it is by entering a password that you have created. (See Chapter 4 on SHEET Window Commands.) If you want to prevent someone else from viewing and changing a worksheet, you use the **S**ecurity selection in combination with the **G**lobal-Protection, the **R**ange **P**rotect, and **F**ormat **O**ther **H**idden commands of the SHEET menu. Another type of security is provided by **S**ettings **G**lobal-Protection for protecting ranges in the worksheet. (See Chapter 4.) Finally, through the SERVICES **S**ettings selection, you can automatically load a communications configuration file. (Communications is discussed in Chapter 12.)

New

If you finish working in a worksheet and want to begin a new one, as well as a new file, you select **N**ew from the SERVICES menu. Be certain that you save your current worksheet before selecting **N**ew. Once you have selected **N**ew, you will be asked whether you want to erase everything. The current worksheet data will be lost, unless you first use the **F**ile **S**ave command.

Exit

The **E**xit selection will return you to the main Symphony ACCESS SYSTEM. Here again, you need to make sure that you have saved your work before exiting. Symphony does not automatically save your file, so you must select **F**ile **S**ave before exiting the program.

MENU

*New
with
Symphony*

Although the SERVICES menu is used for all windows and remains the same no matter which one you are working in, the second kind of menu, the command MENU, changes with each type of window. (See fig. 2.14.) The primary command MENU for each window can be retrieved by pressing the F10 function key. (When working within a SHEET window, you can retrieve the command MENU either by pressing the F10 function key or by pressing the / key in the lower right corner of the alphanumeric keyboard.)

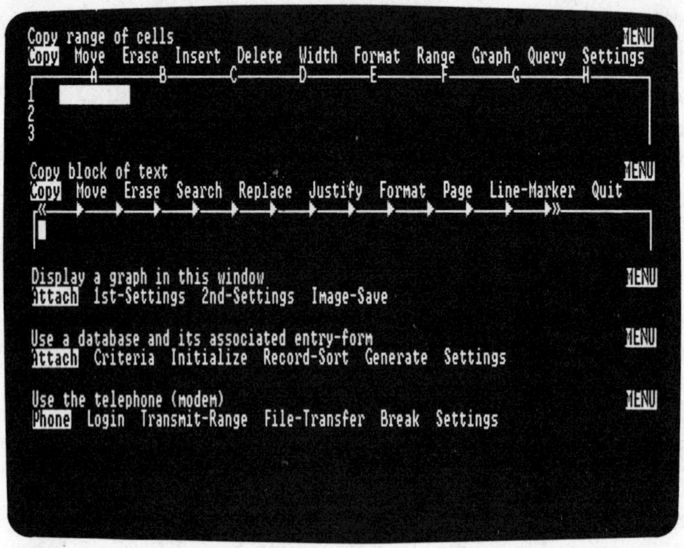

```
Copy range of cells                                              MENU
Copy  Move  Erase  Insert  Delete  Width  Format  Range  Graph  Query  Settings
      A       B        C        D      E       F      G        H
1
2
3

Copy block of text                                              MENU
Copy  Move  Erase  Search  Replace  Justify  Format  Page  Line-Marker  Quit


Display a graph in this window                                  MENU
Attach  1st-Settings  2nd-Settings  Image-Save

Use a database and its associated entry-form                    MENU
Attach  Criteria  Initialize  Record-Sort  Generate  Settings

Use the telephone (modem)                                       MENU
Phone  Login  Transmit-Range  File-Transfer  Break  Settings
```

Fig. 2.14.

Settings Sheets

*New
with
Symphony*

In both the SERVICES menu and the command MENU, you will find settings sheets. (See fig. 2.15.) These settings sheets enable you to store settings for everything from **G**lobal-Protection in a worksheet to **S**pacing settings in a word-processing work area.

Except for the DOC command MENU, all command menus contain settings sheets on the first command line. **S**ettings is the final selection in the SHEET, FORM, and COMM menus; **S**ettings is the

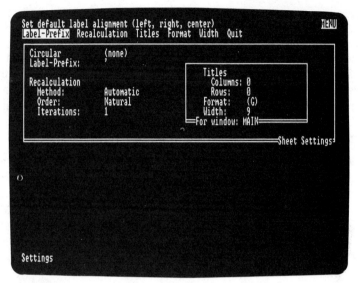

Fig. 2.15.

second and third selection in the GRAPH menu. Special settings sheets, however, are located within first-level commands. For example, the SHEET **G**raph command contains two settings sheets, the SHEET **Q**uery command contains one, and the DOC **F**ormat command contains one.

If you are a 1-2-3 user, be aware that some 1-2-3 commands now operate within Symphony settings sheets. If, for instance, you want to set horizontal or vertical titles in a worksheet, you will find **T**itles within the SHEET **S**ettings window. In addition, numerous kinds of DOC format changes are entered through the **F**ormat **S**ettings sheet, including changes in tabs, margins, and spacing.

1-2-3 users will find that Symphony settings sheets provide two major advantages. Unlike 1-2-3, in which special settings can exist in various locations in the command menus, Symphony displays multiple settings on screen at once. This feature is particularly helpful when you are trying to remember special print or graph settings. Another major advantage of settings sheets is that you can create a catalog of some types of sheets and retrieve them when needed. Such a catalog is useful when you have various kinds of document formats to print, such as memos or letters, each with its own special margin, heading, and spacing formats.

A catalog of print settings sheets can make your job of printing these documents quite easy. As you read other chapters in this book, you will find examples of specific settings sheets and suggestions on how they can be used to make your tasks easier in spreadsheets, word processing, graphics, data management, and communications.

You will find in many cases that settings sheets located in the specific menus of the SHEET, DOC, GRAPH, FORM, and COMM environments contain the same settings as those in the Configuration settings of the SERVICES menu. The effect of SERVICES Configuration settings on settings sheets in the SHEET, DOC, GRAPH, FORM, and COMM windows may be a bit confusing at first. But to help you understand this effect, consider the following example.

Suppose that the SERVICES Configuration settings for the left margin of a DOC window is 5 spaces, and the right margin setting is 65. (See fig. 2.16.) Suppose also that you are just beginning a new worksheet and have created a DOC window for writing a memo. When you create the DOC window, the setting for the left margin is 5 spaces, and for the right margin the setting is 65. If you begin entering text into this DOC window, all lines will be indented 5 spaces on the left, as in figure 2.17.

If, however, you decide to change the default left margin setting to 10 spaces, you do so by changing the settings sheet in the DOC menu. To change the DOC settings sheet, you retrieve the DOC menu by pressing the MENU key (F10), selecting Format from the menu, and then selecting Settings. After you select Settings, Symphony will display a settings sheet containing format settings. If you compare the settings in the settings sheet in SERVICES Configuration Document with the settings in Format Settings, you will see that the settings are the same. After you change the left margin setting in the DOC settings sheet, however, the new setting will override the setting in SERVICES Configuration Document.

When you finish the memo, suppose that you decide to write a letter. You then create another DOC window on the same worksheet.

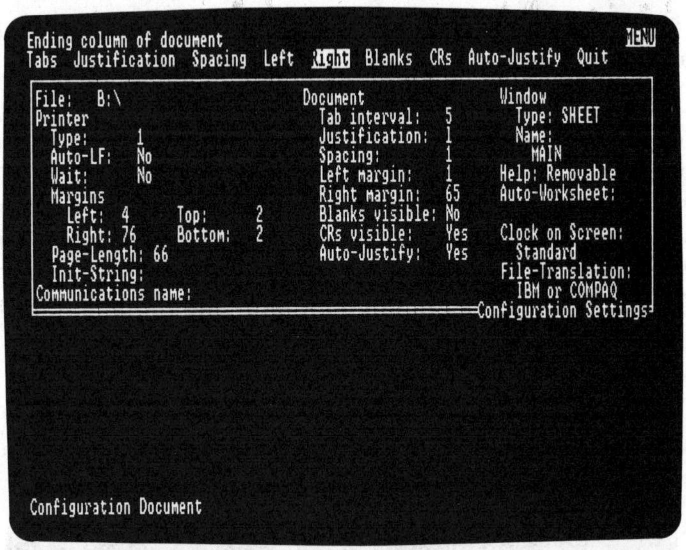

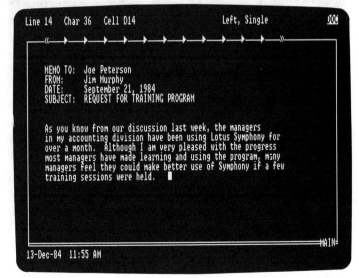

Fig. 2.16.

Fig. 2.17.

When you create the new window, it will inherit the settings sheet of
the previous (memo) window. The DOC settings sheet still overrides

the SERVICES **C**onfiguration settings even though you have shifted to a new window.

It is possible to change the **F**ormat **S**ettings for the second window. When you do, the first DOC window will retain its format settings, and the second DOC window will retain its settings. If a third DOC window is created, it will inherit the format settings of the second window. But once you save the worksheet file and begin a new worksheet in a later session, the SERVICES **C**onfiguration **D**ocument settings will be in effect for the first DOC window in that later session.

TYPE

*New
with
Symphony*

In addition to SERVICES and MENU, one other menu, called TYPE, is part of the Symphony menu tree. (See fig. 2.18.)

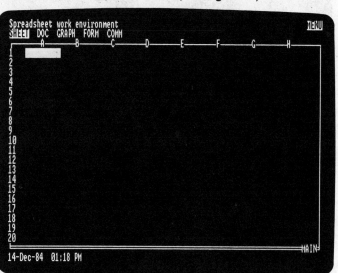

Fig. 2.18.

The TYPE menu enables you to change the window environment in which you are working. To retrieve this menu, you press the TYPE key (Alt + F10), move the cursor to the new window type, and press RETURN (or type the first letter of the window). Besides using the TYPE key to change window type, you can use two other methods.

One is to use the **W**indow **S**ettings **T**ype command. The other method is to press the Switch key (Alt + F9), but only when you have been using different types of windows in one worksheet. The Switch key will return you to a previous window type.

Automatic Exit versus "Sticky Menu"

Like 1-2-3, Symphony contains two ways for exiting from a menu. Many menus return you to the current window mode—SHEET, DOC, GRAPH, FORM, or COMM—once you have finished selecting commands or entered a response. Other menus, however, require that you select **Q**uit in order to exit and return to the current window mode. Selecting **Q**uit, like pressing RETURN, tells Symphony that you have entered a command or changed a setting. To assure yourself that a command has been entered, you need to complete the following:

- Move the cursor to the appropriate selection and press RETURN or type the first letter.

- To change a setting, such as for margins in **P**rint Settings, press RETURN or select **Q**uit after making the change.

Remember that you can move out of a command menu by pressing Esc or Ctrl-Break. If you select either Esc or Ctrl-Break, however, before entering a change in a setting by pressing RETURN or selecting **Q**uit, the change will not be entered.

Suppose, for example, that you are working in Symphony's word-processing environment (a DOC window) and want to change margin settings. You first retrieve the DOC command MENU. Second, you select **F**ormat by moving the cursor to "Format" on the menu and pressing RETURN or by typing **F**. The following menu will appear:

    Create   Edit   Use-Named   Settings

Then you select **S**ettings, again either by moving the cursor and pressing RETURN or by typing **S**. When the next screen appears, you select **L**eft and then enter the new margin when Symphony indicates "Default Left Margin:1". You enter the new margin simply by typing in the number, such as 4, and pressing RETURN. If you were to press Esc or Ctrl-Break at this point instead of RETURN, your new setting would not be entered. Once you have pressed RETURN and Symphony returns to the prior menu (fig. 2.19), you can exit by selecting **Q**uit, pressing Esc three times, or pressing Ctrl-Break.

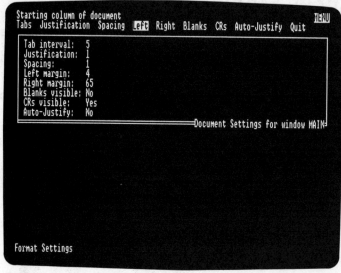

Starting column of document
Tabs Justification Spacing Left Right Blanks CRs Auto-Justify Quit

Tab interval: 5
Justification: 1
Spacing: 1
Left margin: 4
Right margin: 65
Blanks visible: No
CRs visible: Yes
Auto-Justify: No

Document Settings for window MAIN

Format Settings

Fig. 2.19.

The Symphony Keyboard

New with Symphony

Although 1-2-3 made considerable use of all parts of the IBM keyboard, Symphony with its five windows makes even more use of the various keyboard sections, particularly function keys and the Alt and Ctrl keys used in combination with others. The keyboard is divided into three sections: (1) the alphanumeric keyboard in the center, (2) the numeric keypad on the right, and (3) the special-function key section on the left. (See fig. 2.20.)

With this arrangement in mind, you can more easily understand the functions of the Symphony keyboard.

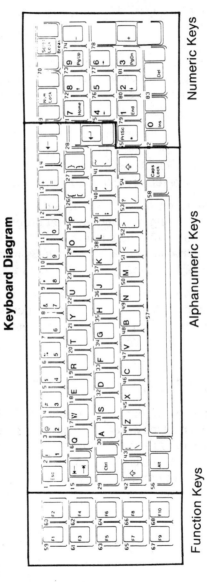

Keyboard Diagram

Function Keys

Alphanumeric Keys

Numeric Keys

Fig. 2.20.

A General Look

If you are familiar with 1-2-3, you will find that the Symphony keyboard is quite different because the functions of certain keys change as you change windows. Apart from the changing functions, however, the Symphony keyboard sections have certain general characteristics.

Most of the keys in the alphanumeric section at the center of the keyboard are found on any common typewriter. These keys maintain their normal functions in Symphony. Keys that take on unique functions, however, are Esc, Tab, Shift, and Alt.

The numeric keypad on the right-hand side of the keyboard is normally used for entering numbers in most programs on the IBM PC and can be used for numbers in the SHEET, DOC, and FORM windows whenever the Num Lock key is set. In Symphony, however, the main purpose for the numeric keypad is cursor movement.

The special-function keys on the left-hand side of the keyboard (on the IBM PC and compatibles) are designed for special uses ranging from getting help (the F1 function key) to retrieving the command menus (the F10 function key).

The Alphanumeric Keyboard

*New
with
Symphony*

Although most of the alphanumeric keys (fig. 2.21) have the same functions as those on a typewriter, in Symphony several keys have special functions, which are listed below. If some of the functions do not make much sense the first time through, don't worry. Their meanings will become clearer as you read more of this chapter and those that follow.

Key	Function(s)
Esc	Erases current entry when you specify a command line or range, erases a command menu, or returns from a help screen; removes a graph from the screen and returns you to the graph menu in SHEET mode

Fig. 2.21.

Tab	Moves the cursor to each tab setting in the DOC mode; moves the cursor to the left when Tab is used with the Shift key; anchors cells or the cursor when you are indicating a range
Alt	When used in combination with the function keys, Alt changes function key operations (fig. 2.24); used simultaneously with other alpha keys to invoke keyboard macros. (Alt is covered in detail in Chapter 13 on keyboard macros.)
Shift	Changes the central section of the keyboard to uppercase letters and characters; allows you to key in numbers by using the numeric keypad on the right when you are working in a SHEET window. (Shift is equivalent to a temporary Num Lock.)

Ctrl   When used with Break, takes you out of
                    a command operation and back to the
                    SHEET, DOC, GRAPH, FORM, or
                    COMM mode

The Numeric Keypad

*New
with
Symphony*

The keys in the numeric keypad on the right-hand side of the
keyboard are used primarily for cursor movement. (See fig. 2.22.)
They are also used for scrolling the screen up or down, deleting
characters, and inserting records into a data base. In some cases a
key's function is specific to the type of window in which you are
working. These specific functions are indicated below.

See the later section on Cursor Movement Keys and the Cell Pointer
for detailed explanations of the use of Home, End, PgUp, and PgDn
keys used alone or in combination with other keys.

Key	Function(s)	Windows
Backspace	When you are defining the contents of a cell, erases the character in the definition; erases characters in DOC and FORM windows	SHEET DOC FORM
/ (Slash)	Retrieves the SHEET command MENU; used in its normal function as a division sign	SHEET
. (Period)	Separates cell addresses when ranges of cells are designated and anchors cell addresses or the cursor when you are pointing. (See the section on Ranges in Chapter 3.) The period is also used as a decimal point.	SHEET DOC FORM GRAPH COMM

Fig. 2.22.

| Home | Returns to cell A1 or the beginning of a restrict range from any location in the worksheet in the SHEET window; used after the End key to position the cursor at the active end of the worksheet or restrict range; used in the EDIT mode to jump to the beginning of the edit line; returns to the beginning of the file or restrict range from any location in the DOC window; returns to the beginning of the first entry line from any location in the entry in the FORM window. (See the section on Cursor Movement and the Cell Pointer.) | SHEET DOC FORM |

PgUp	Moves the cursor 20 rows up in the column where it currently resides in a SHEET window; moves the cursor one window up in a DOC window; moves to a previous record in a FORM window	SHEET DOC FORM
PgDn	Moves the cursor 20 rows down in a SHEET window and one window down in a DOC window; moves to the next record in a FORM window	SHEET DOC FORM
Ins	Inserts a record into the FORM data base; clears form for next entry; used to switch from Insert to Overstrike mode in a DOC window.	FORM DOC

The Lock Key Indicators

Three "lock" keys are on the IBM PC: Num Lock, Caps Lock, and Scroll Lock. (See fig. 2.23.) Whenever any of these keys is used, Symphony indicates that the keys are operating. Each key has its own reverse-video indicator that will appear in the lower right corner of the screen when the key is on.

The Function Keys

New with Symphony

Besides the alphanumeric and numeric keys, the special-function keys in Symphony are somewhat different from those in 1-2-3. Like some of the numeric keys, a few special-function keys change their functions when you change a window environment. On the IBM PC and the Compaq, for example, the F2 function key is used to edit cell entries when you are working in a SHEET window, but this same key is used to justify paragraphs when you are working in a DOC window.

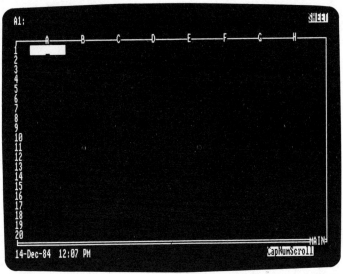

Fig. 2.23.

Lotus Development provides for Symphony users a function key template that fits over the function keys of the IBM PC, with a special version available for Compaq owners. Figure 2.24 is a diagram of the function keys. The figure distinguishes those keys that operate by pressing a function key alone and those keys that operate by pressing simultaneously the Alt key and a function key. On the template, operations in light tan are initiated by pressing the function key alone. Operations with a grey background are initiated by pressing simultaneously the Alt key and the function key. Some function keys, like the lock keys, toggle on and off. In other words, the particular function remains "turned on" until you press the key(s) a second time. Such toggle keys include F5 (Learn), F6 (Zoom), Alt + F7 (Step), and F7 (User).

*New
with
Symphony*

Function Keys Working in All Windows

Some keys operate in all types of windows, whereas other keys function only with specific window types. The three keys that you will probably use most frequently for all window types are the SERVICES key (F9), the TYPE key (Alt + F10), and the MENU key (F10). Function keys operating in all windows include the following:

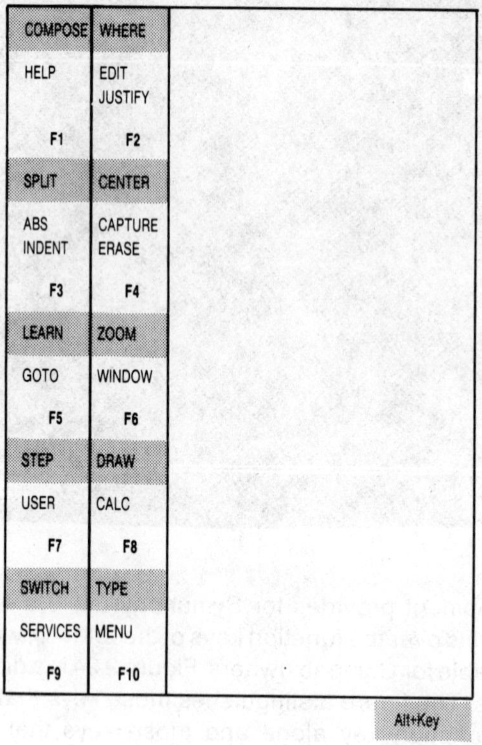

COMPOSE	WHERE
HELP	EDIT JUSTIFY
F1	F2
SPLIT	CENTER
ABS INDENT	CAPTURE ERASE
F3	F4
LEARN	ZOOM
GOTO	WINDOW
F5	F6
STEP	DRAW
USER	CALC
F7	F8
SWITCH	TYPE
SERVICES	MENU
F9	F10

Alt+Key

Fig. 2.24.

Key	Function(s)
F1 (Help)	Retrieves the help screens. (On a system with two disk drives, you need to replace the Symphony Program disk with the Help disk before pressing F1.)
Alt + F1 (Compose)	Creates special characters by combining two standard characters
Alt + F5 (Learn)	Records keystrokes for creating macros
F6 (Window)	Rotates windows; brings a bottom window to the top; moves the cursor from one window to another; rotates the settings sheets for windows of the same type

Alt + F6 (Zoom)	Creates a full screen after isolating a window
F7 (User)	Initiates a macro
Alt + F7 (Step)	Operates a macro in single-step mode for debugging
Alt + F8 (Redraw)	Redraws all windows after making changes
F9 (SERVICES)	Retrieves the SERVICES menu
Alt + F9 (Switch)	Changes window to previous type
F10 (MENU)	Retrieves the command menus for each Symphony environment
Alt + F10 (TYPE)	Retrieves the TYPE menu

New with Symphony

Function Keys for Specific Windows

The function keys listed in the previous section are available for any Symphony window (SHEET, DOC, GRAPH, FORM, and COMM). As mentioned earlier, many function keys have particular uses for specific window types. These keys and their functions are listed below.

Key	Window	Function(s)
Alt + F1 (Compose)	DOC FORM SHEET	Inserts special print commands (such as those for boldfacing and underlining) in the text; creates special characters
F2 (Justify)	DOC	Justifies paragraphs

F2 (Edit)	SHEET FORM	Edits a cell entry in a spreadsheet; edits entries in a form
Alt + F2 (Where)	DOC	Indicates page and line location on printed copy of current on-screen line
F3 (Indent)	DOC	Indents lines
F3 (ABS)	SHEET	Changes a formula to absolute reference
Alt + F3 (Split)	DOC	Splits a line without leaving carriage return
F4 (Capture)	COMM	Captures data to a worksheet range or printer
F4 (Erase)	DOC	Erases a block
Alt + F4 (Center)	DOC	Centers a line
F5 (GoTo)	SHEET DOC FORM	Goes to a range, a line, or page
F8 (Calc)	SHEET	Calculates formulas in a worksheet

Other Special Key Combinations

Besides the special uses of the Alt key with function keys, many other key combinations have special functions, particularly in the DOC and SHEET windows. In many cases these combinations involve moving the cell pointer in a SHEET window or moving the cursor in a DOC or FORM window.

Cursor-Movement Keys and the Cell Pointer

Cursor movement occurs in all Symphony environments. In some cases cursor movement within a window is primarily for identifying ranges; in other windows, cursor movement is important for entering, editing, and deleting data, and for making selections from menus. Cursor movement occurs when you use keys alone and in combination with others, as listed in the tables below. In a SHEET environment the cursor is referred to as the cell pointer.

Moving the Cell Pointer in a SHEET Window

Like 1-2-3, Symphony provides several ways for moving around a worksheet, whether you are entering or changing data, or identifying a range. Eleven keys in all, used alone and in combination, control cell-pointer movement throughout the worksheet. These keys include the following:

> The cursor keys: ←, →, ↓, ↑
> PgDn and PgUp keys
> The Home key
> The End key
> The F5 function key
> The Ctrl key (used only in combination with others)
> The Scroll Lock key (used only in combination with others)

These eleven keys will enable you to move the cell pointer around the worksheet in the ways listed below. (See fig. 2.25.)

- To move the cell pointer: Use the following:

1 cell up	↑
1 cell down	↓
1 cell left	←
1 cell right	→
To the upper left corner	Home
To the lower right corner	End + Home
1 window up	PgUp
1 window down	PgDn

| 1 window left | Ctrl + ← |
| 1 window right | Ctrl + → |

Window up 1 row	Scroll Lock + ↑
Window down 1 row	Scroll Lock + ↓
Window left 1 column	Scroll Lock + ←
Window right 1 column	Scroll Lock + →

- To jump the cell pointer to: Use the following:

Specific cell position or named range	F5 function key
Next filled cell above	End then ↑
Next filled cell below	End then ↓
Next filled cell to left	End then ←
Next filled cell to right	End then →

First row of window restrict range	End then PgUp
Last row of restrict range	End then PgDn
First column of restrict range	End then Ctrl ←
Last column of restrict range	End then Ctrl →
Upper right corner of restrict range	Scroll Lock + Home

Moving the Cursor in a DOC Window

New with Symphony

Moving the cursor in a DOC window is similar to moving the cell pointer in a SHEET window. Many more keys, however, can be used to move the cursor in a DOC window. These keys include the following:

The cursor keys: ←, →, ↓, ↑
PgUp and PgDn keys
The Home key
The End key
The Ctrl key (used only in combination with others)
The Scroll Lock key (used only in combination with others)
The F2 function key (used with the End key)
The Alt + F2 keys (used with the End key)
RETURN (used with the End key)
Any typed character (used with the End key)

Cursor-Movement Keys

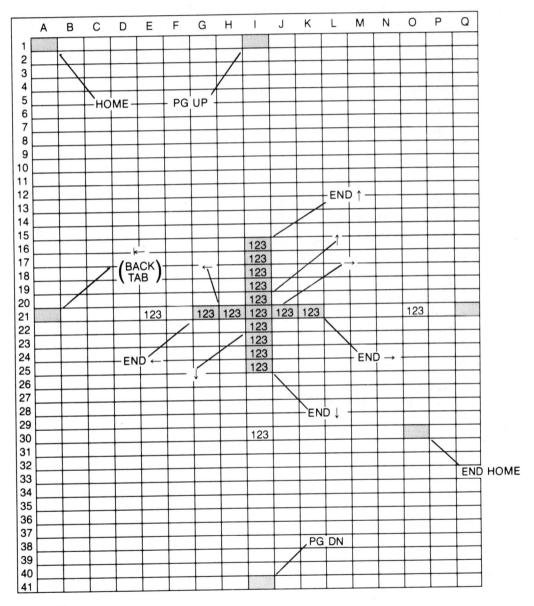

Fig. 2.25.

These keys will enable you to move the cursor around a DOC worksheet in the following ways.

- To move the cursor: Use the following:

  1 line up   ↑
  1 line down   ↓
  1 format line up   End then Alt + F2
  1 format line down   End then F2

  To preceding character   ←
  To next character   →
  To any specific character   End then specific
                                               character

  To the next word   Ctrl + →
  To the preceding word   Ctrl + ←

  To beginning of paragraph   End then ↑
  To end of paragraph   End then ↓

  One window up   PgUp
  One window down   PgDn
  Window up 1 line   Scroll Lock + ↑
  Window down 1 line   Scroll Lock + ↓
  Window 25% to left   Scroll Lock + ←
  Window 25% to right   Scroll Lock + →

  To upper left corner of a
     document or restrict range   Home
  To end of a document or
     restrict range   End then Home

  To next carriage return   End then RETURN

Moving the Cursor in a FORM Window

*New
with
Symphony*

Cursor movement is important not only for operating within a SHEET or DOC window, but also for the work you do in a FORM window. When you enter information into data forms and criterion records, the following keys are used for cursor movement:

The cursor keys: ←, →, ↓, ↑
The Tab key

The Home key
The End key
The Ctrl key (used only in combination with others)

These keys will enable you to move the cursor in a FORM window in the following ways.

- To move the cursor: Use the following:

To the previous field   ↑ or ←
To the next field   ↓ or → or Tab

To the first field of a file   Ctrl + ←
To the last field of a file   Ctrl + →

New
with
Symphony

The Symphony Display

Descriptions of the Symphony display, like those of many other features of the program, vary according to the type of window being used. Some general remarks, however, can be made about the Symphony display. For all types of windows, the work or display area is bordered on all four sides. This border can be changed or removed completely by using the **W**indow **S**ettings **B**order command. The border for a SHEET window, like the reverse-video border of 1-2-3, contains letters and numbers that mark columns and rows. Unlike the spreadsheet border in 1-2-3, the border in Symphony surrounds all four sides. (See fig. 2.26.)

A particularly important part of the border of any window is the bottom line. When it is displayed as a double line, the bottom line indicates the current window. Important areas outside the window border include the mode indicator, the date-and-time indicator, the error message area, and the lock key indicator.

The Control Panel

The area directly above the top line of the border is the menu area for all windows. In Symphony, the command menu line appears in this position, but the explanation of the command appears on the first line above the command menu line. (See fig. 2.27.)

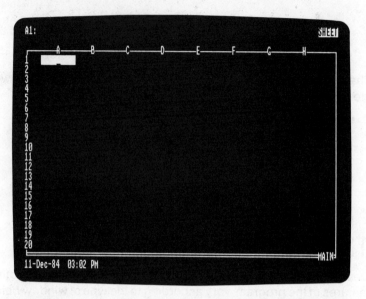

Fig. 2.26.

```
"A" setting: Allow changes to cells even if Global Protection = Yes    MENU
Allow-Changes  Prevent-Changes
         A              B         C   D     E      F       G          H
 1
 2  Balance Sheet
 3  ===================================================================
 4
 5         Assets                                31-Jul-83    Common
                                                               Size
 6
 7  Cash                                           $255,000      8%
 8  Marketable Securities                            29,000      1%
 9  Accounts Receivable              1,256,000
10     Allowance for Doubtful Accounts   8,000
11     Net Accounts Receivable                     1,127,500    37%
12  Inventory                                        323,000    11%
13  Prepaid Expenses                                  60,000     2%
14  Other                                             21,000     1%
15                                                -----------
16     Total Current Assets                        1,815,500    60%
17
18  Property, Plant, and Equipment      956,700
19     Accumulated Depreciation         123,700
20     Net Property, Plant, and Equipment           833,000    27%
                                                              =MAIN=
Range Protect
```

Fig. 2.27.

Whenever a SHEET, DOC, or FORM window is in the mode ready to receive data, the area above the top border contains information about the data or the operations that must be completed before data can be entered.

In the SHEET window mode, this first line contains all the information about the current cell, and the second line contains the characters that are being entered or edited. A current cell is the cell where the pointer is currently located. The first item is the address of the cell. And the second item is the display format, which is always displayed in parentheses. (Display formats are covered in detail in Chapter 4.) In the first line, the last item is the actual contents of the current cell. (See fig. 2.28.)

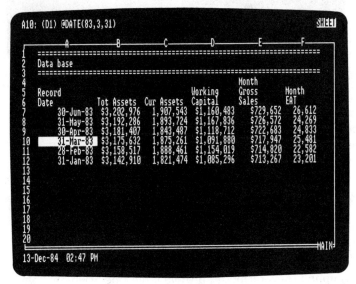

Fig. 2.28.

In the DOC window mode the first line indicates the line, character, and cell position of the cursor, as well as the type of justification and spacing that are set. (See fig. 2.29.) Whenever an asterisk (*) appears in the middle of the control panel, the asterisk indicates that the cursor is positioned on data which was entered in another type of window, or positioned on a special DOC format symbol. (See Chapter 7.)

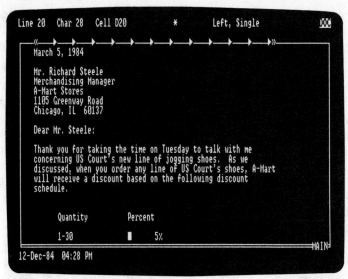

Fig. 2.29.

In the FORM window mode, the control panel is reserved as a special message area. (See fig. 2.30.) For example, it informs the user that a range needs to be set for creating a form. But more important, this area tells the user which record is being entered or edited and indicates the entry slot where the cursor is currently positioned.

The Mode Indicators

New
with
Symphony

In Symphony several modes are available, one of which is always in effect, depending on what you are doing. The mode indicator is located in the upper right corner of the screen and always shows the current mode. The mode indicators and related modes include those listed below.

Modes Indicating Current Window

Mode	Indicator
SHEET	You can enter a command or make a cell entry in the spreadsheet.

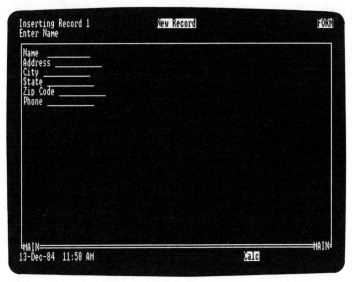

```
Inserting Record 1              New Record                        FORM
Enter Name

Name
Address
City
State
Zip Code
Phone




MAIN                                                               MAIN
13-Dec-84  11:58 AM                                    Calc
```

Fig. 2.30.

DOC	You can enter a command or text or perform editing operations in a word-processing window.
GRAPH	You can enter a command to create graphs and charts and attach them to a GRAPH window.
FORM	You can enter a command or data and change data in the forms you have created in a FORM window.
COMM	You can enter a command or data in the COMM window.

Modes Working in All Windows

Mode	Indicator
MENU	Select from the TYPE menu, SERVICES menu or from a SHEET, DOC, GRAPH, FORM, or COMM menu. (Or you can press Esc to return to a window mode.)

POINT	A range is being pointed to.
HELP	You are using a help screen.
ERROR	An error has occurred, and Symphony is waiting for you to press Esc or RETURN to acknowledge the error.
WAIT	Symphony is in the middle of an operation and cannot respond to commands.
EDIT	A settings sheet or cell entry is being edited.
CMD	CMD appears in front of the mode indicators during the execution of a keyboard macro. (Keyboard macros are covered in Chapter 13.)
SST	SST appears instead of CMD when Symphony is in single-step execution of a keyboard macro.

SHEET Window Modes

Mode	Indicator
VALUE	Number or formula is being entered.
LABEL	Label is being entered.
FIND	Symphony is in the middle of a **Q**uery **F**ind operation and cannot respond to commands.

FORM Window Mode

Mode	Indicator
CRIT	A criterion record is being edited.

Other Indicators

In addition to the mode indicators in the top right corner, other indicators are displayed in the area at the bottom of the screen. (See fig. 2.31.) On the left, date and time are displayed whenever you are in a window mode. The bottom of the screen is also reserved for other indicators. When you have selected a command, the command name is displayed in the bottom left corner. Also displayed here are error messages and the "Memory full" message. In the bottom right corner a number of other indicators are displayed. These inform the user of certain conditions, such as lock keys being on, and also of operations for creating, editing, and using macros.

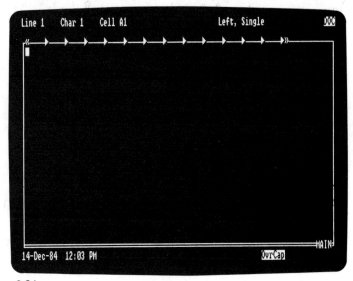

Fig. 2.31.

Following is a list of other indicators:

Mode	Indicator
Calc	You need to recalculate the worksheet.
Capture	Data from a COMM environment is being logged in a worksheet range to the printer.
Circ	A circular reference has been found in the worksheet.
Draw	Windows need to be updated because of changes in one of them.

End	The End key is on.
Macro	A macro is in operation.
Mem	Only a small amount of memory remains.
New Record	A new record is being entered (FORM window).
Num	The Num Lock key is on.
OnLine	In the COMM window a connection with another computer is signified.
Ovr	You are in the Overstrike mode in a DOC window.
Pause	You need to input something so that a macro can continue.
Scroll	The Scroll Lock key is on.
Step	Step mode is set for running macros.
User	You can execute a macro by entering the macro name.
Learn	Keystrokes can be stored automatically for creating macros.

Using the Tutorial Disks

Whether you are a veteran Lotus user or new to Lotus software, the Tutorial Lessons disk and the Help and Tutorial disk will acquaint you with Symphony and enable you to understand better its command structure, capabilities, and operations.

The Tutorial Lessons Disk

The Tutorial Lessons disk is an excellent introduction to the Symphony program. The tutorial is comprehensive in its treatment of all Symphony applications—spreadsheet, word processing, graphics, data base management, and communications. A series of lessons covering the five applications are presented in separate sections of the disk. You can select any one of the five applications as well as particular lessons within that application. If, for example, you want to view the lessons on data base management, you can select that item from the menu. You can then choose to begin with either the basic lessons or the more advanced lessons. The Symphony Tutorial disk is excellently conceived, written, and presented.

The following applications and lessons are included on the disk:

A	Introduction	Included are (1) an introduction to what Symphony can do and directions for using the tutorial; and (2) an introduction to windows, menus, and setting sheets.
B	Spreadsheets	Lessons include (1) Working with a Spreadsheet, (2) Editing and Copying Entries, (3) Writing and Copying Formulas, (4) Organizing Your Work, and (5) Saving Steps: Functions and Macros.
C	Word Processing	Lessons include (1) Working with the Word Processor, (2) Handling Text, and (3) Formatting a Document.
D	Graphing	Included are (1) Working with Graphs and (2) Creating More Graphs.
E	Data Management	Lessons include (1) Working with Entry Forms, (2) Creating an Entry Form, and (3) Data Base Features on a Worksheet.
F	Communications	Included are (1) Entering Communications Settings, (2) Using Your Phone, (3) Sending a Range of Data, and (4) Receiving Data.

If you work through Symphony's tutorial, you are guaranteed a complete introduction to all the major operations and features of the program. And unlike the 1-2-3 tutorial, Symphony's tutorial does include an introduction to keyboard macros.

The tutorial is too long and detailed to review all in one sitting. You will do best if you work on one section at a time, particularly since the organization of lessons enables you to begin and end at any point. A number of features make the tutorial an excellent learning aid; it often presents a clearer introduction to the program than does the documentation, which includes the *Introduction, The How-To Manual,* and *The Reference Manual.* Following are a few of the tutorial's features:

- The tutorial emphasizes the integrated features of the program by introducing all of Symphony's capabilities.

- Each lesson is based on hands-on exercises that enable you to practice using many of Symphony's keys, commands, and operations.

- At the end of each lesson, you are encouraged to practice on your own the commands and operations covered in the lesson. (Moving back and forth from the Tutorial Lessons disk to the Symphony Program disk is fairly easy.)

- The introduction to windows, menus, and setting sheets can help 1-2-3 users understand quickly the differences between 1-2-3 and Symphony.

- Each exercise clearly explains what the goal of each procedure is, what keys you should press, and what part of the screen you should focus on as changes occur. (See fig. 2.32.)

- The tutorial is user friendly, not only because it provides clear and complete instructions, but also because it acknowledges the needs of different users, both beginning and advanced.

- If you want to speed up the process of working through a lesson, you can press the space bar, which will enter each of the keystrokes for you. Thus, you get the benefit of the tutorial without having to do all the work.

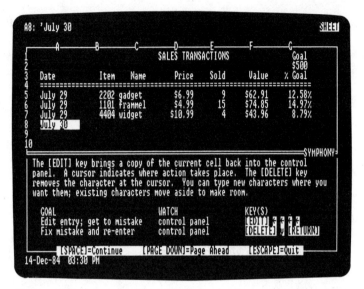

Fig. 2.32.

If you want to pass through part of a lesson even more quickly, pressing the PgDn key will enable you to do so. One problem, however, is that you cannot return to a prior screen without starting again at the beginning of a lesson and scrolling through each screen until you reach the screen you want to review.

The Symphony Tutorial disk is highly recommended as one resource for introducing you to the general capabilities, menus, commands, and operations of Symphony.

New with Symphony

Accessing the Tutorial

Accessing Symphony's tutorial is somewhat more complicated than accessing 1-2-3's tutorial. To access Symphony's tutorial, you must take the following steps:

1. Load the Symphony Program disk.

2. Access the Symphony Program.

For a system with two disk drives, you must also do the following: after Symphony is loaded and the screen appears as in figure 2.4 shown earlier, replace the Symphony Program disk with the Help and Tutorial disk, then press RETURN.

3. With a worksheet on the screen, press SERVICES and select **A**pplication in the menu.

4. Select **A**ttach and then move the cell pointer to TUTORIAL.APP.

5. Select SERVICES and **A**pplication again.

6. Select **I**nvoke.

For a system with two disk drives: replace the Help and Tutorial disk with the Tutorial Lessons disk, then press RETURN.

7. When the tutorial menu appears, select Introduction or any of the lesson sections.

The Help and Tutorial Disk

Like 1-2-3, Symphony makes available a series of help screens that you can easily refer to while working in the program. If you are using a system with two disk drives, you need to replace the main Symphony Program disk with the Help and Tutorial disk and press the F1 function key to access a help screen while working in the program. If you are in the middle of entering or changing data, don't forget to save your file before exiting from the Symphony program.

Each screen contains information on a topic listed in the Help Index. (See fig. 2.33.) To retrieve the Help Index, you simply move the cursor to the bottom of the screen, position it over "Help Index," and press RETURN. When the Help Index appears, you will notice that it is arranged alphabetically according to general topics. To select a help screen topic, you position the cursor over a heading, then press RETURN.

Each heading within the Help Index consists of a series of screens, which are organized in two ways. First, screens are organized

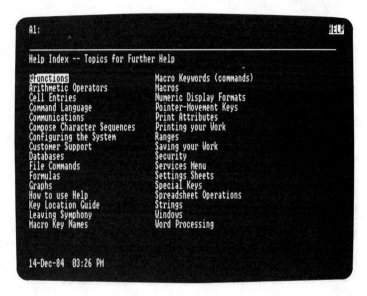

A1:   HELP

Help Index -- Topics for Further Help

@Functions   Macro Keywords (commands)
Arithmetic Operators   Macros
Cell Entries   Numeric Display Formats
Command Language   Pointer-Movement Keys
Communications   Print Attributes
Compose Character Sequences   Printing your Work
Configuring the System   Ranges
Customer Support   Saving your Work
Databases   Security
File Commands   Services Menu
Formulas   Settings Sheets
Graphs   Special Keys
How to use Help   Spreadsheet Operations
Key Location Guide   Strings
Leaving Symphony   Windows
Macro Key Names   Word Processing

14-Dec-84 03:26 PM

Fig. 2.33.

according to the topics in the Help Index; the @Function help
screen, for example, lists all of the types of functions. Second, many
help screens contain cross references listed in the bottom left
corner of the help screen. (See fig. 2.34.) If, for example, you select
the Database Statistical function help screen, it contains cross
references to Database Ranges and Criterion Ranges. By positioning the cursor on either of these cross references, you can retrieve
the help screen for either Database Ranges or Criterion Ranges.

Conclusion

This chapter has provided information for helping you begin to use
Symphony. The chapter has covered the important maintenance
procedures for getting started, including copying your Symphony
disks, adding DOS, and installing your disks. Also presented was an
overview of Symphony: the Symphony ACCESS SYSTEM, the Help
and Tutorial disk, the menu structure, the keyboard, the display, and
the window feature. Now that you have had a chance to discover

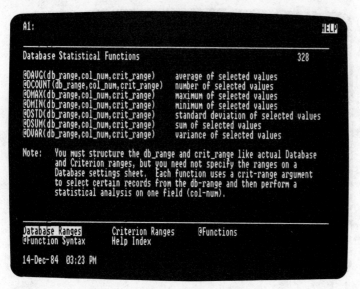

Fig. 2.34.

Symphony, read the following chapters for a closer view of Symphony's capabilities. These include creating spreadsheets; using file commands; using word processing; printing reports; creating and displaying graphs; and using data management, communications, and macro features.

3

The Symphony
SHEET Window

If you have used 1-2-3, the Symphony spreadsheet application (SHEET window) will be familiar to you. Examining this feature is a good way to begin learning about the program. Entering and editing data, moving the cell pointer, and identifying and using ranges are much the same in 1-2-3 and Symphony. Like its counterpart in 1-2-3, Symphony's spreadsheet application is the foundation of the program. And even without the other applications—word processing, data management, graphics, and communications—Symphony is an amazingly powerful program.

Some significant differences, however, exist between the spreadsheet applications of 1-2-3 and Symphony. These differences include the following:

- Larger worksheet size in Symphony
- Different command menu structures
- Differences in function keys
- Differences in display
- Ability in Symphony to create formulas (new string arithmetic functions) that will join words, phrases, or sentences

- Ability in Symphony to integrate the spreadsheet application with other applications through use of the window feature

The spreadsheet is the basis for the whole Symphony product because all command menus operate similarly, just as they do in 1-2-3. And even when you are working in the word-processing window (DOC) or the data form window (FORM), all data is stored within the worksheet boundaries. Because of this arrangement, entries and changes in a DOC or FORM window can affect a spreadsheet that is entered on the same worksheet.

Some of Symphony's other applications depend on the spreadsheet also. For instance, to create a data form, you enter the form in a spreadsheet window, place the cursor at the beginning of the form, and then switch to a FORM window. The data base created from form entries is viewed within the spreadsheet environment and can be changed in a SHEET window. Although a separate GRAPH window exists, the spreadsheet menu contains its own commands for creating graphs. In fact, all commands for displaying graphs refer to entries in the spreadsheet and use these entries to draw graphs on the screen. Finally, the macro, or command language, depends on the SHEET environment. To edit a macro, then, you need to work in a SHEET window.

Worksheet Size and Its Effect on RAM

One of the major differences between the 1-2-3 and Symphony spreadsheet components is the worksheet size. Compared to 1-2-3's worksheet with 2,048 rows and 256 columns (524,288 cells), Symphony's worksheet contains 8,192 rows and 256 columns (2,097,152 cells). Each column is assiged a one- or two-letter value ranging from A for the first column to IV for the last. A good way to visualize the worksheet is to imagine a giant sheet of gridded paper containing 1/4" x 1" cells and being about 21 feet wide and 171 feet high!

New
with
Symphony

Compared to the tremendous overall size of the Symphony worksheet, the video display is capable of showing only 20 rows and 8 columns at a time on the screen. As illustrated in figure 3.1, the screen represents one small window on the Symphony worksheet. Because of the worksheet's size, you have plenty of room to create many windows within the same worksheet: windows containing different kinds of spreadsheets; data bases; and notes, memos, or short reports.

The Symphony worksheet is four times the size of the 1-2-3 worksheet. And like 1-2-3, Symphony has some limitations to using the entire sheet. In practical terms, memory limitations must be considered when you are determining the size and complexity of a spreadsheet or data base.

New with Symphony

The Symphony program alone requires approximately 300K of RAM. Its large size stems primarily from the programming required for all the extra features that Symphony provides. Such features as windows and settings sheets, as well as increased use of ranges, all expand the memory requirements of Symphony, compared to those of 1-2-3. Some information is saved automatically by Symphony, but some information must be saved by the user.

In addition to the size of the Symphony program, the size of the worksheet in RAM must be considered. The number of active cells in a worksheet cannot simply be equated to its RAM requirements because the contents of cells can vary greatly. Perhaps the best way to get a realistic notion of the potential size of a worksheet is to conduct two simple tests. In the first test, you can relate the size of the worksheet to the number of standard 8 1/2 x 11-inch pages that can fit into the worksheet. In the second test, you can experiment with filling cells in the worksheet, using the Copy command, and then seeing when you run out of main memory. From these two tests, you can draw realistic conclusions about the worksheet size.

To begin the first test, use a configuration of 512K of RAM. After subtracting the 300K for the Symphony program, a worksheet size of 212K remains. If you divide the remaining RAM by the number of characters on a standard 8 1/2 x 11-inch page, with pica type (66 lines by 80 characters = 5,280), you get approximately 40 pages. In theory, then, this figure points out the capacity of the Symphony sheet. In the second test, you'll use again the configuration of 512K. Begin by entering the label ABCDEF in cell A1. Then duplicate this

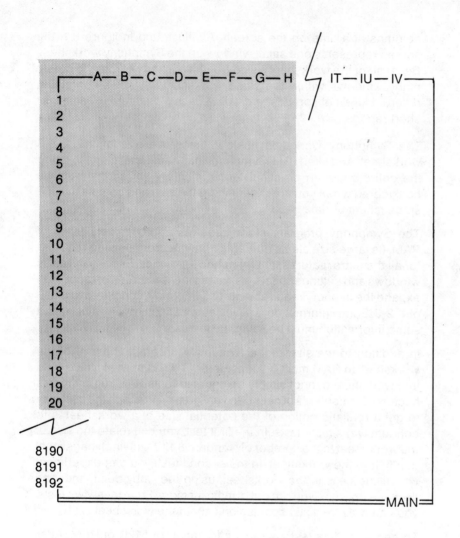

Fig. 3.1.

cell until you run out of main memory. These tests indicate that you can fill columns A and B to the bottom, approximately 16,000 cells.

As you can see, an important consideration in using Symphony is the size of the worksheets you will be creating. Symphony requires a computer with at least 320K of memory; if you are operating Symphony with 320K, you will be limited in the amount of space you can use on your worksheet. You will particularly find memory limited when you are creating multiple windows in various sections of your worksheet. A few guidelines, however, will help you get the most from the amount of memory you have available.

First, try to monitor your use of memory by periodically checking how much memory is available for your worksheet. You can easily check memory by selecting **S**ettings from the SERVICES menu.

Second, keep your active worksheet areas as close as possible to cell A1. If you scatter your model about, you may find yourself running out of memory because RAM is required to store the contents of cells between entries, even though only blanks may be in the cells. For example, the spreadsheets in figures 3.2 and 3.3 contain the same information, but the first spreadsheet requires nearly one and a half times more RAM than the second.

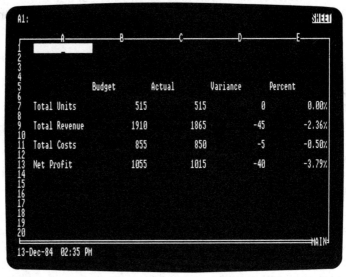

Fig. 3.2.

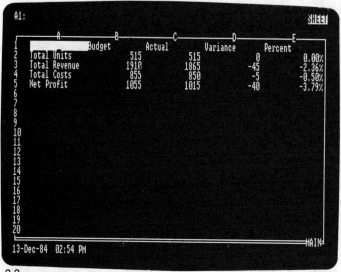

Fig. 3.3.

Finally, remember that when you delete a part of a worksheet, the main memory requirements for that worksheet do not diminish until you save it to your disk, then load the worksheet back into RAM. Symphony's optimization routines are not activated until you store a worksheet. (The commands for storing and retrieving worksheets are covered in Chapter 6 on File Operations.)

Speed

Although claimed to be somewhat faster than 1-2-3, Symphony's speed of recalculation isn't noticeably faster. Nevertheless, the speed is an outstanding feature of the program. And like the recalculation speed of 1-2-3, Symphony's speed is much faster than that of spreadsheet-only programs.

The speed of Symphony's cursor movement is also quite remarkable if you take into account Symphony's larger worksheet size. Moving the cursor from the top left corner of the worksheet to the bottom right corner occurs instantly with almost no visible delay. In contrast with several other spreadsheet programs in which the screen flickers each time the cursor is moved, Symphony shows almost no flickering. The screen reacts fast enough for you to move quickly to a cell without overshooting your mark and ending up several cells beyond.

If you have used 1-2-3 and thought the loading time was long, you will find the loading time for Symphony to be even longer. This period of time is understandable when you consider the size of the system program. On a per-byte basis, however, loading time is relatively fast. Of course, this fact doesn't do you much good when you are waiting to get started. Our tests indicate that loading time takes almost 30 seconds.

Entering Data

If you have worked with spreadsheets before, you will recall that three different types of cell entries can be made: labels, numbers, and formulas (including functions). Data is entered in a cell simply by positioning the cell pointer in the cell and typing the entry. From the first character that you enter, Symphony reads the type of cell entry you are making. If you start with one of these characters

0 1 2 3 4 5 6 7 8 9 + - . (@ # $

Symphony will treat your entry as either a number or a formula. If you begin by entering a character other than one of those listed, Symphony will treat your entry as a label.

Entering Labels

In spreadsheets, labels are commonly used for row and column headers. They can be up to 240 characters long and can contain any string of characters and numbers. If a label is too long for the width of a cell, the label will continue across the cells to the right for display purposes, as long as there are no other entries in the neighboring cells. (See fig. 3.4.)

When you enter a value into a cell, and the first character is not one of those listed above for entering numbers and formulas, Symphony assumes that you are entering a label. As you type the first character, Symphony shifts to the LABEL mode.

One advantage of Symphony is that you can left-, center-, or right-justify labels when you display them. (See fig. 3.5.) The label must be preceded by one of the following label-prefix characters:

Character	Action
´	Left-justifies
^	Centers
"	Right-justifies
\	Repeats

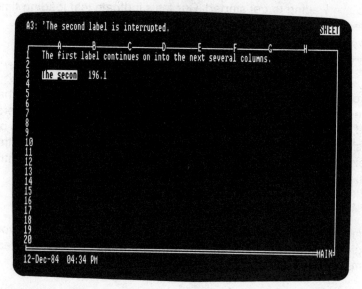

A3: 'The second label is interrupted.   SHEET

```
      A        B        C        D        E        F        G        H
 1  The first label continues on into the next several columns.
 2
 3  The secon   196.1
 4
 5
 6
 7
 8
 9
10
11
12
13
14
15
16
17
18
19
20
```

12-Dec-84 04:34 PM   MAIN

Fig. 3.4.

The default for displaying is left justification. Symphony automatically enters the label prefix, as indicated below:

What You Enter	What Symphony Stores
Net Income	´ Net Income

If you want to enter a header that begins with a numeral, such as *1983 Sales*, you must enter the prefix before 1983 (´ 1983 Sales). Symphony will then interpret 1983 as a label and will automatically left-justify, as Symphony does for other labels. If you want to center this header, you enter ^*1983 Sales.*

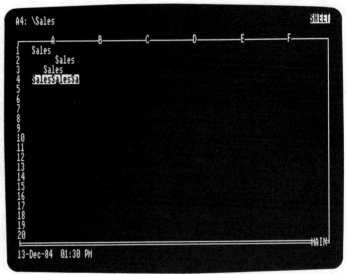

Fig. 3.5.

The most unusual label prefix is the backslash (\), which is used for repetition. One of the most frequent uses of this prefix is to create a separator line. The first step is to enter \= into the first cell (in fig. 3.6, cell A3). This entry causes the equal sign to appear across the entire cell. Once you have set up the first cell, you then use the Copy command from the SHEET menu to replicate the cell across or to other parts of the worksheet. (See fig. 3.7.) For more information about the Copy command and replication, see Chapter 4.

Label prefixes can be controlled in several ways. For example, suppose you have entered a series of labels, using the standard default of left justification, but you decide that you would rather have the labels centered. You can manually change all label prefixes, or you can change them all at once with the Range Label-Alignment command. When you select this command, you are given the following choices:

Left   Right   Center

Each choice gives you the label prefix that its name indicates. If you select Center, Symphony will ask you to designate a range of cells to change. When you specify a range and hit RETURN, the cells will be displayed as centered.

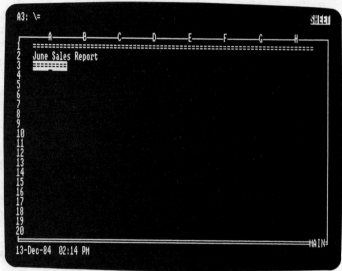

Fig. 3.6.

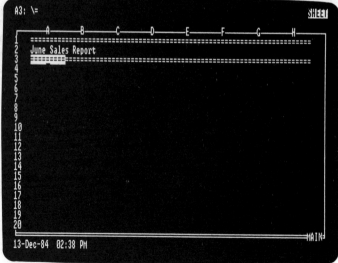

Fig. 3.7.

Another option for changing label prefixes is to change the default
setting for text justification. The command to do this is **S**ettings
Label-Prefix from the SHEET command MENU. This command

gives you the same options as **R**ange **L**abel-Alignment. But after you change label justification with the **S**ettings **L**abel-Prefix command, the labels entered before you changed the setting will remain as originally aligned. Labels entered after you changed justification will appear as set until you change **L**abel-Prefix again.

Entering Numbers

If you begin an entry with any of the characters in the previous list, Symphony will interpret the entry as a number, and you can use cell entry to perform numerous operations. The following are simple rules for entering numbers:

1. You cannot begin a number with any character except 0 through 9, a decimal point, or a dollar sign ($).

2. You can end a number with a percent sign (%), which indicates to Symphony to divide by 100 the number that precedes the sign.

3. You cannot have more than one decimal point in a number.

4. Although you may not use commas or spaces when you enter a number, it can be displayed with them. You can also suppress the display of a number, or you can display the formula rather than the value itself. (See Chapter 4.)

5. You can enter a number in scientific notation.

If you do not follow these rules, Symphony, like 1-2-3, will beep when you hit RETURN while trying to enter numbers into the spreadsheet. Symphony also will automatically shift to the EDIT mode just as if you had hit F2. (See the section on Editing for an explanation on how to respond.)

Entering Formulas

A special formula feature of Symphony is that it can process formulas relating values as well as formulas connecting strings, such as words, phrases, and sentences.

The ability to process formulas involving strings is uncommon in spreadsheet programs; the ability to process mathematical formulas, however, is primary to spreadsheet programs. Generally, electronic spreadsheets allow mathematical relationships to be created among cells. For example, if a cell named C1 contains the formula

$$C1 = +A1+B1$$

then C1 will display the sum of the contents of cells A1 and B1. The cell references serve as variables in the equation. No matter what numbers are entered in A1 and B1, cell C1 will always return their sum. For example, if cell A1 contains the number 5 and cell B1 contains the number 10, the formula in C1 will return the value 15. If the number in cell A1 were changed to 4, C1 would also change to 14. Of course, spreadsheet formulas can be much more complex than in this simple example. A cell can be added to any other cell, subtracted from it, multiplied by it, or divided by it. Spreadsheet functions may also be applied to the cells.

To enter a formula into a cell, you need to follow certain rules. Suppose, for example, you want to create a formula that adds a row

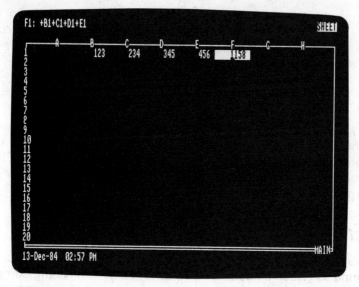

Fig. 3.8.

of numbers—in figure 3.8, the amounts in cells B1, C1, D1, and E1—and place the result in cell F1.

One formula that will perform the addition is +B1+C1+D1+E1. The plus sign (+) at the beginning of the formula tells Symphony to interpret the entry as a formula, not a label. Remember that for Symphony to recognize an entry as a formula, the entry must begin with one of the following characters:

$$0 \quad 1 \quad 2 \quad 3 \quad 4 \quad 5 \quad 6 \quad 7 \quad 8 \quad 9 \quad + \quad - \quad . \quad (\quad @ \quad \# \quad \$$$

Entering Cell Addresses in Formulas

Two methods can be used to enter cell addresses in formulas: typing and pointing. Both accomplish the same result, and you can mix and match the two techniques within the same formula. Typing cell addresses is self-explanatory, but pointing to cell addresses requires some explanation. The method used is the same as that used in pointing to cell ranges (see the section on Ranges in Chapter 4), but in this case the range is only a single cell.

In the example C1 = +A1+B1, to enter the formula by pointing, you move the cell pointer to B1 after entering the first plus sign. Notice that the address for the cell appears after the plus in the second line of the control panel—that is, +B1. The mode indicator in the upper right corner of the screen shifts from VALUE to POINT mode as you move the cell pointer to cell B1.

To continue to the next address in the formula, you type another plus sign. The cell pointer will move immediately from cell B1 back to the cell where the pointer was located when you began entering the formula—in this case, cell F1. Also, the mode indicator will shift back to VALUE. You continue this sequence of pointing and entering plus signs until you have the formula you want. Remember that nothing prohibits you from using a combination of the two methods of pointing and typing. Use whatever works best for you.

Usually, you will find that it is easier to point to cells that are close to the cell you are defining, but to type references to distant cells. Symphony, however, makes pointing to distant cells quite simple because of the End, PgUp, PgDn, and Tab keys that help you move quickly around the spreadsheet.

Operators

Operators indicate arithmetic operations in formulas. These operations can be classified as three types: mathematical, logical, and string. Logical operators are discussed in Chapters 5 and 11. The mathematical and string operators are listed here:

Operator	Meaning
^	Exponentiation
+,-	Positive, Negative
*,/	Multiplication, Division
+,-	Addition, Subtraction
&	String Concatenation

Important to understanding operators is knowing their order of precedence. The list above is arranged in order of precedence. Operators with the highest order of precedence are at the top, and operators with equal precedence are listed on the same line. Operators with equal precedence are evaluated from left to right. You can always use parentheses, though, to override the order of precedence.

Determine the order of precedence in the following formulas, where B3 = 2, C3 = 3, and D3 = 4. Are your answers the same as those given? In the first two formulas, notice particularly how parentheses affect the order of precedence as well as the answer.

Formula	Answer
+C3-D3/B3	1
(C3-D3)/B3	(.5)
+D3*C3-B3^C3	4
+D3*C3*B3/B3^C3=25/5	(2)

Symphony has the capability of processing complex formulas that involve many levels of nested parentheses. The number of levels is limited, however. If Symphony is unable to process a formula because it contains too many levels of nested parentheses, ERR is displayed instead of the answer. If the formula is too long, the computer will beep and the EDIT indicator will appear. In the unlikely event that this message occurs, you should split the formula into one or more intermediate calculations.

Functions

New
with
Symphony

Symphony includes all the functions available in 1-2-3 as well as some new ones. Specifically, Symphony contains a group of functions for performing string arithmetic, such as @STRING, @CHAR, and @MID. Other new special functions are @CELL, @CELLPOINTER, @COLS, and @ROWS. New time functions are available also.

All Symphony functions are considered formulas by Symphony. In fact, the functions are simply abbreviations for long or complex formulas. Each function consists of three parts: the "@" sign, a function name, and an argument or range. The @ sign signals to Symphony that a function is being entered, the name indicates which function is being used, and the argument or range is the data required by Symphony to perform the function. (Ranges are discussed later in this chapter and also in Chapter 4.) Although Chapter 5 provides a detailed discussion of Symphony's functions, a brief illustration is provided here to help you begin to understand them.

In figure 3.8, four cell references were used to create the desired formula. But the @SUM function could have been used to "sum" the numbers in the example. (The concept of ranges is important to the @SUM function. For now, think of a range as simply a continuous group of cells.) When you use the @SUM function, the equivalent to the +B1+C1+D1+E1 formula is @SUM(B1..E1). The only difference between the two formulas is one of convenience. Had several more entries extended down the row, the @SUM function would change only slightly in order to use the address of the last cell to be summed. For example, @SUM(B1..Z1) would sum the contents of the first row all the way from B to Z.

The following formulas perform the same function in this example, yet they all look slightly different:

@SUM(B1..E1)	@SUM($B$1..$E$1)
@SUM($B1..$E1)	@SUM($B$1..$E1)
@SUM(B$1..E$1)	@SUM($B1..E1)

Notice the dollar signs in the formulas. These signs are strategically placed to distinguish between relative, absolute, and mixed addressing. (These concepts are discussed extensively in the section on Copying in Chapter 4.)

String Formulas

New
with
Symphony

As mentioned earlier, Symphony's string arithmetic permits the user to create formulas for joining words, phrases, or even sentences. Special functions enable you to perform various operations on strings, including joining them together, converting strings to numbers, and indicating the total number of characters in a string. (These special functions are discussed in Chapter 5 and Chapter 11.)

String formulas can join words, phrases, and sentences originally entered in SHEET, DOC, FORM, or COMM windows; the string formula, however, must be entered in a SHEET window. String formulas are also discussed in Chapters 5 and 11, but the following general principles can be mentioned here:

- Like formulas involving values, formulas involving strings use cell addresses. For example, if you enter "John" in cell B1 and "Smith" in cell B2, the formula +B1&B2 will result in "JohnSmith". Like formulas for values, formulas containing strings must begin with a plus sign (+). The ampersand (&), which is the special operator for strings, tells Symphony to join items together.

- To add a space between the first and last name, you indicate within the formula that a space belongs between the two cell entries, as in

    +B1&" "&B2

    Whenever you want to include in a formula an element that is not the cell address itself or a range name, you must enclose that element in double quotation marks. In the example above, the space is enclosed in quotation marks, telling Symphony to add a space between B1 and B2.

- You can indicate cell addresses by either typing or pointing.

- String formulas involving functions follow the same rules as mathematical formulas. That is, string functions begin with an @ sign, followed by the function name and an argument or range in parentheses.

Symphony's string arithmetic will enable you to apply many types of functions to strings stored in data bases, in spreadsheets themselves, and in text produced through Symphony's word-processing capability. In the following chapters, you will find specific explanations of the many string arithmetic functions and suggested applications for using these functions.

Editing

Because of the complexity of Symphony, four kinds of editing are possible. First, you can edit data that you are entering in response to a command. For example, you can edit range names, cell addresses, or special entries that you are making in settings sheets. This data can be edited if you have not pressed RETURN and "locked in" the entry. The other three kinds of editing involve editing data that you are entering or have already entered in SHEET, DOC, and FORM windows. This section covers the keys and procedures for editing in a SHEET window, which includes editing labels, values, and formulas. (Erasing ranges and deleting rows and columns are discussed in Chapter 4.)

Editing an entry in a SHEET window is easy to do in Symphony. (This task is the same as editing an entry in a 1-2-3 worksheet.) To edit an entry in a Symphony worksheet, you begin by moving the cursor to the appropriate cell and pressing the F2 function key (the Edit key), or simply by pressing F2 if you are in the process of typing the entry. Remember, however, that the F2 function key only activates the EDIT mode in a SHEET window. Therefore, make sure that you are in a SHEET window when trying to edit data entered in a SHEET window.

When you press F2, Symphony switches from the SHEET mode to the EDIT mode. In the EDIT mode the following keys function differently than they do in the SHEET mode:

Key	Action
←	Moves the cursor one position to the left
→	Moves the cursor one position to the right
Home	Moves the cursor to the first character position of edit line
End	Moves the cursor one position to the right of the last character
Backspace	Deletes the character just to the left of the cursor
Del	Deletes the character above the cursor
Esc	Clears the edit line. Esc will also cancel data that you haven't finished typing.

After you press F2, the mode indicator in the upper right corner of the screen will change to EDIT. The contents of the cell will be duplicated in the second line of the control panel (in this book, called the "Edit Line") and will then be ready for editing.

To show how these keys are used, let's consider two examples. First, suppose you want to edit an entry in cell E4 that reads "Sales Comparisson." After you position the cursor to cell E4, the actions to take are these:

Key	Edit Line	Explanation
F2	'Sales Comparisson_	The cursor always appears at the end of the edit line when you press F2.
← ← ←	'Sales Comparisson	The cursor now appears below the extra *s*.
Del	'Sales Comparisson	The Del key deletes the character above the cursor.

RETURN   You must hit RETURN to
                                update the entry in the
                                spreadsheet and return to the
                                READY mode.

One thing to remember about using the EDIT mode is that you can
also use it when you are entering a cell for the first time and you
make a mistake. With the EDIT mode, you can eliminate retyping.

Now suppose you want to change a formula in cell G6 from
+D4/H3*(Y5+4000) to +C4/H3*(Y5+4000). After you move the
cursor to cell G6, do the following:

Key	Edit Line	Explanation
F2	+D4/H3*(Y5+4000)_	Again, the cursor always appears at the end of the edit line when you first press F2.
Home	+D4/H3*(Y5+4000)	The Home key takes you to the first position in the edit line.
→	+D4/H3*(Y5+4000)	The → key moves the cursor one position to the right.
C	+CD4/H3*(Y5+4000)	Whenever you enter a character in the EDIT mode, the character is inserted to the left of the cursor. Entering a character will never cause you to write over another one. Unwanted characters can be eliminated with the Del and Backspace keys.
Del	+C4/H3*(Y5+4000)	The Del key deletes the character above the cursor.
RETURN		Again, you must hit RETURN to update the entry in the spreadsheet and return to the SHEET mode.

The Edit (F2) and Calc (F8) function keys can be used together to convert a formula stored in a cell to a simple number. As indicated in figure 2.20 in Chapter 2, F8 is normally used for recalculating when **S**ettings **R**ecalculation in the SHEET menu is set to **M**anual. (The **R**ecalculation command is covered in Chapter 4.) However, when you are in the EDIT mode, pressing F8 will cause a formula to be converted to a number, which is its current value.

For example, suppose you want to use F8 to convert the formula in the previous example to its current value (assumed to be 64,000) and to store the result. You should take the following steps:

Key	Edit Line	Explanation
F2	+C4/H3*(Y5+4000)_	F2 puts Symphony in the EDIT mode.
F8	64000_	F8 converts the formula to its current value (64,000).
RETURN		RETURN stores the entry in the current cell and shifts back to the SHEET mode.

Ranges

In Symphony, as in 1-2-3, the commands and functions often require that you deal with a group of cells in aggregate. And as in 1-2-3, in Symphony this group is called a range. A *range* is one or more cells in a rectangular group. One cell is the smallest possible range, and the largest range is the size of the worksheet itself.

In Symphony, using ranges will definitely make your work easier and faster. Because of the worksheet size and the possibility that you may have spreadsheets, data bases, and word-processing text in various parts of the worksheet, using range names and indicating ranges in settings sheets will save you from having to hunt all over your worksheet for ranges. Ranges also allow you to process blocks of cells in commands and formulas at the same time. Although you can choose when to use ranges, you will soon learn that using ranges frequently can simplify and speed up many operations. (Ranges are covered in more detail in Chapter 4.)

The Shape of Ranges

Ranges are rectangles, as illustrated in figure 3.9. The expanding-cursor feature allows you to see the shape of ranges in Symphony. When you designate a range, Symphony displays it in reverse video. Creating a range is easy because you can tell where its borders are. As the cursor moves, the reverse-video rectangle expands. (See fig. 3.9.)

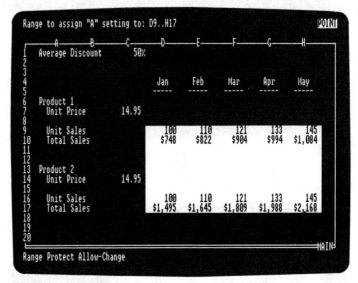

Fig. 3.9.

Designating Ranges

Ranges can be designated in three ways: entering cell addresses, pointing to cells, and naming ranges. These methods allow you to indicate the diagonally opposite corners of the rectangular group of cells that the range represents. (See fig. 3.10.)

Ranges are specified by diagonally opposite corners—usually the upper left-hand and lower right-hand cells. The other set of corners, however, is also permissible. For example, the range shown in figure 3.11 can be identified as A1..F16 or F1..A16.

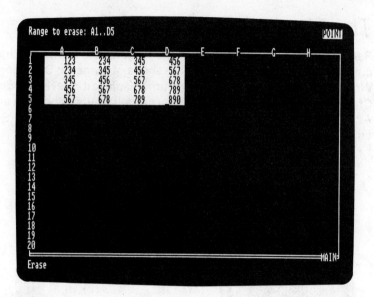

Fig. 3.10.

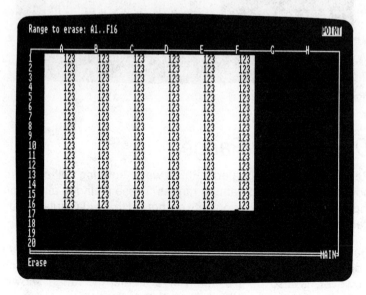

Fig. 3.11.

Cell addresses that specify the corners are usually separated by one or more periods, as in

A7..D10
AA1.AB20
J2...K4

If you separate cell addresses with one period or with three or more, Symphony will automatically change the periods to two.

Ranges will be referred to frequently in the following chapter. Once you begin using Symphony extensively, you will find that the range feature is more than a convenience; ranges are often necessary for processing commands and moving to various parts of the worksheet. All the commands that use ranges in a SHEET window will be included in the next chapter.

New with Symphony

Integrating SHEET Windows with Other Applications

So far, most of this chapter has focused on the SHEET window as a separate application in the Symphony program. But even though the SHEET window can be used apart from the DOC, FORM, GRAPH, and COMM environments, you will get the most out of Symphony by integrating your spreadsheet work with the four other applications.

Many possibilities are available for integrating SHEET windows with other types of windows. Following are some suggestions for integrating the work that you do in a SHEET window with your work in other kinds of windows:

- SHEET windows can be integrated with DOC (word-processing) windows in two ways. First, you can draft reports directly from the data you have collected in a SHEET window. Having a SHEET window with a spreadsheet or data base on the screen at the same time that you are drafting a report will help you organize your thoughts and present your analysis in the report. (See fig. 3.12.) Second, as you draft a report in a DOC window, you can easily incorporate figures

and charts by using spreadsheets and data bases
stored in SHEET windows. (See fig. 3.13.)

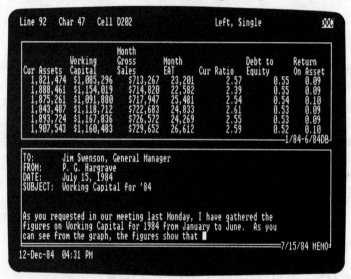

Fig. 3.12.

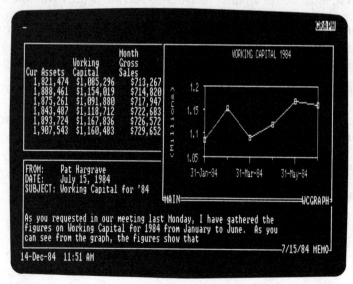

Fig. 3.13.

- If you have used 1-2-3 before, then integrating SHEET and GRAPH windows won't be new to you. Like 1-2-3, Symphony provides the capability for instantly creating graphs from data collected in spreadsheets and data bases. GRAPH windows, however, offer the capability of displaying two or more graphs on the screen at once. Depending on your equipment and the driver set, you can display a SHEET window and GRAPH window(s) on the screen simultaneously. (See fig. 3.14.)

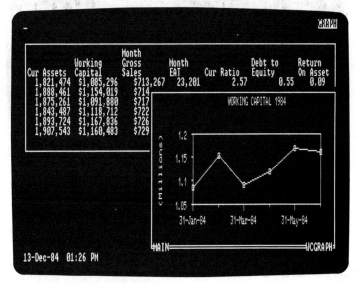

Fig. 3.14.

- Once you begin using the FORM you will quickly see how FORM and SHEET environments are integrated. In fact, you will see that getting the most out of Symphony's data form capability requires working in both environments. These environments are related for two reasons. First, you begin the creation of a data form in a SHEET window. Second, the data base created in a FORM window is viewed in a SHEET window. (See fig. 3.15.) Also within the SHEET command menu, discussed in Chapter 4, are the primary data management commands.

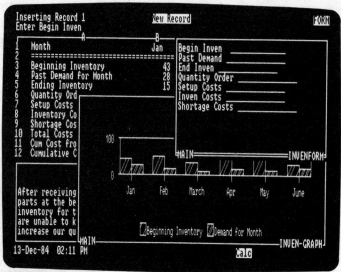

Fig. 3.15.

- Symphony's COMM capability depends on the SHEET environment. To use fully this capability, you will need to read-in data transferred through the COMM environment into a SHEET window.

Conclusion

As an overview of the Symphony SHEET environment, this chapter has defined its capabilities and described the general procedures for working in a SHEET window. Using these procedures, you will be able to enter and format labels and values easily, build various kinds of sophisticated formulas, edit any cell entry, and integrate SHEET windows with other types of windows. Chapter 4 shows specifically how you can use Symphony's SHEET environment and the SHEET window commands.

4

SHEET Window Commands

Symphony, like 1-2-3, has a sophisticated command system that provides the full capability of spreadsheet-only programs. Commands are the instructions you give Symphony to perform a variety of tasks, such as formatting a worksheet, creating graphs, or accessing a data base. These commands also include replicating formulas, inserting and deleting rows and columns, and moving data. Unlike 1-2-3, Symphony has a spreadsheet command menu that enables you to switch rows and columns, easily change formulas to values, and "hide" cell contents.

If you frequently use 1-2-3 for creating spreadsheets, you will find that Symphony's spreadsheet application is much like 1-2-3's. Procedures are similar for entering and editing data, moving the cell pointer, and identifying and using ranges. One major difference should be kept in mind as you use Symphony's SHEET environment: operations that you complete in a SHEET window can affect other windows which you have created on your worksheet. Suppose, for example, that you have created a SHEET window, a DOC window, and a second SHEET window containing a data base. Unless you restrict the ranges for each of these windows, changes in one of the SHEET windows can affect the data in the other two. In the discussion of the spreadsheet commands, mention will be made of those operations that can affect data in other windows.

SHEET Command MENU

Command menus, which are the devices used by Symphony to present command alternatives to the user, allow you to complete a spreadsheet operation easily. You select spreadsheet commands by first retrieving the SHEET command MENU. This is done by pressing the MENU key (F10), hereafter referred to as the SHEET menu key, or by pressing the slash key (/).

Selecting commands is fairly easy, but locating a command can be a complicated process. In some ways, though, locating spreadsheet commands in Symphony is easier than in 1-2-3. First, the Symphony SHEET menu pertains only to spreadsheet operations. Unlike the 1-2-3 Worksheet menu, the Symphony SHEET menu does not include File and Print commands; commands controlling file and print operations are located in the SERVICES menu. (Throughout this book the first letter of each word in a command name appears in boldface, emphasizing that the first letter can be used to select the command.) Second, Lotus has also made the Symphony spread-sheet menu easier to work with because frequently used commands, such as Column-Width in 1-2-3 and Erase, are now located at the first level of Symphony's SHEET menu. Third, settings sheets enable you to view all settings items at once.

New with Symphony

Another feature of the Symphony command-menu system that makes it easy to use is the display. As shown in figure 4.1, the menu is visible on the second line of the control panel, while an explanation appears on the line above. Once you have selected a command, the command name appears in the lower left corner until you have completed all selections or responses.

To select a command, you can either point to the option you want or enter the first letter of the command name. To point to the command-menu item, use the left and right cursor keys on the right-hand side of the keyboard. When the cursor is positioned at the proper item, hit RETURN. If you move the cursor to the last item on the list and strike the → key again, the menu cursor will "round the horn" and reappear on the first item in the list. Similarly, if the menu cursor is on the first

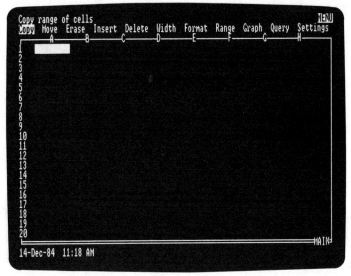

Fig. 4.1.

item in the menu, typing the left arrow will move the cursor to the last option.

Entering the first letter of the command-menu item is another way to select a command. For example, to select the **Range T**ranspose command to switch a column and a row, you press the SHEET menu key (F10) or type /, then type **R** to select **R**ange. At this point, the menu in figure 4.2 appears.

From the line in the menu, you select **T**ranspose by typing **T**. You are then asked to provide information so that Symphony can complete the operation.

If you find that you have made the wrong command selection, you can hit Esc at any time to return to the previous command menu. For instance, if you meant to enter **D**istribution instead of **F**ill, press Esc to return to the SHEET **R**ange menu. To move to prior command menus or to move out of the menu mode altogether, you enter a series of escapes. You can also press the Ctrl and Break keys to move out of the menu mode and back to the SHEET mode.

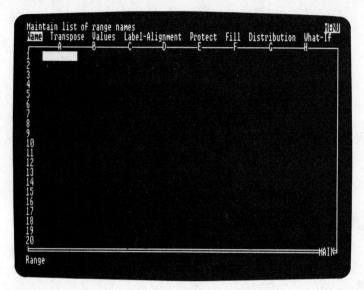

Maintain list of range names   MENU
Name Transpose Values Label-Alignment Protect Fill Distribution What-If

Fig. 4.2.

Spreadsheet Commands

If you look back at the Symphony SHEET command MENU, you will see that it includes commands specifically related to creating spreadsheets (**C**opy, **M**ove, **E**rase, **I**nsert, **D**elete, **W**idth, **F**ormat, **R**ange, and **S**ettings) and graphs (**G**raph), and to conducting data base query and/or sort operations (**Q**uery). This chapter contains the commands for creating spreadsheets. Graphics commands are covered in Chapter 9, and data base commands are explained in Chapter 11.

This discussion of spreadsheet commands does not follow the order in which they appear in the menu. The **R**ange commands are discussed first because setting and storing ranges through range names are fundamental tasks in many spreadsheet operations. Following **R**ange commands, the SHEET commands discussed are **E**rase, **M**ove, **I**nsert, **D**elete, **W**idth, **F**ormat, **T**itles, and **R**ecalculation.

Range Commands

The commands that operate on ranges are organized in Symphony under the SHEET **R**ange menu. These commands give you the ability to name, protect, or change label justification in a range. In the SHEET mode, when you press the SHEET menu key (F10) or type /, then type **R**, the menu appears as shown in figure 4.3.

The Label-Prefix command is covered in Chapter 3 in the section on Labels. The other range commands are discussed here.

```
Maintain list of range names                                    MENU
Name Transpose Values Label-Alignment  Protect  Fill  Distribution  What-If
         A        B        C     D        E      F        G          H
1
2  Balance Sheet
3  ===========================================================================
4                                                              Common
5         Assets                                  31-Jul-83     Size
6
7  Cash                                            $255,000      8%
8  Marketable Securities                             29,000      1%
9  Accounts Receivable                 1,256,000
10     Allowance for Doubtful Accounts     8,000
11     Net Accounts Receivable                     1,127,500    37%
12 Inventory                                         323,000    11%
13 Prepaid Expenses                                   60,000     2%
14 Other                                              21,000     1%
15                                                 ----------
16     Total Current Assets                        1,815,500    60%
17
18 Property, Plant, and Equipment        956,700
19     Accumulated Depreciation          123,700
20     Net Property, Plant, and Equipment            833,000    27%
                                                               MAIN
Range
```

Fig. 4.3.

Naming Ranges

In Symphony a name can be assigned to a range of cells. Range names can be up to 15 characters long, and they should be descriptive to help you recall what range the name represents. The advantage to naming ranges is that range names are easier to understand than cell addresses, and range names allow you to work more intuitively. For example, describing gross margin with the phrase "Sales - COGS" is more understandable than using B = +A17-B10.

Creating Range Names

Range names are created with the **R**ange **N**ame **C**reate and **R**ange **N**ame **L**abels commands. Once names are established, they can be easily applied in both commands and formulas. The **R**ange **N**ame **C**reate command allows you to specify a name for any range, even one cell. In executing this command, you can specify range names by one of two methods: entering the cell address or pointing. You can also use **R**ange **N**ame **C**reate to respecify a range if its location has changed. If minor changes occur to the range, however, such as a column or row of numbers being deleted from the range, Symphony will handle these changes internally without any respecification.

Range names can also be used in naming macros. A macro is named with **R**ange **N**ame **C**reate, as is any other range. Keyboard macros are discussed in detail in Chapter 13.

The **R**ange **N**ame **L**abels command is similar to **R**ange **N**ame **C**reate except that with **R**ange **N**ame **L**abels, the names for ranges are taken directly from adjacent label entries. (See fig. 4.4.)

If you use the **R**ange **N**ame **L**abels command and specify that the appropriate name for cell B1 is to the left in cell A1, you can assign

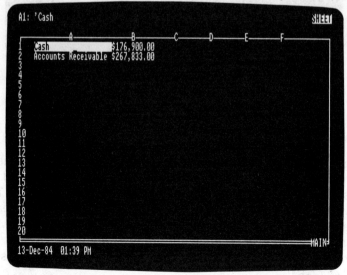

Fig. 4.4.

the name "Cash" to the range B1. If you assign the label "Accounts Receivable" as a range name, Symphony will store "Accounts Receiv". Symphony accepts only up to 15 characters (including spaces) for any range name or range name label.

Deleting Range Names

Range names can be deleted individually or all at once. The **R**ange **N**ame **D**elete command allows you to delete a single range name. The **R**ange **N**ame **R**eset command causes all range names to be deleted. Because of its power, **R**ange **N**ame **R**eset should be used with caution.

New with Symphony

Creating a Table of Range Names

A range name option included in Symphony but not in 1-2-3 is the **R**ange **N**ame **T**able command. With this command, you can create a list of range names on the current worksheet. The **R**ange **N**ame **T**able option enables you to print a list of range names or to see very quickly on the screen all the range names you have created. (See fig. 4.5.)

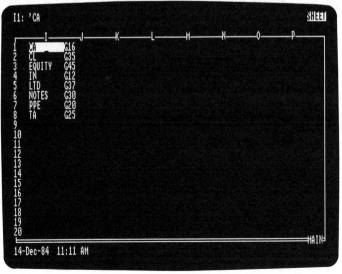

Fig. 4.5.

Creating a range name table is simple, although you should be careful about where you tell Symphony to put the table. To create it, you select the **R**ange **N**ame **T**able command. Then when Symphony asks for the location for the table, indicate the range on your worksheet where you want the table located and press RETURN. Be certain that you tell Symphony to place the table in an area which won't interfere with any other worksheet data. Otherwise, the table will overwrite previously entered data.

Using Range Names

After range names have been created, they can be useful tools in processing commands and generating formulas. In both cases, whenever a range must be designated, a name can be entered instead. This often eliminates the repetitive task of either entering cell addresses or pointing to cell locations each time a range specification is called for. Suppose you had designated "SALES" as a range name for the range A5..J5 in one of your worksheets. The simplest way to compute the sum of this range is to use the formula @SUM(SALES). Similarly, to determine the maximum value in the range, you can use the formula @MAX(SALES). Range names can always be used in place of cell addresses, functions, and formulas.

Symphony also allows you to use multiple names for the same range. For example, a cell can be given the range names "1978 Sales" and "Sales Prev Yr" in the same worksheet.

Still another advantage is that once a range name has been established, Symphony will automatically use that name throughout the worksheet in place of cell addresses. If a range name is deleted, Symphony will no longer use that name but will revert to cell addresses. The following example shows the effect of assigning the name "Revenues" to the range A5..J5.

Prior to Creating Range Name   After Creating Range Name

@SUM(A5..J5)   @SUM(REVENUES)

The first example, which uses range names, is illustrated in figure 4.6. The example shows a simple case of adding together two rows of numbers.

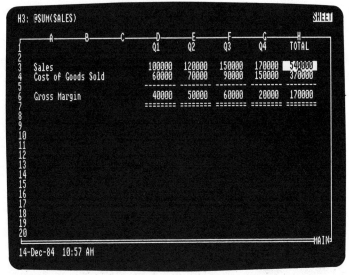

Fig. 4.6.

If the range name "SALES" is assigned to the range D3..G3 and the name "CGS" to range D4..G4, cell H3 can be defined with the formula

@SUM(SALES)

Similarly, cell H4 can be assigned the formula

@SUM(CGS)

Finally, cell H6 can contain the formula

@SUM(SALES)-@SUM(CGS)

Another example uses names to designate the ranges of cells to be printed or saved. Suppose you set up special names corresponding to different areas and want to print, or save to another worksheet, the corresponding portions of the current worksheet. When Symphony prompts you for a range, you can enter a predefined name rather than actual cell addresses. For example, in response to the print range prompt, you can enter the range name *Page 1* or the name *Page 5*.

A third example using range names involves the GoTo key (F5). You will recall that the GoTo key allows you to move the cell pointer directly to a cell when you specify the cell's address. Another alternative is to provide a range name instead of a cell address. For example, you can enter *Instruct* in response to "Address to go TO: ". If "Instruct" is the range name for a set of cells that includes a set of instructions, you may get the results shown in figure 4.7.

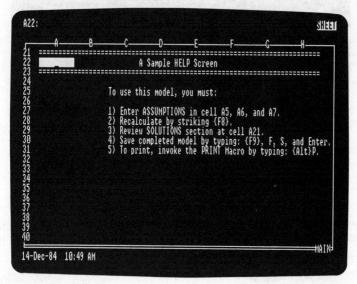

Fig. 4.7.

Using the SALES example again, suppose you assign the name CGS to the range D4..G4. You can erase this portion of the worksheet by pressing the SHEET menu key (F10) or typing /, and selecting **E**rase, then entering the range name *CGS* instead of cell coordinates D4..G4.

To see how this function works, look at the example in figure 4.6. Suppose that after you select the **E**rase command, you cannot remember the name of the range you want to erase. You can press the SHEET menu key to produce a list of the range names in the current worksheet. If you have more range names than will fit across the control panel, press the SHEET menu key a second time. Symphony will display a complete list of range names on the screen. Figure 4.8 shows the screen at this point. After the list appears, you can use the cursor to point to the first alternative (CGS) and select it by pressing RETURN.

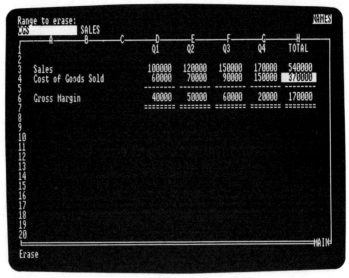

Fig. 4.8.

Transposing Rows and Columns (Range Transpose)

New with Symphony

Another **R**ange command new to Symphony but not included in 1-2-3 is **R**ange **T**ranspose. With this command you can transpose rows to columns or columns to rows. This added feature is particularly useful if, for example, you want to take a monthly inventory sheet with items listed in Column A, as shown in figure 4.9, and create a data base that will display each item in a separate column with its monthly figure totaled below it.

As indicated by this example, the **R**ange **T**ranspose command allows you to copy labels, values, and formulas, and to reverse their positions from rows to columns or from columns to rows. To use this command, select **R**ange **T**ranspose, indicate the range of the original column or row, and finally indicate the range for the new column or row.

When using the **R**ange **T**ranspose command, you should be aware of the following possibilities. First, if you are transposing values or

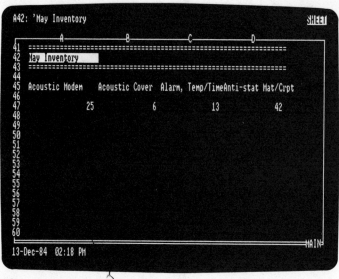

A42: 'May Inventory   SHEET

```
        A           B           C           D
41  ==================================================
42  May Inventory
43  ==================================================
44
45  Acoustic Modem   Acoustic Cover  Alarm, Temp/TimeAnti-stat Mat/Crpt
46
47             25              6              13              42
48
49
50
51
52
53
54
55
56
57
58
59
60
```
                                                          MAIN
13-Dec-84 02:18 PM

Fig. 4.9.

formulas, Symphony will recalculate or indicate that you should press the Calc key when copying is completed. If, however, the range you are transposing contains relative cell addresses (discussed in the section on Copying), Symphony cannot convert the cell addresses. In this case, formulas will not recalculate correctly. Second, make sure that the "copy TO" range won't interfere with other worksheet data. Otherwise, the transposed columns and rows will overwrite previously entered data.

Using the *Range Values Command*

New with Symphony

The **R**ange **V**alues command is another **R**ange command not included in 1-2-3. With **R**ange **V**alues, you can copy a range of values from one part of a worksheet to another. This feature is useful in a worksheet when you want to preserve current values that will be changed when new values are entered. What is particularly important about the **R**ange **V**alues command is that it converts formulas to values. You don't have to worry, therefore, about formulas that depend on cell references. (Copying formulas with cell addresses is discussed in more detail in the section on Copying.)

Now consider the following illustration of the use of the **R**ange **V**alues command. Suppose you calculate monthly totals from values entered into an income statement, as in figure 4.10. As you change the sheet every month, the Year-to-Date (Y-T-D) totals will change as well. If, however, you want to save the Y-T-D totals to compare them with previous years or quarters, the **R**ange **V**alues command enables you to do so, as illustrated in figure 4.11.

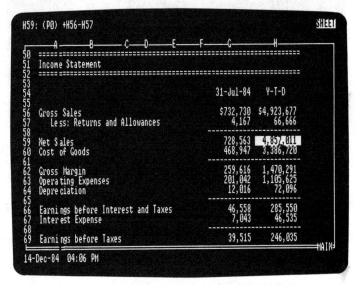

Fig. 4.10.

With 1-2-3 you can extract values like those above, but Symphony's **R**ange **V**alues command will save you both steps and time. To copy values in Symphony, select the **R**ange **V**alues command. When Symphony asks for "Range to copy FROM:", indicate what range of values you want moved. Then indicate where you want values moved, being careful that the newly copied values don't overwrite previously entered data.

To complete the same operation in 1-2-3, you have two options, both of which require additional steps and are much more complicated than using Symphony's **R**ange **V**alues command. The two 1-2-3 operations are described here only briefly.

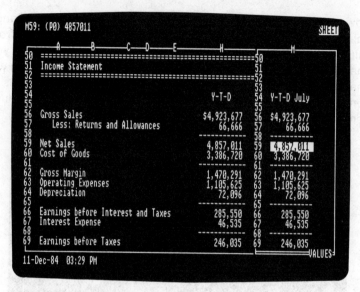

Fig. 4.11.

In the first option, copying values in 1-2-3 requires using the Edit and Calc keys to change formulas to values, and then using the **C**opy command to copy the values to another part of the worksheet. Besides having many steps, this procedure has another disadvantage: it requires that you change your original worksheet, thus changing original formulas to values.

The second option will leave the original worksheet as it is, but requires that you use the **F**ile **X**tract command to copy a range of values. When you use **F**ile **X**tract, you must create a file to which you can extract the new values. If you wish to keep the new values in the original worksheet, you must add those values by using the **F**ile **C**ombine command.

Using the Range Label-Alignment Command

The **R**ange **L**abel-Alignment command is discussed in Chapter 3 in the section on Labels.

Protecting Ranges

The ability to protect ranges is a special feature of 1-2-3. Symphony also includes the **R**ange **P**rotect feature although a few changes have expanded this capability. In Symphony the **R**ange **P**rotect command can be used simply to "freeze" a range, thus preventing changes. In addition, Symphony's **R**ange **P**rotect command, when used with the **S**ettings **S**ecurity **G**lobal-Protection and **F**ormat **O**ther **H**idden commands, permits you to hide a range of cells and prevent anyone from making changes in these cells unless the person enters a password especially created by the user. (See the section on Security in Chapter 1.)

In Symphony, as in 1-2-3, you can use a series of commands to set up ranges of cells that cannot be changed without special effort. In fact, rows and columns containing protected cells cannot be deleted from the worksheet. The **R**ange **P**rotect command is particularly beneficial when you are setting up worksheets that other people will use but which you don't want changed.

When a worksheet is first created, every cell has the potential of being protected, but no cell is protected unless you invoke the **R**ange **P**rotect command along with the **G**lobal-Protection command in the SERVICES menu. Lotus uses the analogy of a series of electric fences being set up around all the cells in the worksheet. The "juice" to these fences is turned off when the sheet is first loaded. In other words, all the cells in the worksheet can be modified. This arrangement is appropriate because you will want to have access to everything in the worksheet while you are creating it. Once you have finished creating the worksheet, however, you may have areas that you don't want modified, or you may want to set up special form-entry areas and not allow cursor movement anywhere else.

To protect a range of cells in your worksheet, you need to take certain steps. First, you must provide cell protection for your worksheet by setting the **G**lobal-Protection option in **S**ettings of the SERVICES menu. To set **G**lobal-Protection, press the SERVICES key (F9), select **S**ettings, then select **G**lobal-Protection. Next, position the cursor on "Yes" in response to "Allow changes only to cells with 'A' setting." Once you have issued this command (**Y**es), any cell can be protected.

To continue the "electric fence" analogy, the **G**lobal-Protection command is the switch that activates all the electric fences in the worksheet. After you turn on this switch, your next step is to tell Symphony which fences should be "turned off" so that data can be entered.

To turn off the protection on certain cells, choose the **R**ange **P**rotect command and then select **A**llow-Changes. You next indicate the range to mark the cells where changes are to be allowed. You can reprotect these cells at any time by issuing the **R**ange **P**rotect **P**revent-Changes option. If you want to make changes possible in any cell in the worksheet, you select the **G**lobal-Protection **N**o option in **S**ettings of the SERVICES menu. The chart in figure 4.12 may help you understand the relationship between the **G**lobal-Protection and **R**ange **P**rotect commands if sufficient memory is available.

	SERVICES **G**lobal-Protection **N**o: allow changes to all cells	SERVICES **G**lobal-Protection **Y**es: allow changes to cells with only "A" setting
SHEET **R**ange **P**rotect **A**llow-Changes "A" setting: Allow changes to cells even if **G**lobal-Protection = **Y**es	No Restriction Changes can be made in all cells	Restricted Changes can be made in only "A" cells
SHEET **R**ange **P**rotect **P**revent-Changes Remove "A" setting: Prevent changes to cells when **G**lobal-Protection = **Y**es	No Restriction Changes can be made in all cells	Restricted The "A" marker is removed; no changes can be made

Fig. 4.12.

Suppose you create a worksheet that includes a number of long and important formulas. You may want to protect these formulas against accidental deletion by using Symphony's protection capability. But what if you need to make a change in several of these formulas? You can move around the sheet, allowing the formulas to be changed, then preventing the cells from being changed again. Or you can use the **G**lobal-Protection **N**o setting to "lower the fences" around all the cells. After you make the necessary changes, the **G**lobal-Protection **Y**es setting will restore the protection to all cells.

*New
with
Symphony*

For even more protection, you can limit the movement of the cursor by using the **W**indow **S**ettings **R**estrict selection from the SERVICES menu. Setting a restrict range will allow cursor movement only to those cells within the range you set. Suppose, for example, that you want to restrict cursor movement within the area occupied by the data in figure 4.13. To restrict this area, you select **W**indow from the SERVICES menu, then **S**ettings, then **R**estrict, and finally **R**ange. When Symphony asks "Restrict range for this window: ", you type E1..G12 or move the cursor to highlight that range. (Press Esc to move the cursor back to the beginning of your worksheet.)

```
Restrict range for this window: A51..H76                      POINT

       A       B       C       D       E       F       G       H
 57   Less: Returns and Allowances                     4,167    66,666
 58
 59   Net Sales                                       728,563 4,857,011
 60   Cost of Goods                                   468,947 3,386,720
 61
 62   Gross Margin                                    259,616 1,470,291
 63   Operating Expenses                              201,042 1,105,625
 64   Depreciation                                     12,016    72,096
 65
 66   Earnings before Interest and Taxes               46,558   285,550
 67   Interest Expense                                  7,043    46,535
 68
 69   Earnings before Taxes                            39,515   246,035
 70   Income Taxes                                     10,342    62,816
 71
 72   Earnings after Taxes                             29,173   183,219
 73   Cash Dividends                                        0    76,389
 74
 75   Net Income                                      $29,173  $106,830
 76                                                   =================
                                                                   MAIN
 Window Settings Restrict Range
```

Fig. 4.13.

The restrict range will remain in effect in the window where you have set the range until you reset **R**estrict. The **W**indow **S**ettings **R**estrict and the **R**ange **P**rotect commands are important features for eliminating the possibility of data being lost because new data overwrites it, or the possibility of values or formulas being changed.

Filling Ranges with Numbers (Range Fill)

The **R**ange **F**ill command has a number of uses throughout the Symphony program, particularly in any SHEET environment where you require a range of values listed in sequence. This range of values can include simply a table of numbers listed in increments of one, or a list of years, as in figure 4.14. Although the **R**ange **F**ill command must be used in a SHEET mode, you can apply it in a number of projects: reports that contain long itemized lists, or anything involving a sequence of values or dates. You will particularly find the **R**ange **F**ill command valuable when you have created data bases.

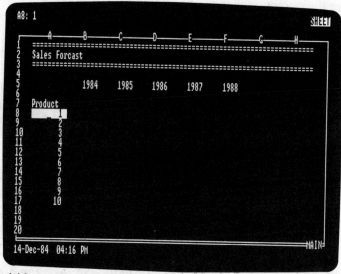

Fig. 4.14.

The **R**ange **F**ill command first prompts you for the number where you want the sequence to start. The command then asks for the step or incremental value that you want to add to the previous value. Finally, the command asks for the ending value at which to stop the filling operation.

To enter a sequence of numbers, you retrieve the SHEET menu, select **R**ange, and then select **F**ill when the **R**ange menu appears. After you select **F**ill, Symphony will ask "Fill Range: ". Here you indicate the range in the worksheet where the numbers should be listed. In our example in figure 4.14, you indicate A7..A17. Next, Symphony asks for the Start Value, for which you enter 1. Following that is Step Value, or the increments. Here you enter 1. Finally, you must respond to Stop Value. Here you enter 10. The Symphony default stop value is set at 8191, so it is possible to create a list running the length of the total worksheet area.

One valuable use for the **R**ange **F**ill command is for data bases that will be sorted. When you use this command, if you attach consecutive numbers to each record in a data base (thereby placing the numbers in a separate field), no matter how much you change the original order of the data base, you can re-create the original order. You simply sort your data base according to the numbers listed by using the **R**ange **F**ill command. Using **R**ange **F**ill in this way is particularly helpful if the data base you began with has a relational order rather than a numeric one, such as the names of the months in a year. Figures 4.15 and 4.16 show an example before and after resorting.

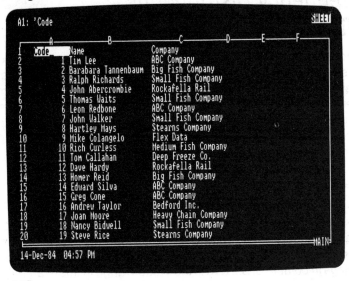

Fig. 4.15.

```
Sort data records                                                      MENU
Settings  Find  Extract  Unique  Delete  Record-Sort  Parse  Quit
     ┌A────────────B────────────┬C─────────D─────E─────┬F──────
  1  Code    Name               Company
  2       16 Andrew Taylor      Bedford Inc.
  3        2 Barabara Tannenbaum Big Fish Company
  4       12 Dave Hardy         Rockafella Rail
  5       14 Edward Silva       ABC Company
  6       15 Greg Cone          ABC Company
  7        8 Hartley Mays       Stearns Company
  8       13 Homer Reid         Big Fish Company
  9       17 Joan Moore         Heavy Chain Company
 10        4 John Abercrombie   Rockafella Rail
 11        7 John Walker        Small Fish Company
 12        6 Leon Redbone       ABC Company
 13        9 Mike Colangelo     Flex Data
 14       18 Nancy Bidwell      Small Fish Company
 15        3 Ralph Richards     Small Fish Company
 16       10 Rich Curless       Medium Fish Company
 17       19 Steve Rice         Stearns Company
 18        5 Thomas Waits       Small Fish Company
 19        1 Tim Lee            ABC Company
 20       11 Tom Callahan       Deep Freeze Co.
                                                                   MAIN
Query
```

Fig. 4.16.

Frequency Distributions (**R**ange **D**istribution)

Another SHEET command that is valuable when working with data bases is the **R**ange **D**istribution command, used to create frequency distributions. For those who are not familiar with this term, a *frequency distribution* is a representation of the relationship between a set of measurement classes and the frequency of occurrence of each class. A simple example of a frequency distribution and the use of the **R**ange **D**istribution command is shown in figure 4.17. This example contains a list of consumers and their product preferences.

To create the frequency distribution in this example, you need to take the following steps. First, select the **R**ange **D**istribution command from the SHEET menu. Then specify a Values range, which corresponds to the range of numbers listing the "Taste Preference" ratings in column B. B3..B18 is the Values range in this example. The next step is to set up the range of intervals, or what Symphony calls

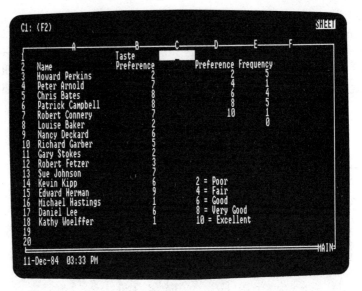

Fig. 4.17.

the Bin range. Here the Bin range is D3..D7. If you want evenly spaced intervals, you can use the **R**ange **F**ill command to specify the values to be included in the Bin range. The example above does not have evenly spaced intervals, so the **R**ange **F**ill command was not used to list the values.

When you specify these ranges and enter the **R**ange **D**istribution command, Symphony returns the Results column to the right of the Bin range (E3..E8). The Results column is a frequency distribution, which is always in the column segment to the right of the Bin range and extending one row down.

The values in the Results column represent the frequency of occurrence of numbers in the Values range that fall within the interval. The first interval in the Bin range is for values greater than zero and less than or equal to one, the second interval is for values greater than one and less than or equal to three, and so on. In the Results column the last value, in cell D6, just below the corresponding column segment, is the frequency of what is left over (that is, the frequency of anything that doesn't fit into an interval classification).

The **R**ange **D**istribution command can be used to create under-standable results from a series of numbers, particularly in the analysis of surveys. The results are easily graphed, as shown in figure 4.18. According to this graph, the manufacturer of the product should be searching for another product, or at least improving the taste of the current one.

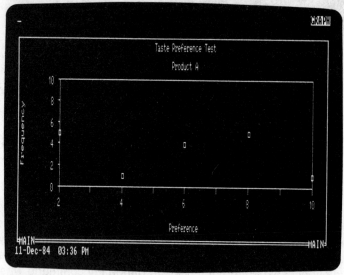

Fig. 4.18.

"What If" Analysis (**R**ange **W**hat-If)

Symphony's SHEET **R**ange **W**hat-If command enables you to make a very extensive analysis with a minimal amount of effort. With the command, you can perform the kind of thorough analysis that you might not do otherwise.

The SHEET **R**ange **W**hat-If command works through iteration. That is, Symphony takes sets of values and substitutes them one at a time into the worksheet. The results of the substitution are automatically recorded by Symphony. You provide Symphony with the values to substitute and also tell it where to substitute them.

This procedure may sound mysterious, but it is actually very simple. Most of the work is done internally by Symphony. All you have to know is how to set the appropriate ranges. Symphony takes care of the rest.

You may find the SHEET **R**ange **W**hat-If command difficult to use at first. But once you have learned how to use it, you will find that it is one of the most powerful commands in Symphony's SHEET command MENU. In fact, the power of this command rivals similar commands in some of the most sophisticated mainframe decision systems. When you consider the ease of implementation, the SHEET **R**ange **W**hat-If command can be one of your most frequently used SHEET commands.

The purpose of the SHEET **R**ange **W**hat-If command is to structure the "what if" process. The command allows you to build a table of input values and have Symphony substitute them one at a time into a model you have developed. Symphony then records the results in the table, next to the input values.

A simple example of how the command works can be illustrated in a table of interest rates and their effects on the monthly payments of a thirty-year mortgage, as shown in figure 4.19.

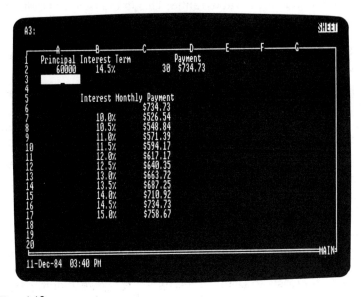

Fig. 4.19.

By using the SHEET **R**ange **W**hat-If **1**-Way command, you can have Symphony substitute the interest rates you have entered in a column into the appropriate input cells above. After a short wait, Symphony will list the monthly payments in the column, next to the interest rates.

Before entering the SHEET **R**ange **W**hat-If command, you must enter the principal, interest, and term values in cells A2, B2, and C2, respectively. Then enter the formula for calculating payment in cell D2: @PMT(A2,B2/12,C2*12). Next, you must enter the interest rate values in a column. (You can use the SHEET **R**ange **F**ill command, covered in the section on Filling Ranges with Numbers.) Cells B7..B18 hold the interest rates.

The next step is to enter the appropriate formula for calculating the results, or cell address from which to draw them, next to the column of interest rates and one row above the first entry. As shown in figure 4.19, +D2 has been entered in cell C6, but the actual formula used to compute the value in cell C6—@PMT(A2,B2/12,C2*12)—could have been entered.

When the SHEET **R**ange **W**hat-If command is executed, Symphony asks you to indicate a Table range. This is the range of cells that includes the column of interest rates to be substituted as well as the column where you want the results to appear. The entry here is B6..C18. Notice that the formula's row has also been carefully included in the range specification. B2 is the Input cell 1.

While Symphony is calculating the results, a WAIT sign will flash in the upper right corner of the screen. When Symphony has finished— and sometimes it takes a while—the screen will return to the SHEET mode. At this point, the table is complete with all the payment values.

A more involved example uses the SHEET **R**ange **W**hat-If **2**-Way command. This command requires two input variables instead of one. The advantage to this command is the increased breadth-of-sensitivity analysis.

The next example is designed to show the effects on total cost of changes in order quantity and order point. You are after that combination of order point and order quantity that minimizes "Cumulative Costs to Date" at the end of a twelve-month period. Figure 4.20 illustrates this example.

Month	Jan	Feb	Mar	Apr	May	Jun	Jul	Aug	Sep	Oct	Nov	Dec
Beginning Inventory	43	51	35	60	42	30	46	33	45	35	59	40
Past Demand for Month	28	16	11	18	12	20	13	24	10	12	19	22
Ending Inventory	15	35	24	42	30	10	33	9	35	23	40	18
Quantity Ordered	36	0	36	0	0	36	0	36	0	36	0	36
Setup Costs ($10 per order)	10	0	10	0	0	10	0	10	0	10	0	10
Inventory Costs ($.2/unit)	$3.00	$7.00	$4.80	$8.40	$6.00	$2.00	$6.60	$1.80	$7.00	$4.60	$8.00	$3.60
Shortage Costs ($1/unit)	$0.00	$0.00	$0.00	$0.00	$0.00	$0.00	$0.00	$0.00	$0.00	$0.00	$0.00	$0.00
Total Costs for Month	$13.00	$7.00	$14.80	$8.40	$6.00	$12.00	$6.60	$11.80	$7.00	$14.60	$8.00	$13.60
Cum Cost From Last Month	$0.00	$13.00	$20.00	$34.80	$43.20	$49.20	$61.20	$67.80	$79.60	$86.60	$101.20	$109.20
Cumulative Costs to Date	$13.00	$20.00	$34.80	$43.20	$49.20	$61.20	$67.80	$79.60	$86.60	$101.20	$109.20	$122.80

```
Order Quantity Input Cell->   36
Order Point Input Cell---->   28
```

Order Quant	Cumulative Cost		Order Quant	Cumulative Cost	25	26	27	28	29	Average
	+M12			+M12						
25	$137.40		15	$150.40	$150.40	$150.40	$150.40	$150.40	$150.40	$150.40
26	$136.00		16	$163.60	$163.60	$163.60	$163.60	$163.60	$163.60	$163.60
27	$144.60		17	$143.00	$149.80	$160.00	$160.00	$160.00	$154.56
28	$137.60		18	$154.80	$154.80	$154.80	$154.80	$154.80	$154.80
29	$140.20		19	$141.40	$145.20	$149.00	$149.00	$149.00	$146.72
30	$130.40		20	$148.40	$148.40	$148.40	$152.40	$152.40	$150.00
31	$131.80		21	$132.40	$136.60	$136.60	$150.80	$150.80	$141.44
32	$122.80		22	$138.00	$142.40	$142.40	$142.40	$142.40	$141.52
33	$130.00		23	$138.60	$138.60	$143.20	$143.20	$147.80	$142.28
34	$130.40		24	$133.20	$133.20	$133.20	$138.00	$138.00	$135.12
35	$123.40		25	$132.40	$137.40	$137.40	$137.40	$142.40	$137.40
36	$122.80		26	$136.00	$136.00	$136.00	$136.00	$141.20	$137.04
37	$129.20		27	$123.80	$134.60	$144.60	$144.60	$144.60	$138.44
38	$128.00		28	$120.80	$126.40	$132.00	$137.60	$137.60	$130.88
39	$124.20		29	$128.60	$128.60	$128.60	$140.20	$140.20	$133.24
40	$130.40		30	$124.40	$124.40	$124.40	$130.40	$142.40	$129.20
41	$128.40		31	$131.80	$131.80	$131.80	$131.80	$131.80	$131.80
42	$134.40		32	$122.80	$122.80	$122.80	$122.80	$129.20	$124.08
43	$123.20		33	$130.00	$130.00	$130.00	$130.00	$130.00	$130.00
44	$128.80		34	$110.00	$116.80	$130.40	$130.40	$130.40	$123.60
45	$134.40		35	$116.40	$116.40	$116.40	$123.40	$123.40	$119.20
46	$121.60		36	$122.80	$122.80	$122.80	$122.80	$122.80	$122.80
47	$126.80		37	$121.80	$121.80	$129.20	$129.20	$129.20	$126.24
48	$122.00		38	$110.40	$118.00	$118.00	$128.00	$128.00	$120.48
49	$127.20		39	$116.40	$116.40	$124.20	$124.20	$124.20	$121.08
50	$122.40		40	$122.40	$122.40	$122.40	$130.40	$130.40	$125.60

Fig. 4.20.

The lower left portion of figure 4.20 shows how the SHEET **R**ange **W**hat-If **1**-Way command is used in the example and indicates the effect on cost of several different order quantities. To the right is a much more extensive table, which is the result of executing the SHEET **R**ange **W**hat-If **2**-Way command. Here several additional order points are used to make the analysis more complete. The SHEET **R**ange **W**hat-If **2**-Way command can be quite useful.

To use the SHEET **R**ange **W**hat-If **2**-Way command, you enter the values for Variable 2 (order point) in the row just above the first entry of Variable 1 (order quantity.) You also enter +M12, the address of the formula for "Cost to Date," in the row directly above the first entry of Variable 1.

When executed, the SHEET **R**ange **W**hat-If **2**-Way command calls for a Table range and Input cells for Variables 1 and 2. Following is the information you enter for these parameters:

Table range	F21..K47
Input cell 1	B15
Input cell 2	B16

After you enter this information, Symphony begins building the table of results. The waiting time for the SHEET **R**ange **W**hat-If **2**-Way command is substantial, but when you consider what Symphony is actually doing, the wait is worth it. To duplicate manually what Symphony does would take quite a bit longer.

The advantages of the SHEET **R**ange **W**hat-If command are the abilities to conduct extensive sensitivity analysis and to display the results in a tabular format. The SHEET **R**ange **W**hat-If command lets you do the kind of thorough analysis that you might not do otherwise, given the time required to perform the analysis. Furthermore, the power of the command in combination with macros and special data base statistical functions can be outstanding.

Cutting and Pasting

Four primary commands from the SHEET command MENU cover the operations that "electronically cut and paste" a spreadsheet. In other words, these commands accomplish what cutting and pasting did in the days of manual spreadsheets: moving and deleting data around on the worksheet. Symphony's cut-and-paste commands include **Move**, **Erase**, **Insert**, and **Delete**.

With these four commands, you have complete control over the appearance of worksheets because the commands allow you to rearrange items in almost any manner. The **M**ove command, as its name indicates, moves the contents of cells. The **E**rase command deletes a single cell, row, column, or range of cells. Insert enters blank rows and columns in the worksheet, and **Delete** deletes rows and columns.

Moving Cell Contents

With **M**ove you can move ranges of cells from one part of the worksheet to another. For example, suppose you created the same sheet shown in figure 4.21. Furthermore, suppose you want to move the contents of range C1..D3 to the range E1..F3. After you select **M**ove from the SHEET command MENU, "Range to move FROM: " is displayed by Symphony. You will notice that a range is already specified after this message. If the cursor was at cell D7 when you started, the range specified is D7..D7.

To help you enter ranges, Symphony, like 1-2-3, indicates the cell where the cursor is presently positioned. If the range is different from the range where the cursor is positioned, you can enter the new range in two different ways: either type the addresses in the upper left and lower right corners, or move the cell pointer to indicate the range. To designate the proper FROM range for our example, enter C1..D3, followed by RETURN.

Symphony will then ask you to indicate "Range to move TO: ". Again, a range is already specified for you, and just as before, it corresponds to the address of the cell where the pointer is when you initiate the command.

D7..D7 will again appear. To enter your own range, start typing again. For the TO range, you can specify just the single cell E1. Symphony will know that E1 refers to the beginning of the range where you want your list of numbers placed. As soon as you finish

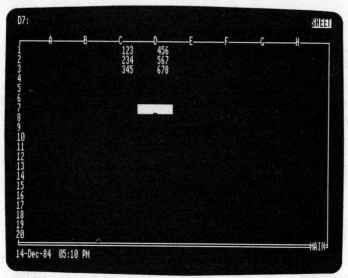

Fig. 4.21.

designating the TO range and you press RETURN, the pointer will
return immediately to where it was when you initiated the command.
Figure 4.22 shows the results of the **M**ove operation.

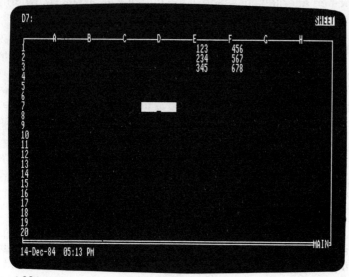

Fig. 4.22.

When setting ranges, remember that you don't have to position the cursor at the beginning of the TO or FROM ranges when you initiate a command. You can designate a range while the cursor is positioned anywhere on the sheet.

A Warning about Move

Whenever you move a range that includes formulas, all of them are updated automatically. For example, suppose you define a simple three-cell worksheet that contains the following data:

    A1 = +D1*100
    C1 = 15
    D1 = +C1

Now suppose you move the contents of cell D1 to cell E1. The formulas become the following:

    A1 = +E1*100
    C1 = 15
    E1 = +C1

As with the Copy command, you must be careful about the finality of the Move command. When you move a range of cells into other cells, the TO range is completely overwritten by the FROM range, and the previous contents of those cells are lost forever. If there are other cells whose formulas depend on the cell addresses of the lost cells, those cells will be given the value ERR instead of the cell addresses. For example, if you add the cell

    E2 = +E1

to the example above and repeat the move operation (Move D1..E1), the value of cell E2 will change from 0 to ERR, and the contents of that cell will become ERR. The cell E2, once referred to as E1, has been removed and replaced as a result of the move operation.

Pointing to Cells: The Expanding Cursor

Chapter 2 provides a discussion of the keys used for moving the cell pointer in a SHEET window. A few tips and techniques are offered here for defining ranges by pointing to cells.

Suppose you want to shift the contents of the range C1..D3 to E1..F3, but this time you don't want to enter the cell addresses from the keyboard. Again, you can assume that the cursor was positioned in cell D7 before you initiated the command. When Symphony asks for the FROM range, press Esc.

Esc is used because cell D7 has been automatically "anchored" for you by Symphony. In other words, Symphony has automatically designated D7 as one corner of the FROM range. If you do not press Esc and move the cursor, you will see the reverse-video field begin to expand, starting at cell D7. Because you do not want to have cell D7 as one corner of the range, you press Esc.

You can also anchor cells yourself by entering a period (.) or by pressing the Tab key when you are entering a range. Because you do want C1 to be one corner of the FROM range, move the cursor to this cell. As you move the cursor upward from cell to cell, you will see a change in the address designation in the command field. After you move the cell pointer to C1, press the period key to anchor the cell. (Cell C1 may be referred to as the anchor cell, and the cell diagonally opposite the anchor cell is called the free cell.)

You will notice that the free cell contains the blinking underscore character in the middle of it. At this point, cell C1 is both the anchor cell and the free cell. But as you move the cursor down to cell E3 to point to the other corner of the range, you will see the reverse-video expand while you shift the free cell. You will also see a change in the second part of the range designation as you move from cell to cell. For example, C1..D1 will appear when the cursor is at cell D1.

When you reach cell C3 from cell C1, start moving over to cell D3. Now you will see the cursor expand in a columnar manner. The designation of the FROM range will appear, as though you entered it from the keyboard. When you reach cell D3, lock in the range by hitting RETURN.

The process for designating the TO range is similar. Once you have specified the FROM range, the cursor will automatically return to cell D7. Move the cursor over to E1 and hit RETURN. You can designate the TO range by pointing to the entire range, but remember that Symphony knows what you are implying when you enter just E1.

The Esc key can also be used when you are in a command but a cell has not been anchored. Pressing Esc will return you to the previous command step. If you are in the middle of a formula, pressing the Esc key will erase the cell address from the end of the formula and return the cursor to the current cell.

The Backspace key can also be used in pointing to ranges. Pressing Backspace will cancel the range specification, whether or not a cell has been anchored, and return the cell pointer to where you began the command or formula. The Backspace key is slightly more powerful than the Esc key in returning Symphony to where you started from (when you began entering a command or formula).

Using the End Key to Point

By using the End key, your job of pointing to ranges is made fairly easy. Suppose, for example, that you want to move the contents of range A1..C5 to the range that begins at cell A7. When the range prompt A1..A1 appears after you select the **M**ove command, press the End key followed by →. The cursor will jump to cell C1, and the prompt will read A1..C1. Next, move the cursor by pressing End ↓. The prompt will then read A1..C5.

The End key can speed up the process of pointing to ranges. In this example, you were able to define the range with only four keystrokes. If you had used the two arrow keys instead of the End key, the process would have taken seven keystrokes. The difference becomes even more dramatic when you work with larger ranges.

The End key can even be used in some cases when it appears to be of little value. For example, figure 4.23 shows a worksheet consisting of two rows of information: one continuous and one broken. Suppose you want to erase the contents of the broken row. Select the **E**rase command, and Symphony then prompts you for a range to delete. You can enter the range by either typing the coordinates or pointing with the cursor.

If you point, you may want to try using the End key. But because the range is not continuous, the End key will not easily move you from one end of the range to the other. Try this trick. When you specify the range, first move the cursor up one row to cell A1, use End and → to

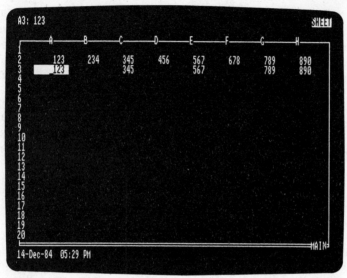

Fig. 4.23.

move the cursor to the end of the range, then move the cursor down
one row. Presto! The correct range is specified. Figures 4.24A, B,
and C show this process. Although the technique appears to waste

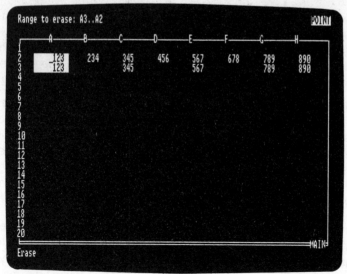

Fig. 4.24A.

keystrokes, it is actually much more convenient than simply using the → to point. You should use this technique often when you define ranges.

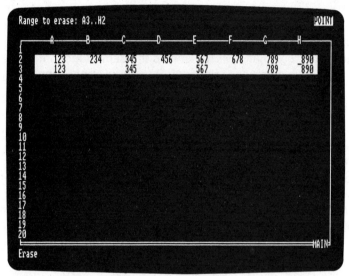

Fig. 4.24B.

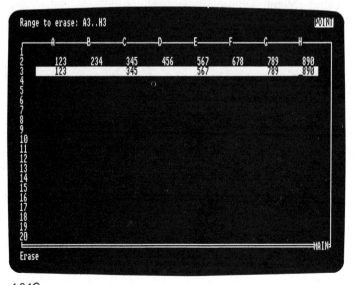

Fig. 4.24C.

Erasing

In 1-2-3 two types of erasing commands are available through the command menu: **W**orksheet **E**rase and **R**ange **E**rase. In Symphony, however, the SERVICES **N**ew command replaces the **W**orksheet **E**rase command of 1-2-3. And in Symphony the **E**rase command in the SHEET command MENU serves the same function as 1-2-3's **R**ange **E**rase command. Although Symphony places the two types of **E**rase commands in different menus, both commands are comparable to 1-2-3's.

Like 1-2-3's **W**orksheet **E**rase command, Symphony's SERVICES **N**ew command is used to clear the entire worksheet. When you select the SERVICES **N**ew command, it not only erases the worksheet but also restores all global settings to their default condition, erases range or graph names, and clears any title lock or windows in the sheet. The SERVICES **N**ew command can be used in any window environment to wipe the worksheet clean.

On the other hand, the Symphony **E**rase command erases only those cells that are within the range you set and which are unprotected. But **E**rase will not alter any of the global settings, including column widths or label prefixes.

To use the **E**rase command, simply retrieve the SHEET command MENU, select **E**rase, indicate the range you want to erase, and press RETURN. When you erase a range, values are recalculated. Whenever a value has been erased that is used in a remaining formula, the formula will, depending on the type of address, read ERR. (See the later section on Copying.)

Keep in mind the differences between the two types of commands. Remember also that the SERVICES **N**ew command restores the Symphony worksheet to its default configuration. Symphony does reduce your chances of mistakenly selecting **N**ew instead of **E**rase. Unlike 1-2-3, Symphony has the two commands in different menu systems. Symphony also has changed terminology, further reducing your chances of confusing the two types of erasing.

Inserting Blank Columns and Rows

Insert, the fourth command in the SHEET command MENU, is quite valuable for inserting blank rows and columns. Suppose you have finished building a model in a worksheet, but you want to "dress up" its general appearance before you show it to anyone. One technique for improving a worksheet's appearance is to insert blank rows and columns in strategic places to highlight headings and other important items.

With the Insert command, you can insert multiple rows and columns. After you select Insert, you are asked whether you want to insert a column or a row. Insert also gives you two options: (1) to insert a column or a row only within the *restrict range* of the window in which you are working, or (2) to insert the column or row beyond the restrict range. If you want to insert the column or row within the restrict range, select either Columns or Rows and then enter the range. If you want to insert the column or row beyond the window's restrict range, select Global, then indicate whether you want a column or row inserted, and finally enter the range.

Symphony's capability of inserting columns and rows only within restrict ranges is a tremendous advantage. Restricting the insert prevents you from unknowingly changing data in windows other than the one you are currently working in. If you have created multiple windows, and you insert a row or column in one of them, using Columns or Rows will limit the inserted column or row to the currently active window. Using Global, on the other hand, will insert columns or rows in all windows. Remember also that the Insert Global command will affect those windows displayed on the screen as well as "hidden" windows. (See the discussion of the Window Hide command in Chapter 2.)

Inserted columns appear to the left of the specified range, and inserted rows appear above the specified range. For example, let's assume you created the worksheet shown in figure 4.25. If you issue the Insert Columns command and enter an insert range of A10..A10, you will get a single blank column inserted to the left of the values in column A, as shown in figure 4.26. Symphony automatically shifts everything over one column and modifies all the cell formulas for the change. If you then repeat the command, but specify the Rows option and a range of A10..A10, Symphony will insert one blank row below row 9. Figure 4.27 illustrates the results of this operation.

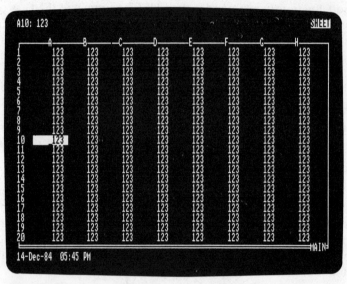

Fig. 4.25.

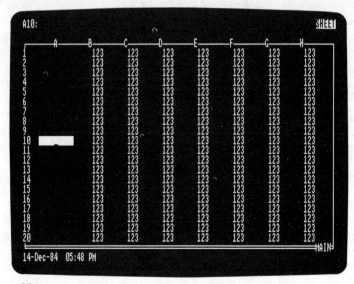

Fig. 4.26.

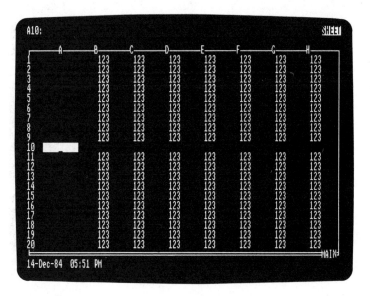

Fig. 4.27.

Whenever you insert a column or row, Symphony automatically adjusts range settings. Suppose, for example, that you have created two named ranges in the spreadsheet shown in figure 4.28. These range names include CA at cell G16 for "Current Assets" and TA at cell G25 for "Total Assets." Once you have entered these range names, Symphony remembers the cell address for each name.

If, however, you decide to insert a column at column D, Symphony will automatically change CA and TA to cells H16 and H25, respectively. This adjustment of remembered ranges occurs whether you use the **G**lobal **I**nsert or the **R**estrict **R**ange **I**nsert, with one exception: only the **I**nsert **G**lobal command changes the restrict range of a window.

Earlier spreadsheet programs, such as VisiCalc, allow you to insert only one column or row at a time. This method can be very time-consuming, especially when you want to rearrange a spreadsheet completely. Symphony, like 1-2-3, allows you to insert more than one row or column.

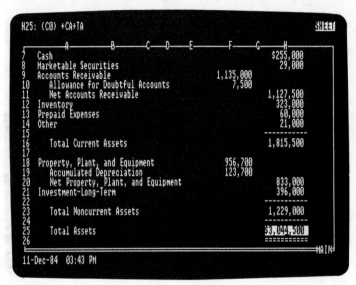

Fig. 4.28.

Deleting Columns and Rows

The opposite of the Insert command is the **D**elete command. It deletes columns and rows either in restrict ranges of a window or throughout the whole worksheet. The **D**elete command allows you to delete multiple columns or rows at the same time. After you select this command, you then choose **C**olumns, **R**ows, or **G**lobal from the menu. Like the Insert command, **D**elete allows you to restrict the column or row deletion to the current window, or to delete columns or rows globally. If you have created multiple windows, the **D**elete **G**lobal command will affect all windows, whether or not they are displayed on the screen at the time you initiate the **D**elete command.

If you choose **R**ows, Symphony then asks you to indicate the range within the window restrict range to be deleted. As with the Insert command, the range you specify should include one cell from a given row. For example, to delete rows 2 and 3 in the worksheet in figure 4.29, you enter A2..A3. Other acceptable range designations are B1..B2, A1..B2, and C1..G2. The results of the deletion are shown in figure 4.30.

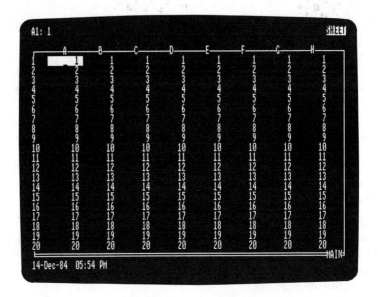

Fig. 4.29.

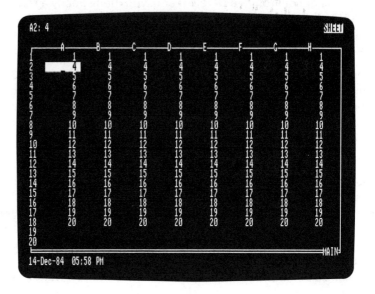

Fig. 4.30.

The easiest way to designate the range to be deleted is by pointing to the appropriate cells. You can also enter the cell addresses from the keyboard. Pointing to cells, however, helps you to avoid choosing inadvertently the wrong range. Remember that when you use the **D**elete command, the rows or columns you delete are gone for good. If you choose **C**olumns or **R**ows from the first menu, the cells in the columns or rows of the window restrict range are deleted. If you choose **C**olumns or **R**ows after choosing **G**lobal, all the cells in the rows or columns are deleted, not just the range you specify. You may be able to get the values back if you have previously saved a copy of the model on disk. But if you have not saved a copy, the rows and columns are lost.

Notice that the worksheet in figure 4.30 is automatically readjusted so that all the contents below row 3 are shifted up. In addition, all the formulas, command ranges, and named ranges are adjusted for the deletion. Formulas that contain references to the deleted cells are given the value ERR.

The process of deleting one or more columns is very similar to the process discussed earlier for deleting rows. After you select the **C**olumns option from the **D**elete menu, you then specify a range of columns to delete within the window's restrict range. The range you specify should correspond to one or more cells in each column to be deleted.

For example, suppose you want to delete column B in figure 4.31. A suitable range to designate for the **D**elete command is B1..B1. Again, pointing is the best way to designate the range so that you can avoid selecting the wrong column. Figure 4.32 shows the worksheet after column B is deleted.

Remember that just as you have two options for deleting rows, you also have two options for deleting columns: within a window's restrict area only, or throughout the worksheet. To delete columns throughout the worksheet, use the **G**lobal command in the **D**elete menu. After selecting **G**lobal, select **C**olumns and indicate the range to be deleted. Here again, be cautious in using the **G**lobal command. If you have various kinds of data on your worksheet, using the **D**elete **G**lobal **C**olumns command may affect areas that you want to keep intact.

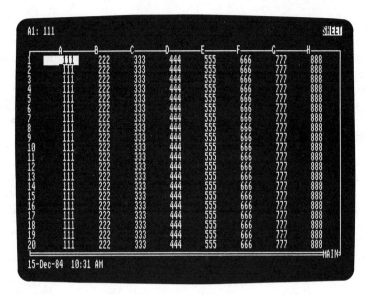

Fig. 4.31.

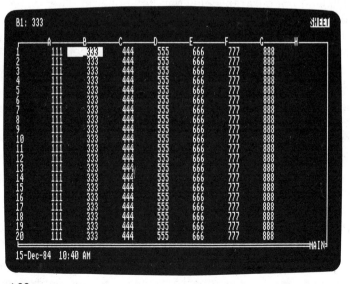

Fig. 4.32.

In Symphony, two differences exist between deleting cells with **D**elete and erasing cells with **E**rase. First, the **D**elete command deletes entire columns and rows within a worksheet, but the **E**rase command erases particular ranges of cells that may be as small or large as you wish. Second, when you use the **D**elete command, the worksheet is automatically readjusted to fill in the gaps created by the deleted columns or rows. But with **E**rase, the cells in the range that has been erased are merely blanked.

The **D**elete command is very different from the **E**rase command. The difference is best illustrated by using the analogy of a paper spreadsheet. The manual equivalent of **D**elete is to use scissors to cut apart the columnar sheet and remove the unwanted columns and/or rows. Then the sheet is pasted back together again. The **E**rase command, on the other hand, is similar to an eraser that erases ranges of cells in the sheet. Don't forget the difference between these powerful commands.

Copying

The first command in the SHEET command MENU is **C**opy. This command not only replicates data to appear in other parts of the worksheet, but also copies formulas from one cell to another. You will find yourself frequently using the **C**opy command to copy the contents of cells to other locations in a worksheet. The uses of the **C**opy command can be divided into four categories.

The first type of copy operation is to copy *from one cell to another*. In the worksheet shown in figure 4.33, you can copy the contents of cell A1 to cell A2. Just issue the **C**opy command. Symphony then prompts you to supply a FROM range with the message "Range to copy FROM: ".

Because you want to copy from cell A1, enter A1. (If the cursor is on cell A1, you can instead press RETURN.) Next, Symphony will prompt for a TO range with the message "Range to Copy TO: ". Because you want to copy the contents of cell A1 to cell A2, enter A2 as the TO range. Figure 4.34 shows the results of this operation.

As illustrated in this example, the steps required for all copy operations are basically these: (1) issue the **C**opy command, (2)

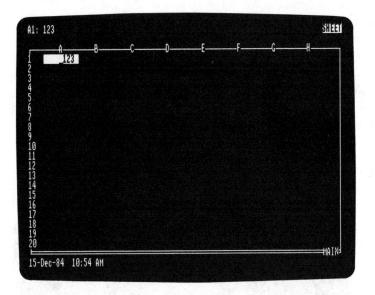

Fig. 4.33.

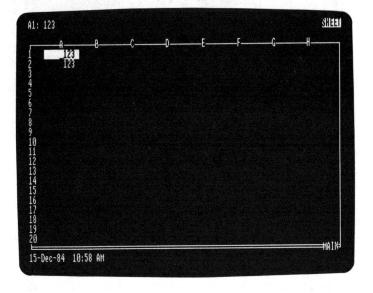

Fig. 4.34.

specify the FROM range, and (3) specify the TO range. The only elements that will change from time to time are the size, shape, and locations of the TO and FROM ranges.

A second type of copy operation is to copy *from one cell to a range of cells*. Using the same worksheet shown in figure 4.33, let's suppose you want to copy the contents of cell A1 into the range B1..H1. To do this, issue the **C**opy command, specify A1 as the FROM range and B1..H1 as the TO range. Remember that you can either type the coordinates of the TO range from the keyboard or point to the range by using Symphony's POINT mode. The results of this copy operation are shown in figure 4.35.

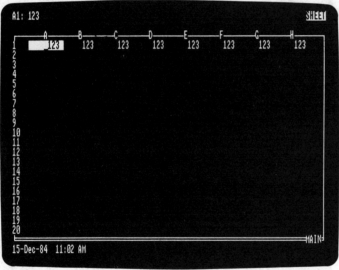

Fig. 4.35.

The third type of copy operation is a little more complicated. You may want to copy *a range of cells to another place* in the worksheet. Using the results of your copy in figure 4.34 as an example, now suppose you want to copy the range A1..H1 to the range A2..H2. As always, you begin by issuing the **C**opy command. Then you specify the FROM range—in this case, A1..H1. (Remember that you can either type the coordinates or point to the range by using the cursor keys.) Next, you must specify the TO range. Now things get a bit tricky. Even though you are copying to the range A1..H2, the TO range is the single cell A2. The result of this command is shown in figure 4.36.

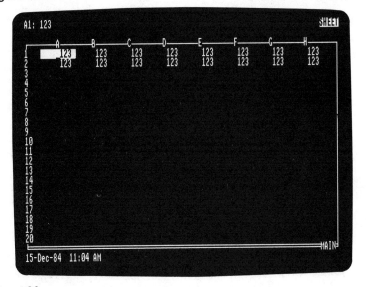

Fig. 4.36.

Although the TO range does not seem to make sense, it really is perfectly logical. Think about it in this way. You want to Copy to the eight-cell partial row A2..H2. Because the FROM range is an eight-cell partial row, the TO range must also be an eight-cell partial row. Since the TO range must be an eight-cell partial row, the first cell in that partial row is sufficient to define the range. Given a starting point of A2, the only possible destination for the copy is the range A2..H2. Similarly, to specify the single cell H3 as the TO range implies a destination of H3..O3. In other words, Symphony deduces the rest of the destination from the single cell provided as the TO range.

The same principle applies to copying partial columns. Look back at figure 4.34, which shows the results of the first copy example. Now suppose you want to copy the range A1..A2 to the range B1..B2. The first two steps should be familiar by now. Issue the Copy command and specify the FROM range A1..A2. What should the TO range be? Because you want to copy the two-cell partial column A1..A2 into the two-cell partial column B1..B2, you need to supply only the starting point of the target, which is B1, for the TO range in order to create figure 4.37.

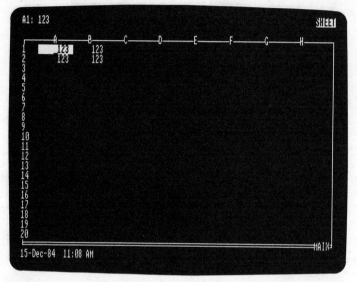

Fig. 4.37.

Finally, in the fourth kind of copy operation, you may want to copy *a range of cells to an even larger range of cells* somewhere else in the worksheet. Using figure 4.34 once again as an example, let's assume you want to copy the range A1..H1 into the rectangular block A2..H20. As before, you issue the command Copy and specify the FROM range as A1..H1, and the TO range as A1..A20. Figure 4.38 shows the results of this copy.

You can think of this last kind of copy operation as an extension of the preceding type. Essentially, the copy you made in figure 4.38 can also be created by repeating the Copy command 19 times and specifying 19 different single-row TO ranges. The first TO range will be A2, the second will be A3, the third will be A4, and so on. Regardless of which method you use, the result is the same, but you can save much time by using the A2..A20 range shown in figure 4.38.

The concept of TO ranges can be complicated. The best way to become familiar with the effects of different TO and FROM ranges is

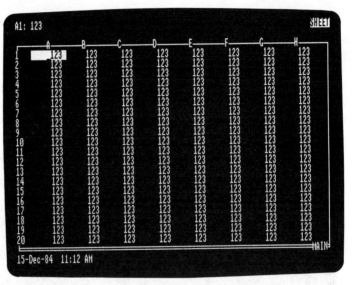

Fig. 4.38.

to experiment on your own. After a while, the rules of copying will become "old hat."

Relative versus Absolute Addressing

In Symphony, as in 1-2-3, one of the important features of the **C**opy command is its ability to copy formulas and to adjust the formula whenever necessary. But for Symphony to know how to adjust a formula as it is copied to another part of the worksheet, the original formula must contain the right kind of address. Two different methods of addressing cells can be used in replication: relative and absolute. These two methods are also important in building formulas. In fact, a discussion of either method of addressing is difficult unless you treat both topics at once. Following are general definitions of these two types of addressing. ,

In *relative addressing*, when a formula is copied, the cells in the formula change relative to the new cell(s) where the formula has been copied. Suppose, for example, that cell A5 contained the formula +A2+A3, meaning that Symphony should add the contents of the cells located two and three cells above A5. If we copy +A2+A3 to cell B5, the formula (in cell B5) will read +B2+B3, as indicated in figure 4.39. When the formula +A2+A3 is copied to cell B5, Symphony interprets the copy in this way: the cells located two and three cells above B5 should be added. One way to understand relative addressing is to remember that when formulas are copied, their operators, their functions, and the relationships of cells are copied, but not the specific cell addresses of the original formulas.

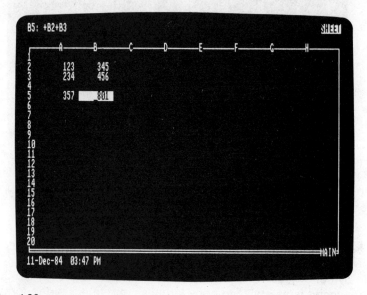

Fig. 4.39.

In *absolute addressing*, when the formula is copied, the operators, functions, and relationships of cells are copied as well as the original cell addresses. For example, if you want to copy the formula in cell A5 (+A2+A3) to cell B5 and have the formula remain as originally entered, you enter the original formula in this way: +$A$2+$A$3. When you copy this formula to cell B5, you still have +$A$2+$A$3, as indicated in figure 4.40. The dollar signs tell Symphony to copy the formula with its original cell addresses.

Now let's explore the concepts of relative addressing and absolute addressing in a bit more detail.

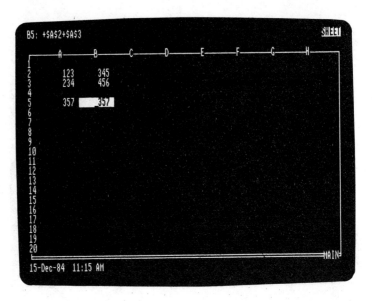

Fig. 4.40.

Relative Addressing

Suppose you want to sum the contents of several columns of cells, but you don't want to enter the @SUM function over and over again. Figure 4.41 shows a sample worksheet with five columns of numbers. Only column C has been summed, with the formula @SUM(C3..C7) in cell C8.

You want to add the contents of the cells in columns D, E, F, and G in the same way in which the contents of the cells in column C were added. To perform this addition, use the Copy command, which is the command for replicating cells, no matter what their contents.

To initiate the command, choose Copy from the main command menu. Symphony then asks for a range of cells to copy FROM, and you enter C8 for the range, followed by RETURN. Next, Symphony asks for a range of cells to copy TO. Here you enter D8..G8 by either pointing to or entering the cell addresses. When you hit RETURN, Symphony will replicate the @SUM formula in cell C8 to the other cells, as shown in figure 4.42.

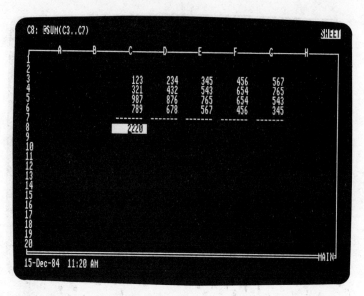

Fig. 4.41.

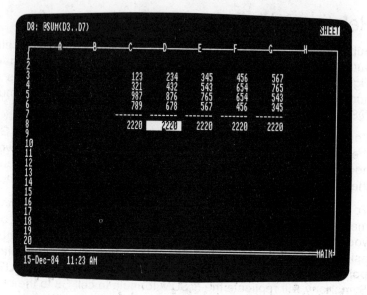

Fig. 4.42.

If you look at the formula in the first line of the control panel, you will see that the formula contains the proper cell addresses for adding cells in column D but not in column C. Symphony knows that you actually meant the relative addresses of cells in column B and not their absolute addresses.

Absolute and Mixed Addressing

Sometimes a formula has an important address that can't be changed as the formula is copied. In Symphony you can create an address that will not change at all as it is copied. Remember that this address is called an absolute address. But you can also create a mixed address, which will sometimes change, depending on the direction of the copy. The following examples will help make clear the concepts of absolute and mixed addresses.

Mixed Cell Addressing

Mixed cell addressing refers to a combination of relative addressing and absolute addressing. Because a cell address has two components—a row and a column—you can fix (make absolute) either portion while leaving the other unfixed (relative). For example, suppose that for Product 1 you want to do a projection of monthly sales in dollars. In the first pass, you want to use a specific retail price, an average discount rate, and a unit volume for the projection. Later you will want to change these parameters to see what happens. Figure 4.43 shows how you can set up the projection.

Notice the dollar signs in the formula for cell D10 in the first line of the control panel. The dollar signs signal Symphony to use absolute addressing on the column portion of the addresses. Because dollar signs do not appear in front of the row portion of the addresses, Symphony will use relative addressing there.

To see the importance of this type of referencing, now Copy the contents of cell D10 into the range E10..H10. As before, you first issue the Copy command and designate the FROM range (D10) and the TO range (E10..H10). Figure 4.44 shows the results of this operation.

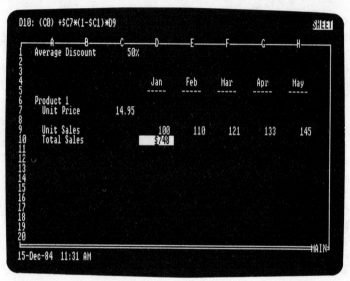

Fig. 4.43.

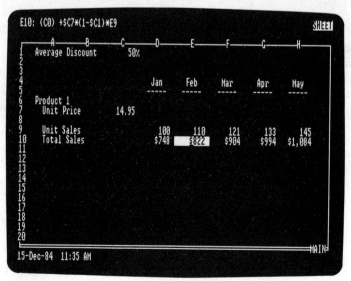

Fig. 4.44.

Now compare the formula in cell E10 with the original formula in cell D10:

E10 = $C7*(1-$C1)*E9
D10 = $C7*(1-$C1)*D9

Notice that the formulas are identical except for the last item. Symphony holds constant the addresses for C7 and C1. Only the reference to cell D9 is altered. Essentially, this formula says: using a constant price (C7) and a constant discount (C1), compute the dollar sales for Product 1 at each month's sales volume (D9..H9).

Now suppose you want to create a projection for a second product. You duplicate the labels in column A and change the product name to Product 2. Finally, you copy the contents of the range C7..H10 to the range C14..H17. Figure 4.45 shows the results of this copy operation.

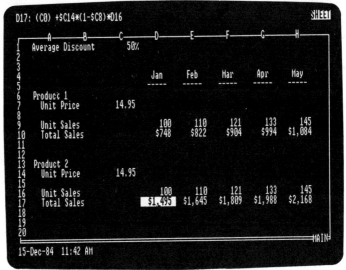

Fig. 4.45.

Notice that the numbers in row 17 are not correct. Even though the same price and unit sales volumes have been assigned to Product 2, that product shows monthly dollar sales which are double those for Product 1. To figure out why, look at the formula in cell D17:

+$C14*(1-$C8)*D16

The references to cell C14 and cell D16 are correct—these cells contain the unit price and unit sales for Product 2. But notice that the reference to cell C1 has changed so that it refers to cell C8. This change occurred because the row designation (8) in that address was relative and not absolute. When you copied the formulas containing the address $C1 down the worksheet, Symphony assumed you wanted to adjust the row component of the address.

Absolute Addressing

You can correct the problem by changing the reference to cell C1 from a mixed to an absolute reference. Going back to the model in figure 4.44, you will see that you edited cell D10 and changed the formula to

    +$C7*(1-$C$1)*D9

The only difference between this formula and its predecessor is the addition of a dollar sign in front of the 1 in the address $C$1. The added dollar sign changes this address from mixed to absolute.

Now you must copy the new formula in cell D10 to the range E10..H10 so that all the formulas in the row are the same. You can then recopy the area D9..H10 into the range D16..H17. Figure 4.46 illustrates the adjusted worksheet.

Notice that the numbers in cells D17..H17 are now correct. If you look at the following formula in cell D17

    +$C14*(1-$C$1)*D16

you will see that the reference to cell C1 has remained fixed as it was copied.

Note to VisiCalc users: To use absolute addressing to copy cells in Symphony (as in 1-2-3), you must prepare the cell to be copied prior to initiating the command. That is, you must enter dollar signs in strategic places when the cell is defined. In this way Symphony's method of replication differs from earlier spreadsheet programs, including VisiCalc. In VisiCalc you normally designate the method of addressing, either relative or absolute, at the time of the Replicate(/R) command.

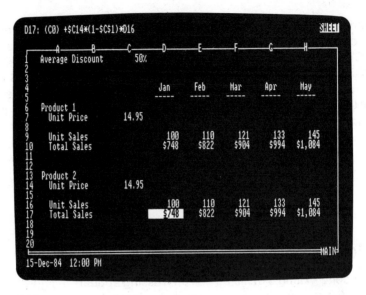

D17: (C0) +$C14*(1-$C$1)*D16   SHEET

```
     A        B        C        D      E      F      G      H
 1  Average Discount   50%
 2
 3
 4                             Jan    Feb    Mar    Apr    May
 5                             ----   ----   ----   ----   ----
 6  Product 1
 7    Unit Price        14.95
 8
 9    Unit Sales                100    110    121    133    145
10    Total Sales              $748   $822   $904   $994 $1,084
11
12
13  Product 2
14    Unit Price        14.95
15
16    Unit Sales                100    110    121    133    145
17    Total Sales              $748   $822   $904   $994 $1,084
18
19
20                                                          MAIN
```

15-Dec-84 12:00 PM

Fig. 4.46.

Earlier spreadsheet programs, such as VisiCalc, do not have mixed cell addressing. To accomplish the replication in figure 4.44 in VisiCalc, you have to use a hodgepodge of indicators for relative and absolute addressing at the end of the replication command and issue the command several times.

Setting Absolute and Relative References

In the example above, the dollar signs in the formula for cell D10 can be entered in two ways. You can type them in as you enter the formula, or you can use the ABS key (F3) to have Symphony automatically enter the dollar signs for you. One limitation of the ABS key is that you must be in the POINT mode to use it. As you will recall from the section on Formulas in Chapter 3, in POINT mode you must use the cell pointer to enter addresses.

Here is the procedure for using the ABS key for entering dollar signs. Using the formula in figure 4.43, begin by entering the first part of the formula; in this case, enter +. To change the formula to an absolute address, shift to the POINT mode by moving your cursor to cell C7 and then pressing the ABS key. The formula in the control panel shows $C$7. Pressing the ABS key again will change the address to C$7. Next, a third press of the ABS key will change the address to $C7, which is the result you want. Finally, you again use the ABS key to make Symphony automatically enter dollar signs into formulas for both absolute and mixed addressing. Notice what happens to a cell address when you press the ABS key in the POINT mode:

First press	$C$7
Second press	C$7
Third press	$C7
Fourth press	C7

More Examples

A second example of mixed cell addressing appears in figure 4.47. This figure contains a table for exploring the effect of different interest rates and years-to-maturity on the present value of an annuity that pays $1,000 a year. (See the @PV built-in function in Chapter 5 for an explanation of present value.) The general form of the function is

@PV(payment, interest, term)

The object of this example is to use a single formula for the entire model and to copy the formula, with mixed cell addressing, as shown in figure 4.47.

Once again, if you look at the command line, you will see the special places where the dollar signs appear. The idea in this example is to use absolute addressing on the column portion of the interest rate address, and relative addressing on the row portion ($A4). Conversely, you want to use relative addressing on the column portion of the years-to-maturity address, and absolute addressing on the row portion (B$2).

Compare the B4 cell formula in the control panel in figure 4.47 with the formula for cell D8 in figure 4.48. Notice that column A for the interest rate and row 2 for the years-to-maturity have not changed, but the other portions of the addresses have.

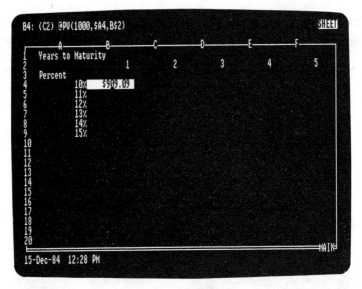

Fig. 4.47.

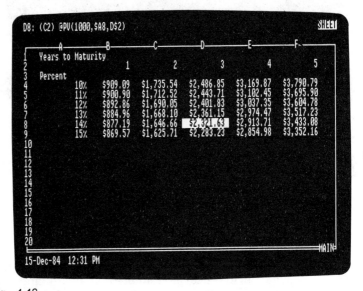

Fig. 4.48.

A third way that mixed cell addressing can be used is to accumulate
a running total across a row of numbers. You can use the formula
@SUM($A$1..B1) in cell A2 and copy the formula across cells B2
through F2. In figure 4.49 notice the formula in the first line of the
control panel for cell B2 and see how the relative address in the
formula changes as you copy it.

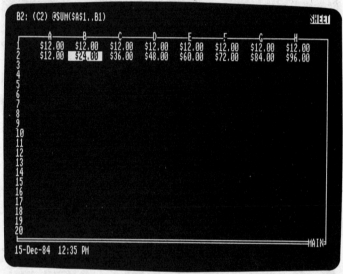

Fig. 4.49.

The best way to become comfortable with mixed cell addressing
is to experiment with it. Try several different uses and examine
your results.

Miscellaneous Comments on Copying

In using the **C**opy command from Symphony's SHEET menu, keep
the following points in mind:

1. When you copy a cell, Symphony automatically copies
    the format of the cell with it. (See the section on
    Formats for more information.) This copying saves you
    from having to preset the format for an entire range of
    cells before copying them.

2. Sometimes the TO and FROM ranges will overlap when you copy. The general rule is this: If you do not overlap the end points for the FROM and TO ranges, you will be okay; if you do overlap them, you may get mixed results. The one time that it is legitimate to overlap the ranges is when the FROM and TO ranges have the same upper left boundary.

3. Note particularly the finality of the **C**opy command. If you copy over the contents of a cell, even a cell in another window, you cannot retrieve the contents. Make sure that you have your ranges designated properly before you hit RETURN.

4. You can copy between two windows, from one SHEET window to another SHEET window, or even from a SHEET window to a DOC window and vice versa. To copy from one SHEET window to another, you select **C**opy and indicate the FROM range. When Symphony asks for the TO range, you indicate the range within the other window. If you want to copy from a DOC window to a SHEET window, shift the window type from DOC to SHEET, initiate the **C**opy command, indicate the FROM range, and then indicate the TO range within the spreadsheet area. If you want to copy from a SHEET window to a DOC window, you must switch from DOC to SHEET.

Adjusting Column Width

One of the problems in earlier spreadsheet programs was that the widths of worksheet columns could be controlled only as a group. If you were setting up a projection of expenses for the next five years and wanted to display the full descriptions of the expense items (some of them 20 characters), you would have to set all the columns to a width of 20 characters. To avoid doing this, you had to abbreviate or truncate the labels.

In Symphony, as in 1-2-3, you don't have this problem. You can separately control the width of each column. You can set the first column of your projection of expenses to be 20 characters wide and the rest of the columns to whatever you wish. If a value is wider than the column in which the value is being entered, then it will be displayed as a series of asterisks (********). On the other hand, a label that is wider than the column in which the label is being entered will be displayed in its complete form as long as blank columns appear to the right of the label.

The command used to set individual column widths is SHEET Width Set. (This command functions the same as the Worksheet Column-Width command in 1-2-3.) You can set one column width at a time by either entering a number or using the ← and → cursor keys, followed by RETURN. The advantage of the ← and → cursor keys is that the column width actually expands and contracts each time you press these keys. To get a good idea of what your width requirements are, try experimenting when you enter the command.

Two things should be remembered about the SHEET Width Set command. First, you must locate the pointer in the proper column before you initiate the command. Otherwise, you will have to start over. Second, to reset the column width to the standard setting, you must use the SHEET Width Restore command. This command will change a column width to the width value stored within the window's settings sheet. (See the following discussion of the SHEET Settings Width command.)

As in earlier spreadsheet programs, including 1-2-3, in Symphony you can control all the column widths at once. The command is SHEET Settings Width (in 1-2-3, the Worksheet Status Column-Width command). The standard setting for column width is 9, but you can change this setting to whatever width you want for the current worksheet.

Any column width set previously by the SHEET Settings Width command will not be affected by a change in the global setting. For example, if you use the SHEET Width command to set the width of column A to 12, and then you use the SHEET Settings Width command to change all the columns in the worksheet to a width of 5, every column except A will change to 5. Column A will remain at a width of 12 and have to be reset to 5 with the SHEET Width Set command.

*New
with
Symphony*

Both the SHEET **W**idth and SHEET **S**ettings **W**idth commands affect only the current window in which you are working. Note, for example, the three windows in figure 4.50. Each window contains different column widths. The column widths in window 1 are set at the default setting of 9. The column widths in window 2 are set at a width of 6. And the column widths in window 3 are set at various widths. Each window also has a different width setting for its settings sheet. If you were to scroll each window, you would find that the column width of one does not affect the column width of another. Each window will maintain its width setting until you either delete the window by using the **W**indow **D**elete command or change the width in the settings sheet.

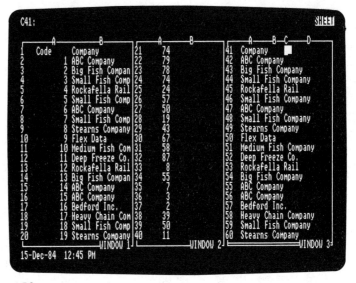

Fig. 4.50.

Formats

Format, the seventh command on the SHEET menu, controls how cell contents are displayed on the screen. And although 1-2-3's format capability surpasses earlier spreadsheet programs, Symphony has surpassed them even more by improving and expanding its format capability. In all, Symphony offers eleven format settings, here compared with those of 1-2-3:

Symphony Formats	1-2-3 Formats
Currency	Currency
Punctuated	, (Comma)
Fixed	Fixed
% (Percent)	Percent
General	General
Date (Including two new options for International formats)	Date
Time	
Scientific	Scientific
Other	
Bar-Graph	+/-
Literal	Text
Hidden	

As you can see, Symphony includes several new formats, expands on 1-2-3's Date format, and uses names that are different from those in 1-2-3. Unlike 1-2-3, Symphony also has settings sheets for controlling formats.

Settings Sheets and Commands for Controlling Formats

New with Symphony

The basic command for changing formats in a worksheet is the SHEET Format command. However, the SERVICES Configuration Other International and SHEET Settings commands also control formats. Before beginning a discussion of the various formats, a brief explanation is provided of the functions of the SERVICES Configuration Other International, SHEET Settings, and SHEET Format commands.

The SERVICES Configuration Other International selection from SERVICES Configuration controls the display of punctuation, including decimal points and commas, within numeric values and functions. This command allows you to use either a dot or a comma to separate the integer part of a number from the fraction part. The command also provides three format options for displaying thousands. Finally, **C**onfiguration **O**ther International contains various options for displaying Currency, Date, and Time formats. Although you may not find it necessary to change any of the default settings provided by Lotus, you should know that Symphony gives you the flexibility of changing standard numeric value, Currency, Date, and Time formats if you need to.

While the SERVICES **C**onfiguration **O**ther International selection controls numeric, Date, and Time formats globally, SHEET **S**ettings **F**ormat enables you to set a controlling format for each SHEET window you create. For example, suppose you create two different SHEET windows: one containing values in Currency format with no decimal places, and one containing values in Percent format with two decimal places. (See fig. 4.51.)

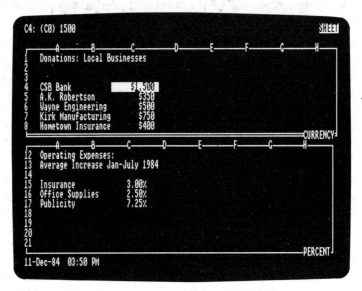

Fig. 4.51.

For each window, you can enter a separate setting in the settings sheet. If you do not change the setting for each window, Symphony accepts the default setting or the setting entered for the first window as the setting for all others. Keep in mind, though, that settings sheets are controlled by the SERVICES **C**onfiguration **O**ther International option.

Generally, you will use the SHEET Settings Format option when you are just starting to enter a worksheet in a particular window. You will want to choose the format that the majority of cells will take. Once you have set all the cells to that format, you can use the SHEET Format command to override the window format setting for specific cell ranges.

The SHEET Format command enables you to set the format for any range, regardless of the format in SHEET Settings. In the example above (fig. 4.51), columns B and C in window 1 contain values in Currency format. These values are formatted automatically because the settings sheet for window 1 has been adjusted for the "currency with no decimal places" format, represented in the sheet as (CO). If, however, you need to enter values in column D that are displayed in Percent format, the SHEET Format command enables you to set the Percent format for column D in window 1.

The SHEET Format command has precedence over the SHEET Settings Format command. That is, whenever you change the SHEET Settings Format, all the numbers and formulas affected will change automatically unless they were previously formatted with the SHEET Format command. If, however, you have changed the format of a range of numbers by using the SHEET Format command, you can restore the range to the window's SHEET Settings Format by selecting Reset on the SHEET Format menu.

In addition, the SHEET Format command will affect the format of values entered in other windows. In the example above (fig. 4.51), suppose you want to format column C in window 1 in the format for currency with no decimal places. The range for column D in window 1 is C4..C8. If, however, you accidentally type in the range TO format as C4..C18, cells C15..C17 in window 2 will also be displayed in the format for currency with no decimal places. When you select the SHEET Format command, the menu appears as in figure 4.52.

General

Although General is the fifth command in the SHEET Format menu, the discussion begins with General because it is the default setting for all new worksheets. That is, once you begin a new worksheet, the

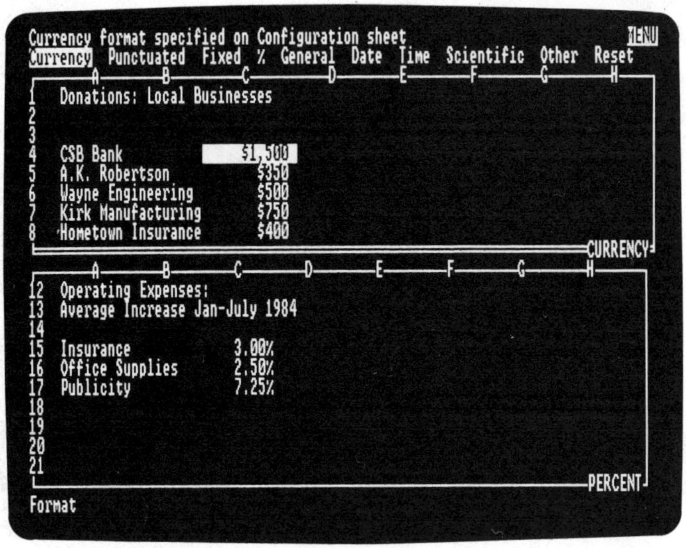

```
Currency format specified on Configuration sheet              MENU
Currency Punctuated  Fixed  %  General  Date  Time  Scientific  Other  Reset
      A------B------C------D------E------F------G------H
1   Donations: Local Businesses
2
3
4   CSB Bank                $1,500
5   A.K. Robertson            $350
6   Wayne Engineering         $500
7   Kirk Manufacturing        $750
8   Hometown Insurance        $400
                                                            CURRENCY
      A------B------C------D------E------F------G------H
12  Operating Expenses:
13  Average Increase Jan-July 1984
14
15  Insurance               3.00%
16  Office Supplies         2.50%
17  Publicity               7.25%
18
19
20
21
                                                            PERCENT
Format
```

Fig. 4.52.

SHEET **S**ettings **F**ormat entry will be General, represented on the settings sheet as (G).

When numbers are displayed in the General format, insignificant zeros to the right of the decimal point are suppressed. If numbers are too large or too small to be displayed normally, scientific notation is used. Following are some examples of the General format:

123.456
5.63E+14
-22.1
1.9E-09

In the General format, labels are displayed as left-justified. Each is preceded by a single quotation mark that signals Symphony to left-justify. As mentioned earlier, you can use the SHEET **S**ettings **L**abel-Prefix or **R**ange **L**abel-Alignment command to change the default of left justification.

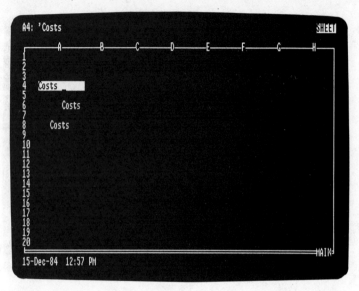

Fig. 4.53.

*C*urrency

The Currency format can be changed and controlled by the two
settings sheets and the SHEET **F**ormat command mentioned earlier.
First, the **C**onfiguration **O**ther **I**nternational **C**urrency option enables
you to change the currency sign and position. If, for example, you
need to create a worksheet with British pound currency values
entered, you can change the default currency sign from $ to £ by
following these steps: (1) choose **C**onfiguration from the SERVICES
menu; (2) when the **C**onfiguration menu appears, select **O**ther;
and (3) select **I**nternational. Then you will have four choices:
Punctuation, **C**urrency, **D**ate, and **T**ime.

When you choose **C**urrency, Symphony will display "Currency Sign:
$" in the top left corner. To change the sign from $ to £, press the
Backspace key to erase $. Next, press the Compose key (Alt + F1) to
tell Symphony that you want to create a special figure. Then type the
letter "l" and the hyphen "-". The Compose key, and the letter "l" and
hyphen tell Symphony you want to create the British pound sign.
After changing the currency sign to £, press RETURN. Symphony

New
with
Symphony

will then give you the option of having the currency sign placed before or after the value.

In some cases, you may want to place the currency sign after the value. To change the position of the currency sign, select **S**uffix when Symphony displays the options "Prefix Suffix." If you want to update **C**onfiguration to the new currency setting, select **U**pdate from the **C**onfiguration menu.

The other settings sheet that controls the Currency format is SHEET **S**ettings **F**ormat **C**urrency. Using this, you can set a worksheet or a specific window's default format setting to Currency, represented in the settings sheet as (C0), (C2), and so on, depending on the number of decimal places. If you enter into the settings sheet the format for currency with 2 decimal places, values in the worksheet or window will be displayed in this format unless you use the SHEET **F**ormat command to change the format of a range within the worksheet or window.

The SHEET **F**ormat **C**urrency command enables you to format a range in the worksheet or window and to override the SHEET **S**ettings **F**ormat. If, for example, you format a range by using the SHEET **F**ormat **C**urrency command, then setting the SHEET **S**ettings **F**ormat to Percent will not affect the range with Currency format.

Both SHEET **S**ettings **F**ormat **C**urrency and SHEET **F**ormat **C**urrency give you the option of controlling the number of places to the right of the decimal point. This can be helpful if you are having trouble displaying values because they are a little too large for the column width. One solution is to override the default of two places to the right of the decimal point.

If the value you want to display in the Currency format is too large for the column width, a series of asterisks will appear across the cell instead. In fact, these asterisks will appear for all formats when values exceed column widths. The problem of space is particularly acute with the Currency format because the dollar sign and commas take up quite a bit of space. The best way to handle this problem is to experiment with the formatting parameters and the column width until you get the appearance you want.

You will recall that column width is controlled through either the SHEET **W**idth or SHEET **S**ettings **W**idth command. The former controls specific columns in the worksheet or window, and the latter controls all the columns at the same time.

When numbers appear in the command line after they are entered, they are preceded by the format indicator for Currency. In fact, all number formats other than General show format indicators in the command line. You do not have to enter them yourself. Symphony automatically provides these indicators, based on the number of decimal places you have specified.

The format indicator for Currency is C, followed by an integer to indicate the number of decimal places you have chosen; both the C and the integer appear in parentheses. Following are some examples of how numbers appear in the command line after you have entered them, and how they are displayed in the worksheet with the Currency format.

In the Command Line	In the Worksheet
(C2)45	$45.00
(C2)1612.3	$1,612.30
(C3)22.805	$22.805
(C1)105.56	$105.6
(C2)-201.99	($210.99)

Cell formats are controlled with SHEET **S**ettings **F**ormat or SHEET **F**ormat, depending on how cell-specific you want the control to be.

Punctuated

*New
with
Symphony*

If you have used 1-2-3, you are probably familiar with the Comma (,) format command. **P**unctuated in Symphony's SHEET **F**ormat menu provides the same display format as 1-2-3's Comma format, but with a few added options for changing punctuation.

Symphony's Punctuated format, like the Currency format, is controlled by three different commands: the SERVICES **C**onfiguration **O**ther **I**nternational **P**unctuated command, the SHEET **F**ormat **P**unctuated command, and the SHEET **S**ettings **F**ormat **P**unctuated command. The **C**onfiguration setting provides the global settings for the type of punctuation to be used in values. (See **C**onfiguration **O**ther **I**nternational **P**unctuated below.) The SHEET Format **P**unctuated command enables you to format a range of values as punctuated, within the worksheet or window. And the SHEET **S**ettings Format **P**unctuated command allows you to set **P**unctuated as the default setting for a worksheet or specific window.

The SERVICES **C**onfiguration **O**ther **I**nternational **P**unctuated command gives you eight options for the punctuation used both to display values and to separate arguments in functions. The default setting uses the period (.) to separate the integer part of a number from its fraction part; the comma (,) is used to separate arguments in functions; and the comma (,) is also used to separate thousands. You will probably use most frequently the default setting, but keep in mind that the other settings are available, all listed in a menu that appears after you retrieve the command.

When Symphony's Punctuated format is used in its default setting, this format, like 1-2-3's **C**omma format, displays values in the same way as in the Currency format except that in Punctuated no dollar signs appear. Commas separate hundreds from thousands, thousands from millions, and so on.

This format can be particularly useful in financial statements for displaying all numbers (except those on the very top and bottom of the statement) with commas but without dollar signs. For example, a portion of a balance sheet is shown here:

Cash	$1,750
Receivables	3,735
Inventories	9,200
Current Assets	$8,685

The numbers corresponding to Receivables and Inventories are displayed with the Punctuated format, and those corresponding to Cash and Current Assets are displayed with the Currency format.

Fixed

In some ways the Fixed format is similar to the General format in that Fixed does not display commas or dollar signs. The difference is that the Fixed command lets you control the number of places to the right of the decimal point. When you select Fixed, Symphony prompts you for the number of decimal places you want displayed. After you choose a number, Symphony will pad the cells you have selected with zeros to the right of the decimal to the number of places you indicate. Conversely, if you decide to display fewer than the number of decimal places you have entered, the number will be rounded to the specified number of places. Following are examples of how numbers appear in the Fixed format.

In the Command Line	In the Worksheet
(F0) 15.1	15
(F2) 1000.2145	1000.21
(F3) -21.405	-21.405

You do not have to enter the format indicator (for example, F0) in the command line because Symphony automatically enters the indicator for you.

The Fixed command can be useful when you want to control specifically the number of places to the right of the decimal point without the automatic removal of insignificant digits, which occurs in the General format. The Fixed format is particularly appealing when you have columns of numbers and want all the numbers to show the same number of decimal places.

Percent

The Percent format is used to display percentages, with the number of decimal places controlled by you. The values displayed in the worksheet are the result of what you enter multiplied by 100 and followed by a percent sign.

In the Command Line	In the Worksheet
(P0) .12	12%
(P4) 12.134	1213.4000%
(P2) .5675	56.75%

One of the difficulties with this format is that it seems natural to want to enter integers instead of decimals (such as 12 instead of .12 in the first example above). Symphony, however, persists in its method of storing cell contents in only one way and allowing you to control only the display of the output.

Date

Symphony, like 1-2-3, represents any given Gregorian date as an integer equal to the number of days from December 31, 1899, to the given date. For example, January 1, 1900, is represented by 1; December 31, 2099, which is the last date in Symphony's calendar, is represented by 73050. To enter a date into the worksheet, you use one of the date functions: @DATE, @DATEVALUE, or @NOW.

To display a date in its proper Date format, use either the SHEET **F**ormat **D**ate or SHEET **S**ettings **F**ormat **D**ate commands. When you use the SHEET **F**ormat **D**ate command, any range you have set using the Date format will appear in one of five ways. When you use the SHEET **S**ettings **F**ormat **D**ate command, dates, as well as integers between 1 and 73050, entered in any cell in the worksheet or window will also be displayed in one of these five ways. You choose one of the five formats after you select **D**ate. The five formats include the following:

1.	(DD-MMM-YY)	Day-Month-Year	11-Jul-84
2.	(DD-MMM)	Day-Month	11-Jul
3.	(MMM-YY)	Month-Year	Jul-84
4.	Full International (See paragraph below.)		
5.	Partial International (See paragraph below.)		

New with Symphony

The Full and Partial International formats are two new Date formats that are not available in 1-2-3. If you choose either of these formats, the date is displayed according to the setting entered in **C**onfiguration **O**ther International **D**ate of the SERVICES menu. Four options for Full International and four options for Partial International format are available, all displaying numerical values for months rather than month abbreviations. For more information on date functions and Date formats, see Chapter 5.

Time

*New
with
Symphony*

The Time format is very much like Symphony's Date format. Time, like Date, is represented as an integer. To tell Symphony that you are entering a time value into the worksheet, you use one of the time functions: @TIME, @TIMEVALUE, or @NOW.

To display time in hour, minutes, and seconds, use either the SHEET **F**ormat **T**ime command or the SHEET **S**ettings **F**ormat **T**ime command. Four options are available for **T**ime formats, including two International formats. These International Time formats are determined by the setting in the **C**onfiguration **O**ther **I**nternational **T**ime option of the SERVICES menu. The Time formats available in SHEET **F**ormat **T**ime and SHEET **S**ettings **F**ormat **T**ime are the following:

1. (HH:MM:SS AM/PM)   Hour-Minute-Second   11:37:43 PM

2. (HH:MM AM/PM)   Hour-Minute   6:33 PM

3. Full International
   (See paragraph below.)

4. Partial International
   (See paragraph below.)

Four Time formats are available in the International settings. These differ from the first two settings listed above according to the punctuation separating hours, minutes, and seconds. Also available is a Time format using h, m, and s abbreviations following hours, minutes, and seconds. For more information on time functions and Time formats, see Chapter 5.

Scientific

The Scientific format causes Symphony to display numbers in exponential scientific notation. You will recall that this notation is used in the General format when numbers are too large or too small to be displayed any other way. One small difference between the way the General format defaults and the way the Scientific format controls scientific notation is found in their treatment of precision. You control the number of decimal places in Scientific, whereas Symphony controls them in General. Following are some examples.

In the Command Line	In the Worksheet
(S2) 27.1	2.71E+01
(S4) 453.235	4.5324E+02
(S1) -21	-2.1E+01
(S0) -1	-1E+00

Bar-Graph

The Bar-Graph format, located in the **O**ther option of the SHEET **F**ormat and SHEET **S**ettings **F**ormat commands, creates a horizontal bar graph of plus or minus signs, depending on the value of the number you enter in the cell. Asterisks are displayed if the size of the bar graph exceeds the column width. If zero is entered in a cell, a "." will be displayed on the graph.

In the Command Line	In the Worksheet
(+) 6	++++++
(+) -4	————
(+) 0	

Unless you develop some unusual applications, you will probably not find much use for the Bar-Graph format. Because Symphony's graphics capability is available, you can create a high-quality bar graph as easily as you can a simple graph with the **B**ar-Graph command.

Literal

The Literal format (1-2-3's **T**ext format) is located in the **O**ther option of the SHEET **F**ormat and SHEET **S**ettings **F**ormat commands. Literal displays formulas as they are entered in the command line, not the computed values that Symphony normally displays. Numbers entered by using this format are displayed in the same way as in the General format. In addition, range names rather than cell addresses are displayed on the worksheet whenever a formula in the Literal format involves range names.

One important application of the Literal format is debugging. Because you can display all the formulas on the screen by using

Literal, you can more easily find problems and correct them. Some examples of the Literal format are given here.

In the Command Line	In the Worksheet
(L) +C4/B12	+C4/B12
(L) (A21*Sales)	(A21*Sales)
(L) 567.6	567.6

Hidden

An option of the **Format O**ther command, **H**idden is not included in 1-2-3. This option is a very powerful addition to Symphony's spreadsheet environment. Used by itself, **H**idden enables you to keep a cell's contents from being displayed on the screen. The cell's contents will appear, however, in the control panel unless you use the SERVICES **S**ettings **S**ecurity selection in combination with **H**idden. (See the section on Security in Chapter 1 for more on protecting a worksheet's contents.)

Hidden will suppress the display of cell contents for any range that you indicate after you have retrieved the **Format O**ther **H**idden selection from the SHEET menu. If you want to "hide" all cell contents in a window, select **S**ettings **F**ormat **O**ther **H**idden from the SHEET menu. Even though a cell's contents are not displayed on the screen when you have used the Hidden format, all formulas and values can nevertheless be calculated and readjusted when values are changed.

Titles

The **S**ettings **T**itles command is similar to Symphony's **W**indow **C**reate command. Both commands allow you to see one area of a worksheet while working on another. The unique function of the **T**itles command, however, is that it freezes all the cells to the left and/or above the current cell pointer position so that they cannot move off the screen.

If you use the **W**indow **C**reate command with the **S**ettings **T**itles command, you can view two different parts of the worksheet while

New with Symphony

freezing one section in one of the windows. This setup is particularly useful when you want to keep row or column labels in view as you continue to work away from these labels. The **S**ettings **T**itles command is also useful whenever you simply want to freeze part of the worksheet without having to create a new window to do so.

A classic illustration of the advantage of this option can be seen when you are entering the items on a pro forma Balance Sheet and Income Statement. Suppose you are trying to set up a budget to project the level of the financial statement items, month by month, for the next year. Because the normal screen (without any special column widths) shows 20 rows by 7 columns, you will undoubtedly have to shift the screen so that cell A1 is no longer in the upper left corner. In fact, if you enter the month headings across row 1 and the Balance Sheet and Income Statement headings down column A, as shown in figure 4.54, you have to scroll the screen several times in order to enter all the items.

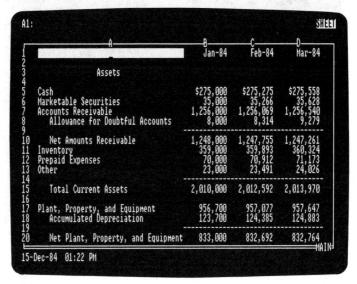

Fig. 4.54.

To keep the headings in view on the screen, even when you scroll, enter **S**ettings **T**itles when the cursor is in cell B2. When you enter this command, the following menu items appear:

Both   Horizontal   Vertical   Clear

If you select **B**oth, it freezes the rows above the cell pointer and the columns to the left of the cell pointer. That is, neither the rows nor columns move off the screen when you scroll up and down or left and right. If you select **H**orizontal, the rows on the screen above the cell pointer become frozen. If you select **V**ertical, the columns to the left of the cell pointer are frozen and move only when you scroll up and down (but not when you move left and right). **C**lear unlocks the previously set **T**itles.

In the pro forma example, the **B**oth option was selected. In this case, when you scroll right and left as well as up and down, the headings always remain in view. Figure 4.55 shows an example of how **B**oth works.

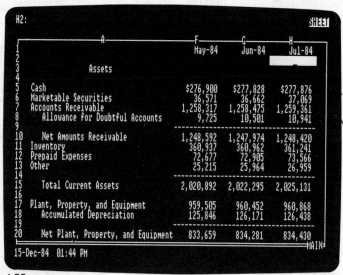

Fig. 4.55.

When you freeze rows or columns, you cannot move the cursor into the frozen area. Again, in the pro forma example, if you try to move the cursor into cell A2 from cell B2, Symphony will beep and not allow the cursor to move into the locked area. Similarly, using the Home key will move the cursor to the upper cell in the unlocked areas—in the example, cell B2. Normally, the Home key moves the cursor to cell A1.

There is one exception to the restriction on cursor movement. If you use the GoTo key (F5) to jump to cell A1, you will see two copies of the title rows and/or columns. Figure 4.56 shows the result when you use the GoTo key to go to cell A1. Seeing two copies of the rows or columns can be very confusing.

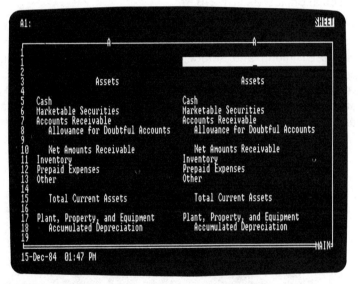

Fig. 4.56.

Recalculation

Recalculating all the cells in a worksheet when a value or a formula in one of the cells changes is a primary function of any spreadsheet program. 1-2-3 advanced the **R**ecalculation function far beyond that of earlier spreadsheet programs. And **R**ecalculation is an important part of Symphony's sophisticated spreadsheet capabilities.

Symphony's **R**ecalculation, however, is one of those groups of settings that 1-2-3 users may have trouble finding at first. Although the specific settings themselves haven't changed, **R**ecalculation's location in Symphony is somewhat obscure. This function is located in **S**ettings of the SHEET menu.

In addition, the **R**ecalculation selections are organized at different menu levels rather than one main level, as in 1-2-3. Once you get used to **R**ecalculation's location, you will find that this group of settings enables you to adjust the method, order, and iterative recalculation, just as in 1-2-3.

A study of the **R**ecalculation selections may help you to understand all the settings. First, to get to the **R**ecalculation setting, you retrieve the SHEET menu and select **S**ettings. After the **S**ettings menu appears, you choose **R**ecalculation. (Selecting **S**ettings also causes Symphony to display the default settings for **R**ecalculation in the bottom left quarter of the sheet, as shown in fig. 4.57.) Choosing **R**ecalculation leads to the following three selections:

     Method   Order   Iteration

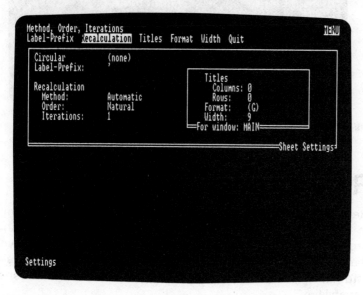

Fig. 4.57.

Method: Automatic versus Manual Recalculation

The **Method** setting tells Symphony that either you want to be recalculated automatically when changes are made, or you want to recalculate manually by pressing the Calc key (F8).

When you are working on a large worksheet that involves many formulas, the worksheet may require some time to recalculate. This delay occurs whenever a new entry is made or a value is changed. One way to get around the problem is to change from the standard **Automatic** to **Manual** recalculation.

With **Manual** recalculation, you can control Symphony so that it recalculates only when you press the Calc key. This advantage is useful with large worksheets in which you change many values. Otherwise, Symphony is so fast that recalculation occurs almost instantly.

Order: Natural versus Column-by-Column or Row-by-Row

If you choose **Order** from the three selections listed above, you can change the order of recalculation from **Natural** to **Column-by-Column** or **Row-by-Row**, or vice versa. The default setting is **Natural**. Symphony normally recalculates in what Lotus calls a "natural order." In other words, all the active cells in a worksheet are interrelated, and Symphony does not recalculate any given cell until the cells on which it depends have been recalculated first. Because the relationship is rarely linear, the method of recalculation is not linear. Instead, recalculation occurs in a "topological" manner, starting at the lowest level and working up.

```
             C3
       B1   B3   B4
   A1  A2   A4   A7   A9
```

With **Natural** recalculation, you no longer have to worry about the order of recalculation and the problem of forward references when a cell refers to another cell that is lower in the worksheet. For example, imagine that you created a sheet with four cells: A1, C1, C2, and C3. Assume that these cells have the following contents:

```
A1 = +C3
C1 = 100
C2 = 200
C3 = +C1+C2
```

Here A1 and C3 both have the value 300. Now suppose that the number in cell C2 is changed to 100.

If the cells are recalculated by using forward reference, here's what happens. Recalculation starts in the upper left corner of the worksheet, and cell A1 is evaluated first. Since the prior value of C3 (300) has not changed, A1 retains the value 300. Recalculation continues, either column by column or row by row, across the sheet until Symphony comes to cell C3. Because the value of cell C2 has changed, the value in C3 changes to 200.

Clearly, the forward reference order of recalculation causes the value of A1 to be different from that of C3, although the cells are defined to be equal. Even though recalculating the sheet again would eliminate the inequality, it would not remove the basic problem. In large and complex models, undetected forward references are possible.

In one instance you must change from Symphony's **N**atural order of recalculation to **C**olumn-by-Column or **R**ow-by-Row. The change is needed when importing a VisiCalc file that is built around either order of recalculation.

Iteration

Usually, only one pass is needed to recalculate a worksheet. But when a worksheet contains a circular reference, one pass will not work. A classic example of a circular reference occurs when you try to determine the amount of borrowing required by a firm. The thought process that is required is the following:

1. Borrowings = Assets - (Total Liabilities + Equity).
    Borrowings represent the difference between projected

asset requirements and the sum of total projected liabilities and equity.

2. But the level of equity is a function of net income and dividends.

3. And net income is a function of gross margin and interest expense.

4. Interest and expense and gross margin are a function of borrowings.

In this line of thinking you can see the circular pattern. When this kind of circular reference occurs, Symphony displays a CIRC indicator in the lower right corner of the screen. When you recalculate this type of sheet, using natural recalculation, Symphony will not accurately recompute all the values. Because each value in the circular set depends directly or indirectly on all the other values, Symphony cannot find a "toehold." That is, Symphony cannot find the most fundamental cell in the worksheet because no such cell exists.

Iterative recalculation allows Symphony to overcome this problem. When Symphony is in the Iterative mode, the sheet will recalculate a specified number of times each time you strike the Calc key. Normally, the sheet will recalculate only once, each time the Calc key is struck. The default number of iterations is 1, but you can alter this number in the Iteration options of the Recalculation setting. If you have circular references in your sheet, you should keep the number of recalculation passes high.

Iterative recalculation overcomes a circular reference because each recalculative pass through the sheet causes the actual values of the cells to approach more closely their correct values. For example, suppose you built a sheet with the following set of relationships:

    A3 = .05*A5
    A4 = 100
    A5 = +A3+A4

When you first enter this formula, A3 has a value of 0, A4 equals 100, and A5 equals 100. Assume that the number of iterations is set to 5. Following are the values of each cell after each recalculative pass:

	A3	A4	A5
1	5	100	105
2	5.25	100	105.25
3	5.2625	100	105.2625
4	5.263125	100	105.2631
5	5.263156	100	105.2631

Notice that on each pass, the difference between the prior and the current value of cells A3 and A4 becomes smaller. After only five passes, the difference is small enough to be insignificant. After 20 passes, the difference would probably be too small for Symphony to recognize. At that point, the problem with the circular reference is eliminated.

Two points should be noted about iterative recalculation. First, it is possible to create a set of circular references that is too complicated for Symphony to sort out, even in 20 passes. If such a circumstance arises with one of your models, simply set the Iteration count to 40. Remember that 20 (and certainly 40) calculations of a large sheet take a long time. Be patient. Control over Symphony will be returned to you soon enough.

Conclusion

Using the SHEET environment alone, you will find Symphony an incredibly powerful program. Like 1-2-3, Symphony enables you to build very sophisticated spreadsheets and data bases by using the SHEET window commands. Symphony's real power, however, can best be seen when you integrate SHEET window applications with the other environments. In the following chapters, you will discover just how the DOC, GRAPH, FORM, and COMM environments can be integrated with Symphony's SHEET window.

5

@Functions

Lotus has added several new @functions to increase the power of Symphony over earlier integrated packages, including 1-2-3. As you may recall, functions (also called built-in functions) can be thought of as abbreviations of formulas and are actually quick ways of performing tasks that would otherwise take much longer (or in many cases could not be done at all) using standard mathematical and string concatenation symbols, such as +, /, and &. Although many of Symphony's new functions are used for timekeeping, most are used for string processing (all the tasks associated with manipulating alphanumeric data).

When Symphony's new functions are combined with those initially offered with 1-2-3, the result is a very comprehensive set of built-in functions. And if you use Symphony's functions with some of its more high-powered features, such as its data base or Command Language, you will find that the program has many of the ingredients of a sophisticated programming language.

This chapter begins an examination of some of the basics of Symphony's functions. These are treated by application: mathematical, statistical, financial, logical, special, string processing, date,

213

and time. In each of the following sections, the new functions are designated *"New with Symphony."* The notation is used also for functions that are available in 1-2-3 but which have been improved in Symphony. If you are already an experienced 1-2-3 user, you will probably want to concentrate on these designated areas.

The Basics of the Functions

Symphony's functions are announced to the computer by typing @ before the function name. The @ distinguishes the formula from a normal label entry.

To obtain the values of functions, most functions refer to one or more arguments. An *argument* fits one of three different types: a single numeric value, a single string value, or a range. In Symphony, arguments are always written in parentheses after the function. For example, the following function (which we'll assume lies in cell B21) computes the total of a range of 8 cells:

@SUM(B12..B19)

Here @ signals that the entry is a function; SUM is the name of the function being used; and the range B12..B19 is the argument. This function tells Symphony to compute the sum of the numbers located in cells B12, B13, B14, B15, B16, B17, B18, and B19, and to display the result in cell B21.

A few functions, such as @ERR and @NA, do not take arguments. These functions are discussed in detail later in the chapter.

Following are examples of different functions with the three argument types:

@SUM(A2..H14)	Computes the sum of the numbers in the rectangular range A2..H14.
@COUNT(TOTALS)	Returns the number of nonblank cells in the range called TOTALS.
@MAX(C15..H32)	Returns the maximum value in the rectangular range C15..H32.
@SUM(A2..H14,A15)	Computes the sum of the numbers in the range A2..H14 and in cell A15.

@DATEVALUE(AA1)   Converts the string value in cell AA1 (such as "12/23/85") to a serial number representing the number of days since December 31, 1899.

@NPV(.15/12,A1..A17)   Computes the net present value of the 17-month range A1..A17 at the monthly rate of 1.25 percent.

@LOWER("TIMES")   Converts the word TIMES to lowercase.

Like mathematical and string concatenation formulas, functions can be much more complex than those shown above. For example, several functions can be combined in a single cell by using functions as the arguments for the original function. Having one function use another function in the same cell is called *nesting*. In practice you will find that you nest functions quite frequently.

Mathematical Functions

Symphony contains several functions that are used to perform mathematical operations. These functions include the following:

@ABS(number)

Computes the absolute value of a number or cell reference. For example, the function @ABS(-4) returns the value 4, and the function @ABS(-556) returns the value 556. The function @ABS(3) returns 3.

@EXP(number)

Computes the value of the constant *e* (approximately 2.718) to the power specified by the number; often used to reverse the @LN function. For example, the function @EXP(5) returns 148.4131. If cell A1 contains the value 2.75, the function @EXP(A1) returns 15.64263. Also, if @LN(2) is placed in cell AA1, the number that appears in that cell will be 0.693147. If @EXP(AA1) is then placed in cell AB1, the number that appears in that cell is 2. If the number used with @EXP is greater than 230, Symphony returns all asterisks.

@INT(number)

Computes the integer portion of the number. For example, the function @INT(4.356) returns the value 4. If cell A1 contains the value 55.666, the function @INT(A1) returns the value 55. Notice that unlike the @ROUND function (explained in the next section), @INT simply truncates all the digits to the right of the decimal.

@LN(number)

Computes the natural logarithm (base *e*) of the number or cell reference. For example, the function @LN(17.634) returns the value 2.869828. The number must be positive; otherwise, the function will return the ERR message. (Refer back to the description of the @EXP to see how the two functions work.)

@LOG(number)

Computes the logarithm (base 10) of the number or cell reference. For example, the function @LOG(4.56) returns the value 0.658964. If cell A1 contains the value 3.555, the function @LOG(A1) returns the value 0.550839.

@SQRT(number)

Computes the square root of the number or cell reference. For example, the function @SQRT(5) returns the value 2.236067. If cell A1 contains the value 16, the function @SQRT(A1) returns the value 4.

Special Mathematical Functions

The following mathematical functions in Symphony require special explanation:

@RAND	Used for random number generation
@ROUND	Rounds numbers to a given precision
@MOD	Returns the remainder (the modulus) from division

Random Number Generation

The @RAND built-in function requires no argument and is used for random number generation. The function generates random numbers between 0 and 1, with up to eight decimal places. If you enter the function @RAND in a cell, that cell will display a different value between 0 and 1 each time the worksheet is recalculated. The following two examples show the same sheet filled with @RAND functions (fig. 5.1). Notice that in the second sheet, each cell has a different value from that in the first. The reason is that the second sheet has been recalculated.

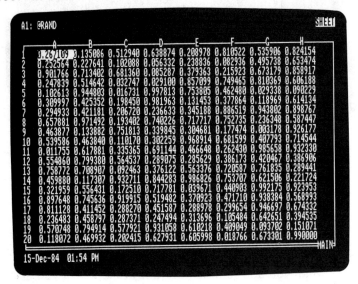

Fig. 5.1A.

Rounding Numbers

The @ROUND built-in function is used to round numbers to a specified precision. The general form of the function is

$$@ROUND(x, numb\_digs)$$

where x is the number to be rounded, and numb_digs is a number between 15 and -15, representing the number of digits to the right of the decimal. The following are examples of this function:

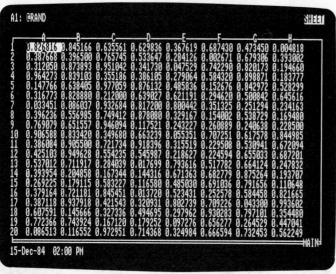

Fig. 5.1B.

@ROUND(123.456,3) = 123.456
@ROUND(123.456,2) = 123.46
@ROUND(123.456,1) = 123.5
@ROUND(123.456,0) = 123
@ROUND(123.456,-1) = 120
@ROUND(123.456,-2) = 100

The advantage of the @ROUND function over the **Format Fixed** command is that with @ROUND you avoid the errors that may appear when you add rounded currency amounts. If you add the following two sets of numbers, the numbers in the right column will appear to have the wrong total.

Cell	Value Stored	Value Displayed in Currency Format to Nearest Cent
A1	123.025	$123.03
A2	123.025	$123.03
A3	———	———
A4	246.05	$246.05

The @ROUND built-in function gets around this problem by making the columns total properly.

Cell	Value Stored	Value Displayed in Currency Format to Nearest Cent
A1	123.025	$123.03
A2	123.025	$123.03
A3	————	————
A4	246.05	$246.06

The total on the right uses the formula @ROUND(A1+A2,2) in cell A4.

Returning a Remainder

The @MOD function returns the remainder (the modulus) from division. Its general form is

@MOD(number,divisor)

The following examples illustrate how @MOD is used:

@MOD(7,3) =   1
@MOD(71.3,21) 8
@MOD(31,0) =   ERR

If you specify 0 as the divisor, Symphony will issue an ERR message.

The @MOD function is helpful in determining the number of parts that will be left over if you run equal-sized batches of 33 items, and if the total demand for a product is expected to be 500 items during the course of a year. The result will be five items, as in

@MOD(500,33) = 5

Trigonometric Functions

Symphony also has a complete set of trigonometric functions. Many Symphony users will never use these functions because they have little application in the world of accounting or finance. But those who use Symphony to solve engineering problems will find that these

functions are invaluable. Symphony's trigonometric functions
include the following:

@PI

> This function, which requires no argument, returns the
> value of the constant pi, accurate to 10 decimal places,
> or 3.1415926536.

@SIN(number), @COS(number), @TAN(number)

> These functions compute the common trigonometric
> functions. The values returned are expressed in
> radians. For example, the value of the function @SIN(2)
> = 0.909297 (radians). The value of @TAN(136) is
> 1.290401 (radians).

@ASIN(number), @ACOS(number), @ATAN(number),
  @ATAN2(number)

> These functions compute the arc sine, arc cosine, arc
> tangent, and four-quadrant arc tangent of a number or
> cell reference. The @ASIN, @ACOS, and @ATAN
> functions reverse the @SIN, @COS, and @TAN
> functions, respectively. For example, for the @ACOS
> function, you specify a number between 1 and -1,
> representing the cosine of an angle; the value of the
> function is the size of the angle in radians. The value of
> @ACOS(.33) is 1.234492 in radians. To convert to
> degrees, you multiply the value by 180/@PI. Therefore,
> the value of @COS(.33)*180/@PI is approximately 71
> degrees.

Statistical Functions

Symphony has several functions that perform simple statistical
analyses. Symphony's statistical functions are typically used with an
argument consisting of a range of cells. As you may recall, a range is
a series of contiguous cells, either by row or column. Symphony's
statistical functions include @SUM, @MAX, @MIN, @COUNT,
@AVG, @STD, and @VAR.

@SUM

Perhaps the most important statistical function is the @SUM built-in function. @SUM(range) computes the sum of a range of entries. The range is usually a partial row or column, but the range can also be an entire block of cells consisting of several rows and columns. For example, in the simple sheet in figure 5.2, the function @SUM(A1..A2) returns the value 1115. The function @SUM(A1..C2) returns the value 3330, which is the total of all the numbers in the six-cell range. Notice that the range in this case consists of two partial rows.

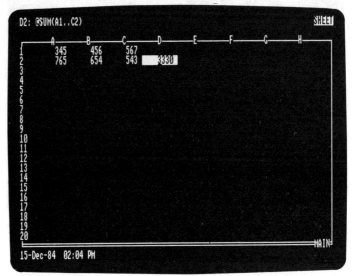

Fig. 5.2.

You can even define the argument of the @SUM function as a discontinuous set of cells. For example, the function @SUM (A1,B2,C1) returns the value 1566. This function is equivalent to the formula +A1+B2+C1. A more useful hybrid is the function @SUM(A1..B2,C1), which computes the total of the range A1 to B2 plus the value in C1, or a total of 2787.

In the example above, using @SUM will take about the same amount of time as using the long-hand arithmetic +A1+A2+B1+B2+C1. But in a case where the range is very long, this function can save time.

Another advantage of the @SUM function (and other range functions as well) is that it is more adaptable than a formula to changes
made in the sheet with cut-and-paste commands. For example, in
the sheet in figure 5.2, the function @SUM(A1..C1) is equivalent to
the formula +A1+B1+C1. But if you use the SHEET window's **D**elete
Column command to delete column B, the sheet will look like that in
figure 5.3. The formula has changed to +A1+ERR+B1, which returns
the message ERR. The function, on the other hand, has changed to
@SUM(A1..B1) and returns the correct answer: 912.

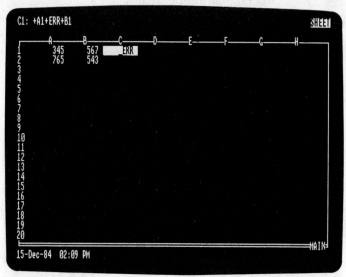

Fig. 5.3.

In this example, if you go the other way and insert a column using the
SHEET window's **I**nsert **R**ow command, what will happen? The
sheet will look like that in figure 5.4. The formula is +A1+C1+D1 and
still has the value 1368. The function will now be @SUM(A1..D1). If
you insert a number in the new cell B1, the function will include that
number in the new total, but the formula will not.

Modeling Tip: There is one very practical application for this insert
feature. Whenever possible, a sum range is defined to include an
extra cell at the end of the function. Frequently this can be done by
including the cell that contains the underline to mark the addition in

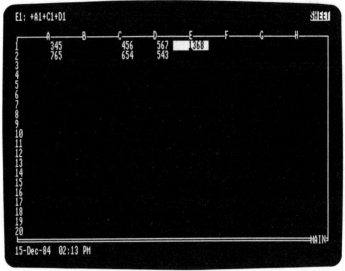

Fig. 5.4.

the range. For example, in the sheet shown in figure 5.5, you can enter the formula @SUM(A1..A4) in cell A5. Because the label in cell A4 has a mathematical value of 0, it does not affect the sum. But because you include the label in the formula, you can add an extra item in the list simply by inserting a row at row 5. The sheet will then look like that in figure 5.6.

The formula in cell A6 is now @SUM(A1..A5). If you insert the number 111 in cell A4, the formula will immediately pick it up and display the value 2100 in cell A6.

@MAX and @MIN

Other simple statistical functions include @MAX, @MIN, @COUNT, and @AVG. The @MAX and @MIN functions return the maximum and minimum values in a range. As with the @SUM function, the range can be a partial row or column, a block or several partial rows and columns, a named range, or a discontinuous group of cells joined by commas. Both @MAX and @MIN assign a value of 0 to labels but completely ignore empty cells. For example, in the simple sheet in figure 5.7, the function @MAX(A1..A5) returns the value 777.

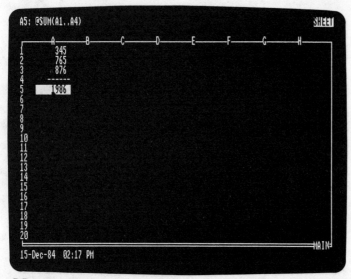

Fig. 5.5.

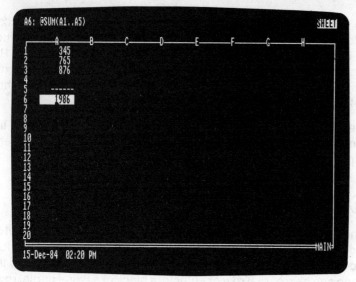

Fig. 5.6.

The function @MIN(A1..A5) returns the value 134, and the function
@MIN(A1..A6) also returns 134 because cell A6 is blank. But if the

label ABCD is entered in cell A6, the function @MIN(A1..A6) will return the value 0.

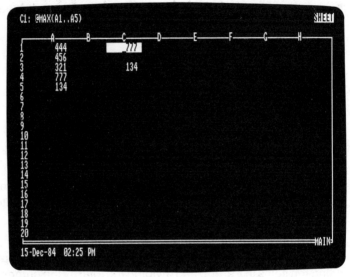

Fig. 5.7.

@COUNT

The @COUNT function is similar to the @MIN, @MAX, and @SUM functions. @COUNT returns the count of the number of nonblank entries in a range. In the previous example the function @COUNT(A1..A6) returns the value 5. If a label or number had been entered in cell A6, the value of the function would be 6.

One interesting feature of the @COUNT function is the way it reacts to a single blank cell. If cell A1 is blank, the function @COUNT(A1) will return the value 1. However, the function @COUNT(A1..A1) returns the value 0. In fact, every @COUNT function that refers to a single cell without using the range format (such as A1..A1) will have a value of 1. The most reliable technique for avoiding the single-cell problem is always to use the range format with the @COUNT function. Cells with spaces will increment the @COUNT.

@AVG

Another simple statistical function is @AVG. This function computes the mean, or average, of all the cells in a range. Essentially, the @AVG function is similar to the @SUM function divided by the @COUNT function. Because blank cells are ignored by @AVG, an @AVG function that refers to a range with all blank cells will return the value of ERR.

A Quick Review of Statistics

A quick review of statistical concepts may be worthwhile at this time. If you are already quite familiar with the concepts of mean, variance, and standard deviation, as well as population and sample statistics, you may want to skip to the next section.

The *mean,* often called the arithmetic average, is commonly used to mark the midpoint of a group of data items. The mean is calculated by adding the items in a group and dividing the total by the number of items. Don't confuse the mean with the median or mode, which are also measures of central tendency. The *median* is the value midway between the highest and lowest value in the group in terms of probability. Half the items in the group have values above the median, and half have values below. The *mode* is the most commonly found value in a group of items (that is, the value you see most often).

Variance and *standard deviation* are related dispersion statistics. To calculate the variance, you subtract the mean of a group of numbers from each number in the group and square each result. You then add the squares and divide the total by the number of items in the group. To compute the standard deviation, you take the square root of the variance. Symphony's @VAR and @STD functions automatically make these calculations for you.

What does the standard deviation tell you? As a general rule, about 68 percent of the items in a normally distributed population will fall within a range that is plus or minus one standard deviation of the mean. About 95 percent of the items fall within plus or minus two standard deviations of the mean.

To understand Symphony's @VAR and @STD statistical functions, you should know the difference between population and sample statistics. Population statistics are used when you know the values of all the items in a population. However, when the number of items is quite large and you don't know them all (which is usually the case), you cannot compute the population statistics. You must instead rely on sample statistics as estimates of the population statistics. (For more information on statistics, see Donald Harnett, *Statistical Methods*, Addison-Wesley Publishing Company, Philippines, 1982.)

More Complex Statistical Functions

Two slightly more complex statistical functions are the following:

@VAR(list)	Computes the population variance
@STD(list)	Computes the standard deviation of a population

A very simple example that uses both functions is shown in figure 5.8. Here is a list of salespeople, showing the number of items they sold during a given period. The list of the number of items sold is the population in this example. The population is used as the range for all the statistical functions.

The mean of the population (about 101) is computed by using the @AVG function. The standard deviation is about 24, which means that roughly 68 percent of the salespeople sold between 77 and 125 items.

Assuming that you do not have the entire population of sales figures but only a small portion of it, you can compute the sample statistics. This approach is more realistic because you are more likely to be told that the actual population is all the monthly sales for the year, and be given only one month's worth of sales. You can see that moving into the realm of sample statistics involves more sophisticated concepts.

To calculate the sample variance for the sales data used above, you multiply the population variance by n/n-1 (degrees of freedom), where *n* equals the number of items in the sample. Multiplying by n/n-1 adjusts the variance for the size of the sample used in the

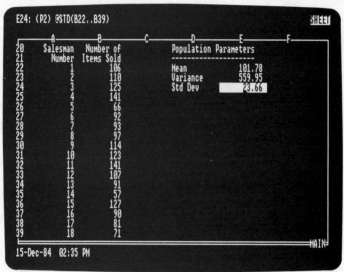

Fig. 5.8.

calculation. Since n/n-1 is always less than one, multiplying it by the population variance has a conservative influence on the sample variance. The results of this calculation are shown in figure 5.9.

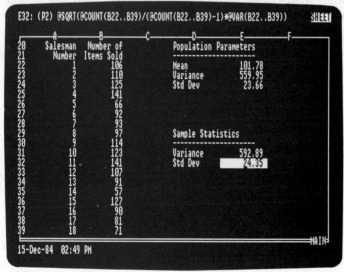

Fig. 5.9

To compute the sample variance in figure 5.9, you can use @COUNT to determine the degrees of freedom, as in

Sample Variance = @COUNT(list)/(@COUNT(list)-1)
   *@VAR(list)

To compute the standard deviation of the sample, you can take the square root of the sample variance. A convenient way to do this is to use the built-in @SQRT function, as in

Sample Standard Deviation = @SQRT(Sample Variance) =
   @SQRT(@COUNT(list)/(@COUNT(list)-1)*@VAR(list))

Financial Functions

Symphony also has several financial functions. One example is the @NPV function, which computes the net present value of a stream of flows. The form of this function is

@NPV(discount_rate,range)

The discount rate is the interest rate that Symphony will use to compute the net present value. And the range is the stream of flows to be discounted. The interval between the flows must be constant. It is determined by the specified rate. For example, if the flows occur one year apart, an annual discount rate should be used. If the rates occur every month, a monthly rate should be used.

The @NPV function can be used to evaluate a variety of investment opportunities. For instance, suppose you have an opportunity to buy a piece of property that will create the following stream of income in the next five years:

Year 1	100,000
Year 2	120,000
Year 3	130,000
Year 4	140,000
Year 5	50,000

To evaluate this investment, you can create a simple worksheet, as illustrated in figure 5.10. The function @NPV(A3,A1..E1) will return the value 368075.1, which is the net present value of that stream at the discount rate of 15 percent. If this rate accurately represents the

rate you earn on the investment, and the price of the property is
equal to or less than $368,075, you can see that the property would
be a good investment.

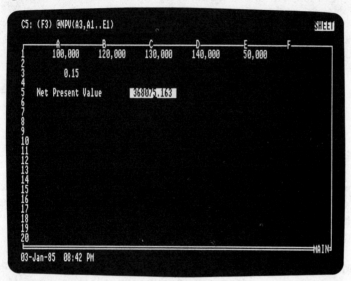

` Fig. 5.10.

Notice that a cell reference, A3, is used to enter the discount rate into
the function. Because the formula @NPV(.15,A1..E1) is just as easy
to enter, why wasn't it used instead? In fact, neither method has an
advantage until you want to make a change in the rate.

For example, assume that you want to evaluate this same investment, using a rate of 14 percent. With the method just used, all you
need to do is enter the number .14 in cell A3, and Symphony will
automatically recalculate the worksheet. If you embedded the rate in
the formula, you would have to edit the cell, replacing the .15 with
.14. As you can see, if several changes are required, this operation
would unnecessarily consume much time. The simple technique of
using a cell reference to enter a rate can be applied in a variety of
situations to facilitate changing a worksheet.

Present Value of an Annuity

The @PV built-in function is used to calculate the present value of an ordinary annuity, given a payment per period, an interest rate, and the number of periods. An *ordinary annuity* is a series of payments made at equally spaced intervals, and *present value* is the value today of the payments to be made or received later, with the value discounted at a given interest or discount rate. Calculating the present value of an ordinary annuity gives you a way to compare different investment opportunities or potential obligations while taking into account the time value of money. The general form of the @PV formula is

@PV(payment,interest,term)

The actual equation for calculating the present value of an ordinary annuity is

$$PV = payment * \frac{(1-(1+interest)^{-n}}{interest}$$

Figure 5.11 shows an example of how the @PV built-in function is used.

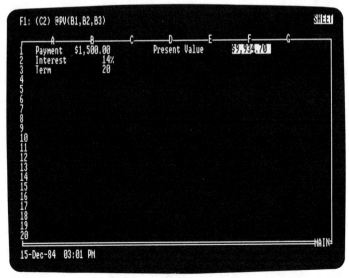

Fig. 5.11.

The difference between @NPV, the built-in function for net present value, and @PV stems from the difference in cash flows and the way they are laid out in the worksheet. @NPV calculates the net present value of a series of flows that may or may not be equal, but which are all contained in a range of cells in the worksheet. The cash flows in the @PV function must all be equal, and the amount of the flows must be contained in a single cell or entered as a value in the @PV function.

Future Value of an Annuity

The @FV built-in function is similar in form to the @PV function, but @FV is used to calculate the future value of an ordinary annuity. *Future value* is the value at a given day in the future of a series of payments or receipts, discounted at a given interest or discount rate. Calculating the future value of an annuity allows you to compare different investment alternatives or potential obligations. The form of the @FV function is

> @FV(payment,interest,term)

The equation for calculating the future value of an ordinary annuity is

$$FV = payment * \frac{(1+interest)^{-n}}{interest}$$

An example using the @FV built-in function is shown in figure 5.12.

Symphony's method of computing the future value of an annuity is similar to its method of computing the present value, except that the future value equation is used.

Internal Rate of Return

Internal rate of return (IRR) is the discount rate that equates the present value of the expected cash outflows with the present value of the expected inflows. In simple terms, IRR is the rate of return, or profit, that an investment is expected to earn. Like the other financial calculations, IRR determines the attractiveness of an investment opportunity.

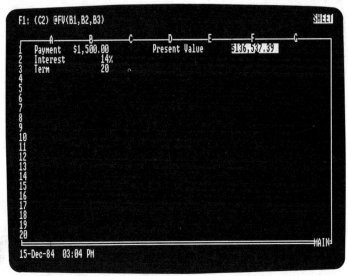

F1: (C2) @FV(B1,B2,B3)   SHEET

	A	B	C	D	E	F	G
1	Payment	$1,500.00		Present Value		5136,537.39	
2	Interest	14%					
3	Term	20					

15-Dec-84 03:04 PM

Fig. 5.12.

The function for internal rate of return is built around an iterative process whereby you provide an initial "ballpark" guess for a discount rate (somewhere between 0 and 1), and Symphony calculates the actual discount rate that equates the present value of a series of cash outflows with the present value of a series of inflows. Symphony's method may seem awkward, but it is actually very logical. The same iterative method is used to calculate IRR manually.

Given the format of the equation, all the inflows and outflows must be in the same range. The general form of the @IRR function is

@IRR(guess,range)

Symphony should reach convergence on a discount rate within .0000001 after 20 iterations, or ERR is returned. Figure 5.13 shows an example of how the @IRR built-in function is used. The internal rate of return, or profit, for the project illustrated in figure 5.13 is about 16 percent.

You may encounter two possible problems with the @IRR function. First, as indicated earlier, Symphony may not converge on a value for one of two reasons. One reason is that you have more than a

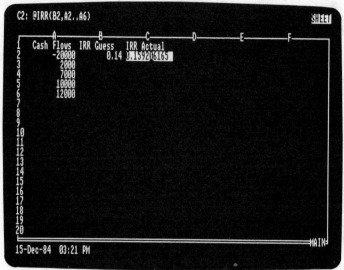

Fig. 5.13.

single sign change between negative and positive cash flows. For example, you may have the sporadic cash flows that appear in figure 5.14. Because Symphony is unable to reach convergence on a single IRR value, Symphony returns ERR.

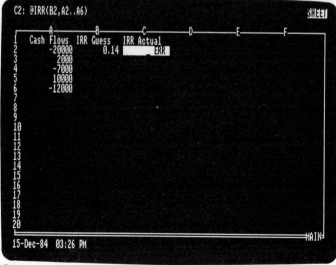

Fig. 5.14.

Another possible problem with the @IRR function is that, depending on the guess value which you enter, the value returned may be unreasonable. For example, Figure 5.15 shows a series of 11 cash flows, an IRR guess of .20, and an actual IRR of approximately - 289 percent. Even though Symphony has not reached the proper convergence, the ERR message is not displayed. The proper IRR for this series of cash flows is approximately 138 percent. In order to get Symphony to display 138%, your guess must be between .74 and 1.0.

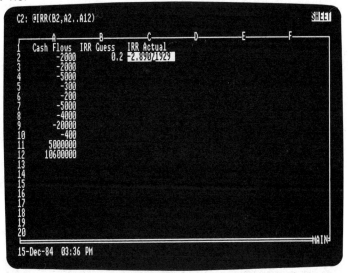

Fig. 5.15.

A good way to avoid this problem with the @IRR function is to guess on the high side. You should also double-check any answer you get by trying two or more guess values.

Payment per Period

The last financial function provided by Symphony calculates the mortgage payment required for a given principal, interest rate, and number of periods. The format of this function is

> @PMT(principal,interest,n)

where n equals the number of periods.

Again, the formula behind the function calculates the present value of an ordinary annuity, but the formula is rearranged to yield the period payment as the result:

$$PMT = principal * \frac{interest}{1-(1+interest)^n}$$

@PMT is a slight variation of the @PV built-in function discussed earlier. You can use @PMT to build a table of mortgage rate payments similar to those in the SAMPLES.BAS program supplied with DOS. Such a table is very easy to construct and appears in figure 5.16.

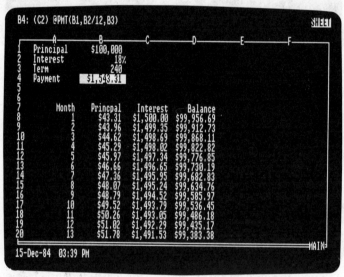

Fig. 5.16.

Data Management Functions

Symphony has four simple data management functions: @CHOOSE, @VLOOKUP, @HLOOKUP, and a new function called @INDEX. These functions are called "special" functions by Lotus, but in this book they are called data management functions because the functions retrieve data from lists and tables. These functions should not be confused with Symphony's data base statistical functions, which operate only on data bases. (Data base statistical functions are discussed in Chapter 11.)

@CHOOSE

The @CHOOSE function uses a key value provided by the user to select a number from a list. The form of this function is

@CHOOSE(key,argument0,argument1,...,argumentN)

wherein the first argument is 0, the second argument is 1, and so on.

@CHOOSE displays the argument whose position in the list matches the key. For example, the function

@CHOOSE(2,3,4,5)

returns the number 5 because 5 is in the second argument position in the list. If the key is changed to 1, as in

@CHOOSE(1,3,4,5)

the function will return 4.

As with other functions, the arguments in the @CHOOSE function can be numbers, formulas, or functions. @CHOOSE can also be used to select formulas that will vary in different situations. For example, the percentage rate used to compute depreciation under the ACRS depreciation system varies with the useful life of the asset. Thus, an asset with a three-year life would be depreciated in the first year of the asset's life at a rate that is different from that of an asset with a five-year life. A function like the following one dramatically simplifies the computation:

@CHOOSE(Year of Life,Rate for 3 year asset,Rate for 5
    year asset...)

*New
with
Symphony*

Variations of @LOOKUP

@VLOOKUP and @HLOOKUP are two variations of the basic @LOOKUP function pioneered by VisiCalc. As their names suggest, these functions "look up" a value from a table based on the value of a test variable. The forms of these functions are

@VLOOKUP(test variable,range,column offset-number)

@HLOOKUP(test variable,range,row offset-number)

The first argument, which is the test variable, can be either a number or a string. (1-2-3 aficionados should take note that Symphony now allows not only "numeric" lookups but "string" lookups as well.)

The second argument is a range containing at least two partial rows or columns. This range includes the entire lookup table from the top left corner of the comparison column to the bottom right corner of the last data column. (A range name can also be used here instead of the actual cell references.)

The third argument, called the offset-number, determines which data column should supply the data to the function. In every case the comparison column has an offset-number of zero, the first data column has an offset-number of 1, and so on. If you are well versed in 1-2-3, you may recall that an offset-number must always be positive and cannot exceed the actual number of rows or columns in the table. In Symphony, however, these restrictions have been lifted. An offset-number can be negative in Symphony, and the number can also exceed the number of columns or rows in the lookup table. (Some examples of negative and excessive offset-numbers will be shown later on.)

If you want to use the lookup functions, the worksheet needs to have a lookup table. This table must consist of two or more adjacent partial rows or columns. An example of a numeric vertical lookup table is illustrated in figure 5.17.

What differentiates this table from a string vertical lookup table is the contents of the first column, M. (The first column in a vertical lookup table is called the comparison column.) In a numeric vertical lookup table, the comparison column must contain numbers arranged in ascending order. In a string vertical lookup table, the comparison column can contain labels in any order.

In figure 5.17 the comparison column contains the values that will be used to look up the data shown in the second and third columns (N and O). To access this columnar table, you use the @VLOOKUP or vertical lookup function.

In this table the function @VLOOKUP(5,M61..O70,1) will return the value 54999. To return this result, Symphony searches the comparison column for the largest value that is not greater than the key and returns the value in the data column with an offset-number of 1

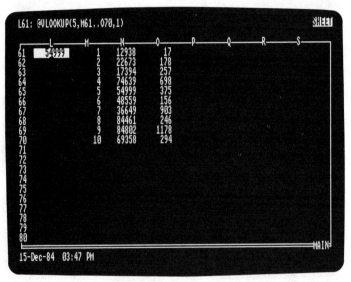

Fig. 5.17.

(in this case, column N). Remember that the comparison column has an offset-number of 0. Column N, therefore, has an offset-number of 1, and column O has an offset-number of two.

Because the lookup table does not search for a specific match, but for the largest key in the table that is not greater than the search variable, the function @VLOOKUP(5.5,M61..O70,1) also returns 54999. Similarly, a key of 100 returns 69358, the number that corresponds to the largest key in the list. If 0 is used as the key, an ERR message will appear because no key in the table is less than or equal to 0.

The data in column O can also be looked up with @VLOOKUP. For example, the function @VLOOKUP(10,M61..O70,2) returns the value 294.

Lookup tables must follow specific rules. As mentioned earlier, the comparison column values for numeric lookups must be arranged in ascending order. (In other words, a comparison value cannot be repeated.) For example, the lookup table in figure 5.18 does not work because the comparison values in column M are not in ascending order. The table in figure 5.19 is also not allowed because the key 5 is repeated twice.

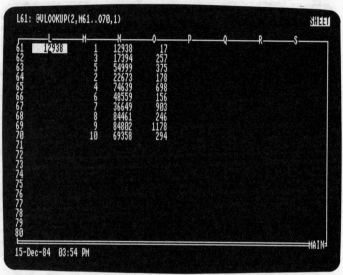

Fig. 5.18.

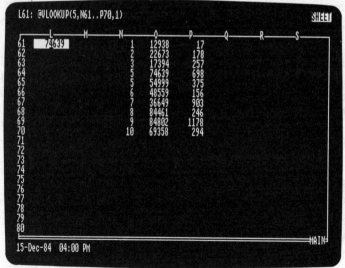

Fig. 5.19.

A slight modification of the table in figure 5.17 illustrates the effects of using a negative offset-number. Using the statement @VLOOKUP(5,N81..P90,-1) for the vertical lookup table in figure

5.20, you can see that Symphony selects the appropriate value from the column just to the left of the lookup table. Here the value returned from the table lookup is "Shelf 8" (cell L81).

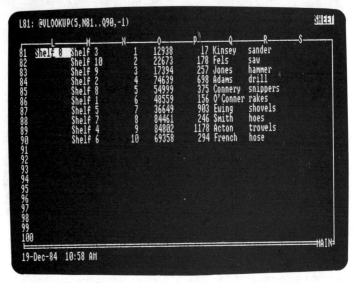

Fig. 5.20.

Similarly, an offset-number that exceeds the last column in the lookup range is also acceptable. Figure 5.21 shows the result from setting the offset-number to 4. In this case the value returned is "snippers", a value taken from the column that is two columns to the right of the rightmost column in the lookup table.

Besides numeric table lookups, Symphony is also capable of performing string table lookups. Some early spreadsheet programs have had this feature for quite a while, but it is not included in 1-2-3. Including string table lookups in Symphony adds power to the program.

In performing string table lookups, Symphony looks for a perfect match between a value in the comparison column and the test variable. For example, in figure 5.21, Symphony uses the function @VLOOKUP("rakes",M101..O110,1) to search for the value in column N corresponding to rakes. Notice that the string argument is enclosed in double quotation marks.

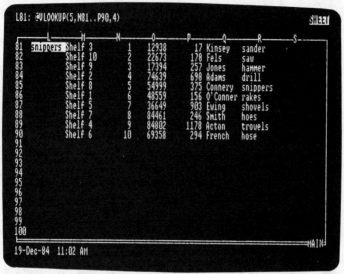

L81: @VLOOKUP(5,N81..P90,4)   SHEET

```
        L        M       N        O        P       Q         R        S
81  snippers Shelf 3     1      12938     17 Kinsey    sander
82           Shelf 10    2      22673    178 Fels      saw
83           Shelf 9     3      17394    257 Jones     hammer
84           Shelf 2     4      74639    698 Adams     drill
85           Shelf 8     5      54999    375 Connery   snippers
86           Shelf 1     6      48559    156 O'Conner  rakes
87           Shelf 5     7      36649    903 Ewing     shovels
88           Shelf 7     8      84461    246 Smith     hoes
89           Shelf 4     9      84802   1178 Acton     trowels
90           Shelf 6    10      69358    294 French    hose
91
92
93
94
95
96
97
98
99
100
```

19-Dec-84 11:02 AM   MAIN

Fig. 5.21.

If 0 is used as the offset-number for the @VLOOKUP statement above, the value returned will be 5. This number corresponds to the position of the matched string in the lookup range. The first entry ("nails") is 0, the second entry ("hammers") is 1, and so on. If the search of the lookup table fails to produce a match, the value returned is ERR.

The @HLOOKUP function is essentially the same as @VLOOKUP, except that @HLOOKUP operates on tables arranged across rows instead of columns. The rules here are the same as those for vertical tables. Now look at an example of how the @HLOOKUP function works for a numeric lookup. (Again, the same rules apply for a string lookup). If you build the table in figure 5.22, the function @HLOOKUP(5,L123..S125,1) will return the value 567. The function @HLOOKUP(8,L123..S125,1) will return the value 890. And the function @HLOOKUP(3,L123..S125,2) will return the value 765.

A useful application for the @VLOOKUP and @HLOOKUP functions is to create tax tables that automatically retrieve the appropriate rate base on income. In fact, this application is the one for which the function was originally developed. These functions can also be used for simple data management, such as handling inventory and

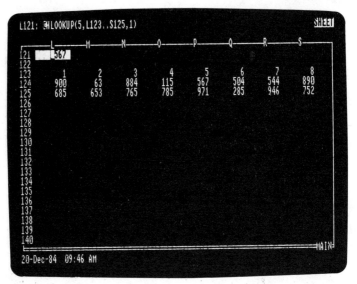

Fig. 5.22.

employee lists, although in Symphony these functions can be performed better with the data base commands.

New
with
Symphony

@INDEX

The last data management function, @INDEX, was introduced with Symphony. This function is similar to the table lookup functions described earlier; however, it has some of its own unique features. The general form of the function is

@INDEX(range,column-number,row-number)

Like the table lookup functions, the @INDEX function works with a table of numbers. But unlike the table lookup functions, the @INDEX function does not use a test variable and a comparison column (or row). Instead, the @INDEX function requires you to indicate the row-number and column-number of the range from where you wish to retrieve data. For example, if you use the function @INDEX(L142..S145,3,2) in figure 5.23, you get the value 2625.

Notice that the number 0 corresponds to the first column, 1 corresponds to the second column, and so on. The same numbering

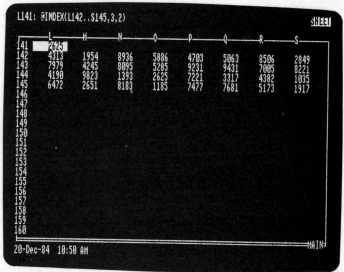

Fig. 5.23.

scheme applies to rows. Therefore, using 3 for the column-number and 2 for the row-number indicates that you want the item from the fourth column, third row.

Although the behavior of the @VLOOKUP and @HLOOKUP functions may lead you to believe otherwise, you cannot use column and row numbers that fall outside the relevant range with the @INDEX function. Using either negative numbers or numbers too large for the range will cause Symphony to return the ERR message.

The @INDEX function is useful when you know the exact position of a data item in a range of cells and wish to locate the item quickly. For instance, the @INDEX function works well for rate quotation systems. Figure 5.24 shows an example of a system for quoting full-page magazine advertising rates.

In this example the function @INDEX(L167..Q171,M163,M164) returns a value of $2,085. This value corresponds to the amount in the first column and the second row of the index range. If a 6 is entered for the frequency, the ERR message will appear instead of a valid dollar amount.

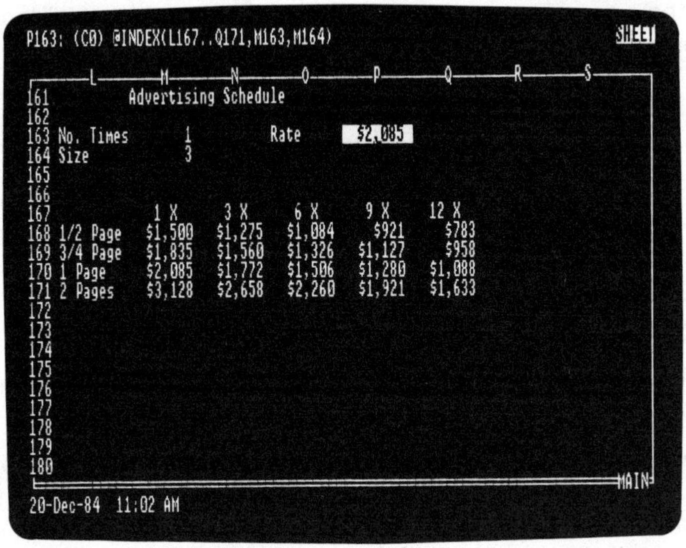

```
P163: (C0) @INDEX(L167..Q171,M163,M164)                    SHEET
├───L────M────────N────────O────────P────────Q────────R────────S──
161              Advertising Schedule
162
163 No. Times        1              Rate      $2,085
164 Size             3
165
166
167                 1 X      3 X      6 X      9 X     12 X
168 1/2 Page       $1,500   $1,275   $1,084    $921     $783
169 3/4 Page       $1,835   $1,560   $1,326   $1,127    $958
170 1 Page         $2,085   $1,772   $1,506   $1,280   $1,088
171 2 Pages        $3,128   $2,658   $2,260   $1,921   $1,633
172
173
174
175
176
177
178
179
180                                                          MAIN
20-Dec-84  11:02 AM
```

Fig. 5.24.

Logical Functions

Symphony, like its predecessor 1-2-3, includes logical functions. These can be thought of as a subset of the mathematical functions. In all cases, Symphony analyzes logical functions as either true or false. If a logical function is true, it has a numeric value of 1. But if the logical function is false, it has a numeric value of 0. The importance of a logical function's numeric value will be made clear shortly.

Logical functions are advantageous because they allow you to build conditional tests into cells. These tests return different values depending on whether they are true (1) or false (0). Symphony's primary conditional function is @IF. Several new logical functions, however, have been added to increase the power of the program over earlier integrated packages.

Logical Operators

In many instances, conditional functions require *logical* operators. These help to determine the relationship between two different numbers or among several. The following is a list of "simple" logical operators and their meanings:

Operator	Meaning
=	Equal
<	Less than
<=	Less than or equal to
>	Greater than
>=	Greater than or equal to
<>	Not equal

Simple logical operators have lower precedence than any mathematical operator, but all logical operators have equal precedence within their group.

As mentioned earlier, logical functions are either true (1) or false (0). Conditional statements also follow this same line of reasoning. For example, the statement 5<3 is clearly false (0), whereas the statement 16<27 is true (1). Symphony's @IF function tests the conditional statement as either true (1) or false (0) and then assigns a cell value based on the results of the test.

@IF

New
with
Symphony

Let's create a logical statement using the @IF built-in function. The general form of this function is

@IF(a,vtrue,vfalse)

where the first argument "a" is tested as true or false. If the result of the test is true (1), the function assigns the cell the value of the second argument, vtrue. If the value of the first argument is false, however, the function assigns the cell the value of the third argument, vfalse. Following are examples of logical statements that use the @IF function, along with their English-language equivalents. 1-2-3 users should take note that Symphony, unlike 1-2-3, now allows strings in @IF functions.

@IF(B4>=450,B5,C7)
> If the value in cell B4 is greater than or equal to 450, then use the value in cell B5. Otherwise, use the value in cell C7.

@IF(A3<A2,5,6)
> If the value in cell A3 is less than the value in cell A2, then assign the number 5. Otherwise, assign the number 6.

@IF(G9<>B7,G5/9,G7)
> If the value in cell G9 is not equal to the value in cell B7, then use the value in cell G5 divided by 9. Otherwise, use the value in cell G7.

@IF(A9<>"January",45,"wrong entry")
> If the value in cell A9 is not the string "January", then assign the number 45. Otherwise, assign the string "wrong entry". Note that if a string value is entered in cell A9, either the vtrue or the vfalse argument is assigned. Note also that January must be entered with quotation marks in A9. However, if a number is entered in cell A9, or if the cell is left blank, Symphony returns the ERR indicator.

@IF(@FALSE,"ok","not ok")
> If false (0), then assign "not ok"; otherwise, assign "ok". The value of this function is always "not ok" because the value of @FALSE is always 0. (See a discussion of the @FALSE function.) This example emphasizes the numeric character of the @IF function.

Complex Operators

Relationships get more complicated when another set of logical operators, the *complex* operators, is introduced:

Operator	Meaning
#NOT#	Not (logical)
#AND#	And (logical)
#OR#	Or (logical)

The complex logical operators have lower precedence than the simple logical operators. Among the complex operators, the #AND# and #OR# have equal precedence.

Now that we have a complete set of logical operators, we can combine simple and complex operators to create the following @IF functions:

@IF(A1<>1#AND#G5="yes",E7,E6)

> If the value in cell A1 is not equal to 1, and the value in cell G5 is "yes", then use the value in cell E7. Otherwise, use the value in cell E6. The values in cells E6 and E7 can be either numbers or strings.

@IF(#NOT#(COST=50)#AND#A1=1,L10,K10)

> If the amount entered in the cell named COST is not $50 and the value in cell A1 is equal to one, then use the value in cell L10. Otherwise, use the value in cell K10.

Symphony's conditional functions are quite sophisticated and can be very complicated. The @IF function can be used in a wide variety of instances to allow Symphony to make decisions. Figure 5.25 provides an example of how the @IF function can be used.

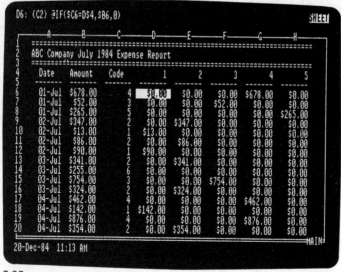

Fig. 5.25.

Figure 5.25 shows a simple worksheet that summarizes a company's expenditures for the month of July, 1984. Column A contains the date of each expenditure, and column B contains the amounts of the disbursements. Notice that column C has been labeled "Code" and that row 4 contains a sequence of numbers, beginning with 1 in column D and ending with 3 in column H. The label "Accounts" can be used for these numbers. Now suppose that the following formula is entered in cell E6:

@IF($C6=E$4,$B6,0)

Similarly, the formula

@IF($C6=F$4,$B6,0)

is entered in cell F6. These formulas can be translated as: If the number in cell C6 (the code) equals the number in cell E4 (or cell F4) (the account), then enter the value in cell B6 here. Otherwise, enter 0 here.

Let's assume that similar formulas existed in all the cells in range D6..H20. Suppose that you enter a code for each check recorded in column A. The code for each disbursement should be a number less than six. With all the proper codes entered, the result will look like that in figure 5.26.

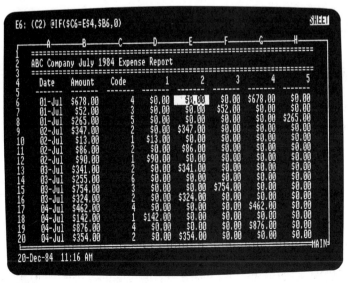

Fig. 5.26.

Notice that in each cell, Symphony has compared each code to the accounts located above in row 3. In the cells where the code and account match, Symphony has recorded the amount of the disbursement. In all the other cells, Symphony has entered zero. This result is exactly what can be expected from the conditional tests that were used in these cells.

Notes on Strings

*New
with
Symphony*

Strings have created an additional level of complexity in Symphony's logical functions. When using strings in conditional functions, be aware of how Symphony reacts to your entering numbers or leaving cells blank. The results can be quite different from those of similar numeric conditional tests. The cases that follow illustrate some of the differences:

In case 1, cell C1094 is left blank:

Function	Value Displayed on Screen
@IF(C1094="1","lambda","beta")	ERR
@IF(C1094=1,"lambda","beta")	beta
@IF(C1094=1#OR#C1094="1","lambda","beta")	ERR

In case 2, cell C1094 has the numeric value 1:

Function	Value Displayed on Screen
@IF(C1094="1","lambda","beta")	ERR
@IF(C1094=1,"lambda","beta")	lambda
@IF(C1094=1#OR#C1094="1","lambda","beta")	ERR

In case 3, cell C1094 has the string "1":

Function	Value Displayed on Screen
@IF(C1094="1","lambda","beta")	beta
@IF(C1094=1,"lambda","beta")	ERR
@IF(C1094=1#OR#C1094="1","lambda","beta")	ERR

Some of these results may seem counterintuitive when you first look at them, particularly the final function in case 3. You might expect that Symphony would display "lambda" instead of the ERR message. However, these examples illustrate that you need to have a good idea of what type of entry you are using in a logical function (numeric or string) before you use it. The @ISSTRING, @ISNUMBER, and @CELL functions that follow should help you evaluate entries.

Error-Trapping Functions

Error-trapping functions are used to test for and to evoke NA and ERR messages in a spreadsheet. NA can be translated as "Not Available" and ERR as "Error."

@NA and @ERR

If you have an instance in which you simply don't know what number to use for a value, but you don't want to leave the cell blank, you can use NA instead. Simply enter @NA in the cell. Symphony will then display NA in that cell and in any other cell that depends on the cell displaying NA.

Another problem you may run across, particularly when you are setting up templates for other people to use, is unacceptable values for cells. For example, suppose you are developing a checkbook-balancing macro, and checks with values less than or equal to zero are unacceptable. One way to indicate your dislike for these kinds of checks is to use ERR to signal that fact. You might use the following version of the @IF built-in function:

@IF(B9<=0,@ERR,B9)

In simple English, this statement says that if the amount in cell B9 is less than or equal to zero, then issue ERR on the screen; otherwise, use the amount. Notice that the @ERR function has been used to control the display in almost the same way as @NA above.

ERR is also used as a signal when Symphony finds unacceptable numbers—for example, a division by zero or mistakenly deleted cells. ERR will often show up temporarily when you are reorganizing the cells in a worksheet. If ERR persists, however, you may have to do some careful analysis to figure out why.

Just as for NA, Symphony displays ERR in any cells that depend on a cell with an ERR value. Sometimes many cells will display ERR after only one or two small changes have been made to a worksheet. To correct this problem, you must trace back down the chain of references to find the root of the problem.

@ISERR and @ISNA

@ISERR and @ISNA relate closely to the @ERR and @NA functions. @ISERR and @ISNA, which are commonly used with the @IF function, allow you to test the value in a cell for the value ERR or NA.

The @ISERR and @ISNA functions are like the logical operators discussed earlier; they are always either true (1) or false (0). The function @ISERR(A1) is false (0) if cell A1 does not contain the value ERR, and true (1) if cell A1 is equal to ERR. Similarly, the @ISNA function is true (1) if the cell that the function refers to contains the value NA, and false (0) if the cell does not.

The @ISERR function is frequently used to keep ERR messages that result from division by 0 from appearing in the worksheet. For example, at one time or another as you use Symphony, you will create a formula that divides a number by a cell reference, as in

    23/A4

If A4 contains a value, the formula will simply return the value of the division. But if A4 contains a label or a 0, or if A4 is blank, the function will return the value ERR. The ERR will be passed along to other cells in the sheet, creating an unnecessary mess.

Using the formula

    @IF(@ISERR(23/A4),0,23/A4)

will eliminate the ERR result. This function says that if the value of 23/A4 is ERR, then enter a 0 in this cell; otherwise, enter the value of the division 23/A4. The function effectively traps the ERR message and keeps it from displaying on the worksheet.

@ISNA works in much the same way. For example, the formula

    @IF(@ISNA(A4),0,A4)

tests cell A4 for the value NA. If the value of A4 is NA, the formula returns a 0. Otherwise, the formula returns the value in A4. This type of formula can be used to keep an NA message from spreading throughout a worksheet.

New with Symphony

Determining the Aspect of a Cell

Before you use the contents of a cell, you will sometimes want to use functions to test its *aspect*. One part of a cell's aspect is its type—whether the data it contains is a number or a label, or is empty. Other parts of a cell's aspect are its address, the row and column it resides in, its label prefix (if any), the width of its column, and its format. Depending on the characteristics of a cell's aspect, you may need to use different methods to process the cell.

As many readers are aware, 1-2-3 has a limited ability to determine a cell's aspect. One way to determine the contents of a cell is to use the @COUNT function. This function lets you determine when a number has been entered. However, the function does not let you distinguish between blank cells and ones with a label entry. The only other option to guarantee the contents of cells in 1-2-3 is to use the /XN and /XL macro commands. These commands work effectively for assuring numeric and label entries, but you have to invoke a macro in order to use them, which is not a convenient option in many cases.

Symphony, on the other hand, has several different functions for determining the aspect of cells. Which functions you use will depend on the particular situation. Symphony does, however, provide some redundancy in this area; usually, you can accomplish what you need to do in more than one way.

New with Symphony

@ISSTRING and @ISNUMBER

Two new functions that are used for determining the type of value stored in a cell are @ISSTRING and @ISNUMBER. Both of these functions are most often used with the @IF function. But they can be used with other types of functions as well.

The @ISNUMBER function is used to verify whether a cell entry is a number. The general format of the function is

@ISNUMBER(argument)

If the argument is a number, the numeric value of the function is 1. But if the argument is a string, including the blank string " ", the numeric value of the function is 0.

As a simple example, suppose you want to test whether the value entered in cell B3 is a number. If the value is a number, then you want to show the label "number" in the current cell; otherwise, you want to show the label "string". The function you can use is

@IF(@ISNUMBER(B3),"number","string")

With this function you can be fairly certain that the appropriate label will appear in the current cell. Besides numbers, however, the @ISNUMBER function also gives blank cells a numeric value of 1. Obviously, the function is incomplete as it stands because it will assign the label "string" to the current cell if cell B3 is empty. The function must be modified to handle the case of blank cells before it is fully reliable.

At this point you may consider using the @ISSTRING function. @ISSTRING works in nearly the same way as @ISNUMBER. However, @ISSTRING determines whether a cell entry is a string value. The general format of the command is

@ISSTRING(argument)

If the argument for the @ISSTRING function is a string, then the value of the function is 1. However, if the argument is a number or blank, the value of the function is 0. One nice feature of @ISSTRING is that it stops what Lotus calls the "ripple-through" effect of NA and ERR.

Returning to the earlier example, you can now complete the function with the help of @ISSTRING by using the following formula:

@IF(@ISSTRING(B3),"string",@IF(@COUNT(B3..B3)>0,
    "number","blank"))

The first step that this function performs is to test whether string data is present. If it is, then the function assigns the label "string".

Otherwise, the @COUNT function is used to test for a number. If the data is a number, then the label "number" is assigned. Otherwise, the label "blank" is assigned.

Notice that the @ISNUMBER has been eliminated from the function. Since @ISNUMBER does not recognize the difference between numbers and blank cells, the @COUNT function has been used instead. (Recall that @COUNT assigns to blank cells a value of 0 and to cells with an entry a value of 1 when the argument used has the range rather than single-cell format. See the @COUNT function earlier in this chapter for more explanation.) @ISNUMBER's inability to recognize blank cells is its principal weakness. In many applications, however, @ISNUMBER provides sufficient testing of values, especially when you are certain that a cell is not blank.

Special Functions

These functions are included in a separate category because of their special power to give you detailed information about the contents of cells (or ranges) and their locations in a spreadsheet. @CELL and @CELLPOINTER are two of Symphony's most powerful special functions.

*New
with
Symphony*

@CELL

Another more efficient way of determining the aspect of a cell is to use the @CELL function. This function is one of the most comprehensive of all the Symphony functions since it gives you many different options to choose from. The general form of the @CELL function is

@CELL(string,range)

The first argument is a string value that you code into the function to indicate to Symphony what aspect of the cell you are interested in. The second argument represents a cell in the range format (such as A1..A1). If you use just the single-cell format, Symphony returns the ERR message. In addition, if you specify a range that is larger than a single cell, Symphony uses the upper left corner cell for evaluation.

Table 5.1 shows all the string arguments you can use with @CELL and the results that the strings will elicit from Symphony.

Table 5.1

String	Result
address	The address of the current cell expressed in absolute terms (for example, $G$19)
row	The row number (1 to 8192)
col	The column number (1 to 256)
type	The type of value stored in a cell
	What Symphony returns:
	b — Indicates a blank cell (even if the cell is formatted)
	v — Indicates a number or numeric formula
	l — Indicates a label or string formula
prefix	The label prefix of the current cell
	What Symphony returns:
	' — Indicates a left-aligned label
	" — Indicates a right-aligned label
	^ — Indicates a centered label
	blank — Indicates a number, formula, or blank cell
	(Note: Formula may be a label formula.)
width	Indicates the column width of the column that the cell resides in (1 to 240)
	(Note: Width may be different for each window.)
format	Indicates the numeric display format

What Symphony returns:

G	General format
F0 to F15	Fixed decimal (0 to 15 decimal places)
P0 to P15	Punctuated (0 to 15 decimal places) (Equivalent to 1-2-3's comma [,] format)
C0 to C15	Currency (0 to 15 decimal places)
S0 to S15	Scientific (0 to 15 decimal places)
%0 to %15	Percent (0 to 15 decimal places)
D1 to D5	Date (formats 1 to 5)
T1 to T4	Time (formats 1 to 4)
L	Literal (Equivalent to 1-2-3's Text format)
H	Hidden format

The following are some examples of how the @CELL function may be used:

@CELL("address",SALES)

If the range named SALES is C187..E187, Symphony returns the absolute address $C$187. This is a convenient way of listing the upper left corner of a range's address in the worksheet. To list all the range names and their addresses, see the SHEET **R**ange **N**ame **T**able command.

@CELL("prefix",C195..C195)

If the cell C195 contains the label 'Chicago, Symphony will return ' (indicating left alignment). If, however, cell C195 is blank, Symphony will return nothing; in other words, the current cell will appear blank.

@CELL("format",A10)
> Symphony will return the ERR indicator because the second argument is not in the range format.

@CELL("width",B12..B12)
> Symphony will return the width of column B as viewed in the current window regardless of whether that width was set using the SHEET **W**idth command (for the individual column) or the SHEET **S**ettings **W**idth command (for the default column-width).

@CELLPOINTER

New with Symphony

The @CELLPOINTER function is similar to the @CELL function, except @CELLPOINTER works with the current cell. The *current* cell is the cell where the cell pointer was sitting at the time the worksheet was last recalculated. The general format of the command is

@CELLPOINTER(string)

For this function the strings you can use are the same as those for the @CELL function. (See table 5.1.) For example, to determine the address of the current cell, you can enter @CELLPOINTER("address") in cell B22. If recalculation is set to automatic, the value displayed in that cell will be the absolute address $B$22. This same address will remain displayed until you make another entry somewhere else in the sheet or hit the Calc key. Either action will cause the worksheet to be recalculated, and the address that appears in cell B22 will change to reflect the position of the cell pointer when the sheet was recalculated. If recalculation is set to **M**anual, hitting the Calc key is the only action that will cause the address to change.

@ROWS and @COLS

New with Symphony

@ROWS and @COLS are two other special functions that Symphony offers. They are both used to describe the dimensions of ranges. The general form of these commands is

@ROWS(range)   @COLS(range)

Suppose you want to determine the number of columns in a range called EXPENSES and to display that value in the current cell. The function you enter is @COLS(EXPENSES). Similarly, you can enter @ROWS(EXPENSES) to display the number of rows in the range.

One rule to remember about @ROWS and @COLS is that you cannot specify a single cell as the argument unless it is in the range format (for example, C3..C3). Otherwise, Symphony will display the ERR message.

New
with
Symphony

@TRUE and @FALSE

Symphony's remaining two special functions are @TRUE and @FALSE. Neither one of these functions requires an argument. The numeric value of @TRUE is 1, and the numeric value of @FALSE is 0. Typically, these functions are used with @IF and @CHOOSE, mainly for documentation purposes. For example, the function @IF(B3<30,@TRUE,@FALSE) is exactly equivalent to @IF(B3<30,1,0). In this case, the @TRUE and @FALSE functions provide better documentation than their numeric equivalents.

String Functions

Symphony has a variety of new string functions that give the user significantly more power to manipulate strings than do earlier integrated packages, including 1-2-3. (As former 1-2-3 users are well aware, 1-2-3 has very limited power to manipulate strings and offers no string functions whatsoever.) Particular caution is necessary, however, in using Symphony's new string functions to guard against mixing data types. For instance, some functions produce strings, and others produce numeric results. You must be careful not to combine functions from these two different groups unless you have taken all the necessary precautions. The proper techniques for mixing data types are discussed throughout this section on string functions.

One other thing to consider about string functions is the numbering scheme used for the positions of characters in a label. These positions are numbered beginning with zero and continuing on to a number that corresponds to the last character in the label. For example, the character that follows shows the position numbers for a long label:

```
        1111111111122222
       Ø1234567890123456789Ø1234
       ' two chickens in every pot
```

Notice that the label prefix (') at the beginning of the label does not have a number because the prefix is not considered part of the label. Nor are negative position numbers allowed. The importance of position numbers will become clear in the next section.

Locating the Position of One String within Another: @FIND

*New
with
Symphony*

One of the simplest string functions is @FIND. It is also one of the most convenient functions for illustrating the use of position numbers in strings. The @FIND function is used to locate the starting position of one string within another string. For instance, using the string that is shown above, suppose you want to find at what position the string "every" occurs in this string. The general format of @FIND is

@FIND(search-string,overall-string,start-number)

The search-string is the string you want to locate. In the example the search-string is "every". The overall-string is the target string to be searched. In the example, "two chickens in every pot" is the overall-string. Finally, the start-number is the position number in the overall-string where you wish to start the search. Suppose you want to start the search at position 6. If the overall-string you are using is located in cell B5, the function you use is

@FIND("every",B5,6)

The result of this example is the number 16 because this is the position of the first (and only) occurrence of "every" in the overall-string. If the search-string "every" had not been found in the overall-string, then Symphony would have displayed the ERR message.

Notice that in this example the choice of a start-number of 6 had no bearing on the outcome of the function. You could just as easily have chosen 0, or any other number less than or equal to 16, for the starting position of the search-string. Had "every" appeared more than once in the overall-string, however, you could have used the start-number to locate its occurrence elsewhere. Suppose the following overall-string appeared in cell B5:

'two chickens in every pot, two cars in every garage

Now suppose you want to locate all the occurrences of "every" in the overall-string. You can start with the function @FIND("every", B5,0). Just as before, this function returns a value of 16. You can then change the start-number by adding 1 to the result of the original function (as in 1 + 16 = 17). The appropriate function is then @FIND("every",B5,17). This function returns the number 39, which is the starting location of the second occurrence of "every". Next, you can add 1 to the second result (1 + 39 = 40) and use @FIND("every",B5,40). The result of this function is ERR. When you see the ERR message, you can be sure that you have found all the occurrences of the search-string.

One rule to remember about @FIND, and generally about strings, is that the maximum number of characters in a string is 240. Another rule is that Symphony truncates the start-number to a whole number if the number includes a decimal portion.

You should also be aware that @FIND does not perform approximate searching as does the DOC Search command. In the example above, if you had used a search-string of "Every" instead of "every", you would get the ERR message instead of a number value. See Chapter 7 for more information on the DOC Search command.

New with Symphony

Extracting Strings: @MID

Whereas @FIND helps you to locate one string within another, the @MID function lets you extract one string from another. This operation is called *substringing*. The general form of the function is

@MID(string,start-position,length)

The start-position is a number representing the character position in the string where you wish to start extracting characters. The length argument indicates the number of characters you wish to extract. For example, if you wish to extract the first name from a label containing the full name "Laura Mann", you can use @MID("Laura Mann",0,5). This function extracts the string starting in position 0 (the first character) and continuing for a length of 5 characters.

Now suppose you have a column with a list of full names running down it, and you want to extract the first and last names, putting them into separate columns. To accomplish this task, you can use the @MID and @FIND functions together. Since you know a blank space will always separate the first and last names, you can use @FIND to locate the position of the blank in each full name. With this value, you can then set up the functions to extract the first and last names.

Suppose cell A1 contains the full name "Gerald Frankel". In cell B1 you place the function @MID(A1,0,@FIND(" ",A1,0)). The value of this function will appear as "Gerald" since FIND(" ",A1,0) will return a value of 6 for the length argument. Next, you place in column C the function @MID(A1,@FIND(" ",A1,0)+1,99). With the @FIND function, you are indicating that the start-position is one character beyond the blank space. In addition, the length of the string to be extracted is 99 characters. Obviously, using a length of 99 is overkill, but there is no penalty for this excess. The string that Symphony extracts is "Frankel".

Now that you have seen how to use the @MID and @FIND functions to separate first and last names, you may want to try using these functions in a case with a name containing a middle initial.

@LEFT and @RIGHT

New
with
Symphony

@LEFT and @RIGHT are special variations of the @MID function and are used to extract one string of characters from another, beginning at the leftmost and rightmost positions in the underlying string, respectively. The general format of the functions is

@LEFT(string,length)   @RIGHT(string,length)

The length argument is the number of character positions in a string that you wish to extract. For example, if you are given the string "Cincinnati, Ohio 45243", and you want to extract the ZIP code, you can use @RIGHT("Cincinnati, Ohio 45243",5).

@LEFT works the same way as @RIGHT except that @LEFT extracts starting at the beginning of a string. For instance, you can extract the city in the above example by using @LEFT("Cincinnati, Ohio 45243",10).

New
with
Symphony

Replacing Characters in a String: @REPLACE

The @REPLACE function is used to remove a group of characters from a string and to replace them with another string. @REPLACE uses the same numbering scheme as @FIND. That is, @REPLACE numbers the character positions in a string, starting with zero and continuing to the end of the string (up to a maximum of 239). The general form of the command is

@REPLACE(original-string,start-number,length,
    replacement-string)

The start-number argument indicates the position where Symphony is to start removing characters in the original-string. The length indicates how many characters to remove, and the replacement-string contains the new characters that will replace the removed ones. For example, suppose the string "Now is the time for all good men" appears in cell C1, and you want to replace "men" with "people". The function to use is

@REPLACE(C1,29,3,"people")

Instead of starting at 0 and counting up the 30 positions of the start-number, you may want to use the @FIND function instead. For instance, you can enter

@REPLACE(C1,@FIND("men",C1,0),3,"people")

This example is just one of many in which combining functions can save you much time and effort.

Finding the Length of a String: @LENGTH

New with Symphony

The @LENGTH function simply returns the length of strings. The general form of the function is

@LENGTH(string)

For example, suppose cell E9 contains the string "Credit policy"; then the value of @LENGTH(E9) is 13. If, in the same spreadsheet, cell J6 contains the formula E9&" "&"respondents", the value of @LENGTH(J6) is 25.

A rule to remember about the @LENGTH function is that the length of numeric strings, as well as empty or null sharings, is ERR.

Comparing Strings: @EXACT

New with Symphony

The @EXACT function is used to compare two strings. If the strings are alike, @EXACT returns a value of 1. If the strings are not alike, the function returns a value of 0. The general form of the function is

@EXACT(string1,string2)

The method of comparison for @EXACT is similar to the = operator that is used in formulas. Whereas the = operator checks for an approximate match, the @EXACT function checks for an exact match. For example, if cell A2 contains the string "Marketing Function", and cell B2 contains the string "marketing function", the numeric value of A2=B2 is 1 because the two strings are an approximate match. Conversely, the numeric value of @EXACT(A2,B2) is 0 because the two functions are not an exact match.

One rule must be remembered when you use @EXACT. The function cannot be used to compare nonstring arguments. For instance, if you are comparing two cells—A2, which is empty, and B2, which contains a valid string—the value of @EXACT(A2,B2) is ERR. In fact, if either argument is a nonstring value of any type (including numbers), Symphony will return the ERR message.

*New
with
Symphony*

Converting Case: @LOWER, @UPPER, and @PROPER

Symphony offers three different functions for converting the case of a string value. First, @LOWER converts all the letters in a string to lowercase. If letters are already in lowercase, they remain so. For instance, if cell B3 contains the string "ALL iN GooD tiME", the value of @LOWER(B3) is "all in good time".

Second, @UPPER is nearly the opposite of @LOWER because it converts all the letters in a string to uppercase. For example, the value of @UPPER(@lower("ALL iN GooD tiME")) is "ALL IN GOOD TIME".

Finally, @PROPER capitalizes the first letter in each word of a label. Words are defined as groups of characters separated by blank spaces. @PROPER also converts all other letters in each word to lowercase. For example, the value of @PROPER("when IS tHE meeTING?") is "When Is The Meeting?"

As you might expect, none of these three functions work with nonstring values. For instance, if cell E9 contains a number or a null string, Symphony will return ERR for each of these functions.

*New
with
Symphony*

Repeating Labels: @REPEAT

@REPEAT is used to repeat strings within a cell much as the backslash (\) is used to repeat characters. But @REPEAT has some distinct advantages over the backslash. The general form of the function is

@REPEAT(string,number)

The number argument indicates the number of times you wish to repeat a string in a cell. For example, if you want to repeat the string "COGS" three times, you can enter @REPEAT("COGS",3). The resulting string will be "COGSCOGSCOGS". This string follows Symphony's rule for long labels. That is, if the width of a column is 9 (the default column-width), the string will display beyond the right-hand boundary of the column, provided no entry is in the cell to the right. The technique for repeating labels with \ is different from that of @REPEAT because with \, Symphony will fill the column to exactly whatever the column width may be.

By using the @CELL and @LENGTH functions, you can set up a function to fill a cell almost exactly. If A3 is the cell you wish to fill by repeating the string "COGS", the first step is to enter @CELL ("width",A3..A3) in an out-of-the-way cell, say K4. The next step is to enter @LENGTH("COGS") in K5, another out-of-the-way cell. The final step is to enter @REPEAT("COGS",K4/K5) in cell A3. If the width of column A is 9 (the default column-width), the label that appears in cell A3 is "COGSCOGS". Notice that since @REPEAT uses only the integer portion of the "number" argument, "COGS" is repeated only twice, rather than 2.25 times.

Trimming Unwanted Blank Spaces: @TRIM

New with Symphony

The @TRIM function is used to trim unwanted blank spaces from a string. The spaces may occur at the beginning, end, or middle of a string. If more than one consecutive space occurs in the middle of a string, Symphony removes all but one of the blank spaces. For instance, if the string " When in the course of human events" resides in cell A3, @TRIM(A3) will appear as "When in the course of human events". Notice that the extra blank spaces have been removed. Notice also that whereas the value of @LENGTH(A3) is 40, the value of @LENGTH(@TRIM(A3)) is 34. (For trimming other characters besides blank spaces, see the section later in the chapter on the @CLEAN function.)

Converting Strings to Numbers and Numbers to Strings

New with Symphony

Two of the most important and powerful functions that Symphony offers are @STRING and @VALUE. The @STRING function is used to convert a number to a string, and @VALUE is used to convert a string to a number.

@STRING

You can use @STRING to override Symphony's automatic right-hand justification of numbers and to display a number justified to the left. The general form of the @STRING function is

@STRING(number-to-convert,decimal-places)

Since Symphony uses the fixed-decimal display format for the @STRING function, the decimal-places argument represents the number of places that you wish to display in the string. For example, if the number-to-convert argument is 9.482 and resides in cell J7, you can enter @STRING(J7,2) in the current cell. The result of this function is 9.48, displayed with left-hand justification.

If the number-to-convert argument is 9.478 instead of 9.482, Symphony will round the number upward to 9.48, just as Symphony rounds any number displayed in the fixed-decimal format.

If you wish to display a number in its string version, using a percentage sign or punctuated format, you can use the {CONTENTS} statement in the Symphony Command Language. See Chapter 13 for more information on the {CONTENTS} statement.

@VALUE

You may want to use the @VALUE function when you have been entering string data in a FORM window but later decide that you prefer to use the data as numbers. For example, suppose you enter part numbers and their quantities, using "Label" as the default setting. (If you are not familiar with the FORM window at this point, see Chapter 11.) Now suppose that the information on part numbers works fine in the string format, but you want to change the format of the quantity data in order to add together different part quantities. You can convert the quantity data with @VALUE. The general form of the function is

@VALUE(string)

If cell K11 contains a data base entry for the quantity data in the string format, you can enter @VALUE(K11) in an out-of-the-way cell in the worksheet, say, Z11. If the string in cell K11 is "23", then the number displayed in cell Z11 is 23. You can now use the number in cell Z11 in any kind of numeric operation. For more examples of converting data base entries, see Chapter 11.

Another nice feature of @VALUE is that besides converting strings, which appear in the standard number format (for example, 23.445), you can also convert strings with decimal fractions and numbers displayed in scientific format. For example, if cell T10 contains the string "12 31/32", @VALUE(T10) will appear as 12.96875. Even if cell T10 contains the string "12 54/32", @VALUE will still perform the appropriate conversion of the string to the number 13.6875. Similarly, if a number is displayed as the string "1.37E+1", @VALUE will convert the string to the number 13.7.

A few rules should be remembered when you use @VALUE. First, if you leave extra spaces in a string, Symphony does not object. The program, however, has trouble with some extra characters, such as trailing percent signs, although currency signs (such as $) that precede the string are okay. If you are interested, you should experiment with different character signs to see how Symphony reacts. Finally, if you use numbers as the argument (string) for @VALUE, Symphony does not object. It simply returns the original number value.

Functions Used with the ASCII/LICS

Symphony offers a few special functions for interfacing with the Lotus International Character Set (LICS), what Lotus calls "an extension of the ASCII printable character set." (Be aware that the ASCII code number for a given character may not correspond to its LICS code number.) Actually, the LICS can best be thought of as a new character set created by Lotus and superimposed on top of the ASCII character set.

The complete set of LICS characters is listed at the back of Symphony's *Reference Manual* and includes everything from the copyright sign to the lowercase e with the grave accent. Actually, more characters are available than you will probably ever use, but you should still know how to use them if the need ever arises.

@CHAR

The @CHAR function is used to produce on the screen the LICS equivalent of a number between 0 and 255. The general form of the function is

@CHAR(number)

Suppose you want to make the trademark sign (™) appear on the screen. You can enter @CHAR(184) in a cell, and the trademark sign should appear. What is more, you can use a string formula to concatenate the trademark sign to a product name. For instance, you can enter the formula +"Symphony"&@CHAR(184) to produce the string "Symphony™".

You should remember only two simple rules when using @CHAR. First, if the numeric argument you are using is not between 1 and 255, then Symphony returns the ERR message. Second, if the argument you use is not an integer, Symphony disregards the noninteger portion of the argument.

Nonprintable Characters in the LICS

Be aware that not all the LICS characters are printable, nor will they always show up on the screen. More specifically, codes 1 through 31 are the problem area. But since these codes include all the characters necessary for making boxes and arrows in Symphony, you may want to gain access to these characters.

You can get at these nonprintable characters in one of two ways. First, you can use the Edit key while you are in a SHEET window. You start with a SHEET window in a new worksheet. Next, you use the **R**ange **F**ill command to enter the numbers 1 through 31, starting in cell B1 and moving down column B. Then, after moving one column to the left, you enter @CHAR(B1) in cell A1 and copy that function to the cells below. Finally, you use the **R**ange **V**alues command to convert the cells in column A to their actual string values. Even though the cells in column A appear blank, you can see any one of the characters by moving the cursor to any cell in column A and pressing Edit. Figure 5.27 shows how the screen should appear.

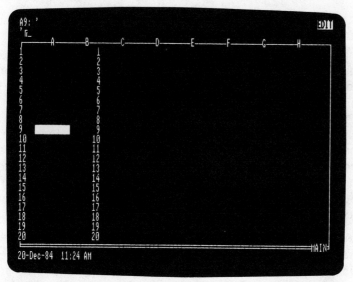

Fig. 5.27.

Another way to see the nonprintable characters is to use the SHEET window as it appears in figure 5.27 and change it to a DOC window. Now you will see all the nonprintable characters corresponding to ASCII/LICS codes 1 to 31. You can continue to use these characters in a DOC window, but because they are nonprintable, only blanks will appear when you try to print them out.

@CODE

New with Symphony

The @CODE function is nearly the opposite of @CHAR. Whereas @CHAR takes a number between 0 and 255 and returns an ASCII/LICS character, @CODE goes the other way. That is, it examines an ASCII/LICS character and returns a number between 0 and 255. The general form of the function is

@CODE(string)

Suppose you want to find the ASCII/LICS code number for the letter *a*. You enter the @CODE("a") in a cell, and Symphony returns the number 97. If you had entered @CODE("aardvark"), Symphony would still return 97, the code of the first character in the string.

Remember that if you specify a number as the argument for @CODE (expressed as a number and not a string), Symphony returns the ERR message.

New with Symphony

Cleaning Unwanted Characters Other Than Blanks: @CLEAN

Sometimes when you receive strings during a communications session, the strings arrive with nonprintable characters (ASCII codes below 32) interspersed throughout. The @CLEAN function removes the nonprintable characters from the strings. The general format of the function is

@CLEAN(string)

Another useful function of @CLEAN is that you can use it to remove the carriage return characters from a string created in a DOC window. (Since a carriage return symbol is actually the equivalent of an ASCII/LICS code 20, @CLEAN removes the symbol quite nicely.) Before you use a string that is created in a DOC window in a concatenation formula or a function, a good practice is always to use @CLEAN first.

Date and Time Arithmetic

One of Symphony's most advanced features is its ability to manipulate dates and times. This feature can be used for such things as mortgage analysis, aging of accounts receivable, and time management. As former 1-2-3 users well know, 1-2-3 uses a serial numbering system for manipulating dates, but it is incapable of handling time. Symphony has taken 1-2-3's original serial numbering system and expanded it to handle time.

Symphony's Serial Numbering System

All aspects of Symphony's date-handling capability are based on Symphony's ability to represent any given date as a serial integer equal to the number of days from December 31, 1899, to the date in question. With this scheme, January 1, 1900, is represented by the number 1; January 2, 1900, is represented by the number 2; and so on. The maximum date that Symphony can handle is December 31, 2099, represented by the serial number 73050.

Symphony's time-handling capability is based on fractions of serial numbers. For instance, 8:00 a.m. is represented by the decimal fraction 0.333333 (or 1/3). Similarly, the decimal fraction for 10:00 p.m. is 0.916666. Symphony's serial numbering system allows you to devise an overall number representing both date and time.

Date	Time	Serial Number
January 3, 1900	01:00 AM	3.041666666
December 9, 1935	12:00 PM	13127
December 30, 1983	12:00 AM	30680
June 25, 1984	09:21 AM	30858.38958
December 31, 2099	11:00 PM	73050.95833

The serial numbering system also allows you to manipulate dates and times just as you would any other number in Symphony. For example, after setting the beginning date for a project and adding to that date the number of days that the project should take, you can easily determine the completion date. Time values are just as easy to work with. For example, you can set up a complete schedule for the day by dividing it up into hour increments.

Date Functions: @DATE

Perhaps the most commonly used date function is @DATE. This function allows you to convert a date into an integer that Symphony can interpret. The form of the @DATE function is

@DATE(year-number,month-number,day-number)

Following are examples showing how the @DATE built-in function can be used:

@DATE(55,12,30)=	20453
@DATE(12,1,1)=	4384
@DATE(C7,C8,D10)=	integer equivalent of the date represented by these cells. If the cells contain the values 83, 12, and

25, respectively, the function will have the value 30675.

The numeric arguments have certain restrictions. First, the year-number must be between 0 (indicating the year 1900) and 199 (2099). Second, the month-number must be between 1 and 12. Third, the day-number must be one of the actual values for a given month (for example, 30 days for September and 31 days for December). Finally, Symphony truncates all but the integer portion of the numeric arguments.

Once a date has been interpreted by Symphony as an integer, you can then use the Format command to display the date in a more recognizable way (such as 06/26/84). For a discussion of Symphony's Date and Time formats, see the sections in this chapter on Displaying Dates and Displaying Times and also Chapter 4.

New
with
Symphony

Converting a String to a Date: @DATEVALUE

@DATEVALUE is a variant of @DATE because, like it, @DATE-VALUE produces a serial number from the month, day, and year information that you give to the function. But unlike @DATE, which expects numeric arguments, the argument that you give @DATE-VALUE is a string. The general form of the function is

> @DATEVALUE(date-string)

The date-string must be in any one of the available Date formats—D1, D2, or D3. (See the section on Displaying Dates.) If the string conforms to one of the appropriate formats, Symphony will display the appropriate serial integer.

Function	Date Format	Number
@DATEVALUE("26-JUN-84")	D1	30859
@DATEVALUE("26-JUN")	D2	30859
@DATEVALUE("JUN-84")	D3	30834

Notice that for the second function, Symphony automatically supplied 84 as the year. You can assume that a date in 1984 was entered when DOS prompted the user for a date at the start of the day's session. Notice also that for the third function, Symphony defaults to the first day in June as the day value.

You may prefer to enter the date-string in one of what Lotus calls the International Date formats. (These formats are called D4 and D5 in Symphony. See the section on displaying dates.) The default separation character for the International Date formats is / (for example, 6/26/84). But you can also use periods or dashes as the separation characters. To indicate to Symphony that you are going to use something other than the default setting for the International formats, however, you must modify one of the configuration settings. To modify the setting, you must use the SERVICES Configuration Other International Date command; then you can select the format you like.

Suppose for now that you have chosen the default setting for the separation character, and you want to enter the date-string in the D4 (MM/DD/YY) format. You can enter @DATEVALUE("6/26/84"), and Symphony will display the number 30859. If you enter @DATEVALUE("6-26-84"), Symphony will return the ERR message. (Symphony does not expect the hyphen [-] as the separation character unless you change the configuration settings.)

Extracting the Day, Month, or Year

The built-in functions of @DATE, @MONTH, and @YEAR allow you to extract parts of a date in integer form. In the example

```
@DAY(30284) =      29
@MONTH(30284) = 11
@YEAR(30284) =      82
```

the three functions, taken together, are nearly the reverse of the @DATE built-in function because they allow you to convert from the integer format back into Gregorian format. You can use these functions for various time-related chores, such as aging accounts receivable and setting up a table for amortizing a loan.

Displaying Dates

The five date functions discussed thus far are extremely useful for entering dates in the worksheet in a form that Symphony can understand. But there is a problem. The results of these functions are integers that don't look like dates and are therefore hard to comprehend. For example, do you know the dates represented by the numbers 30124 and 32988?

The SHEET **F**ormat **D**ate command allows you to display dates in five different forms. As indicated earlier, dates are represented as integers that equal the number of days which have elapsed since December 31, 1899. The Date format displays these integers in one of the following five arrangements (Lotus calls them D1 through D5), depending on which one you select.

Number	Arrangement	Example
1	DD-MMM-YY	26-Jun-84
2	DD-MMM	26-Jun
3	MMM-YY	Jun-84
4	MM/DD/YY	06/26/84
5	MM/DD	06/26

Note that for all the examples shown above, the integer which is displayed in the worksheet prior to formatting is 30859.

Notice, too, that the first option (D1) creates a string which is 9 characters long—too long to be displayed in a column with the default width of 9. In general, you will need to expand any column containing dates formatted in the DD-MMM-YY format so that the column width is 10 or more characters. Because the other date formats can be displayed in normal width columns, these formats can be used frequently (especially D4) in place of the more detailed, but wider, DD-MMM-YY format.

New
with
Symphony

Today's Date and Time: @NOW

The @NOW function returns today's date and time as an integer representing the number of days since December 31, 1899, and a fraction representing the time elapsed since 12:00 a.m. of the previous day. This built-in function is particularly useful for taking advantage of an IBM PC's (and compatible's) timekeeping capability. If you have a clock that automatically supplies the date and time, or if you simply enter the date and time when you are prompted by DOS at the start of the day, the @NOW function will give you access to the date and time in the current worksheet. For example, if you enter the date 6-26-84 in response to the DOS date prompt and 16:00 to the DOS time prompt (corresponding to 4:00 p.m.), the @NOW function will have the value

@NOW = 30859.66

Because the @NOW function is dependent on the PC DOS or MS-DOS system date and time for its value, you must always remember to enter at least the date, and more preferably the date and time, in response to the operating system prompt before you enter Symphony. (If you want to modify the operating system date and time while you are in midsession, see the discussion on **A**pplication **A**ttach in Chapter 2 for exiting to DOS.)

Former 1-2-3 users may recognize @NOW as being very similar to 1-2-3's @TODAY function. The only difference between the two functions is that @NOW includes the time as well as the date. 1-2-3 users should take note that the @TODAY built-in function is not available in Symphony. The best way to reproduce this function is to use @INT(@NOW).

Time Functions

Until this point, the discussion of how Symphony deals with time has been brief. As mentioned earlier, time is expressed in fractions of serial numbers between 0 and 1. For example, .5 is equal to twelve hours (or 12:00 p.m.). In addition, you should think of Symphony as a military timekeeper. That is, 10:00 p.m. in normal time is 22:00 in military time.

Symphony's timekeeping system may seem a little awkward at first, but you should get used to it quickly. Here are some general guidelines to help you along:

1 hour =	0.041666
1 minute =	0.000694
1 second =	0.000011

*New
with
Symphony*

@TIME

The @TIME built-in function is used to arrive at a serial number for a specified time of day. The general form of the function is

@TIME(hour-number,minute-number,second-number)

The following are examples of how the @TIME built-in function is used:

@TIME(3,12,30)=	0.133680
@TIME(23,0,0)=	0.958333
@TIME(C7,C8,D10)=	integer equivalent of the time represented by these cells. If the cells contain the values 23, 12, and 59, respectively, the function would have the value 0.967349.

The numeric arguments have certain restrictions. First, the hour-number must be between 0 and 23. Second, both the minute-number and second-number must be between 0 and 59. Finally, Symphony truncates all but the integer portion of the numeric arguments.

Once a time has been interpreted by Symphony as a fraction of a serial number, you can then use the Format command to display the time in a more recognizable way (for example, 10:42 PM). See the section on Displaying Times for a discussion of Symphony's Time formats.

*New
with
Symphony*

Converting a String to a Time: @TIMEVALUE

Just like @DATEVALUE and @DATE, @TIMEVALUE is a variant of @TIME because @TIMEVALUE produces a serial number from the hour, minute, and second information you give to the function. But, unlike @TIME, which uses numeric arguments, @TIMEVALUE uses string arguments. The general form of the function is

@TIMEVALUE(time-string)

The time-string must appear in one of the two Time formats, T1 or T2. (See the section on Displaying Times.) If the string conforms to one of the appropriate formats, Symphony will display the appropriate serial number fraction. (If you then format the cell, Symphony will display the appropriate time of day.)

Function	Time Format	Number
@TIMEVALUE("12:30:59")	T1	0.521516203
@TIMEVALUE("12:30")	T2	0.520833333

Notice that the time used for the functions is 12:30 p.m. and 59 seconds.

Two other Time formats, called the International Time formats, are available in Symphony. (Formats T3 and T4 correspond to the International Time formats.) As for the T1 and T2 formats shown earlier, the International formats use the colon as the default separation character. But you can also use periods, commas, or other characters as separation characters. When you change the separation characters, you must modify one of the configuration settings, as you do for the Date formats. To modify the setting, you must use the SERVICES Configuration Other International Time command. Afterward, you can select the separation characters you prefer.

Extracting the Second, Minute, or Hour

The @SECOND, @MINUTE, and @HOUR built-in functions allow you to extract different units of time from a numeric time fraction. In the example

    @SECOND(30284.4432) =12
    @MINUTE(30284.4432) = 38
    @HOUR(30284.4432) =   10

notice that the argument includes both an integer and decimal portion. Although the integer portion is important for date functions, it is disregarded for time functions. You can use these functions for various time-related chores, the most important of which is developing a time schedule.

Displaying Times

You have now examined all the time functions that Symphony has to offer, but the results of these functions are serial number fractions that don't look at all like the times you usually see. The SHEET Format Time command allows you to display times in a more recognizable format. Lotus offers the following four different formats, called T1 through T4:

Number	Arrangement	Example
1	HH:MM:SS AM/PM	11:51:22 PM
2	HH:MM AM/PM	11:51 PM
3	HH:MM:SS (24 hours)	23:51:22
4	HH:MM (24 hours)	23:51

Note that for all the examples shown above, the fractional number displayed in the worksheet prior to formatting is 0.994.

Notice also that the first option (T1) creates a string that is 11 characters long and requires a column width of 12 in order to display the time in this format. For this reason, and also because we do not use seconds very often, we prefer the T2 format. Depending on your needs, you may prefer another format.

General Comments on Date and Time Arithmetic

Notice that Symphony's date and time arithmetic capabilities actually incorporate both a set of functions and a set of formats. Don't be confused by this mix. The functions, like @DATEVALUE, enter dates or times in the worksheet; the formats display these functions in an understandable form. Although the format can be used without the function, or the function without the format, the two tools are not very meaningful when used alone.

In most cases date and time arithmetic will require simply subtracting one number from another. By subtracting, you can easily determine the number of days between dates, or hours between times. For example, subtracting @DATE(84,7,31) from @DATE(84,8,15) results in the value 15 (days). Similarly, subtracting @TIME(10,4,31) from

@TIME(12,54,54) results in a value of 0.11832175 (2 hours, 50 minutes, and 23 seconds). To Symphony these problems are as simple as subtracting the serial number for @DATE(84,7,31)+ @TIME(10,4,31)(30894.4198) from the serial number for @DATE (84,8,15)+@TIME(12,54,54)(30909.5381).

You can even determine the number of minutes, hours, weeks, and years between two serial numbers by dividing the difference by an appropriate number. If you need only a rough idea, you can use the banker's convention of 7 days in a week, 30 days in a month, and 360 days in a year. If you want to be more exact, you can use the @MOD function for remainders. You can even build in odd-numbered months and leap years. Symphony's date keeping and timekeeping will allow you to simplify the analysis or make it as sophisticated as you like.

The selection of December 31, 1899, as the starting date for date and time arithmetic may seem arbitrary, but when you actually use Symphony's date formats and built-in functions, you will find that this choice is a good one. The selection of an ending date is more important. The date has to be far enough in the future to allow you to perform long-term analysis. The choice of December 31, 2099, seems to work just fine.

As mentioned earlier, besides using date and time functions in arithmetic calculations, you can also use them in logical expressions, such as @IF(@DATE(84,15,05)>B2,C3,D4). In simple English this statement says: If the serial number that is equivalent to May 15, 1984, is greater than the value in cell B2, then assign the value in cell C3 to the current cell; otherwise, use the value in D4. This kind of test can be used to help keep track of investment portfolios or time performance.

Conclusion

In this chapter you have seen examples of Symphony's SHEET functions at work. Many of the functions are completely new (especially the string processing and time functions), but most are either directly borrowed from 1-2-3 or are slight variants of 1-2-3 functions. In the next chapter you'll examine Symphony's file-handling commands. You will learn how to save and retrieve worksheet files and how to use the program's other, more sophisticated, file management tools.

6

File Operations

One of the commands you will use quite often is the **F**ile command from the SERVICES menu. **F**ile provides the important operations for storing, retrieving, and deleting files to and from disks. In addition, Symphony's file operations, like those of 1-2-3, enable you to combine entire files, to combine a range from one file with a range in another file, to extract part of a file and place it in another file, and to import text or numbers.

Getting Started

If you have used 1-2-3, you will find that Symphony's file commands, with the exception of two that are new, are the same as 1-2-3's. Two major differences between the file operations of 1-2-3 and Symphony are the location of the file commands and the application of file operations. In 1-2-3 the **F**ile command is located in the worksheet menu along with the various spreadsheet, data management, graphics, and print commands. In Symphony the command **F**ile is located in the SERVICES menu, which provides global operations for all five Symphony environments.

The other difference between the file operations of 1-2-3 and Symphony is found in their application. In 1-2-3 such file commands as **File Combine** and **File Xtract** operate solely with data in the spreadsheet environment of the program. In Symphony the same commands operate with data not only in a spreadsheet environment, but also in a word-processing environment. This capability expands the application of these commands in Symphony.

A General Description of Symphony Files

Before you use the file commands, keep in mind several rules concerning files. Symphony file names can be up to eight characters long; that is, Symphony will store only eight characters. In addition to the eight-character name, all files are designated with a three-character extension. Following are three basic rules for file names:

1. File names may not include blank spaces.

2. You can use either letters (A through Z) or numbers (0 through 9) to create file names because Symphony will not accept many other characters, including < > , . *

3. Lowercase letters are automatically converted to uppercase in file names.

Although you determine the eight-character name, the extension is controlled by Symphony and will vary with the type of file. The six possible file extensions are the following:

.WRK	For worksheet files
.PRN	For print files
.PIC	For graph files
.CCF	For communications configuration files
.CTF	For character-code translation files
.APP	For add-in application files

If you have used 1-2-3, you will notice that the file extension for 1-2-3's worksheet files is different from the extension used in Symphony. 1-2-3 uses .WKS. When you use a 1-2-3 file in Symphony, you will need to change the file extension. (See the section on Transferring Files later in this chapter.)

Note that there is only one worksheet to a file and that you work on a worksheet only when it is in main memory. Note also that you can create many windows within one file. As explained in Chapter 2, you can set up your worksheet so that it contains a window for entering a spreadsheet, a window for word processing, a window for graphics, a window for data management, and a window for communications. When you save your file after having created and entered data in all five windows, the file will store all window settings. When you next retrieve the file, the windows will be available with their individual settings. But if you use the **Window Delete** command to delete any windows before saving your file, those windows will be lost.

New with Symphony

File Management

The following file commands in the SERVICES **File** menu are available to enable you to perform several file-checking and management operations: File **Bytes**, File **List**, and File **Table**. These commands are particularly important to perform before initiating the File **Save**, File **Erase**, and File **Combine** commands.

File Bytes

The File **Bytes** command provides a quick and simple way for you to check the available disk space on the current disk drive. File **Bytes** is important for checking disk space when you are creating new files on a disk that already has on it many files or a few large files.

Because the File **Bytes** command is not included as a separate command in 1-2-3, File **Bytes** is considered an addition to Symphony. In 1-2-3, however, this command's function, that of displaying available disk space, is accomplished through the File **List** command. As a separate File command in Symphony, File **Bytes** provides a reminder to check available disk space every time you select **File**.

File List

When you use **File List**, Symphony will display one of four types of file lists on the screen: a list of all worksheet files (.WRK), all print files (.PRN), all graph files (.PIC), or all files including those not created by Symphony. For instance, after you select **File List Worksheet**, Symphony displays all worksheet files on the screen.

Figure 6.1 presents an example of a file list. Notice in the control panel that Symphony displays in the top line the current drive and directory. The second line of the control panel displays the file name of the file where the cursor is positioned, as well as the date and time when the file was last modified.

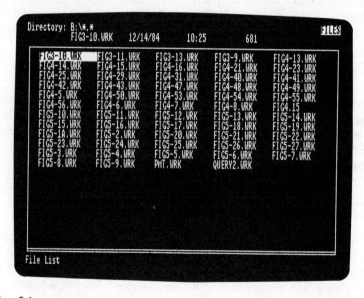

Fig. 6.1.

To return to your current window, press RETURN. Remember that a command such as **File List** replaces a current SHEET, DOC, FORM, GRAPH, or COMM window, but only temporarily. The command does not affect the data that has been entered into that window.

*New
with
Symphony*

File Table

You may find it convenient at times to have a printed copy of the file names on a particular disk or to have a list available within your worksheet area. The **File Table** command will create a list of files in a worksheet area specified by you. You can therefore save the list you have created or print a copy to keep with your floppy disks.

When you use **File Table**, Symphony gives you two different options for the list. First, after you select **File Table**, Symphony asks you to specify the directory from which you want the list created. If you press RETURN, Symphony accepts the current directory. The second option is to create a list of worksheet files (.WRK), print files (.PRN), graph files (.PIC), or all files, including those not created in Symphony.

To place the file table into the worksheet, Symphony will ask you to indicate a range for the table. Here you need only to indicate the first cell where the table should begin. Be careful when indicating where the table should be located because it will overwrite the existing cell contents. Keep in mind that each entry in the table occupies three columns, as illustrated in figure 6.2. The first column contains the file

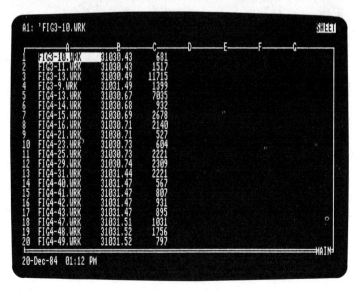

Fig. 6.2.

name, the second column contains the date and time when the file
was last modified, and the last column contains the number of bytes
in the file.

Simple Storage and Retrieval

In Symphony the basic file functions of storing and retrieving entire
files are easy to perform. The **F**ile **S**ave command in the SERVICES
menu allows you to save an entire worksheet in a disk file.

When you enter **F**ile **S**ave, Symphony will display the file name for
the worksheet in which you are currently working if you have
previously created a file. (See fig. 6.3.)

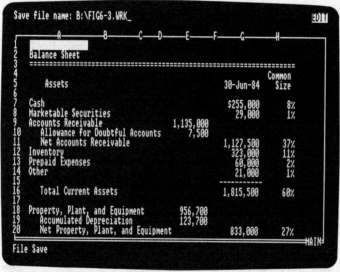

Fig. 6.3.

To save all data entered into the worksheet since you last saved it,
press RETURN. When Symphony asks

> A file with that name already exists—replace it?
> No Yes

type **Y** or move the cursor to "Yes," if you are sure that you do want
your previously saved file replaced by the worksheet currently on
the screen.

If you want to create a new file, type the file name after the B:\. If you want to change the disk drive or create the file in another directory, press Esc or Backspace and then indicate the disk drive, followed by a colon (:), a backslash (\), the directory name, another backslash, and finally the name of the file. As mentioned earlier, when you enter a file name, you do not need to type the period (.) or supply a .WRK extension. These items are supplied automatically by Symphony. The **File S**ave command makes an exact copy of the current worksheet, including all the formats, range names, and settings that you have specified.

To call a file back into main memory from the disk, use the **File Retrieve command. When you enter this command, Symphony will display a menu of all .WRK file names currently on the disk. Often the list will extend beyond the single line on the first page.

You have two options for seeing the entire list of file names. In the first option, you can move the cursor to the right, beyond the last file name in the current line. The Home and End keys are useful tools in locating a file name. Home will return you to the first file name on the list, and End will send you to the last file name.

The second option is to have Symphony list within the display a complete menu of all file names. (See fig. 6.4.) To have a complete list of files displayed, select **File R**etrieve and then press the SERVICES key a second time after the "Name of file to retrieve" message appears in the control panel.

Just as for saving a file, when you retrieve a file, you can override the default disk and indicate a directory. To change the disk drive and to indicate a directory, select **File R**etrieve. When Symphony displays "Name of file to retrieve: B:*.WRK", press Esc and the Backspace key to erase "B:*.WRK". Then indicate the disk drive, the file directory, and finally the file name, as in

A:\SALES\JUNETOT

Notice that the disk drive is indicated by the A: and that the drive and directory are separated by the backslash (\), as are the directory name and file name.

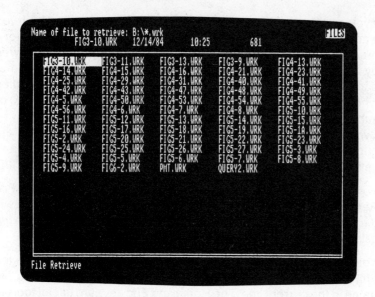

Fig. 6.4.

Making Backup Copies of Files

As mentioned earlier, Symphony, unlike 1-2-3, does not contain a file operations program within the ACCESS SYSTEM. The file copy operation available through 1-2-3's ACCESS SYSTEM is therefore not directly available in Symphony.

Two procedures can be used in Symphony for making backup copies of files. The first procedure involves running the **F**ile **S**ave operations on two separate disks. The second procedure involves copying files by using the **A**pplication **A**ttach option in the SERVICES menu. As discussed in Chapter 2, using the **A**pplication option to copy files requires first copying DOS to your Symphony Program disk and/or Help and Tutorial disk. (See Chapter 2 for the directions for adding DOS and for using the SERVICES **A**pplication command.) Either of the two alternatives discussed below may be used for making backup copies.

In the first procedure, you can use the **F**ile **S**ave command to make backup copies of files whenever you want to copy files one at a time.

First, save your file once by following the directions given earlier for File Save. After Symphony has saved your file, remain in the Symphony program. Then insert another "formatted" blank disk (or a disk that has enough space for the file you want to save) into the disk drive. Finally, repeat the File Save operation, thus saving the file to the disk you just inserted.

The second procedure for making backup copies is to use the Application command from the SERVICES menu whenever you want to copy one or more files. First, make sure that you have saved a file of your current worksheet. Second, retrieve the SERVICES menu and select Application. (If you are using a system with two disk drives and are using your Help and Tutorial disk for attaching DOS, replace your Symphony Program disk with the Help and Tutorial disk. But if you have copied DOS onto the Symphony Program disk so that DOS can be attached, proceed to the next step.)

The third step is to select Attach, unless you have set DOS to attach automatically as soon as you select Application. (See Chapter 2 for directions on automatically attaching an add-in program.) Fourth, select Invoke and press RETURN; the words "Application to invoke: " will appear in the control panel. A menu of add-in programs will also appear in the second line of the control panel. Fifth, move the cursor to DOS and press RETURN, or simply press RETURN if DOS is the only program or the first one listed in the menu. Finally, once the prompt appears, follow the specific directions for copying files, using your DOS COPY command.

Partial Loads and Saves

Often you will want to store only a part of a worksheet (such as a range of cells) in a separate file on the disk. Symphony enables you to extract part of a worksheet that has been created in either a SHEET or DOC environment. For example, you may want to extract outlays from an expense report of revenues from an income statement. One of the best uses for partial storage is breaking up worksheet files that are too large to be stored on a single diskette. Likewise, you may want to extract parts of a DOC file to be used to create new reports or form letters.

The **F**ile **X**tract command allows you to save a part of a worksheet file. This command saves either the formulas that exist in a range of cells or the current values of the formulas in the range of a SHEET window, depending on which of these you select. Either option creates a worksheet file that can be reloaded into Symphony with the **F**ile **R**etrieve command. If you decide to save only the current values, however, the resulting worksheet file will contain numbers but no formulas. Selecting the formula options creates a file with all the formulas intact.

The **F**ile **X**tract command also requires that you specify the worksheet portion you want saved, whether or not that portion includes a range from a SHEET or DOC window. As is generally the case with Symphony, the range to be saved can be as small as a cell or as large as the entire worksheet.

If you are extracting a range from a DOC window, you will notice that Symphony automatically shifts from the DOC window to a SHEET window when Symphony asks you to indicate the range to be extracted. Symphony views the text entered in a DOC window in terms of cell contents. If, for example, you were to extract the two paragraphs above, you would select the **F**ile **X**tract command and press RETURN in response to "Preserve Formulas." (Although this option doesn't apply to extracting text, you nevertheless must make a selection in order to set the **F**ile **X**tract range.)

Next, you must either select an existing file to which the range can be extracted, or create a new file. After selecting a file or typing the name of a new file, you must then indicate the range you want extracted. To extract the two paragraphs above and have them copied to another file, you indicate A219..A233 as the range. In a SHEET window Symphony reads DOC lines as "long labels" entered into column A cells.

If you select an existing file to extract a range to, remember that the file's contents will be lost, replaced by the contents of the extract range. Symphony will remind you of losing the original by displaying the following:

    A file with that name already exists—replace it?
    No Yes

Extracting ranges from DOC windows is covered in more detail in Chapter 7.

Using Symphony's **File Xtract** command is different from using 1-2-3's **File Xtract** command in one important respect. Unlike 1-2-3's command, Symphony does not require the **File Xtract** command to create a values-only range within the same worksheet. If you want to create a values-only range in the same worksheet in 1-2-3, you must use **File Xtract** and then **File Combine** to copy the extracted range back into your worksheet. In Symphony, however, you perform the same operation by using the **Range Values** command from the SHEET menu. Symphony's **Range Values** command will save you steps and time when you want to create a values-only range in the same worksheet. (See "Using the **Range Values** Command" in Chapter 4.)

Combining Files

Another function you will want to perform is to make copies of certain ranges of cells from other worksheets and place these ranges into strategic spots in the current worksheet. For example, if you work for a large firm, you may want to combine into one all-encompassing worksheet the balance sheets and income statements from different divisions.

A very simple technique for accomplishing this kind of consolidation is to keep a copy of an "empty master." Then when the time comes to perform a consolidation, you will always have an empty master to work from. In addition, when you start with an empty master, you can copy the first divisional worksheet onto the master and leave untouched the original copy of the divisional worksheet.

Copying a range of cells can also be helpful when you want to combine quarterly data into a yearly statement. Again, the forms must be compatible, and you will benefit by keeping an empty master. The command used to combine data is **File Combine**. This command gives you the following options:

Copy   To pull in an entire worksheet or a named range into a worksheet and have the new contents write over the existing area

Add   To pull in the values or formulas from an entire worksheet or a named range and to add the new contents to the existing cell contents. (**A**dd is the option you use for combining worksheets, as in the earlier examples.) Incoming values are either added to the existing cell values or entered into an empty cell. Instead of having values overlay labels and formulas, Symphony retains any labels and formulas that exist.

Subtract   To pull in an entire worksheet or a named range of cells and to subtract its contents from the existing cell contents. When an existing cell is empty, the incoming value is subtracted from zero, and the result is entered in the cell. As is true for **A**dd, Symphony does not allow incoming values to overlay existing labels and formulas.

For any of these options listed above, place the cursor in the upper left corner of the area in the worksheet where you want the incoming data to be entered. Suppose, for example, that you want to add values from the two spreadsheets in figure 6.5, which are contained in separate files. Because the values in both spreadsheets are stored in the same cells, you position the cursor in cell A1 before initiating the **F**ile **C**ombine **A**dd command.

If you want to use **F**ile **C**ombine **C**opy to add a file or named range into a DOC window, you should position the cursor in the upper left corner of the area where the incoming data should begin, as in figure 6.6.

Because incoming information will overwrite existing cell contents, you need to be particularly careful with positioning the cursor and to make sure that the incoming data won't overwrite anything that you want to save in the worksheet. One way of assuring yourself that important data won't be lost is to use cell protection. Before you use

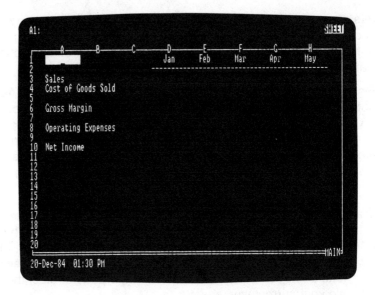

Fig. 6.5.

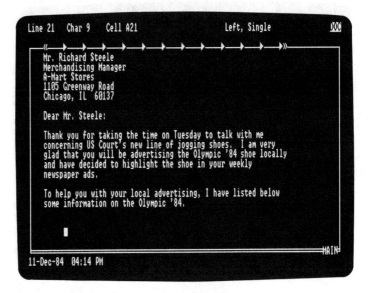

Fig. 6.6.

File Combine, first use the SHEET Range Protect command, allowing changes only to that part of the worksheet where incoming data will be overlaid. (In Chapter 4 see the section on Protecting Ranges.)

Figures 6.7, 6.8, 6.9, and 6.10 show examples of the Copy and Add options. Figure 6.7 shows a worksheet that was created and stored on disk. Figure 6.8 shows another worksheet that is stored in Symphony's memory. Figure 6.9 shows the results of combining these two sheets through the Copy option, and figure 6.10 shows the results of the Add option. The Subtract option is similar enough to the Add option that Subtract has not been included here.

In addition to using the File Combine command to copy the contents of a spreadsheet into an existing file, you can also use File Combine to copy text entered in a DOC environment. Combining the File Xtract and File Combine commands enables you to create special form letters or document files and to combine parts or all of these files into your current worksheet.

*New
with
Symphony*

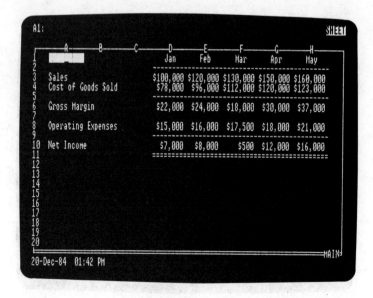

Fig. 6.7.

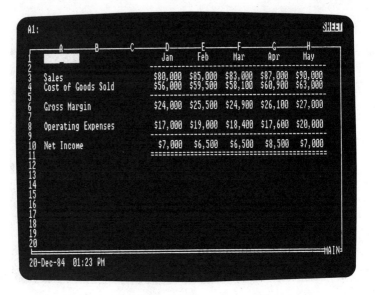

Fig. 6.8.

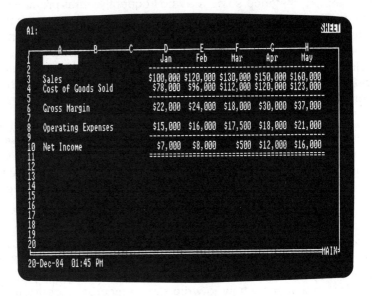

Fig. 6.9.

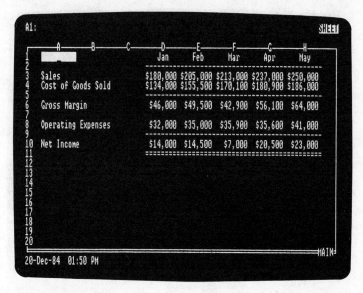

Fig. 6.10.

Consider, for instance, someone who frequently writes promotional material or sales correspondence using the same product description. The paragraph(s) containing this product description can be stored in a special file that can then be combined into the individual sales or promotional letters. (See figs. 6.11 and 6.12.) For a more detailed discussion of using the **F**ile **X**tract and **F**ile **C**ombine commands in a DOC environment, see Chapter 7.

For word processing and spreadsheet work, the three **F**ile **C**ombine options are useful in combining worksheets. The **F**ile **C**ombine **A**dd command is especially helpful for consolidating two worksheets. For instance, a user in a business with several divisions can use the **F**ile **C**ombine **A**dd command to consolidate the income statements for each division into a company-wide statement.

Keep in mind also that the **F**ile **C**ombine commands, if used frequently, can be easily converted into keyboard macros to reduce **F**ile **C**ombine operations to one keystroke. In Chapter 13 on Symphony's Command Language (macros), some examples are presented that show how to write simple macros to perform **F**ile **C**ombine operations.

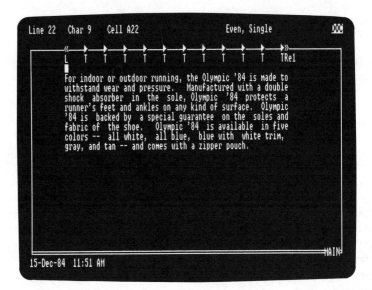

Fig. 6.11.

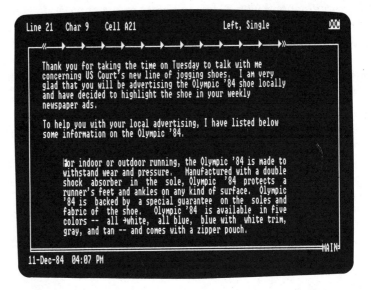

Fig. 6.12.

Deleting Files

When you save files, you may sometimes find that the disk is full. Symphony will inform you of this condition by indicating "Disk full" in the lower left corner of the screen. You can do one of two things when this occurs: swap disks, or delete one or more of the current files that occupy space on the disk.

Deleting files, like making backup copies of files, can be accomplished by either of two procedures. The first is to use the **A**pplication command from the SERVICES menu, attach and invoke DOS, and then use the DOS ERASE command to erase files. If you want to erase a number of files at one time, this first procedure is easier. The other procedure for erasing a file is to use the **F**ile **E**rase command from the SERVICES menu. When you select **F**ile **E**rase and enter the name of the file to be deleted, it will be erased from the disk. You are given a chance to halt the deletion process when Symphony asks

Are you sure you want to erase this file?
No Yes

Once you respond with **Y**, the complete file will be deleted, and it cannot be recovered by conventional means. Always check and double-check before you delete a file to be sure that you really want to delete it. Be careful, too, when you tell Symphony which file to delete. Make sure that the cursor is positioned on the file you want deleted or that you have correctly typed its file name.

When you name files, make file names clearly distinguishable from one another to minimize accidental deletion of the wrong file. For example, consider the following file names:

SALESA.WRK SALESB.WRK SALESC.WRK SALESD.WRK

Because of the different sixth character, all these files are correctly stored by Symphony. But the similarity in names increases the possibility that the user might accidentally delete the wrong file.

Changing a Drive and Directory

When you select **C**onfiguration from the SERVICES menu, you will notice that the first item on the **C**onfiguration sheet displayed on the screen is **File**. This indicates the default setting for the disk drive where files are to be saved and retrieved. In Symphony the default setting is drive B. This drive, then, is the active disk drive for storing and retrieving files. The **C**onfiguration **F**ile setting also permits you to enter a default file directory.

You may sometimes find that you must override temporarily the default disk drive. Suppose that drive B malfunctions, but you still want to continue using Symphony. In this case, use the **File Directory** command. When you select **File Directory**, the words "Current directory: " followed by the default drive and directory will appear in the control panel, as in

    Current directory: B:\DRAFT

If you want to change either the drive or the directory or both, you can press Esc to erase the drive and directory entry, or you can use the Backspace key to erase part of the entry. Next, type in the new directory and/or drive, then press RETURN. At this point, the drive and/or directory will be changed but only until you exit from the Symphony program. Later, when you reenter the program, **File Directory** will be reset to its default setting.

Transferring Files

With its expanded capabilities, Symphony gives you access to the most frequently used applications: spreadsheet, word processing, data management, graphics, and communications. Another component of Symphony's integration is the ability to transfer files created from programs outside Symphony. In some cases, the transfer procedure is fairly easy, as in the case of transferring 1-2-3 files into Symphony. At other times, transferring files is a bit more complex. Symphony nevertheless enables you to transfer files into the program and also to convert Symphony files for use in other programs.

Specifically, the File Import and Print Settings commands from the SERVICES menu and the Translation utility provide the operations for transferring files back and forth between Symphony and another program. As in 1-2-3, the kinds of files that can be transferred with these techniques are limited. This setback, however, is a minor one because most files can be converted to the proper format by using one of the available techniques. The methods described in this section work well and, with a few exceptions, are very easy to use.

Transferring Files with File Import

The File Import command is used to copy standard ASCII and LICS files to specific locations in the current worksheet. .PRN (print) files are one example of standard ASCII text files created to print after a current Symphony session. (.PRN files and their uses are covered in detail in Chapter 8.) Other standard ASCII files include those produced by different word-processing programs and BASIC programs. LICS files, on the other hand, are those files created with the Lotus International Character Set. These files are created by using the Configuration Other File-Translation command.

Transferring Standard ASCII Files

A standard ASCII text file must have a .PRN extension before it can be transferred. If a file doesn't have an appropriate extension, you must rename the file by using the DOS RENAME command. If you have added DOS to either your Symphony Program disk or your Help and Tutorial disk, renaming is a fairly easy process.

Once you have a file properly named, return to the worksheet and position the cursor at the cell where you want the upper left corner of the imported file to be located. Then invoke the File Import command with either Text or Structured. These two options have quite different effects on the worksheet.

The Text designation causes Symphony to create a separate left-justified label in the first cell of a new row for each line of imported text. In other words, everything in a line gets placed in just one worksheet cell, called a long label. If you need to justify labels, switch from a SHEET window to a DOC window. Then use the Format Create command to create a format line for justifying labels.

Whereas the Text option treats numbers as text, the Structured option treats numbers as numbers. The rules for the Structured option are that (1) only text enclosed in double quotation marks is valid, and (2) each valid item in a line must be placed in its own cell within a row.

Note that regardless of which option you choose for File Import (Text or Structured), when the file items are imported into the worksheet, everything in the space to be occupied by the file items will be written over. Be sure that there isn't anything important in the affected range of cells.

Transferring Files with the Translation Utility

Lotus Development retains the Translation utility originally included in 1-2-3's ACCESS SYSTEM. Symphony's Translation utility operates like 1-2-3's, permitting you to import files from VisiCalc (in either VC or DIF format) or dBASE II into Symphony. In addition, the Translation utility enables you to translate Symphony worksheet files (.WRK) to either DIF or dBASE II files. This translation capability is one of many demonstrating the program's flexibility. In Symphony, as in 1-2-3, the Translation utility is a valuable asset. For example, the utility is a helpful aid to users who are creating dBASE II files and want to process that data through Symphony. The Translation utility is also an important part of Symphony's communications applications.

Before you begin to use the Translation utility, make sure that the files you want to transfer have the correct file name extensions. If the extension is different from those listed above, use the DOS RENAME command for changing the extension. (Refer to your system's directions for using DOS and the RENAME command.)

Symphony's Translation utility will make the following types of conversions:

Source	File Name Extension	Destination	File Name Extension
VisiCalc	.VC	Symphony	.WRK
DIF (Data Interchange Format)	.DIF	Symphony	.WRK
dBASE II	.DBF	Symphony	.WRK
Symphony	.WRK	DIF	.DIF
Symphony	.WRK	dBASE II	.DBF

After you have checked the file extensions and made corrections if necessary, the translation operation is fairly simple. Take the following steps:

1. Access the Translation utility in one of two ways: through the system prompt or through the Symphony ACCESS SYSTEM menu. If you access the utility at the system prompt, type *trans* after the prompt or *trans* and the driver name if you are using a driver name other than the default name "Lotus." (If you are using a system with two disk drives, remember to insert the Symphony Install disk into drive A before you begin to access the utility.)

2. After you access the utility, Symphony will display a menu of the file translation options listed above. (See fig. 6.13.) Select one of the displayed options.

3. When Symphony asks, "Please enter source path: ", indicate the disk drive and/or the directory of the files that you want translated.

4. Specify which file should be translated by moving the cursor to the file name appearing in the file list on the screen.

5. Indicate the drive and directory where the source file should be translated.

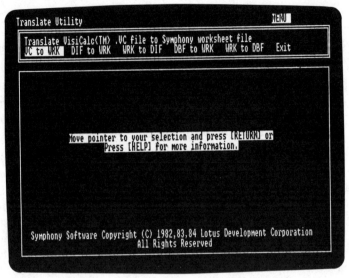

```
Translate Utility                                          MENU
Translate VisiCalc(TM) .VC file to Symphony worksheet file
VC to WRK   DIF to WRK   WRK to DIF   DBF to WRK   WRK to DBF   Exit




               Move pointer to your selection and press [RETURN] or
                      Press [HELP] for more information.




        Symphony Software Copyright (C) 1982,83,84 Lotus Development Corporation
                              All Rights Reserved
```

Fig. 6.13.

6. Select one of the special format options below.

   a. Select either **C**olumnwise or **R**owwise translation if
      you are translating a .DIF file to a .WRK file.
      Symphony switches columns and rows only if your
      selection here is different from the selection
      you made when you created the .DIF file.

   b. Select **E**ntire **W**orksheet of **N**amed **R**ange if you are
      translating a .WRK file to a .DBF file.

7. Initiate the translation operation (or return to the
   original file list) by selecting **Y**es or **N**o. Selecting **Q**uit
   returns you to the translation menu.

Transferring Symphony and WordStar Files

With Symphony's word-processing capability, you may find that you
want to transfer WordStar files or sections of text from WordStar files
to Symphony. On the other hand, you may sometimes want to

transfer Symphony worksheet files (.WRK) to WordStar. The possibility of transferring files between the two programs can be quite an advantage when you want to use existing WordStar files to create new documents that incorporate data created in Symphony.

Transferring a WordStar file for use in Symphony requires two operations. First, create a custom character-translation table; enter and save it in Symphony's Configuration Settings sheet. Then you can transfer WordStar files by means of File Import.

To create a custom character-translation table in Symphony, you must understand how Symphony uses the Lotus International Character Set (LICS) to display characters. Each character in LICS is represented by one of 256 codes (using the numbers 0 through 255). The numbers 32 through 127 represent the same codes as their ASCII equivalents. For example, the LICS (and ASCII) code for the character *b* is 98. (See the Symphony reference manual for a listing of the LICS characters and their related codes.) For most ASCII files the conversion from ASCII to LICS requires almost no change in code numbers, but this is not true for WordStar files.

Before Symphony can transfer WordStar files, you need to create the custom character-translation table pictured in Table 6.1. The left side of Table 6.1 shows the default character-code-translation table that appears in the worksheet when you use the SERVICES Configuration Other File-Translation Generate Custom command and choose cell A1 as the location for the upper left corner of the table.

Column A of the default table shows the codes that Symphony uses when it sends a character to a print file or a remote computer during a communications session. Column B of the same table shows the default codes used when a file is imported into the program or read in during a communications session. When you are importing WordStar files, you are most concerned with changing the values in column B.

To determine the code that Symphony uses when it receives a character, add one (1) to the LICS code number. Symphony uses this number as a row number to look up the appropriate item. For example, to look up the code that corresponds to LICS code 226, Symphony goes to row number 227 and finds code 153—the box or unknown character.

Table 6.1

The Default Table			A Special Table for Reading in WordStar Files		
A	B	C	A	B	C
1	0	0	1	0	0
2	32	1	2	32	1
3	32	2	3	32	2
4	32	3	4	32	3
.	.	.	.	.	.
.	.	.	.	.	.
32	32	31	32	32	31
33	32	32	33	32	32
34	33	33	34	33	33
35	34	34	35	34	34
.	.	.	.	.	.
.	.	.	.	.	.
127	126	126	127	126	126
128	127	127	128	127	127
129	63	199	129	63	0
130	63	252	130	63	1
131	63	233	131	63	2
.	.	.	.	.	.
.	.	.	.	.	.
226	160	223	226	160	97
227	131	153	227	131	98
.	.	.	.	.	.
.	.	.	.	.	.
253	129	153	253	129	124
254	152	178	254	152	125
255	63	153	255	63	126
256	63	153	256	63	127

To change the code table to handle WordStar files, use the SHEET Range Fill command to enter the numbers 0 through 127 in cells B129..B256. (See the right side of Table 6.1.) This change causes Symphony to convert the last character in each word to a readable LICS character. Use the SERVICES Configuration Other File-Translation Generate Save command to save the new table under a special name, for example, WORDSTAR.CTF. (The .CTF extension indicates a custom character-code-translation file.) Then use the

SERVICES Configuration Other File-Translation Custom command to activate the custom table.

Transferring a Symphony .WRK file to WordStar requires the following steps. First, convert the Symphony .WRK file to a .PRN file (a print file). To make this conversion, retrieve the Symphony file to be converted, then select Print Settings from the SERVICES menu. Choose Source, select Range, and then indicate the range for the print file. If you want to transfer the complete file, simply set the range to the end of the file by using the End and Home keys.

After indicating the range of the source, select Destination and choose File. When Symphony asks for the file name, type the name of the file you want to transfer, but type only the first part of the name, not the extension. Next, change the right margin setting to 240 by selecting Margins; then after the prompt, select No-Margins. After changing the right margin setting, select Quit twice to return to the main Print menu. Then select Go from the Print menu and wait as Symphony saves the print file. Finally, press Quit to exit from the SERVICES menu. You have now created a .PRN file ready to be used in WordStar.

Conclusion

As you use Symphony, you will find yourself frequently performing not only the "necessary" file operations—that is, File Save and File Retrieve—but also many others. Some File commands you will use for file management. For instance, as you begin to create worksheet files containing valuable spreadsheets and data bases, you will want to make copies of these files for safekeeping. And as the number of worksheet, print, and graph files increases, you may use File List, File Bytes, and File Erase to keep track of files and disk space and clean out files. Finally, you will want to use such commands as File Combine, File Xtract, and File Import as you apply Symphony to numerous spreadsheet, data management, and word-processing applications.

*New
with
Symphony*

Word Processing: Working in a Symphony DOC Window

What are the advantages of having a fully integrated software package that includes word processing? Once you begin to use Symphony's word-processing capability, the Symphony DOC environment, you will find numerous advantages to having this feature. The first is simply one of convenience. Not having to access another program or to change disks whenever you have to compose a letter or memo, draft a report, or put a few notes together is one kind of convenience. But there's also the convenience of learning one program but having five applications available at any time.

Learning to use Symphony's word-processing environment is similar to learning to use the other program applications—spreadsheet, graphics, data management, and communications. The Symphony DOC environment shares a number of features with the other applications, including similarities in the display screen, in the use of command menus, and in the way Symphony stores text. Except for handling special format lines or print commands within the text, you don't need to master a new way of entering commands in Symphony's DOC window environment; the approach is the same as that for a SHEET, FORM, GRAPH, or COMM window.

The second advantage to having word processing along with spreadsheet, data management, graphics, and communications capabilities is Symphony's ability to integrate word processing with the other applications. For instance, you can be working in a DOC window and at the same time have a SHEET or GRAPH window on the screen. You will find that this capability alone may make switching from a single word-processing program to Symphony well worth it.

The third advantage to using Symphony's word-processing capability is the simplification of many DOC operations through the use of macros, which are discussed in Chapter 13. In that chapter, you are shown how to create macros for many moving, erasing, and copying operations. After becoming familiar with Symphony's DOC environment and the process of creating Symphony macros interactively, you will be able to reduce operations involving many keystrokes to one keystroke.

This chapter introduces you to Symphony's word-processing capabilities so that you can make the DOC window environment a regular part of using the program. Included are the following topics:

- Creating a DOC window
- The DOC display
- The DOC function keys
- Getting started in a DOC window
- Entering text and moving the cursor
- Erasing and editing text
- Searching and replacing
- Formatting your document
- Integrating the DOC environment with other Symphony applications

Creating a DOC Window

Various methods can be used to create a DOC window. First, if you will be working within a DOC window more frequently than other types of windows (SHEET, GRAPH, FORM, or COMM), then you can

begin every work session with a DOC window by updating the
SERVICES Configuration Window Type setting to DOC. To change
the setting for the window type, retrieve the SERVICES menu by
pressing the SERVICES key, select Configuration on the menu, then
choose Window. Next, select Type. When the five types of windows
are displayed, move the cursor to DOC and press RETURN, or type
D to create a DOC window. Finally, press Update in the Configuration menu. The default window will then be set to DOC. Every time
you access the Symphony program or create a new worksheet, the
window type will be DOC.

If, however, the default window type is SHEET, GRAPH, FORM, or
COMM, you can shift to a DOC window by pressing the TYPE key
(Alt + F10) and selecting DOC. One other procedure can be used for
setting the window type. Whenever you create a new window by
using the Window Create command from the SERVICES menu,
Symphony will ask you to choose a window type. If the current
window is not DOC, you can select it.

The DOC Display

When you enter the Symphony program for the first time, a SHEET
window will be the type of window to appear first. Symphony has set
the default setting for initial window type to SHEET. As mentioned in
Chapter 2, the SHEET window is similar to the 1-2-3 display in that
columns are represented by letters at the top, and rows are
indicated by numbers down the left side. The SHEET window, which
is bordered on all four sides, contains an indicator area in the top
right and left corners. When you shift to a DOC window, either by
selecting TYPE or by creating a new window with the Window
Create command, the display remains much the same as for the
SHEET window—still bordered on all four sides and containing
indicators in the upper right and left corners.

In addition, DOC commands are displayed exactly as those for
SHEET, GRAPH, FORM, and COMM. (See fig. 7.1.) When you select
the DOC command MENU, it appears above the top line of the DOC
border, and the explanation of the cursor-highlighted command
appears above the menu line.

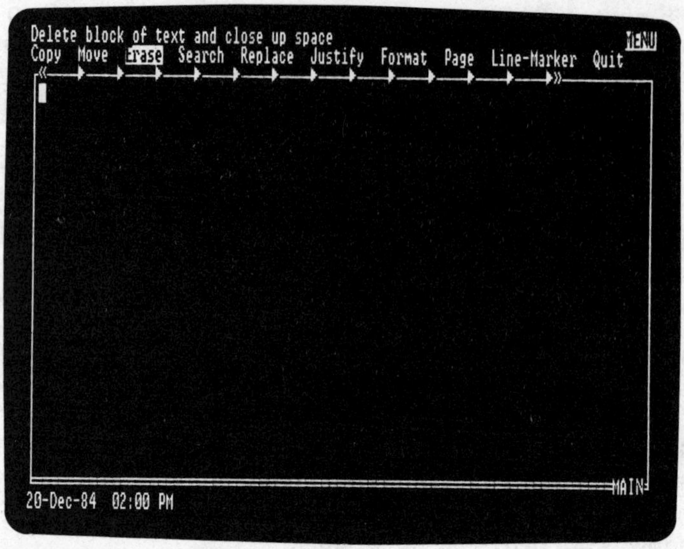

```
Delete block of text and close up space                           MENU
Copy  Move  Erase  Search  Replace  Justify  Format  Page  Line-Marker  Quit
«───►───►───►───►───►───►───►───►───►───►──»




















                                                                    ─MAIN─
20-Dec-84  02:00 PM
```

Fig. 7.1.

The DOC display screen has some special features, however. First, the top line of the border indicates the left and right margins and all tab settings. The default setting (shown in the SERVICES Configuration settings sheet) for the left margin is 1 and for the right margin is 72. Tabs are set five spaces apart. The top line indicating margins and tabs is always displayed unless you change the border from Standard to Line or None by selecting Window Settings Border.

Above the top line are three indicators: the cursor position (line, character, and cell), the type of justification and spacing, and the mode indicator. If an asterisk appears in the middle of the control panel, the asterisk indicates that the cursor is presently located on data which has been entered in another type of window.

If you are working in a DOC window and move the cursor to data that you have already entered in a SHEET environment, Symphony will display an asterisk to remind you that DOC commands and operations and SHEET commands and operations are not interchangeable. You cannot edit, for example, labels and numbers entered in a SHEET window by using the Backspace and Del keys while you are working in a DOC window. If you include special format lines (discussed later) in your text, an asterisk will appear when the cursor is positioned at these format lines, again telling you that this text cannot be changed as other data can.

One other indicator to note particularly is the Calc indicator in the bottom right corner. Calc indicates that changes in the DOC window may affect calculations in spreadsheets created in other areas of your worksheet. If you do have spreadsheets in the worksheet, press the Calc key to recalculate cell values.

DOC Function Keys

Whenever you begin word-processing operations in a DOC window, eight function keys are available, ranging from a key for justifying paragraphs to a key for jumping the cursor from one part of the text to another. (See fig. 7.2.)

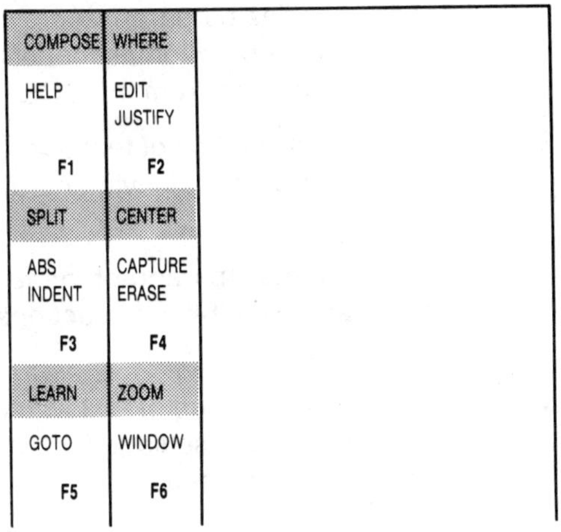

COMPOSE	WHERE
HELP	EDIT JUSTIFY
F1	F2
SPLIT	CENTER
ABS INDENT	CAPTURE ERASE
F3	F4
LEARN	ZOOM
GOTO	WINDOW
F5	F6

Fig. 7.2.

Two of these keys—Justify (F2) and Erase (F4)—perform the same operations as comparable commands from the DOC command MENU. The cursor keys (for the IBM PC and compatibles) that have special uses for DOC operations are the following:

Key	Function
Alt + F1 (Compose)	Used for indicating special "print attribute" symbols. For example, to indicate that you want text underlined, press together Alt and F1 at the beginning of the text; then type B , then A, then the symbol for underlining (U). At the end of the text you want underlined, press Alt and F1 again; then type E, then A. Compose is also used for creating special characters not included on the keyboard. To create these, press Alt + F1; then press the key(s) for the symbol.
Alt + F2 (Where)	Indicates in the lower left corner of the screen the page and line location of the cursor's present position
F2 (Justify)	Justifies paragraphs; completes the same operation as that of **J**ustify **P**aragraph from the DOC menu
Alt + F3 (Split)	Divides a line of text or creates blank lines without leaving hard carriage returns
F3 (Indent)	Indents a paragraph or section of text. (See the later sections on special formatting.)
Alt + F4 (Center)	Centers a line of text with respect to the margin settings for the line where Center is used
F4 (Erase)	Initiates the **E**rase command; completes the same operation as that of the **E**rase command from the DOC menu
F5 (GoTo)	Used for jumping the cursor to another line on the same page, to a line on another page, or to a named line. (See the later section on GoTo and

Line-Marker Names.) When you press F5 and then the MENU key, a list of all marked lines appears.

Getting Started in a DOC Window

What do you need to know as you begin using Symphony's word processor? You will probably want to know how text is displayed, stored, and finally printed. You will also want to know how to enter text on the screen and how to edit and change text.

The DOC Command MENU

Getting started in a DOC window requires that you understand the organization of the DOC command MENU (fig. 7.3), the kinds of special commands that are inserted within the text, and the different kinds of settings sheets that affect a DOC window.

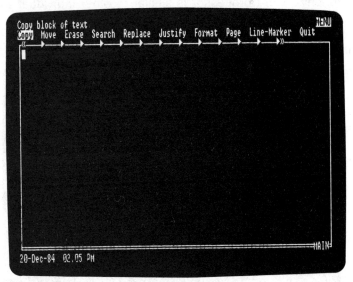

Fig. 7.3.

Using the DOC command MENU requires the same operations as using the command menus for other windows. You simply press the

MENU key (F10), move the cursor to the command, and complete
the operations required by that command. The DOC commands fall
into the following primary categories:

1. **C**opy, **M**ove, and **E**rase commands

2. **S**earch and **R**eplace commands

3. Format commands, including those for paragraph
   justification, spacing, margins, tabs, and operations
   connected with creating special "format lines,"
   naming lines, and inserting page breaks.

Format Lines and Print Attributes

Working in a DOC window is different from working in other types of
windows in one respect: not only do you control the entering,
displaying, and changing of text by using the DOC command MENU,
but you also control text by placing special commands on the
screen within the same area as the text you are entering. In this way
Symphony's word processor is similar to other individual word-
processing programs that require entering special format or print
commands into the text and which are displayed on the screen. (See
fig. 7.4.)

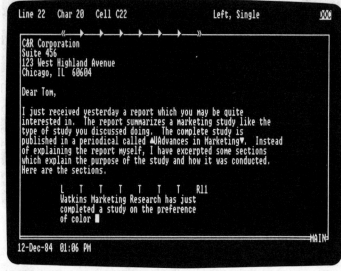

Fig. 7.4.

Besides being controlled by the command menu above, text is also controlled by format lines and print attributes entered into the worksheet itself. Format lines and print attributes always appear on the screen, as in figure 7.4, unless you delete them.

Format lines are inserted into the text whenever you want to change the margins, tabs, justification, or spacing of the text that follows. (See the later section on Creating, Editing, and Storing Format Lines.) For example, suppose you want to indent your text on both sides and to center a section of a report that you are composing, as in figure 7.5.

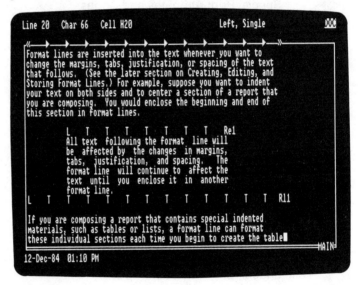

Fig. 7.5.

If you are composing a report that contains special indented materials, such as tables or lists, a format line can format these individual sections each time you begin to create the table or list. (See also the directions later on using the Indent key.)

Special print attributes (boldface, italics, underlining, superscript, subscript, and combinations of these) can be placed within the text. For example, you tell Symphony to boldface characters, letters, or words by enclosing them in three special characters:

1. Signal the beginning of a special print attribute by pressing the Compose key, then typing B and then A. This sequence of presses creates the triangle (▲).

2. Type directly after the triangle (▲) one of the codes listed below.

3. Signal the end of the print attribute by pressing the Compose key, then typing E and then A. This sequence of presses creates the inverted triangle (▼).

Special Print Attributes and Codes

Attribute	Code
Boldface text	B or b
Italics	I or i
Underline	U or u
Superscript	+
Subscript	-
Strike through	X or x
Boldface italics	0 (Zero)
Boldface underline	1
Boldface italic underline	2
Italic underline	3
Bold superscript	4
Italic superscript	5
Boldface subscript	6
Italic subscript	7
Boldface italics	8
Boldface italic superscript	9

| Include spaces in print attributes (for example, underlining) | S or s |
| Do not include spaces | Q or q |

Before using these print attributes, make sure that your driver is set for the right printer. (In Chapter 2 see the section on Installing Drivers.)

Format Settings

The first step in using Symphony's DOC environment is to adjust special format settings. Besides inserting format lines in the text, Symphony provides two ways for controlling the format of a DOC environment: the default format settings stored in Symphony's configuration file (SYMPHONY.CNF), and the format settings that can be entered for each DOC window you create.

Format Settings in Symphony's Configuration File

The SERVICES Configuration Document setting establishes the default settings for tabs, justification, spacing, margins, display of hard spaces between words, display of carriage returns and automatic justification of paragraphs. When you first enter Symphony, the following default settings are in operation:

Tab interval: 5
Justification: 1
Spacing: 1
Left Margin: 1
Right Margin: 72
Blanks visible: No
CRs visible: Yes
Auto-Justify: Yes

You can change any or all of these settings by selecting Configuration from the SERVICES menu, choosing Document, selecting each item to be changed, and then entering the new settings. Once you have changed the Configuration Document settings, you need to update the settings sheet by selecting Update from the Configuration menu. If you do not update the sheet, the new settings that you enter will be in effect only until you finish your current work session and exit from the program.

The SERVICES Configuration Document settings are useful for storing format settings for documents that you frequently work on. You will need to remember that Configuration Document settings control the format settings for the first DOC window that you create in any given file. You may therefore want to change the SERVICES Configuration Document settings to the kind of format you will be using most frequently. For example, if you find that you will often be using the DOC environment for creating one-page memos, you may want to change the Configuration Document settings for the particular format required by the memos you will be creating.

DOC Window Format Settings

You can override Configuration Document settings, however, by changing the Format Settings in the DOC menu. When you change Format Settings, then the format of text you enter is controlled by these settings. Also, whenever you change Format Settings in one DOC window and then create another DOC window, the second window inherits the format settings of the previous window unless you have deleted that window.

After you enter a DOC window, the next step is to determine whether you need to change format settings. As mentioned earlier, the top line of the border tells you where margins and tabs have been set. Above the top line in the control panel, Symphony indicates the type of justification and spacing. For example, "Left,Single" tells you that the window is set for left justification and single-spacing.

Whenever you need to change format settings for the current DOC window, use the Format Settings command from the DOC menu. The Format Settings command allows you to enter settings for the current window and to save those settings along with the window. Suppose, for example, that you are creating a table, as shown in figure 7.6. In the window (named Table 1 at the bottom), you are creating a table with a left margin of 15, a right margin of 60, and double-spacing. (Double- and triple-spacing do not appear on the screen but in printed copy. See Setting Tabs, Spacing, and Margins.)

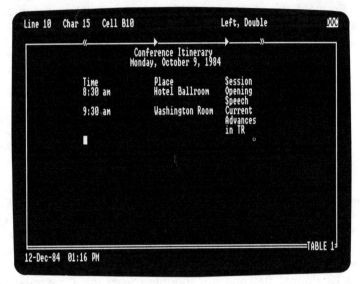

Fig. 7.6.

In addition to checking the settings for margins, tabs, justification, and spacing before you begin to work in a DOC window, you can also check three other settings by retrieving the Format Settings sheet from the DOC menu. (These three settings can also be changed in the SERVICES Configuration Document settings.) The settings are the following:

- **B**lanks. If you select **Yes**, Symphony will display periods on the screen for every space. Because the default setting is **No**, you need to change this setting only when you want spaces marked.

- **C**Rs. Symphony will display hard carriage returns. **Yes** is the default setting.

- **A**uto-Justify. When **A**uto-Justify is set to **Yes**, which is the default setting, Symphony will automatically justify paragraphs every time you use the **C**opy, **M**ove, **E**rase, or **R**eplace command.

Guidelines for Using Format Settings

When you use the SERVICES Configuration Document settings, the DOC Format Settings, and format lines, keep the following guidelines in mind:

1. The Configuration Document settings provide the default settings; however, DOC Format Settings can override Configuration Document settings.

2. A DOC Format Settings sheet is stored with each window you create, and the settings remain with that window until you change them.

3. Blanks, CRs, and Auto-Justify settings will override format lines.

Some examples can help clarify the relationships of the SERVICES Configuration Document settings, a DOC Format Settings sheet, and format lines. You can also note the effect that creating different windows will have on these three methods for adjusting format. When you create the first DOC window for a particular worksheet, the DOC Format Settings are inherited from the Configuration Document settings.

Figure 7.7 shows the Configuration Document settings stored in the Symphony configuration file (SYMPHONY.CNF). The DOC Format Settings for the DOC window, shown in figure 7.8, are the same as those in the Configuration Document settings.

The Configuration Document settings, like the DOC Format Settings, are the following:

Tab interval: 5
Justification: l (l = Left)
Spacing: 1
Left Margin: 1
Right Margin: 72
Blanks visible: No
CRs visible: Yes
Auto-Justify: Yes

When you create a second DOC window on the screen, that window inherits the DOC Format Settings from the first window. You can,

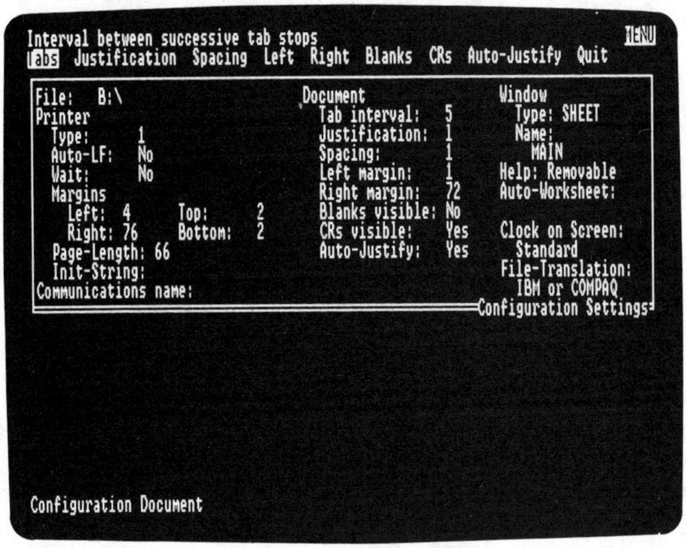

```
Interval between successive tab stops                          MENU
Tabs Justification  Spacing  Left  Right  Blanks  CRs  Auto-Justify  Quit

File:   B:\              Document              Window
Printer                    Tab interval:    5      Type: SHEET
  Type:     1             Justification:   1     Name:
  Auto-LF:  No            Spacing:         1         MAIN
  Wait:     No            Left margin:     1     Help: Removable
  Margins                 Right margin:    72    Auto-Worksheet:
    Left:   4   Top:    2  Blanks visible: No
    Right: 76   Bottom: 2  CRs visible:    Yes   Clock on Screen:
  Page-Length: 66          Auto-Justify:    Yes     Standard
  Init-String:                                   File-Translation:
Communications name:                               IBM or COMPAQ
                                           ═Configuration Settings═

Configuration Document
```

Fig. 7.7.

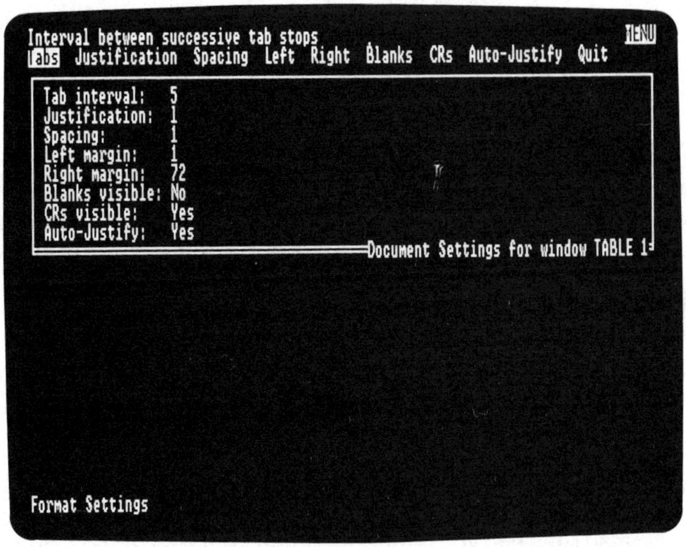

```
Interval between successive tab stops                          MENU
Tabs Justification  Spacing  Left  Right  Blanks  CRs  Auto-Justify  Quit

Tab interval:    5
Justification:   1
Spacing:         1
Left margin:     1
Right margin:    72
Blanks visible: No
CRs visible:    Yes
Auto-Justify:    Yes
                          ═Document Settings for window TABLE 1═

Format Settings
```

Fig. 7.8.

however, change the settings in DOC **F**ormat **S**ettings for the particular window in which you are working. In the example in figure 7.6, the DOC **F**ormat **S**ettings are changed to these:

Tab interval: 18
Justification: I (I = Left)
Spacing: 2
Left Margin: 15
Right Margin: 60
Blanks visible: No
CRs visible: Yes
Auto-Justify: No

New settings will affect text in other windows unless you set **W**indow **S**ettings **R**estrict outside the area of other DOC windows. Figure 7.9A, for example, contains a window with a left margin of 1, a right margin of 65, and a tab setting of 5. If we add to the screen a second DOC window, which has different format settings, these settings will affect our first window. That is, the settings of window 2 will affect window 1, if we do not restrict each window to *different* worksheet areas.

If you look at figure 7.9B, you will notice that the lines in window 1 have been readjusted. This readjustment happened because the restrict range (A1..M80) for window 2 was set to include window 1. When the DOC **F**ormat **S**ettings were changed for window 2, they affected the text in window 1 as well.

So that the DOC **F**ormat **S**ettings in window 2 do not affect window 1, you should restrict window 2 to an area below or to the right of the text in window 1. When window 2 was restricted to range A30..M80, the DOC **F**ormat **S**ettings did not affect window 1. (See fig. 7.10.)

Notice that the top line of the border of window 2 indicates the tab and margin settings, and the control panel indicates the type of justification and spacing. Notice also that the second DOC window in an earlier figure (fig. 7.4) contains a format line. All text before the format line is controlled by DOC **F**ormat **S**ettings; all text after the format line is controlled by it until you reset the line or create a new one.

You can also return to your original format settings (those displayed in the top line of the window border of fig. 7.27, for example) by using

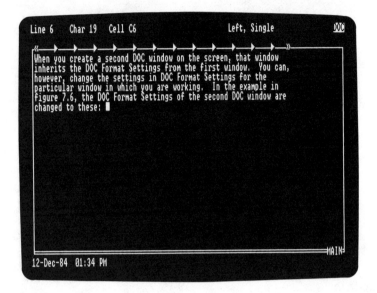

Fig. 7.9A.

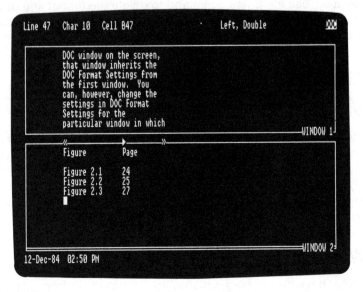

Fig. 7.9B.

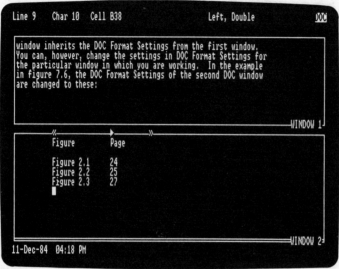

Fig. 7.10.

the Format Edit Current Reset command. (See Creating, Editing, and Storing Format Lines.) If you decide that you don't need the format line at all, use the Erase command to delete the format line or the format line marker. Whenever you erase a format line that you have given a name, the name is also deleted.

Entering Text and Moving the Cursor

After you have made changes in the Configuration Document settings and/or the DOC Format Settings, you are ready to begin entering text in the DOC window. Actually, entering words from the keyboard isn't much different from typing words on a typewriter keyboard, except for "word wrap" and "insert/overstrike mode" capabilities.

Word Wrap

If you have used word-processing programs before, you are probably familiar with word wrap. As in other word-processing programs, in Symphony word wrap is the capability of maintaining automatically the right margin and moving the cursor to the succeeding line. Whole words, then, are not divided but "wrap around" to the next line. In other words, you do not have to press the carriage return to begin a new line. When word wrap occurs, Symphony formats each line according to the controlling justification setting—**L**eft, **E**ven, or **C**enter.

At times, you may want two words (or letters and numbers separated by spaces) to remain on the same line, instead of one word being at the end of a line and the other word appearing at the beginning of the next line. In this case, you can insert a "hard space" between the two lines.

For example, you may want a trademark, product name, or company name, such as "J. P. McMurphy," to appear all on one line. (See fig. 7.11.) To have the name wrap around to the next line, you take the following steps. Type J., press the Compose key (Alt + F1), then the space bar twice. Next, type P., press the Compose key, and again press the space bar twice. Symphony will insert a dot in both spaces, indicating that a hard space is inserted. When margins are justified because of word wrap, J. P. McMurphy will remain on the same line.

```
 Line 13   Char 4    Cell A13                  Left, Single         DOC

 the beginning of the next line.  In this case, you can insert a
 "hard space" between the two lines.  For example, you may want a
 trademark, product name, or company name, such as "J. P.
 McMurphy," to appear all on one line.

 In order to have the name wrap around to the next line, you do
 the following.  Type J., then press the Compose key (Alt + F1),
 then the spacebar twice.  Next, type P., then press the Compose
 key, and again press the spacebar twice.  Symphony will insert a
 dot in both spaces, indicating that a hard space is inserted.
 When margins are justified because of word wrap, then
 J. P. McMurphy will wrap around to the next line.




                                                             MAIN

 12-Dec-84  02:57 PM
```

Fig. 7.11.

Insert and Overstrike Modes

The Insert mode is the default setting for entering characters from the keyboard. Whenever you enter characters in Insert mode, you can delete or insert any character or a space to the immediate left of the cursor. Also, whenever the DOC environment is set in Insert mode, word wrap is in effect.

The Overstrike mode is the opposite of the Insert mode. Overstrike is turned on by pressing the Ins key in the lower left corner of the numeric keyboard. In Overstrike mode, you can change characters or add spaces directly over the character or space where the cursor is positioned. Also, in Overstrike mode word wrap is turned off. Whenever Overstrike mode is on, an "Ovr" indicator is displayed in the bottom right corner of your screen.

Using the Backspace key in both Insert and Overstrike modes erases the character to the left of the cursor. In Insert mode, however, characters to the right are shifted to the left when you press the Backspace key. In Overstrike mode, characters to the right remain in their original positions.

Except for the features of word wrap and Insert/Overstrike mode, entering text into a DOC window is much like typing text at a typewriter keyboard. The real differences between the two activities are noticeable when you use Symphony's word processor for performing many kinds of editing and formatting operations. These operations range from word-level changes, like correcting spelling, to much larger changes, such as moving blocks of text or transferring text from other files.

Moving the Cursor in a DOC Window

An essential part of performing many editing and formatting operations is being able to move the cursor within a DOC window. You will find cursor movement to be quite convenient when you are working not only in the DOC mode as you enter and change text, but also in the POINT mode when you are completing such commands as Copy, Move, and Erase.

Moving the cursor in a DOC window is similar to moving the cell pointer in a SHEET window; you use many of the same keys for both kinds of movements. Many more keys, however, can be used to move the cursor in a DOC window. (See fig. 7.12.)

The keys for moving the cursor in a DOC window include the following:

> The cursor keys: ←, →, ↑, ↓
> The PgUp and PgDn keys
> The Home key
> The End key
> The Ctrl key (used only in combination with others)
> The Scroll Lock key (used only in combination with others)
> The F2 key (used with the End key)
> The Alt + F2 keys (used with the End key)
> The RETURN key (used with the End key)
> Any typed character (used with the End key)

Using these keys in a DOC worksheet will enable you to move the cursor from one character or space to another, from one word to another, from one line to another, from the beginning of the paragraph to the end (and vice versa), from one screen to another, and from the beginning of the window restrict range to the end (and vice versa). The sections that follow describe in detail each of these types of cursor movement.

Moving the Cursor: Character or Space

You may at times want to move the cursor backward or forward one character or space, particularly when you need to correct a misspelling in a previous word on the current line. The keys listed here are used for moving from one character to another.

To move the cursor:	Use the following:
To preceding character	←
To next character	→
To any specific character	End then specific character

You will find the last option particularly convenient when you want to move forward to a specific spot in your text. Although using the **S**earch command is similar to using the End key and a specific

Keyboard Diagram

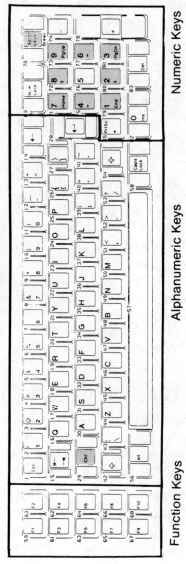

Function Keys

Alphanumeric Keys

Numeric Keys

Fig. 7.12.

character, the latter method will save you keystrokes. The **Search** command requires six keystrokes, including one to return to the DOC mode; the End key followed by a character requires only two.

Suppose you want to move the cursor forward to a sentence that ends with a question mark. If you use **S**earch, you first retrieve the DOC menu by pressing the Compose key (F10) and then selecting **S**earch. Next, you type the character—in this case, a question mark (?)—press RETURN, and then indicate whether the search should be **F**orward or **B**ackward. Finally, after the cursor moves to the specific character, select **Q**uit to move out of the MENU mode and back to the DOC mode. With the End key, you accomplish the same operation by pressing End and then pressing the Shift and question mark keys at the same time.

Using the End key followed by another character is also convenient when you are highlighting a block for completing the **C**opy, **M**ove, or **E**rase commands. For example, suppose you want to erase the beginning of the sentence shown in figure 7.13A, erasing from "Although" to the comma after "character." To erase this part of the sentence, first place your cursor at the beginning of the sentence, then select the **E**rase command from the DOC menu, or press the

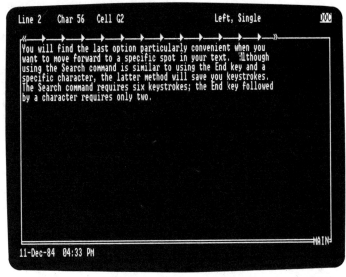

Fig. 7.13A.

Erase key (F4). When the "Erase what block?" prompt appears,
press End, then press the comma key (fig. 7.13B), and finally press
RETURN.

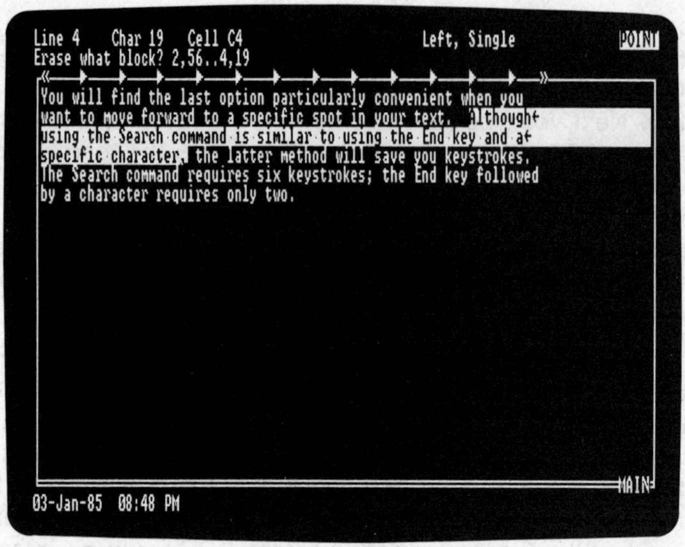

```
Line 4    Char 19   Cell C4                Left, Single        POINT
Erase what block? 2,56..4,19
«————►——►——►——►——►——►——►——►——►——»»
You will find the last option particularly convenient when you
want to move forward to a specific spot in your text.  Although◄
using the Search command is similar to using the End key and a◄
specific character, the latter method will save you keystrokes.
The Search command requires six keystrokes; the End key followed
by a character requires only two.




03-Jan-85  08:48 PM                                           MAIN
```

Fig. 7.13B.

Search does, however, have one major advantage over the End key
followed by a character. The Search command enables you to
complete not only a forward search but also a backward search.
End followed by a character operates only for forward movement.

Moving the Cursor: Word to Word

Moving the cursor from the beginning of one word to the beginning
of the next or preceding word is convenient when you want to move
quickly to the middle of a line or to edit a character at the beginning
or end of a word. The keys for moving the cursor from one word to
another are listed here.

To move the cursor: Use the following:

    To the next word   Ctrl + →
    To the preceding word   Ctrl + ←

Moving the Cursor: Line to Line

Two types of cursor movement from one line to another are available in Symphony. These include moving the cursor from one line of text to another and moving the cursor from one format line to another.

To move the cursor:	Use the following:
1 line up	↑
1 line down	↓
1 format line up	End then Alt + F2
1 format line down	End then F2

Moving the Cursor: Beginning and End of Lines

To move the cursor to the beginning or end of a line, use the keys listed here.

To move the cursor:	Use the following:
To the beginning of a line	End then ←
To the end of a line	End then →

Moving the Cursor: Beginning and End of Paragraphs

To move the cursor to the beginning or end of a paragraph, use the following keys.

To move the cursor:	Use the following:
To the beginning of a paragraph	End then ↑
To the end of a paragraph	End then ↓

Moving the cursor to the beginning or end of a paragraph is particularly useful when you want to copy, erase, or move a whole paragraph. Suppose you want to erase a paragraph. First, you place the cursor at either the beginning or the end of the paragraph. If you place the cursor at the beginning of the paragraph, you next select **E**rase from the DOC menu. Symphony will ask, "Erase what block?" You then press the End key and the ↓ key to highlight the paragraph, and finally press RETURN.

Moving the Cursor: Screen to Screen

Sometimes you will want to move quickly to a previous or later screen. One thing to keep in mind is that Symphony will move the cursor exactly one screen. There is no overlap of a previous or later screen when you use the keys listed here. (See figs. 7.14A and 7.14B.)

To move the cursor:	Use the following:
One window up	PgUp
One window down	PgDn

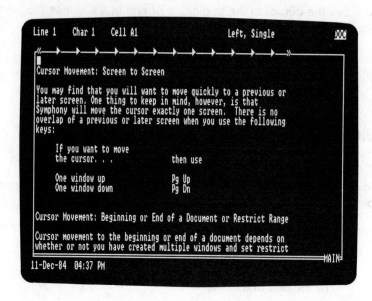

```
Line 1    Char 1    Cell A1                    Left, Single          DOC
«──▸──▸──▸──▸──▸──▸──▸──▸──▸──▸──▸──»
▉
Cursor Movement: Screen to Screen

You may find that you will want to move quickly to a previous or
later screen. One thing to keep in mind, however, is that
Symphony will move the cursor exactly one screen.  There is no
overlap of a previous or later screen when you use the following
keys:

      If you want to move
      the cursor. . .          then use

      One window up            Pg Up
      One window down          Pg Dn


Cursor Movement: Beginning or End of a Document or Restrict Range

Cursor movement to the beginning or end of a document depends on
whether or not you have created multiple windows and set restrict
                                                            ─MAIN─
11-Dec-84  04:37 PM
```

Fig. 7.14A.

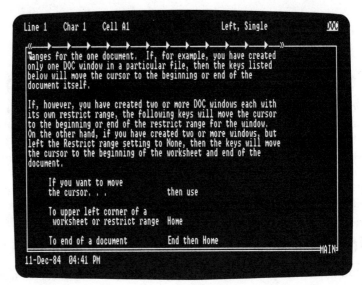

Fig. 7.14B.

Moving the Cursor: Beginning or End of a Document or Restrict Range

Cursor movement to the beginning or end of a document depends on whether or not you have created multiple windows and set restrict ranges for the document. If, for example, you have created only one DOC window in a particular file, then the keys listed below will move the cursor to the beginning or end of the document itself.

If you have created two or more DOC windows, each with its own restrict range, these same keys will move the cursor to the beginning or end of the restrict range for the window. On the other hand, if you have created two or more windows but left the restrict range setting to None, then the keys will move the cursor to the beginning of the worksheet and the end of the document.

To move the cursor:	Use the following:
To upper left corner of a worksheet or restrict range	Home

To end of a document
or restrict range   End then Home

Moving the Cursor: Next Carriage Return

If you have hard carriage returns in your text, particularly in key places, such as at the ends of paragraphs or after headings, this method is useful for quickly moving the cursor to key spots in the text. For instance, you may want to highlight an area of text when you are using the Copy, Move, or Erase commands. To move the cursor to the next carriage return, press the End key and then press RETURN.

Moving the Cursor: Using the GoTo Key

In addition to using the keys listed above for moving the cursor from one part of your text to another, you can use the GoTo key for jumping the cursor from one line to another or from one page to another. To move the cursor this way, first press the GoTo key (F5). Symphony will ask, "Go to where?" In response, you enter the line number to which you want to move the cursor. If your cursor is positioned at line 535 and you want to jump to line 555, enter 555 and press RETURN.

You can also enter a page number when Symphony asks, "Go to where?" You must enter a line number in addition to the page, however. Using the GoTo key is particularly useful when you are comparing a printed copy of your text with the text on the screen. If, for example, you want to move the cursor to the middle of page 3, enter 3 and then the line number by dividing the SERVICES Print Settings Page Length setting in half. If the setting is 66, you enter 3,33 at the prompt.

The GoTo Key and Line-Marker Names

The GoTo key can also be used to move the cursor to lines that have been named with the Line-Marker command from the DOC menu. You first must create a line marker and name at key points in your document. You may want to create a line marker and name for every major heading of a document, as we did for this chapter. (See fig. 7.15.)

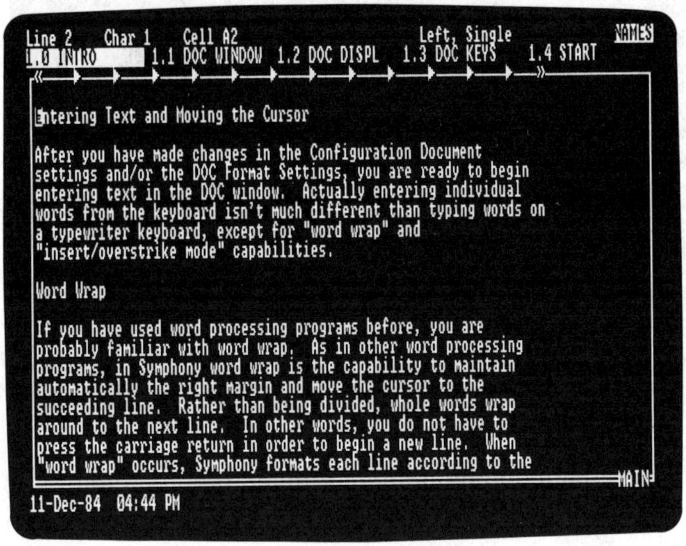

```
Line 2    Char 1     Cell A2                    Left, Single      NAMES
1.0 INTRO          1.1 DOC WINDOW   1.2 DOC DISPL   1.3 DOC KEYS   1.4 START

Entering Text and Moving the Cursor

After you have made changes in the Configuration Document
settings and/or the DOC Format Settings, you are ready to begin
entering text in the DOC window.  Actually entering individual
words from the keyboard isn't much different than typing words on
a typewriter keyboard, except for "word wrap" and
"insert/overstrike mode" capabilities.

Word Wrap

If you have used word processing programs before, you are
probably familiar with word wrap.  As in other word processing
programs, in Symphony word wrap is the capability to maintain
automatically the right margin and move the cursor to the
succeeding line.  Rather than being divided, whole words wrap
around to the next line.  In other words, you do not have to
press the carriage return in order to begin a new line.  When
"word wrap" occurs, Symphony formats each line according to the          MAIN

11-Dec-84   04:44 PM
```

Fig. 7.15.

Keeping a menu of line-marker names for key headings in a document has two applications. First, line-marker names enable you to move back and forth between sections by pressing the GoTo key and entering the name at the prompt (or pressing F10, then moving the cursor to the name). Second, a menu of line-marker names can provide you with a key outline to your document. (See fig. 7.16.) If you create line-marker names for major headings of your text, you will need to place numbers before them to keep them in their text order; otherwise, Symphony will organize all names alphabetically. (Symphony will order numbers between 1 and 9, including those with one or more decimal places.)

Here are some guidelines for creating and using line-marker names:

1. Line-marker names can contain up to 15 characters.

2. Names can consist of any type of characters and can include spaces within a name.

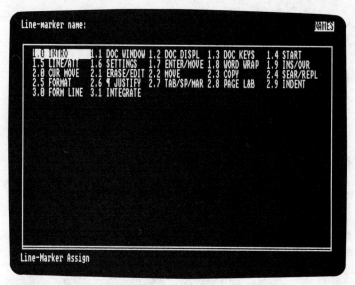

Fig. 7.16.

3. Symphony will store names either alphabetically or by number, with numbers taking precedence over letters.

4. You can display a menu of line-marker names by pressing the GoTo key, then pressing the DOC menu key.

5. You can display a complete list of line-marker names by pressing the DOC menu key after line-marker names appear in the control panel. (See fig. 7.16.)

As illustrated in figure 7.15, when you establish a line marker and create a name, Symphony stores each name. In some ways the Line-Marker command is like the Range Name command in the SHEET menu. Both allow you to create a name for a specific location on the worksheet and then to use the name for moving the cursor to that location.

To create a line marker, place the cursor at the beginning of the line you want named. Next, select Line-Marker from the DOC menu. When the "Assign Remove" prompt appears, choose Assign if you are creating a line-marker name; select Remove if you want to delete a name. When creating a name, you can either enter a new name by typing it in or move the cursor to a name that already exists. If you select a name that already exists, Symphony assigns the existing name to the line where the cursor is currently located. (See also the section on Creating, Editing, and Storing Format Lines.)

Although range names have many other functions in spreadsheets, line-marker names are limited to these two primary functions:

1. Using line-marker names with the GoTo key as described earlier; that is, you press the GoTo key and then enter the line-marker name.

2. Using line-marker names to create a file of format lines, which can be stored and then retrieved whenever you need to change a DOC window's format to a previously created format. If you store format lines in a separate file, you can use the SERVICES File Combine command to add these format lines into your text.

Erasing and Editing Text

As you become accustomed to processing text, you will find yourself juggling many of the following tasks: (1) entering words, sentences, and paragraphs on the screen; (2) correcting misspellings and typographical errors and making other word-level corrections; (3) keeping your sentences, paragraphs, and sections organized; and (4) editing your text to improve its development and organization.

Symphony's DOC environment enables you to handle all four of these tasks easily and efficiently. The tools you will need for completing each of these tasks can be found in combining the cursor-movement keys; the format settings; and the Erase, Move, Copy, and Search commands. This section describes the tools Symphony provides for completing different types of editing and erasing tasks.

Erasing and Editing: Characters and Words

For the most part, simple editing consists of moving the cursor to a character or word and deleting, changing, or moving that character or word. To delete and/or change individual characters, use the cursor-movement keys, Backspace key (←), and Del key. The editing functions of the cursor key and Backspace key depend on whether or not you are in Insert or Overstrike mode. (See the earlier section on Insert and Overstrike Modes.)

To move individual characters, you can use the **Move** command from the DOC menu. In most cases, however, using the **Move** command for this purpose will require as many, if not more, keystrokes than are required for simply deleting the character, moving the cursor (in the Insert mode) to the right of where you want the character moved, and typing the character again. But if you find that you often have to correct letter reversals, such as reversing the *i* and *e* in the misspelled word *recieve,* then you can create a simple macro that will reverse letters for you whenever you invoke the macro. (See Chapter 13 for an explanation of how to create this macro.)

Erasing and Editing: Groups of Words, Lines, Sentences, and Paragraphs

When you have to erase or edit segments of text larger than individual characters, use the **C**opy, **M**ove, or **E**rase commands from the DOC menu. These commands, when used with the various cursor-movement keys, will make your job of changing and correcting text quite easy.

The **Erase** Command and Key

When you need to erase a group of words, one or more lines, sentences, paragraphs, or larger segments of text, the **Erase** command from the DOC menu and the Erase (F4) key make the procedure easy. **E**rase also enables you to delete format lines and print attributes from the text. When you use **E**rase, keep the following points in mind:

1. Once you erase a block of text, you cannot retrieve the erased text in the current worksheet.

2. Because the **E**rase command can erase data outside the DOC window area in which you are working, be careful when you indicate the block to be erased. To prevent accidentally erasing data, set a restrict range for your DOC window and make sure that the restrict range doesn't overlap data that you don't want changed.

3. You can place the cursor at either the beginning or end of the block you want to erase.

4. If **A**uto-Justify is turned on, paragraphs will be automatically justified after you complete the **E**rase operation.

The procedure for erasing blocks of text requires four steps. First, position the cursor at the beginning or end of the block you want to erase. Second, initiate the **E**rase command by pressing the Erase key or selecting **E**rase from the DOC menu. Third, indicate the block you want to erase by moving the cursor to the end or back to the beginning of the block. (See the lists below for ways to move the cursor to the end of a block.) Fourth, press RETURN.

If you are erasing a format line, Symphony will automatically highlight the whole line. You cannot erase, move, or copy only part of a format line. When erasing text, use the appropriate cursor-movement key for highlighting the area you want erased.

Use the following:	To erase:
Ctrl →	A word
End →	A line
End then the end punctuation of the sentence (. ? !)	A sentence (which doesn't contain these marks inside the sentence

End ↓	A paragraph or portion of text from anywhere in a paragraph to the end of the paragraph
End then Home	A section that ends with the end of your text or the end of the window's restrict area

Moving Text within the Same File

The **M**ove command from the DOC menu enables you to move characters, words, sentences, or larger blocks of text to any area (1) within the DOC window's restrict range if you have set one, or (2) within the worksheet if the restrict range is set to **N**one. Be careful, however, when you are using the **M**ove command because it can affect data in other windows.

Using **M**ove, like using the **C**opy command, requires following these guidelines:

1. The area where you are moving TO must be within the DOC window's restrict range. If, for example, you are moving 20 lines of text to the end of your present text located at line 590, and you have set your restrict range at 600, Symphony will display the message "Not enough room in the Restrict range." To correct this problem, change **W**indow **S**ettings **R**estrict.

2. Whenever you are moving text to an area within other text, Symphony will move all existing text down. Symphony will also automatically justify the text, if **F**ormat **S**ettings **A**uto-Justify is set to **Y**es. Otherwise, you must justify the text by pressing the Justify key (F2) or using the **J**ustify command in the DOC menu.

3. Using the **Move** command can affect data entered in other types of windows on the same worksheet. For example, a spreadsheet entered below the DOC window area can be affected by **Move** if you do not restrict the range for the DOC window.

4. When you use the DOC **Move** command, it does not overwrite other data, as does the SHEET **Move** command.

With these guidelines in mind, you will find that using the **Move** command is fairly easy. To move any portion of text, you must position the cursor at the beginning of the text you want moved. (See fig. 7.17A.) Then select **Move** from the DOC menu. When "Move FROM what block?" appears, indicate the area to be moved by moving the cursor. (See fig. 7.17B.) Use the appropriate cursor-movement keys for highlighting the area you want moved.

Use the following:	To move:
Ctrl →	A word
End →	A line
End then the end punctuation of the sentence (. ? !)	A sentence (that doesn't contain these marks inside the sentence)
End ↓	A paragraph or a portion of text from anywhere in a paragraph to the end of the paragraph
End then Home	A section of text that ends with the end of your text or the end of the window's restrict range

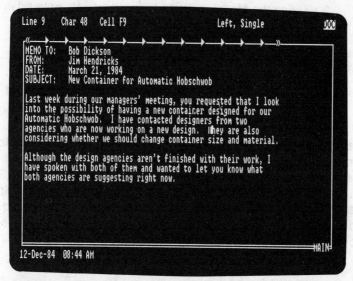

Fig. 7.17A.

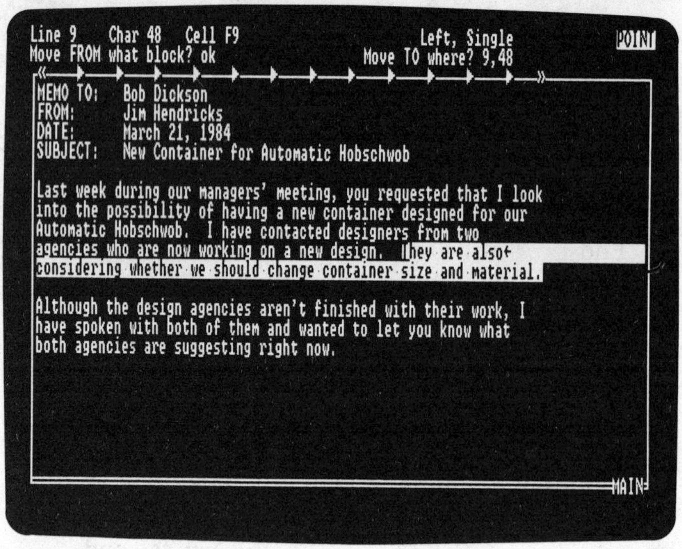

Fig. 7.17B.

After you indicate the move FROM area, you next indicate move TO
by moving the cursor to the place where you want the text to begin.

Then you press RETURN. If **A**uto-Justify is set to **N**o in **F**ormat **S**ettings of the DOC menu, you may need to justify the paragraph by pressing the Justify key or by selecting **J**ustify from the DOC menu. (See fig. 7.17C.)

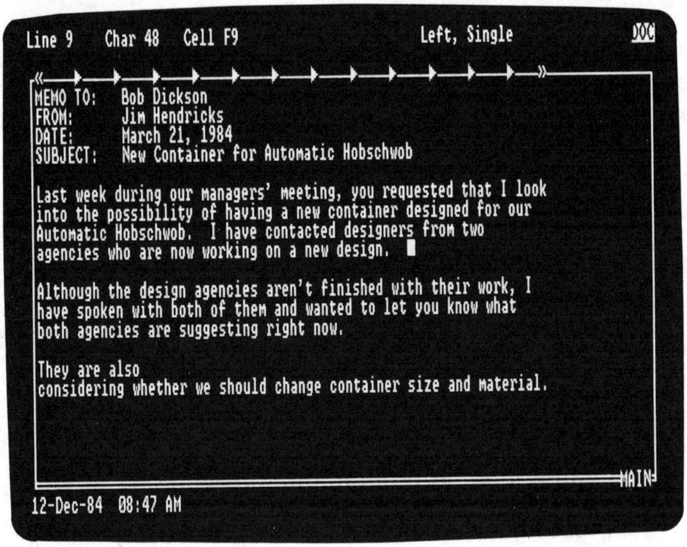

```
 Line 9    Char 48   Cell F9                    Left, Single         DOC
«───►───►───►───►───►───►───►───►───►───►───►───»
MEMO TO:   Bob Dickson
FROM:      Jim Hendricks
DATE:      March 21, 1984
SUBJECT:   New Container for Automatic Hobschwob

Last week during our managers' meeting, you requested that I look
into the possibility of having a new container designed for our
Automatic Hobschwob.  I have contacted designers from two
agencies who are now working on a new design. ▮

Although the design agencies aren't finished with their work, I
have spoken with both of them and wanted to let you know what
both agencies are suggesting right now.

They are also
considering whether we should change container size and material.

                                                              ═MAIN═
 12-Dec-84  08:47 AM
```

Fig. 7.17C.

If you want to move text to an area in another DOC window, when the "Move TO where?" prompt appears, press the Window key (F6). You may need to press the Window key several times until the window appears where you want the text copied. Once the cursor is positioned in the correct window, move the cursor to the place where the text should begin. Press RETURN to complete the move operation.

Moving Text to a Document in Another File

If you want to move text to a document in another file, you can use the procedure described below in the section on Copying Text from One File to Another, with one additional step. After you copy a block from one file to another, you can then delete the original block if it isn't needed in the file where the block was first located.

Copying Text within the Same File

Copy, the first command on the DOC menu, enables you to copy characters, words, lines, or larger blocks of text to another blank area of the worksheet. Following are a few guidelines for using the Copy command:

1. The area where you are copying to must be within the DOC window's restrict range, and the restrict range should be large enough to accommodate the copied text. When you use the Copy command, text following the copied portion will move down; enough room should be available within the restrict range for the text to move down.

2. After you copy text to another part of the window, Symphony will automatically justify the text and all the following paragraphs if Format Settings Auto-Justify is set to Yes. Otherwise, you must justify the text by pressing the Justify key or using the Justify command in the DOC menu.

3. Using the Copy command can affect data entered in other types of windows on the same worksheet. For example, a spreadsheet entered below the DOC window area can be affected by Copy if you do not restrict the range for the DOC window.

4. When you use the DOC Copy command, it does not overwrite other data, as does the SHEET Copy command.

If you follow these guidelines when you use the Copy command, the procedure will be fairly easy. To copy any portion of text, position the cursor at the beginning of the text to be copied. Then select Copy from the DOC menu. When "Copy FROM what block?" appears, indicate the area to be copied by moving the cursor. (See fig. 7.18A.) Use the appropriate cursor-movement keys to highlight the areas you want copied.

Use the following:	To copy:
Ctrl →	A word
End →	A line
End then the end punctuation of the sentence (. ? !)	A sentence (that doesn't contain these marks inside the sentence)
End ↓	A paragraph or text from anywhere in a paragraph to the end of the paragraph
End then Home	A section of text that ends with the end of your text or the end of the window's restrict range

After you indicate the copy FROM area, you next indicate copy TO by moving the cursor to the place where you want the copied text to begin. (See fig. 7.18B.) Then you press RETURN. If Auto-Justify is set to No in Format Settings of the DOC menu, you may need to justify the paragraph by pressing the Justify key or by selecting Justify from the DOC menu. (See fig. 7.18C.)

If you want to copy to an area in another DOC window, when the "Copy TO where?" prompt appears, press the Window key (F6). You will need to press the Window key a few times until the window appears where you want the text to be copied. Once the cursor is positioned in the correct window, move the cursor to the place where the copied text should begin. Press RETURN to complete the copy operation.

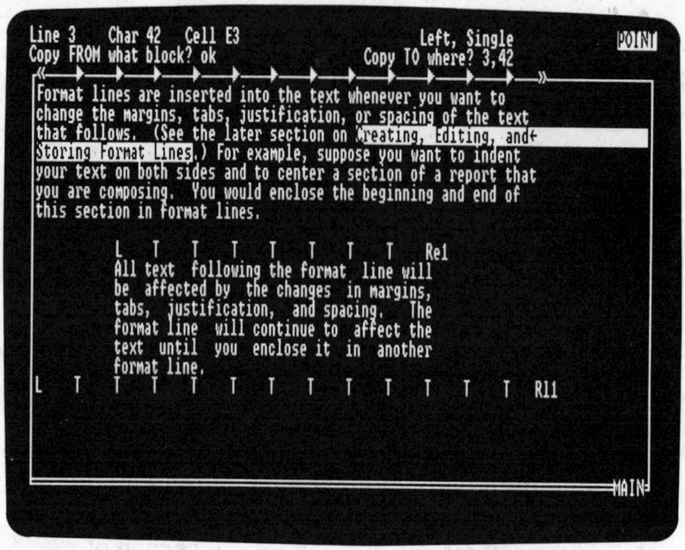

Fig. 7.18A.

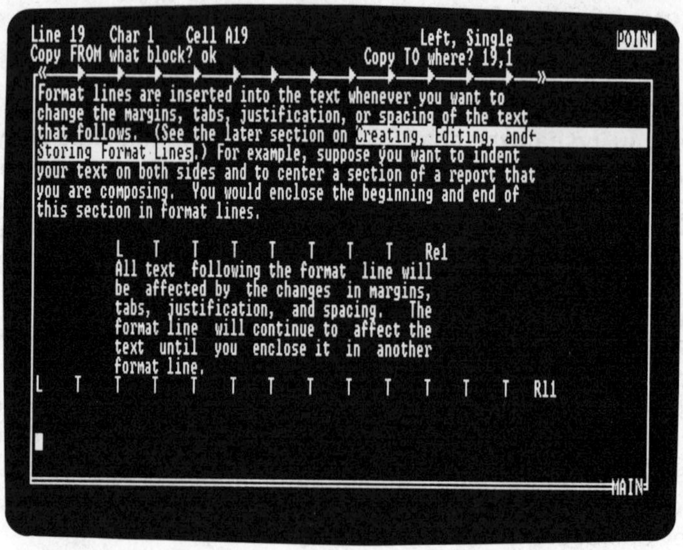

Fig. 7.18B.

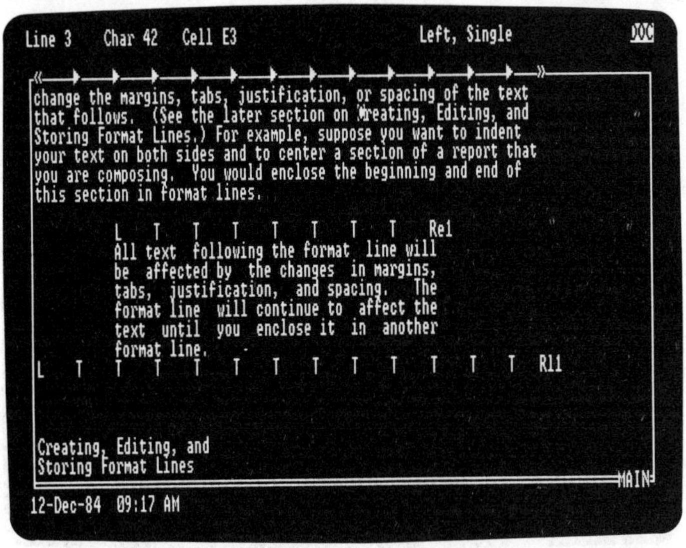

Fig. 7.18C.

Copying Text from One File to Another

In addition to copying text from one area to another within the same window or from one window to another, you can also copy text to other files. You may want to copy text from an existing file to another existing file. Or you may want to copy text from an existing file to a new file.

The first procedure described here should be followed for copying text from one file to another existing file. Suppose, for example, you are writing a letter to a client to promote a new product your company is introducing. (See fig. 7.19A.) As you begin writing the letter, you realize that a paragraph from text in another file will fit well into your letter.

Follow these steps for copying the paragraph into your letter:

1. Using SERVICES File Save, save the current worksheet that contains the beginning of the letter to a client.

2. Using SERVICES File Retrieve, retrieve the file containing the paragraph you want to copy into the letter.

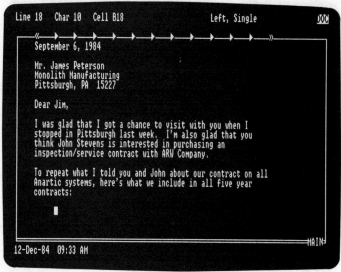

Line 18   Char 10   Cell B18   Left, Single   DOC

«—→—▶—→—▶—→—▶—→—▶—→——»
September 6, 1984

Mr. James Peterson
Monolith Manufacturing
Pittsburgh, PA 15227

Dear Jim,

I was glad that I got a chance to visit with you when I
stopped in Pittsburgh last week. I'm also glad that you
think John Stevens is interested in purchasing an
inspection/service contract with ARW Company.

To repeat what I told you and John about our contract on all
Anartic systems, here's what we include in all five year
contracts:

    ▮

                                                        MAIN
12-Dec-84 09:33 AM

Fig. 7.19A.

3. When the worksheet for the second file appears, move
   your cursor to the paragraph you want to copy. (See
   fig. 7.19B.)

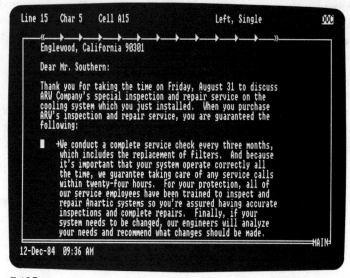

Line 15   Char 5   Cell A15   Left, Single   DOC

«—→—▶—→—▶—→—▶—→—▶—→——»
Englewood, California 90301

Dear Mr. Southern:

Thank you for taking the time on Friday, August 31 to discuss
ARW Company's special inspection and repair service on the
cooling system which you just installed. When you purchase
ARW's inspection and repair service, you are guaranteed the
following:

    ▮ →We conduct a complete service check every three months,
         which includes the replacement of filters. And because
         it's important that your system operate correctly all
         the time, we guarantee taking care of any service calls
         within twenty-four hours. For your protection, all of
         our service employees have been trained to inspect and
         repair Anartic systems so you're assured having accurate
         inspections and complete repairs. Finally, if your
         system needs to be changed, our engineers will analyze
         your needs and recommend what changes should be made.

                                                        MAIN
12-Dec-84 09:36 AM

Fig. 7.19B.

4. Switch from a DOC to a SHEET window by pressing the TYPE key and selecting SHEET.

5. Retrieve the SHEET command MENU, select **R**ange, then select **N**ame **C**reate. (See the section on Range Names in Chapter 4.)

6. Enter a range name for the paragraph when the prompt "Range name: " appears.

7. Indicate the range for the paragraph you want to copy. (Notice that in SHEET mode, word-processing text appears as long labels originating in column A.) (See fig. 7.19C.)

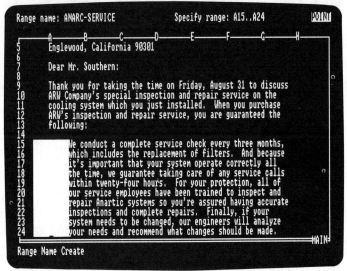

Fig. 7.19C.

8. Using SERVICES **F**ile **S**ave, save the file with its new range name.

9. Using SERVICES **F**ile **R**etrieve, retrieve the file containing the letter into which you want to copy the paragraph.

10. Place the cursor at the beginning of where you want to copy the paragraph. Make sure enough blank space is below the cursor to accommodate the paragraph.

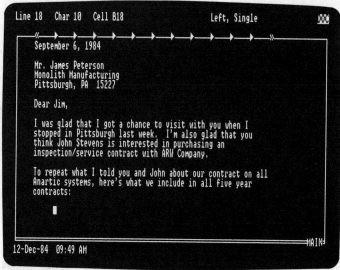

```
 Line 18   Char 10   Cell B18            Left, Single        DOC
 «──►──►──►──►──►──►──►──►──►──►──►──►──»
   September 6, 1984

   Mr. James Peterson
   Monolith Manufacturing
   Pittsburgh, PA  15227

   Dear Jim,

   I was glad that I got a chance to visit with you when I
   stopped in Pittsburgh last week.  I'm also glad that you
   think John Stevens is interested in purchasing an
   inspection/service contract with ARW Company.

   To repeat what I told you and John about our contract on all
   Anartic systems, here's what we include in all five year
   contracts:

       ▌




 12-Dec-84  09:49 AM                                          MAIN
```

Fig. 7.19D.

Otherwise, the paragraph will overwrite existing text. (See fig. 7.19D.)

11. Select SERVICES **F**ile **C**ombine, select **C**opy, select **R**ange name, and finally type in the range name for the paragraph.

12. Next, indicate whether you want to preserve line markers in the paragraph text.

13. Select the file where the paragraph is stored and press RETURN.

The paragraph should now be copied into your letter. (See fig. 7.19E.)

If you find that you frequently copy a particular section of text from one file to another, you may want to create a separate file for the section of text that you frequently want copied into other files. Copying a section of text involves using the SERVICES **F**ile **X**tract command and requires the following steps:

1. To copy a section of text, retrieve the file containing the text you want to copy (use SERVICES **F**ile **R**etrieve), and place the cursor at the beginning of that text.

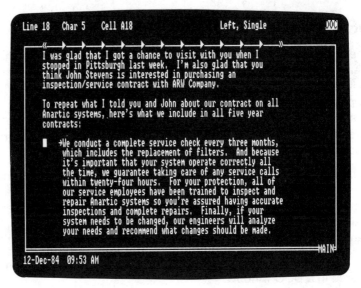

Line 18   Char 5   Cell A18   Left, Single   DOC

I was glad that I got a chance to visit with you when I
stopped in Pittsburgh last week. I'm also glad that you
think John Stevens is interested in purchasing an
inspection/service contract with ARW Company.

To repeat what I told you and John about our contract on all
Anartic systems, here's what we include in all five year
contracts:

■   →We conduct a complete service check every three months,
    which includes the replacement of filters. And because
    it's important that your system operate correctly all
    the time, we guarantee taking care of any service calls
    within twenty-four hours. For your protection, all of
    our service employees have been trained to inspect and
    repair Anartic systems so you're assured having accurate
    inspections and complete repairs. Finally, if your
    system needs to be changed, our engineers will analyze
    your needs and recommend what changes should be made.

                                                        MAIN
12-Dec-84 09:53 AM

Fig. 7.19E.

2. Select the **F**ile **X**tract command from the SERVICES menu.

3. If you are *not* extracting any spreadsheet data, press RETURN at the "Preserve Formulas" prompt.

4. When the "Xtract file name: " prompt appears, enter a name for the file where the text will be copied.

5. Indicate the range of the text you want copied and press RETURN.

Your section of text is then copied into the new file. (If you don't supply an extension, .WRK will be used.) Whenever you want to copy this text into another document, use the SERVICES **F**ile **C**ombine command, described earlier in this section. If you are copying the entire file into your current file, select **E**ntire-File instead of **N**amed-Area after you select **F**ile **C**ombine **C**opy.

As with many Symphony word-processing operations, you can also create macros for the copy operations described in this section. (See Chapter 13 for an explanation of creating such macros.)

Searching and Replacing

One feature that distinguishes word-processing programs is their search and replace capabilities. Programs differ in their speed for completing search and replace operations, in the options available for performing these operations, and in the ease of using them. In most respects, Symphony's search and replace capabilities compare favorably to similar capabilities of many sophisticated word-processing programs.

Symphony, for example, provides both forward and backward search, performs search and replace operations quickly, and makes using search and replace operations quite easy. **S**earch and **R**eplace are separate commands located in Symphony's DOC menu.

You can search for and replace the following types of strings entered in a DOC window:

- A single character, including those characters in the Lotus International Character set: a, 4, &, *

- A cluster of characters (for example, prefixes and suffixes such as *ed*), with no cluster containing more than 50 characters and spaces

- A single word

- Groups of words and characters, with no group containing more than a total of 50 characters and spaces (See fig. 7.20.)

When the string to be searched for is composed of words, the search is affected by whether the words are entered in uppercase or lowercase.

If you search for:	Symphony finds:
1. All lowercase	Any combination of uppercase and lowercase letters
Example:	
tutorial program	tutorial program Tutorial Program Tutorial program

Color Section of Graphs and Charts

See related text in Chapters 9 and 10.

COLOR ADDED

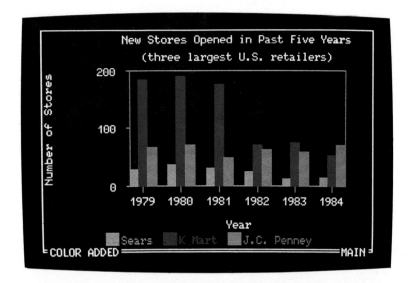

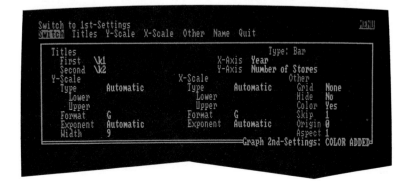

CHANGE COLOR

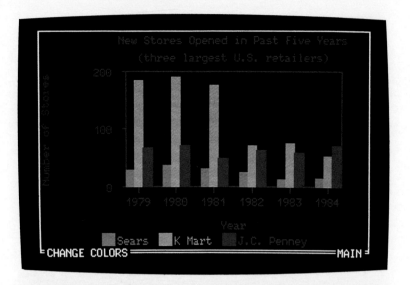

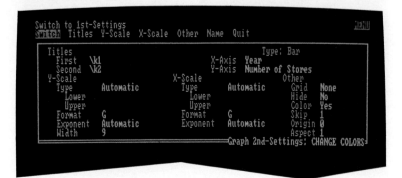

PIE COLORS

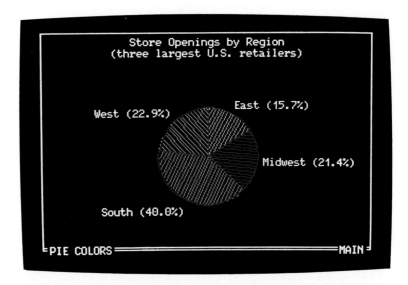

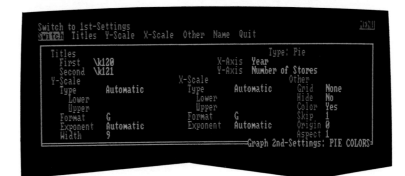

ALTERNATE COLOR

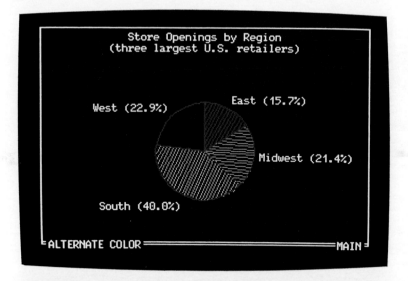

Store Openings by Region
(three largest U.S. retailers)

West (22.9%)

East (15.7%)

Midwest (21.4%)

South (40.0%)

ALTERNATE COLOR ══════════════════════ MAIN

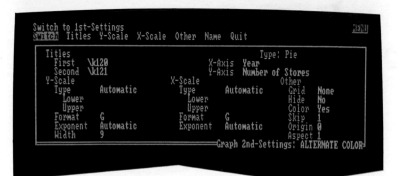

Switch to 2nd-Settings   MENU
SWITCH Type Range Hue Format Data-Labels Legend Cancel Name Quit

     Type: Pie

Range   Hue Format Data-Labels   Legend

X J145..J148   1
A K145..K148   2
B M145..M148   3
C   4
D   5
E   6
F   7
                              Graph 1st-Settings: ALTERNATE COLOR

Switch to 1st-Settings   MENU
SWITCH Titles Y-Scale X-Scale Other Name Quit

  Titles   Type: Pie
    First   \k120   X-Axis   Year
    Second   \k121   Y-Axis   Number of Stores
  Y-Scale   X-Scale   Other
    Type   Automatic   Type   Automatic   Grid   None
    Lower   Lower   Hide   No
    Upper   Upper   Color   Yes
    Format   G   Format   G   Skip   1
    Exponent Automatic   Exponent Automatic   Origin 0
    Width   9   Aspect 1
                              Graph 2nd-Settings: ALTERNATE COLOR

EXPLODED WEST

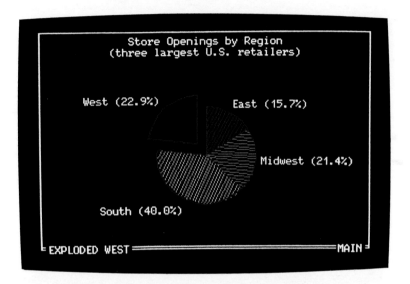

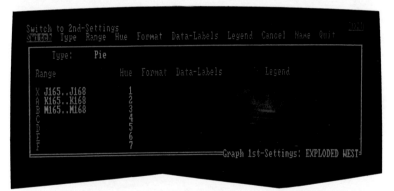

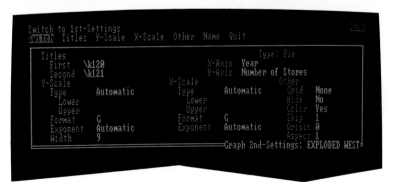

EXPLODE TWO

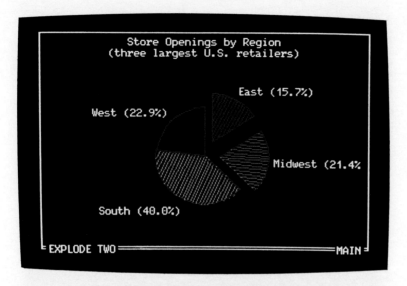

```
                Store Openings by Region
                (three largest U.S. retailers)

                                    East (15.7%)

        West (22.9%)


                                          Midwest (21.4%


        South (40.0%)

  ⊢EXPLODE TWO═══════════════════════════════MAIN ⊣
```

```
Switch to 2nd-Settings                                    MENU
Switch  Type  Range  Hue  Format  Data-Labels  Legend  Cancel  Name  Quit

     Type:    Pie

  Range              Hue  Format  Data-Labels     Legend

  X J185..J188        1
  A K185..K188        2
  B M185..M188        3
  C                   4
  D                   5
  E                   6
  F                   7
                                          ═Graph 1st-Settings: EXPLODE TWO═
```

```
Switch to 1st-Settings                                    MENU
Switch  Titles  Y-Scale  X-Scale  Other  Name  Quit

  Titles                                     Type: Pie
    First   \k120              X-Axis  Year
    Second  \k121              Y-Axis  Number of Stores
  Y-Scale                    X-Scale                    Other
    Type    Automatic          Type    Automatic          Grid    None
    Lower                      Lower                       Hide    No
    Upper                      Upper                       Color   Yes
    Format  G                  Format  G                   Skip    1
    Exponent Automatic         Exponent Automatic          Origin  0
    Width   9                                              Aspect  1
                                          ═Graph 2nd-Settings: EXPLODE TWO═
```

XY GRAPH

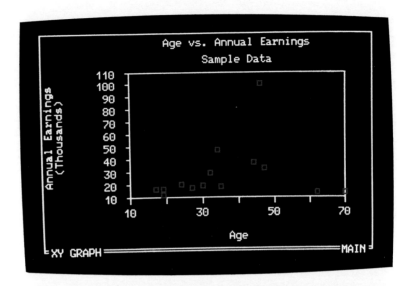

Switch to 2nd-Settings
Switch Type Range Hue Format Data-Labels Legend Cancel Name Quit

```
     Type:    XY

Range                  Hue  Format  Data-Labels        Legend

X  J206..J219           1
A  L206..L219           2   Symbols
B                       3   Both
C                       4   Both
D                       5   Both
E                       6   Both
F                       7   Both
                                            ═Graph 1st-Settings: XY GRAPH═
```

Switch to 1st-Settings
Switch Titles Y-Scale X-Scale Other Name Quit

```
                                                    Type: XY
 Titles
   First    \j200                 X-Axis   Age
   Second   \j201                 Y-Axis   Annual Earnings
 Y-Scale                  X-Scale                  Other
   Type      Automatic      Type      Automatic      Grid     None
   Lower                    Lower                    Hide     No
   Upper                    Upper                    Color    Yes
   Format    G              Format    G              Skip     1
   Exponent  Automatic      Exponent  Automatic      Origin   0
   Width     9                                       Aspect   1
                                            ═Graph 2nd-Settings: XY GRAPH═
```

HIGH GRAPH

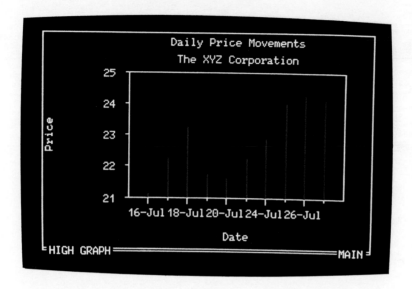

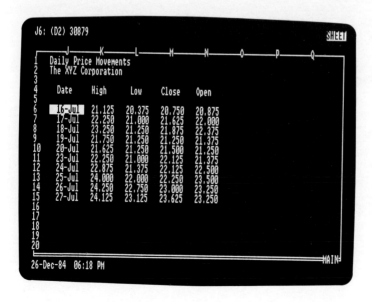

HIGH-LOW GRAPH

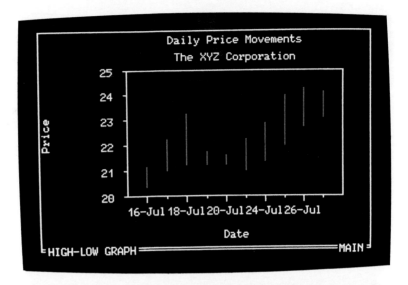

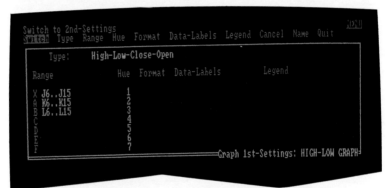

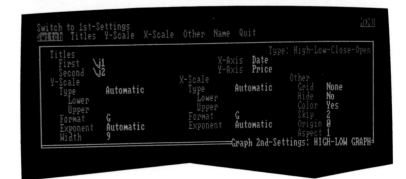

HI-LO-CLOS-OPEN

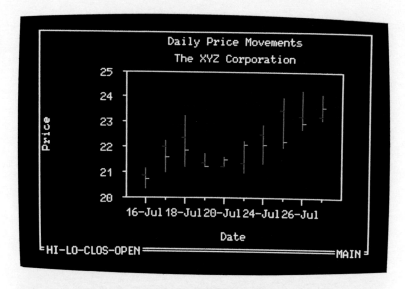

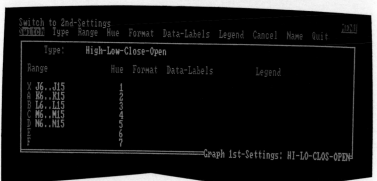

BILLIONS

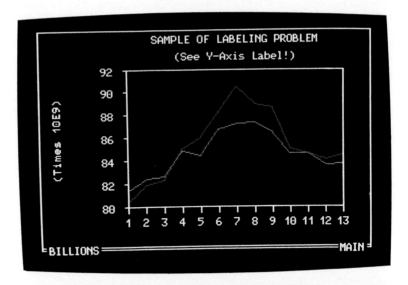

BILLIONS2

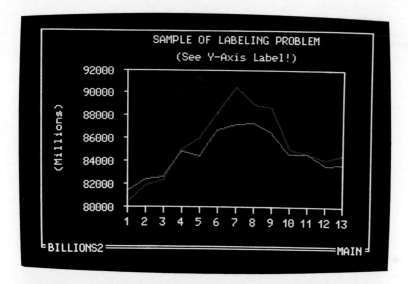

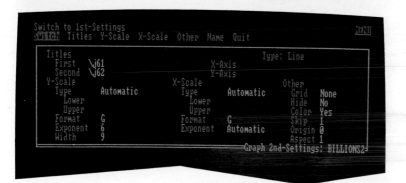

HIDE OUTSIDE

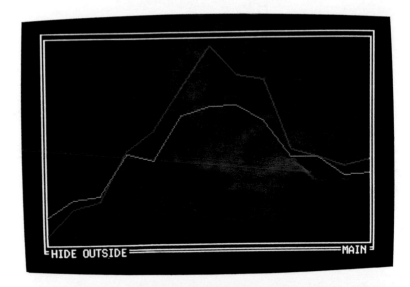

HIDE SCALES

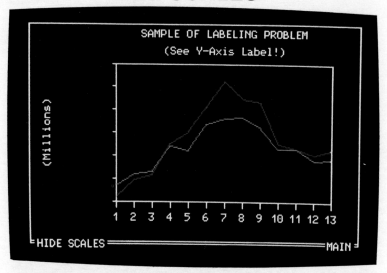

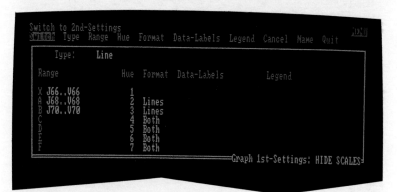

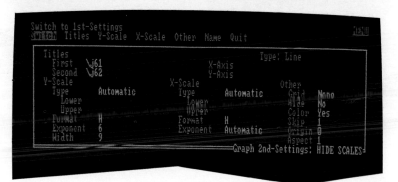

DATA

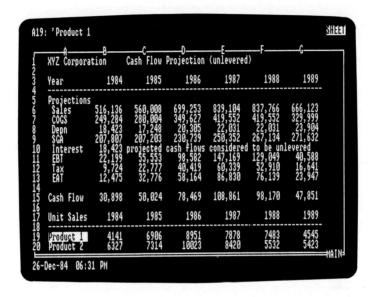

```
A19: 'Product 1                                                    SHEET
      A          B         C         D         E         F         G
  1  XYZ Corporation   Cash Flow Projection (unlevered)
  2
  3  Year          1984      1985      1986      1987      1988      1989
  4  --------------------------------------------------------------------
  5  Projections
  6  Sales      516,136   560,008   699,253   839,104   837,766   666,123
  7  COGS       249,284   280,004   349,627   419,552   419,552   329,999
  8  Depn        18,423    17,248    20,305    22,031    22,031    23,904
  9  SGA        207,807   207,203   230,739   250,352   267,134   271,632
 10  Interest    18,423  projected cash flows considered to be unlevered
 11  EBT         22,199    55,553    98,582   147,169   129,049    40,588
 12  Tax          9,724    22,777    40,419    60,339    52,910    16,641
 13  EAT         12,475    32,776    58,164    86,830    76,139    23,947
 14
 15  Cash Flow   30,898    50,024    78,469   108,861    98,170    47,851
 16
 17  Unit Sales    1984      1985      1986      1987      1988      1989
 18  --------------------------------------------------------------------
 19  Product 1     4141      6906      8951      7878      7483      4545
 20  Product 2     6327      7314     10023      8420      5532      5423
                                                                   MAIN
26-Dec-84  06:31 PM
```

This is the data used to create the graphs that follow in this section.

SIMPLE BAR

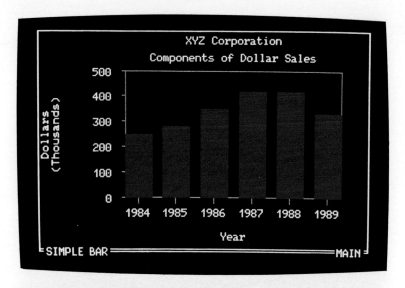

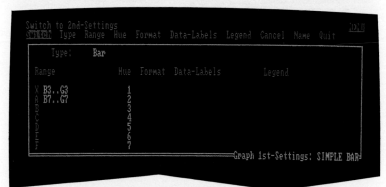

MORE BARS

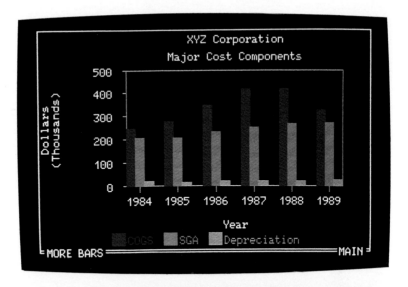

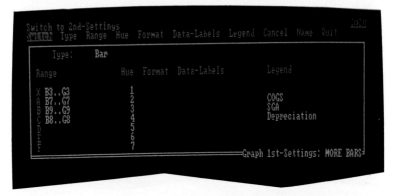

STACKED BAR

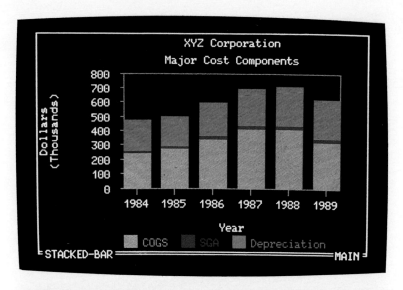

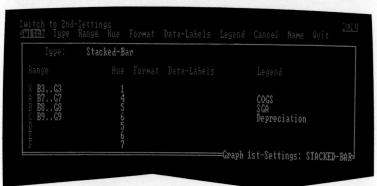

PIE

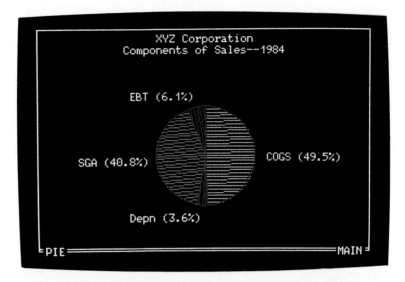

PIE2

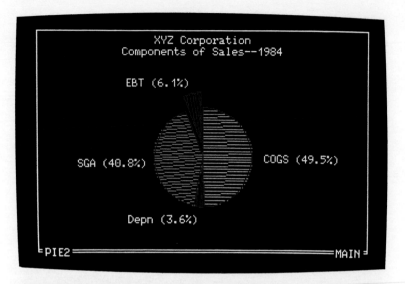

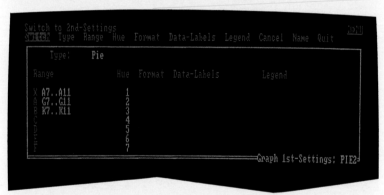

XY GRAPH

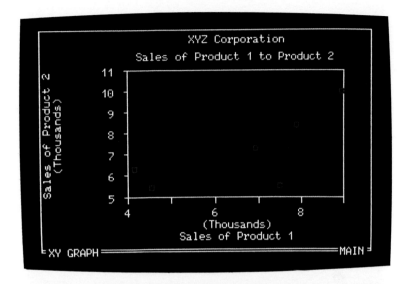

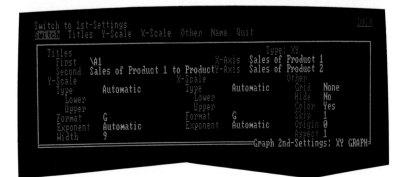

LINE

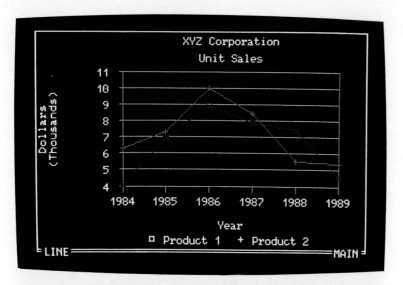

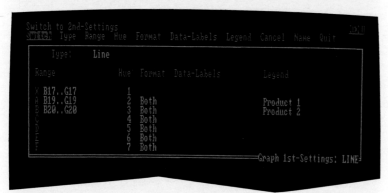

```
Replace this occurrence and resume typing                        MENU
Once Continue Skip All-Remaining Quit
«‹—►—►—►—►—►—►—►—►—►—►—►—►—►——»›
Format lines are inserted into the text whenever you want to
change the margins, tabs, justification, or spacing of the text
that follows.  (See the later section on Creating, Editing, and†
Storing Format Lines.) For example, suppose you want to indent
your text on both sides and to center a section of a report that
you are composing.  You would enclose the beginning and end of
this section in format lines.

        L    T    T    T    T    T    T    T   Re1
        All text  following the format  line will
        be  affected by  the changes  in margins,
        tabs,  justification,  and spacing.   The
        format line  will continue to  affect the
        text until  you  enclose it  in  another
        format line.
L    T    T    T    T    T    T    T    T    T    T    T   R11

If you are composing a report that contains special indented
materials, such as tables or lists, a format line can format
these individual sections each time you begin to create the table
                                                            MAIN
Replace
```

Fig. 7.20.

2. Initial letter capitalized	Initial letter capitalized, but other letters can be either uppercase or lowercase
Example:	
Tutorial Program	Tutorial Program
3. All uppercase	Only all uppercase
Example:	
TUTORIAL PROGRAM	TUTORIAL PROGRAM

When you are searching once for a single character, use the End key and then type the character if you are performing a forward search. If, however, you want to search more than once, or if you want to search backward for a single character, you need to use the Search command in the DOC menu. Although the Search command performs both forward and backward searches, the Replace command will only search for and replace a string by working forward through the text. To overcome this limitation, you can create a simple macro that will automatically move the cursor to the beginning of your document and initiate the **R**eplace command. (See Chapter 13.)

The **S**earch Command

If you follow the guidelines provided earlier, you will find the **S**earch command quite easy to use. To begin the search, retrieve the DOC menu and select **S**earch. When the prompt "Search for what?" appears, enter the string you want Symphony to search for and press RETURN. Symphony will then provide the following options for searching the text:

Forward   Backward   Quit

Select either of the first two options to initiate the document search. When Symphony finds the first occurrence of the string, the cursor will highlight it. At this point, you have two options. You can continue the search by selecting either **F**orward or **B**ackward, or you can select **Q**uit. When you select **Q**uit, the cursor remains at the location of the string so that you can edit, move, or delete the string. Pressing Ctrl-Break before **Q**uit, on the other hand, will move the cursor back to its original position where you initiated the **S**earch command.

If Symphony cannot find the string in the direction you indicated, Symphony will display "String not found" in the bottom left corner of your screen. You can then select **B**ackward to begin the search in the opposite direction, or select **Q**uit to move from the MENU mode back to the DOC mode.

The **R**eplace Command

To use the **R**eplace command, you must retrieve the DOC menu and select **R**eplace. When the prompt "Replace what?" appears, enter the string you want Symphony to search for and press RETURN. Symphony will then ask, "Replace it with what?" Next, enter the replacement string and press RETURN again.

Symphony will begin the search at this point for the first occurrence of the string, conducting a forward search from the cursor to the end of the document. If Symphony does not find the string, Symphony will display "String not found" in the bottom left corner of the screen and return you to the "Replace what?" prompt. But if a first occurrence of the string is found, Symphony displays the following menu:

Once   Continue   Skip   All-Remaining   Quit

If you select **O**nce, Symphony replaces the string and returns to the DOC mode. If you select **C**ontinue, Symphony replaces the string and searches for the next occurrence of the string. When the next occurrence is found, Symphony again waits for you to respond by selecting any of the items from the menu. If you select **S**kip, Symphony skips over the string and moves on in its search for the next occurrence. When you select **A**ll-Remaining, Symphony finds and replaces every occurrence of the string, beginning at the position of the cursor and ending at the end of the document. After completing the search and replace operations, Symphony displays "No more occurrences found." You then select **Q**uit from the menu to return to the DOC mode.

While writing this chapter, when we discovered that we had misspelled *occurrence* as *occurence,* we began a search-and-replace operation. We entered *occurence* at the "Search for what?" prompt, then entered *occurrence* at the "Replace with what?" prompt. After Symphony found the first occurrence of the misspelled word, we chose **A**ll-Remaining, and Symphony then replaced all other misspellings of this word to the end of the document.

Formatting Your Document

For text entered in Symphony's DOC window, you can set the format in three ways. First, you can control format through the SERVICES **C**onfiguration **D**ocument settings. Second, you can control format through **F**ormat **S**ettings in the DOC menu. Third, you can control format by creating format lines within the DOC window.

Configuration **D**ocument settings, **F**ormat **S**ettings, and format lines were discussed earlier, including the effects they have on one another. This section describes the different kinds of format commands and how they affect text as it appears on the screen and as it is printed.

Paragraph Justification

You can set and regulate paragraph justification in a number of ways. The **J**ustification setting in both SERVICES **C**onfiguration **D**ocument settings and DOC **F**ormat **S**ettings controls paragraph justification within each window. Remember that **F**ormat **S**ettings overrides **C**onfiguration **D**ocument settings. However, in the DOC window in a worksheet, the format settings are inherited from the **C**onfiguration **D**ocument settings of the SERVICES menu. Whatever justification setting is in effect in DOC **F**ormat **S**ettings or a format line controls automatic justification when turned on, and controls the changes made when you invoke the Justify key and the **J**ustify command.

Auto-Justify

You can set paragraph justification to an **A**utomatic or **M**anual setting. The default setting is **A**utomatic, set in **C**onfiguration **D**ocument **A**uto-Justify of the SERVICES menu. The **A**uto-Justify setting in **F**ormat **S**ettings in the DOC menu inherits the default setting. You can override the **A**uto-Justify setting in **C**onfiguration **D**ocument by changing the setting in the DOC **F**ormat **S**ettings.

Whenever **A**uto-Justify is set to **Y**es in the DOC **F**ormat **S**ettings, paragraphs are automatically justified when you disturb the original justification by using the **C**opy, **E**rase, **M**ove, or **R**eplace commands from the DOC menu. Paragraphs are justified according to the margin settings and justification settings that control margins— either DOC **F**ormat **S**ettings or a format line. If you change the margins and/or justification manually for any part of your text, the **A**uto-Justify setting can affect that text, changing it to the margins and justification controlling the text around that portion.

For example, suppose you need to indent a section of text. Instead of using a format line or the Indent key (described later), you format the section manually by using the Tab key to indent the beginning of each line. If you use the **C**opy, **M**ove, **E**rase, or **R**eplace commands in this section of text, and you have set **A**uto-Justify to **Y**es, the text will be justified to the setting controlling the text around the section of text to be indented. (See figs. 7.21A and 7.21B.)

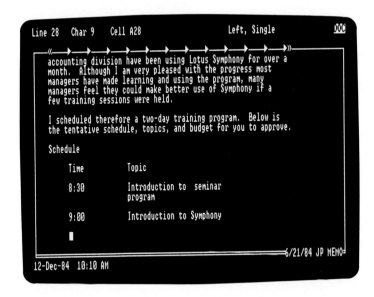

Fig. 7.21A.

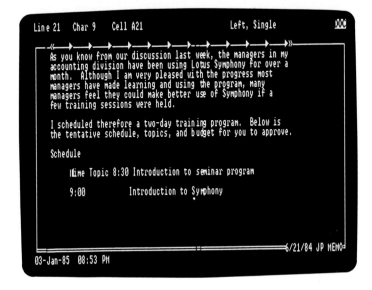

Fig. 7.21B.

The Justify Key and Command

In addition to justifying paragraphs automatically, you can justify paragraphs or larger units of text by using the Justify key (F2) or the Justify command in the DOC menu. If, for example, you decide to turn off **A**uto-Justify (**N**o), you can then use the Justify key or the Justify command every time you need to justify a paragraph. Suppose you want to erase the second sentence of the paragraph shown in figure 7.22A. If **A**uto-Justify is turned off, then after you erase the sentence, you need to press Justify. (See fig. 7.22B.)

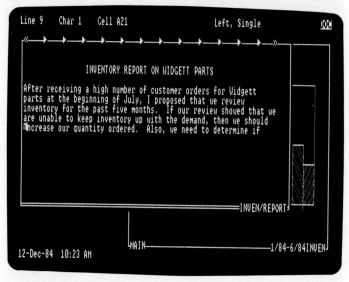

Fig. 7.22A.

The **J**ustify command in the DOC menu is different from the Justify key in one respect. When you select **J**ustify from the DOC menu, you have two choices: **P**aragraph and **A**ll-Remaining. Selecting **P**aragraph performs the same operations that are performed by the Justify key. Selecting **A**ll-Remaining justifies not only the paragraph where the cursor is located but all following paragraphs, to the end of the document. Even when you have **A**uto-Justify turned on (**Y**es), you will still need to use the Justify key or the **J**ustify command. Whenever you delete characters, words, or larger sections of text,

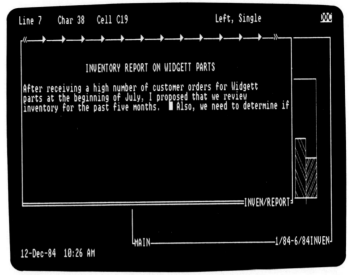

Fig. 7.22B.

using the Backspace or Del keys, you must either press the Justify key or select **J**ustify **P**aragraph.

Setting Paragraph Justification

As mentioned earlier, the Justify key, **J**ustify command, and **A**uto-Justify command operate according to the justification setting controlling a section of text. Justification can also be controlled by DOC **F**ormat **S**ettings **J**ustification or by the justification setting for a format line. DOC **F**ormat **S**ettings **J**ustification can be determined by either SERVICES **C**onfiguration **D**ocument **J**ustification, by the DOC **F**ormat **S**ettings **J**ustification of a previously created DOC window, or by you.

The **J**ustification setting for a format line, on the other hand, is determined by you if you are creating a new format line or editing one. Also, the **J**ustification setting for a format line can be determined by the DOC **F**ormat **S**ettings **J**ustification whenever you choose to reset a format line to the DOC **F**ormat **S**ettings. In any case, when you want to change justification, you are given the following four options:

None   Left   Even   Center

Whatever option is set in DOC **F**ormat **S**ettings will control justification for your DOC window unless you create a format line within the text. If you do, the format line will override **F**ormat **S**ettings **J**ustification. Keep the differences between DOC **F**ormat **S**ettings and format lines in mind.

If you change the DOC **F**ormat **S**ettings **J**ustification after you have entered text, the setting will affect all text, except text preceded by a format line. For example, the DOC **F**ormat **J**ustification setting for the text shown in figure 7.23 is **L**eft. All paragraphs in the text have the same format, so no format lines are entered. If we changed DOC **F**ormat **S**ettings **J**ustification to **E**ven, the justification automatically changes throughout the text. (See fig. 7.24.)

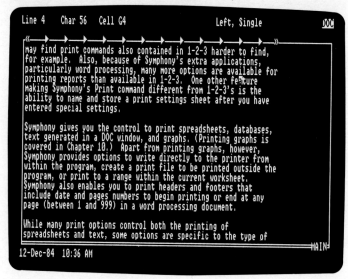

```
Line 4    Char 56   Cell G4                   Left, Single           DOC
»————►——►——►——►——►——►——►——►——►——————»
may find print commands also contained in 1-2-3 harder to find,
for example.  Also, because of Symphony's extra applications,
particularly word processing, many more options are available for
printing reports than available in 1-2-3.  One other feature
making Symphony's Print command different from 1-2-3's is the
ability to name and store a print settings sheet after you have
entered special settings.

Symphony gives you the control to print spreadsheets, databases,
text generated in a DOC window, and graphs. (Printing graphs is
covered in Chapter 10.)  Apart from printing graphs, however,
Symphony provides options to write directly to the printer from
within the program, create a print file to be printed outside the
program, or print to a range within the current worksheet.
Symphony also enables you to print headers and footers that
include date and pages numbers to begin printing or end at any
page (between 1 and 999) in a word processing document.

While many print options control both the printing of
spreadsheets and text, some options are specific to the type of
                                                              MAIN
12-Dec-84  10:36 AM
```

Fig. 7.23.

If, however, our original text contains a format line, as in figure 7.25, changing DOC **F**ormat **S**ettings **J**ustification affects all text except the text after the format line. (See fig. 7.26.)

When either the DOC **F**ormat **S**ettings or format line is set at **N**one, then automatic justification, the **J**ustify key, and the **J**ustify command are turned off. When all three are inactive, entering text on the

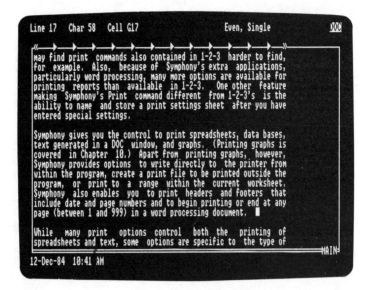

Fig. 7.24.

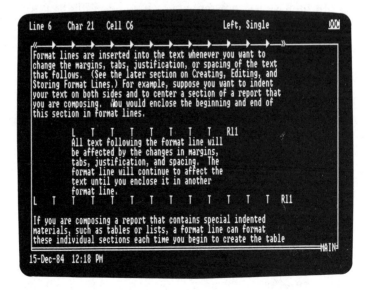

Fig. 7.25.

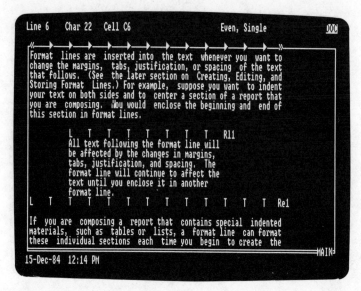

Fig. 7.26.

screen is like entering text at a typewriter. You can continue typing to the right-hand limit. In a Symphony DOC window this limit is a total of 240 characters and spaces.

With the **J**ustification **N**one setting, you control the carriage return and can thus format the section of text however you want. But if you change the **J**ustification setting from **N**one to **L**eft, **E**ven, or **C**enter, then all text, except text following format lines, will be changed.

Left is the default **J**ustification setting in **C**onfiguration **D**ocument **J**ustification in the SERVICES menu. When **J**ustification is set to **L**eft in DOC **F**ormat **S**ettings or in a format line, text is left-justified against either the default margin (1) or your margin setting. When the **J**ustification setting is **L**eft, lines on the right are ragged. (See fig. 7.27.)

As with the other three options, you can set **J**ustification to **L**eft in DOC **F**ormat **S**ettings or in a format line.

When you use the **J**ustification **E**ven setting, Symphony justifies text along both the left and right margins. (See fig. 7.28.) To justify the text on both sides, Symphony enters extra spaces within each line. In

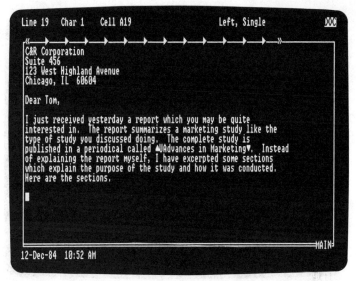

Fig. 7.27.

documents where the lines are short, **E**ven justification may leave **a** number of large spaces within the text. (See fig. 7.29.)

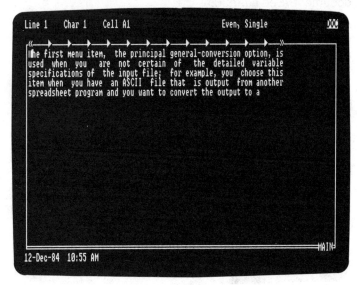

Fig. 7.28.

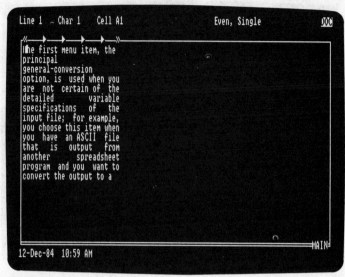

Fig. 7.29.

Center, which is the last option for **J**ustification, centers every line of text according to the left and right margins controlling the section of the document. (See fig. 7.30.)

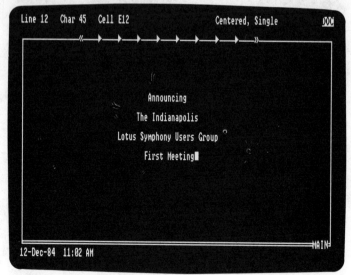

Fig. 7.30.

Setting Tabs, Spacing, and Margins

Like justification, the tab, spacing, and margin settings can be regulated by entering new settings in the **C**onfiguration **D**ocument settings of the SERVICES menu, in **F**ormat **S**ettings of the DOC menu, or in a format line. For all three types of settings, the options for changing tabs, spacing, and margins are the same. Also, the effect of one type of setting on another (for example, the effect of DOC **F**ormat **S**ettings on SERVICES **C**onfiguration **D**ocument settings) is the same as that mentioned earlier for **J**ustification.

If you want to change the tab setting, you can change the default setting of 5 (SERVICES **C**onfiguration **D**ocument **T**abs), change the tab setting for a specific DOC window (DOC **F**ormat **S**ettings **T**abs), or change the tab setting for a section of text by using a format line (**F**ormat **C**reate or **E**dit **M**argins/**T**abs). Whenever you decide to change any of these tab settings, Symphony enables you to set the spaces between tabs to any number between 1 and 240. Tab settings are indicated in the top line of the standard border of a DOC window by right arrows positioned between the left and right margin indicators.

The default setting for spacing is 1. You can, however, change spacing to double or triple in the SERVICES **C**onfiguration **D**ocument settings, in DOC **F**ormat **S**ettings, or in a format line. Whenever you change from single-spacing to double- or triple-spacing, Symphony does *not* display either double- or triple-spacing on the screen. (See figs. 7.31A and 7.31B.) Spacing is one of the few settings that control print format but not the screen display.

Even though double- or triple-spacing does not appear on the screen, you can nevertheless determine how many printed pages your text will be or how many lines are on a page. You check lines and pages by pressing the Where key (Alt + F2).

The margin settings (indicated as **L**eft and **R**ight on the command menus) in SERVICES **C**onfiguration **D**ocument settings and in DOC **F**ormat **S**ettings are displayed in the top line of the standard DOC border as two less-than and greater-than signs (<< and >>). In a format line, margins are indicated by the L and R indicators on each side of the line. (See fig. 7.32.)

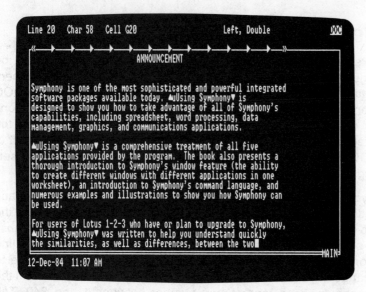

```
Line 20    Char 58    Cell G20              Left, Double           DOC
«‹═►─►─►─►─►─►─►─►─►─►─►─►─►─►─►─►─►─►═»›
                        ANNOUNCEMENT

Symphony is one of the most sophisticated and powerful integrated
software packages available today. ◢uUsing Symphony▼ is
designed to show you how to take advantage of all of Symphony's
capabilities, including spreadsheet, word processing, data
management, graphics, and communications applications.

◢uUsing Symphony▼ is a comprehensive treatment of all five
applications provided by the program.  The book also presents a
thorough introduction to Symphony's window feature (the ability
to create different windows with different applications in one
worksheet), an introduction to Symphony's command language, and
numerous examples and illustrations to show you how Symphony can
be used.

For users of Lotus 1-2-3 who have or plan to upgrade to Symphony,
◢uUsing Symphony▼ was written to help you understand quickly
the similarities, as well as differences, between the two■
                                                           ═MAIN═
12-Dec-84  11:07 AM
```

Fig. 7.31A.

If you want to set margins in either SERVICES **C**onfiguration **D**ocument settings or DOC **F**ormat **S**ettings, select **L**eft and / or **R**ight from the appropriate menu. When you are changing the left margin, Symphony will display the prompt "Default Left Margin: ". At this prompt, enter a figure between 1 and 240. When you are changing the right margin, select **R**ight. Two other prompts will appear: **S**et and **R**eset. Use **S**et when you want to enter a right margin between 1 and 240. Use **R**eset when you want the right margin adjusted to the width of the DOC window you are working in.

To set left and right margins in a format line, you delete the original L and R indicators, and enter new settings by typing **L** and **R** where you want margins set.

The left margin on your screen may be different from the left margin on printed pages. Here's how left margin settings for screen and print affect one another. If you have set the left margin for text on the screen to 1 and have set the left margin print setting to 4, Symphony will print a left margin of 5. In other words, Symphony adds the DOC left margin setting to the left margin setting for print. (See Chapter 8 for an explanation of print commands.)

ANNOUNCEMENT

Symphony is one of the most sophisticated and powerful integrated software packages available today. Using Symphony is designed to show you how to take advantage of all of Symphony's capabilities, including spreadsheet, word processing, data management, graphics, and communications applications.

Using Symphony is a comprehensive treatment of all five applications provided by the program. The book also presents a thorough introduction to Symphony's window feature (the ability to create different windows with different applications in one worksheet), an introduction to Symphony's command language, and numerous examples and illustrations to show you how Symphony can be used.

For users of Lotus 1-2-3 who have or plan to upgrade to Symphony, Using Symphony was written to help you understand quickly the similarities, as well as differences between the two programs. In every chapter, the authors explain how Symphony has expanded on and changed aspects of 1-2-3's spreadsheet, graphics, and data management capabilities.

Fig. 7.31B.

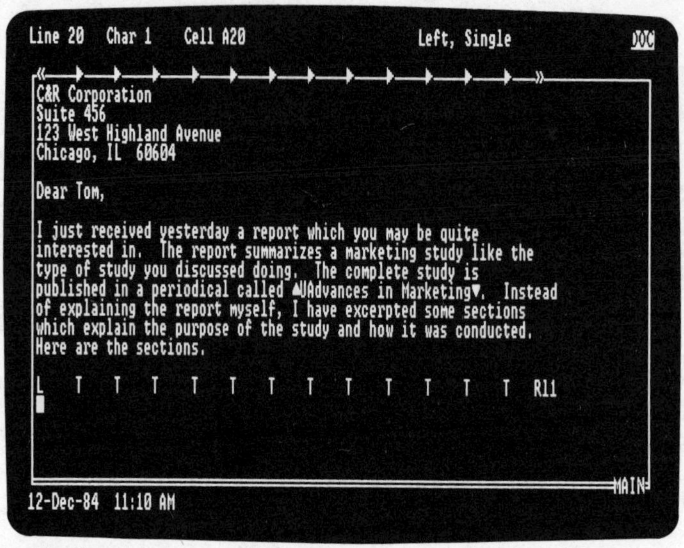

```
 Line 20   Char 1    Cell A20              Left, Single          DOC

 «——▶——▶——▶——▶——▶——▶——▶——▶——▶——▶——▶——»
 C&R Corporation
 Suite 456
 123 West Highland Avenue
 Chicago, IL  60604

 Dear Tom,

 I just received yesterday a report which you may be quite
 interested in.  The report summarizes a marketing study like the
 type of study you discussed doing.  The complete study is
 published in a periodical called ▲▼Advances in Marketing▼.  Instead
 of explaining the report myself, I have excerpted some sections
 which explain the purpose of the study and how it was conducted.
 Here are the sections.

 L    T    T    T    T    T    T    T    T    T    T   R11


                                                              ═MAIN═
 12-Dec-84  11:10 AM
```

Fig. 7.32.

Controlling Page Length and Page Breaks

Two settings in the SERVICE menu are available for controlling the number of lines of text for each printed page. First, the default value for page length is set in SERVICES Configuration Printer Page-Length. This page-length setting is stored in Symphony's configuration file (SYMPHONY.CNF). Second, you can change page length for any document you are creating by changing SERVICES Print Settings Page Length.

SERVICES Print Settings Page Length overrides SERVICES Configuration Printer Page-Length for the particular window in which you are working. If you do not change SERVICES Print Settings Page Length, the page-length setting is inherited from either SERVICES Configuration or the SERVICES Print Settings created for another window in the same worksheet.

Whenever you press the Where key (Alt + F2), Symphony will display in the bottom left corner of your screen the page and line number where the cursor is positioned. (See fig. 7.33.) The page and line numbers are determined by the setting in SERVICES **P**rint **S**ettings **P**age **L**ength. Consider the example shown in figure 7.33. If the setting for SERVICES **P**rint **S**ettings **P**age **L**ength is 66, Symphony will display "Printed page 12, Line 51" when you press the Where key. If you change the page-length setting to 33, however, Symphony will then display "Printed Page 29, Line 23" when you press the Where key.

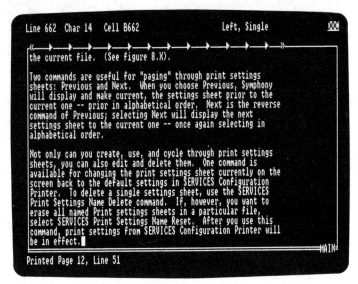

```
Line 662  Char 14   Cell B662              Left, Single        DOC
«—→—→—→—→—→—→—→—→—→—→—→—»
the current file. (See figure 8.X).

Two commands are useful for "paging" through print settings
sheets: Previous and Next. When you choose Previous, Symphony
will display and make current, the settings sheet prior to the
current one -- prior in alphabetical order. Next is the reverse
command of Previous; selecting Next will display the next
settings sheet to the current one -- once again selecting in
alphabetical order.

Not only can you create, use, and cycle through print settings
sheets, you can also edit and delete them. One command is
available for changing the print settings sheet currently on the
screen back to the default settings in SERVICES Configuration
Printer. To delete a single settings sheet, use the SERVICES
Print Settings Name Delete command. If, however, you want to
erase all named Print settings sheets in a particular file,
select SERVICES Print Settings Name Reset. After you use this
command, print settings from SERVICES Configuration Printer will
be in effect.█
                                                           MAIN
Printed Page 12, Line 51
```

Fig. 7.33.

When you print text entered in a DOC window, Symphony automatically ends one page and begins another according to the page-length setting in SERVICES **P**rint **S**etting **P**age **L**ength. But if you want to control where a page ends and a new one begins, use the DOC **P**age command.

Suppose, for example, that you want to keep on separate pages certain sections of a report, as in figure 7.34. To break the page between the two sections, place the cursor on the line where you want the break to occur, and then select **P**age from the DOC menu. When you select DOC **P**age, Symphony will place a marker (::) in the left margin to indicate that the page will break there. If you want to change a page break, simply erase the break by using the Erase key or the **Erase** command in the DOC menu.

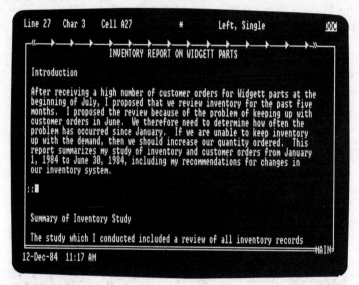

Fig. 7.34.

Indenting Sections and Varying Format within the Text

If you are composing a letter, memo, or report in which the format is consistent—that is, the text contains all paragraphs of the same margins, spacing, and so on—then setting format will be easy. But if your document contains sections of text that vary from the regular format (for example, with paragraphs, tables, or lists that are indented), you can simplify your job by using Symphony's Indent key and format lines.

You may want at times to indent a section of text underneath another section, as shown in figure 7.35. To indent this way, use the Indent key (F3). To indent a whole section, change from Insert to Overstrike mode if you are not already in that mode. Next, move the cursor to the space where you want each line of indented text to begin. Press the Indent key, then type the section of text. When you finish typing, press the Justify key or use the Justify command to justify the section of text.

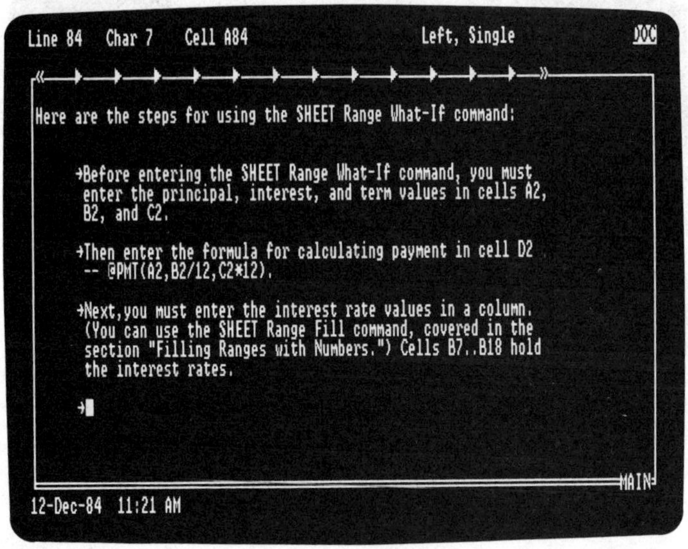

```
Line 84   Char 7   Cell A84              Left, Single        DOC

«──►──►──►──►──►──►──►──►──►──►──►──►──►──»

Here are the steps for using the SHEET Range What-If command:


  →Before entering the SHEET Range What-If command, you must
   enter the principal, interest, and term values in cells A2,
   B2, and C2.

  →Then enter the formula for calculating payment in cell D2
   -- @PMT(A2,B2/12,C2*12).

  →Next,you must enter the interest rate values in a column.
   (You can use the SHEET Range Fill command, covered in the
   section "Filling Ranges with Numbers.") Cells B7..B18 hold
   the interest rates.

  →█


══════════════════════════════════════════════════MAIN═
12-Dec-84  11:21 AM
```

Fig. 7.35.

The Indent key is also useful whenever you want to include an itemized list that contains items which are preceded by numbers, letters, or bullets. (See fig. 7.36.) Using the Indent key to create such a list, follow the steps listed above, with one variation. Instead of pressing the Indent key before you begin typing a section of text, first type the number, letter, or bullet, and then press Indent. Repeat this procedure for each item in your list.

Creating, Editing, and Storing Format Lines

If you find that you repeatedly change format in the documents you write, then you can create, name, and store format lines for changing format whenever you want. As mentioned earlier, format lines enable you to change the format settings in a DOC window anytime

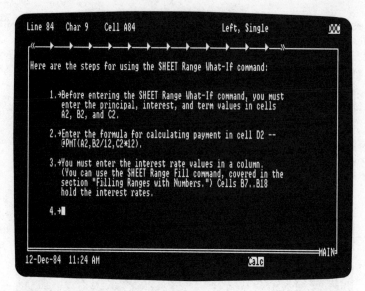

Fig. 7.36.

while you are entering text on the screen. Format lines are particularly useful, for example, whenever you want to indent a block of text or create special lists or tables. Keeping a file of format lines will enable you to retrieve special formats without having to re-create these lines each time. This section describes how to create, name, store, retrieve, and edit format lines.

Format lines can be created wherever in your text you want to change margins, tabs, paragraph justification, or spacing. For example, whenever you want to indent on both the left and right a section of quoted text, you can use a format line to set off the text, as shown in figure 7.37.

To create a format line, you retrieve the DOC menu and select Format, then choose Create. Symphony will ask, "Where should format line(s) be inserted?" Move the cursor to the line just before the line where newly formatted text is to begin, and press RETURN. On this preceding line, Symphony will place a format line with the same settings as those controlling the text preceding the format line. For example, if you are creating a format line for the first time in the DOC window, the format line will inherit the settings controlling that

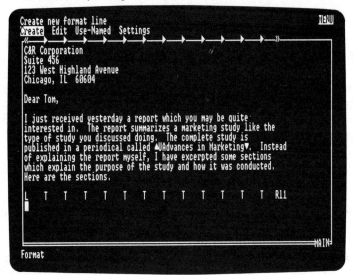

```
Line 22   Char 20   Cell C22              Left, Single          DOC
 «——→——→——→——→——→——→——»
C&R Corporation
Suite 456
123 West Highland Avenue
Chicago, IL  60604

Dear Tom,

I just received yesterday a report which you may be quite
interested in.  The report summarizes a marketing study like the
type of study you discussed doing.  The complete study is
published in a periodical called ▲UAdvances in Marketing▼.  Instead
of explaining the report myself, I have excerpted some sections
which explain the purpose of the study and how it was conducted.
Here are the sections.

         L   T   T   T   T   T   T   R11
         Watkins Marketing Research has just
         completed a study on the preference
         of color ■


                                                        ═MAIN═
12-Dec-84  11:28 AM
```

Fig. 7.37.

window. In figure 7.38 the format line settings duplicate the margin and tab settings indicated in the top line of the border, and the justification and spacing settings indicated in the control panel.

```
Create new format line                                   MENU
 Create Edit Use-Named Settings
 «——→——→——→——→——→——→——→——→——»
C&R Corporation
Suite 456
123 West Highland Avenue
Chicago, IL  60604

Dear Tom,

I just received yesterday a report which you may be quite
interested in.  The report summarizes a marketing study like the
type of study you discussed doing.  The complete study is
published in a periodical called ▲UAdvances in Marketing▼.  Instead
of explaining the report myself, I have excerpted some sections
which explain the purpose of the study and how it was conducted.
Here are the sections.

L   T   T   T   T   T   T   T   T   T   T   T   R11
■

                                                        ═MAIN═
Format
```

Fig. 7.38.

After displaying a format line on the screen, Symphony provides a menu for changing, naming, and storing format lines; using them; or removing the name of a format line. (See fig. 7.39.)

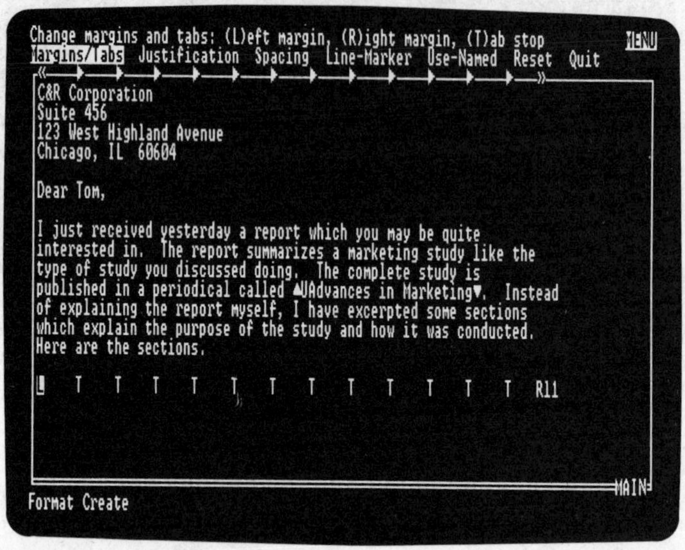

```
Change margins and tabs: (L)eft margin, (R)ight margin, (T)ab stop      MENU
Margins/Tabs Justification Spacing Line-Marker Use-Named Reset  Quit
┌«─────►──►──►──►──►──►─┬──►──►──►──►──►──►──►──►──»─────────────────────┐
│C&R Corporation                                                       │
│Suite 456                                                             │
│123 West Highland Avenue                                             │
│Chicago, IL 60604                                                    │
│                                                                     │
│Dear Tom,                                                            │
│                                                                     │
│I just received yesterday a report which you may be quite            │
│interested in.  The report summarizes a marketing study like the     │
│type of study you discussed doing.  The complete study is            │
│published in a periodical called ▲▼Advances in Marketing▼.  Instead  │
│of explaining the report myself, I have excerpted some sections      │
│which explain the purpose of the study and how it was conducted.     │
│Here are the sections.                                               │
│                                                                     │
│L  T  T  T  T   T  T  T  T  T  T  T  T  T   T  R11                    │
│                                                                     │
│                                                                     │
│                                                                     │
│                                                          ═════MAIN═  │
│Format Create                                                        │
```

Fig. 7.39.

To change a format line, select either **M**argins/Tabs, **J**ustification, or **S**pacing. Then press RETURN. When you choose **M**argins/Tabs, for example, the control panel will clear, and your next step is to change margins and tabs on the format line. To set new margins and tabs, delete the existing ones and enter **L** (left), **T** (Tab), or **R** (right) where you want the new settings. After you have changed margin and tab settings, press RETURN. The format line menu will appear again. At this point, you can make other changes (such as paragraph justification or spacing), assign a name to the format line, or exit from the menu.

If you want to change justification or spacing, simply select one of these choices from the menu and enter the appropriate setting. Symphony indicates justification by displaying the first letter of the type of justification (n = None, l = Left, e = Even, c = Center) after the R (right margin) indicator. Spacing is indicated directly after justification (1 = Single, 2 = Double, 3 = Triple).

Once you have entered all settings for the format line, you have two options. First, you can exit from the DOC menu and return to the text by choosing **Q**uit. Second, you can create a name for the format line. When you create a name, the format line settings are stored with that name and can be retrieved and reused whenever you need them.

To create a name and to store the format line, select **L**ine-Marker from the format line menu. When Symphony displays two options (**A**ssign and **R**emove), choose **A**ssign and enter a name when the "Name to assign: " prompt appears. At this point, the format line settings will be stored with the line's assigned name. Finally, select **Q**uit to exit from the menu and go back to the DOC mode.

After you have assigned a name to a format line, you can reuse the line when needed. Just select **F**ormat from the DOC menu, then **U**se-Named. Symphony will ask, "Where should format line(s) be inserted?" Move the cursor to the place where you want the line(s). Afterward, press RETURN. Symphony will display the name of your format line with an @ sign preceding it. All named format lines are displayed this way when you reuse them.

In addition to creating and naming format lines, you can also edit either a named format line or one that is currently in the DOC window but not named. To edit either type, select **F**ormat **E**dit, then either **C**urrent or **N**amed. Whenever you edit either type of format line, you can change any of the format settings (**M**argins/Tabs, **J**ustification, or **S**pacing), or have Symphony change the format line to the DOC window's default format settings. To change a format line to the window's default format settings, select **R**eset.

Integrating Symphony's DOC Window with Other Types

One of the advantages of Symphony's word-processing capability, as mentioned earlier, is the ability to integrate word processing with the applications of spreadsheet, data management, graphics, and communications. In Chapter 14, you will see how all five applications work together in one model. But for now, here's an example of how you can integrate a DOC window with a SHEET, FORM, and GRAPH window.

In figure 7.40, you will see four separate windows created on the screen. The first is a FORM window containing the data form. The second window, a SHEET window, displays the data base created from form entries. The third window, GRAPH, is the graphics representation of one part of the data base—column D, "Working Capital." Finally, you will notice the long rectangular DOC window at the bottom of the screen.

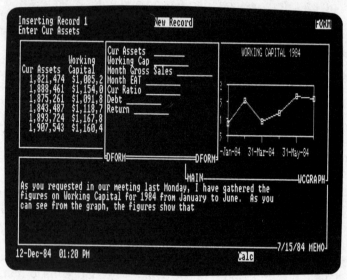

Fig. 7.40.

What's the connection of the DOC window to the others? From the text in the DOC window, you'll see that the user is beginning to write a report summarizing important conclusions from the data entered and presented in other windows. Having both a SHEET and a GRAPH window at hand helps the writer analyze and organize text. In addition, the writer can make a report more effective by combining either the data base or the graphics into the text. To combine the data base or part of the data into the text, the writer can use the SERVICES File Combine command at the point in the document where the data base is to appear. To integrate the graph, the user can print a copy of the graph and then insert it into the printed copy of the report.

8

Printing Reports

If you have used 1-2-3, then printing a report or creating a print file in Symphony may seem like breaking new territory. You may find, for example, that print commands which are also contained in 1-2-3 are harder to find in Symphony. Because of Symphony's extra applications, particularly word processing, many more options are available for printing reports than are available in 1-2-3. One other feature making Symphony's **P**rint command different from 1-2-3's is the ability to name and store a print settings sheet after you have entered special settings.

Symphony lets you control the printing of spreadsheets, data bases, text generated in a DOC window, and graphs. (Printing graphs is discussed in Chapter 10.) As explained in that chapter, printing graphs requires that you use a separate disk, the PrintGraph disk, instead of the Symphony Program disk. Except in the case of printing graphs, Symphony provides options for writing directly to the printer from within the program, creating a print file to be printed outside the program, or printing to a range within the current worksheet. Symphony also enables you to print headers and footers that include dates and page numbers to begin printing or to end

379

printing at any page (between 1 and 999) in a word-processing document.

Although many print options control both the printing of spreadsheets and text, some options are specific to the type of application. For example, within the Print menu are the options for printing spreadsheets as displayed or as cell formulas. You can tell Symphony to repeat the printing of column and/or row headings for each page of a spreadsheet you print. Special print options related to printing documents include regulating underlining, boldface characters, superscript, and subscript in text.

SERVICES Configuration Printer and SERVICES Print

If you will be sending data directly to the printer, you will want to make sure that the correct printer driver is set and that you have accessed the Symphony program with the correct driver. (See Chapter 2 for an explanation of setting drivers.) Apart from setting drivers, however, two other types of settings affect the output to the printer, print file, or worksheet range (the three output choices you have when using SERVICES Print). These two settings are SERVICES Configuration Printer settings and SERVICES Print settings. (See fig. 8.1.)

SERVICES Configuration Printer contains the default settings for single sheet versus continuous feed, and for margins, page length, and initialization string. These settings are inherited by the first SERVICES Print Settings sheet in a worksheet. For example, if your SERVICES Configuration setting for the left margin is 5 and for the right margin is 65, the first SERVICES Print Settings sheet you retrieve in a worksheet will display these margins. In addition, SERVICES Configuration Printer contains settings for printer type (parallel or serial) and automatic line feed, which are necessary settings for sending output directly to the printer.

You can, however, change the SERVICES Configuration Printer settings and update the Symphony configuration file to include new settings. Several options are provided by the SERVICES Configura-

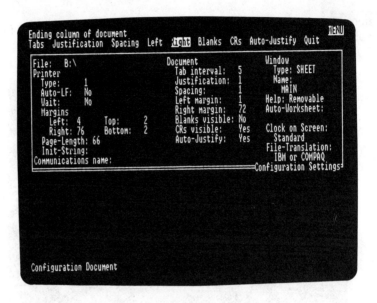

Fig. 8.1.

tion **P**rinter settings. Four of these options are available for parallel or serial interface between Symphony and your printer (**C**onfiguration **P**rinter **T**ype). Settings are also available for having either Symphony or your printer automatically advance the paper at the end of each line (**C**onfiguration **A**uto-LF). When determining which **C**onfiguration **P**rinter settings to change and how to change them, consult the manual that comes with your printer.

Through SERVICES **C**onfiguration **P**rinter, you can also regulate whether the printer continuously loads paper after finishing a page or whether the printer waits (**C**onfiguration **P**rinter **W**ait). SERVICES **C**onfiguration contains settings for left, right, top, and bottom margins (SERVICES **C**onfiguration **P**rinter **M**argins) and page length (SERVICES **C**onfiguration **P**rinter **P**age-Length). Finally, print type and size are controlled by the setting in SERVICES **C**onfiguration **P**rinter **I**nit-String. (See the later section on Sending an Initialization String to the Printer.)

As figure 8.2 indicates, SERVICES **P**rint contains many types of options. These include selections for regulating format for printing

spreadsheets to selections for regulating naming and using print
settings sheets.

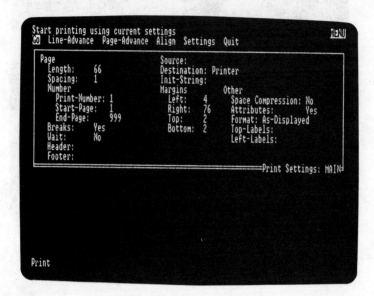

```
Start printing using current settings                           MENU
  Go Line-Advance Page-Advance Align Settings Quit

  Page                        Source:
    Length:    66             Destination: Printer
    Spacing:   1              Init-String:
  Number                      Margins        Other
    Print-Number: 1             Left:   4      Space Compression: No
    Start-Page:   1             Right:  76     Attributes:        Yes
    End-Page:     999           Top:    2      Format: As-Displayed
  Breaks:       Yes             Bottom: 2      Top-Labels:
  Wait:         No                             Left-Labels:
  Header:
  Footer:
                                           ======Print Settings: MAIN=

  Print
```

Fig. 8.2.

The Print Menu

The examples in this chapter provide explanations of many of the
options in the SERVICES Print menu. (See fig. 8.2 earlier.) A general
introduction to the types of commands that are available may help
you understand Symphony's print capabilities. Print commands fall
into the following categories:

1. Commands for indicating what should be printed,
    stored in a print file, or entered into a range in the
    worksheet (Settings Source)

2. Commands for having source data printed directly,
    stored in a print file, or entered into a range in the
    worksheet (Settings Destination)

3. Commands regulating the format of the page

   A. Numbers of lines per page (**S**ettings **P**age **L**ength)

   B. Spaces between lines in spreadsheets or data bases (**S**ettings **P**age **S**pacing)

   C. Headers on each page (**S**ettings **P**age **H**eader)

   D. Footers on each page (**S**ettings **P**age **F**ooter)

   E. Margins (**S**ettings **M**argins)

   F. Boldface, underlining, superscript, and subscript (**S**ettings **O**ther **A**ttributes)

   G. Printing of spreadsheet data—as displayed on screen versus cell formulas (**S**ettings **O**ther **F**ormat)

   H. Printing of worksheet labels (**S**ettings **O**ther **T**op-Labels, **S**ettings **O**ther **L**eft-Labels, and **S**ettings **O**ther **N**o-Labels)

   I. Numbers printed on each page (**S**ettings **P**age **N**umber)

4. Commands controlling printer operations

   A. Page breaks (**S**ettings **P**age **B**reaks)

   B. Paper feed (**S**ettings **P**age **W**ait)

   C. Print size and type (**S**ettings **I**nit-String)

*New
with
Symphony*

5. Commands for creating, naming, using, and deleting print settings sheets

   A. Creating and naming print settings sheets (**S**ettings **N**ame **C**reate)

   B. Using print settings sheets (**S**ettings **N**ame **U**se, **S**ettings **N**ame **P**revious, and **S**ettings **N**ame **N**ext)

   C. Deleting print settings sheets (**S**ettings **N**ame **D**elete)

The SERVICES **P**rint menu is one of Symphony's "sticky" menus. The only way to exit from it is to specify the **Q**uit option. Whenever you perform one of the functions from the **P**rint menu, it returns to exactly where you were before. Be careful not to hit the RETURN key again at this point unless you want the same function to be executed twice. You will find that it is particularly disconcerting to return from printing the worksheet by using the **G**o function only to hit RETURN again accidentally and have the file printed a second time. If you want to interrupt a print operation, press Ctrl-Break.

Whenever you are creating a print file or are printing to a range in a worksheet (that is, whenever you select SERVICES **P**rint **S**ettings **D**estination **F**ile or **R**ange), you must press SERVICES **P**rint **G**o before exiting from the menu. SERVICES **P**rint **G**o has three important functions: (1) it initiates sending output to the printer to begin printing, (2) it initiates the storing of a print file, and (3) it sends output to a range in the worksheet.

When and How to Print

The first choice you make in printing a file is whether to print it now or later, or whether to create a print file to send through communications lines. If the system you are working on doesn't have a printer, if your printer isn't working, or if you want to create a file whose output you can send over data communications lines, then you can set up a print file. The SERVICES **P**rint **S**ettings **D**estination **P**rint command is used if you want to go directly to the printer in the current Symphony session. And the SERVICES **P**rint **S**ettings **D**estination **F**ile command is used to store output in a file either to be sent or to be printed later with the DOS TYPE command or special printing routine.

Symphony, unlike 1-2-3, offers an alternative to creating a print file if your printer isn't working or if you don't want to print now. In Symphony you can name and store print settings and then retrieve those settings later when you want to print a spreadsheet or word-processing text. Being able to save print settings alleviates having to reset print commands and also enables you to use a print settings sheet for other documents or spreadsheets in your worksheet. (See the section on Naming, Using, and Deleting Print Settings Sheets.)

Print Files (.PRN)

Files created with the SERVICES **P**rint **S**ettings **D**estination **F**ile command have a .PRN file name extension. Portions of .PRN files can be called back into Symphony from the disk and entered into specific locations in a worksheet with the **F**ile **I**mport command. Creating a .PRN file also enables you to transfer a Symphony file to another word-processing program, such as WordStar. Importing .PRN files is not as straightforward as it sounds, however. (Chapter 6 provides more information on importing .PRN files.)

New
with
Symphony

Printing to a Range

In addition to the options of sending data directly to the printer or creating a print file, Symphony provides one other option. You can send print data to a range in the worksheet. "Printing" data to a range in ther worksheet is particularly valuable when you want to import SHEET data into a DOC window. For example, when you transfer spreadsheet data into the DOC window of a worksheet, you can edit the data or use DOC commands on the data as you would with data originally entered in the DOC mode.

Printing to a range in the worksheet is different from using the SHEET **C**opy command. If you use the SHEET **C**opy command, you can copy a spreadsheet or parts of a spreadsheet into a DOC window. Even though the spreadsheet section is copied into a DOC area, however, you cannot use the Del or Backspace keys to change the entries. But if you copy the spreadsheet data into the DOC area by using the SERVICES **P**rint **S**ettings **D**estination **R**ange command, the spreadsheet data can then be changed just as any data originally entered in a DOC window can be changed.

Printing Reports: A Few Examples

Shown here to help you understand Symphony's print capabilities are three examples of reports and how they can be printed. The first example is a spreadsheet (Mom's Root Beer Company Cash-Flow Projection) printed with the minimum number of print options. In this case, the spreadsheet is printed very much as it appears on the screen, without using any of the special options. Figure 8.3 shows a portion of the screen display of the spreadsheet.

```
A1: 'Mom's Root Beer Company -- Cash Flow Projection          SHEET
     ╔═════A═══════B═══════C═══════D═══════E═══════F═══════G═══
   1  Mom's Root Beer Company -- Cash Flow Projection
   2
   3  Year          1982    1983    1984    1985    1986    1987
   4  ──────────────────────────────────────────────────────────
   5  Growth Assumptions (as % of Sales)
   6  Sales        actual   1.085   1.085   1.085   1.085   1.085
   7  CGS           0.483   0.500   0.500   0.500   0.500   0.500
   8  SGA           0.403   0.370   0.350   0.350   0.350   0.350
   9
  10  Plant and Equipment: 22% of sales; cap exp = 30% of Sales Change + Deprecia
  11  Depreciation: 14% of plant and equipment; all depreciation reinvested
  12  Working Capital: Change = 15% of Sales change
  13  Tax Rate = 41%
  14
  15  Projections
  16  Sales        516,136 560,008 607,608 659,255 715,292 776,091
  17  COGS         249,284 280,004 303,804 329,627 357,646 388,046
  18  Depn          18,423  17,248  18,714  20,305  22,031  23,904
  19  SGA          207,807 207,203 212,663 230,739 250,352 271,632
  20  Interest      18,423 projected cash flows considered to be unlevered
                                                                 MAIN
12-Dec-84  03:09 PM
```

Fig. 8.3.

The second example of a report (Inventory Report on Cattuna) has been created in a DOC window; again, the report is printed very much as it appears on the screen. Double spacing does not, however, appear on the screen. (See fig. 8.4.) Finally, the third example of a report (The Cattuna Distributing Inventory), shown in figure 8.5, illustrates how to use the special options for printing spreadsheets.

For the first sample report, called Mom's Root Beer Report, you will be more interested in the figures on the cash-flow projection for the next ten years than in the format of the printed page. (See fig. 8.6.) The only thing special you might do for the printing of this report is to print all ten years on one standard 8 1/2 x 11-inch page.

Whether you decide to print the report immediately or create a print file and print it later, you begin either operation by selecting **Print** from the SERVICES menu.

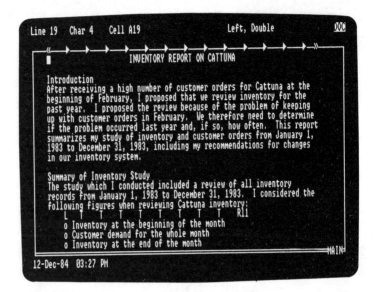

Fig. 8.4.

```
A1: 'Month                                                       SHEET

         _____A_____ ___B___ ___C___ ___D___ ___E___ ___F___
1        Month                     Jan     Feb     Apr     May    June
2        =========================================================
3        Beginning Inventory         43      51      60      42      30
4        Past Demand for Month       28      16      18      12      20
5        Ending Inventory            15      35      42      30      10
6        Quantity Ordered            36       0       0       0      36
7        Setup Costs ($10 per order) $10.00  $0.00   $0.00   $0.00  $10.00
8        Inventory Costs ($.2/unit)  $3.00   $7.00   $8.40   $6.00   $2.00
9        Shortage Costs ($1/unit)    $0.00   $0.00   $0.00   $0.00   $0.00
10       Total Costs for Month       $13.00  $7.00  $14.80   $6.00  $12.00
11       Cum Cost from Last Month    $0.00  $13.00  $20.00  $43.20  $49.20
12       Cumulative Costs to Date    $13.00 $20.00  $34.80  $49.20  $61.20
13
14
15       Order Quantity Input Cell ->   36
16       Order Point Input Cell ---->   28
17
18                               Order   Cumulative    Order   Cumulative
19                               Quant     Cost        Quant     Cost
20                               -----   ----------    -----   ----------
                                                                      MAIN

12-Dec-84  03:42 PM
```

Fig. 8.5.

```
A1: 'Mom's Root Beer Company -- Cash Flow Projection              SHEET
   ┌───A────────B────────C────────D────────E───────F───────G──────────
 1 │Mom's Root Beer Company -- Cash Flow Projection
 2 │
 3 │Year         1982     1983     1984     1985     1986     1987
 4 │--------------------------------------------------------------------
 5 │Growth Assumptions (as % of Sales)
 6 │  Sales    actual    1.085    1.085    1.085    1.085    1.085
 7 │  CGS       0.483    0.500    0.500    0.500    0.500    0.500
 8 │  SGA       0.403    0.370    0.350    0.350    0.350    0.350
 9 │
10 │Plant and Equipment: 22% of sales; cap exp = 30% of Sales Change + Deprecia
11 │Depreciation: 14% of plant and equipment; all depreciation reinvested
12 │Working Capital: Change = 15% of Sales change
13 │Tax Rate = 41%
14 │
15 │Projections
16 │  Sales   516,136  560,008  607,608  659,255  715,292  776,091
17 │  COGS    249,284  280,004  303,804  329,627  357,646  388,046
18 │  Depn     18,423   17,248   18,714   20,305   22,031   23,904
19 │  SGA     207,807  207,203  212,663  230,739  250,352  271,632
20 │  Interest 18,423 projected cash flows considered to be unlevered
                                                                    MAIN
12-Dec-84  03:59 PM
```

Fig. 8.6.

Designating a Print Range

One of the first steps in printing any report is to designate a range of cells to be printed. As indicated earlier, the command used to designate a range is SERVICES **P**rint **S**ettings **S**ource **R**ange. In addition to **R**ange, Symphony provides another option for indicating the source of the print output: **D**atabase. You choose **D**atabase whenever the source is a report specified in the data base settings sheet. (See Chapter 11.)

In the first and second print examples, setting the range requires selecting SERVICES **P**rint **S**ettings **S**ource **R**ange, then indicating the range to be printed. If the range begins with the upper left corner of the window's restrict range and ends with the lower right corner of the restrict range, then you move the cursor to the upper left corner and select SERVICES **P**rint **S**ettings **S**ource **R**ange. Symphony will ask, "Range to be printed: ". You next press the period key followed by the End key, then the Home key. The cursor will highlight the complete restrict range.

In the third print example, setting the print range is somewhat more complicated. Printing the spreadsheet part of this document requires setting multiple ranges in order to print the inventory on two 8 1/2 x 11-inch pages. These ranges must be designated and printed one at a time.

Because a print file has been created for this third example of a report, the ranges will be appended one after the other in the file. Symphony lets you control the format of each range that is written. This feature is helpful when you want to control the printing of each part of the inventory. Each time a range is designated and print options are changed, you must select **G**o from the SERVICES **P**rint menu in order to send the range to the print file. **G**o is also required to send a range to the printer.

If, on the other hand, you are printing a large range, as in Mom's Root Beer Report, you will want to use the special-function keys (PgUp, PgDn, End, etc.). One particularly useful sequence for pointing to a print range when the range is the entire sheet is pressing the End key followed by the Home key.

Setting Print Options

Aside from the task of designating print ranges, the only other task that requires any kind of detailed explanation in printing reports is that of setting print options. Several print options will be designated for the Cattuna Distributing Inventory, whereas only a few options will be used for Mom's Root Beer Report (to get everything on one page) and the Inventory Report on Cattuna.

Special print options are available for both spreadsheets and text. The options for spreadsheets include the following:

- Spacing (The DOC **F**ormat **S**ettings **S**pacing command controls spacing for printing text created in a DOC window.)

- Printing column and row labels along the top and left on every page

- Printing cell formulas rather than cell entries as displayed

For DOC text, special print options include printing of special print attributes: underlining, boldface characters, and superscript or subscript characters.

Setting Headers and Footers

For the third report, the first step after designating a print range is to set the header and footer options. These options allow you to specify up to 240 characters of text in each of three positions—left, center, and right—in the header and footer. Realistically, you should use only enough text to fit on an 8 1/2 x 11-inch page.

You can enter all of the text yourself, but Symphony offers some special characters that control page numbers, the current date, and the location where text is printed in the header and footer lines. These special characters are the following:

This character automatically prints page numbers starting with the number entered in SERVICES **P**rint **S**ettings **P**age **N**umber. If you use **P**rint **A**lign, the page number will be reset to the number in SERVICES **P**rint **S**ettings **P**age **N**umber.

@ This character automatically includes the current date in the format stored in Symphony's configuration file, and takes the date from what you entered when you loaded DOS—that is, the current date.

| Headers and footers have three separate segments: left-justified, centered, and right-justified. Use this character to separate one segment from another. Notice the following examples of entries for header or footer lines.

What you type:

    Cattuna Distributing Co. Inventory| |page #
    |Cattuna Distributing Co. Inventory, page #
    Cattuna Distributing Co. Inventory, @, page #|

What appears on the page:

Cattuna Distributing Co. Inventory   page 1

Cattuna Distributing Co. Inventory, page 1

Cattuna Distributing Co. Inventory, 07/24/84, page 1

These symbols (@ | #) can be used in either headers or footers. Also, date appears in the format for month, day, and year (MM/DD/YY). Figure 8.15B at the end of this chapter shows how the header and footer options are set up with the special characters for the third report. For the header and footer options to work, you must set SERVICES Print Settings Page Breaks to Yes. Otherwise, your header and footer entries will be ignored.

Although no headers or footers are used for Mom's Root Beer Report, two things should be noted about the report. First, Symphony always places two blank lines below the header and two above the footer line. Second, if you use the # special character for page numbers, and if you want to print a report a second time, you must reset the print settings by selecting SERVICES Print Align. After you have reset Settings, you can respecify them before the second printing. (See the section on Naming, Using, and Deleting Print Settings Sheets.) Otherwise, the page counter will pick up where it left off.

Neither headers nor footers can be changed in the middle of a report. If you want to print different headers and footers in different sections of a report, you must create a separate print settings sheet, enter the new header or footer, and set Print Settings Page Number Page-Start to the number of the first page of the new section.

Setting Margins

Margin settings controlling the size of margins on text as it is printed are located in the following three settings sheets:

1. SERVICES Configuration Printer Margins, which contains default margin settings

2. SERVICES Print Settings Margins, which contains the specific margin settings you enter for a specific print output

3. DOC **F**ormat **S**ettings **L**eft, which affects the left margin for text entered in a DOC window. When printing the left margins of text created in a DOC environment, Symphony adds the margin settings in DOC **F**ormat **S**ettings **L**eft to those in SERVICES **P**rint **S**ettings **M**argins **L**eft.

New
with
Symphony

If you are retrieving the **P**rint **S**ettings Sheet (SERVICES **P**rint) for the first time in a worksheet, you will notice that the sheet contains the margin settings stored in SERVICES **C**onfiguration **P**rinter **M**argins. When setting your margins for data entered in a SHEET or DOC window, you can either use those provided by SERVICES **C**onfiguration **P**rinter **M**argins or enter new margin settings. The SERVICES **P**rint **S**ettings **M**argins option will override SERVICES **C**onfiguration **P**rinter. The default margin settings (from the edge of the paper) stored in SERVICES **C**onfiguration **P**rinter **M**argins are the following:

Left 4
Right 76
Top 2
Bottom 2

Right and left margin settings can be changed to settings between 0 and 240; top and bottom margin settings can be changed to settings between 0 and 10. Whenever you change margin settings in SERVICES **C**onfiguration **P**rinter **M**argins, you can update the Symphony configuration file to these new settings by selecting **U**pdate from the SERVICES **C**onfiguration menu.

The SERVICES **P**rint **S**ettings **M**argins command operates on both spreadsheets and text entered in a word-processing window. The same margin settings, however, can result in different margins when you are printing a spreadsheet or when you are printing text from a DOC window.

For the first example, Mom's Root Beer Report, you will want to get everything on an 8 1/2 x 11-inch page. But there are 12 active columns of data in the worksheet, which, when combined, form a total worksheet width of 108 characters. The only way to fit everything on one page is to use compressed print on a dot-matrix printer. You can get up to 136 characters on a line with this type of print. With the 5 characters for the left margin and the worksheet width of 108, you can just stay under the limit of 136. The right margin should be set at 136, and an Init-String should be sent to the printer. (See the section on Sending an Initialization String to the Printer.)

An alternative to the compressed print is to use the current defaults. You can let the printer print up to 80 columns on one page with either pica or elite type, then continue on to later pages with what is left over. This solution is not an ideal one, but it is the only other choice.

For the second example, the Inventory Report on Cattuna, you will want a left margin of 5 and a right margin of 72. As you'll recall, for text from a DOC window, Symphony adds the left margin settings from DOC Format Settings Left to the left margin settings in SERVICES Printer Settings Margins. The original setting in DOC Format Settings for the left margin is 4; the setting in SERVICES Print Settings Margins is 1. Symphony will therefore print a left margin of 5.

For the third example, the Cattuna Distributing Inventory, the top and bottom margins are set at 8. These margin settings, which are the distance from the top of the page to the header and from the bottom of the page to the footer, should give you a good appearance. The left margin is set at 4 for this report, and the right margin at 76. You may have to try several different combinations to get the setup you want.

Repeating Labels on Multipage Printouts

Like 1-2-3, Symphony allows you to print column and/or row headings on a multipage printout, such as for the spreadsheet in the third example. If, for instance, you want to print a comparative income statement that has several columns of monthly figures carrying beyond the first page, you can have the row headings that usually occur in the first column of the first page repeated on each page. SERVICES Print Settings Other Top-Labels is the option used to repeat column labels. SERVICES Print Settings Other Left-Labels is used to repeat row labels.

You can also use SERVICES **P**rint **S**ettings **O**ther **T**op-Labels or **L**eft-Labels whenever you want to extract part of a data base and have the correct column and row headings printing with it. For example, suppose that you want to print only one section from a data base you have created, such as the one shown in figure 8.7, which extends from column A to column J.

```
===================================================================================================
Data base
===================================================================================================
                                            Month
Record                          Working      Gross     Month             Debt to    Return
Date         Tot Assets  Cur Assets  Capital     Sales     EAT    Cur Ratio  Equity     On Assets   DSO
     30-Jun-83  $3,202,976  1,907,543  $1,160,483   $729,652  26,612    2.59      0.52      0.10       53
     31-May-83  $3,192,286  1,893,724  $1,167,836   $726,572  24,269    2.55      0.53      0.09       53
     30-Apr-83  $3,181,407  1,843,487  $1,118,712   $722,683  24,833    2.61      0.53      0.09       53
     31-Mar-83  $3,175,632  1,875,261  $1,091,880   $717,947  25,481    2.54      0.54      0.10       54
     28-Feb-83  $3,158,517  1,888,461  $1,154,019   $714,820  22,582    2.39      0.55      0.09       55
     31-Jan-83  $3,142,910  1,821,474  $1,085,296   $713,267  23,201    2.57      0.55      0.09       57
```

Fig. 8.7.

If you want to print only the range from A10..J12 and also print labels with it, follow this procedure. First, you select SERVICES **P**rint **S**ettings **S**ource and indicate the range of the data base that you want to print. In this case, enter A10..J12. After indicating the range, select **D**estination **P**rinter and make any page or margin changes that are necessary.

To have labels printed, select SERVICES **P**rint **S**ettings **O**ther **T**op-Labels. To indicate which labels should be your top labels, enter the row range or highlight the row where column headings are located. In figure 8.7, for example, you highlight A4..J6. To indicate which labels should be your left labels, select SERVICES **P**rint **S**ettings **O**ther **L**eft-Labels and indicate the column of labels you want printed. You are now ready to begin printing, unless you first want to name the settings sheet you just created so that you can use it again. The printed data base is shown in figure 8.8.

When you are using the SERVICES **P**rint **S**ettings **O**ther **T**op-Labels or **L**eft-Labels commands to print labels on consecutive pages after the first page, be careful that you do not include the column and row labels when you set the **S**ource Range. If you set the **S**ource **R**ange to include column and row borders and also enter a range in

Record Date	Tot Assets	Cur Assets	Working Capital	Month Gross Sales	Month EAT	Cur Ratio	Debt to Equity	Return On Assets	DSO
31-Mar-83	$3,175,632	1,875,261	$1,091,880	$717,947	25,481	2.54	0.54	0.10	54
28-Feb-83	$3,158,517	1,888,461	$1,154,019	$714,820	22,582	2.39	0.55	0.09	55
31-Jan-83	$3,142,910	1,821,474	$1,085,296	$713,267	23,201	2.57	0.55	0.09	57

Fig. 8.8.

Top-Labels and **L**eft-Labels, Symphony will print labels twice on the first page. (See fig. 8.9.)

```
================================================================================
Balance Sheet                      Balance Sheet
================================================================================
                                                                     Common
                                                          31-Jul-84  Size
            Assets                        Assets

Cash                          Cash                          $275,000   8%
Marketable Securities         Marketable Securities           35,000   1%
Accounts Receivable           Accounts Receivable         1,256,000
   Allowance for Doubtful Accounts   Allowance for Doubtful Accounts    8,000
   Net Accounts Receivable      Net Accounts Receivable    1,248,000  39%
Inventory                     Inventory                      359,000  11%
Prepaid Expenses              Prepaid Expenses                70,000   2%
Other                         Other                           23,000   1%
                                                          ------------
   Total Current Assets          Total Current Assets     2,010,000  62%


Property, Plant, and Equipment  Property, Plant, and Equipment  956,700
   Accumulated Depreciation       Accumulated Depreciation     123,700
   Net Property, Plant, and Equipment   Net Property, Plant, and Equipment  833,000  26%
Investment-Long-Term          Investment-Long-Term           396,000  12%
                                                          ------------
   Total Noncurrent Assets       Total Noncurrent Assets   1,229,000  38%
                                                          ------------
   Total Assets                  Total Assets             $3,239,000 100%
```

Fig. 8.9.

Sending an Initialization String to the Printer

If you want to control either print size or type, you can regulate both through the Init-String (Initialization String) commands. Two separate Init-String settings are available: one in SERVICES **C**onfiguration **P**rinter and one in SERVICES **P**rint **S**ettings. The SERVICES **C**onfiguration **P**rinter Init-String is stored in Symphony's configuration file (.CNF) and controls SERVICES **P**rint **S**ettings Init-String unless you change the SERVICES **C**onfiguration.

The Init-String option sends a string of up to 39 characters to the printer every time you select **G**o from the SERVICES **P**rint menu. All printers are different, so you will have to look carefully at your printer's manual to see what is required for your printer. The string is made up of backslashes (\) followed by the decimal equivalent of special characters in ASCII code.

You can change the print size and/or type by selecting SERVICES **P**rint **S**ettings Init-String. Once you have selected this command, Symphony will ask you to enter the printer-control sequence. (See fig. 8.10.) At the printer-control sequence prompt, you should enter the special control code(s) for your printer. (Again, consult the manual that comes with your printer.)

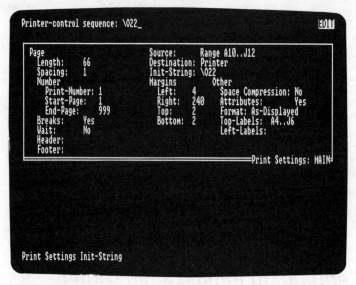

```
Printer-control sequence: \022_                              EDIT

  Page                    Source:      Range A10..J12
    Length:     66        Destination: Printer
    Spacing:    1         Init-String: \022
  Number                  Margins         Other
    Print-Number: 1         Left:    4    Space Compression: No
    Start-Page:   1         Right: 240    Attributes:        Yes
    End-Page:   999         Top:     2    Format: As-Displayed
  Breaks:     Yes           Bottom:  2    Top-Labels:  A4..J6
  Wait:        No                         Left-Labels:
  Header:
  Footer:
                                         ═Print Settings: MAIN═

  Print Settings Init-String
```

Fig. 8.10.

Like the other SERVICES **P**rint **S**ettings commands, the Init-String is a temporary override of the SERVICES **C**onfiguration **P**rinter setting, unless you name the settings sheet. If you name the settings sheet, it will be saved for you to use again. (For a more detailed description of this option, refer to the *Symphony Reference Manual*, with your printer manual also in hand, and experiment.) If you don't expect to use your printer's special features and just want regular printing, then don't worry about this command.

Remember that if you are using compressed print, you should change the right margin to get the full 136 characters. Otherwise, you may not get all the columns to print on one page.

Setting the Page Length

The SERVICES Configuration Printer setting for the number of lines printed on one page is 66. You can change this number temporarily or store a new page length in a named SERVICES Print Settings sheet. Page length can be set to any number between 20 and 100 with the SERVICES Print Settings Page Length option. This option is useful when you use special forms, paper, or type sizes. Because standard 8 1/2 x 11-inch paper has been used for the examples, however, this option will default to 66 in all three examples.

Printing Cell Formulas

Like 1-2-3, Symphony enables you to print cell contents in more than one way. For the sample reports in this chapter, the contents are printed just as they are displayed on the screen (except for spacing in the second example); also printed is a one-line-per-cell listing of the cell formulas for the Mom's Root Beer Report.

The command SERVICES Print Settings Other Format controls the way cell formulas are printed. When you enter this command, you are given the following choices:

As-Displayed   Cell-Formulas

The Cell-Formulas option is used to create the one-line-per-cell listing of the contents of a worksheet. This option is very convenient for debugging and also can be useful for re-creating formulas in other worksheets. Figure 8.11 shows the Cell-Formulas listing of Mom's Root Beer Report.

The As-Displayed option works with Cell-Formulas to reverse the Cell-Formulas option. As-Displayed returns to printing the format on the screen.

```
A1: 'Mom's Rootbeer Company -- Cash Flow Projection     G8: (F3) 0.35
A3: 'Year                                               H8: (F3) 0.35
B3: 1982                                                I8: (F3) 0.35
C3: 1983                                                J8: (F3) 0.35
D3: 1984                                                K8: (F3) 0.35
E3: 1985                                                L8: (F3) 0.35
F3: 1986                                                A10: 'Plant and Equipment: 22% of sales; cap exp = 30% of Sales Change + Depreciation
G3: 1987                                                A11: 'Depreciation: 14% of plant and equipment; all depreciation reinvested
H3: 1988                                                A12: 'Working Capital: Change = 15% of Sales change
I3: 1989                                                A13: 'Tax Rate = 41%
J3: 1990                                                A15: 'Projections
K3: 1991                                                A16: ' Sales
L3: 1992                                                B16: (P0) 516136
A4: \-                                                  C16: (P0) +B16*C6
B4: \-                                                  D16: (P0) +C16*D6
C4: \-                                                  E16: (P0) +D16*E6
D4: \-                                                  F16: (P0) +E16*F6
E4: \-                                                  G16: (P0) +F16*G6
F4: \-                                                  H16: (P0) +G16*H6
G4: \-                                                  I16: (P0) +H16*I6
H4: \-                                                  J16: (P0) +I16*J6
I4: \-                                                  K16: (P0) +J16*K6
J4: \-                                                  L16: (P0) +K16*L6
K4: \-                                                  A17:    COGS
L4: \-                                                  B17: (P0) 249284
A5: 'Growth Assumptions (as % of Sales)                 C17: (P0) +C16*C7
A6: ' Sales                                             D17: (P0) +D16*D7
B6: (F3) *actual                                        E17: (P0) +E16*E7
C6: (F3) 1.085                                          F17: (P0) +F16*F7
D6: (F3) 1.085                                          G17: (P0) +G16*G7
E6: (F3) 1.085                                          H17: (P0) +H16*H7
F6: (F3) 1.085                                          I17: (P0) +I16*I7
G6: (F3) 1.085                                          J17: (P0) +J16*J7
H6: (F3) 1.085                                          K17: (P0) +K16*K7
I6: (F3) 1.085                                          L17: (P0) +L16*L7
J6: (F3) 1.085                                          A18: ' Depn
K6: (F3) 1.085                                          B18: (P0) 18423
L6: (F3) 1.085                                          C18: (P0) +C16*0.22*0.14
A7: ' COGS                                              D18: (P0) +D16*0.22*0.14
B7: (F3) +B17/B16                                       E18: (P0) +E16*0.22*0.14
C7: (F3) 0.5                                            F18: (P0) +F16*0.22*0.14
D7: (F3) 0.5                                            G18: (P0) +G16*0.22*0.14
E7: (F3) 0.5                                            H18: (P0) +H16*0.22*0.14
F7: (F3) 0.5                                            I18: (P0) +I16*0.22*0.14
G7: (F3) 0.5                                            J18: (P0) +J16*0.22*0.14
H7: (F3) 0.5                                            K18: (P0) +K16*0.22*0.14
I7: (F3) 0.5                                            L18: (P0) +L16*0.22*0.14
J7: (F3) 0.5                                            A19: ' SGA
K7: (F3) 0.5                                            B19: (P0) 207807
L7: (F3) 0.5                                            C19: (P0) +C16*C8
A8: ' SGA                                               D19: (P0) +D16*D8
B8: (F3) +B19/B16                                       E19: (P0) +E16*E8
C8: (F3) 0.37                                           F19: (P0) +F16*F8
D8: (F3) 0.35                                           G19: (P0) +G16*G8
E8: (F3) 0.35                                           H19: (P0) +H16*H8
F8: (F3) 0.35                                           I19: (P0) +I16*I8
```

Fig. 8.11.

New
with
Symphony

Naming, Using, and
Deleting Print Settings Sheets

As mentioned several times throughout the book, one of the advantages of Symphony over 1-2-3 is the ability to name (and thus save) settings sheets. When settings sheets are named, you can retrieve them and reuse the settings again in the worksheet. Settings sheets, however, can be saved only if you save the file in which they were created.

SERVICES **P**rint **S**ettings provides the flexibility of entering the print settings for two different documents at the same time. After you have finished printing the first document, simply retrieve the named settings sheet, align or advance paper if needed, and then select **G**o to begin printing.

To use the options provided by naming print settings sheets, choose SERVICES **P**rint **S**ettings **N**ame. When you select **N**ame, the following menu will appear:

    Use   Create   Delete   Previous   Next   Initial-Settings   Reset   Quit

Here's how you use the SERVICES **P**rint **S**ettings **N**ame command. After having entered all the settings—margins, headers, footers, and so on—you select **N**ame from the SERVICES **P**rint **S**ettings menu. From the **N**ame menu, choose **C**reate. When Symphony asks "Name for new Print settings sheet: ", you enter a name, preferably one that will remind you of the document for which the name was created.

Before exiting from the file, you need to save the file by using the SERVICES **F**ile **S**ave command; having saved the file, you also retain the print settings sheet. Whenever you decide to use the print settings sheet again, you select SERVICES **P**rint **S**ettings **N**ame **U**se. A list of named print settings sheets will be displayed in the control panel of your screen. If you want to see a complete listing of print settings sheets, press the SERVICES key (F9), and Symphony will display a complete listing of sheets for the current file. (See fig. 8.12.)

Two commands are useful for "paging" through named print settings sheets: **P**revious and **N**ext. When you choose **P**revious, Symphony will display and make current the settings sheet prior to the current one, in alphabetical order by name. The **N**ext command

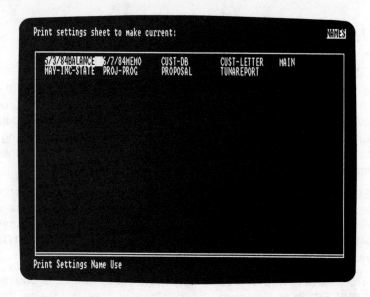

Print settings sheet to make current: NAMES

5/3/84BALANCE 5/7/84MEMO   CUST-DB   CUST-LETTER   MAIN
MAY-INC-STATE PROJ-PROG   PROPOSAL   TUNAREPORT

Print Settings Name Use

Fig. 8.12.

is the reverse of **Previous**; selecting **Next** will display the settings sheet next to the current one—once again, selecting in alphabetical order.

You can not only create, use, and cycle through print settings sheets, but also edit and delete them. One command is available for changing the print settings sheet currently on the screen back to the default settings in SERVICES **C**onfiguration **P**rinter. To delete a single settings sheet, use the SERVICES **P**rint **S**ettings **N**ame **D**elete command. If, however, you want to erase all named print settings sheets in a particular file, select SERVICES **P**rint **S**ettings **N**ame **R**eset. After you use this command, **P**rint **S**ettings from SERVICES **C**onfiguration **P**rinter will be in effect.

Controlling the Printer

Symphony makes it possible for you to control the printer. In fact, Symphony provides so much control that you hardly ever have to touch the printer except to turn it on just prior to printing and turn it off when you are done.

The ability to control the printer is important in printing the Cattuna Inventory. Between some of the different sections and text to be printed for this report, you will need to space down several lines. The SERVICES **P**rint Line-Advance makes the printer skip a line each time the command is entered. The command will be used several times in a row to skip between some of the sections.

You will also need to skip often to a new page by using SERVICES **P**rint **P**age-Advance. Like the SERVICES **P**rint Line-Advance command, the SERVICES **P**rint **P**age-Advance command causes the printer to skip to a new page each time you enter the command. When **P**age-Advance is used at the end of a printing session, the footer will be printed on the next page. If you **Q**uit from the SERVICES **P**rint menu before issuing the **P**age-Advance command, the last footer won't be printed.

Finally, when you start printing this report, you will need a way to signal to the printer where the top of the page is. The command used to align the page is SERVICES **P**rint **A**lign. Again, this command saves you from having to touch the printer control buttons.

The SERVICES **P**rint **G**o command must be entered to start the printer. This command also allows you to send a range to a print file (SERVICES **P**rint **S**ettings **D**estination **F**ile) and to a worksheet (SERVICES **P**rint **S**ettings **D**estination **R**ange).

If you want to interrupt the printing of a report in midstream, simply press the Ctrl key and the Break key simultaneously. The print buffer may take some time to clear, depending on its size, but Symphony will return you to the worksheet.

Now that you understand how to set print options, let's take a look at the three examples.

In figures 8.13A, 8.13B, 8.14A, 8.14B, 8.15A, and 8.15B, you will see the SERVICES **P**rint **S**ettings sheet and the final printed copy of each of the three examples of reports. Each example requires different commands for printing, which are listed below.

To print the Mom's Root Beer Company Cash-Flow Projection (figs. 8.13A and 8.13B), you enter the following commands*:

*Note: The ~ signifies RETURN.

1. SERVICES **P**rint **S**ettings **S**ource **R**ange A1..L30~
2. SERVICES **P**rint **S**ettings **I**nit-String \O19~
3. SERVICES **P**rint **S**ettings **M**argins **R**ight 136~
4. SERVICES **P**rint **S**ettings **M**argins **Q**uit
5. SERVICES **P**rint **S**ettings **Q**uit
6. SERVICES **P**rint **G**o

The only special entries made in the **P**rint commands for the Mom's Root Beer Report are **I**nit-String and **M**argins. Otherwise, printing this report requires setting the range and selecting **G**o when you are ready to begin printing.

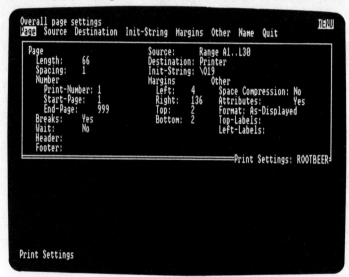

Fig. 8.13A.

To print the Inventory Report on Cattuna (figs. 8.14A and 8.14B), you enter the following commands:

1. SERVICES **P**rint **S**ettings **P**age **F**ooter |#~
2. SERVICES **P**rint **S**ettings **P**age **Q**uit
3. SERVICES **P**rint **S**ettings **S**ource **R**ange 22..50~
4. SERVICES **P**rint **S**ettings **M**argins **L**eft 1~
5. SERVICES **P**rint **S**ettings **M**argins **Q**uit
6. SERVICES Print **S**ettings **Q**uit
7. SERVICES **P**rint **G**o

```
Mom's Root Beer Company -- Cash Flow Projection

Year         1982     1983     1984     1985     1986     1987     1988     1989     1990     1991     1992
--------------------------------------------------------------------------------------------------------------
Growth Assumptions (as % of Sales)
  Sales     actual    1.005    1.005    1.005    1.005    1.005    1.005    1.005    1.005    1.005    1.005
  CGS        0.483    0.500    0.500    0.500    0.500    0.500    0.500    0.500    0.500    0.500    0.500
  SGA        0.403    0.370    0.350    0.350    0.350    0.350    0.350    0.350    0.350    0.350    0.350

Plant and Equipment: 22% of sales; cap exp = 30% of Sales Change + Depreciation
Depreciation: 14% of plant and equipment; all depreciation reinvested
Working Capital: Change = 15% of Sales change
Tax Rate = 41%

Projections
  Sales    516,136  560,000  607,600  659,255  715,292  776,091  842,059  913,634  991,293 1,075,553 1,166,975
  COGS     249,284  280,004  303,804  329,627  357,646  388,046  421,030  456,817  495,647  537,776  583,487
  Depn      18,423   17,248   18,714   20,305   22,031   23,904   25,935   28,140   30,532   33,127   35,943
  SGA      207,807  207,203  212,663  230,739  250,352  271,632  294,721  319,772  346,953  376,444  408,441
  Interest   18,423 projected cash flows considered to be unlevered
  EBT       22,199   55,553   72,427   78,583   85,263   92,510  100,373  108,905  118,162  128,206  139,103
  Tax        9,724   22,777   29,695   32,219   34,958   37,929   41,153   44,651   48,446   52,564   57,032
  EAT       12,475   32,776   42,732   46,364   50,305   54,581   59,220   64,254   69,716   75,641   82,071

  Cash Flow 30,898   50,024   61,446   66,669   72,336   78,485   85,156   92,394  100,247  108,769  118,014

  Cap Expend 64,757  30,410   32,995   35,799   38,842   42,144   45,726   49,612   53,829   58,405   63,369
  Work Cap             6,581    7,140    7,747    8,405    9,120    9,895   10,736   11,649   12,639   13,713

  Net CF             13,034   21,312   23,123   25,089   27,221   29,535   32,045   34,769   37,725   40,931
```

Fig. 8.13B.

The only special entry for printing the Inventory Report is the footer entry |#. Through this entry the page number is centered and printed at the bottom of the first page. (See fig. 8.14B.)

New with Symphony

If you compare figure 8.14A (the Inventory Report as it appears on the screen) with figure 8.14B (the printed copy), you will notice a difference in spacing. On the screen the report appears with single-spacing (except for the extra spaces added manually after the first paragraph and after the itemized list). The report, however, is printed with double-spacing. Double- and triple-spacing settings do not affect the text on the screen. If DOC Format Settings Spacing or a format line is set with double- or triple-spacing, these settings will control the spacing during printing.

In addition, for any text created in a DOC window, spacing in the printed copy is controlled by DOC Format Settings Spacing or a format line rather than SERVICES Print Settings Page Spacing. Keep in mind that if you want your document printed with double- or triple-spacing, enter the setting in DOC Format Settings Spacing instead of SERVICES Print Settings Spacing. Also keep in mind that spacing which you add manually to your document will also be added to the spacing setting, as in figure 8.14B.

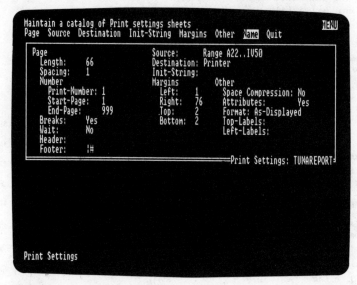

```
Maintain a catalog of Print settings sheets                          MENU
Page  Source  Destination  Init-String  Margins  Other  Name  Quit

Page                        Source:      Range A22..IV50
  Length:      66           Destination: Printer
  Spacing:     1            Init-String:
Number                      Margins           Other
  Print-Number: 1             Left:    1        Space Compression: No
  Start-Page:   1             Right:   76       Attributes:        Yes
  End-Page:     999           Top:     2        Format: As-Displayed
Breaks:       Yes             Bottom:  2        Top-Labels:
Wait:         No                               Left-Labels:
Header:
Footer:       !#
                                        ═══════Print Settings: TUNAREPORT═



Print Settings
```

Fig. 8.14A.

To print the Cattuna Distributing Inventory (figs. 8.15A and 8.15B), enter the following commands:

1. SERVICES **P**rint **S**ettings **P**age **S**pacing 2
2. SERVICES **P**rint **S**ettings **P**age **H**eader Cattuna Distributing Inventory Report||Page#~
3. SERVICES **P**rint **S**ettings **P**age **Q**uit
4. SERVICES **P**rint **S**ettings **S**ource **R**ange A1..G12~
5. SERVICES **P**rint **S**ettings **D**estination **F**ile Cattuna
6. SERVICES **P**rint **S**ettings **M**argins **T**op 8~
7. SERVICES **P**rint **S**ettings **M**argins **B**ottom 8~ **Q**uit **Q**uit
8. SERVICES **P**rint **G**o

This third example requires six special options as indicated by the list of commands above. First, to make the sheet easy to read, you must change spacing from single to double. Second, you enter a header identifying the report on the left side and the page number on

INVENTORY REPORT ON CATTUNA

Introduction

After receiving a high number of customer orders for Cattuna at the

beginning of February, I proposed that we review inventory for the

past year. I proposed the review because of the problem of keeping

up with customer orders in February. We therefore need to determine

if the problem occurred last year and, if so, how often. This report

summarizes my study of inventory and customer orders from January 1,

1983 to December 31, 1983, including my recommendations for changes

in our inventory system.

Summary of Inventory Study

The study which I conducted included a review of all inventory

records from January 1, 1983 to December 31, 1983. I considered the

following figures when reviewing Cattuna inventory:

    o Inventory at the beginning of the month
    o Customer demand for the whole month
    o Inventory at the end of the month
    o Quantity ordered at the end of the month
    o Setup costs at $10 per order
    o Inventory costs at $.20 per unit
    o Shortage costs at $1.00 per unit

Using the setup, inventory, and shortage costs, I calculated the total

costs for each month and the cumulative costs from month to month. See

Appendix A for a complete listing of inventory figures and costs for

January to December 1983.

Fig. 8.14B.

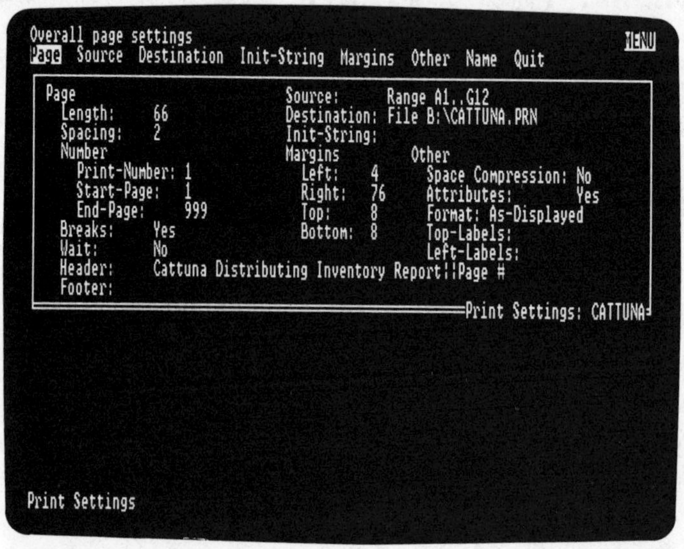

```
Overall page settings                                                    MENU
Page  Source  Destination  Init-String  Margins  Other  Name  Quit

  Page                        Source:       Range A1..G12
    Length:      66           Destination: File B:\CATTUNA.PRN
    Spacing:      2           Init-String:
  Number                      Margins          Other
    Print-Number: 1             Left:    4       Space Compression: No
    Start-Page:   1             Right:  76       Attributes:       Yes
    End-Page:   999             Top:     8       Format: As-Displayed
  Breaks:      Yes              Bottom:  8       Top-Labels:
  Wait:        No                               Left-Labels:
  Header:      Cattuna Distributing Inventory Report!!Page #
  Footer:
                                          ═══Print Settings: CATTUNA═

Print Settings
```

Fig. 8.15A.

the right. Third, if this report is not to be printed immediately, you can create a print file. Finally, to center the report evenly on the page, you change the top and bottom margins to 8.

Conclusion

This chapter has presented an introduction to printing reports and other documents with Symphony's SERVICES Print command. Covered here are all the major print operations that you will need

Cattuna Distributing Inventory   Page 1

Month	Jan	Feb	Apr	May	June	July
Beginning Inventory	43	51	60	42	30	46
Past Demand for Month	28	16	18	12	20	13
Ending Inventory	15	35	42	30	10	33
Quantity Ordered	36	0	0	0	36	0
Setup Costs ($10 per order)	$10.00	$0.00	$0.00	$0.00	$10.00	$0.00
Inventory Costs ($.2/unit)	$3.00	$7.00	$8.40	$6.00	$2.00	$6.60
Shortage Costs ($1/unit)	$0.00	$0.00	$0.00	$0.00	$0.00	$0.00
Total Costs for Month	$13.00	$7.00	$14.80	$6.00	$12.00	$6.60
Cum Cost from Last Month	$0.00	$13.00	$20.00	$43.20	$49.20	$61.20
Cumulative Costs to Date	$13.00	$20.00	$34.80	$49.20	$61.20	$67.80

Fig. 8.15B.

when you begin printing spreadsheets and word-processing documents. Symphony's print capabilities, however, extend beyond what is discussed in this chapter. For example, Symphony is capable of printing data base reports, labels, and form letters. These operations require integrating the print functions with Symphony's data management capabilities (Symphony's FORM window). In Chapter 11, Data Management, you will find a discussion of the special print functions connected with using Symphony's FORM window.

9
Creating and Displaying Graphs

Since 1-2-3's introduction, several major computer magazines have carried articles that compared 1-2-3's graphics with stand-alone graphics packages. 1-2-3 has been rated favorably against, and sometimes even as outperforming, many of these packages. 1-2-3's graphics typically score highest in their ease of use and immediacy: data is taken directly from the spreadsheet and graphed. 1-2-3's graphics score lowest in their scope and variability: the program offers limited display options and graph types (what can be called "business" graphs).

Symphony builds on the foundation of 1-2-3's strong graphics. Just as with 1-2-3, Symphony's graphics are designed for quick and easy implementation. Graphs are an integral part of the program, and data can be converted to a graph without transferring data from one program to another. Instead, the graph can easily be displayed by means of one or two simple commands.

Symphony has a good set of graphics commands, but it is not as powerful as some of the dedicated graphics packages, and it is only

409

moderately more powerful than 1-2-3. However, if your graphics needs are principally business-related, Symphony may have all the power you need.

1-2-3 and Symphony

Symphony has some graphics features not found in 1-2-3. For example, two new graph types have been added: exploded pie and high-low-close-open charts. The exploded pie chart is a variation of 1-2-3's standard pie chart with one or more of the slices separated from the pie for emphasis. High-low-close-open charts are good for graphing the prices of stocks over time and for evaluating trends. With the addition of these two graph types, Symphony has a nearly complete set of business graph types.

Other options found in Symphony graphics but not in 1-2-3 are manual control over scaling factors, new cross-hatchings, nonzero origins, and logarithmic graph scales.

SHEET and GRAPH Windows

All the changes that have been mentioned are minor, though, compared to Symphony's ability to display graphs and text at the same time on the same screen. If you select the Shared mode of display when you create your driver set, Symphony can show a graph in one window and text in another. (See Chapter 2 for more on setting up drivers.) In fact, Symphony does not restrict the number of windows you can create; you can show as many different graph or text windows as you can fit on the screen at any one time.

Just as with 1-2-3, you can access all of Symphony's graphing capabilities by using the **G**raph command within the SHEET environment (the equivalent of 1-2-3's spreadsheet environment). You can also set up a separate GRAPH window specifically designed to display graphs. The GRAPH window has all the capabilities of a SHEET window. What's the difference then? When do you want to use a SHEET window for graphing, and when is a GRAPH window more appropriate?

New with Symphony

*New
with
Symphony*

The difference between a SHEET window and a GRAPH window is how long a graph remains displayed on the screen. When you are in a SHEET window, you enter **P**review from the main **G**raph menu to display a graph on the screen. The main **G**raph menu appears below:

Preview   1st-Settings   2nd-Settings   Image-Save   Quit

By selecting **P**review, you can display a graph temporarily. The graph will remain displayed only until you press another key. Then you return to the SHEET environment, and the main **G**raph menu appears in the control panel again.

On the other hand, when you are in a GRAPH window, you use the **A**ttach option to display a graph on the screen. The GRAPH window menu appears below:

Attach   1st-Settings   2nd-Settings   Image-Save

When you select **A**ttach, any graph that you name will remain displayed in the window indefinitely. The only way you can eliminate the graph from the window is to attach another graph or delete the graph name. (See Deleting Graphs.)

Otherwise, all the commands in the **G**raph menu of the SHEET environment are exactly the same as those in the main menu of the GRAPH environment. You can even pass settings back and forth between the two environments. For example, you can create a pie chart in the SHEET environment and give those settings a name, such as SALESPIE. You can then use the same settings to display SALESPIE in a GRAPH window. Because the settings are shared by the two windows, any changes you make in one environment will also be made in the other.

Most of the examples in this chapter illustrate commands that are available for graphing in both SHEET and GRAPH windows. However, the sections on More on GRAPH Windows and More Examples (at the end of the chapter) include several examples in which you will need to choose one environment.

Types of Graphs

*New
with
Symphony*

Regardless of the environment, SHEET or GRAPH, Symphony offers six basic types of graphs:

Line
Simple Bar
Stacked Bar
XY
Pie Charts
High-Low-Close-Open Charts

Bar Graphs

Suppose that you want to create a simple worksheet containing data about store openings over the last five years for the three biggest retailers in the United States, as shown in figure 9.1. You can create many interesting graphs that will help make the data more understandable. For example, you can make a simple bar chart to illustrate the data on Sears alone. This graph is illustrated in figure 9.2.

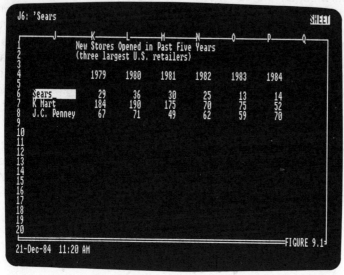

Fig. 9.1.

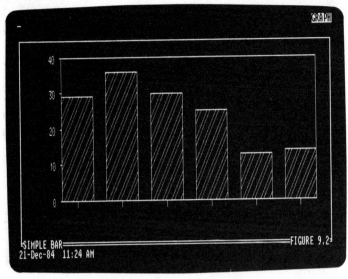

Fig. 9.2.

Making a Simple Bar Graph
in a SHEET Window

Bar graphs are used to compare different sets of data. A typical bar graph consists of vertical bars that show value by the height of the bar. To create a bar graph, start in a new SHEET window that occupies the entire screen and select the **G**raph option from the main SHEET menu.

Selecting the Type of Graph

After you select **G**raph, then **1**st-Settings, you must choose the **T**ype of graph you want to produce. Select **T**ype from the 1st-Settings menu. Figure 9.3 shows the 1st-Settings menu and settings sheet.

When you choose **T**ype, the following menu will appear:

Line Bar Stacked-Bar XY Pie High-Low-Close-Open

Because you are creating a bar graph, select **B**ar from this menu. Notice that Symphony automatically returns you to the 1st-Settings

Switch to 2nd-Settings
MENU
Switch Type Range Hue Format Data-Labels Legend Cancel Name Quit
Type: Line
Range Hue Format Data-Labels Legend
X 1
A 2 Both
B 3 Both
C 4 Both
D 5 Both
E 6 Both
F 7 Both
Graph 1st-Settings: MAIN
Graph 1st-Settings

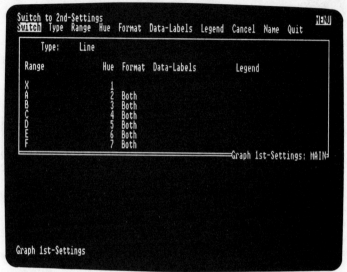

Fig. 9.3.

menu and settings sheet. In figure 9.4 you can see that the graph **T**ype has changed from the default setting of **L**ine to **B**ar.

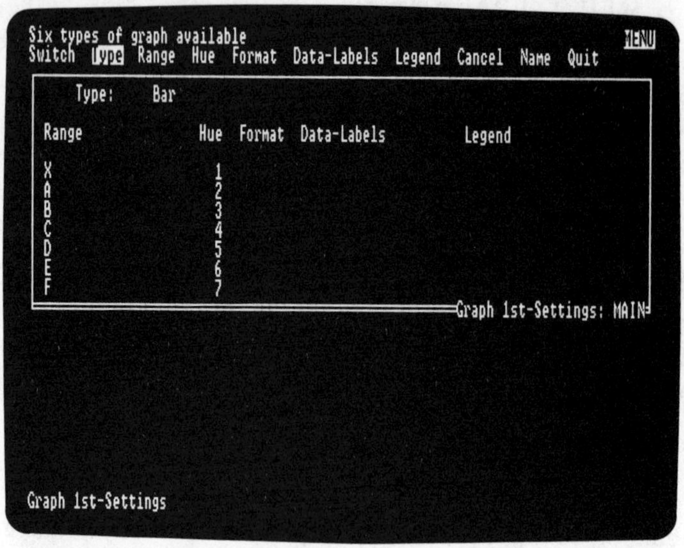

Six types of graph available
MENU
Switch Type Range Hue Format Data-Labels Legend Cancel Name Quit
Type: Bar
Range Hue Format Data-Labels Legend
X 1
A 2
B 3
C 4
D 5
E 6
F 7
Graph 1st-Settings: MAIN
Graph 1st-Settings

Fig. 9.4.

*New
with
Symphony*

Entering Data

Now that you have told Symphony what type of graph to create, you must give the program information to use in creating the graph. You begin this process by selecting **R**ange from the 1st-Settings menu. (**R**ange is the third item in the 1st-Settings menu, which appears in fig. 9.3.) Selecting **R**ange brings up the following menu:

X A B C D E F Quit

The appropriate range for the simple bar graph is **A**. After this option is selected, Symphony prompts for a range definition.

Choosing the Data Range

The range can be defined with cell references or a range name. In this example, the coordinates are K6..P6. Remember that this reference can be entered by typing the cell coordinates from the keyboard or by using the POINT mode. (If you are in the GRAPH environment when you want to designate a range, Symphony temporarily shifts to the SHEET environment.)

The simple bar graph in the example requires only one range, but Symphony lets you specify as many as six data ranges per graph. The letters **B** through **F** on the **R**ange menu represent the other ranges.

The data range for the sample graph consists of a partial row of data, but there is no reason why the data range cannot be a partial column. The graphs at the end of this chapter include examples of both vertical and horizontal data ranges. Remember, however, that the range must be a continuous set of cells. (This same rule applies in 1-2-3.) The ranges A2..A6, D3..F3, and F14..F30 are legal ranges; but the ranges A2,A4,D7 and E5,E8,F17,L4 are not.

Viewing the Graph

The final step in producing the graph is to enter **P**review from the main **G**raph menu. The results of entering **P**review depend on your hardware and how you configured it during installation. (For more on installing the system, see Chapter 2.) If you have a nongraphics screen, nothing happens; all you get is a beep. But don't worry;

although you can't see the graph on the display, it still exists in your computer's memory. You can use the PrintGraph program (see the next chapter) to save and print your graph.

If you have a graphics card and either a black-and-white or color monitor, you will see the bar graph displayed on the screen after you enter **P**review. If you have a Hercules Graphics Card (or equivalent) for your monochrome display, the graph will appear on the display. Notice that in both cases the temporary GRAPH window, which is created by your selecting **P**review, replaces the SHEET window on the screen. (This always happens when you are in the SHEET environment regardless of whether you selected Shared or Toggle mode during installation.) You can return to the screen by pressing any key.

Finally, if you are fortunate enough to have a dual monitor system with both a graphics monitor and a monochrome display (and you selected the Dual mode during installation), the bar chart will appear on the graphics monitor, and the worksheet will remain on the monochrome display. If your graphics monitor can display color, you can format the graph to take advantage of that capability, too.

Adding Titles and Labels

New
with
Symphony

Although the picture created so far has graphics appeal, it does not offer much information. To complete the graph, you must add titles and labels. For instance, you can enter titles for the graph itself and for the X and Y axes. You first access the **G**raph **2**nd-Settings command menu. Figure 9.5 shows the command menu in the control line above the **G**raph **2**nd-Settings sheet.

You then select **T**itles from the **2**nd-Settings command menu (as it appears in fig. 9.5). The **T**itles option lets you assign a main title and a subtitle that will appear at the top of the graph (the **F**irst and **S**econd options in the menu below) and also titles for the X and Y axes (the **X**-Axis and **Y**-Axis options). The **G**raph **2**nd-Settings **T**itles command menu gives you the following choices:

    First   Second   X-Axis   Y-Axis   Quit

For the **X**-Axis and **Y**-Axis commands, you may enter the labels "Year" and "Number of Stores," respectively. To enter the X-axis

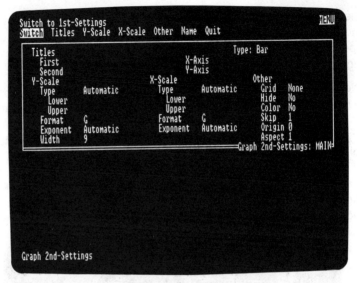

Fig. 9.5.

label, you select the **X**-Axis option and simply type the title *Year*. The Y-axis title is similarly specified. Figure 9.6 shows the original bar graph with the titles added.

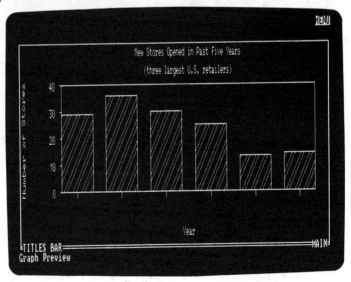

Fig. 9.6.

The graph titles at the top of figure 9.6 were entered using the **F**irst and **S**econd options. **F**irst was used for the main title "New Stores Opened in Past Five Years," and **S**econd for the subtitle below it, "(three largest U.S. retailers)".

These titles are usually entered by typing the title from the keyboard. In this case, however, we used the special backslash (\) feature made available to the **G**raph **2**nd-Settings **T**itles commands (and **L**egends commands). This feature lets you enter the contents of cells instead of typing in text. To use the contents of a cell for a title (or legend text), place a backslash (\) before the cell address when Symphony asks you for a title. For instance, you enter \K1 for **F**irst and \K2 for **S**econd. Notice that these selections appear in the **2**nd-Settings sheet. (See fig. 9.7.)

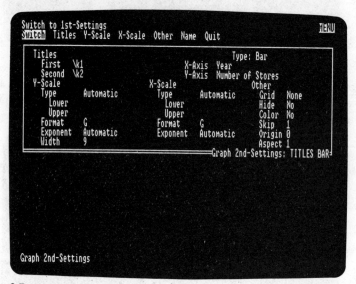

Fig. 9.7.

A range can also be used to create a title or label. To do this, you enter the range name instead of the cell reference after the backslash. Incidentally, just as with 1-2-3, a Symphony graph title can be no longer than 39 characters.

You should be aware of two particulars of Symphony's graph titles. First, Symphony always disregards label prefixes when setting up titles, so the program automatically centers the **F**irst and **S**econd graph titles when it displays the graph. Second, the **F**irst and **S**econd titles look very much alike in size and intensity on the screen, but the PrintGraph program prints the **F**irst title much larger than the **S**econd. (This facility is explained in the following chapter.)

Another enhancement you may make is to add labels along the X-axis to define the data items you are plotting. Figure 9.8 shows the basic bar graph to which X-axis labels have been added.

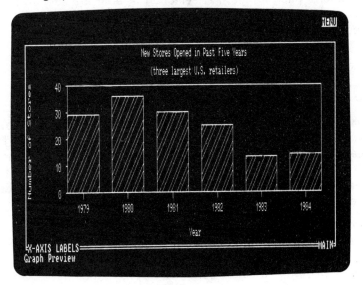

Fig. 9.8.

You add these labels by selecting **X** from the **1st-Settings R**ange menu and pointing to the appropriate range of labels in the worksheet. In this example, the labels are in the range K4..P4 (fig. 9.1). Symphony uses the contents of the cells in the indicated range as the X labels. (The values in the range K4..P4 are actually stored as numbers; however, Symphony uses them as labels in this instance.) Symphony automatically centers the X labels.

Switching between 1st- and 2nd-Settings Sheets

You can get from the **2**nd-Settings menu to the **1**st-Settings menu (as in the example above) by entering **Q**uit from the **2**nd-Settings command menu to return to the main **G**raph menu. You can then select **1**st-Settings. There is an easier way, though. Symphony offers a **S**witch option as the first selection in both the **1**st- and **2**nd-Settings command menus. **S**witch lets you automatically switch back and forth between the two graph settings sheets without having to return to the main **G**raph menu.

Changing the Automatic Scale Settings

Like 1-2-3, Symphony automatically sets the scale (upper and lower limits) of the Y-axis according to the range you designate. This feature is extremely convenient. Symphony uses a scale that shows all the data points in the graph with the graph filling as much of the window as possible. If Symphony did not automatically set the scale, creating graphs would be much more cumbersome.

Sometimes you will want to change the scale that Symphony has chosen for a graph. For example, you may want to focus attention on a certain range of values, such as those surrounding a target goal, or you may want to create a series of graphs that all have the same scale.

Overriding Automatic Scaling

You can override Symphony's automatic scaling in several ways. The commands for overriding automatic scaling are accessed through the **2**nd-Settings **Y**-Axis and **X**-Axis commands. Suppose you have selected the **2**nd-Settings **Y**-Axis command. The following menu appears:

New with Symphony

     Type   Format   Exponent   Width   Quit

The **T**ype option selects the kind of scale overriding that you wish. Symphony usually uses linear scales, but you can also set logarithmic scales. The options that appear once you have selected **T**ype are

Manual-Linear   Automatic-Linear   Logarithmic

The **M**anual-Linear option manually overrides Symphony's automatic scaling in a linear fashion. With **M**anual-Linear, you must manually set the lower and upper boundaries of the scale. Logarithmic, on the other hand, lets you override Symphony's automatic linear scaling in a logarithmic fashion; however, Symphony still sets the upper and lower boundaries on its own. (See Advanced Graphics Options at the end of the chapter for more on logarithmic scaling.)

Invoking Linear Scale Override

When you choose the **M**anual-Linear option, Symphony requests upper and lower boundaries for the scale limits. Figure 9.9 shows how this function works. This figure uses the same data as figure 9.8, except that the scale has been changed to show an upper limit of 50 and a lower limit of -50.

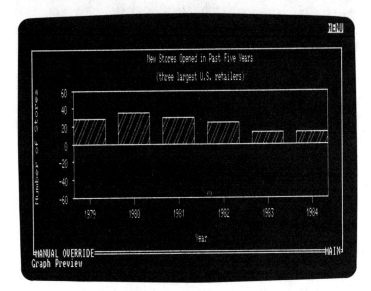

Fig. 9.9.

If you decide that you want to eliminate the manual overrides which you have set up, you can select the **A**utomatic-Linear option to reset the scaling to automatic.

Formatting Numbers

The **F**ormat option of the **2**nd-Settings **X**- and **Y**-Scale commands allows you to change the way the numbers on the X-axis and Y-axis are displayed. The alternatives under this option are the same as those for the SHEET **F**ormat. You can specify that the numbers be displayed with a fixed number of digits, with a $ or embedded command, or as a percentage with an appended % sign. For example, figure 9.9 shows the same graph as figure 9.10, except that the scale has been assigned the Fixed 2 format.

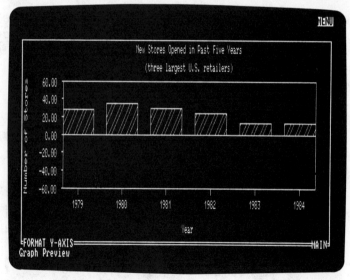

Fig. 9.10.

Fitting the Graph to the Scales

Symphony will always try to fit the graph into the scales you have specified. If you set the upper limit of a scale too low, the resulting graph will simply show as much of the data as can be squeezed into the allotted space. For example, if you set the upper limit at 10 and the lower limit at 0 and try to graph the sample data, the result will be the graph in figure 9.11.

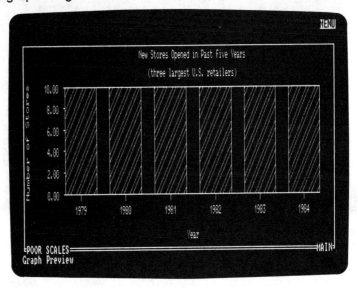

Fig. 9.11.

New
with
Symphony

Changing to Nonzero Origin

When you use the **M**anual-Linear option, Symphony always ignores a positive lower limit or a negative upper limit on the Y-axis scale; this feature ensures that zero (the origin) is always on the scale. However, Symphony offers another option that lets you change the origin of a graph. This new option is accessed through the **2**nd-Settings **O**ther **O**rigin command. For example, you can change the origin of the graph in figure 9.8 from 0 to 10. Figure 9.12 shows how the graph changes.

Using Other Scale Options

You have several other scale options for formatting a graph. These include logarithmic scaling, controlling the width of Y-axis scale numbers, and controlling Symphony's scaling messages. However,

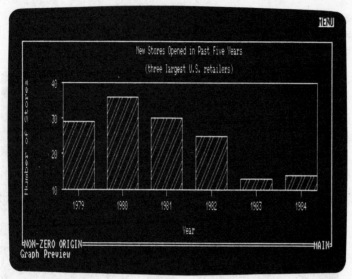

Fig. 9.12.

these options are best applied to more complex graphs and therefore are discussed in the section on Advanced Graphics Options at the end of the chapter.

Saving and Recalling Graph Settings

Only one set of graph settings can be the *current* graph settings. Before you can build a new set of graph settings sheets, you must store the old ones.

By issuing the **N**ame option from either the **1**st- or **2**nd-Settings command menus, you can instruct Symphony to remember the parameters stored in the current graph settings sheets. (The option resides in both menus.) The **N**ame command menu is

Use Create Delete Previous Next Initial-Settings Reset Quit

With the **C**reate option, you can create a 15-character name for the current settings. All the settings in both the **1**st-and **2**nd-Settings sheets—the data range settings, graph titles, and axis titles—are saved under this name. The new name appears in the lower right corner of both the **1**st- and **2**nd-Settings sheets; and when you save

New
with
Symphony

the Symphony file, the name will also be saved. (Notice in fig. 9.7 that the name of the settings sheets for that figure is TITLES BAR.)

You can recall a named set of **1**st- and **2**nd-Settings sheets at any time by issuing the **N**ame **U**se command. When the command is issued, Symphony presents a list of all the named sets of graph settings stored in the current worksheet (the *settings catalog*). You can select the set you want by typing the name from the keyboard or pointing to the name in the list. The **N**ame **U**se command will retrieve the **1**st- and **2**nd-Settings sheets of the named set and make them the current set.

1-2-3 is incapable of recalling graph settings if you do not give them a name before saving the file. Symphony is not quite so strict. If you save a file without naming the current graph settings, Symphony will still keep your current graph settings.

New with Symphony

Using Graph Settings Catalogs

Several different graph settings sheets can be created for a single file, even for a single window. The entire group of settings in a worksheet file is called a catalog. The **N**ame **C**reate and **N**ame **U**se commands make it easy to create and use a catalog of settings sheets. For example, the settings sheets for all the various graphs in this chapter are contained in a single catalog. After each settings sheet was created, it was attached to a GRAPH window and a picture of the graph was taken.

Two other options available in the **N**ame menu help you select settings sheets from a catalog. These commands are **P**revious and **N**ext. When you select **P**revious, Symphony automatically selects the settings sheet that alphabetically precedes the current settings sheet in the catalog. For example, suppose you had the following catalog of settings names:

FORMAT Y-AXIS	MANY PARTS
LOGARITHMIC	NONZERO ORIGIN
MAIN TEXT	POOR SCALES
MANUAL	SIMPLE BAR
OVERRIDE	X-AXIS LABELS

If the current settings name is SIMPLE BAR and you select **P**revious, Symphony will shift the current settings to POOR SCALES. However, if the current settings name is FORMAT Y-AXIS, Symphony will use the last entry in the list, X-AXIS LABELS. The **N**ext option works just the opposite from **P**revious.

Deleting Graph Settings

New with Symphony

To delete a single settings name from the worksheet, you use the **1**st- or **2**nd-Settings **N**ame **D**elete command. As with the **N**ame **C**reate command, Symphony will prompt you with a list of all the settings names in the current worksheet file. You can point to the name you want to delete or type the name from the keyboard.

To delete all the settings names, you can issue the **N**ame **R**eset command. This command automatically deletes all the settings names in the catalog. Be careful. When the settings names are deleted, all the settings for all the graphs in the current file are lost. A "Yes / No" confirmation step in the **G**raph **R**eset command gives you a second chance if you accidentally type **R** for **R**eset. However, once you enter **Y**es, all the settings for all the graphs are gone.

1-2-3 users will recognize that up to this point Symphony resembles 1-2-3 in regard to deleting graph names. However, Symphony has two rules that 1-2-3 doesn't. First, you cannot delete the current settings name. For example, suppose FORMAT Y-AXIS is the current graph settings name. You must make another settings name current before you can delete FORMAT Y-AXIS.

A second thing to remember about deleting settings names in Symphony is that there is no barrier to deleting a settings name that is attached to a GRAPH window. The GRAPH window will simply appear blank on the screen, and the settings for the GRAPH window will reset to the default configuration settings.

Resetting All the Current Graph Settings

New with Symphony

Instead of deleting a settings name, you can completely reset all the settings associated with that name by using the **N**ame **I**nitial-Settings command. When you select the **I**nitial-Settings option, Symphony resets the current settings sheet to the default settings.

For example, suppose you have created what you thought were the correct settings for a graph of revenue projections and named the settings PROJECT REVENUE. Suppose also that you later discover that the settings in PROJECT REVENUE are all wrong. You can go through a detailed sequence of making another settings name current, deleting PROJECT REVENUE with the **N**ame **D**elete command, and finally re-creating PROJECT REVENUE with **N**ame **C**reate. However, a much easier way to reset all the settings for PROJECT REVENUE is to use the **I**nitial-Settings command while the name is still current.

New
with
Symphony

Resetting a Portion of the Current Graph Settings

Besides resetting all the current settings for a particular name, you can also delete selected settings with the **1**st-Settings **C**ancel command. In fact, all or just a portion of the **1**st-Settings can be deleted with this command. Settings that can be deleted include range addresses, formats, data labels, legends, and hues (colors). For example, suppose you have the first settings sheet, which appears in figure 9.13.

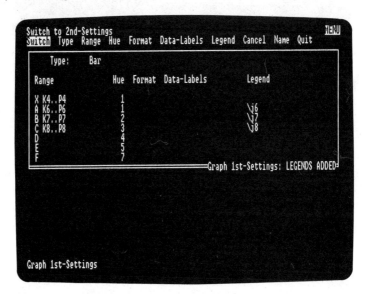

Fig. 9.13.

To delete the A range addresses, you select **C**ancel from the **1st-**Settings menu. The following menu will then appear:

Entire-Row   Range   Format   Data-Labels   Legend   Hue

To delete the A range, you select **R**ange from the menu. The following menu then appears:

Graph   X   A   B   C   D   E   F   Quit

To cancel the A range, you select **A**. The **1st-**Settings sheet then appears as shown in figure 9.14.

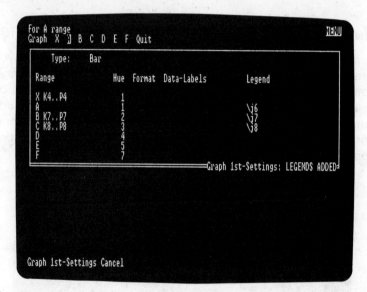

Fig. 9.14.

If you want to delete all the entries for the A range, you select the **1st-**Settings **C**ancel **E**ntire-Row **A** command. This selection will cause the **1st-**Settings sheet to appear as in figure 9.15.

To delete all the settings for the entire graph, you select the **C**ancel **E**ntire-Row **G**raph command. All the settings in the **1st-**Settings sheet will be reset to the default settings.

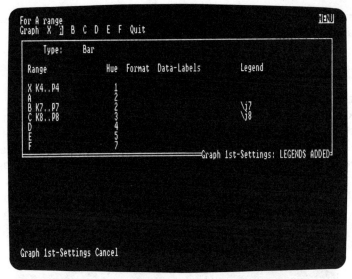

Fig. 9.15.

Saving Graphs for Printing

As mentioned earlier, the main Symphony program does not have the ability to print graphs. The PrintGraph program must be used to print graphics. Before a graph can be printed with PrintGraph, however, it must be saved. The Image-Save option from the GRAPH menu or SHEET Graph menu causes Symphony to save the current graph settings, including all the selected formatting options. All graph files saved have the extension .PIC.

Once you have created a .PIC file, you can no longer access it from the main Symphony menu other than to list its name. The .PIC file is accessible only from the PrintGraph program. If you want to re-create the graph on the screen from within Symphony, you must give the settings a name in the current worksheet file.

Creating a More Complex Bar Graph

Increasing the complexity of the bar graph in figure 9.8 will help you understand the following explanations. You can build a more complex bar graph by including the data for the two other major U.S. retailers, K Mart and J. C. Penney, with the data for Sears.

Adding More Data Ranges

After you create a new settings name (by using **N**ame **C**reate), your next step is to inform Symphony that the new graph will include two additional data ranges. To do this, you must first access the **1**st-Settings **R**ange menu. Because one data range has already been created, the next set of data goes into the B range. To enter the data range, you select **B** from the **R**ange menu and tell Symphony that the data is located in the range K7..P7 (fig. 9.1). To enter the third data set, you select **C** and indicate the location of the data: K8..P8. If you are in a SHEET window, use **G**raph **P**review to draw the graph. The graph will appear as shown in figure 9.16.

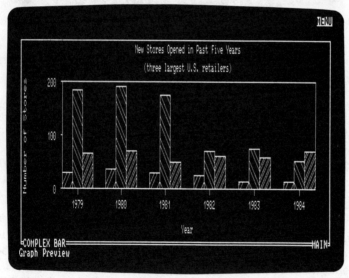

Fig. 9.16.

The graph groups the data sets. The first data items from each range are grouped together; similarly, the second and third data items are grouped together. This grouping makes it easy to compare the data in each data set.

For an additional challenge, you may try creating a special graph window. To do this, use the SERVICES **W**indow **C**reate command and enter a window name; you may want to use *FIGURE 9.16* for the name. You can then call up the GRAPH menu by selecting the MENU key (F9 on IBM PCs and compatibles). Finally, use the **A**ttach option from the GRAPH menu to attach the COMPLEX BAR settings to the window.

Notice the different crosshatches with the bars in figure 9.16. There were crosshatches in the earlier bar graphs in this chapter, but because there was only one set of data, only one pattern of crosshatches appeared. Because this graph has several sets of data, the contrast between crosshatches is much greater. Cross-hatching makes it easy to distinguish among different data sets when they are graphed in black and white. Normally, Symphony controls the crosshatches for you.

*New
with
Symphony*

Controlling Bar Graph Cross-Hatchings

Although most of the time you will want Symphony to control the cross-hatching, the program does allow you to select patterns yourself. Symphony offers 7 different cross-hatching patterns with a numbering scheme of 1 through 7. Figure 9.17 shows the patterns and their respective numbers.

Suppose you prefer the patterns numbered 5 through 7. To change the patterns for the data sets, you use the **1**st-Settings **H**ue command. If you want to change the patterns for data set A to pattern 5, you use **1**st-Settings **H**ue **5**; to change data set B to pattern 6, you use **H**ue **5**; etc. Figures 9.18A and 9.18B show the **1**st-Settings sheet and associated bar graph.

On the **1**st-Settings sheet, the **H**ue for range X is 1. Changing the **H**ue selection for range X will have no effect when you are displaying a graph in black and white. When you are using color, though, the **H**ue selection allows you to change the color of the labels below the X-axis.

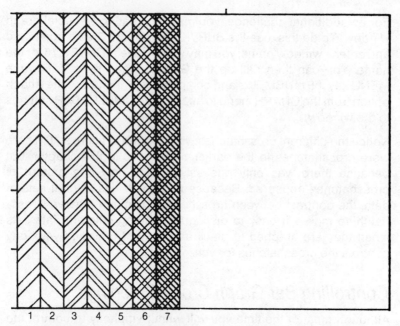

Fig. 9.17.

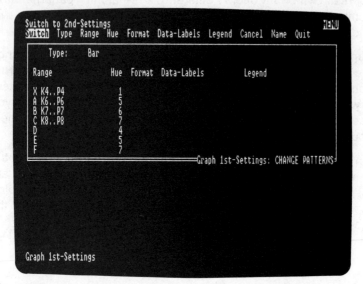

Fig. 9.18A.

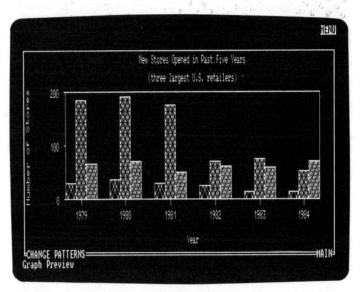

Fig. 9.18B.

Using Legends

Whenever you have more than one set of data on a graph, you need some method to distinguish one set from another. Symphony has several ways to help you distinguish data sets. Line graphs provide different symbols to mark the different data points. Bar charts use different patterns of cross-hatchings. If your display is a color monitor, Symphony can also use color to make the distinction.

Even with the different patterns of color or cross-hatchings, legends to label the patterns are also useful. At the bottom of figure 9.19B, below the X-axis, are three different legends corresponding to the three different ranges of data already graphed. These legends are entered by the **1**st-Settings **L**egend command. Once you have selected this option, you can type the actual legend text. For example, you can enter *Sears* for legend A. See figures 9.19A and 9.19B, respectively, for the **1**st-Settings sheet and associated graph when legends are added.

Like titles, legends can also be entered with \ and a cell reference or a range name. For example, you can enter \J6 for **1**st-Settings

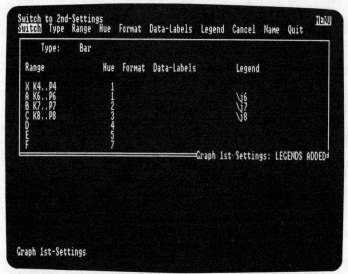

Fig. 9.19A.

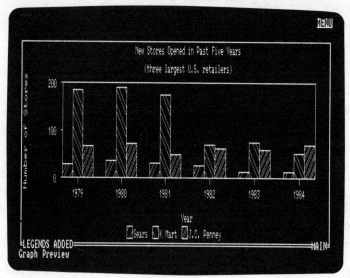

Fig. 9.19B.

Legend **A**, \J7 for **B**, and so on. The legends that appear in figure
9.19B were entered using this method.

Displaying the Graph in Color

If you have a color monitor, you can instruct Symphony to display graphics in color. The ability to produce colors is one of the nicest features of the program. Just what colors Symphony uses depends on your hardware. If you have an IBM PC/XT, Symphony can display graphics in only three different colors (white, red, and blue). These colors are not to be confused, however, with the large selection of colors the program can actually use for printing graphs if you have the appropriate printer or plotter. (Printing graphs and the additional colors available are covered in the following chapter.)

To display the graph from figure 9.19B in color, you select **C**olor **Yes** from the **2**nd-Settings **O**ther menu. The bars and lines for the data and label ranges can then be set to different colors. Symphony offers the following hues for the IBM PC/XT and compatibles:

Hue Number	Actual Color
1	White
2	Red
3	Blue
4	White
5	Red
6	Blue
7	White

The list of colors available for the IBM PC is obviously somewhat limited, and the colors for your particular machine may be different. You should consult your dealer if you have any questions about what colors Symphony can produce on your machine.

The COLOR ADDED graph shows the same graph as in figure 9.19B but in color. To produce this graph, Symphony's standard default settings were used. COLOR ADDED and all other graphs in color appear in the color section of this book. They are referred to by name rather than figure number in both the text and the color section.

Changing Colors in Bar Graphs

If you don't like the colors that Symphony chooses for the different ranges, you can change them. For example, suppose that you prefer the outside scales and numbers to be red and the bars to be blue for data range A, white for B, and red for C. You use the **1st-Settings H**ue command to make the appropriate changes. To select red for the outside scales and numbers, you use the **1st-Settings H**ue **R**ange **X 2** command; to have blue for range A, you use **H**ue **R**ange **A 3**. The CHANGE COLOR graph shows the graph, and CHANGE COLOR 1st-Settings sheet shows the new colors.

The **H**ue option is also used to control the cross-hatchings. Whether Symphony uses colors or cross-hatchings for filling in the bars in a bar graph depends on whether color has been invoked. Unfortunately, you cannot have colors and cross-hatchings at the same time on bar graphs. (You can with pie charts; see Pie Chart Cross-Hatchings.)

Stacked Bar Graphs

A slight variation of the basic bar graph is the stacked bar graph. Stacked bar graphs are frequently used to compare different sets of data while showing the components and total of each data set. In these graphs, the totals are created by stacking the component data items one on another.

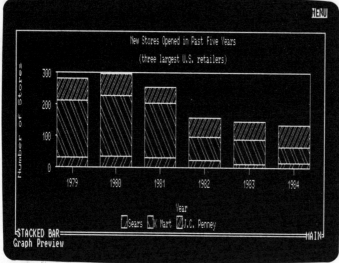

Fig. 9.20.

In figure 9.20, you can see the total number of store openings for the three largest U.S. retailers. This graph was created in much the same way as the graph in figure 9.19B. In fact, the same settings were used to produce both, except the 1st-Settings **T**ype was changed to **S**tacked-Bar in the second graph. **P**review draws the graph in the SHEET environment. Notice that legends, X-axis labels, and titles have also been added. They, too, were added in the same way as they were in the simpler examples.

Line Graphs

Symphony also offers line graphs. They are particularly useful for showing time-series data but are by no means restricted to this use. Consider the data on "Interest Rate Movements for February 1983" that appears in figure 9.21.

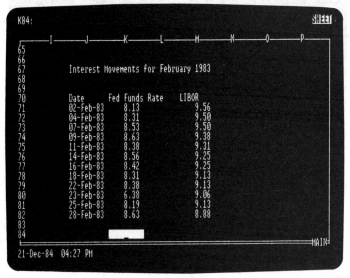

Fig. 9.21.

This data, taken from *The Wall Street Journal,* reflects the Federal Funds Rate and London Interbank Offering Rate (LIBOR) for the indicated dates.

Making a Line Graph

To create a line graph of the Federal Funds Rate plotted against time, you first select the **L**ine option from the **1**st-Settings menu. Next, you select **A** from the **1**st-Settings **R**ange command and enter the range K71..K82 as the A range. As always, the graph is drawn with **P**review when you are in the SHEET environment; however, when you are in the GRAPH environment, you must attach a name to the window before the graph will appear. Figure 9.22 illustrates this line graph.

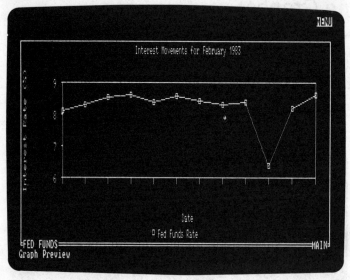

Fig. 9.22.

Once again, titles have been added to the graph. To do this, you select **T**itles from the **2**nd-Settings menu and enter the titles shown for **F**irst, **S**econd, **X**, and **Y** selections. Figure 9.23 shows the **1**st- and **2**nd-Settings sheets for the graph in figure 9.22.

Notice also that the line chart in figure 9.22 has no X-axis labels. The next step is to enter the range of dates in column J as the X range. As with the bar graphs shown earlier, you enter X labels by selecting the **X** option from the **1**st-Settings **R**ange command. In this example, you use the range J71..J82. When this graph is redrawn (by the **P**review command), you will see figure 9.24.

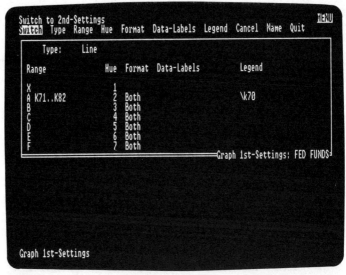

Fig. 9.23A.

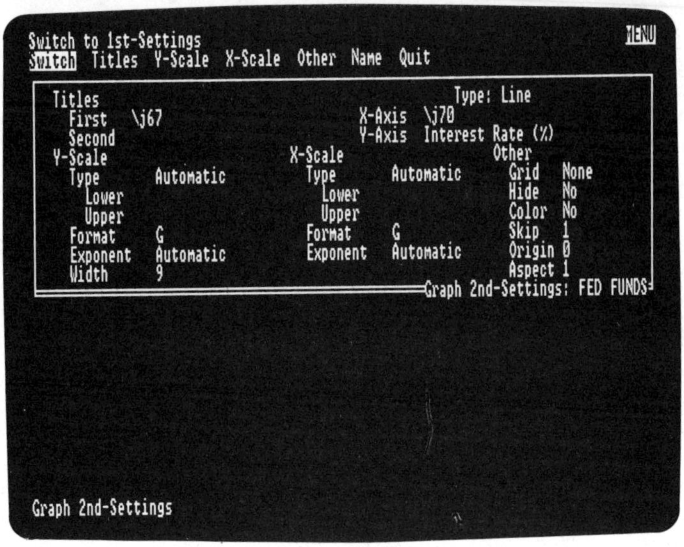

Fig. 9.23B.

Using the entire set of data labels in column J causes a problem because there is simply not enough room on the graph to display all

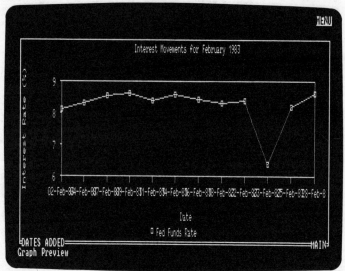

Fig. 9.24.

the labels without overlapping. This can happen anytime the X labels are unusually long or there are a great many of them.

Symphony offers two solutions to this problem. One option is to reformat the dates in a shorter form (for instance, format D2—DD/MMM). If you prefer not to change the format, however, you can use the **2**nd-Settings **O**ther **S**kip command to skip every nth X label when the graph is displayed. After you enter the command, Symphony will prompt you for the skipping factor. In most cases, as in the example in figure 9.25, skipping every other label will be sufficient to clean up the graph. This is done by specifying a factor of 2. On some graphs, however, it may be necessary to choose a much larger factor. Actually, Symphony has the ability to skip as many as 8,192 X labels.

The fact that the date labels are ordered sequentially doesn't matter to Symphony. It could just as easily have plotted against any other set of labels. Although cells containing date functions were used for the X-axis labels, Symphony can use numbers, labels, or functions for these labels.

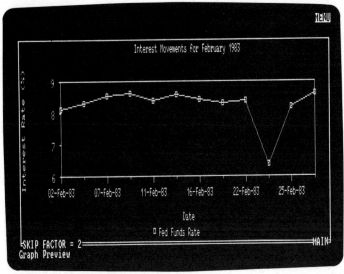

Fig. 9.25.

Making a More Complex Line Graph

The data set that appears in figure 9.21 suggests a second line graph that compares the variations in the Federal Funds rate to the changes in LIBOR during the same period. This graph is really a simple extension of the previous one. To continue the example, you must first create a B range that captures the data in range M71..M82. Figure 9.26 illustrates the new graph.

Formatting the Line Graph

Notice the different symbols at the points of intersection on the graph (box and plus). So far, you have seen only one of the four ways of displaying a line graph. The command that controls the lines and symbols at the points of intersection on a line graph is **1st-Settings Format <A through F>**. This command has the following menu:

Lines   Symbols   Both   Neither

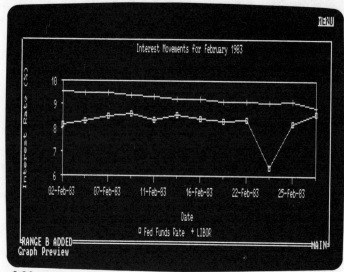

Fig. 9.26.

*L*ines

Lines signals Symphony to connect the different data points with straight lines and no symbols. Figure 9.27 shows the graph from figure 9.26 with lines only.

*S*ymbols

The **S**ymbols option tells Symphony to leave out the straight lines and use different graphic symbols for each of up to six data ranges. The symbols are

A □	D △
B +	E x
C ◇	F ▽

Figure 9.28 shows the graph with symbols but no lines. Although this format can be used with line charts, it is more commonly used with XY plots.

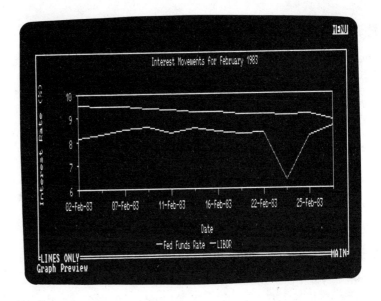

Fig. 9.27.

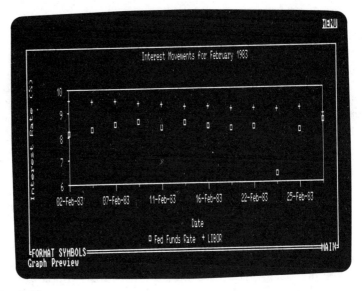

Fig. 9.28.

*B*oth Lines and Symbols

The third choice, **B**oth, is the default used in figures 9.22 through 9.26 to produce both lines and symbols. Because it is difficult to tell one data set from another without using both lines and symbols, in most cases **B**oth is the preferred option.

*N*either Lines nor Symbols

Neither suppresses both lines and symbols. You may wonder how points of intersection can be shown if neither lines nor symbols appear on the graph. The answer is through **D**ata-Labels.

*D*ata-Labels

Symphony's **D**ata-Labels command uses data from a SHEET window as labels in a graph. These labels are placed in the graph near the data points on the graph. The **D**ata-Labels option is a part of the **G**raph **O**ptions menu. After the **1**st-Settings **D**ata-Labels selection is made, the following menu appears:

    A B C D E F Quit

Notice that the options here correspond to the data range options; there is one set of data labels for each set of data. In general, you will want to use the same coordinates to define the data labels and the data range. For example, in the latest sample graph, the data labels for data range A are entered by selecting the label range K71..K82. Symphony then presents the option of placing the data labels above or below the data point, centered on the data point, or to the left or right.

The data labels can be numbers, values, or text. All data labels are converted to labels before they are placed in the worksheet. In most cases, you will want to use numbers as data labels. If you use text, be sure to keep the strings short to avoid cluttering the graph.

Data labels can be used in a line chart that includes lines and symbols, as well as in a graph that contains no lines or symbols. If you are not using lines or symbols (on a line graph), you will probably want to center the data labels on the data points.

Otherwise, you'll want to choose one of the other options to avoid cluttering the graph.

Figures 9.29A and 9.29B show the first sample line graph (one data set) with data labels and without symbols or lines; the 1st-Settings sheet is also included (fig. 9.29A). Of course, data labels can also be used in graphs with symbols and lines. In fact, in line charts with multiple data sets, lines or symbols are necessary to differentiate the various data sets. Otherwise, the graph will look like a jumble of numbers. Figure 9.30 shows another line graph (with two data sets) with data labels.

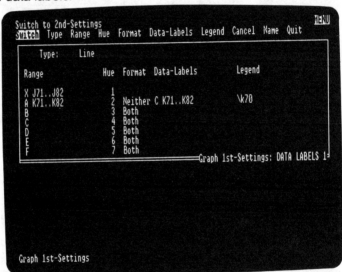

Fig. 9.29A.

Data labels also work with bar graphs. In bar graphs, the labels are centered above each bar. As with line charts, data labels can be helpful in identifying the numeric value associated with each data point.

Sometimes it is easy to get confused about the difference between the X-axis titles, the X labels, and the data labels. An X-axis title usually describes the units of measure used on the X-axis (like dollars or years). X labels distinguish the different data points (for example, 1981 and 1982 data). Data labels describe individual data items.

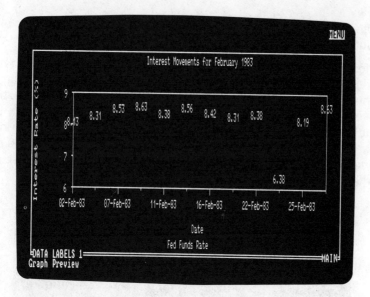

Fig. 9.29B.

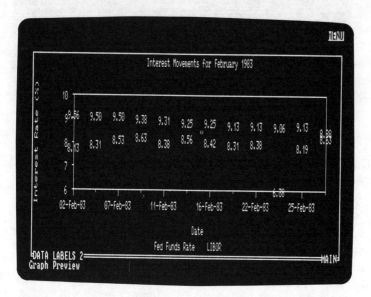

Fig. 9.30.

Grids

Symphony offers still another option for formatting graphs: grids. This option lets you impose a grid on a Symphony graph. The command to create a grid is **2**nd-Settings **O**ther **G**rid. The submenu under this command offers the following options:

Horizontal   Vertical   Both   None

The first option creates a horizontal grid over the graph; the second, a vertical grid. Option 3, **B**oth, causes both types of grids to be displayed, as in figure 9.31. The last option, **N**one, eliminates all grids from the current graph settings.

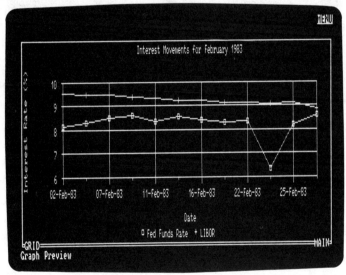

Fig. 9.31.

Although grids can be useful, they also can clutter the graph unnecessarily. You may find that using data labels works better than grids for many applications.

Pie Charts

Symphony also provides simple pie charts. They show relationships within a single set of data items. Each data item is a slice of the pie, and the entire pie represents the sum of the slices.

In many ways, a pie chart is the simplest of Symphony's graphs. Only one data range can be represented by a pie chart, so only the **1st-Settings R**ange **A** option is needed to define a pie. Because a pie chart has no axes, the X- and Y-axis titles cannot be used. Similarly, grids, scales, and data labels are not used with pie charts.

One convenient way to show the advantages of a pie chart, as well as its limitations, is to add data to figure 9.1. As you can see in figure 9.32, the additional data is simply the regions and their respective store openings for 1979.

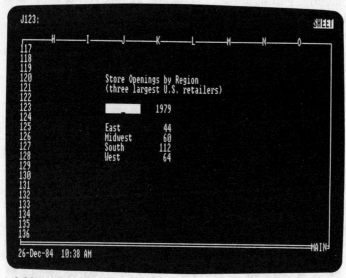

Fig. 9.32.

To create the pie chart shown in figure 9.33, you first select **P**ie from the **1st-Settings T**ype menu. Next, you enter K125..K128 for the A range. Because pie charts do not have an X- or a Y-axis, Symphony adopts the convention of using the X labels as the captions for the slices of the pie. Here you designate J125..J128 as the X label range. Figure 9.33 shows the resulting graph.

In this pie chart, you should notice the number of slices in the pie and the percentages next to the labels. The number of slices in the pie corresponds to the number of data items in the A range, in this case, four. The most important limitation on the number of data items used

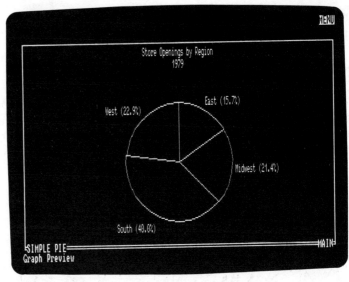

Fig. 9.33.

in a pie chart is that the labels tend to get bunched up if you use too many. Each situation is different, but you might collect some of the smaller slices into an "Other" category if you have too many data items.

The point of a pie chart is to show the relationship of each data item to the whole. Symphony automatically calculates the percentage of each label and places it next to the appropriate label. It would be nice, however, if there were also a way to display the value of each data item next to the percentage. Unfortunately, the basic Symphony program does not offer this feature.

The Aspect Ratio

The aspect ratio is the ratio of height to width in a graph. For most graph types, changing the aspect ratio slightly has no adverse visual effect. However, when you change the aspect ratio in a pie chart, the pie may be noticeably *not* round. In fact, even with the same aspect ratio, some computers may show a round pie chart, but others will show the same pie as an ellipse. Therefore, Symphony offers a special command to control the aspect ratio of pie charts, 2nd-

Settings **O**ther **A**spect. If you find that your pie charts do not look round, you may want to use this command.

Pie Chart Cross-Hatchings

If you are familiar with 1-2-3, you may recall that the program does not give you the option of using cross-hatchings in pie charts. Symphony does. In Symphony, pie charts have the same number of cross-hatching patterns as bar charts, but the patterns themselves are different. Figure 9.34 shows Symphony's pie chart cross-hatching patterns.

New
with
Symphony

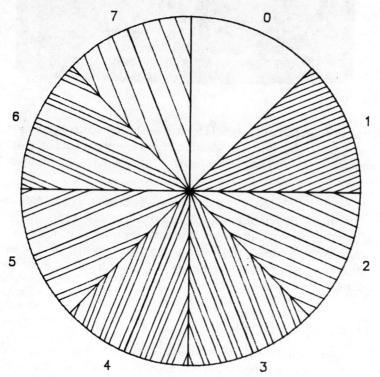

Fig. 9.34.

When setting up cross-hatching patterns for a bar chart, you use the **H**ue option from the **1**st-Settings menu. With pie charts, you must set up a special range of values containing hatching pattern numbers.

(Lotus also calls them "hue" numbers.) You then assign the range of pattern numbers to the B range of the pie chart. Because pie charts do not use the B range for assigning other data, the range is free for pattern numbers.

For example, suppose you want to assign pattern 1 to the first slice of the pie chart. Then, starting at the top of the pie chart and moving clockwise, pattern 2 is assigned to slice 2; pattern 3 to slice 3; etc. To get the proper cross-hatching patterns, you must place the pattern numbers in the worksheet (as they appear in the range M125..M128 in fig. 9.35) and assign them to the B range. If you set **C**olor to **N**o, using the **2**nd-Settings **O**ptions **O**ther command, the pie chart will then appear as illustrated in figure 9.36.

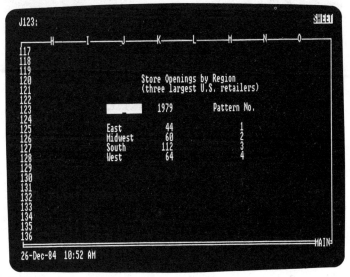

Fig. 9.35.

Color in Pie Charts

Unlike a bar graph, you can use both color and cross-hatchings in a pie chart; but whenever you use color in a pie chart, Symphony automatically draws all slices with the same cross-hatching pattern. When color is used, the values you code in the B range control the color of the slices but not their hatching patterns.

For example, suppose you want to reproduce in color the pie chart
shown in figure 9.34. If you have an IBM PC/XT (or compatible), you
assign the colors just as you do for bar charts.

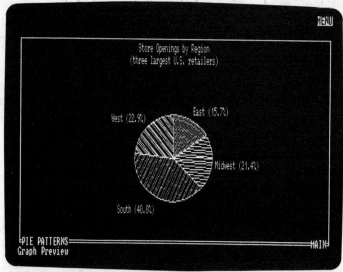

Fig. 9.36.

B-Range Value	Actual Color
0 or blank	No color, no hatchings
1	White
2	Red
3	Blue
4	White
5	Red
6	Blue
7	White

Notice that a B-range value of 0 causes Symphony to omit both color
and cross-hatchings.

The PIE COLORS chart shows the graph that is produced with the
same data that appears in figure 9.36 but with Color set to Yes.

Symphony draws the labels, titles, and percentages, using the Hue
designated for the X range. (In PIE COLORS the Hue is 1 for white.)
The slices are outlined according to the Hue for the A range (in this

case, red). Suppose you want to change the sequence of colors in the graph to red, blue, white, and no color. You must change the B-range values as they appear in M125..M128. The ALTERNATE COLOR 1st-Settings sheet shows the new values required for the new color scheme, and the ALTERNATE COLOR graph shows what the new values produce.

Remember that the 1st-Settings **H**ue numbers have no bearing on the colors in a pie chart. The values in the B range are what count.

New
with
Symphony

Exploded Pie Charts

Exploded pie charts allow you to draw emphasis to one or more slices in a pie chart. By adding a value of 100 to the normal B-range value, you can have Symphony set a slice apart from the others. For example, suppose you want to produce the same graph as in ALTERNATE COLOR but have the slice for the West Coast region exploded. The EXPLODED WEST 1st-Settings sheet shows how you must change the B range, and the EXPLODED WEST graph shows the exploded pie chart.

You can also explode more than one slice in a pie chart. The EXPLODE TWO 1st-Settings sheet shows the data and EXPLODE TWO shows the graph for exploding the slices for the East and the Midwest as well.

XY Graphs

Symphony also offers XY graphs, which are sometimes called scatter plots. In an XY graph, two or more data items from the same data range can share the same X value. Obviously, this is not possible with a line chart. XY graphs are not used to show time series data. Instead, they help to illustrate the relationships between different attributes of data items, such as age and income or educational achievements and salary.

In an XY graph, the X labels become more than simple labels on the graph. They are, in fact, the X-axis scale. This means that an XY graph requires as a minimum of information an X range and an A range.

In every other respect, an XY plot is like a line graph. In fact, a line graph can be thought of as a specialized type of XY graph. For an example of an XY graph, look at the data in the XY GRAPH 1st-Settings sheet and the XY GRAPH. (The X range is J206..J219, and the A range is L206..L219 in these figures.)

Notice that titles, X labels, and a grid have been added to this graph. Notice also that the format has been set to show only symbols instead of both lines and symbols. To do this, you select the **F**ormat option from the 1st-Settings menu and specify **S**ymbols. Typically, XY graphs are formatted to display only symbols instead of symbols and lines. You can display the symbols, however, using any format you wish. If you format an XY graph to include lines between the data points, be sure that at least one of the data sets is sorted in ascending or descending order. Otherwise, the lines that connect the data points will cross one another and make the graph difficult to read.

Frequently, scatter plots also include a line, called the *regression line*, which is an approximation of the trend suggested by the data in the graph. Unfortunately, Symphony cannot produce an XY graph with a regression line. Perhaps this capability will be included in a future special graphics add-in program.

High-Low-Close-Open Charts

New with Symphony

Finally, Symphony offers high-low-close-open graphs. This type of graph is most often used for graphing the daily price movements of stocks. However, you can also track commodities or other financial data that experiences price fluctuations.

When setting up the high-low-close-open graph, you should think of it as a special kind of bar graph. For example, to create a bar graph of just the high prices for a series of days, you enter those values as the A range and enter the graph **T**ype as **B**ar. To change the bars to lines, you simply change the graph **T**ype to **H**igh-Low-Close-Open. HIGH GRAPH shows some typical stock quotation data and the graph you produce by designating the A range as K6..K15.

However, the HIGH GRAPH chart is really no more useful than a bar chart of the same data. To add more information to the graph, you must designate a B range. Once again, if the graph were a bar chart, including a B range would simply add another series of bars to the graph. However, because the Type is High-Low-Close-Open, adding a B range has a different effect. Both the high and low prices for each day are combined into a single vertical line. The HIGH-LOW GRAPH shows what happens when you designate the B range as L6..L15.

By adding a third and fourth range to the graph (the C and D ranges), you combine the opening and closing price information into the graph. The HI-LO-CLOS-OPEN chart shows what happens when you choose a C range of M6..M15 and a D range of N6..N15.

Notice that the closing prices are represented by the right tick mark and the opening prices by the left tick mark on each vertical line in the HI-LO-CLOS-OPEN graph.

A good technique to remember when organizing the data for a High-Low-Close-Open chart is to arrange the data in parallel columns in the same sequence as the graph name: high, low, close, open. This technique helps prevent confusion when you have to designate ranges for the graph.

New with Symphony

Advanced Graphics Topics

Symphony also has several advanced options relating to GRAPH windows and special command options. 1-2-3 users should be aware that all the options that follow were created specifically for Symphony.

New with Symphony

More on GRAPH Windows

When you start out with a new file, attaching graph settings to a GRAPH window is fairly simple. You usually have only one graph settings name and one GRAPH window. However, once you have several graph settings names and GRAPH windows, matching the proper settings name with the proper window can be a problem.

Using Current Graph Settings

*New
with
Symphony*

A typical method for creating graphs is to start in the SHEET environment with the **G**raph command. Then, once you have all the settings and have decided that you want to **A**ttach the settings to a GRAPH window, the first step is to create the new GRAPH window. Interestingly enough, when you create a new graph window, Symphony automatically attaches the current settings to the new window. Although this automatic feature saves work in many cases, it can also create problems in other situations.

For example, suppose you have created all the graph settings for a pie chart and named the settings PIE1. You then decide that you want to create a second pie chart, PIE2, which is the same as PIE1 but uses color. The first step you take to create the new PIE2 graph settings is to use the **1**st- or **2**nd-Settings **N**ame command to create the new name, PIE2. (If you do not create the new name before modifying the current settings, all the changes will be made to the PIE1 settings.) You can then make changes to the current settings that will apply to PIE2.

Now, suppose you want to **A**ttach the named settings to GRAPH windows. If you start by creating a new GRAPH window to display the PIE1 settings, Symphony will automatically attach the current settings to the new window. Because the current settings are actually those for PIE2, the new window will show those settings immediately. This can be confusing. Once you attach the PIE1 settings to the new GRAPH window, though, the new window will appear as you originally intended. Note: You must always remember the name of the current graph settings. If you are not careful, you may wind up using the wrong graph settings.

Changing from One GRAPH Window to Another

*New
with
Symphony*

When you are changing from one GRAPH window to another, the current graph settings travel with you. Even though the new window usually has named graph settings of its own, those settings do not appear in the **1**st- and **2**nd-Settings sheet unless you use the **N**ame **U**se command.

A frequent mistake is to change windows and immediately start altering graph settings. Again, be careful not to make changes to the wrong graph settings.

*New
with
Symphony*

Deleting a GRAPH Window

As you may recall, Symphony does not allow you to delete the current named graph settings. However, there are no barriers to deleting the current GRAPH window. If you do delete the current GRAPH window, the next most recently accessed window will appear on the screen.

Unfortunately, Symphony does not have a **W**indow **R**ename option. Therefore, the best technique to rename a GRAPH window is to start from the original graph window and create a new window with the desired name. If you start from the original window, Symphony will use all its settings when you create the new window. You can then delete the old window, using the SERVICES **W**indow **D**elete command.

"What If" Graphing

Symphony's graphics can be an integral part of "what if" analysis. You can use graphics extensively to fine-tune projections, budgets, or projects. You'll be amazed at how graphics will help you understand the impact of changes in your data on the results of your models.

If your hardware has graphics capability, you can use Symphony's windowing to perform outstanding "what if" analysis. For example, you can set up one window to display spreadsheet data and another window with a related graph; you can then display both windows simultaneously on the screen. When you make a change in the data, the GRAPH window will immediately reflect the change. You can even show multiple GRAPH windows on the screen at once. Figure 9.37 shows SHEET and GRAPH windows that appear simultaneously on the screen. (See Chapter 2 for more on windows.)

Notice the SHEET window and accompanying GRAPH window in Figure 9.37. In figure 9.37 the value for 1984 is $190,311. If you

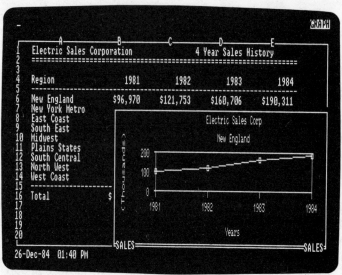

Fig. 9.37.

change the value for 1984 by 200 thousand, the change will immediately be reflected in the graph. (See fig. 9.38.)

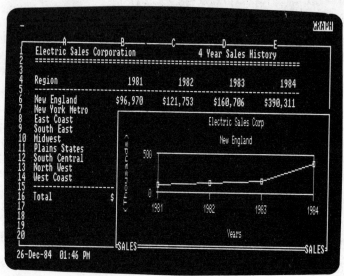

Fig. 9.38.

Keep in mind that using graphs is a good way to verify the reasonableness of your data. You may be surprised at how much help a simple graph can be for checking your work.

New
with
Symphony

The Draw Key

GRAPH windows have only one special key associated with them—the Draw key (Alt + F8 on IBM PC/XTs and compatibles). 1-2-3 users are forewarned that the function of this key is only remotely similar to 1-2-3's GRAPH key. Pressing the Draw key causes Symphony automatically to redraw all the windows that appear on the screen, GRAPH windows included.

The Draw key is normally used with the **A**uto-Display option of the SERVICES **W**indow **S**ettings command. If you set a GRAPH window's **A**uto-Display to **N**o, Symphony will not redisplay that window unless you press Draw (or unless that window is made the current window). For example, suppose you have the windows appearing on the screen as shown in figure 9.37, and you want to change the data as shown in figure 9.38. If you have set the **A**uto-Display option to **N**o for the GRAPH window on the right side of the screen (fig. 9.37), when you make the change in the data for the SHEET window on the left (fig. 9.38), the GRAPH window does not reappear. However, if you press the Draw key, the updated GRAPH window reappears on the right just as in figure 9.38.

Special Command Options

Symphony offers several other special command options. Most of these options are related to controlling Symphony's numeric scaling. However, some relate to Symphony's ability to hide certain parts of a graph.

Using Logarithmic Scale Override

The advantage of logarithmic scaling is that it allows you to compare very large and very small numbers in a reasonable fashion. Sometimes, when you use linear scaling in Symphony, very large numbers in a range can dwarf their smaller companion numbers.

For example, suppose you want to create a bar graph of the number
of parts produced on a new production process during the first eight
months of 1984. Figure 9.39 shows how the graph might appear.

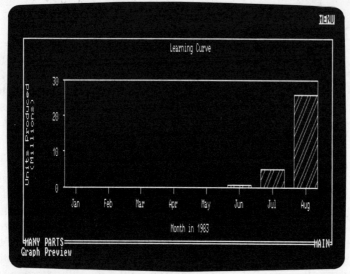

Fig. 9.39.

Because of the relatively large number of parts produced in August
(26 million), the smaller quantities for January through April (53 to
7,420) cannot be seen. Figure 9.40 shows the same numbers
graphed with the **2**nd-Settings **Y**-Scale **T**ype command set to
Logarithmic.

Notice that Symphony creates evenly spaced tick marks along the
Y-axis; however, the numbers that are assigned to the marks are not
evenly distributed numerically. Each tick mark corresponds to a
power of 10. For example, the first tick mark corresponds to
$10^1=10$, the second mark to $10^2=100$, the third to $10^3=1,000$, and
so on. The **2**nd-Settings **Y**-Scale **A**utomatic-Linear command
resets the Y-axis to automatic linear scaling.

Changing the Y-Axis Scale Width

Looking at figure 9.40, you notice that the largest Y-axis scale
number appears in Symphony's scientific format as 1.0E+08.

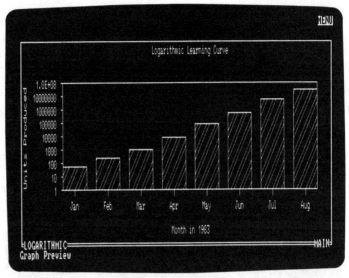

Fig. 9.40.

Because the default width of Symphony's scale numbers is 9 characters, Symphony is incapable of displaying 100,000,000 (the fixed format equivalent of 1.0E+08). Therefore, Symphony opts for the scientific format. If you want the 100 million scale number to appear in its full fixed format, you can use the **W**idth option of the **2**nd-Settings **Y**-Scale command to change the width to 10 or greater. Conversely, if you set the width to less than 9 characters, Symphony shows asterisks. Note: Width is not an option for the **2**nd-Settings **X**-Scale command.

New with Symphony

Controlling Symphony's Automatic Scaling Labels

Anyone who has graphed very large numbers in 1-2-3 has experienced problems with the program's automatic scaling labels. (Scaling labels are the messages that appear below the X- and Y-axis labels when the values being graphed are in the thousands or greater.) For example, when you graph numbers in the billions, 1-2-3 uses a scaling factor label of "(Times 10E9)" instead of "(Billions)".

Symphony has corrected the scaling-label problem to some degree. If you don't like the automatic scaling labels that Symphony offers, you can select your own—up to a point. The technique used is to have you specify manually an exponent (power of ten) representing the number of zeros to be truncated when a range is graphed.

For example, suppose you have the graph in figure 9.41, and you want to change the scaling message from "(Times 10E9)" to something more readable. By using the **M**anual option of the **2nd**-Settings **Y**-Scale **E**xponent command, you can get Symphony to display "(Millions)" by selecting an exponent of 6. (See fig. 9.42.) Although Symphony will not show the label "(Billions)", "(Millions)" certainly beats "(Times 1E9)".

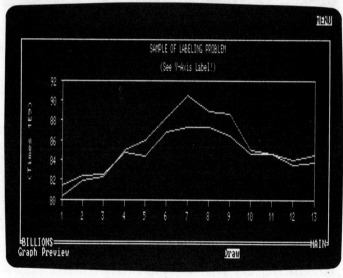

Fig. 9.41.

Hiding Parts of a Graph

*New
with
Symphony*

Symphony allows you to hide all the different elements of a graph that reside outside the box containing the graph. These elements include titles, scale numbers, exponents, and legends. When you select the **H**ide option from the **2nd**-Settings **O**ther command, the box portion of the graph occupies the entire window. The HIDE

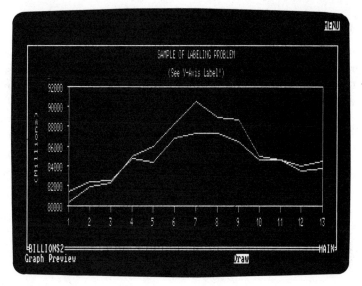

Fig. 9.42.

OUTSIDE chart shows the same graph as in figure 9.42 but with **H**ide set to **Y**es.

You can also hide the X- and Y-axis scale numbers by selecting the **H**idden option from the **2**nd-Settings <X- or Y-Scale> **F**ormat **O**ther command. The HIDE SCALES chart shows the same graph as in figure 9.42 but with the Y-axis scale formatted to **H**idden.

More Examples

The examples in the color section in the middle of this book illustrate each type of graph that has been discussed, along with the commands that were used to create each. In some cases, multiple windows are used. The DATA chart shows the sample data set used to create the graphs that follow. Study all these examples for more information about Symphony's graphics.

Conclusion

Although Symphony's basic graphics capability is not very different from 1-2-3's, Symphony's windowing feature adds a new dimension to the term *business graphics*. To get a good feel for Symphony's power, you should start working with graphics at the earliest possible point in your introduction to Symphony. The more you work with Symphony's graphics, the more you will realize the benefits of the program's integration.

10
Printing Graphs

Even though you can show graphs and text on your screen simultaneously with Symphony, your printer cannot print graphs and text in the same operation. Some software packages are capable of printing graphs and text together, but the results lack sufficient detail for presentation purposes; these programs use graphics block characters that often do not give graphs clear resolution.

Lotus chose, however, the greater detail offered by bit-mapped graphics. This choice means that Symphony can produce presentation-quality graphics, but some trade-offs were necessary. For one thing, the main program itself is incapable of printing graphics. To print a graph, you must first save the graph to a graph file with a .PIC extension. Then you exit from Symphony and enter the PrintGraph program. Finally, you select the file and the options for printing.

Just as in the case of 1-2-3, Lotus decided to deviate from its customary all-in-one style for reasons of size. By making Print-Graph a separate program, Lotus decreased the total size of the main program. Unfortunately, this move also limited interactive capability in printing graphs in Symphony.

Still, the PrintGraph program has many strengths; for one, it is easy to use. The menus and command structure are similar to Symphony's main program. (Some might even argue they are a great deal simpler.) The PrintGraph program is capable of batch processing, so the program can print several graphs consecutively. Finally, PrintGraph has many special features that would not otherwise be available because of size restrictions. PrintGraph produces high-resolution output on special graphics printers and plotters, makes enlargements and reduction, allows rotations, and offers several colors and font types.

1-2-3 and Symphony Compared

Those familiar with 1-2-3 may be surprised at how closely Symphony's PrintGraph program resembles 1-2-3's. Only a few changes have been made.

1. Additional font types have been added, including Forum, Bold, and Lotus.

2. More graphics devices are supported.

3. Some of the command names have been changed, although their functions are the same.

4. Colors (called *hues*) are assigned by means of a number scheme.

5. The set of graphics-device types is chosen when PrintGraph is installed, not when the program is running.

Access to the PrintGraph Program

New with Symphony

Like 1-2-3, Symphony's PrintGraph program can be accessed through the ACCESS SYSTEM. Most often you will probably use PrintGraph immediately after a Symphony session. First, you will want to make sure that you have saved the graph file by using the Image-Save option from either the SHEET Graph or the GRAPH menu (as explained in the previous chapter). After you use the SERVICES **E**xit command to leave Symphony, instead of exiting to DOS, use the ACCESS SYSTEM menu to go into the PrintGraph program.

If you have sufficient RAM, you can also go into the PrintGraph program through the SERVICES DOS command. The advantage of this technique is that you do not have to reload Symphony after leaving PrintGraph; you can go directly back into Symphony by typing *EXIT* after the system prompt. Be careful, though. Always save your files before trying this technique.

To use this technique, you must first attach the DOS.APP file (as explained in Chapter 2). Next, you should check how much RAM is available by using the SERVICES **S**ettings command. If you have approximately 150K left (a conservative estimate), you should be able to run PrintGraph simultaneously with Symphony and not worry about overwriting Symphony files. You may, however, require more RAM to print several graphs at one time. Once you have left Symphony (using the SERVICES DOS command), you then enter *PGRAPH* plus the appropriate driver-set name (for example, PGRAPH DRIVS1) from the system prompt. At this point, you will move into PrintGraph.

If you are starting directly from DOS, you can go into PrintGraph directly or go through the ACCESS SYSTEM. To go into the program directly, simply enter *PGRAPH* plus the appropriate driver-set name after the operating system prompt. To go through the ACCESS SYSTEM, enter *ACCESS* plus the appropriate driver-set name.

*New
with
Symphony*

Configuration of PrintGraph

To configure PrintGraph, you must first select the appropriate driver set during installation. (See Chapter 2.) The graphics devices you have access to when you run PrintGraph depend entirely on the devices you select during installation. If you do not select any graphics device during installation, you cannot run PrintGraph. (This is different from 1-2-3, where the graphics-device selection takes place in the PrintGraph program itself.)

You can select more than one graphics device during installation. For example, if you have an HP plotter and an Epson FX80 printer, you can select both as graphics output devices. The only restriction is that a device must be supported by Symphony. If your printer or plotter is not on the list of Symphony-supported graphics devices, you may want to call Lotus Development to see whether a device driver has been released for it.

The second stage of configuring PrintGraph occurs after you are in the program; you need to indicate your particular hardware setup. Figure 10.1 shows an example of the PrintGraph screen when you are running the program for the first time.

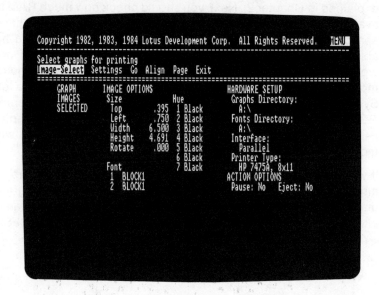

Fig. 10.1.

Notice that "HP 7470A" appears below the "Printer Type: " message on the right side of the screen. This device, which is chosen during installation, is automatically activated in PrintGraph. You will never need to change this setting unless you install an additional or different graphics device.

Printer Selection

If you selected more than one device type during installation, your first selection is automatically activated when you enter PrintGraph. Suppose you selected an HP 7470A plotter and an Epson FX80 printer, in that order. When you go into PrintGraph, the program automatically chooses the HP 7470A. To change to the Epson, you select **S**ettings from among the PrintGraph main menu choices:

> Image-Select   Settings   Go   Align   Page   Exit

After you have selected **S**ettings, the following menu choices will appear:

> Image   Hardware   Action   Save   Reset   Quit

You choose **H**ardware to tell PrintGraph you wish to change the hardware setting. Finally, you select **P**rinter from the following menu items:

> Graphs-Directory   Fonts-Directory   Interface   Printer   Quit

After you have chosen **P**rinter, a menu of the two graphics devices selected during installation will appear on the screen. (See fig. 10.2.)

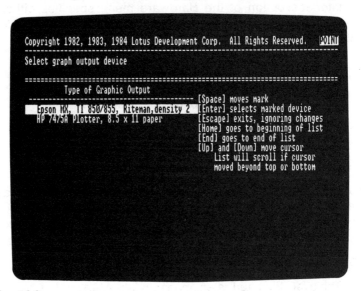

Fig. 10.2.

To change to the Epson, just move the cursor to the appropriate line and press the space bar. This action makes the change and marks the selected printer with a # symbol. When you press RETURN, PrintGraph will return to the main PrintGraph **S**ettings sheet.

Graph and Font Directories

When you configure PrintGraph to your hardware, you must also indicate the directories for the graph and font files. The information you supply for the **G**raphs-Directory and **F**onts-Directory will tell PrintGraph which directories to search for the graph and font files. Because PrintGraph normally resides in drive A on a two-diskette system, A:\ is the default for finding the graph and font files. If you have a hard disk and have stored all the PrintGraph files in a directory, you will need to change this default setting. (On systems with two disk drives, change the graph directory to B:\)

Interface

The **I**nterface option of the **H**ardware menu specifies either a parallel or a serial interface card for your system. You are given four choices:

1. A parallel interface—the default.

2. A serial interface (RS-232-C-compatible)—optional. You must specify a baud rate. (See below.)

3. A second parallel interface—optional.

4. A second serial interface (RS-232-C-compatible)— optional. You must specify a baud rate. (See below.)

If you specify a serial interface, you will need to select a baud rate, which determines the speed at which data is transferred. Because each printer has its own requirements, you will need to consult your printer's manual for the appropriate rate. Many printers will accept more than one baud rate, so a general guideline is to choose the fastest baud rate that the printer will accept without corrupting the data. The available baud rates appear in table 10.1.

Table 10.1

Setting	Baud rate
1	110
2	150
3	300
4	600
5	1,200
6	2,400
7	4,800
8	9,600
9	19,200

*New
with
Symphony*

Configurations to Save and Reset

To save the hardware settings, select **S**ave from the **Settings** menu. The saved settings will then be active for subsequent PrintGraph sessions. PrintGraph saves the settings in a file called PGRAPH.CNF, which is read each time PrintGraph is loaded. You will probably not want to change hardware settings unless you change your hardware.

Another option in the **S**ettings menu, **R**eset, provides a function almost the opposite from **S**ave. **R**eset will cancel all the **Settings** made during the current session and return to the options that were present when PrintGraph was loaded or the options **S**aved during the current session, whichever occurred last.

The Image Settings

Besides settings for your hardware configuration, there are other settings that affect the way graphs appear on the printed page. These Image settings will apply to all the graphs printed in a batch. All the Image settings are saved when you update the .CNF file. If you want different Image settings for different graphs, you must select and print the graphs one at a time.

To specify the Image settings, select Image from the Settings menu. The following choices are then displayed:

    Size   Font   Hue   Quit

Adjusting Graph Size and Orientation

The Size option in the Image menu allows you to adjust the sizes of graphs and to decide where they will be printed on a page. This Image option also allows you to rotate the axes by as much as 90 degrees. The menu for the Size option gives you the following menu choices:

    Full   Half   Manual   Quit

Full means that the graph will occupy an entire page, and Half that the graph will take up a half page. PrintGraph automatically handles all the spacing and margins for both these choices unless you specify Manual.

The following choices appear for Manual:

    Top   Left   Width   Height   Rotation   Quit

Top, Left, Width, and Height are used to adjust the respective margins. The numbers you supply are converted from base 10 to base 2 after you enter them, so don't be concerned if they seem to be different when they are displayed. Rotation adjusts the number of counterclockwise degrees of rotation. You must choose a number between 0 and 90. On the one extreme, 0 will not cause any rotation, and the X-axis will appear on the page as it normally does. At the other extreme, a full 90 degrees of rotation will shift the X-axis to a vertical position.

Interestingly enough, if you choose the Full option, Symphony will print graphs rotated 90 degrees. The X-axis of a bar graph will run along the long edge of an 8 1/2 x 11-inch page. If you choose the Half option, Symphony considers the degree of rotation 0, and the X-axis of a bar graph will run along the short edge of a sheet of paper so that you can get two graphs on a single page.

You will need to expriment to get the results you want from Rotation. The default settings for Height and Width when Half is selected are 6.500 and 4.691. This setting gives an aspect ratio of approximately 1 (X-axis) to 1.385 (Y-axis). If you change the aspect ratio, distortion can, and often will, occur when PrintGraph fits a rotated graph into the specified height and width. Distortion in bar and line graphs is usually not a problem. Distorted pie charts, however, will probably look like ellipses instead of pies. When you change the setting for height and width, the best policy to avoid distortion is to maintain the 1 to 1.385 aspect ratio.

*New
with
Symphony*

Choosing Fonts

Symphony allows you to print in different character types (fonts). (This includes printing with a dot-matix printer.) The **F**ont option lets you choose from among 11 different character types. The number after the font name (see fig. 10.3) indicates the density, that is, how dark the printed character will be. The fonts followed by a 2 are identical to the fonts with the same names followed by a 1, but the number-2 fonts are darker.

You can even set the first line of text, the graph title, in one font and the remaining lines of text in another. If you specify only one font, it will be used for all the text in the graph.

An example is the exploded pie chart of retail-store openings from the previous chapter; a dark Italic typeface is used for the first graph title and a lighter Italic for the other lines. To get these fonts, you specify ITALIC2 for Font 1 (the first line of the title line). If another font had not been chosen for Font 2, it would have automatically taken on the same value as Font 1. Once the fonts are specified, ITALIC2 appears in the settings sheet for Font 1, and ITALIC1 for Font 2. (See fig. 10.4.)

*New
with
Symphony*

Choosing Colors

If you have a color printing device, you can select the **H**ue from the Image menu. This option sets the colors (hues) for printing or plotting different parts of graphs. If the device you are using does not support color graphics (most printers do not), of course, you have no choice of colors.

PrintGraph assigns a default color of black to every data range and
to the grid, axes, and scales. However, the program can handle nine
other colors: red, green, blue, orange, lime, gold, turquoise, violet,
and brown. You may assign any of these colors to any data range, or
you may assign the same color to more than one data range.

When you select **H**ue, PrintGraph asks you to assign colors to the
hue numbers you assigned to data ranges in Symphony. (See the
previous chapter for assigning hue numbers to graph data ranges.)
Each time you specify a hue number (1 through 7), Printgraph will
display a list of colors from which you can choose. The colors you

This is BOLD type

This is FORUM type

This is LOTUS type

This is SCRIPT1 type
This is SCRIPT2 type

This is BLOCK1 type
This is BLOCK2 type

This is ITALIC1 type
This is ITALIC2 type

This is ROMAN1 type
This is ROMAN2 type

Fig. 10.3.

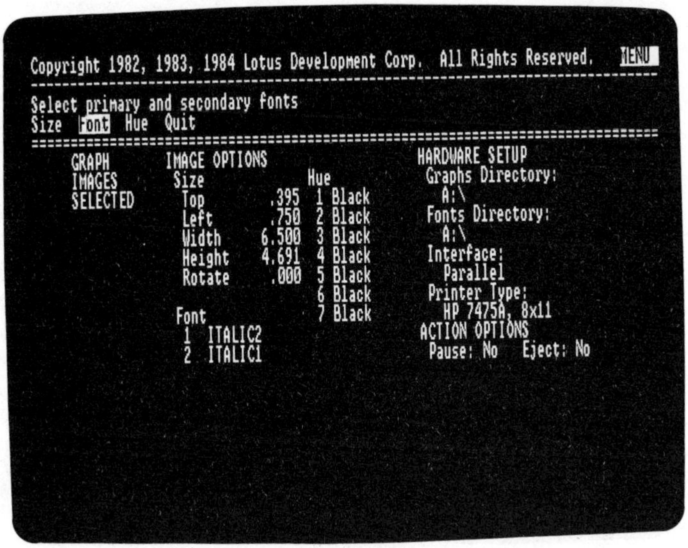

```
Copyright 1982, 1983, 1984 Lotus Development Corp.  All Rights Reserved.  MENU

Select primary and secondary fonts
Size  Font  Hue  Quit

   GRAPH      IMAGE OPTIONS              HARDWARE SETUP
   IMAGES     Size          Hue         Graphs Directory:
   SELECTED   Top      .395 1 Black       A:\
              Left     .750 2 Black      Fonts Directory:
              Width   6.500 3 Black       A:\
              Height  4.691 4 Black      Interface:
              Rotate   .000 5 Black       Parallel
                            6 Black      Printer Type:
              Font          7 Black       HP 7475A, 8x11
               1 ITALIC2                 ACTION OPTIONS
               2 ITALIC1                  Pause: No  Eject: No
```

Fig. 10.4.

use in PrintGraph do not have to be the same colors you use in the main Symphony program. In fact, you don't have to have a color monitor to print color graphs.

After you have assigned colors to the hues, the screen will look as it does in figure 10.5.

You may save the color settings by means of the **S**ave option from the **S**ettings menu. This choice saves hue settings (and all other image and hardware settings) to PGRAPH.CNF so that the settings will be available for the next PrintGraph session.

Selection of Files for Printing

After you have configured PrintGraph, you can return to the main PrintGraph menu and choose **I**mage-Select. After you use Print-Graph the first time, **I**mage-Select will probably be the first step every time you use the program. This option gives you a list of all the .PIC files on the current **G**raphs-Directory. A typical list of graph files is shown in figure 10.6.

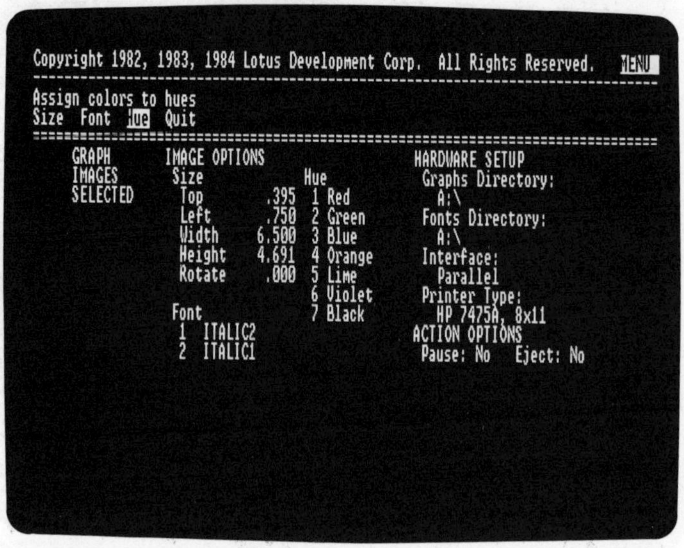

```
Copyright 1982, 1983, 1984 Lotus Development Corp.  All Rights Reserved.  MENU
--------------------------------------------------------------------------------
Assign colors to hues
Size Font Hue Quit
================================================================================
     GRAPH    IMAGE OPTIONS                HARDWARE SETUP
     IMAGES   Size              Hue        Graphs Directory:
     SELECTED Top      .395  1 Red           A:\
              Left     .750  2 Green       Fonts Directory:
              Width   6.500  3 Blue          A:\
              Height  4.691  4 Orange      Interface:
              Rotate   .000  5 Lime          Parallel
                             6 Violet      Printer Type:
                             7 Black         HP 7475A, 8x11
              Font                         ACTION OPTIONS
              1 ITALIC2                    Pause: No   Eject: No
              2 ITALIC1
```

Fig. 10.5.

```
Copyright 1982, 1983, 1984 Lotus Development Corp.  All Rights Reserved.  POINT
--------------------------------------------------------------------------------
Select graphs for output

================================================================================
  PICTURE    DATE    TIME   SIZE
  -------------------------------------
  BARHUES1  06-12-84         3405    [Space] turns mark on and off
  BARHUES2  06-12-84         4865    [Enter] selects marked pictures
  COLORBAR  01-01-80         1001    [Escape] exits, ignoring selections
  EXPLOPIE  01-01-80         1755    [Home] goes to beginning of list
  NORMPIE   01-01-80         1001    [End] goes to end of list
  XYGRAPH   01-01-80         1001    [Up] and [Down] move the cursor
                                         List will scroll if cursor
                                         moved beyond top or bottom
                                     [Draw] displays highlighted picture
```

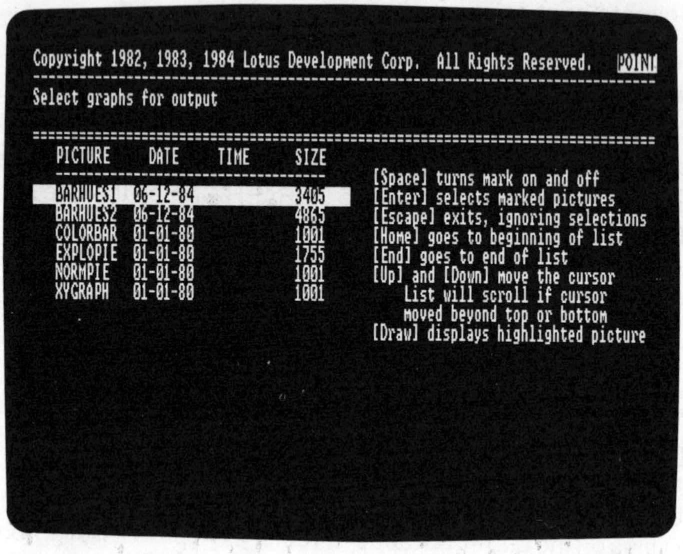

Fig. 10.6.

The directions for selecting files are on the right side of the display. To select a graph file to print, you use the Up and Down arrow keys to position the cursor at the appropriate entry; then you press the space bar. Pressing the space bar causes PrintGraph to place a # next to the graph name to indicate that the graph has been selected for printing. Finally, you press RETURN to get back to the main PrintGraph menu.

You can select as many graphs as you wish before you press RETURN. A # will appear next to each graph you select. To confirm your choice, press DRAW (Alt + F8 on the IBM PC and compatibles) to see the graphs as they were created and displayed in Symphony. (Actually, the graphs will look slightly different when you view them in PrintGraph because the special font types are used on the printed copies.)

Batch Printing

The way you print graphs in batch will depend on your particular graphics device. For instance, if you have a graphics device that accepts only single sheets of paper, such as the HP 7470A plotter, you can configure PrintGraph to run unattended except when you have to load a new piece of paper. Many graphics devices, such as the HP plotter, are smart enough to know when you have room to print the next graph. If you do have room, the device will print. Otherwise, it will pause for you to load another piece of paper.

If, on the other hand, you have a graphics device that accepts continuous-form paper, such as the IBM Color Graphics Printer, you can have graphs printed continuously and unattended. You simply elect not to have the printer pause between graphs. (Set **P**ause to **N**o as discussed below.)

Individual Print Options

If the configuration settings that you have set are inappropriate for one of your graphs, you can easily override them. For example, suppose you want to change the **S**ize settings. You simply call up the **S**ize menu and choose the settings you need. These new settings will remain in effect until you change them or exit from the program.

The Pause and Eject Options

Another Settings menu selection is Action, which controls the interval between graphs when you are printing in batch mode. The two choices for Action are Pause and Eject. Pause makes the printer pause between graphs so you can change settings, and Eject controls whether the printer stops for you to change paper. Your choices of these options will depend on how many graphs you are printing and what size they are. For example, if you are printing several full-size graphs on a dot-matrix printer, you will probably want the Eject option set so that the paper will advance automatically between graphs.

Align and Advance Options

The Align selection in the main PrintGraph menu sets the program's built-in, top-of-page marker. When you choose the Align option, PrintGraph assumes that the paper is correctly aligned in the printer with the top of the form in the right place. PrintGraph then inserts a form feed at the end of every page, using the page-length information you provided when installing the graphics device.

Note: Many printers have controls that allow you to scroll the paper up and down one line at a time. PrintGraph does not recognize these controls. If you, for example, scroll the paper up three lines without realigning, PrintGraph will be three spaces off when it next issues a form-feed command.

Page selection advances the paper one page at a time. This useful option advances continuous-form paper to help you remove the printed output at the end of a printing session.

The Finished Product

To print a graph, you must select Go from the main PrintGraph menu. After you have done so, PrintGraph will start printing. If you have several graphs, you may as well go have lunch while you wait because PrintGraph's high-resolution printing takes a long time. Printing the graph shown in figure 10.7 in full size on an HP 7470A plotter took about four minutes.

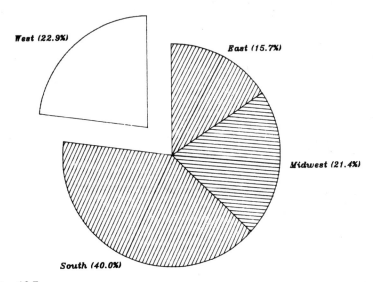

Fig. 10.7.

Exit from PrintGraph

Exiting from PrintGraph is similar to exiting from any other Symphony module. You simply choose **E**xit from the main PrintGraph menu. After you select **E**xit, you will be returned to the ACCESS SYSTEM or to DOS, depending on which you entered from.

Conclusion

The Symphony PrintGraph program is surprisingly similar to the 1-2-3 PrintGraph program. This similarity is an advantage for many users. As pointed out, to produce high-resolution, presentation-quality graphics, Lotus had to make some compromises. For instance, PrintGraph is a separate program from Symphony, which deviates slightly from Lotus' integrated approach. However, the results produced by the PrintGraph program are outstanding, and the program is easy to use.

11

Data Management

Data management involves all the commands and procedures for creating and manipulating a data base. There are three distinct areas in data management: the FORM window, the data base commands in the SHEET environment, and data base statistical functions. Data management in a FORM window is used for setting up and manipulating individual records. The SHEET commands are used for working with groups of records. Finally, data base statistical functions are used for determining statistics about groups of records within a data base.

These three areas are closely interrelated. For example, you can create a data base of all your customers' names and addresses by means of a special form you have set up in a FORM window. Once the data base is created, you can then use the data base commands in the SHEET environment to extract the names of all your customers who operate in a specific location, like Washington, D.C. (Many of the settings used in the FORM window can also be used in the SHEET window.) Finally, you can use data base statistical functions to determine the number of customer names you've extracted and their average monthly orders from your company.

Symphony's data management program has many strengths. First, it's easy to create forms and to add or modify records. Second, when you are using a FORM window, you can hide from the user everything in the data base except the input form. Therefore, you can set up a data entry environment for someone who does not know, or care to know, Symphony. Third, Symphony's data management is fast. Because all the operations are RAM-based, you can perform rapidly almost any data base manipulation you want. Finally, the data management is integrated; you can use data management techniques in all of Symphony's working environments—SHEET, DOC, GRAPH, FORM, and COMM.

New with Symphony

Although Symphony's data management is strong in several respects, it is weak in others. Most notably, like everything else in Symphony, the fact that data management is RAM-based places strict limitations on the size and the kinds of applications it can be used for. However, indications are that Lotus may soon (perhaps as early as the end of 1984) offer a disk-based data management add-in that will virtually eliminate the size restriction.

Another drawback is that Symphony's data management is hard to learn. It is probably one of the most complex operations in the program. As you will soon see, many special rules apply. However, you will probably find that you need to know only some of those rules to accomplish what you want.

The structure of this chapter follows the three natural divisions inherent in Symphony's data management: the use of FORM windows, SHEET data base commands, and data base statistical functions. Included at the end of the chapter is a section on printing data base reports. This is a particularly good topic to end with because it incorporates many different aspects of Symphony's data management capability.

1-2-3 and Symphony

If you are an experienced 1-2-3 user, you have a distinct advantage in learning Symphony's data management—provided you keep an open mind. Many of the important techniques are the same in both programs, but Symphony has added several new techniques. Most of them are associated with Symphony's FORM window, so mastering this window requires patience.

New with Symphony

The structure of the FORM environment may seem rigid at first, as though Lotus has removed some of the flexibility and user-control that was so appealing in 1-2-3. However, once you get to know the FORM environment, you will learn to use it to your advantage. For example, the FORM window has several special ranges. Some are new; others will look familiar; and all have special locations that are automatically chosen by the program. However, after you have learned all the rules for these special ranges, you don't have to stick to Symphony's locations. You can put the special ranges anywhere you want.

You can use Symphony's data management in a way remarkably similar to 1-2-3's data management if you want to. All the same capabilities are there. However, you miss the full power of Symphony's data management if you limit yourself to 1-2-3's old ways. You can now let Symphony handle many routine chores for you (for instance, setting up data base ranges, criterion ranges, and output ranges). You will learn quickly when to let Symphony do the work for you and when to do it yourself.

If you are an experienced 1-2-3 user, you may want to go directly to the section Creating a Data Base in a FORM Window. You will notice clear differences and similarities in the two programs. You can expect the FORM window to be somewhat different from what you are used to. However, by the time you come to the SHEET commands and the data base statistical functions, you will feel at home. You will want to give special attention to the ranges used in the SHEET environment and the locations of the **Q**uery commands in the menu structure, but data base statistical functions should require only a cursory review. Finally, you will want to pay close attention to the information about printing data base reports, particularly if you intend to print form letters or mailing lists.

Keep in mind that Symphony has more severe RAM limitations than 1-2-3. Because the main program requires approximately 300K of RAM, you have only about 340K left for applications. (This figure assumes you have 640K on your computer—the maximum amount of usable memory on PC/XTs manufactured after January, 1983.

For machines manufactured before this date, the maximum amount of usable memory is 544K.)

Data Base Fundamentals

A data base is a collection of related pieces of information. In its simplest form, a data base is a list that can contain any kind of information from addresses to tax-deductible expenses.

In Symphony, a data base is a range of cells that spans at least one column and at least two rows. This basic definition alone contains nothing that sets a data base apart from any other group of cells. However, because a data base is actually a list, another important aspect is its method of organization. Just as a list must be properly organized before you can gain information from it, a data base must also be properly organized. However, remembering that in Symphony there is an underlying similarity between a data base and any other group of cells will help you learn about the different commands that are presented in this chapter. You will begin to see many other instances where these commands can be used in what might be considered nondata-base applications.

Organization of a Data Base

As mentioned above, an important aspect of a data base is the way it is organized. This organization relies heavily on the composition of the data base itself. To understand this composition, you need certain general definitions. First, data bases are made up of *records*. Each record corresponds to an item in a list. In Symphony, a record is a row of cells within a data base. Second, records are made up of *fields*. In Symphony, a field is a single cell (or column) within a record. Finally, *field names* are used at the tops of columns to identify fields; field names are required for nearly every data base operation.

In figure 11.1, a typical data base, the second record resides in row 4. The name that is highlighted, "Cotter, James F.", is one of the four fields for that record. The field name for the items in column I is "Name."

```
I4: 'Cotter, James F.                                                    SHEET

I━━━━━━━━━━━━━━━━━━━J━━━━━━━━━━━━━K━━━━L━━━━
1   Addresses database
2   Name                    Address                         Code  Phone
3   Ahmad, Shamim Sultana   Ashton Ctr, Weatherly Hall 202  123  337-1559
4   Cotter, James F.        1003 Tulip Tree House           453  332-0617
5   Englert, Michael        224 Greenup St.                 735  423-4351
6   Harding, Edward         2400 Central Parkway            645  871-6223
7   Harrington, James T.    238 High St.                    837  871-4900
8   Holland, Earl           3712 Drake Road                 324  561-4870
9   Horton, Robert          9980 Yale Ave.                  143  339-6731
10  Owen, David J.          612 Knight Ridge Road           812  339-8770
11  Schumann, Fritz W.      100 E. Miller Dr.               532  334-1873
12  Sharpe, Sarah           7897 Providence St.             315  339-4662
13  Sikes, William L.       3751 Clifton Ave.               632  241-8445
14  Simpson, Jeremy         3509 Ludlow Ave.                976  321-7362
15  Stone, Betty            700 Vine St.                    545  321-9000
16  Timmerman, Chuck        7900 Castleway Drive            812  984-9745
17  Tuke, John              531 Remington Road              754  332-6742
18  Yeagar, Patrick         4237 Mariemont Ave.             516  561-2145
19  Zakon, Steven           3549 Keene St.                  534  332-6773
20  Zealear, Mathew         2909 Fresno St.                 532  334-9008
                                                            ━━━━━ADDRESSES━
17-Dec-84   04:24 PM
```

Fig. 11.1.

What You Can Do with a Data Base

If the data base in figure 11.1 were your own data base, what would you use it for? You might want to *sort* it by last name to find an address. You might also want to *query* the data base for a name or group of names. For example, you could search out the street address for a particular person or select all the people in the data base with the same telephone exchange. Sorting and querying are the chief methods used in Symphony to extract information from a data base. Symphony offers several ways to sort and query, depending on whether you are in a SHEET or a FORM window.

New with Symphony

The FORM Window for Creating Data Bases

One of Symphony's nicest features in creating a data base in a FORM window is the amount of work the program does for you behind the scenes. While you are in a FORM window, you rarely see the entire data base; yet Symphony constantly keeps track of the data base. You just browse through the data base, looking at one record at a time. You view the records through the use of a special form that you build with Symphony's help.

In order to gain a better understanding of Symphony's FORM window, suppose you are a manufacturer of special accessory chips for the semiconductor market, and you want to build a "Customer Priority" data base for one of your best-selling but difficult-to-manufacture computer chips. Because demand is far higher than you can supply, you want the data base to be the foundation for a priority system that allocates chips as fairly as possible but at the same time maximizes your profit.

Building a Simple Input Form

New with Symphony

In planning the data base, you've decided that you want to use Symphony's forms capability, and you've also decided that the data base should contain the following fields:

Field Name	Type	Length	Example Value
Order number	Label	6 characters	PO1435
Customer name	Label	20 characters	Amdek Corporation
Phone	Label	12 characters	312-364-1180
Priority	Number	1 decimal	1
Entry date	Serial number	9 decimal	7/23/84
Promise date	Serial number	9 decimal	8/23/84
Amount	Number	8 decimal	23000

The simplest way to build an input form for the data base is to use the **G**enerate command in a FORM window. However, before you can use the **G**enerate command, the first step is to use either a SHEET or DOC window to enter the field names. Figure 11.2 shows how you enter the field names for the "Priority" data base while you are in a SHEET window.

Notice that the field names are entered in a single row across the window. You can also enter them down a column. In a SHEET window, Symphony does not care which way you choose, as long as the field names are placed in consecutive cells. Nonconsecutive cells lead to blank columns in the data base and therefore waste space.

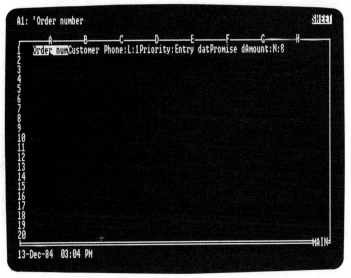

Fig. 11.2.

Figure 11.3 shows you how to enter the field names in a DOC window. When you are using a DOC window, field names must be entered down a column. Before you enter the field names, change DOC Format Settings Justification to None. This prevents Symphony from putting two or more field names on the same line. (When you customize the input form, you will want to combine field names on the same line.)

Notice that some of these records have end-of-paragraph markers after them and some do not. Recall that end-of-paragraph markers are the result of your pressing RETURN when you are in a DOC window and Justification is on. When Justification is off, as it should be when you are creating an input form in a DOC window, these markers do not appear. Because Symphony disregards end-of-paragraph markers, don't worry about them. If you do have them, however, make sure that there are no spaces between the markers and the field-name entries. Otherwise, you will have trouble later on when you try to generate the input form.

Immediately after each field name, for all but the field "Order number," there is a letter followed by a colon and a number. The

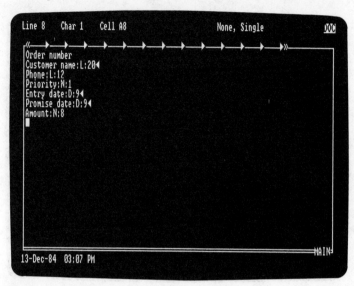

Fig. 11.3.

letters and numbers are used to indicate the field type and the field length, respectively. When you issue the **G**enerate command, Symphony will use the field types and field lengths to set up the data base. If you do not indicate a type or length, as is the case with "Order number," Symphony will use the default settings.

The choices you have for the field type are L (label), N (number), D (date), T (time), or C (computed). The label and number choices tell Symphony whether you want to store entries for those fields as labels or numbers, respectively. The date and time choices are a little different. Symphony uses its special serial-numbering scheme to store date and time values. Therefore, if you enter a date in any one of the valid date formats (D1 through D5), Symphony converts your entry to serial numbers. If you select a computed field type, Symphony will calculate the value based on a formula you supply. (Computed fields are treated in more depth in the section Advanced FORM Features.)

Specifying a field length tells Symphony how wide the columns in the data base should be. For example, if you choose a length of 9 for the "Entry date" field, Symphony uses a column width of 9 for that field in the data base.

*New
with
Symphony*

*Using the FORM **G**enerate Command*

To use the input form you have created, you must change to a FORM window. When you do this, Symphony displays a blank screen with the message at the top (No Definition range defined). Disregard the message this first time; it will soon disappear. To initiate the FORM **G**enerate command, first use the MENU key to display the main FORM window menu, which displays

Attach Criteria Initialize Record-Sort Generate Settings

When you select **G**enerate, Symphony gives you the following menu options:

Label Number Date Time Computed

These choices give the default field type. If you choose **N**umber, for example, you are telling Symphony that any field name without a field-type indicator appearing after the name is to be a number field. After you select a default field type, Symphony asks you for a length. In this case, you choose a default length of 6 because this is the length of the purchase order numbers you will be entering.

After you have selected a length, Symphony asks you for a data base name. The name you choose should be clearly descriptive because it will be used for establishing a series of range names. For this data base, enter *Priority*.

Next, Symphony asks you for a default field length. The length you choose is the value Symphony uses when a field-length number has not been explicitly declared. Enter 6 because this is the default length you want for the "Order number" field. (The lengths for all the other fields have already been explicitly declared in the Field Names range.)

Finally, Symphony asks you for a Field Names range. In order to have you choose the range, Symphony temporarily shifts to the SHEET environment. You can then enter the proper range. In this case, you enter the range A1..A7, which is the column of field names shown in figure 11.3.

After you enter the Field Names range, Symphony immediately shifts to an input form, provided you have entered the field-name information correctly. Figures 11.4A and 11.4B show how the input form appears in both FORM and SHEET mode.

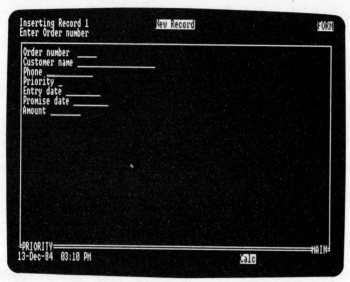

Fig. 11.4A.

As mentioned earlier, Symphony uses the lengths you specify for determining the individual column widths in the data base. However, as illustrated in figure 11.4A, Symphony also uses the field lengths to

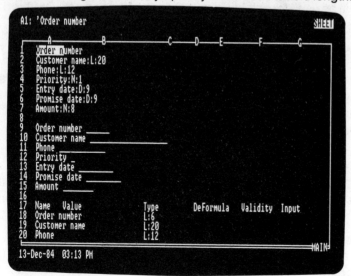

Fig. 11.4B.

determine the number of underscores that follow the field names in the input form.

New
with
Symphony

Entering a Record

At this point you can start entering records. To enter the order number for the first input record, you simply start typing. For example, you enter PO1435 and then press RETURN. When you press RETURN, the cursor shifts down to the second field in the input form, the "Customer name." For this field you type *Amdek Corporation* and press RETURN. Continue this process until you have entered the last value for the last field. Then, to insert the record in the data base, you press the Ins (Insert) key. After you press Ins, Symphony enters the first record in the data base and erases the data from the input form so that you can enter another record.

For a comprehensive guide to important keys for entering and revising data records in a FORM window, see figure 11.5.

Key	Activity
PgDn	Moves sequentially to the next record in the data base. When data is being edited or entered, adds current record to data base and displays next record or new blank record.
PgUp	Moves sequentially to the previous record in the data base. When data is being entered or edited, adds record to data base and displays previous record.
RETURN (or Tab)	Moves cursor to next field
Home	Adds current record to data base and takes you to the first record in data base. If no data is being entered or edited, displays the first record.
End	Adds current record to data base and takes you to the last record in data base. If no data is being entered or

	edited, displays the last record. End followed by PgDn positions you at the end of the data base and generates a blank form ready for input.
GoTo	Jumps directly to a record if you enter the record number
Edit	To revise an existing entry, press Edit to activate the field. You can then use the edit keys, such as Backspace, Esc, and Del, in the same manner as in SHEET mode. (See Chapter 2.)
Esc	If pressed once, clears the current field. Pressed twice, clears all fields and restores their previous values. If pressed three times, removes current entry and returns previous record.
Backspace	Clears the current field
Begin typing	During editing of a field, causes Symphony to erase the current entry and lets you enter a new one
Ins	During entering of data, adds current record to data base and displays new blank form. When editing data, adds current record to data base, leaving record in the form with cursor at first field.
Del	During editing of data, deletes current record from a data base. You are given a Yes/No confirmation step.
Up arrow	Moves cursor to previous field above or to the left of current cell
Down arrow	Moves cursor to next field below or to the right
Right arrow	Moves cursor to next field

Left arrow	Moves cursor to previous field during entry of new data. Moves cursor to next field during revision of data.
Ctrl + ←	Moves cursor to first field in the form
Ctrl + →	Moves cursor to the last field in the form

Fig. 11.5.

When you enter a record in a data base by pressing the Ins key, Symphony places a copy of the record in a special data base area located in the rows below the input form. The exact location of that area is not important for now. What is important is that when you use a FORM window, Symphony automatically does much of the work that you would otherwise have to do yourself.

After you enter a date, Symphony automatically changes the date to the D1 display format. For example, figure 11.6 shows how the screen appears just after you enter the entry date in the D4 (the Full International) format but before you press RETURN. Figure 11.7

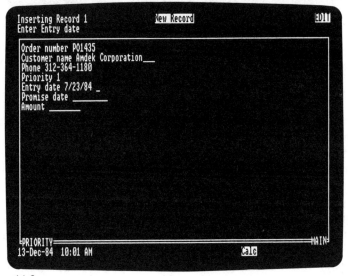

Fig. 11.6.

shows what happens after you press RETURN. Just as with the @DATEVALUE function, you can enter the date in a FORM window

in any one of the valid date formats—D1 through D5. (You cannot use a formula or a function, however.) Later you will learn how to change the date to any display format you like.

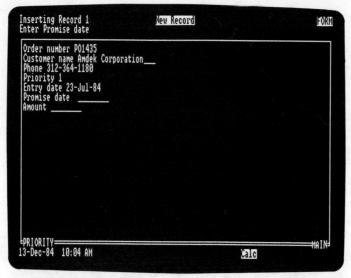

Fig. 11.7.

Modifying the Current Record before Insertion

Sometimes before you insert a record, you will discover a mistake. There are several ways to modify the entry. Suppose you discover the error immediately after entering an order number, and you want to go back and change it. One way is to press the Up arrow, which returns you to the "Order number" field, and start typing. The old entry immediately disappears and clears the way for the new entry. Another method is to use the Edit key. Move the cursor to the "Order number" field and press the Edit key; you can then use the Backspace, Esc, and Del keys just as you would in the EDIT mode in a SHEET window. (See Chapter 2 for more on the Edit key.) Two other alternatives are to use the Backspace or the Esc key. When you press either key, Symphony erases the field where the cursor is. You can then make the correct entry.

Modifying Previous Records

If you have already pressed the Ins key when you find the error in a record, you must make that record current again before you can modify it. One way to make the record current is to use the PgUp key to browse through the records until you reach the one you wish to modify. Another way is to use the GoTo key. If you can remember the number of the incorrect record, simply press the GoTo key and type in the record number. Symphony will immediately go to that record.

Undoing Changes to a Record

If you change a record that was previously inserted in the data base and then decide you don't like the changes you've made, you can always recall the original copy of the record. Simply press the Esc key twice. The first time you press Esc, Symphony clears the field where the cursor resides and restores the original value of the field. The second time you press Esc, Symphony restores the entire original record.

Adding New Records

If, after making the initial entries to the data base, you decide to add more records, first use the End key to go to the last record in the data base. Then press the PgDn key. Symphony will show a "New Record" indicator at the top of the screen and a blank entry form below.

Adding new records is similar to making changes to existing records. Simply enter the value you want in a field and press the RETURN key. When you press RETURN, Symphony shifts the cursor down to the next field in the input form. After entering your last field, press the Ins key to enter the new record in the data base. You can add as many new records as you like up to the practical limitations of RAM. Be sure to press Ins once for each record after you have entered all the fields for that record.

Deleting Records

Deleting records is the easiest operation in a FORM window. Simply use the PgUp and PgDn keys to make current the record you want to delete. Then press the Del key. Symphony completely erases the record from the data base and displays the next record in the form.

Sorting the Data Base

Suppose you have entered several records in the "Priority" data base, and you want to sort the data base by priority number. To sort the data base, you must first select the **S**ettings option from the main FORM menu. Figure 11.8 shows a copy of the FORM **S**ettings sheet with the **S**ettings menu above it.

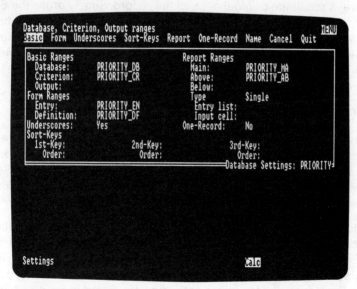

Fig. 11.8.

The next step is to select the **S**ort-Keys option from the **S**ettings menu. When you choose **S**ort-Keys, Symphony gives you three options:

    1st-Key   2nd-Key   3rd-Key

To sort the data base by priority number, you choose **1st-Key** from the menu. Symphony will shift temporarily to the SHEET environment so you can select the proper field. Figure 11.9 shows the Database range A34..G53 (corresponding to PRIORITY_DB in the settings sheet in figure 11.8). This is the same range that would appear if you selected **B**asic **D**atabase from the **S**ettings menu.

```
Database range: A34,.G53                                              POINT
      A           B                C         D     E        F        G
   34 Order nCustomer name      Phone          PrEntry datePromise daAmount
   35 PO1435 Amdek Corporation   312-364-1180 1    30886    30917    23000
   36 PO1436 AST Research Inc.   714-540-1333 1    30887    30918    34000
   37 PO1437 Hercules Computer   415-654-2476 2    30887    30918    12000
   38 PO1438 Quadram Corp        404-923-6666 1    30888    30919    42100
   39 PO1439 Raytronics          800-854-1085 3    30889    30920    12200
   40 PO1440 Seattle Computer    800-426-8936 2    30890    30921    24500
   41 PO1441 Tecmar Inc.         216-464-7410 1    30891    30922    51000
   42 PO1442 Qubie' Distributing 800-821-4479 4    30892    30832    11330
   43 PO1443 Micro Graphics Tech 408-996-8423 4    30894    30925     8190
   44 PO1444 Orchid Technology   408-942-8660 3    30895    30926     4520
   45 PO1445 Maynard Electronics 305-331-6402 2    30897    30928    23500
   46 PO1446 Hayes Microcomputer 404-449-8791 1    30897    30928    19800
   47 PO1447 Apparat, Inc.       303-741-1778 4    30898    30929     3100
   48 PO1448 Data Technology Corp 408-496-0434 3   30899    30930     7890
   49 PO1449 Super Computer, Inc. 714-540-1880 4   30900    30931     6538
   50 PO1450 IDE Associates      617-275-4430 2    30901    30932     2180
   51 PO1451 MBI                 303-279-4628 4    30902    30933     2300
   52 PO1452 Arby Corporation    617-864-5058 3    30903    30934     7892
   53 PO1453 Indigo Data Systems 713-488-8186 2    30904    30935     3290
                                                                          MAIN
Settings Basic Database                              Calc
```

Fig. 11.9.

When Symphony shows you the Database range, you simply point to any item in the "Priority" field (column C) to designate the **1st-Key**. For example, you might point to cell C36. After you point to the **1st-Key**, Symphony asks whether you want **A**scending or **D**escending order. Because you want the priority numbers to appear in ascending order, you select **A** (for **A**scending).

After you set up the **1st-Key**, you return to the main FORM menu and issue the **R**ecord-Sort command. Symphony will ask whether you want to sort **A**ll the records or only the **U**nique records. (If you select **U**nique, Symphony will remove all duplicates.) After you select **A**ll or **U**nique, Symphony rearranges the data according to priority number and returns you to the data base form. Figures 11.10A and 11.10B show the settings and newly sorted data base. Again, the data base appears only when you use the **S**ettings **B**asic **D**atabase command.

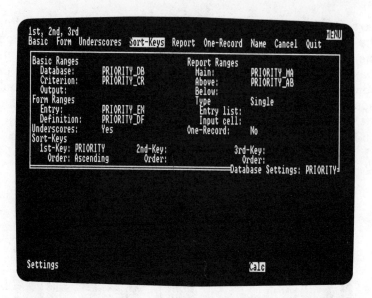

```
1st, 2nd, 3rd                                                    MENU
 Basic  Form  Underscores  Sort-Keys  Report  One-Record  Name  Cancel  Quit
┌─────────────────────────────────────────────────────────────────────┐
│ Basic Ranges                        Report Ranges                     │
│    Database:      PRIORITY_DB           Main:      PRIORITY_MA         │
│    Criterion:     PRIORITY_CR           Above:     PRIORITY_AB         │
│    Output:                              Below:                         │
│ Form Ranges                             Type       Single              │
│    Entry:         PRIORITY_EN           Entry list:                    │
│    Definition:    PRIORITY_DF           Input cell:                    │
│ Underscores:      Yes                One-Record:   No                  │
│ Sort-Keys                                                             │
│    1st-Key: PRIORITY      2nd-Key:                3rd-Key:            │
│       Order: Ascending       Order:                 Order:            │
│                                          Database Settings: PRIORITY  │
└─────────────────────────────────────────────────────────────────────┘



 Settings                                    Calc
```

Fig. 11.10A.

```
Database range: A34..G53                                         POINT
        A         B              C          D     E          F         G
34  Order n Customer name    Phone         Pr Entry date Promise da Amount
35  PO1438  Quadram Corp     404-923-6666  1     30888     30919     42100
36  PO1441  Tecmar Inc.      216-464-7410  1     30891     30922     51000
37  PO1435  Amdek Corporation 312-364-1180 1     30886     30917     23000
38  PO1436  AST Research Inc. 714-540-1333 1     30887     30918     34000
39  PO1446  Hayes Microcomputer 404-449-8791 1   30897     30928     19800
40  PO1440  Seattle Computer 800-426-8936  2     30890     30921     24500
41  PO1453  Indigo Data Systems 713-488-8186 2   30904     30935      3290
42  PO1450  IDE Associates   617-275-4430  2     30901     30932      2180
43  PO1445  Maynard Electronics 305-331-6402 2   30897     30928     23500
44  PO1437  Hercules Computer 415-654-2476 2     30887     30918     12000
45  PO1444  Orchid Technology 408-942-8660 3     30895     30926      4520
46  PO1452  Arby Corporation 617-864-5058  3     30903     30934      7892
47  PO1439  Raytronics       800-854-1085  3     30889     30920     12200
48  PO1448  Data Technology Corp 408-496-0434 3  30899     30930      7890
49  PO1442  Qubie' Distributing 800-821-4479 4   30802     30832     11330
50  PO1443  Micro Graphics Tech 408-996-8423 4   30894     30925      8190
51  PO1451  MBI              303-279-4628  4     30902     30933      2300
52  PO1449  Super Computer, Inc. 714-540-1880 4  30900     30931      6538
53  PO1447  Apparat, Inc.    303-741-1778  4     30898     30929      3100
                                                                    MAIN
 Settings Basic Database                      Calc
```

Fig. 11.10B.

Notice that the priority numbers appear correctly, but you have no way of telling the relative priorities within a group. For example, there are five purchase-order numbers with priority 1, but there are no priorities within that group. If you want to prioritize within each group, you can use the dollar amount of the order (or some other field) as the **2**nd-Key. (See fig. 11.11A.) Figure 11.11B shows what happens when you select cell G34 as the **2**nd-Key with **D**escending order and re-sort the data base with the **R**ecord-Sort command. Symphony allows you to specify up to three different **S**ort-Keys for sorting records.

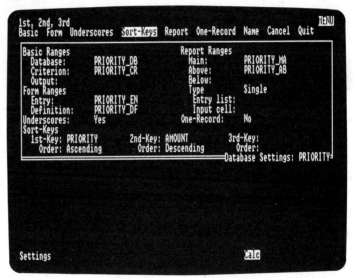

Fig. 11.11A.

Besides using the **S**ettings **B**asic **D**atabase command to see the entire sorted data base, you can also browse through the individual records one at a time to check their order. Remember that when the data base is re-sorted, the first record to appear is the record at the top of the sorting order. (When the data base is sorted according to priority and amount, the first record to appear is the one corresponding to order number PO1441.)

The FORM window is used for looking at individual records, and the SHEET window is used for looking at several records at once. Otherwise, the two windows have a great deal in common when it

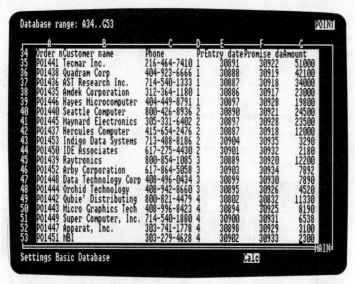

```
Database range: A34..G53                                            POINT
         A           B            C        D     E       F        G
34 Order nCustomer name      Phone        PrEntry datePromise daAmount
35 P01441 Tecmar Inc.        216-464-7410 1    30891   30922    51000
36 P01438 Quadram Corp       404-923-6666 1    30888   30919    42100
37 P01436 AST Research Inc.  714-540-1333 1    30887   30918    34000
38 P01435 Amdek Corporation  312-364-1180 1    30886   30917    23000
39 P01446 Hayes Microcomputer 404-449-8791 1   30897   30928    19800
40 P01440 Seattle Computer   800-426-8936 2    30890   30921    24500
41 P01445 Maynard Electronics 305-331-6402 2   30897   30928    23500
42 P01437 Hercules Computer  415-654-2476 2    30887   30918    12000
43 P01453 Indigo Data Systems 713-488-8186 2   30904   30935     3290
44 P01450 IDE Associates     617-275-4430 2    30901   30932     2180
45 P01439 Raytronics         800-854-1085 3    30889   30920    12200
46 P01452 Arby Corporation   617-864-5058 3    30903   30934     7892
47 P01448 Data Technology Corp 408-496-0434 3  30899   30930     7890
48 P01444 Orchid Technology  408-942-8660 3    30895   30926     4520
49 P01442 Qubie' Distributing 800-821-4479 4   30802   30832    11330
50 P01443 Micro Graphics Tech 408-996-8423 4   30894   30925     8190
51 P01449 Super Computer, Inc. 714-540-1880 4  30900   30931     6538
52 P01447 Apparat, Inc.      303-741-1778 4    30898   30929     3100
53 P01451 MBI                303-279-4628 4    30902   30933     2300
                                                                 MAIN
Settings Basic Database                      Calc
```

Fig. 11.11B.

comes to data base operations. For example, the SHEET **Q**uery
Record-Sort command is almost exactly the same as the FORM
Record-Sort command. The differences between the SHEET and
FORM data base commands are presented later in this chapter.

Working with the Settings Sheets

*New
with
Symphony*

Just as with other types of settings sheets (including GRAPH, DOC,
and COMM), FORM **S**ettings sheets can be named and saved.

Naming Settings Sheets

The settings sheet that appears in figure 11.10A was stored under
the name 1ST-KEY; the sheet that appears in figure 11.11A was
stored under the name 2ND-KEY. (If you look at the lower left
corners of both figures, you will see the settings names.) To save a
group of settings under a name, you use the **C**reate option from the
Settings **N**ame menu that appears as follows:

Use Create Delete Previous Next Initial-Settings Reset Quit

The **N**ame **U**se command recalls the settings.

Attaching Settings Sheets

To have a settings name used with the current data base, you must attach the settings name. For example, if you want to go back and forth in the "Priority" data base between sorting by order number and sorting by priority, you may want to create two different settings sheets: ORDER NUMBER, which contains a Sort-Key from column A, and PRIORITY, which contains a Sort-Key from column F. Depending on how you want the data base sorted at any given time, you use the FORM Attach command to attach the appropriate settings sheet to the data base and then re-sort the data base.

Creating a Catalog of Settings Sheets

Like GRAPH Settings, Symphony offers both Previous and Next options in its Name command menu. These options allow you to browse sequentially through a catalog of settings sheets and select the one you want. Be careful, though. Just because you have made a settings sheet current by using the Next or Previous command, don't assume that the settings sheet will automatically be used the next time you perform a Record-Sort or other data base operation. You must attach the settings name to the current data base before the settings can be used.

Searching for Records

In addition to sorting a data base, Symphony's FORM environment makes it easy for you to search for records. You can search for records individually or in groups. For example, suppose you are given the "Priority" data base sorted by priority number and amount, and you want to find the record for PO1452.

To find a record in the data base, you must enter selection criteria. The criteria can be numbers, labels, or formulas. To enter selection criteria, choose the Criteria option from the main FORM menu. The following options are then given:

> Use   Ignore   Edit

To enter selection criteria and to modify criteria, you choose Edit. Symphony then displays a blank input form with the message

"Editing Criterion Record 1 of 1" at the top. (Symphony lets you enter
as many as four different criterion records.) To select the data base
record for PO1452, you enter that order number in the "Order
number" field. Figure 11.12 shows the input form just after you have
entered the order number.

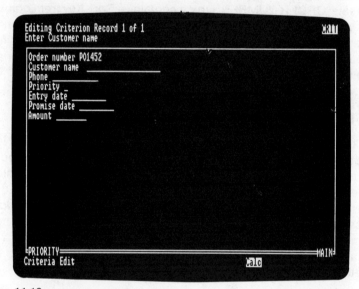

Fig. 11.12.

Next, you press PgUp to return to the data base. Then choose
Criteria **U**se to have Symphony use the selection criteria you have
set up. Symphony selects the record, as illustrated in figure 11.13.

Once you have seen the record for PO1452, and you want to move to
another task, choose **C**riteria **I**gnore. This command returns you to
the data base, but the criteria you have set up remain in effect. If you
want to reinvoke the criteria later, simply press **C**riteria **U**se again.

Using Formulas in Criteria

Besides choosing individual records, you can also set up criteria to
select a group of records. Suppose, for example, that you want to
select all the records in the data base whose amount is greater than

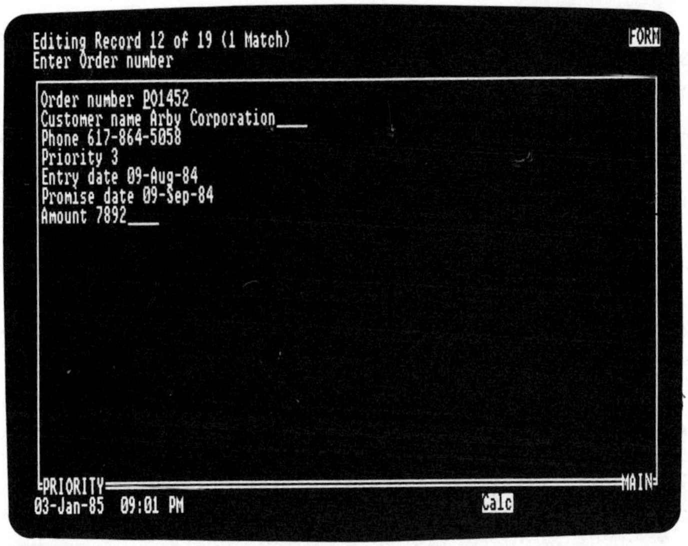

Fig. 11.13.

$10,000. To enter this criteria, you return to the **C**riteria **E**dit command. Because the criteria for the purchase order still reside in the input form, you must first delete the purchase order number from the "Order number" field. To do this, you can enter a blank space or press the Esc key while the cursor is in the "Order number" field. Next, you move to the "Amount" field and enter the formula +?>10000. This entry may not look like a formula, but it has special meaning in a Criterion record.

The question mark in the formula indicates to Symphony that you want the program to supply an address. Symphony then uses one of the special range names that it sets up under the **G**enerate command. If you look back at figure 11.9, you will see the Database range for the "Priority" data base (PRIORITY_DB). When Symphony sets up the data base, it uses the field-name headings as range names for the cells directly below. (See row 34 of fig. 11.9.) In other words, cell A35 is named ORDER NUMBER, cell B35 is CUSTOMER NAME, and so on. Therefore, when you use a question mark in a criterion formula, Symphony automatically substitutes the appropriate range name for the cell where you enter the formula. (In this case, Symphony automatically substitutes AMOUNT for the question mark because the formula was entered in the "Amount" field.)

Because you are actually entering a formula, you must make sure to precede the question mark with a plus (+) sign. Otherwise, the formula will not work correctly.

When you enter the criteria for records with an amount greater than $10,000, press the PgUp key and select Criteria Use, Symphony returns ten records that meet the criteria. Figure 11.14 shows the first of the ten and the message that appears at the top of the screen, indicating which record is in the input form. At this point, the Home, End, PgUp, and PgDn keys let you browse through only those records that match the selection criteria. You must use the Criteria Ignore command to return to the entire data base.

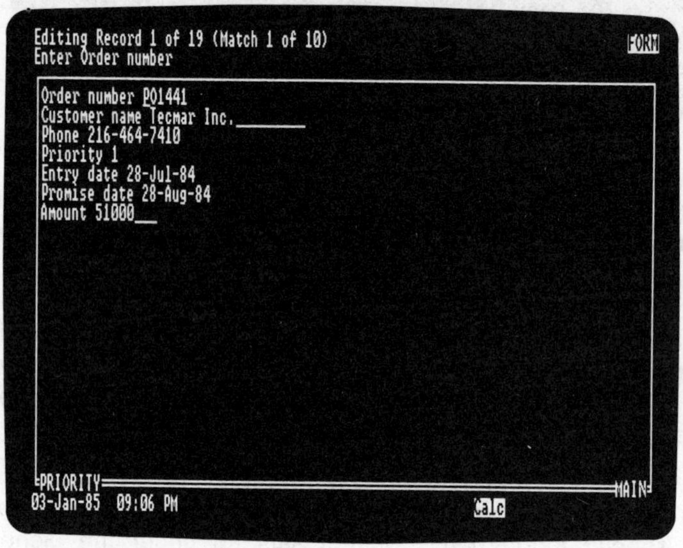

Fig. 11.14.

Combining Criteria with ANDs

Now suppose you want to select in the data base all the records whose amount is greater than $10,000 and whose priority number is 2 or below. First, you use the Criteria Edit command to edit the Criterion record you have constructed. Next, you move to the "Priority" field and enter the formula +?<=2. Do not be concerned if you don't see the entire formula. It can be verified by using the Edit key (F2) even though priority is a 1-position field. Because you still want all the records whose amount is greater than $10,000, you leave the original formula in the "Amount" field (+AMOUNT>10000).

By combining the two formulas in the same Criterion record, you are telling Symphony that you want to combine these two criteria with AND. In other words, for a record to filter through the criteria you have set up, it must pass both tests. Figure 11.15 shows the second record that meets the new criteria.

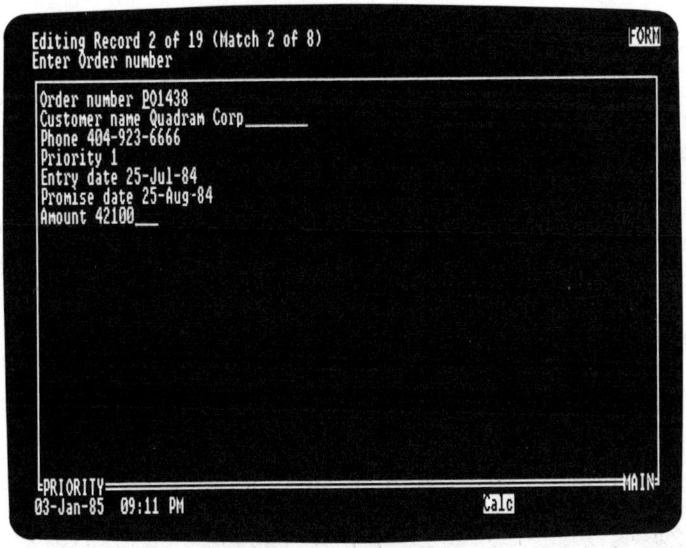

```
Editing Record 2 of 19 (Match 2 of 8)                          FORM
Enter Order number

Order number PO1438
Customer name Quadram Corp_____
Phone 404-923-6666
Priority 1
Entry date 25-Jul-84
Promise date 25-Aug-84
Amount 42100___




PRIORITY                                                       MAIN
03-Jan-85  09:11 PM                              Calc
```

Fig. 11.15.

Combining Criteria with ORs

Suppose, on the other hand, that you want all the records that have a priority of 2 or below or have an amount greater than $10,000. To combine criteria with OR, place them in different Criterion records. You keep the original formula in the first Criterion record (+AMOUNT>10000); then you use the Criterion Edit command followed by PgDn to add the other Criterion record. After placing the proper formula (+?<=2) in the "Priority" field, you press PgUp twice to return to the data base. Finally, you invoke the Criteria Use command again to initiate the search. This time you get 12 records that match the criteria. (See fig. 11.9 to verify this number.)

Adding a Criterion Range

As mentioned earlier, Symphony allows you to construct up to four Criterion records, which can give you fairly complex criteria. There may be times, however, when you want to step outside Symphony's structure. For example, you may want to add a Criterion record. To do this, you must know where Symphony stores the Criterion range.

If you use the **S**ettings **B**asic **C**riterion command, Symphony displays the Criterion range. Figure 11.16 shows the Criterion range for the last example. Notice that the two formulas appear on different lines. Criteria combined with OR reside on different lines in a Criterion range, and criteria combined with AND reside on the same line. Notice also that the formulas are displayed as 1s in the figure. The value of a formula is always true or false (1 or 0). These formulas appear as 1s because both their values are true for the records to which they currently refer. If you shift to the SHEET environment and use the Literal display format on these formulas, they will be displayed in their normal form.

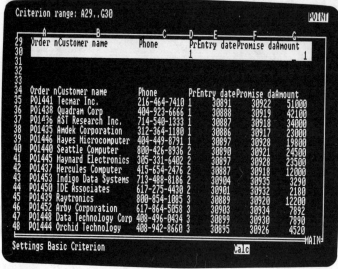

Fig. 11.16.

When you use the **G**enerate command, Symphony automatically sets up the Criterion range and names it according to the data base name you choose. The name of the Criterion range in the example is PRIORITY_CR. When you first use the **G**enerate command, the Criterion range is only one row deep (A29..G29 in the example). However, as you add Criterion records, the range grows. You have added two Criterion records in the current example, so the Criterion range is now three rows deep (A29..G31). Symphony automatically keeps track of the Criterion range, the Database range, and several other important ranges. This is one of the nicest features of building a data base in the FORM work environment.

Constructing Your Own Criterion Range

Symphony automatically sets up the FORM window to allow enough space for four Criterion records. But suppose you want five. For example, suppose you want to select all the records for the following customer names:

> Quadram Corporation
> Indigo Data Systems
> Seattle Computer
> AST Research, Inc.
> Orchid Technology

To select the records for Quadram Corporation, you simply place that name in the "Customer name" field of a Criterion record. However, to use all five names requires five Criterion records.

To add another record to the Criterion range, you first shift to the SHEET environment. Next, move the cursor to the Criterion range by pressing the GoTo key, and enter PRIORITY_CR. This places the cursor at the top left corner of the Criterion range. You can add the record by either of two ways. One way is to use the Insert **R**ow command to insert a blank row below the field-name headings in the Criterion range. The other way is to use the **M**ove command to move the entire Database range (PRIORITY_DB) one row down. (Using the **M**ove command will keep the address of PRIORITY_DB intact.) In either case, once you have added the row, you must update the address of the Criterion range in the FORM **S**ettings **B**asic **C**riterion. In the current example, change the reference for the Criterion range

(PRIORITY_CR) to A29..G33. Figure 11.17 shows the new Criterion range.

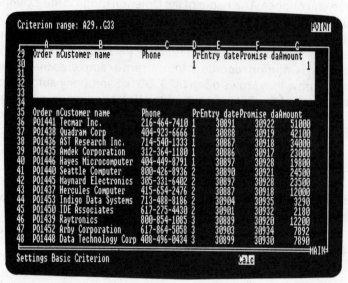

Fig. 11.17.

When you make the appropriate change to the Criterion range, Symphony instantly recognizes five Criterion records.

Approximate Matching

Symphony uses approximate matching when evaluating the labels in a record. (This is the same feature used for the **S**earch command in the DOC environment.) For example, suppose you want to search out all the records in the "Priority" data base whose "Customer name" begins with A. When you enter the formula @LEFT(?,1)="A" in the "Customer name" field of the first Criterion record, Symphony returns four data base records. An alternative is to use the same formula but with lowercase a, @LEFT(?,1)="a". Symphony will return the same results because the program does not recognize the difference between lowercase and uppercase letters when it is matching labels.

Note: If you have leading spaces in front of the @LEFT formula, you must delete them so that your formula will be handled correctly.

Wild Cards

Symphony also has wild-card provisions for matching labels. The characters ?, *, and ~ have special meanings when used in Criterion records.

The ? character instructs Symphony to accept any character in that position (just as it does in DOS). For example, if you want to find the record for order number PO1542 but suspect that you typed a zero instead of a capital O for the second character when you entered the record, you can use the label P?1542.

The * character tells Symphony to accept all characters that follow it. Suppose again that you want to select the records in the "Priority" data base whose "Customer name" begins with A. You can enter A* or a*. Be forewarned. Symphony does not recognize the * character when you put characters after it. For example, "*dek" is an invalid use of the wild-card character.

When placed at the beginning of a label, the ~ character indicates that all the values *except* those that follow it are to be selected. For example, if you want all the records in the "Priority" data base except those that begin with the letter A, you can enter ~A* in the first Criterion record. In this case, Symphony returns 15 records from the "Priority" data base.

Negating Number and Formula Criteria

Although the ~ character works well for labels, it doesn't work for formulas and numbers. To get the same results with a number or a formula, you must use either the <> or #NOT# logical operator. For example, if you want to select all the records in the "Priority" data base *except* those whose priority number is 4, you can enter +?<>4. (Notice that the ? character is not used as the label wild card in this case.) Similarly, you can enter the formula #NOT#?=4. Both formulas give the same results.

Modifying, Adding, and Deleting Records While Searching

New with Symphony

Suppose that while you are searching a data base, you find a record that requires modification. You can stop the search by using the **C**riteria **I**gnore command and return to the data base to edit the record. However, this method is not desirable, because you will have to find the record again before you can modify it. A better technique is to modify the record on the spot.

One of the main drawbacks of the 1-2-3 **/D**ata **Q**uery command is that you cannot modify a record while you are in the middle of a search operation. Lotus has corrected this problem in Symphony. When you are in a FORM window, you can modify any record. If you modify the record to the point where it no longer fits the criteria, Symphony will no longer let you see it during the search operation (unless you change the selection criteria). If, on the other hand, you are performing a search operation in a SHEET window using the **Q**uery command, you cannot modify records.

Besides modifying records while searching in a FORM window, you can also delete records. Simply press the Del key just as you would under normal circumstances. Symphony asks for confirmation before deleting the record.

Under no circumstances can you add a record while you are in the middle of a search operation in a FORM window. This statement holds even if one of the records that conforms to the search criteria is the last record in the data base. (Recall that under normal circumstances you must move to the last record in the data base before adding a record.)

Using Advanced FORM Features

Now that you are familiar with the basics for creating a standard input form and entering a simple data base, you are ready to learn some of the more advanced features of Symphony's FORM window. For example, up to this point Symphony has automatically handled the layout of input forms and has entered all the important ranges with little help from you. You will now learn how to create customized input forms and make other modifications to a data base to suit better your personal data-management needs.

Creating Special Input Forms

Suppose you decide that you want to create a special input form for entering additional records in the "Priority" data base. To begin with, you decide that you want to place two fields on the same line in the input form.

Placing Two Fields on the Same Line

Suppose you want to put the "Phone" field on the same line as the "Customer name" in the input form. To do this, you must be familiar with another special range in Symphony's FORM window, the Entry range.

Modifying the Entry Range

The Entry range is created by Symphony when you issue the **G**enerate command. Figure 11.18 shows the Entry range for the "Priority" data base.

The Entry range (A9..A15) contains a column of label entries, the same labels that appear in the input form when you enter data. If you want to place the "Phone" field on the same line as the "Customer name" field, you must modify the Entry range. Note: This is the entry layout and not the initial data definition. First, use the Type key (Alt + F10) to change to the DOC environment. (You can use the SHEET environment, but the procedure is easier in the DOC environment.) Once again, make sure that **F**ormat **S**ettings **J**ustification is set to **N**one so that Symphony does not try to justify the Entry range.

After you change to the DOC environment, the next step is to use the **M**ove command to move the "Phone" label up to the same line as the "Customer name" label. After moving the label, use the Del key to remove the blank line that is left. Figure 11.19 shows the Entry range after the change.

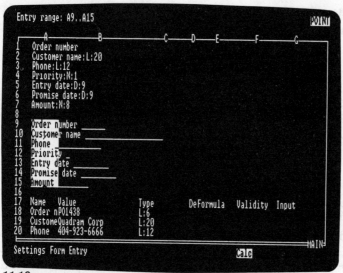

Fig. 11.18.

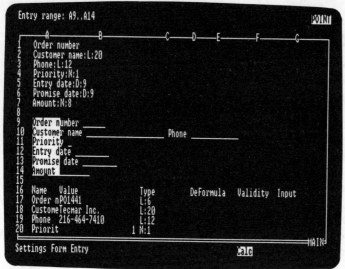

Fig. 11.19.

The address of the Entry range is stored in the settings sheet under the name PRIORITY_EN. (Symphony assigned this name when the **G**enerate command was used.) If you use the MENU **S**ettings **F**orm

Entry command, Symphony highlights the PRIORITY_EN range. You should not have to change this setting unless you change the position of either cell in the range. If you do change the position of either the first or last cell, you must make sure to update the address of the Entry range in the FORM Settings sheet.

Changing the position of the "Phone" field in the input form does not affect the way Symphony enters records in the data base. In fact, you can put several field names on the same line. Symphony will process them sequentially from left to right as though they were all on separate lines. Figure 11.20 shows how the input form appears after this first change.

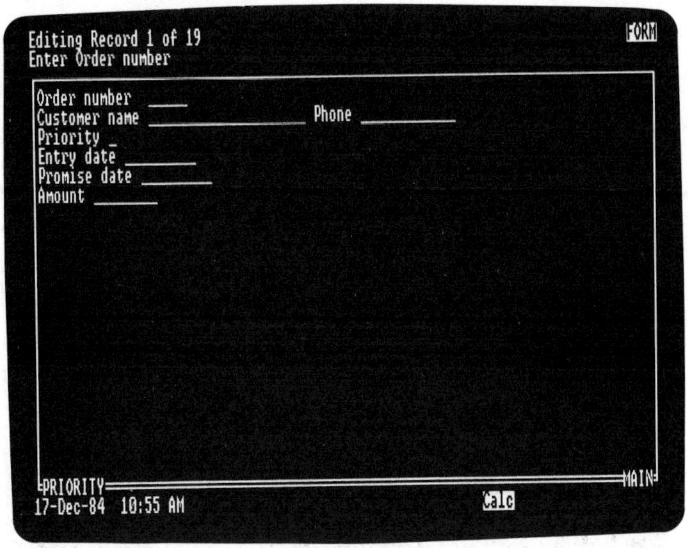

```
Editing Record 1 of 19                                    FORM
Enter Order number

Order number    ____
Customer name   _____        Phone   _____
Priority _
Entry date _____
Promise date _____
Amount _____





















PRIORITY                                                  MAIN
17-Dec-84  10:55 AM                        Calc
```

Fig. 11.20.

Changing Underscores

Suppose you also want to modify the input form to allow longer entries by increasing the size of the "Customer name" field from 20 to 30 characters. To do this, you simply shift to the DOC environment, position the cursor on the "Customer name" label, and add 5 underscore characters to the 20 that are already there. Incidentally, you can stop underscores from appearing at all in the input form. Simply select **S**ettings **U**nderscores **N**o.

Scrolling Characters

If you prefer not to change the input form, but you would still like it to be able to handle longer customer names, Symphony offers the scrolling-characters technique. To use this technique, you have to know how to change the Definition range. The major portion of the Definition range for the "Priority" data base (PRIORITY_DF— A17..H23) appears in figure 11.21.

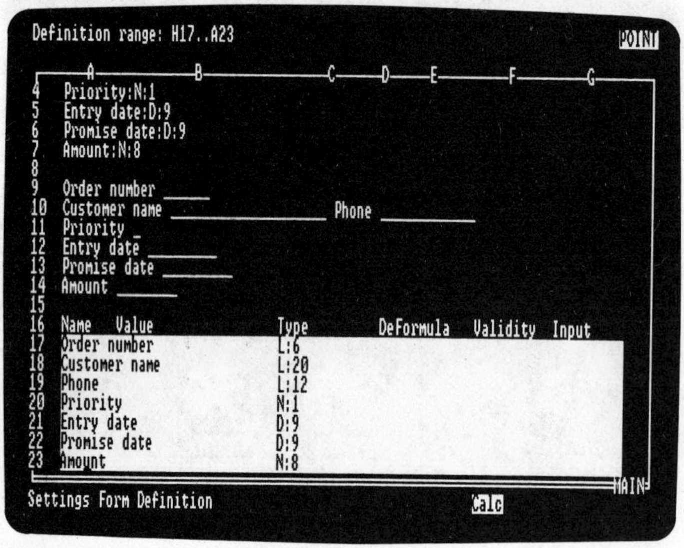

```
Definition range: H17..A23                                              POINT
      A          B              C     D    E        F          G
4    Priority:N:1
5    Entry date:D:9
6    Promise date:D:9
7    Amount:N:8
8
9    Order number _____
10   Customer name _____    Phone _____
11   Priority _
12   Entry date _____
13   Promise date _____
14   Amount _____
15
16   Name    Value              Type       DeFormula  Validity  Input
17   Order number              L:6
18   Customer name             L:20
19   Phone                     L:12
20   Priority                  N:1
21   Entry date                D:9
22   Promise date              D:9
23   Amount                    N:8
                                                                    MAIN
Settings Form Definition                            Calc
```

Fig. 11.21.

Modifying the Definition Range

The Definition range, which is the most comprehensive range in the FORM work environment, contains fields for checking the type of entries made and their *validity*, that is, whether they fall within a certain range of values. The Definition range is also where you control the format for displaying entries and other customization.

To change the number of characters that you can enter in the "Customer name" field but not change the input form, you must switch to the SHEET environment. Next, you move the cursor to the "Type" field in the Definition range. The appropriate "Type" field is cell C18 in figure 11.21. (You can always find the correct cell address by looking at the entries in the Name column, the first column in the Definition range.) Notice that the "Type" field is where Symphony stores the type and length information you provided when you created the data base. Change the value in cell C18 from L:20 (for label, 20 characters long) to L:30. When you switch back to the FORM environment, you can now enter labels up to 30 characters long in the "Customer name" field. However, because there is not enough visible room in the input form to display a 30-character string, Symphony will begin scrolling when you reach the 26th character.

This FORM window scrolling feature also works for number entries. Be forewarned, however, that because Symphony can store numbers with as many as 15 decimal places, the scrolling feature is practical only up to that point. When you get beyond 15 places, Symphony automatically shifts to the Scientific format.

Another mistake to watch out for is eliminating the Definition range address in the settings sheet when you are rearranging the input form. To access the Definition range in the settings sheet, use the **S**ettings **F**orm **D**efinition command. Normally, if you have eliminated the Definition range address, the entry in the settings sheet will be blank. You must restore the correct value in order for the FORM window to work properly.

Creating Defaults

Now that you are familiar with the basic concept of the Definition range, you are ready to make more modifications to the input form. Suppose, for example, that you want to set up the current date as the default entry date in the input form. As the default, the current date will show up every time you create a new record. You then have the option of keeping the current date or overriding it with another date.

To set up a default in the input form, you must make the proper entry in the "Default" field of the Definition range. Although the label in cell

D16 of figure 11.21 is truncated, it actually reads "Default" and indicates the top of the Default column. To have the current date display as the default in the "Entry date" field, enter the formula @INT(@NOW) in cell D21, the cell corresponding to the "Entry date" field in the Default column. [The formula @INT(@NOW) takes the integer portion of the current date/time serial number; see Chapter 5.] Figure 11.22 shows the input form with the new "Entry date" default.

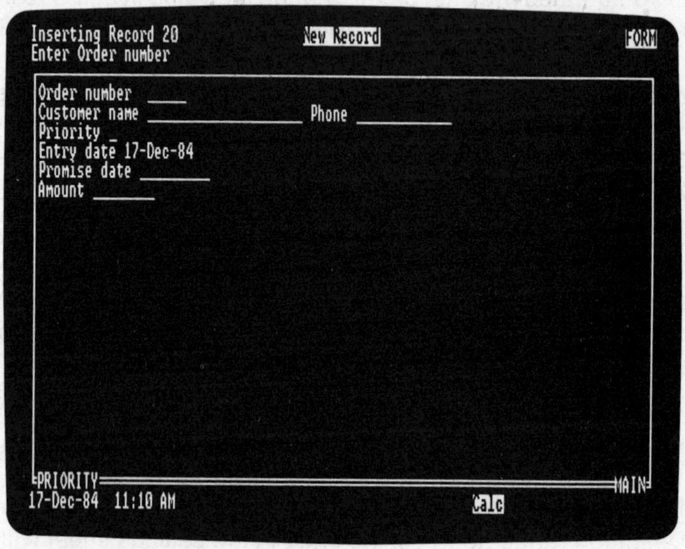

```
Inserting Record 20          New Record                        FORM
Enter Order number

Order number   ____
Customer name  _____    Phone _____
Priority _
Entry date 17-Dec-84
Promise date _____
Amount _____




PRIORITY                                                      MAIN
17-Dec-84  11:10 AM                          Calc
```

Fig. 11.22.

You can also enter labels or numbers as defaults. For example, to have the Priority number default to the highest priority, you can enter the number 1 in cell D20.

No matter what default you use (formula, label, or number), you should always make sure that it is the correct type. Although Symphony performs a validity check on the default value, it does not check to see whether the default is the correct entry type. If you are not careful, you may wind up with character data in a number field, or vice versa.

Computing Fields

Suppose that, as a company policy, you always assign a Promise date of 30 days after the Entry date. Therefore, after you have entered the Entry date, you prefer to have Symphony compute the Promise date. Symphony lets you define a computed field when you first create the data base. This is the best time to do it, but if you decide later that you want to enter a computed field, you simply change the type designation in the Type column of the Definition range to C (for computed). In order to have a computed field, Symphony must show a C in the Type column of the Definition range.

To complete the change, you must enter the formula +B21+30 in cell E22. Column E is labeled "Formula" in figure 11.21. Whenever you enter a formula for computing a field or transforming a field, you always enter the formula in the Formula column of the Definition range. Notice that the formula refers to a value in column B, the Value column. Symphony uses the Value column as a temporary holding place for the current record before writing it to the data base. (Symphony places the result of the formula in the Value column.) You should always make the formulas for computed fields refer to the appropriate cells in the Value column. Figure 11.23 shows the input form after the Promise date is computed from the Entry date.

When you use the input form, you will notice that the cursor jumps past a computed field. Because the field is computed from the values in other fields of the same record, you cannot enter a value manually. Therefore, when you designate a field as the computed type, be sure you will not want to change it manually.

You should also avoid the mistake of trying to compute fields from other records in the data base. The difficulty of creating general formulas for this purpose is beyond the scope of the beginner. You can refer to values outside the Definition range but not formulas; Symphony does not recalculate formulas outside the Definition range during a data base operation.

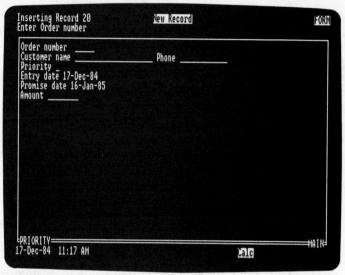

```
Inserting Record 20              New Record                      FORM
Enter Order number

Order number ____
Customer name _____      Phone _____
Priority _
Entry date 17-Dec-84
Promise date 16-Jan-85
Amount _____




PRIORITY
17-Dec-84  11:17 AM                                Calc      MAIN
```

Fig. 11.23.

Transforming Fields

Besides computing fields, you can also transform them. The main difference between the two methods is that transformed fields can be manually modified and computed fields cannot.

Suppose, for example, that you always enter order numbers beginning with PO. Rather than enter the entire order number yourself, you prefer to enter only the number portion and have Symphony enter the initial string for you. To do this, you place the formula +"PO"&G17 in cell E17. Note: Do not be concerned if ERR is generated before the entry of data. This cell resides in the Formula column, the same column used whenever a formula is used for computing or transforming a field. However, this time the formula refers to a cell in the Input column. Figure 11.24 shows the Input and Formula columns in the Definition range.

The entries from the input form are stored temporarily in the Input column. You never actually see values in the Input range; however, any formula that transforms an entry must refer to this column.

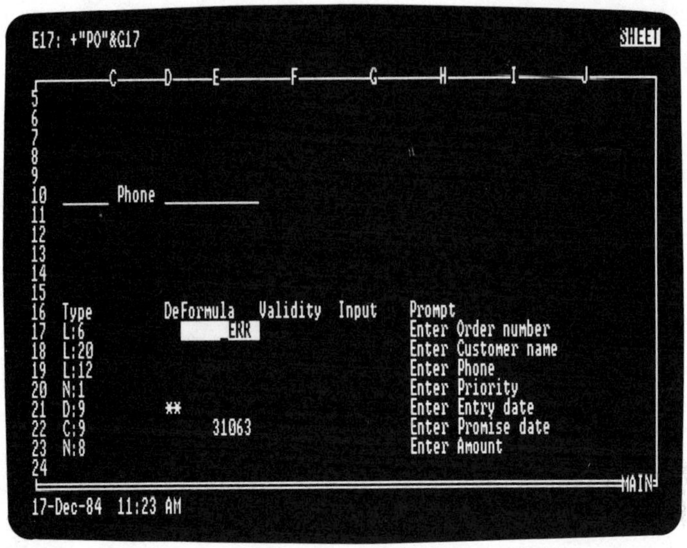

Fig. 11.24.

As another example of transforming an entry, suppose you want to enter customer phone numbers without having to enter the hyphens. To do this, you can enter the following formula in cell E19:

@LEFT(G19,3)&"-"&@MID(G19,4,3)&"-"&@RIGHT(G19,4)

Figure 11.25 shows the input form after a number has been entered but before RETURN has been pressed. Figure 11.26 shows the input form after RETURN has been pressed.

Just as with default and computed entries, transformed entries are stored in the Value column (column B) until the record is placed in the data base.

Performing Edit Checks

Symphony offers some simple edit checks depending on the field-type indicators you use when creating a data base. For example, if you indicate that a field is a date field (by entering a D after the field name), you must enter the date in one of the valid date formats or else Symphony beeps at you. Similarly, time must be entered in one of the valid time formats.

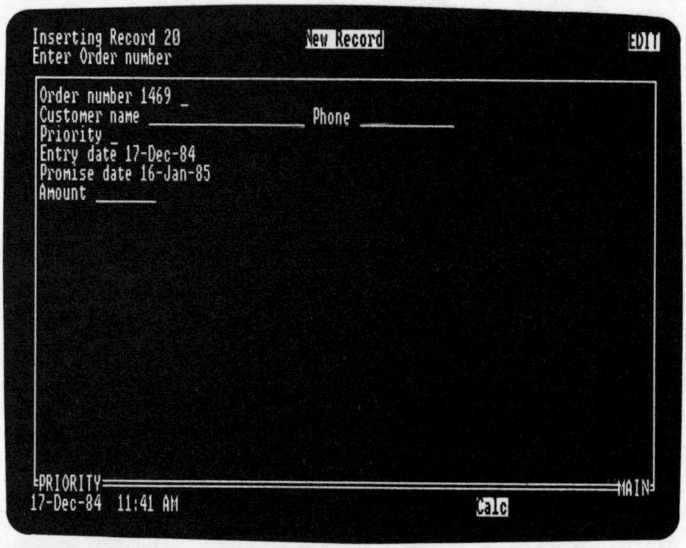

```
Inserting Record 20              New Record                    EDIT
Enter Order number

  Order number 1469 _
  Customer name _____  Phone _____
  Priority _
  Entry date 17-Dec-84
  Promise date 16-Jan-85
  Amount _____




































 PRIORITY                                                    MAIN
17-Dec-84  11:41 AM                              Calc
```

Fig. 11.25.

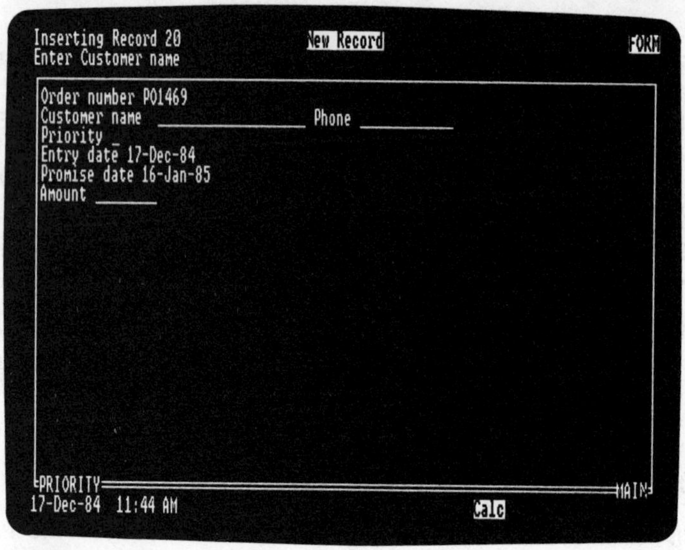

```
Inserting Record 20              New Record                    FORM
Enter Customer name

  Order number PO1469
  Customer name _____  Phone _____
  Priority _
  Entry date 17-Dec-84
  Promise date 16-Jan-85
  Amount _____




































 PRIORITY                                                    MAIN
17-Dec-84  11:44 AM                              Calc
```

Fig. 11.26.

Incidentally, Symphony automatically uses the D1 format for displaying dates in the input form and the Value column of the

Definition range. Times are displayed in the T1 format. If you wish to modify the way in which a date or time is displayed, you must change the format in the Value column of the Definition range. Any change you make will be reflected in the Input range.

Symphony also checks for valid numbers and labels when N and L field-type indicators are used. For example, because the "Priority" field in the example data base is designated as a single-digit number, you must enter a number between 1 and 9. However, when a field is a label field, Symphony will accept just about any entry. About the only edit check that Symphony provides for label fields is to test their length.

Performing Value Checks

Besides the simple edit checks that Symphony provides through field-type indicators, you can also validate inputs by using formulas. For example, suppose you wish to disallow priority numbers greater than four in the "Priority" data base. You can enter the formula +B20<=4 in cell F20 of the Definition range. Notice that the formula is entered in the Validity column of the range and that the formula also refers to a cell in the Value column. Value-checking formulas must always be written this way.

There are two rules to remember when you are using value-checking formulas. First, any default values you use must pass the check; Symphony does not check default values. Second, value-checking formulas test the value in the Value column, not the values actually input.

An example of the importance of this second rule occurs when you want to build a formula to check the four right-hand digits of the order number in the "Priority" data base and also use another formula to enter automatically the "PO" portion of the order number. The formula used to transform the order number is +"PO"&G17. This formula refers to a cell in the Input column, and Symphony places the result in the Value column. Therefore, because the value-checking formula tests the value in the Value column, you must use a formula that works with the transformed order number. The following is such a formula:

@IF(@ISERR(@VALUE(@RIGHT(B17,4)))=0,@TRUE,@FALSE)

This formula converts the four right-hand digits of the order number from characters to numbers. Next, the function tests for an ERR message indicating that the conversion has not taken place. If the conversion does take place, no ERR message is produced, and the value of the function is 1. Otherwise, the value of the function is 0.

Changing Prompts

In column H in figure 11.24, you can see the prompts that Symphony uses when you enter data in the input form. These prompts are supplied automatically when you create the data base.

Suppose you want to change the prompt for the priority number from "Enter Priority" to "Priority?" Simply enter the new label in cell H20 of the Definition range, and Symphony will use it for the next record you enter.

Changing Formats

You can change the format of the "Amount" field in the "Priority" data base to the Currency 0 format. Move the cursor to cell B23 in the Definition range and change the format there. A simple way is to switch to the SHEET environment and use the SHEET Format command. Symphony will now display in the new currency format the amounts you enter in the Input range.

Changing the display format in the input form does not change the format in the actual records stored in the Database range (PRIORITY_DB). However, because most of the time you see the records only as they appear in the input form, you don't really care how they appear in the actual Database range.

Adding a Field to the Data Base

The best place to add a field to an extensive data base is on the right side of the Database range. The best place to add an entry to the input form is at the end of the form. When you add a field, make sure that all the ranges are updated in the settings sheet, and you should have no problem.

If you decide that the new field should be somewhere in the middle of the input form, you must switch to the SHEET environment and issue several **M**ove and/or **I**nsert commands to get the new field where you want it. Remember also that the positions of the fields within the Entry range must correspond exactly to their positions in the Database range. If you change one range, you must change the other. Before you start changing the layout of an input form to add a field, be sure to plan a strategy for modifying the Database range and any other important ranges affected by the change.

Using Multiple Input Forms

When you create an entry form, the **G**enerate command automatically attaches the form to the data base. However, you can activate different input forms for the same data base by means of the **A**ttach command. For example, you can use two different input forms when you need to keep confidential certain fields in a data base. You also need to use the **A**ttach command when you store more than one data base in the same spreadsheet and you want to change from one data base to the other.

The SHEET Data Base Commands

As mentioned earlier, SHEET data base commands are used to manipulate groups of data base records. For data base operations in the SHEET environment, use, if possible, the settings that are automatically created in the FORM environment. This saves your having to re-create the settings yourself. However, you always have the option of creating or modifying the settings in the SHEET environment. Determining when to use Symphony's automatic capabilities and when to use your own is an acquired art. As you become more familiar with Symphony, you should find this choice increasingly easier to make.

A good time to use the SHEET environment is after you have built a data base by using Symphony's FORM environment. For example, suppose you have the name and address data base that was used at the beginning of the chapter and appears again in figure 11.27, and you want to make a copy of all the records whose area code is

812. Symphony's SHEET commands give you a way to accomplish this task.

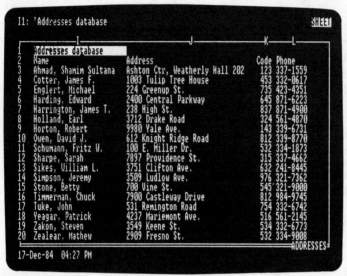

```
I1: 'Addresses database                                          SHEET
        ────────I───────────────────J──────────K──────L
   1  Addresses database
   2  Name                  Address                 Code Phone
   3  Ahmad, Shamim Sultana  Ashton Ctr, Weatherly Hall 202  123 337-1559
   4  Cotter, James F.       1003 Tulip Tree House    453 332-0617
   5  Englert, Michael       224 Greenup St.          735 423-4351
   6  Harding, Edward        2400 Central Parkway     645 871-6223
   7  Harrington, James T.   238 High St.             837 871-4900
   8  Holland, Earl          3712 Drake Road          324 561-4870
   9  Horton, Robert         9980 Yale Ave.           143 339-6731
  10  Owen, David J.         612 Knight Ridge Road    812 339-8770
  11  Schumann, Fritz W.     100 E. Miller Dr.        532 334-1873
  12  Sharpe, Sarah          7897 Providence St.      315 337-4662
  13  Sikes, William L.      3751 Clifton Ave.        632 241-8445
  14  Simpson, Jeremy        3509 Ludlow Ave.         976 321-7362
  15  Stone, Betty           700 Vine St.             545 321-9000
  16  Timmerman, Chuck       7900 Castleway Drive     812 984-9745
  17  Tuke, John             531 Remington Road       754 332-6742
  18  Yeagar, Patrick        4237 Mariemont Ave.      516 561-2145
  19  Zakon, Steven          3549 Keene St.           534 332-6773
  20  Zealear, Mathew        2909 Fresno St.          532 334-9008
                                                      ═══════════ADDRESSES═
  17-Dec-84  04:27 PM
```

Fig. 11.27.

The main command for performing data base operations in the SHEET environment is the **Q**uery command. (*Query* is just another word for search.) The simplest **Q**uery command option is **R**ecord-Sort.

Record-Sort

The only difference between **R**ecord-Sort in the FORM window and in the SHEET window is that in the SHEET window you specify the range to be sorted. Because Symphony does not automatically keep track of the Database ranges while you are in a SHEET window, you must do it yourself. As in the FORM window, the range to be sorted is called the Database range, and the address of the Database range must be entered in the Query settings sheet. Fortunately, if the data base was entered using an input form in the FORM window, the Database range should already be designated correctly.

Unlike 1-2-3, Symphony requires that you include the field name headings in a sort operation. This way you do not have to change the data base designation when you want to sort instead of search for records as you did in 1-2-3.

The *Query Settings Sheet*

The settings sheet for the SHEET **Q**uery commands is invoked by selecting **S**ettings from the main **Q**uery menu. This is the same settings sheet that appears in the FORM window; in fact, the settings that are currently attached to the FORM window also reside in the **Q**uery **S**ettings sheet. If you make a change in the FORM **S**ettings, the same change is immediately reflected in the **Q**uery **S**ettings, and vice versa. Figure 11.28 shows the **Q**uery **S**ettings sheet for the example data base. Notice that the sheet appears exactly as it did in the FORM window. (See fig. 11.11A.)

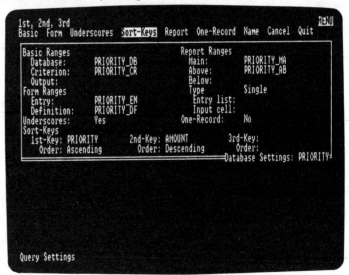

Fig. 11.28.

Symphony does not offer a Query key. In 1-2-3 the Query key can repeat a data base operation using the current settings. With Symphony's settings sheets (and the way the **Q**uery menu is set up), a Query key is no longer necessary. Just by issuing one of the commands in the menu, you invoke a data base operation using the latest settings.

Ways of Searching for Records

Besides **R**ecord-Sort and **S**ettings, **Q**uery is also the host command for a series of other subcommands. They are

Find	Moves down through a data base, locating the cursor at records that match given criteria (similar to issuing **C**riteria **U**se in a FORM window and then browsing through the resulting records)
Extract	Creates copies in a specified area of the worksheet of all or some of the fields in certain records that match given criteria
Unique	Similar to **E**xtract, but recognizes that some of the records in the data base may be duplicates. Includes only unique records.
Delete	Deletes all the records in a data base that match given criteria and shifts the remaining records to fill in the gaps that are left

Before you can execute these **Q**uery commands, however, the following three ranges must be set up:

1. The Criterion range specifying the search criteria

2. The Database range to be searched

3. The Output range—where the output will be written in the worksheet (not required for **F**ind or **D**elete)

The first two of these ranges should look familiar from the FORM window discussion. However, the third is a new range, which is used only for the SHEET environment. The Output range is used with the **Q**uery **E**xtract and **U**nique commands.

Query Find

For the first example of using the SHEET Query commands for searching records, suppose you want to find all the records in the "Priority" data base with a priority of 4. First, make sure that the Database range has been appropriately specified. To check the Database range, use the Settings Basic Database command to verify the address A34..G53.

Next, enter the selection criteria. Recall that the FORM window offers a Criteria command for entering and invoking criteria. The SHEET window does not have this command. Instead, you must manually enter the criteria in the Criterion range. For the current example, enter the number 4 in cell D30. Then make sure the Criterion range is designated as A29..G30 in the Query Settings sheet. Figure 11.29 shows the highlighted Criterion range.

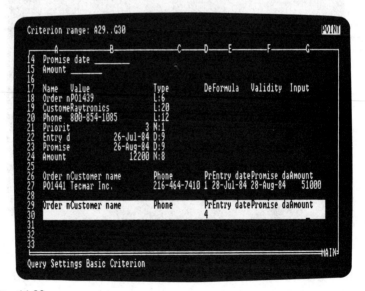

Fig. 11.29.

Notice that figure 11.29 shows the same Criterion range that appears in the examples for the FORM window. (See fig. 11.16.) Symphony retains the Criterion range setting from the FORM window.

Now that the appropriate ranges have been specified, you can issue the **Q**uery **F**ind command. Figure 11.30 shows what happens when you do. The cursor highlights the first record that conforms to the search criteria. By using the down arrow key, you can position the cursor at the next record that conforms to the criteria. By continuing to press the down arrow key, you can browse through the records that conform to the search criteria. The up arrow key works in the opposite direction and moves you to the previous record that conforms to the criteria. The Home and End keys, respectively, take you to the first and last records in the data base, even if these records do not fit the search criteria. To end the **F**ind operation and return to the **Q**uery menu, you can use either RETURN or Esc.

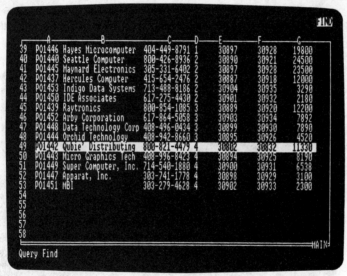

Fig. 11.30.

The Position of Formulas in a Criterion Range

When you manually enter criteria in the Criterion range, you must place numbers and labels below the appropriate field name. The same is not true for formulas. Formulas are written using relative addressing with reference to the first row of the data base. Therefore, in formulas the addresses are important, not what field names they fall under. (Note: You cannot use the ? character to have

Symphony automatically supply the address for you. You may recall that you can use this character in the FORM window.)

Suppose you want to search the "Priority" data base for all the records whose customer name begins with the letter A; the following Criterion ranges are equivalent:

Customer Name	Priority
@LEFT(CUSTOMER NAME,1)="A"	

Customer Name	Priority
	@LEFT(CUSTOMER NAME,1)="A"

Notice that the range name CUSTOMER NAME is used in the examples. When you are building a data base in the FORM window, Symphony automatically creates range names for the first records directly below the field name headings; you should use these names to your advantage in the SHEET environment.

Output Range

The results of a **Q**uery command are sometimes written to a special area of the worksheet called the Output range. All you need to specify for the Output range is a single row containing the names of the fields that you want copied; you do not need to include all the field names. You can specify a larger area for the Output range, but all Symphony actually needs is the field names.

Query **Extract**

Let's say that you want to create copies of all the records in the "Priority" data base whose Promise date occurs after September 3, 1984. The command you use to perform this kind of operation is **Q**uery **E**xtract. Figure 11.31 shows the results. As you can see, the **E**xtract operation copies to the area below the field names all the records that conform to the selection criteria. Incidentally, in order to use the @DATE function in the criteria for this **E**xtract operation, you must place the function outside of the Criterion range and refer to it by means of absolute addressing.

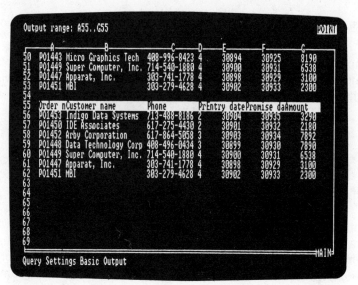

Fig. 11.31.

In figure 11.31, the Output range was set up manually because Symphony does not use the Output range in a FORM window. To create this Output range, use the **C**opy command to copy the field-name headings from the Database range or the Criterion range. When you enter the Output range in the **Q**uery **S**ettings **B**asic **O**utput sheet, enter only the range of the field-name headings (A55..G55 in fig. 11.31).

The advantage of the **E**xtract option is that it allows you to do detailed analysis on a data base. You can use **E**xtract to pull data from one or more records in a data base and perform special processing on the subset. However, you must be careful to designate the Database and Criterion ranges properly.

As mentioned earlier, the theoretical maximum number of records in a data base is about 8,000, but the actual limit is much lower than that. If you are performing an **E**xtract operation, you will require even more space for the Output range; this requirement further restricts the space you can devote to the data base.

Always consider the requirements for the Output range and how they may limit the kind of **E**xtract you can perform. With a fairly small data base, this limitation is not a problem. The larger a data base gets, however, the more you should keep an eye on the amount of RAM available. A frequent check of the SERVICES Settings command will tell you how much RAM is left and allow you to gauge the kinds of Extract operations that are possible with the available RAM.

Query Unique

Another type of search, which uses a variation of the Query command, selects all the *unique* records in a data base. Query Unique can copy all the unique records from an address data base to a separate part of the worksheet. A more popular way to use this command is to focus on specific fields in a data base. To illustrate how this works, let's say that you want to get a listing of all the companies represented in your customer data base, which is organized as shown in figure 11.32; all the records have a "Name" and a "Company" field.

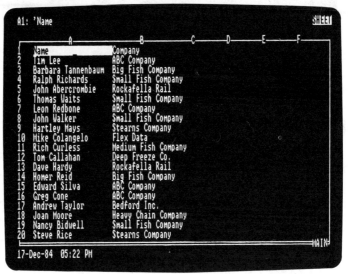

Fig. 11.32.

As you can see, several companies are listed more than once in the data base. To avoid copying duplicate records to the Output range, use the Unique option. The Unique option is set up like the Extract option, but the results can be quite different. Figure 11.33 shows how the **E**xtract and **U**nique options work on the same Criterion range (J2..J3).

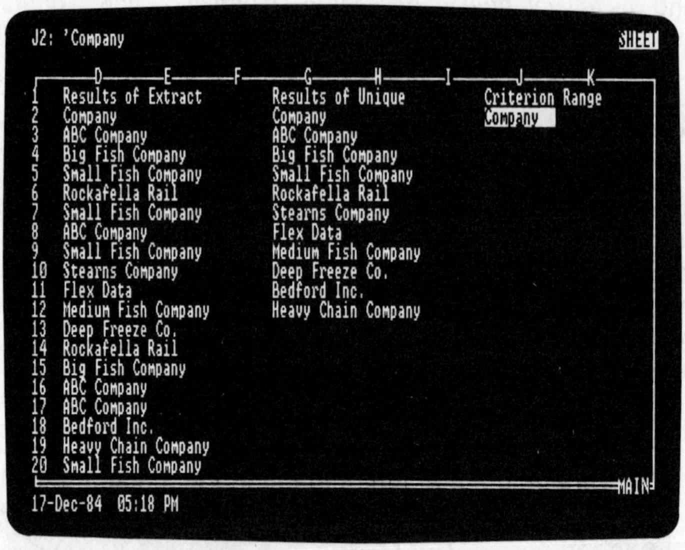

```
J2: 'Company                                              SHEET

    ┌──D────E────F────G────H────I────J────K─┐
  1 │ Results of Extract   Results of Unique   Criterion Range
  2 │ Company              Company             Company
  3 │ ABC Company          ABC Company
  4 │ Big Fish Company     Big Fish Company
  5 │ Small Fish Company   Small Fish Company
  6 │ Rockafella Rail      Rockafella Rail
  7 │ Small Fish Company   Stearns Company
  8 │ ABC Company          Flex Data
  9 │ Small Fish Company   Medium Fish Company
 10 │ Stearns Company      Deep Freeze Co.
 11 │ Flex Data            Bedford Inc.
 12 │ Medium Fish Company  Heavy Chain Company
 13 │ Deep Freeze Co.
 14 │ Rockafella Rail
 15 │ Big Fish Company
 16 │ ABC Company
 17 │ ABC Company
 18 │ Bedford Inc.
 19 │ Heavy Chain Company
 20 │ Small Fish Company
                                                           MAIN
17-Dec-84  05:18 PM
```

Fig. 11.33.

In this example, the Criterion range has only one field name in it ("Company"), and the cell below the field name has been deliberately left blank. For the **E**xtract operation, this allows all the records in the data base to meet the criterion. Therefore, the results of the **E**xtract show copies of the company fields from every record in the data base. The **U**nique operation, however, eliminates all the duplicate listings of the companies. The result of the **U**nique operation is a list of the individual companies in the customer data base.

Query Delete

The last method used to search records is the **D**elete option, which removes unwanted records from a data base. (This option is similar to the **R**ecord-Sort **U**nique operation in the FORM window, except the **D**elete option does not sort the data base.) Figure 11.34 shows a portion of an "Overdue Accounts" data base. Suppose you want to purge all the paid accounts from your "Overdue Accounts" data base, but only after you have verified that they have been paid.

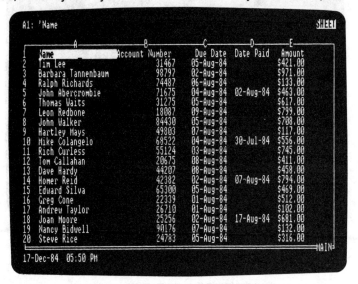

Fig. 11.34.

First, you extract all the paid records to verify their accuracy. To do this, use the **Extract** option with the Criterion range shown in figure 11.35. This figure also shows the results of the **Extract**. After you perform the **Extract** operation and review the results, you can use the same Criterion range for the **Delete** operation. After a confirmation step, the results appear as shown in figure 11.36. Notice that the **Delete** option removes the records that meet the criteria and closes up the gaps that are left in the data base. Like the **Find** operation, the **Delete** operation does not require an Output range.

When you use the **Delete** option, make sure that you are deleting the correct records. The precautionary step of extracting them first is a good idea. This way you can verify that you have set up the right Criterion range. Once you have deleted the records, they are gone from RAM. However, if you make a mistake with the **Delete** option and have not yet saved the file, you can regain the original data base by bringing the file back from storage with the SERVICES **F**ile **R**etrieve command and writing over the current worksheet.

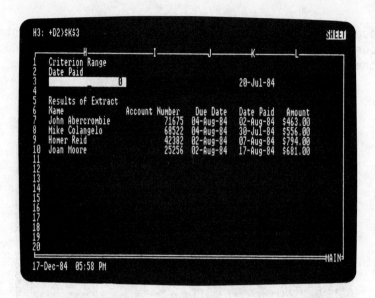

Fig. 11.35.

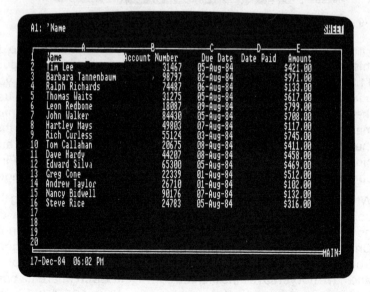

Fig. 11.36.

*New
with
Symphony*

Query Parse

The final option offered in the **Query** menu is **Parse**. Although you may find other uses, **Query Parse** is principally designed to take data entered during a communications session and convert it to a usable form. Because the use of **Query Parse** is so intimately connected with the COMM environment, **Query Parse** will be covered in the next chapter.

Data Base Statistical Functions

Symphony's data base statistical functions are similar to standard statistical functions, but they have been modified to manipulate data base fields. Like the standard statistical functions, the data base statistical functions perform in one simple statement what would otherwise take several statements to accomplish. Because of their efficiency and ease of application, you should take advantage of Symphony's data base functions. The functions include

@DCOUNT	Gives the number of items in a list
@DSUM	Sums the values of all the items in a list
@DAVG	Gives the average value of all the items in a list
@DMIN	Gives the minimum of all the items in a list
@DMAX	Gives the maximum of all the items in a list
@DSTD	Gives the standard deviation of all the items in a list
@DVAR	Gives the variance of all the items in a list

The general form of these functions is

@DFUNC(Database range,offset,Criterion range)

The Database and Criterion ranges are the same as those used by the SHEET **Query** commands and all the commands in the FORM window. You can use the standard settings for the Database and Criterion ranges (the ones in the **Query Settings** sheet that were used to produce the data base), or you can specify different ranges.

As usual, the Database range defines the data base to be scanned, and the Criterion range specifies which records to select from it. The offset, either 0 or a positive integer, indicates which field to select from the data base records. A value of 0 means the first column; a 1, the second column; and so on.

An example that uses the data base statistical functions involves computing the mean, variance, and standard deviation of the average interest rates offered by money market funds for a given week. If you are unfamiliar with the concepts of mean, variance, and standard deviation, refer to Chapter 5, where they are explained.

Figure 11.37 shows a "Money Market Returns" data base and the results of the various data base statistical functions. The functions to find the maximum and minimum rates of return are also included.

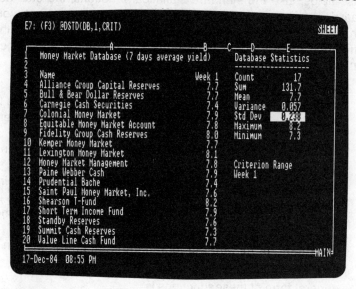

Fig. 11.37.

The equations and their related statistics are

Statistic	Formula
Count	@DCOUNT(A3..B20,1,D13..D14)
Sum	@DSUM(A3..B20,1,D13..D14)

Mean	@DAVG(A3..B20,1,D13..D14)
Variance	@DVAR(A3..B20,1,D13..D14)
Std Dev	@DSTD(A3..B20,1,D13..D14)
Maximum	@DMAX(A3..B20,1,D13..D14)
Minimum	@DMIN(A3..B20,1,D13..D14)

The results, as seen in figure 11.37, indicate that the mean return for the week for the 11 different money market funds is an annual percentage rate of 7.7 (cell E4). The variance is approximately .057 (cell E6), yielding a standard deviation of approximately .238 (cell E7). This indicates that about 68 percent of the money market funds are returning an annual rate of between 7.46 percent and 7.94 percent.

One std dev below mean = 7.7 - .238 = 7.46
One std dev above mean = 7.7 + .238 = 7.94

Summit Cash Reserves returns the lowest rate at 7.3 percent. The 7.3 figure comes from the @DMIN function used in cell E9. This value is approaching two standard deviations below the mean, computed as follows:

Two std devs below mean = 7.7 - (2 x .238) = 7.22

Because approximately 95 percent of the population falls within plus or minus two standard deviations of the mean, Summit Cash Reserves is very close to being in the lower 2.5 percent of the population of money market funds for that week. (5 percent is divided by 2 because the population is assumed to be normal.)

Conversely, the Shearson T-Fund returns the highest rate: 8.2 percent. The @DMAX function is used to determine the highest rate (cell E7), which is just over 2 standard deviations above the mean of the highest 2.5 percent of the population. Obviously, the data base statistical functions can tell you a great deal about the data base as a whole and how to interpret different values in it. These functions are also quite useful for printing data base reports.

Data Base Reports

Symphony has a special feature for printing data base reports. You can print advanced data base reports, like mailing lists and form letters, or something as simple as a listing of your data base as it appears in the spreadsheet. Depending on the criteria that you set up, the data base report can include all or separate portions of a data base; you can use the **P**rint **S**ettings to direct the report to the printer, a file, or a range within the worksheet.

In the first example, you will see how to use the data base reporting feature to print the entire "Priority" data base to the printer. In the second, you will see how to print a portion of the data base and direct it to a range within the current worksheet. In the final example, you will see how to print groups of data base records with each group placed on a separate page. The last example also shows you how to use data base statistical functions with the reporting feature.

Printing a Simple Data Base Report

*New
with
Symphony*

You must be in the FORM environment in order to print data base reports. In some of the examples that follow, you must switch back and forth among the SHEET, DOC, and FORM environments. Always remember to return to the FORM environment before printing the data base. If you forget, the data base reporting feature will not work properly.

Printing the Entire Data Base

To print the entire "Priority" data base, you must be familiar with two Report ranges: the Above and Main ranges. Both ranges are automatically set up when you use the **G**enerate command to create a data base in a FORM window.

The Above Report Range

To access the Above range (and all the other Report ranges), enter the **R**eport option from the FORM **S**ettings command menu. When you do, you select one of four options: **M**ain, **A**bove, **B**elow, or **T**ype.

Figure 11.38A shows the FORM **S**ettings sheet, and figure 11.38B highlights the Above range for the "Priority" data base. As you can see, the Above range contains the same field-name headings as the

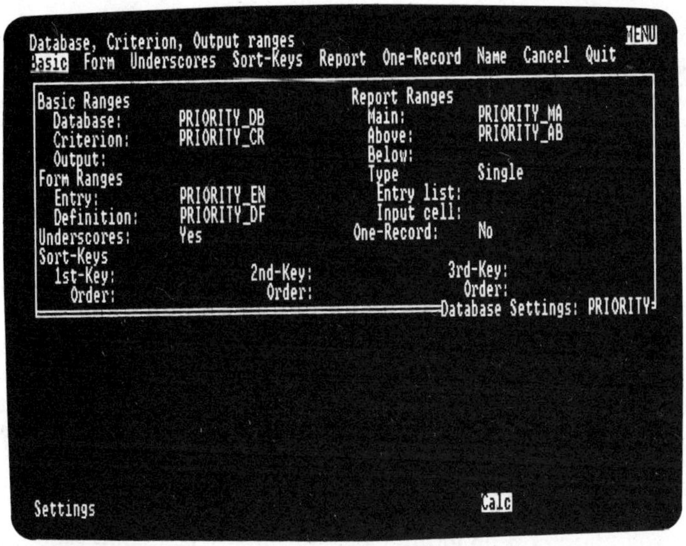

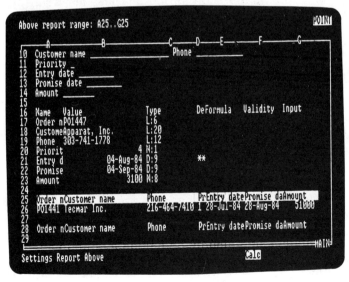

Fig. 11.38A.

Fig. 11.38B.

Database and Criterion ranges. Symphony uses these field names
for the column headings of the report. However, Symphony will print

at the top of the data base report any text you put in the Above range. You can also use the SHEET Move and Insert commands to create an Above range that is deeper than one line. This feature is particularly useful for creating report titles.

The Main Report Range

The Main range is contained in the single row directly below the Above range in the spreadsheet (A26..G26) and is called PRIORITY_ MA. This range contains the cells that are to be printed once for each record in the data base report. If you locate the cursor on the values in the range, you will see that they refer to the fields in the first record of the Database range. For example, cell A26 contains +ORDER NUMBER.

The final step before you use the SERVICES Print command is to enter selection criteria in the Criterion range. (Recall that you use the Criteria Edit command to enter selection criteria in a FORM window.) To print all the records in the data base, make sure that you use the Criteria Ignore command to eliminate any criteria from the Criterion range.

Directing the Report to the Printer

To direct this report to the printer, select the SERVICES Print Settings command. The Source setting is Database, and the Destination setting for this report is Printer, a Destination setting that has not yet been discussed. When you select Database, you must tell Symphony which FORM Settings sheet to use. For this example, suppose the name of the settings sheet is 1ST-KEY. Figure 11.39 shows the Print Settings with the Source set to Database 1ST-KEY. The final step is to select Go from the SERVICES Print menu. Symphony will then produce the data base report, a portion of which appears in figure 11.40.

Notice that the column widths in the report appear just as they do in the data base. To change the column widths in the printed report, you must also change the column widths of the data base. Another alternative is to direct the report to a range in the spreadsheet with the column widths you like, and then print directly from that range.

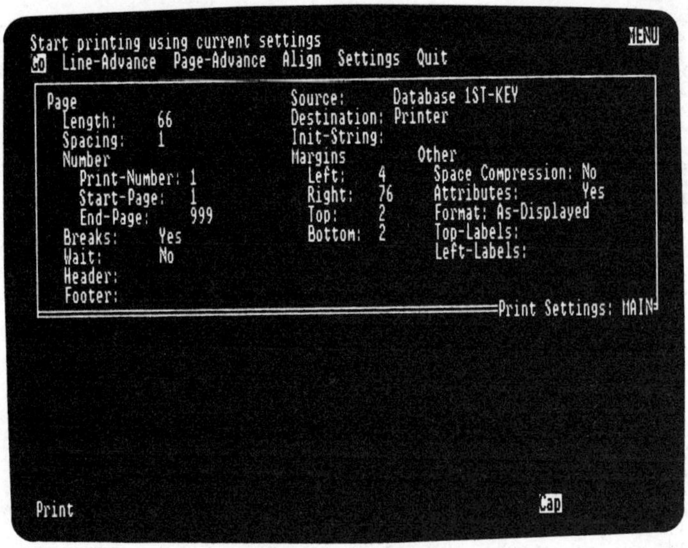

Fig. 11.39.

Printing a Portion of a Data Base

If you want to print just a portion of a data base, you must modify the Criterion range to select only the records you want. For example, suppose you want to print all the records in the data base whose "Amount" field is greater than $10,000. Use the **C**riteria **E**dit command to enter +?>10000 in the "Amount" field. Then issue the **C**riteria **U**se command to get the appropriate records.

Once you have entered the selection criteria, suppose you want to direct the output to a range instead of the printer. In this case, set the **P**rint **S**ettings **D**estination to **R**ange and enter an appropriate range. Figure 11.41 shows how the spreadsheet appears when the data base report has been directed to a range. Notice that the results are long labels.

Data Base Subtotals

As experienced 1-2-3 users are well aware, 1-2-3 has problems creating subtotals. Symphony gives you a way to create subtotals by

Order #	Customer name	Phone	Pr	Entry date	Promise dat	Amount
PO1438	Quadram Corp	404-923-6666	1	25-Jul-84	25-Aug-84	42100
PO1441	Tecmar Inc.	216-464-7410	1	28-Jul-84	28-Aug-84	51000
PO1435	Amdek Corporation	312-364-1180	1	23-Jul-84	23-Aug-84	23000
PO1436	AST Research Inc.	714-540-1333	1	24-Jul-84	24-Aug-84	34000
PO1446	Hayes Microcomputer	404-449-8791	1	03-Aug-84	03-Sep-84	19800
PO1440	Seattle Computer	800-426-8936	2	27-Jul-84	27-Aug-84	24500
PO1453	Indigo Data Systems	713-488-8186	2	10-Aug-84	10-Sep-84	3290
PO1450	IDE Associates	617-275-4430	2	07-Aug-94	07-Sep-84	2180
PO1445	Maynard Electronics	305-331-6402	2	03-Aug-84	03-Sep-84	23500
PO1437	Hercules Computer	415-654-2476	2	24-Jul-84	24-Aug-84	12000
PO1444	Orchid Technology	408-942-8660	3	01-Aug-84	01-Sep-84	4520
FO1452	Arby Corporation	617-864-5058	3	09-Aug-84	09-Sep-84	7892
PO1439	Raytronics	800-854-1085	3	26-Jul-84	26-Aug-84	12200
PO1448	Data Technology Corp	408-496-0434	3	05-Aug-84	05-Sep-84	7890
PO1442	Qubie' Distributing	800-821-4479	4	30-Apr-84	30-May-84	11330
PO1443	Micro Graphics Tech	408-996-8423	4	31-Jul-84	31-Aug-84	8190
PO1451	MBI	303-279-4628	4	08-Aug-84	08-Sep-84	2300
PO1449	Super Computer, Inc.	714-540-1880	4	06-Aug-84	06-Sep-84	6538
PO1447	Apparat, Inc.	303-741-1778	4	04-Aug-84	04-Sep-84	3100
PO1448	STR Corporation	408-665-7893	4	03-Aug-84	02-Sep-84	5600
PO1449	New York Systems	800-321-6745	4	03-Aug-84	02-Sep-84	21000
PO1450	Ashe Electronics	317-665-8734	4	06-Aug-84	05-Sep-84	3670
PO1451	Northwestern Data	412-436-9876	4	09-Aug-84	08-Sep-84	1295
PO1452	Micro Labs	617-864-2321	4	12-Aug-84	11-Sep-84	10200
PO1453	DataServe Inc.	714-553-6584	4	15-Aug-84	14-Sep-84	4500
PO1454	Alton Industries	305-221-0976	4	18-Aug-84	17-Sep-84	3700
PO1455	SPE	800-999-3232	5	21-Aug-84	20-Sep-84	11700
PO1456	Orange Computer	713-432-5643	5	24-Aug-84	23-Sep-84	5420
PO1457	HAL Technology	317-882-7432	5	27-Aug-84	26-Sep-84	6000
PO1458	Midwest Systems	317-456-9087	5	30-Aug-84	29-Sep-84	2400
PO1459	Magnum Corporation	305-972-3456	5	02-Sep-84	02-Oct-84	7200
PO1460	Romar Industries	412-665-4323	5	05-Sep-84	05-Oct-84	8200
PO1461	Neville Electronics	303-884-2123	5	08-Sep-84	08-Oct-84	3710
PO1462	McKee, Inc.	714-908-4632	5	11-Sep-84	11-Oct-84	7050
PO1463	STR Communications	800-233-4126	5	14-Sep-84	14-Oct-84	4250
PO1464	Easterwood, Inc.	713-921-7834	5	17-Sep-84	17-Oct-84	4300
PO1465	Data Control	408-231-0503	5	20-Sep-84	20-Oct-84	6200
PO1466	Becker Corporation	415-885-9193	5	23-Sep-84	23-Oct-84	4900

Fig. 11.40.

using the data base report feature with the data base statistical function @DSUM. For example, suppose you want to create a report with a separate page that presents all the records for each priority in the "Priority" data base. You also want the total dollar amount for each priority.

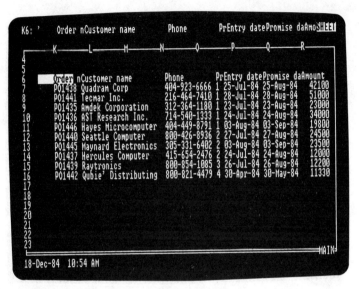

Fig. 11.41.

Up until this point, the two data base report examples have required only a single pass through the data base. Therefore, the FORM **S**ettings **R**eport **T**ype command has been left at **S**ingle, the default setting. However, when you want to produce subtotals (or any other data base statistics), you need to set the **R**eport **T**ype to **M**ultiple. (Familiarity with the SHEET **R**ange **W**hat-If command is helpful for understanding this example. If you have not read about the **R**ange **W**hat-If command, refer to Chapter 4.)

Before you can set the report type to **M**ultiple, you need to switch to the SHEET environment and build a small table of input values (what Symphony calls an Entry list) in an out-of-the-way area of the spreadsheet. The values in the Entry list will be substituted into the Criterion range in order to produce subtotals for each priority. For example, you can use the **R**ange **F**ill command to enter the values in cells C1..C4 in figure 11.42.

When you enter the **S**ettings **R**eport **T**ype **M**ultiple command, Symphony asks for the address of the Entry list you have created. At this point, you enter C1..C4. Symphony then asks for an Input cell, which is the cell where you want Symphony to substitute the values

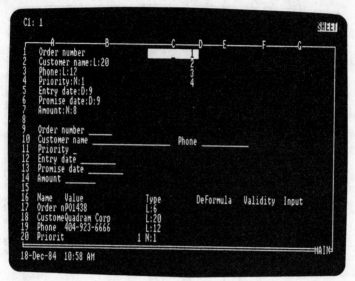

Fig. 11.42.

in the Entry list. You want to have Symphony substitute the values into the Priority column of the Criterion range, so you enter cell D32.

At this point, you have almost all the settings for producing separate report pages. However, you still need to enter the @DSUM function for printing subtotals. To enter the @DSUM function in the proper location, you need to know about the Below range.

The Below Range

The Below range, the final **S**ettings **R**eport range, is used to enter information at the end of a report. The Below range must be located directly below the Main range in the spreadsheet. When you create a data base with the **G**enerate command, Symphony automatically provides enough room to enter a Below range that is one row deep. Symphony does not, however, set up the address of this range; you must do that.

Before you enter the address of the Below range, first decide how you want the bottom of the report to look. As you did for the Above range, you can use the SHEET **M**ove and **I**nsert commands to create a Below range that is deeper than one row. Suppose you want a series of hyphens across the bottom of the report with the subtotals below the hyphens. Figure 11.43 shows how the Below range must appear (A27..G29).

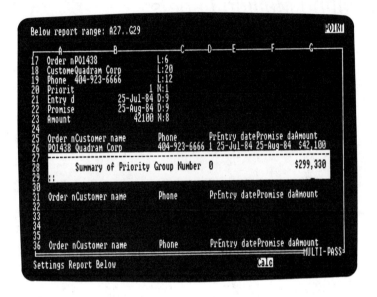

Fig. 11.43.

The @DSUM function appears in cell G28. The actual function is

@DSUM(PRIORITY_ DB,6,PRIORITY_ CR)

Notice also that the formula for cell D28 is +D32. Finally, notice that the third line contains the page-marker characters "::". To enter the marker in the Above range, shift to the DOC and environment and enter the Page command.

Now that you have set the ranges (Above, Main, Below, and Entry), you must switch back to the FORM environment and enter the Print command. The Source for the reports is again Database, but this time the Destination is a file called MULTIPAS.RPN. Figure 11.44 shows a portion of the report when you print MULTIPAS.PRN.

Notice that the format of the "Amount" field appears in the Currency 0 format. To control the format of the display, simply change the format of the cells in the Criterion range.

Printing Mailing Labels

Printing mailing labels is simple once you are familiar with the basics of generating data base reports. A good data base for showing how to print mailing labels is the data base of the name and addresses that appears at the beginning of the chapter. (See fig. 11.1.)

```
Order #  Customer name         Phone         Priority Entry date  Promise date Amount
P01438   Quadram Corp          404-923-6666       1   25-Jul-84     25-Aug-84   $42,100
P01441   Tecmar Inc.           216-464-7410       1   28-Jul-84     28-Aug-84   $51,000
P01435   Amdek Corporation     312-364-1180       1   23-Jul-84     23-Aug-84   $23,000
P01436   AST Research Inc.     714-540-1333       1   24-Jul-84     24-Aug-84   $34,000
P01446   Hayes Microcomputer   404-449-8791       1   03-Aug-84     03-Sep-84   $19,800
-----------------------------------------------------------------------------------------
         Summary of Priority Group Number            1                          $169,900
```

```
Order #  Customer name         Phone         Priority Entry date  Promise date Amount
P01440   Seattle Computer      800-426-8936       2   27-Jul-84     27-Aug-84   $24,500
P01453   Indigo Data Systems   713-488-8186       2   10-Aug-84     10-Sep-84   $3,290
P01450   IDE Associates        617-275-4430       2   07-Aug-84     07-Sep-84   $2,180
P01445   Maynard Electronics   305-331-6402       2   03-Aug-84     03-Sep-84   $23,500
P01437   Hercules Computer     415-654-2476       2   24-Jul-84     24-Aug-84   $12,000
-----------------------------------------------------------------------------------------
         Summary of Priority Group Number            2                          $65,470
```

Fig. 11.44.

To print mailing labels, you must change the position and contents of the Main range. The first step is to shift to the SHEET environment and go to an out-of-the-way area of the worksheet. Then enter the following formulas in three consecutive cells down a column, for example K1..K3:

```
+FIRST&" "&LAST
+ADDRESS
+CITY&", "&STATE&" "&ZIP
```

The next step is to set the Main range. Switch back to the FORM window and enter the **S**ettings **R**eport **M**ain command to designate the range. In order to print one-inch labels, you must include three blank lines below cell K3 (assuming you have six lines for each one-inch mailing label). Therefore, the Main range is K1..K6. The last step before printing is to eliminate the Above and Below ranges (if designated) from the settings sheet. Finally, to print labels, you designate the **P**rint **S**ettings **S**ource as **D**atabase and the **D**estination as **P**rinter. Figure 11.45 shows the results.

As a simple exercise to test your understanding of printing data base reports, see if you can figure out how to print mailing labels by ZIP code. Hint: You need to use the **M**ultiple pass option.

New
with
Symphony

Printing a Form Letter

A final demonstration of Symphony's ability to print data base reports is the form letter. Suppose you are again dealing with the "Priority" data base, and you want to send a letter to all the customers in the data base whose records have been entered on or after August 7, 1984. An example of the letter follows:

Dear IDE Associates:

We are pleased to receive your order and have entered it as PO1450. Please use this number when you contact us about the status of your order. As promised, you should receive your chips on

09/07/84

If there is a change in the status of your order, we will phone you at 617-275-4430. Please inform us if this is not the correct number.

Sincerely,

Tom Perkins

The first step for producing this form letter is to enter its contents in an out-of-the-way area of the spreadsheet. Normally, you start out in the DOC environment, enter most of the contents of the letter, and then switch to the SHEET environment to fill in the variables.

Shamim Ahmad
Weatherly Street
Cincinnati, OH 45243

Sarah Sharpe
7897 Providence St.
Miami, FL 61998

James F. Cotter
1003 Tulip Tree House
Belle Mead, NJ 13120

William L. Sikes
3751 Clifton Ave.
Nashville, TN 42378

Michael Englert
224 Greenup St.
Newport, KY 11166

Jeremy Simpson
3509 Ludlow Ave.
Las Cruces, NM 72814

Edward Harding
2400 Central Parkway
New York, NY 02934

Betty Stone
700 Vine St.
Dallas, TX 64824

James T. Harrington
238 High St.
Boston, MA 02116

Chuck Timmerman
7900 Castleway Drive
Indianapolis, IN 53747

Earl Holland
3712 Drake Road
Columbus, IN 43987

John Tuke
531 Remington Road
Chicago, IL 85677

Robert Horton
9980 Yale Ave.
New Haven, CT 06785

Patrick Yeagar
4237 Mariemont Ave.
Des Moines, IA 63457

David J. Owen
612 Knight Ridge Road
Baltimore, MD 34523

Steven Zakon
3549 Keene St.
Bangor, ME 12392

Fritz W. Schumann
100 E. Miller Dr.
Providence, RI 12344

Mathew Zealear
2909 Fresno St.
Fresno, CA 43645

Fig. 11.45.

However, with this particular letter, it's just as easy to enter the entire
letter in the SHEET environment. The following formulas show how
you enter the letter.

A200:+"Dear "&CUSTOMER NAME &":"
A201:
A202:'We are pleased to receive your order and have entered
A203:+"it as "&ORDER NUMBER&". Please use this number when you"
A204:'contact us about the status of your order. As
A205:'promised, you should receive your chips on
A206:
C207:+PROMISE DATE
A208:
A209:'If there is a change in the status of your order, we
A210:+"will phone you at "&PHONE&". Please inform us if"
A211:'this is not the correct number.
A212:
A213:'Sincerely,
A214:
A215:'Tom Perkins
A216:|::

Notice that the formula for the Promise date is placed on a line by itself. Because the Promise date is a number, it cannot be integrated as easily with text as the label fields "Customer name," "Order number," and "Phone." Note also that while typing in the information above, you will see an ERR message if a blank field is referenced. When you later enter information into this field, the ERR message will disappear.

After entering the contents of the letter, the next step is to designate the selection criteria for the records whose Entry date is on or after August 7, 1984. As mentioned earlier, Symphony has difficulty with the @DATE function when you try to put it in a Criterion range. Therefore, if you want to use the @DATE function, you must enter it outside the Criterion range and refer to it by absolute addressing. Figure 11.46 shows the Criterion range (A28..G29) when you use @DATE. Notice that the formula refers to cell H29, which contains the formula @DATE(84,8,7).

After entering the selection criteria, the final step before using the Print command is to designate the Main range, A200..I215 for this example. This choice allows for the longest lines in the letter. If you choose a range that is narrower, say A200..C215, the lines will be truncated when you print the letter.

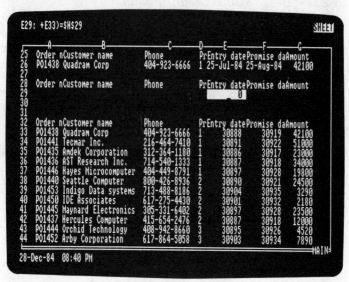

```
E29: +E33)=$H$29                                              SHEET
       A         B              C        D  E        F        G
 25 Order nCustomer name    Phone         PrEntry datePromise daAmount
 26 PO1438 Quadram Corp     404-923-6666  1 25-Jul-84 25-Aug-84  42100
 27
 28 Order nCustomer name    Phone         PrEntry datePromise daAmount
 29                                                    0
 30
 31
 32 Order nCustomer name    Phone         PrEntry datePromise daAmount
 33 PO1438 Quadram Corp     404-923-6666  1  30888     30919    42100
 34 PO1441 Tecmar Inc.      216-464-7410  1  30891     30922    51000
 35 PO1435 Amdek Corporation 312-364-1180 1  30886     30917    23000
 36 PO1436 AST Research Inc. 714-540-1333 1  30887     30918    34000
 37 PO1446 Hayes Microcomputer 404-449-8791 1 30897    30928    19800
 38 PO1440 Seattle Computer 800-426-8936  2  30890     30921    24500
 39 PO1453 Indigo Data systems 713-488-8186 2 30904    30935     3290
 40 PO1450 IDE Associates   617-275-4430  2  30901     30932     2180
 41 PO1445 Maynard Electronics 305-331-6402 2 30897    30928    23500
 42 PO1437 Hercules Computer 415-654-2476 2  30887     30918    12000
 43 PO1444 Orchid Technology 408-942-8660 3  30895     30926     4520
 44 PO1452 Arby Corporation 617-864-5058  3  30903     30934     7890
 28-Dec-84  08:40 PM                                            MAIN
```

Fig. 11.46.

Figure 11.47 shows the settings sheet for printing the letter. Notice that the Above and Below ranges are left blank in this example.

```
Define ranges for database report                           MENU
Basic  Form  Underscores  Sort-Keys  Report  One-Record  Name  Cancel  Quit

Basic Ranges                     Report Ranges
  Database:      PRIORITY_DB       Main:        A200..I215
  Criterion:     PRIORITY_CR       Above:
  Output:                          Below:
Form Ranges                        Type         Single
  Entry:         PRIORITY_EN         Entry list:
  Definition:    PRIORITY_DF         Input cell:
Underscores:     Yes              One-Record:   No
Sort-Keys
  1st-Key:            2nd-Key:              3rd-Key:
  Order:              Order:                Order:
                                    Database Settings: PRIORITY

Settings                              Calc  Cap
```

Fig. 11.47.

If you want to send the letter directly to the printer, from the **P**rint menu, select **P**rinter as the **D**estination and **D**atabase as the **S**ource.

Conclusion

In this chapter you have seen how to use Symphony's FORM window, data base commands in the SHEET environment, and data base statistical functions. You have also seen a demonstration of Symphony's special report-generating capabilities, which are a part of the FORM environment. In Chapter 13, you will find some examples of how to use the Symphony Command Language to help you build input forms and perform other FORM window operations.

12
Communications

Because Symphony has the COMM window for data communications, you can use your personal computer for two-way communicating. For example, your personal computer can receive data base information from a corporate mainframe or a minicomputer. You can also hook up to a time-sharing service to get the latest information on news, stocks, weather, and other current topics. Finally, you can link up with a friend's microcomputer to exchange Symphony models, information, or gossip.

Like many other functions in Symphony, the communications capability is surprisingly strong and rivals the power of many stand-alone packages. However, there are also some weaknesses in the program that you have to watch for. For example, you cannot use Symphony's file-transferring capability in all situations; and unless you build macros to automate the process, sending and receiving messages between microcomputers can be slow and laborious. In general, though, you should be pleasantly surprised at the power of the COMM window.

Symphony enables you to connect with many different kinds of computers; just follow the simple rules outlined in the section

Guidelines for Successful Communications. Because most readers will probably start with Symphony's COMM window by accessing a time-sharing service, the chapter next discusses how to access CompuServe's Executive Information Service (EIS), a typical time-sharing service that is also the source of a new information service called The World of Lotus. This section is followed by an explanation of how to communicate with another person's microcomputer if that person is also running Symphony. These discussions will give you enough background to make good use of Symphony's communications.

Guidelines for Successful Communications

Symphony's COMM window is a powerful feature, but you can easily become discouraged with it if you run into early problems. The following guidelines give you some general background on Symphony's COMM window and let you know what you can expect from the program.

Modems and Acoustic Couplers

For successful communications through Symphony, you must have a modem or an acoustic coupler. (You can also connect two microcomputers with a serial cable, or you can hard-wire your computer to a mainframe or minicomputer, but these tasks are beyond the scope of this book.) A modem (MOdulator-DEModulator) is a device that converts digital signals in your computer into analog tones that travel over telephone lines. Modems can be external devices connecting the serial (RS-232) interface on your computer to a telephone cable, or they can be internal devices on a board that are directly connected to your computer and to a telephone line.

An acoustic coupler, which is actually another type of modem, requires that you place a standard telephone receiver in the rubber cradles of the coupler. Otherwise, acoustic couplers are hooked up like any other external modem. Because the most frequent problems with modems of either type are poor cable connections, take special precautions to make sure your connections are sound.

Asynchronous and Synchronous Transmission

A second important point is that Symphony supports *asynchronous communications transmission*. This means that a clock in the computer is used to time the sampling of incoming data and the recording of the number of bits in each sample. The clock is set according to the transmission speed you specify (the baud rate or bits per second). In general, because the asynchronous transmission technique leaves most of the timing work up to the computer, this type of communications requires relatively inexpensive modems and is simple to use.

Most mainframe computers, however, use *synchronous communications transmission*. Under this kind of communications transmission, the modem provides a clock signal to detect the bits being received. A master-clock signal is also provided by the host computer to its attached modem. For purposes of timing, and for a variety of other reasons too complex to go into here, this type of transmission requires more complex and expensive modems.*

What is the advantage of synchronous communications transmission? The major advantage is that you can transmit data faster. Usually low-to-medium speeds are associated with asynchronous transmission (0 to about 1200 baud), while higher speeds (anything above 1200 baud) are achieved with synchronous transmission.

Perhaps in the future, Symphony will support synchronous transmission communications, but for now any computer with which you use Symphony to communicate must follow the asynchronous transmission method. Most systems designed to communicate with personal computers follow the asynchronous convention, so you should not have much trouble; but you probably cannot communicate with a sophisticated mainframe that is not normally used to communicate with microcomputers.

*Chris DeVoney, *IBM's Personal Computer*, 2nd ed. (Indianapolis: Que Corporation, 1983), pp. 273-77.

XMODEM Protocol

Symphony also supports XMODEM protocol for file transfer. *Protocol* is another name for the rules established for exchanging information between computers. A communications protocol is required to ensure that computers send and receive data accurately.

XMODEM protocol, developed by Ward Christensen, has become a standard in the microcomputer industry. When you are using Symphony's file-transfer capability, both computers must use XMODEM protocol. Unfortunately, most mainframes do not use XMODEM protocol, and Symphony does not allow you to turn it off. Therefore, you are restricted from using Symphony's **F**ile-Transfer command to send files back and forth between a mainframe and your microcomputer. (There is a way to get around this restriction by using Symphony's range-transmitting capabilities; however, because no error checking takes places during this technique, you may end up with garbled results.)

Protocol Parameters

Once these specifics are clear to you, your next step for successful communications with Symphony is to make sure that you set correctly all the parameters for protocol. These parameters include baud rate, byte length, number of stop bits to be transmitted, and parity. Table 12.1 describes each parameter.

Table 12.1

Baud rate Speed at which data is transmitted. Can vary between 0 and 9600, but most frequent settings are 300 and 1200.

Byte length The number of bits (binary digits) to be transmitted in a byte. (Also called the word length.) Can be set to either 7 or 8 bits.

Stop bits The number of bits following each data word. Asynchronous transmission usually requires the addition of stop bits. Choices are 1 or 2.

| Parity | During parity checking, the individual On bits are added, and the total is an odd or even number. Choices are Odd, Even, or None. |

Normally, you don't have to worry about choosing the protocol parameters. They are usually specified by the computer with which you are trying to communicate. A good general guideline, though, is always to match the two computers' settings for baud rate, byte length, stop bits, and parity.

Proper Driver Choice

The final step for successful communications is making sure you have selected the proper driver set during installation. The two options you are given during installation are Hayes and Popcom X100. If you have either of these modems, you are in luck. However, even if your modem is made by another manufacturer, you may still be able to use the modem with one of these driver choices. For example, you can use almost any Western Electric 103 or 212 equivalent modem with the Hayes driver choice. You may not, however, be able to use your modem's auto-dial or auto-answer feature.

Connection to a Time-Sharing Service

The documentation for logging on CompuServe's Executive Information Service (EIS) instructs you to set the following communication standards:

    300 baud or 1200 baud
    7-bit ASCII even parity or 8-bit ASCII no parity
    1 stop bit
    Full duplex

Two terms in these standards may be unfamiliar to you. ASCII (American Standard Code for Information Interchange) is the most common character set used in microcomputer systems. The IBM PC/XT uses a unique 8-bit version of ASCII (in which the 8th bit is 1) for internal processing of data and a standard 7-bit version for communications. However, the full 8-bit-version characters can also be transmitted for communications purposes.* In this application, use the 7-bit version. *Full duplex*, another term that may be unfamiliar, simply means that data flows in both directions between your microcomputer and the information service.

Changing the Default Settings

Now that you are familiar with the standards required for the information service, you are ready to select the first set of COMM window settings. Figure 12.1 shows the settings that appear when you select a COMM window and choose **S**ettings from the main COMM menu.

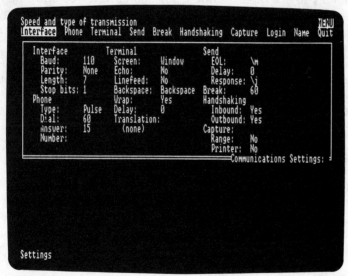

Fig. 12.1.

Lotus provides these default settings with the program. To create new settings, your first step is to create a new settings sheet name. Select **N**ame from the **S**ettings menu and give the new settings the name CEIS (CompuServe Executive Information Service). You will

*Chris DeVoney, *IBM's Personal Computer*, 2nd ed., p. 273.

later use the **N**ame **S**ave command to save the settings to a default Communications Configurations File (recognized by its .CCF extension). This type of file is usually saved on the Symphony Program disk so that you can access it in future sessions. However, the settings in a .CCF file will not come up automatically unless you update the SERVICES **C**onfiguration and save it to the SYMPHONY.CNF file. (See Chapter 2 for more on updating the SYMPHONY.CNF file.)

The Interface Settings

Now that you have named the new settings sheet, you are ready to change the Interface settings. When you select Interface from the main **S**ettings menu, the following choices appear:

Baud   Parity   Length   Stop-Bits

These choices should already be familiar to you. When you enter the **B**aud option, Symphony gives you these choices:

Menu Choice	Baud Rate
1	110
2	150
3	300
4	600
5	1200
6	2400
7	4800
8	9600

For this example, assume you are using a 300-baud modem and select option 3. When you select the **P**arity option, Symphony gives you the choices of 1 (None), 2 (Odd), and 3 (Even). As was mentioned earlier, the 7-bit ASCII code is the standard you want to use, so the information service requires that you choose option 3, Even parity.

For the **L**ength option, Symphony offers you choices 1 (7 bit) and 2 (8 bit). Here again, because you want the 7-bit standard, choose option 1. Finally, select 1 stop bit from the **S**top-**B**its menu. Figure 12.2 shows the COMM **S**ettings menu after all the new Interface settings have been selected.

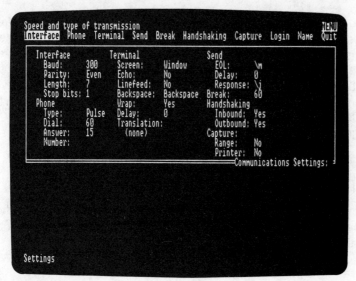

```
Speed and type of transmission                                    MENU
Interface  Phone  Terminal  Send  Break  Handshaking  Capture  Login  Name  Quit

 Interface            Terminal                Send
   Baud:      300      Screen:    Window       EOL:        \m
   Parity:    Even     Echo:      No           Delay:      0
   Length:    7        Linefeed:  No           Response:   \j
   Stop bits: 1        Backspace: Backspace    Break:      60
 Phone                 Wrap:      Yes         Handshaking
   Type:      Pulse    Delay:     0            Inbound:   Yes
   Dial:      60       Translation:            Outbound:  Yes
   Answer:    15         (none)               Capture:
   Number:                                     Range:     No
                                               Printer:   No
                                           Communications Settings:

 Settings
```

Fig. 12.2.

The Phone Settings

After the selection of the Interface settings, your next logical step is to choose the Phone settings. When you select Phone from the Settings menu, the following choices appear:

    Type   Dial-Time   Answer-Time   Number

The Phone settings you want depend on the kind of modem you are using. If your modem has an auto-dial feature, you can select Number and enter the local-area access number for the information service. Symphony will now dial the number for you when you tell it to. However, if your modem is incapable of auto-dialing, you will have to dial the number yourself.

Assume for now that you have a Hayes Smartmodem with auto-dial, and you are calling from a business phone where you have to dial 9 to get an outside line before you dial the number. After Symphony dials the 9, you want the program to pause momentarily before entering the access number. By entering a series of commas between the 9 and the phone number, you can have Symphony pause for as long as you need. The length of the pause that a comma produces is difficult to gauge. However, Lotus recommends five commas as a good starting point. For this example, enter the following string for **P**hone **S**ettings **N**umber:

9,,,,,6382762

You must also indicate the type of phone you are using. (Again, skip this option if your modem is incapable of auto-dialing.) If you have standard rotary-dial service, select **P**ulse. Select **T**one for push-button service.

Dial-Time is the maximum time in seconds that Symphony spends dialing a call and trying to make a connection after you issue **P**hone **C**all, the command that initiates calling. The default setting is 60 seconds, which normally works fine.

Answer-Time is the maximum number of seconds that Symphony spends answering a call when you issue **P**hone **A**nswer. The default here is 15 seconds, which is also sufficient under normal circumstances. These commands work through a modem's auto-dial and auto-answer features, so don't worry about them if your modem does not have these features. Figure 12.3 shows the COMM **S**ettings after all the Phone settings have been made.

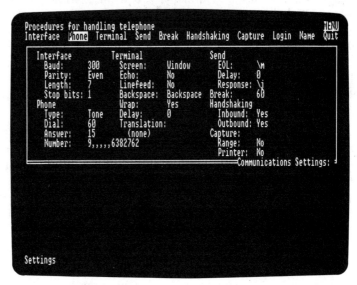

Fig. 12.3.

The Terminal Settings

After you have made the **P**hone settings, the next step is to designate the **T**erminal settings. These are used to match the characteristics of the COMM window in which you are working to the characteristics of the service (or computer) you are calling. In actual practice, you may make several of the **T**erminal settings after you have established a connection with the service. In some cases, you must see how the remote computer reacts to your input before you change the settings. In other cases, you can adjust the settings before you establish the connection. When you select **T**erminal from the main **S**ettings menu, the following selections appear:

Screen Echo Linefeed Backspace Wrap Delay Translation

The **S**creen option lets you eliminate the box enclosing the COMM window. Some remote computers require that you have a full 25-line display (specifically, when you are trying to emulate the VT100 display terminal). However, because you are trying to run a standard IBM PC/XT connection, leave this option set to **W**indow, the default.

The **E**cho option controls whether the characters you type in are displayed on the screen. Normally, you want to have your input displayed so that you can see whether it is correct. Because in this case, the information service standards indicate you are connecting with a full-duplex system, you can leave the setting at **N**o. Full-duplex systems "echo" the characters you type automatically, but half-duplex systems (which allow only one-way communication) do not. Therefore, the echo option is normally set to **Y**es for half-duplex systems.

If you are not sure whether the system you are working on is full- or half-duplex, you can set this option after you have established the connection. If you see two characters for every one you type, set the option to **N**o. If you see no characters when you type, set **E**cho to **Y**es. However, if you see three characters for every character you type, your modem is probably also echoing characters. Turn off this feature on your modem and then set the **E**cho option to **N**o.

Linefeed, the next option, can also be set while you are connected to the remote computer. A few computers do not supply a linefeed. If your messages write over one another on the same line, you need to set Linefeed to Yes. In this example, the remote system supplies a linefeed, so leave this option set to No.

The Backspace option determines whether the Backspace key is destructive. The default setting for this option is for a destructive backspace; that is, whenever you press the Backspace key, the cursor moves one character to the left and erases the character in that space. By setting this option to Delete, you can have the Backspace key delete the character the cursor is on and have all the characters to the right of the cursor shift one place to the left. Normally, you will leave this setting on the default, Backspace.

If long lines that you type or that are returned to you from the other computer do not wrap around to the next line, you need to set the Wrap option to Yes. The default is Yes, so you should keep this setting for the current example.

Delay is used to set the delay between transmissions of characters. The unit of measure is 1/128 of a second, and Lotus says that typical settings range from 30 to 60. You may find, however, that a smaller setting is sufficient. You must set this option by trial and error, as the setting of 10 was for the current example. The Delay option is particularly important for slowing down the transmission of characters while you are logging on to another computer. A good indicator of the need to increase the delay is that the other computer appears to be losing the characters you send it. Of all the Interface options, the Delay option requires the most experimenting. This is one of the most important options you have for controlling the interaction between your microcomputer and a remote computer system.

The final Interface option is Translation, which is used to choose the current character-code translation table. You want to use this option when you are using an International character set to communicate with a remote computer, or if you are an expert user and have devised a special translation table. However, in most cases, including the current example, you will leave the option set to Default. Figure 12.4 shows the COMM settings after the Terminal settings have been made. Only the Delay option has been changed from the default.

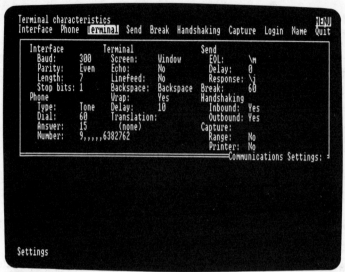

```
Terminal characteristics                                          MENU
Interface  Phone  Terminal  Send  Break  Handshaking  Capture  Login  Name  Quit
  Interface          Terminal                  Send
    Baud:      300      Screen:    Window         EOL:       \m
    Parity:    Even     Echo:      No             Delay:     0
    Length:    7        Linefeed:  No             Response:  \j
    Stop bits: 1        Backspace: Backspace   Break:       60
  Phone                 Wrap:      Yes         Handshaking
    Type:      Tone     Delay:     10            Inbound:   Yes
    Dial:      60       Translation:            Outbound:  Yes
    Answer:    15         (none)              Capture:
    Number:    9,,,,,6382762                     Range:     No
                                                 Printer:   No
                                              Communications Settings:

Settings
```

Fig. 12.4.

Setting Up a Log-in Sequence

Setting up a log-in sequence with a remote computer is one of the most interesting aspects of Symphony's COMM window. You have several options to work with. One has already been mentioned, the **S**ettings **T**erminal **D**elay command. The other options are part of the **S**ettings **L**ogin command. Figure 12.5 shows the settings sheet that appears when you select **L**ogin from the **S**ettings menu. This figure also shows the **L**ogin command menu.

The **L**ogin menu is the place where you store strings to be sent to the remote computer (Send strings) and the responses you are expecting in return (Receive strings). Suppose during the log-in sequence to CompuServe's EIS, you expect the following sequence of events:

1. You enter the local-area access number followed immediately by the string "cps" and RETURN. The "cps" string tells CompuServe that you want the Executive Information Service.

2. CompuServe returns the message "User ID: ".

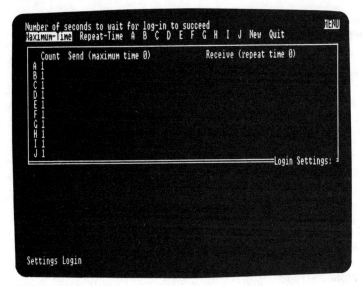

Fig. 12.5.

3. You enter your user ID (for example, 76030.10) followed by RETURN.

4. CompuServe returns the message "Password: ".

5. You enter your password (for example, ralph*morter) followed by RETURN.

After you have gone through this sequence, CompuServe lets you access the various menus of the EIS.

Entering Send and Receive Strings

To automate this sequence, you can enter Send and Receive strings in the **L**ogin menu. First, select the **A** option from the **L**ogin menu. When you do, Symphony shows you the following menu:

Count   Send   Receive   Quit

To enter the first Send string, select **S**end, then enter *cps\013* after the prompt. The \013 signals a RETURN. You must enter \013 after every Send string, or your log-in sequence will not work. (\013 is also equivalent to \m. If you look at the back of Symphony's

Reference Manual, you will see a table of LICS characters and their equivalent codes.)

The Count Option

The **C**ount option designates the number of times you want to transmit the Send string. Because you need to send the string only once for CompuServe, leave **C**ount set to the default of 1.

Note: Some remote computers require that you send a series of RETURNs at the beginning of the log-in sequence. In this case, enter \013 for the **A** option and set the **C**ount option to 3, 4, or however many RETURNs the remote computer expects.

To enter the first Receive string, select **R**eceive, then enter *User ID:* after the prompt. This is the string that you want to appear on the screen before Symphony transmits another Send string. When Symphony reads this string, the next send string (B) will automatically be sent.

You are now finished with the **A** option, so you select **Q**uit from the **A** menu. When Symphony returns you to the **L**ogin menu, select **B** to enter the next set of Send and Receive strings. Enter *76030.10\013* (or whatever your User ID number is) for the Send string and *Password:* for the Receive string. Again, leave the **C**ount option at 1.

Option **C** requires that you enter a Send string (ralph*morter or your password). You do not need a Receive string for this option.

The Maximum-Time Option

After options **A**, **B**, and **C**, you must enter a value for the **M**aximum-Time option of the **L**ogin menu. **M**aximum-Time refers to the maximum number of seconds that Symphony waits for the log-in sequence to succeed. This amount includes all the time needed for sending and receiving during the log-in sequence. The **M**aximum-Time will vary depending on how much sending and receiving you want to accomplish in the log-in sequence. For the current example, a good setting is 30 seconds. You can use a value as small as 10 seconds, but 10 seconds may not be enough time if the Compu-

Serve remote computer is slow in responding. If the **M**aximum-Time setting is reached before the log-in sequence is completed, Symphony interrupts the log-in sequence and issues an error message.

The *Repeat-Time* Option

You may also want to enter a value for the **R**epeat-Time option. The **R**epeat-Time value is the number of seconds that you want Symphony to delay between issuing a Send string and getting a Receive string from the remote computer. If, for example, Symphony issues a Send string and CompuServe responds immediately, Symphony issues the next Send string immediately. However, CompuServe may be slow in responding to the Send string. You don't want Symphony to get ahead of CompuServe by sending another string before receiving a response to the first one. Therefore, you must set the **R**epeat-Time to allow CompuServe enough time to respond. For the current example, a repeat time of five seconds works fine. (The time you require may be less if you are using a 1200-baud modem.)

Striking the right balance between too much and not enough time for the **R**epeat-Time requires some experimenting. Allowing extra time is not a problem if you have the **M**aximum-Time set high enough to allow the entire log-in sequence to be completed. Figure 12.6 shows how the **L**ogin menu appears after you have entered all the settings. Notice that the **M**aximum-Time and **R**epeat-Time appear above the Send and Receive columns, respectively. For a more complete example of this log-in sequence, see the comprehensive model in Chapter 14.

Changing Handshaking Settings

Handshaking refers to whether Symphony uses XON/XOFF (Ctrl-Q/Ctrl-S) protocol when it is communicating with a remote computer. If, after the DOS TYPE command, you have used Ctrl-Q to stop a file from displaying and used Ctrl-S to start displaying again, you have used XON/XOFF. (Don't confuse XON/XOFF with the Christensen XMODEM protocol; the two are entirely different.) Most manufacturers adhere to the XON/XOFF standard, so most remote

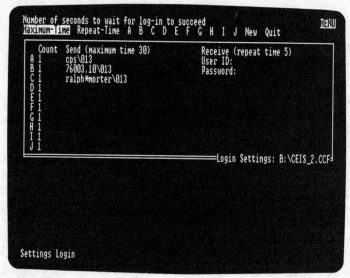

Fig. *12.6.*

computers recognize the Ctrl-Q and Ctrl-S characters. However, some computers have their own variations of handshaking protocol and require different control characters. On a rare occasion you may have to disable Symphony's handshaking in order to communicate with one of these computers. Even if handshaking is disabled, however, you can still manually issue a Ctrl-S to stop the display (not the transmission) of a communications session, and then use Ctrl-Q to start the display again.

There are two controls for **H**andshaking: **I**nbound and **O**utbound. If you set **O**utbound **H**andshaking to **Y**es, you are indicating that Symphony can start and stop a remote computer's transmission by issuing XON/XOFF signals. Similarly, if you set **I**nbound **H**andshaking to **Y**es, the remote computer can stop Symphony's transmission by XON/XOFF signals. The default setting for both **I**nbound and **O**utbound is **Y**es, and you probably will not need to change these settings.

Starting Communications

Now that you have an understanding of most of the COMM settings, you are ready to start communications. You can change any of the COMM settings while you are in the middle of a communications session, so don't worry if you are not sure about a particular setting. Try the settings that you think are most appropriate, and change them one by one if they don't work properly.

Phoning

Let's return to the original example. Suppose you have a Hayes Smartmodem with auto-dial, and you have entered the local-area access number for CompuServe in the **P**hone **N**umber setting. You are now ready to have Symphony dial the number for you. To do this, select **P**hone from the main COMM menu. The following menu choices will appear:

Call Wait-Mode Answer Hangup Data-Mode Voice-Mode

When you select **C**all followed by RETURN, you should hear some strange beeping noises from the modem as it dials the number. A "Dialing..." message appears at the top of the screen. When Symphony makes a connection with the remote system, you should hear a high-pitched tone over the speaker. If Symphony does not make the connection, an error message appears on the screen. After a short while, the high-pitched tone stops, and you are ready to begin the log-in sequence.

Note: If your modem does not have an auto-dial feature, you will have to dial the phone number yourself. When you hear the high-pitched tone over the receiver, flip the switch on your modem from Voice to Data, and you are ready to start the log-in sequence.

Starting the Log-in Sequence

After phoning the remote system, select **L**ogin from the main COMM menu. Symphony will display the letters A through J. You have already entered the log-in sequence in the **L**ogin settings for the current example, so select **A**. Symphony will now start the log-in sequence by transmitting the Send string A and displaying the message "Logging in..." at the top of the screen. If the **L**ogin settings you have chosen are working properly, you should not have to touch the computer again until you are completely logged into the remote computer.

Symphony starts with the Send string A and continues sending strings until it reaches an empty line in the **L**ogin menu. However, if your **L**ogin settings are not correct, you may have to halt the log-in sequence in midstream (by pressing Ctrl-Break followed by Esc) and enter the log-in sequence manually. If this is the case, enter a different value for the **S**ettings **T**erminal **D**elay command, and try logging in again.

Copying to the Printer

While you are in a COMM window, you can have Symphony send to the printer a copy of all data that appears on the screen. This includes all the data that is sent by the remote computer and all the data you type. The command that initiates printing is **S**ettings **C**apture **P**rint. When you have initiated printing, the captured message appears at the bottom of the screen.

Once you have started copying to the printer, you can stop the procedure any time by using the Capture key (F4 on IBM PCs and compatibles). To start copying again, press the Capture key a second time. You must also use the Capture key when capturing data in a range in the worksheet. (The Capture key is the only special key used in a COMM window.)

Capturing Data in a Range

After you have logged into CompuServe's EIS (or any other similar service) and found some interesting data, you may want to capture that data in a range in Symphony. Captured data is stored in a worksheet as labels; therefore, you can immediately use the data in a DOC window. However, if you want to use the data as numbers, you must convert it to a usable form before you can perform calculations with it, make a graph, play "what if," and the like.

Before you can capture data, you must designate in the spreadsheet a Capture range where you want the data placed as it comes in. The Capture range can be located anywhere in the spreadsheet. Just make sure that the range you designate is large enough (both in width and length) to contain all the data you want to capture.

Suppose, for example, that as you are browsing through Compu-Serve, you find some interesting stock data for the XYZ Corporation. In order to capture that data in a range in the Symphony worksheet, you must use the **S**ettings **C**apture **R**ange command with the Capture key. When you issue the **C**apture **R**ange command, Symphony temporarily shifts to the SHEET environment so you can enter a Capture range. A good technique is always to make the Capture range a little larger than you think you need. Otherwise, if the Capture range gets full, you have to erase the Capture range (by using the **S**ettings **C**apture **E**rase command), reset the Capture range to a larger size, reposition CompuServe back to where you were before you tried to capture the data the first time, and start capturing again.

As mentioned, you must use the Capture key to capture data in a COMM window. After you set the Capture range and want to begin capturing data, press the Capture key and choose **R**ange **Y**es to initiate the process. When you have captured all the data you desire, press the Capture key again, followed this time by **R**ange **N**o.

Converting Number Data to a Usable Form

When you have received number data from a remote computer, you need a way to convert it to numbers to be able to use it in calculations, graphs, and the like. There are two ways to accomplish this: to use functions, such as @DATEVALUE, @TIMEVALUE, and @VALUE; or to use the **Q**uery **P**arse command.

Setting the Capture Range Column Widths

Before you can convert the number data to a usable form, you must make sure that you capture the data properly. Suppose you have captured the data that appears in figure 12.7, and you want to convert it for use in a graph.

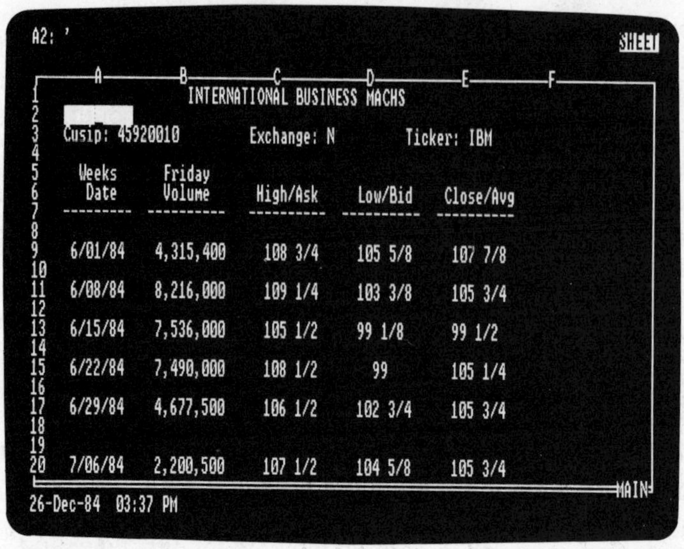

```
A2: '                                                              SHEET
      ----A-------B-------C-------D-------E-------F----
    1              INTERNATIONAL BUSINESS MACHS
    2
    3   Cusip: 45920010        Exchange: N        Ticker: IBM
    4
    5   Weeks       Friday
    6   Date        Volume      High/Ask    Low/Bid     Close/Avg
    7   ---------   ---------   ---------   ---------   ---------
    8
    9   6/01/84     4,315,400   108 3/4     105 5/8     107 7/8
   10
   11   6/08/84     8,216,000   109 1/4     103 3/8     105 3/4
   12
   13   6/15/84     7,536,000   105 1/2     99 1/8      99 1/2
   14
   15   6/22/84     7,490,000   108 1/2     99          105 1/4
   16
   17   6/29/84     4,677,500   106 1/2     102 3/4     105 3/4
   18
   19
   20   7/06/84     2,200,500   107 1/2     104 5/8     105 3/4
                                                            MAIN
   26-Dec-84  03:37 PM
```

Fig. 12.7.

The Capture range for this data is A1..E40. Because the Capture range is several columns wide, Symphony enters the data for Weeks Date, Friday Volume, High/Ask, etc., in separate columns. If the Capture range had been only one column wide (for example, A1..A40), all the data for each row would be written in one long label. Remember to indicate a wide-enough Capture range if you want Symphony to maintain columnar separation.

Another important point to remember about the Capture range is that you must set the column widths to conform to the data you are capturing. If you leave the columns set to the default width of 9, Symphony may not split the data where you want it to. The best way to determine the column widths for your data is to experiment. The column widths for figure 12.7 were set to the following:

Column	Width
A	9
B	13
C	12
D	12
E	12

Using Functions to Convert Data

To use functions to convert the data in figure 12.7 from labels to numbers, switch to a SHEET window and go to an out-of-the-way area of the worksheet. You can then use the following formulas to convert the data in row 9.

Variable	Function
Weeks Date	@DATEVALUE(A9)
Friday Volume	@VALUE(B9)
High/Ask	@VALUE(C9)
Low/Bid	@VALUE(D9)
Close/Avg	@VALUE(E9)

Once you have the formulas for the first row, copy them to succeeding rows. Then use the **R**ange **V**alues command to change the formulas in the out-of-the-way range to numbers and to copy them over the original label data.

Using **Q**uery **P**arse

The second technique for converting string data to numbers, the **Q**uery **P**arse command, is actually much easier than using functions. To use **Q**uery **P**arse, you must be familiar with the FORM window. (See the previous chapter for more on the FORM window.)

Suppose, once again, that you have captured the data in figure 12.7. The first step is to create a simple input form using a DOC window. The best location for entering the fields for the input form is directly to the right of the captured data. Figure 12.8 shows how you enter the fields.

The lengths for the variables are exactly the same as the column widths used for capturing the data. This is necessary for **Q**uery **P**arse to work properly. Next, switch to a FORM window and use the **G**enerate command, which causes Symphony to generate the input form and the important ranges for the data base. You are now ready to issue the **Q**uery **P**arse command.

To enter the **Q**uery **P**arse command, shift from a FORM to a SHEET window. When you enter the command, Symphony asks you for the

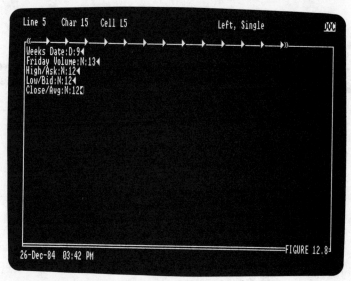

```
Line 5    Char 15   Cell L5                    Left, Single              ☒
‹‹——►——►——►——►——►——►——►——►——►——►——►——►——►——►——►——►——►——►——►——►——►——►——►——►——►——►——►——►——►——►——►——►——►——►——►——►——►»»
Weeks Date:D:9◄
Friday Volume:N:13◄
High/Ask:N:12◄
Low/Bid:N:12◄
Close/Avg:N:12☒


26-Dec-84  03:42 PM                            ═══════════FIGURE 12.8╝
```

Fig. 12.8.

range to be parsed. Enter the address of the Capture range (in this example, A1..E40). Even though the Capture range may contain all kinds of unrelated data (such as titles, and log-in sequences), Symphony conveniently discards all the lines that do not conform to the field definitions you supply. After you enter the range to be parsed, Symphony asks for a Review range. This is the range where Symphony puts all the nonconforming lines. Choose an out-of-the-way place for the Review range. After you enter the Review range, Symphony executes the **Q**uery **P**arse. Figure 12.9 shows the results.

If you try to create the data base directly below the Capture range, **Q**uery **P**arse will not work as expected. When you use the **F**orm **G**enerate command, Symphony adds one space to each column width. For example, the width for the Weeks Date column (column A) is changed from 9 to 10. Therefore, when you use **Q**uery **P**arse, Symphony rejects all the data in the Capture range as non-conforming. The values entered in the Capture range are too wide for the input fields, and Symphony sends them all to the Review range. When you locate the data base directly below the Capture range, you must either subtract one from the length designations when entering the data base (use Weeks Date:D:8 instead of Weeks

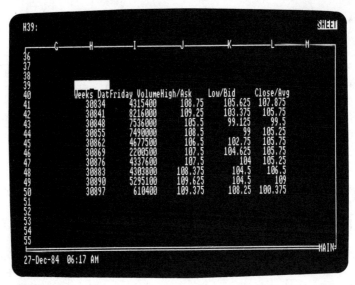

Fig. 12.9.

Date:D:9), or you must manually reset the columns to the proper width after you use the **G**enerate command.

For another example of the use of **Q**uery **P**arse, see the comprehensive model in Chapter 14.

Saving Settings

Before you exit from Symphony, make sure you save your settings for using CompuServe in a Communications Configuration File. To save the settings, issue the **S**ettings **N**ame **S**ave command. Symphony then saves the settings to a .CCF file on the Symphony Program disk. After you have saved your settings, you can retrieve them by the **S**ettings **N**ame **R**etrieve command. If you want Symphony to retrieve the settings for you automatically every time you boot the program, you can enter the name of the .CCF file in the SERVICES **C**onfiguration menu and update the menu. For more on modifying and updating the SERVICES **C**onfiguration menu, see Chapter 2.

Ending a Session

To end the current communications session with CompuServe, log off the service by entering the word *bye*. (Other services may have different commands for logging off.) If your modem has an auto-hangup feature, select **P**hone **H**angup from the main COMM menu. This causes Symphony to signal your modem to hang up the phone. If you do not have an auto-hangup, flip the switch on your modem from Data to Talk.

Communications with Another Microcomputer

In one of your early sessions with Symphony, you will probably want to use the COMM environment to communicate with another Symphony user. In fact, you should make a special point of trying this. Call up a friend who also has Symphony and try passing messages and data back and forth. You will learn a great deal about Symphony's COMM environment by such an experiment.

Settings for Communications with Another Microcomputer

When you are communicating with another microcomputer, your first concern should be that you both have the same Interface settings. For example, if one modem is capable of being set at either 1200 or 300 baud and the other modem can be set only at 300, both must be set at the lower rate. The settings for parity, length, and stop bits must also be the same.

To send files back and forth by means of the **F**ile-**T**ransfer **S**end and **F**ile-**T**ransfer **R**eceive commands (the commands for XMODEM file transfer), Lotus recommends the following settings:

- Interface **L**ength must be set to 2 (8 bits)

- Interface **P**arity must be set to 1 (None)

- Interface **S**top-bits must be set to 1 (1 stop bit)

These are the general standards for XMODEM file transfer. Be careful to use them whenever you transfer files. You may be able to transfer SYMPHONY worksheet files (.WRK) files with the Interface length set to 7, but this practice is not recommended.

Figure 12.10 shows the settings for communicating with another microcomputer when you expect to use the File-Transfer Send and Receive commands. Again, both computers must have the same Interface settings.

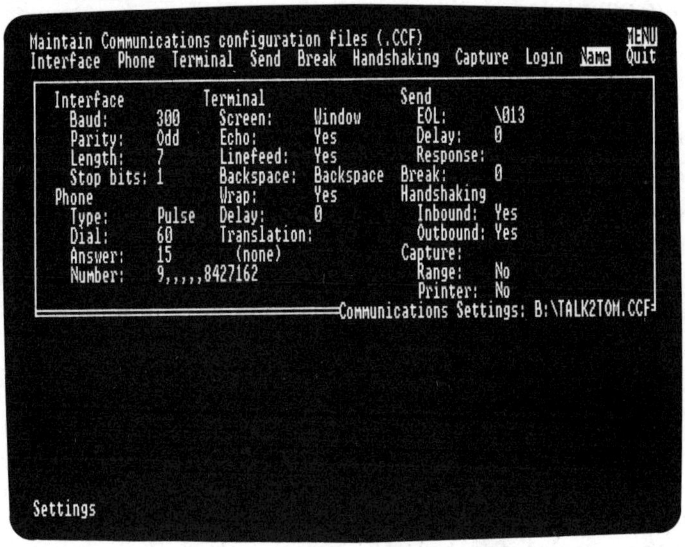

Fig. 12.10.

Making the Connection

Once you have coordinated the Interface settings for both computers, you are ready to make the connection. Suppose your friend is the caller, and you are the receiver of the call. After your friend uses the Phone command to dial your number, you use the Answer command to have Symphony automatically answer the call. While Symphony is working, it displays the message "Answering..." at the top of the screen.

Just how long Symphony will attempt to answer the call depends on the Phone Answer-Time setting that you have entered. The settings sheet in figure 12.10 shows a **P**hone **A**nswer-Time setting of 15 seconds. This is the default setting and is usually more than enough time when you know you are being called.

Because Symphony does not have a special indicator to let you know when you are being called, you have to rely on signals from your modem. If it is equipped with a speaker, you will begin to hear noises when someone is calling. If you are not in a COMM window, you must switch to one to issue the **A**nswer command. (On modems that are not equipped with an auto-answer feature, the **A**nswer has no effect.) You can also have Symphony automatically answer the call for you regardless of what kind of window you are in. To accomplish this, simply set the **P**hone **W**ait-Mode command to **Y**es. This way, your modem will automatically answer a call after a preset number of rings, determined by a setting on the modem.

If your modem is not equipped with the auto-answer feature, you should keep the modem set to Voice mode. Then when someone calls you, just flip the switch from Voice to Data. You should be ready to send messages at that point.

Sending Messages

After you have made the connection, you need to use the **T**ransmit-Range feature to send messages back and forth. To send a message, you must switch to the DOC environment and enter your message in the spreadsheet. Next, you switch back to COMM and enter the **T**ransmit-Range command. When you do, Symphony temporarily shifts to the SHEET environment so that you can designate the range to be sent. Note: If your message stretches across several columns, make sure you designate all the columns involved. If you point to only the first column (as you may do, since your message is actually a long label), Symphony will transmit only the first portion of the message. After you have designated the range and pressed RETURN, Symphony immediately shifts back to the COMM environment and transmits your message.

In general, transmitting messages is awkward in Symphony, but you can automate the process. Chapter 13 shows how to use the Symphony Command Language to make sending messages a simple task.

Sending Ranges

You can also use the **T**ransmit-Range command to send other data. For example, you may want to send a portion of an inventory spreadsheet, or the latest figures you received on T-Bill auction rates.

When you use the **T**ransmit-Range command to send ranges, you must make sure that you have selected the proper options for the **S**ettings **S**end command. When you select **S**ettings **S**end, Symphony returns the following choices:

   End-of-Line   Delay   Response

The **E**nd-of-Line option is used to enter an end-of-line terminator. Symphony uses the terminator between lines of data when you enter the **T**ransmit-Range command. The end-of-line terminator is a three-digit ASCII control code (or letter equivalent) preceded by a backslash. For example, the most common end-of-line indicator is \013 (or its equivalent \m), the carriage-return character. This is the default setting for Symphony and is the end-of-line terminator that you want for communicating with another Symphony user.

The **D**elay option sets the number of seconds you want Symphony to wait before sending consecutive lines of a range. The default setting is 0, the setting you want for communicating with another Symphony user. However, some time-sharing services are slow to accept new data, and you may have to enter a delay time when sending a range to them.

Sometimes you will want to have Symphony read a string from a remote computer before sending a data range. To have Symphony read the string, you must enter it in the **R**esponse setting. For example, suppose the remote computer is running a line editor that is currently in EDIT mode. After you have sent a command to switch the editor from EDIT to **I**nsert mode, you want to have Symphony read the editor's response before sending a range. If the editor's prompt is "Insert", this is the string you enter in the **R**esponse setting. For the current example, leave the Response string blank. When you get into more sophisticated applications later on, such as using the Symphony Command Language to send data ranges, you may want to include a Response string.

Transferring Files—XMODEM

Symphony gives you two options for sending data back and forth between your computer and another Symphony user's. First, you can use the **T**ransmit-**R**ange command for transmitting a portion of a file. Unfortunately, the receiving Symphony user must capture the data as lines of text when you transmit it this way. Second, you can use the **F**ile-**T**ransfer **S**end and **R**eceive commands. These commands are used to transfer entire files by means of Symphony's XMODEM file-transferring capabilities. One of the main advantages of XMODEM file transfer is that you keep the separation between cell entries. Another advantage is that error checking takes place while the file is being transferred.

When you issue the **F**ile-**T**ransfer **S**end command for transferring a file to another Symphony user, Symphony first requests the name of the file you are transferring. (Remember that you are not limited to sending only Symphony files.) Suppose the name of the file you select is SALES.WRK. After you enter this name, Symphony sends that name to the remote computer and displays the following message on your screen:

> Sending file: SALES.WRK
> Waiting for connection...

If the receiving user has already issued the **F**ile **R**eceive command, you will probably not see the second line of the message. Instead, Symphony will show some variation of the following message:

> Sending file: SALES.WRK
> 1024 out of 2048 sent 0 errors corrected

As Symphony transmits the file, the numbers in the second line of the message are constantly updated to reflect the status of the transfer. Incidentally, the receiving user's screen will show the same messages except with the word *Sending* replaced by *Receiving*.

With all the error checking that takes place, transferring a file using the XMODEM capability takes a substantial amount of time; for example, to transfer approximately 5,000 bytes takes three to four minutes.

If the remote computer you are working with does not support XMODEM protocol, you have to use Symphony's **C**apture **R**ange command to transfer a file from the remote computer to Symphony. Sometimes this is the only way to get data from a remote computer into Symphony. Because no error checking takes place when you are capturing data in a range, you may get some strange control characters mixed with your data. If you do, use the @CLEAN function to remove the control characters.

Conclusion

In this chapter you have learned about Symphony's COMM window through two examples: accessing CompuServe's Executive Information Service and communicating with another Symphony user. In many ways Symphony's COMM window is quite sophisticated; however, it can also be awkward at times. In the chapter that follows, you will find some examples of how to use Symphony's Command Language to help streamline some of the COMM window operations. With these Command-Language additions, Symphony provides strong communications capability.

13

Macros—The Symphony Command Language

Before 1-2-3's release, Lotus used the term *the typing alternative* to describe the 1-2-3 macro language. This term was later dropped in favor of *keyboard macros*, a slightly stronger term that better emphasizes the language's power. Actually, both terms are descriptive of the true nature of the 1-2-3 macro language, for its purpose is to automate repetitive keyboard-related tasks. With Symphony, Lotus uses the term *Command Language* to describe the program's macro language; and this term represents a further evolution in the scope and power of Lotus' macro language.

New with Symphony

With the Symphony Command Language, Lotus has introduced a nearly full-featured programming language. Among its features are subroutines, iterative looping (similar to the DO-WHILE structure in PL/1 or the FOR-NEXT structure in BASIC), improved conditional logic (including an IF-THEN-ELSE structure), and error trapping. These tools make it possible to develop special applications programs to run on Symphony.

Another particularly nice feature of Symphony is that you can use the Learn mode to have Symphony automatically store commands. The first step is to use the SERVICES **L**earn command to set up a Learn range where you can store the commands. Then, when you press the Learn key, Symphony executes the commands you type, converts these commands into Command Language statements, and stores them in the Learn range. You will probably find that this is the easiest way to enter most of your macro statements. However, in more complex macros, you will have to enter manually several of the Command Language statements.

New with Symphony

Early in this chapter you will find practical descriptions, with examples, of all the macro commands and keywords available in Symphony. You will also find advice on how to structure macros, where to locate them, and how to use the Learn mode. After the descriptions of commands and keywords, a beginner's library of useful macros is provided. You can use these macros to help you perform tasks in all five of Symphony's working environments.

1-2-3 and Symphony

Experienced 1-2-3 users probably recall their original fascination with the power of 1-2-3's macro language. However, they must also recall many of the problems. Some of the most troublesome problems include cryptic code, limited looping capability, and slow speed. In Symphony, Lotus has corrected many of these problems.

First, 1-2-3's special macro commands have been replaced by more descriptive commands. For example /XI has been replaced by {IF true-false-expression}. As you can see, the macro statement grammar has also changed. All macro keywords must be placed between braces, and sometimes you must also include one or more arguments inside the braces. In this way, the new grammar for macro commands is similar to @function grammar.

Second, 1-2-3 users can also recall the difficulty of building counter macros (macros that execute a specified number of times based on the status of a counter). Symphony provides the FOR command, a single command that replaces the several commands required to build a counter macro in 1-2-3. The FOR command executes a macro the specified number of times, based on a counter that Symphony keeps track of.

One of the principal reasons for the slowness of 1-2-3 macros is the amount of time required for recalculating the entire worksheet. (Recall that you can improve the speed of 1-2-3 macro performance by setting /**W**orksheet **G**lobal **R**ecalculation to **M**anual and re-calculating the entire worksheet only when needed.) Experienced 1-2-3 users may still find macros slow in Symphony. However, with Symphony, you can specify the recalculation of certain parts of the spreadsheet. For example, you can recalculate a range of cells either by row or by column. Controlling the recalculation of ranges can significantly speed up the processing of a Symphony macro.

These are just a few of Symphony's new commands that address problems with 1-2-3's macro language. You will find many other instances as you read through the chapter. In general, you should be pleasantly surprised by the new power and ease of use that the Symphony Command Language affords you.

Many 1-2-3 users are disturbed, though, when they learn that 1-2-3 macros do not work in Symphony. Although you can easily convert .WKS files to .WRK files and use their spreadsheet data, you cannot use their macros. Lotus is working on a macro conversion add-in that will be available soon. In the meantime, however, you will have to convert your old 1-2-3 macros. Try copying your 1-2-3 macros to a range of cells in the Symphony spreadsheet and creating Symphony's equivalent of the 1-2-3 commands in the column to the right. Although this process is slow, it is the only alternative until the add-in is available.

If you are an experienced 1-2-3 user, you may want to go directly to figure 13.1 for a complete list of Symphony's special-key representations and pick up from there. From that point on, you should find the discussion quite useful.

Definition of a Macro

In its most basic form, a macro is simply a collection of keystrokes. A macro is like a storehouse of keystrokes. These keystrokes can be commands or simple text and numeric entries. A macro can be used instead of the keyboard to issue a command or to enter data in the Symphony spreadsheet.

But a macro can be much more than just a collection of keystrokes. Symphony has many special commands that can be used only with macros. These commands do such things as accept input from the keyboard during execution of a macro, perform a conditional test similar to the IF-THEN command of the BASIC language, and create user menus. These and other commands make Symphony's Command Language an actual programming language.

The Complexity of Macros

Lotus calls one section of its 1-2-3 manual "Advanced Topic: Do You Sincerely Want to Become a Programmer?" This question is appropriate for users of 1-2-3 but is even more appropriate for users of Symphony. 1-2-3's macros are complex, but Symphony's can be even more so. Because Symphony's macros can have global effects on the worksheet, the macros should always be used carefully.

If you are a Symphony novice, you may think you should avoid macros until you are fairly comfortable with Symphony in general. But you do not need to know everything about Symphony before you begin to use macros. In fact, the Learn mode makes it possible for you to start entering macros right away; and this chapter contains a number of macros that you can use immediately. Even if you are new to Symphony, there is no reason why you can't begin experimenting with macros.

If you have experience with BASIC or another programming language, you will find the macros easier to learn and use. But even the advanced programmer will encounter some obstacles with Symphony's macros.

This chapter does not explain programming theory. If you are interested in building complex Symphony macros, you should take some time to learn programming theory. A number of excellent books on this subject are available at your local bookstore.

When you start out with Symphony macros, you will be better off using them to automate simple, repetitive tasks. As your knowledge of macros, and Symphony in general, increases, you should take more time to plan and prepare. The greater care you take with the plans for your macros, the less time you will spend coding and debugging.

The Elements of Macros

A macro is one or more specially named *text cells*. All macros are created by entering the keystrokes (or representations of those keystrokes), either manually or by using the Learn mode. The keystrokes are then stored in a worksheet cell. For example, suppose you want to create a simple macro that will format the current cell in the Currency format with no decimal places. The macro will look like this if you start from the SHEET environment:

'{MENU}fc0~~

You can create this macro in the worksheet in two different ways. You can either enter the macro exactly as you enter any other label (by typing all the characters), or you can use the Learn mode to have Symphony type in the macro for you. Using the Learn mode is by far the easier method.

If you decide to enter the macro by typing it in yourself, you do not have to type the label prefix because Symphony interprets the first character, the brace ({), as the beginning of a label entry. When you use the Learn mode, Symphony automatically enters the label prefix (along with everything else) for you.

The other characters in the Currency Format macro represent the command that creates the desired format. {MENU} means the special key command used to access the main SHEET menu. (If you use the Learn mode, Symphony enters {MENU} in the Learn range when you press the MENU key.) {MENU}fc0 is simply shorthand for MENU **F**ormat **C**urrency, and the 0 tells Symphony that you want no digits to be displayed to the right of the decimal.

At the end of the macro are two characters called tildes (~~). When used in a macro, the tilde stands for the RETURN key. In this case, the two tildes signal Symphony to use the RETURN key twice when the macro is invoked. If you enter this command using the Learn mode, remember to press RETURN twice when you format a cell. Press RETURN after supplying 0 for the number of decimals; then press RETURN again to signal that the format applies to the current cell. If you have your Symphony program handy, try entering this simple macro in the Learn mode.

Symphony uses symbols like ~ to stand for other keystrokes as well. For example, look at the following macro:

'{MENU}fc0~{END}{RIGHT}~

This macro is similar to the one previously explained, except that this command also causes the cursor to move. This macro can be used to format an entire row instead of just one cell.

Once again, notice the ' at the beginning of the macro and the ~ at the end. Notice also the phrase {END}{RIGHT} in the macro. {END} stands for the End key on the keyboard; {RIGHT} represents the right arrow key. This phrase, created by pressing these two keys while you are in the Learn mode, causes the cursor to move in the row to the next boundary between blank and nonblank cells.

Symbols like these are used to represent all the special keys on the IBM PC/XT keyboard. In every case, the name of the function key (RIGHT for the right arrow, or CALC for the function key F8) is enclosed in braces. For example, {UP} represents the up arrow key, the symbol {END} stands for the End key, and {DRAW} means the Draw key (Alt + F8). If you are entering the macro statements manually and you enclose in braces a phrase that is not a function name, Symphony will return the error message:

Unrecognized key/range name {...}

Another special-key representation is {?}, which is similar to BASIC's INPUT command. Wherever Symphony has a {?} in a macro, it pauses and waits for the user to enter data from the keyboard. Once data is entered, it is stored in the current cell.

Figure 13.1 is a complete list of special key representations.

Function Keys	Function
{ABS}	Converts relative reference to absolute (same as F3 in a SHEET window)

{CALC}	Recalculates worksheet (same as F8 in SHEET window)
{CAPTURE}	Activates and deactivates capturing of data in the Capture range (same as F4 in a COMM window)
{CENTER}	Centers text (same as Alt + F4 in a COMM window)
{DRAW}	Redraws all the windows on the screen
{EDIT}	Used to edit cell entries (same as F2 in the SHEET environment)
{ERASE}	Erases a designated block of text (same as F4 in a COMM window)
{GOTO}	Sends cursor to a designated cell, range name, or line marker (same as F5)
{HELP}	Activates the help menu facility (same as F1)
{INDENT}	Creates a temporary left margin for the current paragraph when you justify it (same as F3 in a DOC window)
{JUSTIFY}	Justifies a paragraph (same as F2 in a DOC window)
{LEARN}	Activates the Learn mode (same as Alt + F5)
{MENU} or {M}	Brings up the main menu for current window (same as F10)
{SERVICES} or {S}	Brings up the SERVICES menu (same as F9)
{SPLIT}	Splits text in a line (same as Alt + F3)
{SWITCH}	Switches current window to the window type previously chosen

{TYPE}	Sets the current window type (same as Alt + F10)
{USER}	Activates a named macro (same as F7)
{WHERE}	Tells the equivalent number of printed pages (same as Alt + F2 in a DOC window)
{WINDOW}	Cycles between windows (same as F6)
{ZOOM}	Makes the active window occupy the whole screen (same as Alt + F6)

Cursor-Movement Keys

{BIGLEFT}	Same as Ctrl + left arrow key
{BIGRIGHT}	Same as Ctrl + right arrow key
{DOWN}	Down arrow key
{END}	End key
{HOME}	Home key
{LEFT}	Left arrow key
{PGDN} or {BIGDOWN}	PgDn key
{PGUP} or {BIGUP}	PgUp key
{RIGHT}	Right arrow key
{UP}	Up arrow key

Other Special Keys

{BACKSPACE} or {BS}	Backspace key
{BREAK}	Same as Ctrl-Break
{DELETE}	Del key
{ESCAPE} or {ESC}	Esc key
{INSERT}	Ins key
{TAB}	Tab key

{?}	Causes macro to pause and wait for input from keyboard; macro resumes execution after you press RETURN.
~	RETURN key

Fig. 13.1.

Function Key Grammar

To specify more than one use of a special key, you can include repetition factors inside the braces of a special-key phrase. For example, you can use the following statements:

{PGUP 3}	Press the PgUp key three times in a row
{RIGHT JUMP}	Press the right arrow key the number of times indicated by the value in the cell called JUMP

New with Symphony

Macro Commands .

Besides special function-key statements, Symphony has a set of special macro commands. They are also called invisible commands because they cannot be issued from the keyboard, but only from within a macro. Symphony's command set is similar to the commands offered by most higher-level programming languages, such as BASIC.

New with Symphony

Macro Statement Grammar

Macro commands have a special grammar that is similar to @function grammar. The general format of macro commands is

    {KEYWORD}

or

    {KEYWORD argument1,argument2,...,argumentN}

where arguments 1 through N are separated by commas. Examples of macro commands are

> {BLANK SALES}
>
>> Has the same effect as SHEET **E**rase on the range named SALES
>
> {BEEP}
>
>> Causes the speaker to emit a short beep; a good function to indicate when an error has been made by the user
>
> {GETLABEL "Enter label: ",FIRST FIELD}
>
>> Causes macro to stop processing temporarily to allow user to enter a label; places the entry in a cell called FIRST FIELD
>
> {indicate "Bye"}
>
>> Places "Bye" in place of the standard Symphony indicator in the upper right corner of the screen.

In the statements above, the command keywords are BLANK, BEEP, GETLABEL, and INDICATE. Notice that in the last example the keyword is not entered in capital letters. Symphony doesn't care whether you use capital or small letters for entering keywords. However, for the sake of clarity, keywords in this chapter are in capital letters.

Macro statements can have one or more arguments following the macro keyword. Just as in functions, the arguments for macro keyword commands can be of three types: a single number, a single string value, or a range.

The rules for macro keyword command arguments are slightly different from those for functions. The first difference is that you can't use string-value formulas for keyword statements. (Exceptions to this rule are described in the keyword-command descriptions that follow.) Second, you can use a single-cell address for a range. For example, A1 is used in the same way as A1..A1.

New
with
Symphony

Keyword Types

Command Language keywords can be broken down into five different types: keywords for logical operations, keywords for branching and subroutines, keywords for testing keyboard input, keywords for storing and deleting, and a general category of maintenance-oriented keywords. All of Symphony's Command Language keywords have been divided into these categories.

Keywords for Logical Operations

Keywords for logical operations include all the macro keywords used for conditional testing. For example, suppose you want to test the value in a cell before performing a calculation. Symphony provides three different commands for testing the value: the IF, ONERROR, and FOR commands.

The IF Command

The IF command is used to make a macro *branch* as the result of a logical test. By using this command, you can implement the kind of IF-THEN-ELSE logic common to many high-level programming languages. The general form of the command is

{IF logical-expression}{BRANCH range name}

Suppose, for example, that you want to test the value in a single-cell range called NEW RECORD. If the value in NEW RECORD is Y (for Yes), you want to add a new record to a data base. Otherwise, you want to modify an existing record in the data base. The macro includes the following statements:

{IF NEW RECORD="Y"}{BRANCH NEW_ROUTINE}
{BRANCH MOD_ROUTINE}

The first line is contained in a single cell. The part of the cell following the IF portion is called the THEN clause. The THEN clause is executed only if the result of the logical test is true. In this case, the THEN clause contains the keyword BRANCH followed by the range name NEW_ROUTINE. (BRANCH is often used with IF.) The macro will branch to NEW_ROUTINE if the value of NEW RECORD is equal to Y.

The second line contains the ELSE clause, which is executed only if the result of the logical statement in the line above is false. In this case the ELSE clause also contains a BRANCH statement, but the range to branch to is called MOD_ROUTINE. Note: Including an ELSE clause with an IF statement is optional.

The IF statement adds significant strength to Symphony's macro language. However, the one disadvantage of the IF statement is that if you want to execute more than one macro command after the logical test, the THEN clause must always contain some sort of branching statement. What's more, the code to which the THEN clause branches must contain a QUIT command (to end macro processing). If the THEN clause does not contain a branching statement, the macro will continue its execution right through the ELSE clause.

The ONERROR Command

Experienced 1-2-3 users may recall that the processing of 1-2-3 macros is interrupted if a system error (such as "Disk drive not ready") occurs during execution. Symphony, on the other hand, provides the ONERROR command, which lets a macro continue executing even though a system error has occurred. The general format of the command is

{ONERROR branch-location,message-location}

The best place to put an ONERROR statement is directly above where you think an error may occur. For example, suppose your macro is about to copy a portion of the current spreadsheet out to a disk file using the SERVICES **F**ile **X**tract command. A system error will occur if the drive is not ready or the disk is full. Therefore, you should include a strategically placed ONERROR command. (See fig. 13.2.)

In this example, the ONERROR statement will cause the macro to branch to a cell called BAD_DRV if an error occurs. A copy of the error message that Symphony issues is entered in a cell called BAD_DRV_MSG. (This argument is optional.) Then, the first state-

Since there is not enough space on a single typeset line to place all the characters that appear on one line on the screen, carryover lines are indented.

PROC   {ONERROR BAD_DRV,BAD_DRV_MSG}
                        {SERVICES}fxvDATA_4~{BS}A1..G9~

BAD_DRV   {GOTO}OUT_OF_WAY_CELL~
                        Disk drive is not ready{DOWN}
                        Prepare drive and press RETURN to
                            continue~{?}~
                        {BRANCH PROC}

Fig. 13.2.

ment in the BAD_DRV routine positions the cursor to an out-of-the-way cell (cleverly called OUT_OF_WAY_CELL). Next, the message "Disk drive is not ready" is entered in the spreadsheet followed by "Prepare drive and press RETURN to continue." The macro pauses for the user to press RETURN. Finally, the macro branches back to PROC to try again.

As a general rule, you should always make sure that your ONERROR statement is executed by the macro before an error takes place. Therefore, you may want to include an ONERROR statement near the start of your macros. Because you can have only one ONERROR statement in effect at a time, you should take special precaution to write your macros so that the right message appears for each error condition.

Ctrl-Break presents a special problem for the ONERROR statement. Because Ctrl-Break actually causes an error condition, the ONERROR statement is automatically invoked. Therefore, a good technique is to disable Ctrl-Break after you have debugged your macro. (See the section on Eliminating the use of Ctrl-Break.) By disabling Ctrl-Break, you can prevent the confusion that might arise by an untimely error message.

The FOR Command

Symphony offers complete looping capability (or FOR-NEXT logic) in macros. The FOR command is used to control the looping process. The general form of the command is

{FOR counter-location,start-number,stop-number,
    step-number, starting-location}

The start-number, stop-number, and step-number are used to determine how many times a group of macro commands (a loop) is executed. The starting-location indicates where the first macro command in the loop resides. The counter-location is the address where you want to store the counter that Symphony keeps track of.

Suppose, for example, that you want to build a macro that computes factorials. There are several ways to accomplish this, but the FOR command offers one of the easiest alternatives. Figure 13.3 shows a macro that computes a factorial for a number you enter and records the result in the current cell.

```
MAIN              {LET PREVIOUS NUMBER,1}
                  {GETNUMBER "Enter number: ",
                     FACTORIAL}
                  {FOR COUNTER,1,FACTORIAL,1,
                     FACT_RTN}
                  +PREVIOUS NUMBER~

FACT_RTN          {LET PREVIOUS NUMBER,+PREVIOUS
                     NUMBER*COUNTER}
                  {RETURN}
```

Fig. 13.3.

Since there is not enough space on a single typeset line to place all the characters that appear on one line on the screen, carryover lines are indented.

There are several points to notice about this macro. The first line of the MAIN routine uses the LET command. The LET command stores a number (or a string) at a specified cell location; in this case, the number to be stored is 1, and the specified cell location is a cell named PREVIOUS NUMBER. The LET command is particularly useful for initializing variables.

Next, the GETNUMBER command causes a pause for the user to enter a number, which is then stored in a cell called FACTORIAL. Notice that the GETNUMBER command lets you include a string for prompting the user. The string appears in the control panel when the GETNUMBER command is executed.

Symphony begins the FOR command by evaluating the start-, stop-, and step-number values. In this case, they are 1, FACTORIAL, and 1, respectively. Symphony also initializes the counter-location cell, COUNTER, with the start-number value. Next, the program tests the value in the counter-location cell to see if it is less than the stop-number. If the result of the test is true, Symphony executes the routine at the starting-location, FACT_RTN. If the result of the test is false, Symphony proceeds to the next macro command.

The FACT_RTN uses the LET command to reassign the value in PREVIOUS NUMBER. In this case, the value used for reassignment is derived by multiplying PREVIOUS NUMBER by the value in COUNTER.

When Symphony finishes executing the FACT_RTN (that is, when it encounters the RETURN statement, a command specifically designed for ending subroutines), the program returns to the FOR command and increases the value in COUNTER by 1 (the step-number). The entire process of testing the COUNTER against the stop-value, executing the FACT_RTN, and incrementing the value in COUNTER is repeated until the value in COUNTER exceeds the stop-value. When the FOR command is completed, the macro assigns the formula +PREVIOUS NUMBER to the current cell.

If you wish to end the processing of a FOR statement prematurely, you can use the FORBREAK command. When you use this command, Symphony interrupts the processing of the FOR statement and continues execution with the statement following the FOR.

For example, suppose you are using the Factorial model again, and you want to end processing when you reach 15 decimal places of precision, the maximum precision that Symphony is capable of handling. To stop processing, you can use the FORBREAK statement as it appears in figure 13.4.

Since there is not enough space on a single typeset line to place all the characters that appear on one line on the screen, carryover lines are indented.

```
MAIN           {LET PREVIOUS NUMBER,1}
               {GETNUMBER "Enter number: ",
                  FACTORIAL}
               {FOR COUNTER,1,FACTORIAL,1,
                  FACT_RTN}
               +PREVIOUS NUMBER~

FACT_RTN       {LET PREVIOUS NUMBER,+PREVIOUS
                  NUMBER*COUNTER}
               {IF PREVIOUS NUMBER>1E+15}
                  {FORBREAK}
               {RETURN}
```

Fig. 13.4.

Keywords for Branching and Subroutines

Experienced 1-2-3 users may recall that 1-2-3 offers two different techniques for instructing a macro to continue executing, beginning with a particular cell location. One technique is a simple branch (using /XG), and the other is a menu-branch (using /XM). Symphony retains these same techniques (although their related commands are named differently and are much easier to use) and offers subroutines besides.

The BRANCH Command

BRANCH is the simplest macro command for getting Symphony to read keystrokes starting at a new location. The general format of the command is

{BRANCH location}

Suppose, for example, that there are three separate companies under your corporate umbrella, and you have written a macro for adding and modifying records in a corporate personnel data base. Depending on how the user of the macro responds to the "Enter Company (R, A, or C): " prompt, you want the program to branch to a different place in the macro and attach a different set of entry form settings to the FORM window. Figure 13.5 shows a portion of the macro.

The BRANCH statements in the MAIN macro cause the flow of macro execution to shift to the different company routines. After the macro executes a company routine, you may prefer that the flow of execution return to the MAIN macro. Therefore, remove the BRANCH commands and enclose the routine names in braces (for example, {ROTEX}). Removing the BRANCH commands changes the statements to subroutine calls.

There are two important points about BRANCH commands. First, they cause a permanent shift in the flow of statement execution (unless you use another BRANCH statement). Second, BRANCH statements are most often used in combination with IF statements.

Since there is not enough space on a single typeset line to place all the characters that appear on one line on the screen, carryover lines are indented.

```
MAIN          {GETLABEL "Enter Company (R, A, or
                  C): ",COMPANY}
              {IF COMPANY="R"}{BRANCH ROTEX}
              {IF COMPANY="A"}{BRANCH APEX}
              {BRANCH CYTEX}
                 .
                 .
                 .

ROTEX         {TYPE}f{MENU}aROTEX_FORM~
              {QUIT}

APEX          {TYPE}f{MENU}aAPEX_FORM~
              {QUIT}

CYTEX         {TYPE}f{MENU}aCYTEX_FORM~
              {QUIT}
```

Fig. 13.5.

The MENUBRANCH Command

MENUBRANCH is a variant of the simple BRANCH command. Instead of immediately branching to a new location, MENUBRANCH temporarily halts execution of the macro so that you can respond to menu choices. After a choice has been made, the MENUBRANCH command causes the macro to branch accordingly. For example, suppose that you have the corporate personnel data base again, and you have entered the macro in figure 13.6.

```
MAIN          {MENUBRANCH ROTEX_MENU}
              {BRANCH FINISH}

ROTEX_MENU    Production      Financial      Mkt/Sales     Other
              Dept 1 & 2      Dept 3 & 5     Dept 4 & 6    Dept 9
              {BRANCH PROD} {BRANCH FIN}   {BRANCH MKT}  {BRANCH OTHER}
```

Fig. 13.6.

When the MENUBRANCH statement is executed, Symphony displays in the control panel the menu beginning at the cell ROTEX_MENU.

Note: The **R**ange **N**ame **L**abels **R**ight command is used to assign the name ROTEX_MENU to the cell in which Production resides. Production is the first menu item. If the range you name in the MENUBRANCH statement does not refer to the first menu item (or to the entire range of menu items), you will get the error message "Illegal MENUBRANCH/MENUCALL menu."

When Symphony first displays the menu, it appears in the control panel as follows:

    Dept 1 & 2
    Production Financial Mkt/Sales Other

The first line is a capsule description of the highlighted menu item in the line below. As you move the cursor to the right to highlight other menu items, the capsule description changes. For instance, when you move the cursor to **F**inancial, the capsule description "Dept 3 & 5" appears.

Now, suppose you want to select the second menu item (**Financial**). You select it the same way you do any Symphony menu item, by pressing RETURN after you've located the cursor on your choice, or by entering the first letter of the menu item. The menus that you create with the Symphony Command Language are just like the Symphony command menus.

After you've selected **F**inancial from the menu, the next statement to be executed is {BRANCH FIN}. If you press the Esc (Escape) key, however, Symphony executes the line directly below the MENU-BRANCH statement, {BRANCH FINISH}.

Be careful to choose option names that begin with different letters. If you have two or more options in a menu with the same first letter and try to use the first-letter technique, Symphony will automatically select the first option it finds with the letter you specified.

The MENUCALL Command

The MENUCALL option is like MENUBRANCH except that Symphony executes the menu macro as a subroutine. Suppose you replace the MENUBRANCH command in figure 13.6 with a MENU-CALL. (See fig. 13.7.)

```
MAIN    {MENUCALL ROTEX_MENU}
        {BRANCH FINISH}
```

ROTEX_MENU	Production	Financial	Mkt/Sales	Other
	Dept 1 & 2	Dept 3 & 5	Dept 4 & 6	Dept 9
	{BRANCH PROD}	{BRANCH FIN}	{BRANCH MKT}	{BRANCH OTHER}

```
FIN     {DOWN 4}
        {RETURN}
```

Fig. 13.7.

When you use a MENUCALL, Symphony returns to the statement immediately following the MENUCALL whenever it reads a blank cell or a {RETURN}. For example, suppose you select the Financial menu option, which causes Symphony to branch to FIN. The first statement in FIN moves the cursor down four rows. When Symphony encounters the RETURN statement, though, the flow of execution shifts back to the statement following the MENUCALL, the {BRANCH FINISH} statement.

Keep in mind that pressing Esc has the same effect with MENUCALL as it does with MENUBRANCH. Execution shifts to the statement following the MENUCALL statement.

The advantage of MENUCALL is that you can call the same menu from several different places in a macro. This is the advantage you get from using subroutines in general.

Subroutines

The MENUCALL statement should give you some feel for calling subroutines. However, there is usually quite a bit more involved in calling standard (nonmenu) subroutines.

Calling a subroutine is as easy as enclosing the name of a routine in braces (for example, {TOTALS}). When Symphony encounters a name in braces, the program shifts execution to the named routine. Then when the routine is finished (when Symphony encounters a blank cell or a {RETURN}), execution shifts back to where it originally left.

You can duplicate a simple subroutine by using two BRANCH statements. Figure 13.8 shows an example.

Calling a Simple Subroutine		Using Branching to Produce the Same Effect	
MAIN	.	MAIN	.
	.		.
	{TOTALS}		{BRANCH TOTALS}
	{BREAKON}	BACK	{BREAKON}
	{QUIT}		{QUIT}
TOTALS	.	TOTALS	.
	.		.
	.		.
	{RETURN}		{BRANCH BACK}

Fig. 13.8.

By naming the {BREAKON} statement BACK, you can have Symphony branch to BACK when TOTALS is completed. But suppose you want to call TOTALS again from somewhere else in the macro. Unless you want Symphony to branch to BACK again, you must change the BRANCH statement at the end of the routine. This requirement severely restricts the usefulness of the double-branch method. However, by using a subroutine, you can call the subroutine from different places in the macro without having to change the routine's statements each time.

Passing Arguments

Besides including the name of the routine when you make a subroutine call, you can also include arguments. The full form of the command is

{routine-name optional-argument1,optional-argument2...}

Suppose you have an application where you must repeatedly convert strings to numbers and display the numbers in the Currency format. Rather than enter the same code at several different places in the macro, you decide to write a subroutine. Figure 13.9 shows how the subroutine might appear.

Notice that the statement in the MAIN routine refers to a subroutine named STR_2_NO. The arguments that are passed to STR_2_NO

Since there is not enough space on a single typeset line to place all the characters that appear on one line on the screen, carryover lines are indented.

```
MAIN                        .
                            .
                            .
                   {STR_2_NO 123,RETURN_NUMBER}
                            .
                            .
STR_2_NO           {DEFINE SEND_STRING:STRING,
                      RETURN_NUMBER:VALUE}
                   {GOTO}RETURN_NUMBER~
                   +@VALUE(SEND_STRING)~
                   {MENU}fc~~
                   {RETURN}
```

Fig. 13.9.

include the string "123" and RETURN_NUMBER (the location where the formatted number is to be stored).

The STR_2_NO subroutine begins with a DEFINE statement. In fact, any subroutine composed of passed arguments must begin with a DEFINE statement. The DEFINE statement allocates storage locations for subroutine arguments that do not already have them. In this example, the string "123" does not have a location. Therefore, the location named SEND_STRING is used. The location name is used in the body of the subroutine wherever an operation is performed on the string.

Whenever you use a location name, such as SEND_STRING, in the DEFINE statement, make sure that you use the SHEET **R**ange **N**ame **C**reate command to assign the name to an actual cell. Where you locate the cell is up to you. However, if you forget to name a cell SEND_STRING, Symphony will issue the error message "Macro: Missing argument in DEFINE" when the DEFINE statement is encountered.

Notice the :STRING suffix that appears after the location name SEND_STRING in the DEFINE statement. This indicates to Symphony that the argument being passed to the subroutine is a label (123). Another suffix option is :VALUE, which follows the second argument in the DEFINE statement, RETURN_NUMBER. This suffix tells Symphony that it should expect a number as the second argument. (If you do not use a suffix, Symphony expects a label as the argument.)

If you supply the wrong suffix for an argument, Symphony may not work the way you expect. For example, the program may treat your numbers as strings in the formulas that follow the DEFINE. However, you may be able to get away with using what appears to be an improper suffix in certain instances. For example, you can use the :STRING suffix with RETURN_NUMBER in the current example. Symphony still produces the desired results. Try experimenting with the suffix option to see how Symphony reacts to your applications.

When you are passing arguments to a subroutine, always make sure the locations in the subroutine call match exactly the locations in the DEFINE statement. For example, if you use the name RE-TURN_NUMBER as the second argument in the subroutine call above, and you use another name (such as NUMBER) in the DEFINE statement, Symphony will issue the error message "Macro: Missing argument in DEFINE." However, if you use actual values in the subroutine call, you do not have to worry about this problem.

Resetting the Subroutine Stack

Just as you can call subroutines from the main macro program, you can also call one subroutine from another. In fact, as Symphony moves from one subroutine to the next, the program saves the addresses of where it has been. This technique is called *stacking*, or *saving addresses on a stack*. By saving the addresses on a stack, Symphony can trace its way back through the subroutine calls to the main macro program.

If you decide that you don't want Symphony to return by the path it came, you can use the RESTART command to eliminate the stack. You will not need to use this command until you are an expert at writing macros. Once you reach this point, though, this command is very helpful.

Ending a Subroutine

The normal way to end a subroutine is with a RETURN statement. When Symphony reads the RETURN, it returns to the main program (or other subroutine) from which it was called. Do not confuse RETURN with QUIT, however. QUIT ends the macro completely.

Symphony also ends a subroutine when the program encounters a cell that is not a label or a string formula. For example, if Symphony encounters a number, it will leave the subroutine.

Keywords for Testing Keyboard Input

Unlike 1-2-3 macros, Symphony offers several special command keywords for testing keyboard input. These keywords make it easy to perform simple edit checks on the input and to store it in the spreadsheet.

The GET, GETLABEL, and GETNUMBER Commands

Suppose you are writing an inventory macro and want to prompt the user to make a one-keystroke choice to enter data on premium- or regular-quality widgets. Figure 13.10 shows how you might prompt the user.

Since there is not enough space on a single typeset line to place all the characters that appear on one line on the screen, carryover lines are indented.

WIDGETS	{GOTO}MAIN~
	Enter (R)egular or (P)remium~
	{GET CODE}
	{IF CODE="R"#OR#CODE="r"}
	{BRANCH REG}
	{IF CODE="P"#OR#CODE="p"}
	{BRANCH PREM}
	{BEEP}Incorrect entry, press
	RETURN to try again~{?}~
	{BRANCH WIDGETS}
MAIN	Enter (R)egular or (P)remium
CODE	p
REG	{BIGLEFT}{QUIT}
PREM	{BIGRIGHT}{QUIT}

Fig. 13.10.

The GET command is used here to pause for a RETURN key and to store that entry in a cell named CODE. Notice that the macro enters the user-prompt in the cell named MAIN. If you want to have a prompt appear in the control panel rather than in the spreadsheet, you must use the GETLABEL or GETNUMBER keywords.

Suppose in another inventory model you want to prompt the user for a part description. You can use the GETLABEL command to accomplish this. The general form of the command is

> {GETLABEL prompt,location}

Figure 13.11 shows how you can use the command.

          WIDGETS2   {GETLABEL "Enter the description: ",
                               DESC}
                            {IF DESC="Round"#OR#DESC=
                               "round"}{BRANCH WRONG}

          WRONG   {BEEP}
                            {GETLABEL "NO ROUND WIDGETS!,
                               press Return",DESC}
                            {BRANCH WIDGETS2}

          DESC

Since there is not enough space on a single typeset line to place all the characters that appear on one line on the screen, carryover lines are indented.

Fig. 13.11.

As figure 13.11 shows, you can use GETLABEL to inform you when you make an incorrect entry after a GETLABEL (or any other) command. Remember, though, that whatever you enter in response to the prompt is stored in DESC.

Another variant on the simple GET command is the GETNUMBER command. GETNUMBER is exactly like GETLABEL but is used for numbers. According to Lotus, if you enter a value that is not a valid number entry, the GETNUMBER command does not accept the input and reenters the prompt in the command line. We found, however, in the early production version of Symphony that the GETNUMBER command accepted any entry. Check your own copy of Symphony to see how the GETNUMBER command behaves. Figure 13.12 shows how you can use the GETNUMBER in a third inventory model.

Since there is not enough space on a single typeset line to place all the characters that appear on one line on the screen, carryover lines are indented.

WIDGETS3	{GETNUMBER "Enter the part number: ",PART_NO} {IF PART_NO<=0#OR#PART_NO> 9999}{BRANCH WRONG_NO}
WRONG_NO	{GETNUMBER "Invalid number, hit return",PART_NO} {BRANCH WIDGETS3}
PART_NO	23

Fig. 13.12.

The LOOK Command

Typically, after a macro has begun its execution, you can interrupt it only with Ctrl-Break. Otherwise, the characters you enter are stored until the macro completes its execution. However, Symphony offers a special command, the LOOK command, which temporarily interrupts processing. The general form of the command is

{LOOK location}

As a simple example of the LOOK command, try the example in figure 13.13. This macro causes the speaker to beep until you press any key. Each time the LOOK command is encountered, Symphony checks the location called INTERRUPT. If there is no entry there, the macro branches back to MAIN. Otherwise, when you press a key, the message from the GETLABEL command appears in the control panel.

Since there is not enough space on a single typeset line to place all the characters that appear on one line on the screen, carryover lines are indented.

| MAIN | {BEEP}
{LOOK INTERRUPT}
{IF INTERRUPT=""}{BRANCH MAIN}
{GETLABEL "NO MORE, PLEASE!", MESSAGE} |
| MESSAGE
INTERRUPT | |

Fig. 13.13.

A more helpful use of the LOOK command occurs when you want to build a lengthy macro for phoning and logging into a time-sharing service, and you want to be able to interrupt processing at certain points in the macro. You can enter a LOOK statement, similar to the one that appears in figure 13.13, at several different places in the macro. Then, if you press a key, the macro stops. If you do not touch the keyboard, the macro continues processing. In this example, the LOOK command is preferable to the GET command because the GET command always stops the macro to wait for an entry.

Keywords for Storing and Deleting

Symphony has several different commands for storing and deleting the contents of cells. These commands do not work with input directly from the keyboard but with values already in the spreadsheet.

The LET Command

The simplest of the storing commands, the LET command, stores a number or a label entry in a cell. The general form of the LET command is

> {LET location,number} or {LET location,string}

As mentioned earlier, this command is particularly useful for initializing cells used as variables. To show two good uses of the LET command, the Factorial example used earlier is repeated in figure 13.14.

```
MAIN            {LET PREVIOUS NUMBER,1}
                {GETNUMBER "Enter number: ",
                    FACTORIAL}
                {FOR COUNTER,1,FACTORIAL,1,
                    FACT_RTN}
                +PREVIOUS NUMBER~

FACT_RTN        {LET PREVIOUS NUMBER,+PREVIOUS
                    NUMBER*COUNTER}
                {RETURN}
```

Since there is not enough space on a single typeset line to place all the characters that appear on one line on the screen, carryover lines are indented.

Fig. 13.14.

In this example the first LET command uses a simple number to initialize the cell called PREVIOUS NUMBER. In the second LET command a formula is used.

You can also use strings with the LET command. In fact, you can even use a string formula. For example, if the cell named FIRST contains the string "Robert" and LAST holds the string "Hamer", the statement

{LET NAME,FIRST&" "&LAST}

will store "Robert Hamer" in NAME.

Like the DEFINE command, the LET command allows you to specify :STRING and :VALUE suffixes after the string or number argument. If neither suffix is used (which is usually the case), Symphony tries to figure out on its own whether the argument is a string or a number. If Symphony can't determine which the argument is, the program chooses string.

The PUT Command

The LET command works fine for storing a number or label entry in a specific target cell. However, LET does not work when the target location is a range of cells. For this situation, the PUT command is used. The general form of the PUT command is

{PUT location,column-number,row-number,expression}

where location is a range of cells, column- and row- numbers are 0 or a positive integer, and expression is a number or label. Figure 13.15 shows the results of different variations of the command. Keep in mind that the row and column numbers follow the same conventions that functions follow. (The first column is number 0, the second is number 1, etc.)

Statement Result

{PUT A10..H40,0,1,21}	Places the number 21 in the cell A11
{PUT A10..H40,4,6,Jack}	Places the label "Jack" in the cell E16
{PUT A10..H40,7,30,4^2}	Places the number 16 in the cell H40

Fig. 13.15.

The CONTENTS Command

Experienced 1-2-3 users can imagine the many macro statements that would be required to copy a number in one cell to another cell, convert the copied number to a string, and then change the format of the string to display as though it were a formatted number. In Symphony, all these steps are accomplished with one command, the CONTENTS command. The general form of the command is

{CONTENTS destination-loc,source-loc,width-number,
    format-number}

The width-number and format-number are optional.

Suppose, for example, that you want to copy the number 123.456, which resides in cell A21, to cell B25 and change the number to a string while you copy. The statement for this step is

{CONTENTS B25,A21}

The contents of cell B25 will be displayed as the string "123.456" with a left-aligned label-prefix character.

Next, suppose you want to change the width of the string when you copy it. Rather than have the string display as "123.456", you want it to display as "123.4". You will get the desired result if you change the statement to the following:

{CONTENTS B25,A21,5}

This second statement uses a width of 5 to display the string.

Finally, suppose you want to change the display format of the string while you copy it and change its width. The following string will change the display format to Currency 0.

{CONTENTS B25,A21,5,32}

The number used for the format-number in this statement was taken from the list of CONTENTS statement format numbers that appears in figure 13.16. The result of the statement is the number $123.

Code	Destination String's Numeric Display Format
0	Fixed, 0 decimal places
1-15	Fixed, 1 to 15 decimal places
16-31	Scientific, 0 to 15 decimal places

32-47	Currency, 0 to 15 decimal places
48-63	%, 0 to 15 decimal places
64-79	Punctuated, 0 to 15 decimal places
112	+/-
113	General
114	D1 (DD-MMM-YY)
115	D2 (DD-MMM)
116	D3 (MMM-YY)
121	D4 (Full International)
122	D5 (Partial International)
119	T1 (HH:MM:SS AM/PM)
120	T2 (HH:MM AM/PM)
123	T3 (Full International)
124	T4 (Partial International)
117	Literal
118	Hidden
127	Window's default display format

Fig. 13.16.

The following are more examples of the CONTENTS statement with 123.456 as the number in cell A21.

{CONTENTS B45,A21}	Displays the number 123.45 in cell B45 if the width of that cell is 6.
{CONTENTS B25,A21,4}	Displays the number as **** if the default width of the cell is 4 and the display format is Fixed 2.
{CONTENTS B25,A21,5,0}	Displays the number 123.4 in cell B25 if the default width of B25 is 9.

One of the most convenient uses of the CONTENTS statement is to convert a lengthy numeric formula to a string that appears in the Literal format. This ability is particularly useful for debugging purposes.

The BLANK Command

Blanking out a range of cells, A1..A10, for example, can be accomplished by the following macro statement:

{TYPE}s{MENU}eA1.A10~

This statement is fairly simple, but very inconvenient if you are not in a SHEET window. The statement switches you to a SHEET window and then invokes the **E**rase command. You have to use another macro command to return to the previous window type. To blank out a range of cells in a more convenient fashion, you can use the BLANK command. The general form of the command is

{BLANK location}

To blank out the range A1..A10, use the statement

{BLANK A1..A10}.

Maintenance-Oriented Keywords and Commands

Maintenance-oriented keywords form a catch-all group that includes keywords for commands ranging from sounding your computer's speaker to controlling the recalculation of the spreadsheet.

Sounding the Speaker

By using the BEEP command in a macro, you can have Symphony sound your computer's speaker. A good time to use the BEEP command is when the user has made an error in entering data. (For a good example of how and when to use the BEEP command, see fig. 13.9.)

Changing the Indicator

If you want to change the indicator in the upper right corner of the screen to display a message you choose, you can use the INDICATE command. The general form of the command is

{INDICATE string}

where the string can be any length up to five characters. If the string is longer, Symphony uses the last five characters only. Suppose, for example, that you want to display the message START in the upper right corner of the screen. You can use the following INDICATE statement

{INDICATE START}

The START message will remain displayed until you exit from Symphony unless you use another INDICATE statement. For example, to blank out the indicator, you use

{INDICATE""}

To clear the indicator, you use

{INDICATE}

When you use the INDICATE statement, remember that you have to enter the actual string in the statement. You cannot use a cell address.

Using the WINDOWSON and WINDOWSOFF Commands

One of the big problems with 1-2-3, a problem that Symphony has inherited, is that the screen tends to shift around a great deal when you execute macros; and with complex macros, this problem can reach extremes. By using the WINDOWSOFF command, you can freeze the lower part of the screen and have just the control panel show the changes that occur as a result of the macro steps.

This feature is particularly helpful if the purpose of your macro is to produce a multiwindow display. While you are building up the display in the macro, you can use the WINDOWSOFF command to prevent your having to watch all the shifting screens that must take place. After your display is set, you can issue the WINDOWSON command to restore the normal activity of the display screen. Figure 13.17 shows how you can use both the WINDOWSOFF and WINDOWSON commands.

However, if something goes wrong with your macro while the WINDOWSOFF command is in effect, you can get into trouble. Unless you have a simple one-line macro already preset for issuing

```
COMPARE              {WINDOWSOFF}
                     {SERVICES}wuPROFORMA_SALES~
                     {SERVICES}wuACTUAL_SALES~
                     {SERVICES}wuLINE_CHART~
                     {WINDOWSON}
```

Fig. 13.17.

a WINDOWSON statement, you may have to reboot Symphony and start your macro over again.

Using the PANELOFF and PANELON Commands

You can also control the redrawing of the control panel with the PANELOFF and PANELON commands. The PANELOFF and PANELON commands behave exactly the same way as the WINDOWSOFF and WINDOWSON commands.

Eliminating the Use of Ctrl-Break

The easiest way to stop a macro is to issue a Ctrl-Break command. However, Symphony can eliminate the effect of a Ctrl-Break while a macro is executing. By including a BREAKOFF command in your macro statement, you can prevent the user from stopping the macro before its completion. Note: Before you use a BREAKOFF statement, you must be certain that the macro is fully debugged.

To restore the effect of Ctrl-Break, use the BREAKON command. In fact, you will probably want a simple one-line macro that issues a BREAKON, just in case something should happen to your original macro during execution. You also want to make sure that the last statement in your macro before QUIT is BREAKON. Figure 13.18 demonstrates how you can use the BREAKOFF and BREAKON commands.

Using the WAIT Command to Delay Execution

The WAIT command in a macro can delay the execution of the statements that follow the WAIT until an appointed time of the day. The general form of the command is

```
MAIN              {BREAKOFF}
                  {SERVICES}fccerfSAMPLES.WRK~
                  .
                  .
                  .
                  {BREAKON}
                  {QUIT}
```

Fig. 13.18.

{WAIT serial-time-number}

For example, suppose you want to delay until after prime time the execution of a macro that accesses an information service and captures stock information. You can use a macro similar to the one that appears in figure 13.19. You can execute this macro when you leave work at the end of the day, and Symphony will wait until 10:00 p.m. to finish the rest of the statements.

Since there is not enough space on a single typeset line to place all the characters that appear on one line on the screen, carryover lines are indented.

```
WAIT_2_PHONE      {WAIT @TIME(22,00,00)}
                  {PHONE PHONE_NO}{BRANCH
                     NO_GO}
                  {BRANCH MESSAGES}

NO_GO             {GETLABEL "COULD NOT
                     CONNECT!",MSG}
```

Fig. 13.19.

Notice that the serial-time-number is a function in this example. It can also be an equation, such as @NOW+@TIME(0,1,0). This equation will cause Symphony to wait until an hour from the current time before executing the statements that follow the WAIT. (See the comprehensive model in the next chapter for more on the use of WAIT.)

New with Symphony

Phoning from within a Macro

Symphony has a special macro command that allows you to phone a remote computer without having to switch to a COMM window. The command is PHONE, and its general form is

{PHONE phone-number-string}

Figure 13.19 shows an example of how to use the PHONE command. Notice that the phone-number-string is the range name PHONE_NO. You can also use a string formula for the argument.

Notice the BRANCH statement that follows the PHONE statement in figure 13.19. If Symphony is unable to make a connection, it executes the statement following the PHONE statement on the same line (in this case, {BRANCH NO_GO}). However, if a connection is made, the next statement that Symphony executes is on the line below the PHONE statement.

Sending Messages to a Remote Computer

*New
with
Symphony*

You can also send single-line messages to a remote computer without having to switch to a COMM window. The command to send messages is HANDSHAKE, and its general form is

> {HANDSHAKE send-string,receive-string,seconds,
>   capture-location}

Let's expand the example in figure 13.18. Suppose after establishing a connection, you want to send all the log-in messages and menu responses for calling up the stock information on the remote system. The HANDSHAKE statements in figure 13.20 show how you might do this.

```
WAIT_2_PHONE     {WAIT @TIME(22,00,00)}
                 {PHONE PHONE_NO}{BRANCH
                     NO_GO}
                 {HANDSHAKE "CPS\013","User
                     ID:",10}
                 {HANDSHAKE "76030.10\013",
                     "Password:",10}

                     .

                 {HANDSHAKE "\013","!",240,
                     CAPTURE_RANGE}
                 {HANDSHAKE "bye\013","Off",20}

NO_GO            {GETLABEL "COULD NOT
                     CONNECT!",MSG}
```

*Since there is not enough
space on a single typeset line
to place all the characters
that appear on one line on
the screen, carryover lines
are indented.*

Fig. 13.20.

In the first HANDSHAKE statement, notice that the send-string argument (the string you wish to send) includes the string CPS followed by the decimal ASCII code for the RETURN character (\013). Note: Do not forget the decimal ASCII code, or the HAND-SHAKE statement will not work properly.

The second argument, the return-string, is the string you expect from the remote computer in response to the send-string. The third argument is the number of seconds that you want to allocate for sending the send-string and receiving the receive-string. This is the maximum amount of time you want Symphony to take to complete the transaction. Symphony moves immediately to the next statement when the receive-string is read.

The second HANDSHAKE statement is similar to the first. However, it sends the User ID number and receives the next prompt from the remote computer, a prompt to enter the password.

The third HANDSHAKE statement is only slightly different from the first two. Because it includes a capture-location argument, issuing this statement from a COMM window will cause Symphony to save the text that precedes the receive string on the same line (the text that precedes "!") in the capture-location. In actual practice, you will rarely need to include a capture-location argument. Do not confuse this argument with the capture range required for capturing large amounts of data.

The combination of the WAIT, PHONE, and HANDSHAKE statements makes the delayed accessing of remote systems quite easy. See the comprehensive model in the next chapter for more on all three statements.

Controlling Recalculation

1-2-3 users may recall that you cannot recalculate just a portion of the 1-2-3 worksheet. When you press the CALC key in 1-2-3, the program recalculates the entire sheet. Symphony, on the other hand, allows you to recalculate just a portion of the sheet. The commands for recalculation are

{RECALC location}   {RECALCCOL location}

These two commands differ in their method of recalculation. RECALC recalculates the sheet by row, and RECALCCOL recalculates by column. In practical terms, if the formula you wish to recalculate depends on cells that are above and to the right (and whose values you've changed), use the RECALC command. However, if the formula depends on cells that are below and to the left, then use RECALCCOL. There is, however, a situation where neither of the commands works properly: when the formula depends on cells below and to the right. In this case, you must use the CALC key indicator, which recalculates the entire worksheet. Figure 13.21 shows the different situations with the proper commands to use.

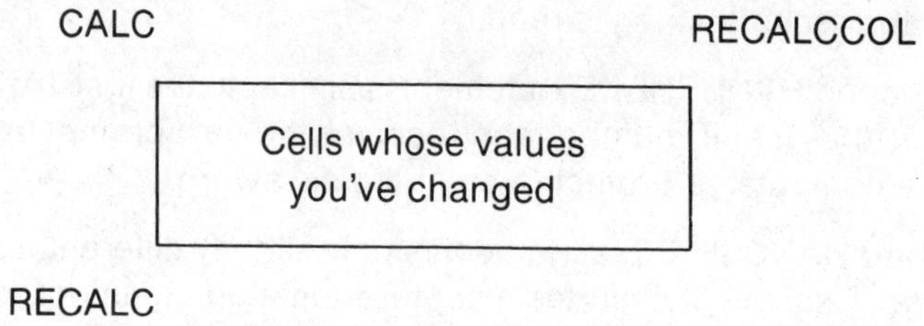

CALC   RECALCCOL

```
            ┌─────────────────────────┐
            │                         │
            │     Cells whose values  │
            │       you've changed    │
            │                         │
            └─────────────────────────┘
```

RECALC

Fig. 13.21.

Recalculating just a portion of the worksheet is risky. You should always make sure that all formulas in a worksheet reflect the changes that you have made. Therefore, the best time to use RECALC and RECALCCOL is only when the CALC key command results in a macro that is unbearably slow. In any case, before you use the special recalculation commands, make sure that you understand fully their effects on your total model.

The RECALC (or RECALCCOL) command is crucial when you use the LET or GETNUMBER macro commands. When you use these commands, Symphony does not reflect the current data in some situations. A good example of when the RECALC command is essential appears in figure 13.27. Without the RECALC statement, that macro will always reflect the data that was entered in a previous loop.

Names of Macros

After the macro has been entered in the worksheet as one or more long labels, the macro must be given a name. Ranges containing macros are assigned names just like every other range. The only difference is that the name assigned to a macro can be of two different types, depending on how you want to invoke the macro.

There are two ways to invoke a macro. The first way is to hold down the Alt key and simultaneously press a single key representing the name of the macro (for example, Alt + A). In order for a macro to be invoked by this technique, the macro's name must be a single alphanumeric character preceded by a backslash (\). Following are several legal and illegal macro names:

Legal Names	Illegal Names
\A	\?
\b	\ABC
\1	ABC

Although naming a macro ABC is illegal when you want to invoke the macro using the Alt key, the name is acceptable for a macro invoked by the second method. By pressing the User key, you can execute a macro with a name up to 15 characters long (the standard limit for range names).

When you press the User key, a User indicator appears at the lower right corner of the screen. You can then enter the name of the macro you want to execute. As you enter the characters in the name, they appear in place of the User indicator at the bottom of the screen. If you enter a macro with a name longer than four characters, the name scrolls across the indicator.

Which of the two techniques is better for naming and invoking macros is open to debate. The Alt key technique is easier for invoking a macro but is not good for documentation purposes. You can easily forget the name of a macro when it is only one character long. On the other hand, the User key does a better job of documenting but is more difficult to invoke. Which one you should use depends on your personal style. You will probably use a mixture of both.

Suppose that you are naming the Factorial macro in figure 13.3. Figure 13.22 shows how the macro might appear in a spreadsheet. To assign the name, invoke the SHEET **R**ange **N**ame **C**reate command. Next, enter the selected name, MAIN, and press the RETURN key. Finally, Symphony prompts you for the range to name. If the cursor is currently on the cell AB1, you can simply press RETURN to assign the name to the cell. Otherwise, you can type the cell coordinates from the keyboard.

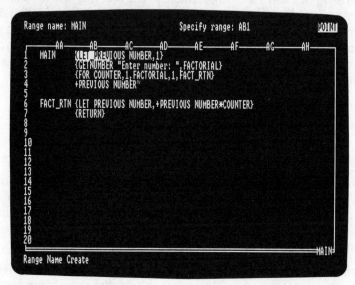

Fig. 13.22.

To name the MAIN macro, you need to assign only the first cell in the range that contains the macro, but there is no reason why a name cannot be assigned to the entire range AB1..AB4 (or even AB1..AB7).

Another variation on the SHEET **R**ange **N**ame command can be useful when dealing with macros. The **R**ange **N**ame **L**abels **R**ight command allows you to name a range, using the contents of the cell immediately to its left. To use this command to name the macro in figure 13.22, position the cursor at cell AA1 and issue the command.

The SHEET **R**ange **N**ame **L**abels command can be used in a variety of ways. If you are documenting your macros properly, you will already have the names in the sheet; so the **L**abels option is a simple and convenient way to name the macros. If you import macros from an external library file, you can use the **L**abels command to create quickly names for the imported macros.

Macro Locations

In most cases, you will want to place your macros outside the area that will be occupied by your main model. This maneuver will help you avoid accidentally overwriting macros as you create your model.

Remember that placing your macros outside the basic rectangle that contains your model can consume large amounts of memory. If you are working with a large model and a relatively small amount of memory, be careful. When the macros are outside the normal rectangle and you press End and then Home, the cursor will move to the lower right corner of the entire spreadsheet, including the macro area, instead of to the lower right corner of the model. This diminishes the usefulness of the End-Home key sequence.

One solution is to put your macros in column AA of your models. This column is a good location for two reasons. Models rarely require more than 26 columns, so you don't have to worry about overwriting the macros with the model; and column AA is not so far from the origin that it causes too much memory to be lost.

There is no rule that says you must place your macros in the same column in every model. In models that you'll use more than once, you'll want to place the macros wherever it is most convenient. In small models, there is no need to waste several columns by placing the macros in column AA. For instance, when all the columns have a width of 9, you may want to put your macros in column I, which lies just off the home screen.

Another good technique is to name the area of your spreadsheet that contains the macros. This measure allows you to access a macro quickly with the GOTO command and the macro's range name.

A Macro Library

You may want to create a macro library to give you easy access to copies of your most useful macros. By saving your macros in a library file, you can easily read them into the current file with the SERVICES **F**ile **C**ombine **C**opy **N**amed-Area command. Just make sure that you have named the area that each macro occupies before you issue the command. Often the copies that you read in will require some minor modifications to make them run in the current model. However, modifying a library macro is usually far easier than re-creating a macro from scratch.

Macro Documentation

Professional programmers usually write programs that are self-documented, or internally documented. This means that the program contains comments that help explain each step. In BASIC, these comments are in REM (REMark) statements.

It is also possible to document your Symphony macros. The best way to do this is to place the comments next to the macro steps in the column to the right of the macro. For example, in the simple macro in figure 13.23, the macro name is in column AA, the macro itself is in column AB, and the comments are in column AD.

Including comments in your macros will make them far easier to use. Comments are especially helpful when you have created complex macros that are important to the overall design of the worksheet. Suppose that you have a complex macro that you have not looked at for a month, and you decide you want to modify the macro. Without built-in comments, you may have a difficult time remembering what each step of the macro does.

Range Names in Macros

One of the biggest problems with Symphony macros is that the cell references included in macros are always absolute. They do not change when cells are moved about or deleted from the sheet. For example, the simple macro

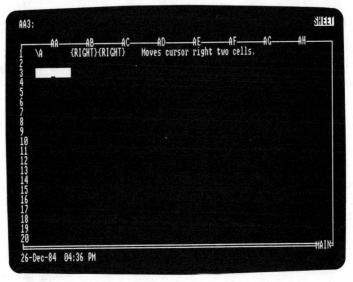

Fig. 13.23.

'{BLANK A6}

erases the contents of cell A6. But suppose you move the contents of cell A6 to cell B6 by means of the macro command

'{MENU}mA6~B6~

Because you will want to blank the same contents from the sheet, you might expect the macro to say

'{BLANK B6}

If you try this, however, you will see that the macro has not changed. Actually, this makes perfect sense. A macro is nothing but a label, and you don't expect other labels to change when the sheet is changed.

The absolute cell references within macros provide a strong argument in favor of using range names. Because a range name remains associated with the same range even if the range is moved, range names within macros (and other formulas) will follow the cells to which they apply.

Macro Debugging

Almost no program works perfectly the first time. In nearly every case, there are errors that will cause the program to malfunction. Programmers call these problems *bugs*, and the process of eliminating them *debugging the program*.

Like programs written in other programming languages, Symphony macros usually need to be debugged before they can be used. Symphony has an extremely useful tool that helps simplify debugging: the STEP function (Alt + F7). When Symphony is in the Step mode, all macros are executed one step at a time. Symphony pauses after each keystroke stored in a macro. This means that the user can follow along step by step with the macro as it executes.

Try running through a macro using Step mode. To invoke the single-step mode, press Alt + F7. Symphony will place a Step indicator at the bottom of the screen. The macro will start executing, but only one step at a time. After each step, the macro will pause and wait for you to type any keystroke before going on.

As you step through the macro, you will see each command appear in the control panel. When an error occurs in a macro, it is easy to pinpoint the location. Once an error is identified, you can exit from the Step mode by pressing Alt + F7 again. Then, abort the macro by pressing Esc.

Sample Macros for the Different Work Environments

Now that you have a feel for all the different macro commands available in Symphony, as well as a good general background with Symphony's work environments, you are probably thinking about ways to apply macros. This section of the chapter should help you conceptualize some of your thoughts. It gives practical, yet simple, examples of macros for all of Symphony's different work environments.

A Macro for the SHEET Environment

Certainly you can think of many situations where you can use macros in the SHEET environment. However, one particularly nice macro for the SHEET environment is a dynamic amortization-table macro. The macro that appears in figure 13.24 will create a variable number of line entries, depending on how many months you want to include in the amortization table in figure 13.25.

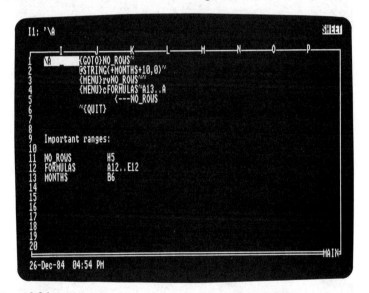

```
I1: '\A                                              SHEET
    I       J        K        L      M     N     O      P
1  \A       {GOTO}NO_ROWS~
2           @STRING(+MONTHS+10,0)~
3           {MENU}rvNO_ROWS~~
4           {MENU}cFORMULAS~A13..A
5                       <---NO_ROWS
6           ~{QUIT}
7
8
9  Important ranges:
10
11 NO_ROWS         H5
12 FORMULAS        A12..E12
13 MONTHS          B6
14
15
16
17
18
19
20
                                                    MAIN
26-Dec-84  04:54 PM
```

Fig. 13.24.

The first step in the macro is to go to the cell called NO_ROWS, cell H5 in the macro, and enter a formula to convert the number of months to a string. The third line in the macro uses the SHEET **R**ange **V**alues command to convert this formula to an actual value. Therefore, when the SHEET **C**opy command is started in the fourth line of the macro, the value that completes it in the fifth line is a string. Figure 13.26 shows an example of the results.

The following conditions are necessary when you use the macro with the spreadsheets in figures 13.25 and 13.26.

Columns B11 to E11 must be set to Currency format set to two decimal places. The width of columns B and E must be set to 11. On a 512K system you will have enough memory for approximately 323 payments before memory is full.

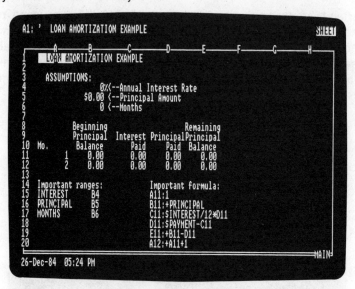

Fig. 13.25.

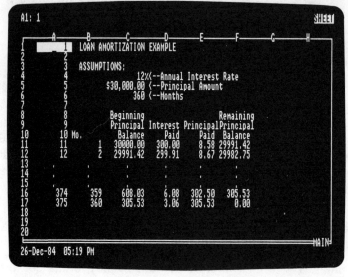

Fig. 13.26.

New
with
Symphony

Macros for the DOC Environment

The Symphony word-processing environment contains most of the operations found in stand-alone word-processing programs. However, you can simplify many word-processing operations when you use Symphony's Command Language to create macros. Many of these macros can be created by Symphony's Learn mode alone; others can be constructed by using Symphony's Learn mode, then editing the macro to make changes and additions. Once you have had an opportunity to experiment with and create Symphony macros, you can begin to design your own. This section provides examples of simple macros that increase the power and capability of Symphony's DOC environment.

All the macros were created using Symphony's Learn mode. Because word-processing macros are easy to create and can be used in many editing operations, we have included more examples of word-processing macros than of other types. You may find experimenting with word-processing macros a good way to introduce yourself to Symphony's macro capability.

As discussed earlier in this chapter, you create macros in the Learn mode by following this general procedure:

1. If you are not already in a SHEET window, switch to a SHEET window by pressing the Type key.

2. Once you are in a SHEET window, select an area of your worksheet where Symphony can record keystrokes as you create each macro. This area should be located where it won't interfere with other data.

3. Set a Learn range where Symphony can create the macros that you enter. You set the Learn range by selecting SERVICES Settings Learn Range. When Symphony asks for a range, enter a range of rows (for example, J1..J25) that is large enough to accommodate all the keystrokes you will make when creating the macro. At first, it may be difficult to tell how much space you will need for the macro(s), so set a fairly large area.

4. After you have set the Learn range, return to your worksheet to begin entering the macro. Because you will be creating macros to use in a DOC environment, shift to a DOC window.

5. Press the Learn key and begin creating the macro. In some cases, it may be best for you to go through a dry run of all the keystrokes before you turn on the Learn mode. Going through a dry run can prevent you from having to do extensive editing on a macro or having to erase a macro and start again.

6. After you have created the macro, turn off the Learn mode by pressing the Learn key again.

7. Shift from the DOC mode to the SHEET mode, move the cursor to the area where the Learn range is located, and check the macro for any extra or wrong keystrokes.

8. In some cases, you may need to edit the macro by inserting {?} so that the macro will stop operations and allow you to enter a command or make a selection from a menu.

9. To assign a name to the macro, select SHEET **R**ange **N**ame. When assigning a name to your macro, you should follow these rules:

   • Assign a name using one of two methods. Either give the macro a descriptive name (for example, P-ERASE) or assign a name consisting of a backslash (\) followed by a letter or a number. If you use a name like P-ERASE, you can invoke the macro with the User key. If you name the macro with a backslash (\) and a letter or number, you can invoke the macro with Alt + the letter or number.

   • Assign a range name to the first cell of the macro.

   You can also name a macro by naming the Learn range before you begin to create the macro.

10. Return to the DOC mode to test the macro. To invoke the macro, press the User key (F7 on IBM and Compaq), enter the name of the macro, and press RETURN.

If you forget to set a Learn range before you begin to create the macro, Symphony will display the message "Learn range has not been defined" in the bottom left corner of your screen. If you don't have enough room in the Learn range for all the keystrokes, Symphony will display the "Learn range full" message at the bottom. When the Learn range is full, Symphony will stop entering keystrokes. To finish creating the macro, take note of the point when the message appears. Shift from the DOC to the SHEET mode and move the cell pointer to the Learn range. Extend the Learn range, and then continue creating the macro, beginning with the keystroke you were entering when Symphony displayed the "Learn range full" message.

The following macros provide automatic editing operations that you can use with Symphony's other editing commands.

Letter Reversal Macro

One useful editing macro is the Letter Reversal macro. With it, you can easily correct typographical errors or misspellings that involve reversed letters, for example, to correct the misspelling of the word *recieve* by transposing the *i* and *e*. (An explanation of the parts of the macro is provided on the right.)

{MENU}m~{LEFT}~   Select MENU; select MOVE; press
                               RETURN; move the cursor one
                               character to the left; press RETURN.

To create this macro, you, of course, use Symphony's Learn mode. After you have set the Learn range, make sure you are in the DOC mode before you begin to create the macro. Next, move the cursor to the second letter of the two that you want transposed. For example, when we created the Letter Reversal macro, we placed the cursor on the second *e* in *recieve*. Then turn on the Learn mode by pressing the Learn key.

With the Learn indicator displayed at the bottom of your screen, select the DOC menu. From the DOC menu, choose the **Move** command. When Symphony asks, "Move FROM what block?" press RETURN; and when Symphony asks, "Move TO where?" move the cursor one character to the left and press RETURN again. Then turn off the Learn mode by pressing the Learn key a second time. The Learn indicator at the bottom of your screen will go off.

With the Learn mode off, shift back to the SHEET mode and move the cell pointer to the Learn range. Next, assign a range name to the macro, as explained earlier. Finally, return to your DOC window to try the macro. When you use the macro, place the cursor on the second letter of the two that you want to reverse, press the User key, and enter the macro name.

Word Reversal Macro

Another useful macro for editing in a DOC window is the Word Reversal macro, which enables you transpose two words located next to each other. Like the Letter Reversal macro described above, the Word Reversal macro is created with the Learn mode.

{LEFT}{MENU}m{END} ~{END} {END} ~   Move cursor left;
                                           select MENU; select Move;
                                           press End, then space bar;
                                           press RETURN; press
                                           End, then space bar;
                                           press End, then space bar;
                                           press RETURN; then space bar.

When you use this macro, place the cursor on the first letter of the first word of the two you want to transpose. Press the User key and enter the macro name. The macro will reverse the words and leave the correct spacing between and around the two.

Line Erase Macro

When you are creating macros, your best strategy is to consider which of Symphony's operations you use over and over. Turning these operations into macros can save you considerable time.

As you recall from Chapter 7, erasing a line by means of Symphony's DOC **E**rase command or function key requires four keystrokes. A

Line Erase macro can reduce this to two keystrokes. Admittedly, this isn't much of a reduction, but you will find that for operations that you use frequently, a reduction of even two keystrokes is significant.

The Line Erase macro is

{END}{LEFT}{ERASE}{END}{RIGHT}~   Move cursor to beginning of line; select Erase; move cursor to end of line; press RETURN.

This macro will work when the cursor is anywhere in a line except on the first character.

Paragraph Erase Macro

The Line Erase macro is just one example of many editing macros you can create. If, for example, you find that you erase complete sentences often, you can create a macro for erasing sentences, depending on the kind of internal punctuation. Another useful erase macro is the Paragraph Erase macro.

{END}{UP}{ERASE}{END}{DOWN}~   Move cursor to beginning of paragraph; select Erase; move cursor to end of paragraph; press RETURN.

You can invoke this macro when the cursor is positioned anywhere in the paragraph except on the first character. Because the macro itself automatically places the cursor at the beginning of the paragraph, you can stop anywhere in a paragraph, invoke the macro, and let Symphony do the rest of the work for you.

Paragraph Move Macro

Like the DOC **E**rase command, the DOC **M**ove command provides many operations that you can simplify through macros. You can, for example, create macros for moving words, phrases, lines, or sentences (depending on the internal punctuation in these sentences). One useful macro involving the **M**ove command is the Paragraph Move macro.

{END}{UP}{MENU}m{END}{DOWN}~{?}

Move cursor to beginning of paragraph; select MENU; then **M**ove; move cursor to end of paragraph; press RETURN; stop for location of move.

Creating the Paragraph Move macro is somewhat different from creating the other macros because you will need to edit this macro. When you edit the macro, first make sure that no other keystrokes except those listed above have been entered after the ~ (RETURN) symbol. Depending on where you stopped the Learn mode when creating this macro, you may need to erase a few keystrokes after the ~. You must also enter the {?}, which stops the macro so that you can enter the location to which you want your paragraph moved.

Keep in mind that any macro involving variable selection, as the paragraph macro does, requires that you have the macro stop at the appropriate place so you can make a selection, enter data, or move the cursor before the macro continues. In some cases, this variable selection may occur at the end of the macro; when this happens, the macro will stop so that you can take over.

Invoke the Paragraph Move macro with the cursor placed anywhere in the paragraph except on the first character. The macro will execute until it reaches the "Move TO where?" prompt. At this point, you should move the cursor to the location in your document to which you want the paragraph moved. Finally, press RETURN to complete the move operation.

File Combine Macro

Chapter 7 discusses how you can combine text into the document you are working on. For example, you can create a file containing a paragraph or paragraphs that you want to use in various letters or other documents. A simple File Combine macro will enable you to copy easily these form paragraphs or sections of text into a letter or document.

Before you begin to create this macro, you should have already created the file containing the form paragraph or sections of text that you want to use repeatedly, for example, a product description you will want to use in many types of letters and promotional materials. The File Combine macro follows.

{SERVICES}fcc{?}~~{?}~	Select SERVICES File Combine Copy; stop for selection; press RETURN; press RETURN; stop for selection; press RETURN.

This macro can be used to copy an entire file into your document or to copy only a named range from a file. The first {?} in the macro lets you select either of the two operations: copying the entire file or copying only a named range.

If you find yourself frequently using the Entire-File option, you can edit the macro so that it no longer stops and waits for you to indicate which kind of copy you want. To edit the File Combine macro so that it automatically copies an entire file, erase the first {?} and replace it with e (Entire-File) or ~ (RETURN).

Start this macro by placing the cursor at the location in your document where you want the copied data to begin. Make sure that there is enough room in your document for the data so that the copied data will not overwrite other information. (See Chapter 6 for guidelines on using the File Combine command.)

Backward Replace Macro

As we mentioned in Chapter 7, Symphony's Replace command in the DOC menu will conduct a search-and-replace operation only forward from the cursor to the end of the DOC window. If you want to have Symphony search and replace from the beginning of your document to the end, the following macro will enable you to do so. Compared to manual operation, this macro saves you five keystrokes.

{HOME}{MENU}r{?}~{?}~a	Move cursor to beginning of the DOC window; select MENU, then Replace; stop for "Replace what?"; press RETURN; stop for "Replace it with what?"; press RETURN; search and replace all occurrences of string.

Like the other macros that contain {?}, the Backward Replace macro must be edited. After you turn off the Learn mode, erase any keystrokes that are not shown in the macro above and enter the two {?}s in their correct places.

There are two points to keep in mind about this macro. First, you can invoke this macro from any location in your text. However, if you want the search-and-replace operation to start from the beginning of your document, the restrict range for your DOC window must start with the beginning of your text. Second, the Backward Replace macro as shown will conduct a nonstop search-and-replace operation throughout the document. Once you invoke the macro and indicate what Symphony should search and replace, the macro will automatically search and replace through the entire document until the macro finds the last occurrence of the string.

Personal Spelling Checker Macro

Although a spelling checker will be available through Lotus Development, you can create your own personal spelling-checker macro. The Personal Spelling Checker macro involves creating a series of search-and-replace operations to check words with which you have difficulty.

This macro is far from a perfect spelling checker, particularly when you consider the limitations on macro length and search capabilities. You will have to keep the spelling checker limited to a small list of words. Also, the Personal Spelling Checker macro works best on short documents; of course, the more words in the macro and the longer the document, the longer it will take for the macro to operate. Finally, the spelling-checker macro is capable of searching for only the spelling variations that you enter.

The spelling checker is practical, however, in the following instance. Suppose, for example, that you have difficulty with the spelling of the following words, which you frequently use in the documents you write: *committee, noticeable, occurred, personnel,* and *receive.* From past experience, you know that you sometimes misspell these words as *commitee, noticable, occured, personel,* and *recieve.* Here's a macro that will check a document for the words listed above.

```
{HOME}{MENU}rcommitee~committee~a
{HOME}{MENU}rnoticable~noticeable~a
{HOME}{MENU}roccured~occurred~a
{HOME}{MENU}rpersonel~personnel~a
{HOME}{MENU}rrecieve~receive~a~~q
```

The operation in each of these lines is as follows. The cursor moves to the beginning of the document (as long as the beginning of your document is A1 or you have set the correct restrict range). Next, the DOC command menu is retrieved, and the Replace command is selected. Symphony searches for occurrences of the misspelled word, and when it finds each one, replaces the word with the correction. The process continues until the last Replace operation is completed.

The Personal Spelling Checker macro is a primitive spelling checker, and its effectiveness depends on the entries you include in the "Replace what?" prompt. However, for the situation described, it can save you (or someone else) editing time.

The word-processing macros presented are only a few examples of the many you can create to simplify your editing tasks. After you become familiar with Symphony's DOC environment, consider which commands and operations you use most frequently. Then, experiment with Symphony's Command Language.

New with Symphony

A Macro for the GRAPH Environment

A simple macro for the GRAPH environment creates a graphics slide show. The following macro displays a new window whenever you enter **Y**.

Since there is not enough space on a single typeset line to place all the characters that appear on one line on the screen, carryover lines are indented.

```
SLIDE       {WINDOW}
            {WAIT @NOW+@TIME(0,0,10)}{GETLABEL"Enter
                another?(Y/N):",Y_OR_N}
            {IF Y_OR_N="Y"#OR#Y_OR_N="y"}{BRANCH
                SLIDE}
            {QUIT}
```

After showing a new window, Symphony waits ten seconds before it asks whether you want to continue. If you enter **Y**, the macro branches back to SLIDE. Otherwise, it quits.

A Macro for the FORM Environment

*New
with
Symphony*

A macro that will help you make more efficient use of the FORM environment is one for building entry forms. Figure 13.27 shows a looping macro that takes field name, length, and type information and builds a range that is ready for the FORM **G**enerate command.

```
MAIN      {WINDOWSOFF}
          {GOTO}Y_OR_N~
          {DOWN 3}{LEFT}
LOOP      {GETLABEL "Enter field name: ",NAME}
          {GETLABEL "Enter (N)umber, (L)abel, or (D)ate: ",
             TYPE}
          {GETLABEL "Enter length: ",LENGTH}
          {RECALC COMBO}
          {MENU}rvCOMBO~~
          {GETLABEL "More fields? (Y/N): ",Y_OR_N}
          {IF Y_OR_N="Y"#OR#Y_OR_N="y"}{DOWN}
             {BRANCH LOOP}
          {WINDOWSON}{QUIT}

NAME
TYPE
LENGTH
COMBO
Y_OR_N
```

Fig. 13.27.

Since there is not enough space on a single typeset line to place all the characters that appear on one line on the screen, carryover lines are indented.

The first line of the macro uses the WINDOWSOFF command to eliminate the shifting of the screen when data is entered. The second command causes the cursor to jump to Y_OR_N, the last location name to appear below the macro. The third macro statement moves the cursor three lines below and one cell to the left of cell Y_OR_N. This is the location where the macro will start collecting the entry form information.

The range name LOOP marks the place in the code to which the macro will branch each time after entering in the spreadsheet all the information associated with a field name. The cell named LOOP contains the first of three GETLABEL commands. The first GET-

LABEL retrieves the field name and places it in a cell called NAME. (NAME and all the other cells used as the target location cells for the GETLABEL commands are listed below the macro.) The second GETLABEL gets the field type designation, and the third GETLABEL, the field length. The RECALC statement is then used to recalculate the cell called COMBO, which is a concatenation of NAME, TYPE, and LENGTH (including the appropriate semicolons), when there are entries in those fields. The RECALC statement is essential here, or else the formula will reflect the entry from the previous loop.

The formula stored in the cell named COMBO is

> +NAME&@IF(TYPE<>"",":"&TYPE&@IF(LENGTH<>""," :
> "&LENGTH,""),"")

Since there is not enough space on a single typeset line to place all the characters that appear on one line on the screen, carryover lines are indented.

This formula concatenates the TYPE and LENGTH strings to the NAME string only if there are entries for TYPE and LENGTH. Otherwise, just the NAME string should appear in COMBO. Note: Do not leave spaces in the formula for documentation purposes, or this formula will generate a syntax error message.

After the RECALC command statement, the next statement uses the SHEET **R**ange **V**alues command to copy COMBO to the cell where the cursor is currently positioned. As you recall, the **R**ange **V**alues command converts the formula to an actual value as the command copies from one location to another.

Next, another GETLABEL command asks whether there are any more fields for this input form. The IF statement that follows the GETLABEL asks whether the answer is Y or y. If either choice is entered, the statements to the right of the IF are executed. Otherwise, the statements on the next line are executed.

New with Symphony

A Macro for the COMM Environment

Although Symphony's communications capability is generally strong, the program does have some weak spots. By using a few simple macros, you can get around many of the COMM window's problems. A particularly helpful macro for the COMM environment is one that automates all the steps necessary to send a message to another microcomputer user.

Recall the steps. First, you have to switch from the COMM window to a DOC or a SHEET window in order to enter the message. Next, you must enter the message in the spreadsheet, then switch back to a COMM window. Finally, you enter the Transmit-Range command followed by the range address. Symphony then transmits the message.

This process makes it difficult to communicate quickly. However, the following macro can speed up the process.

```
\C              {GETLABEL "MSG: ",SAVE_AREA}
                {MENU}tSAVE_AREA~
                {BRANCH \C}
```

This macro assumes that you are starting from a COMM window. When you invoke the macro, the GETLABEL statement stores the message in the location called SAVE_AREA. Next, the Transmit-Range command is called, and the contents of SAVE_AREA are transmitted. Note: You must use the SHEET Range Name Create command to name SAVE_AREA before invoking the macro.

This macro works well for sending single-line messages; however, it does not work when you want to send more than one line. As a good test of your understanding of macros, try writing a macro that will send multiple-line messages.

Conclusion

In this chapter, you have seen all the different commands in the Symphony Command Language. You have also seen examples of macros for each of Symphony's work environments. The discussion here has just brushed the surface of the power (and the potential complexity) of the Command Language. As your knowledge of Symphony grows, you will find more and more applications for the Command Language.

14

A Comprehensive Model

Chapter 1 introduced you to Symphony by presenting a simple integrated model that illustrated the program's data management, spreadsheet, graphics, and word-processing capabilities. The present chapter again provides a model that integrates Symphony's features. But here you will see how Symphony's more sophisticated and special features, particularly its communications and Command Language capabilities, can be part of one integrated model. This chapter, then, shows how all the elements of Symphony can work together to create a unified whole.

The model is designed by Bill Bull, who has become an expert Symphony user and considers himself a part-time expert at analyzing the stock market. Of course, as Bill admits, his stock market expertise is due in great part to using Symphony. Through Symphony, Bill can easily connect to a time-sharing service—in this case, CompuServe Executive Information Service (EIS)—and receive the latest stock information. He can then have the information organized and graphed through Symphony's data management and graphics capabilities. Bill has convinced his uncle, Al Hardnose, to consider investing some of his pumpkinseed business fortune in

Magnum Software Corporation stock. Uncle Al, being the cautious investor that he is, has asked Bill to prepare a thorough analysis of Magnum stocks over a 20-week period.

A General Description of the Model

So that Uncle Al receives all the information he needs, Bill has developed a stock market analysis model that consists of FORM, SHEET, COMM, GRAPH, and DOC windows. All the windows are created on the same worksheet. First, Bill has made a data form that will place in a data base in a SHEET window all data captured through the COMM window.

Knowing that he will want to check Magnum stock often, Bill decides to create a macro. Whenever he wants to connect to CompuServe's Executive Information Service for Magnum stock data, all Bill has to do is enter the macro name. In fact, as you will see later, Bill creates the macro so that it will even dial up CompuServe at the time Bill has set. Besides controlling the time for connecting with CompuServe, the macro performs various functions, from connecting to the time-sharing service to performing a query parse on the data that has been captured.

In addition to using Symphony's FORM and COMM environments and Symphony's Command Language, Bill's model makes use of SHEET window commands for assuring that the data which he receives can be correctly entered into the data base. And knowing that graphics will help Uncle Al to analyze the data that Bill receives, Bill also decides to create two graphs by using Symphony's GRAPH window: a Hi-Lo-Close graph and an XY graph. The final parts of Bill's model consist of a letter to Uncle Al in which Bill includes the data base and graphs. With this description of the whole model Bill has created, let's take a closer look at each of its components.

The Data Form

The first step involved in Bill's model is building the simple input form shown in figure 14.1. The data form is necessary so that with the **Q**uery **P**arse command, Bill can convert to a data base the data

New with Symphony

he has captured. You will notice that figure 14.1 shows the form after it is created in Symphony's SHEET window. First, Bill knows that Uncle Al wants Magnum stock market figures for a 20-week period showing each week's volume, high asking price, low bid, and closing average. Having used CompuServe's time-sharing service before for stock information, Bill knows that one of the options is to receive weekly quotations that provide the volume and high-low-close data he needs.

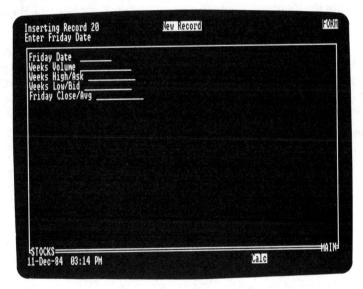

Fig. 14.1.

The data form, then, is arranged with five different fields corresponding to the data captured during the on-line time. These fields consist of (1) the Friday date of the data, (2) the week's volume, (3) the week's high price, (4) the week's low bid, and (5) the Friday closing average. Following each of the fields that Bill enters are the field type and length. The first field (D:9) signifies date type with a length of 9, and the next four fields are number fields. The second field has a length of 13, and the other three fields each have a length of 12.

You need to keep in mind the length of each field in the data form. The reason is that the length of each column in the data base where your information finally ends up must conform to the length of the data form. As mentioned in Chapter 11, if you try to create a data base directly below the Capture range by using the **Q**uery **P**arse command, this command will not work as expected. When you use the **Form G**enerate command, Symphony adds one space to each column width. For example, the width for the Friday Date column (column A) is changed from 9 to 10. Therefore, when you use **Q**uery **P**arse, Symphony rejects all the data in the Capture range as nonconforming. The values entered in the Capture range are too wide for the input fields, and Symphony sends them all to the Review range.

When you locate the data base directly below the Capture range, you must either (1) subtract 1 from the length designations when you enter the data form (use *Friday Date: D:8* instead of *Friday Date:D:9*) or (2) manually reset the columns to the proper width after you use the **G**enerate command.

Once you have entered the field names, types, and lengths in the SHEET window, you then place the cursor on the first field entry and switch to a FORM window. Using the FORM **G**enerate command, your next step is to enter the default field type and length. When Symphony asks for a data base name, Bill enters the name "Stocks." Another important step is indicating the Field Names range; in this model the range is A1..A5.

Bill also has created in his worksheet two range names that are used in the macro for performing the **Q**uery **P**arse operation. For A61..E161 he uses the name CAPTURE_RANGE; this is the "Range to parse." At the "Review range" prompt, Bill enters the name REVIEW_RANGE, which includes A162..E230.

If at this point you were to switch to a SHEET window, you would get a picture of everything contained in figure 14.2.

Communications

New with Symphony

After Bill has created the data form above, his next step is to enter the correct settings in a COMM window so that the macro, discussed later, can operate directly from these settings.

In figure 14.3, you will see the COMM **S**ettings sheet that Bill uses to connect with CompuServe's Executive Information Services (EIS).

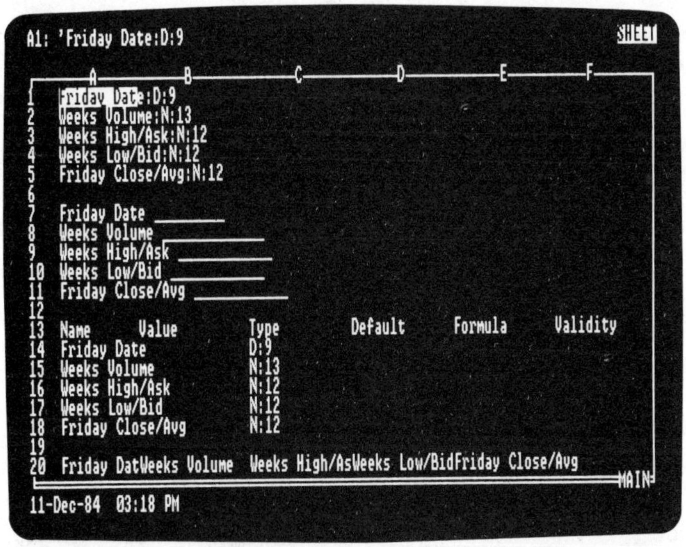

Fig. 14.2.

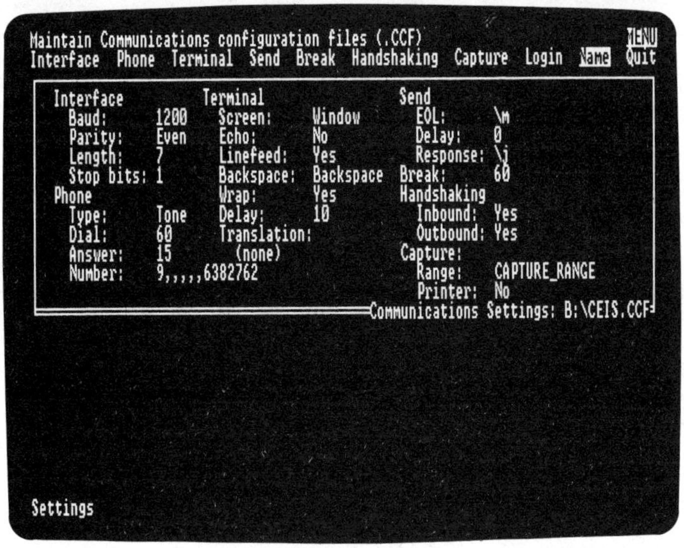

Fig. 14.3.

As explained in Chapter 11, the Interface settings for CompuServe are these: baud rate of 1200, even parity, length of 7, 1 stop bit, and full duplex. Full duplex, you'll recall, simply means that data flows in both directions between your microcomputer and the information service.

Using a Hayes Smartmodem 1200 and push-button phone service, Bill next enters the following **P**hone settings:

> Type: Tone
> Dial: 60

Tone is the correct setting for Bill's push-button service. The **D**ial setting of 60 is the default setting for the time Symphony spends dialing a call and trying to make a connection. (This time is enough for the model.) Although not needed here, the **A**nswer-**T**ime setting (15) is the default setting for maximum seconds that Symphony spends answering a call when **P**hone **A**nswer is used. You will also notice in figure 14.3 that Bill has not entered anything for **N**umber. The macro discussed later contains the specific CompuServe number.

The **T**erminal settings are the following:

> Screen: Window
> Echo: No
> Linefeed: Yes
> Backspace: Backspace
> Wrap: Yes
> Delay: 10
> Translation: (none)

A few points about the **T**erminal settings are important here. First, you don't need to change the default **S**creen setting (**W**indow). The **E**cho setting should be **N**o because Bill is connecting with a full-duplex system, which automatically echoes the characters typed. In receiving the stock information that Bill wants from CompuServe, Bill's **D**elay setting of 10 is sufficient. Finally, no special translation setting is needed for this example.

In the last column of the COMM **S**ettings sheet shown in figure 14.3, you will notice two other kinds of information: **S**end and **C**apture. **S**end has been left at its default settings because, as you will see in the macro, these settings are controlled by the macro itself. On the other hand, Bill must first indicate whether incoming data should be captured in a worksheet range or sent to the printer. Because Bill is capturing incoming data to a range in the worksheet where his data form was created, he sets a named range called CAPTURE_RANGE. He particularly needs to make sure that the range is large enough to capture the twenty weeks of stock quotations he wants. He also needs to enter \013 for an EOL (end of line) character.

These settings, then, include all those that Bill needs to connect with CompuServe. Bill does not enter any settings for Login because, as you will see in the next section, the log-in sequence is also controlled through the macro that Bill has created.

Before leaving the COMM window, however, Bill saves the settings sheet he has just created. He names the settings CEIS so that he will know these are the settings for CompuServe's Executive Information Service.

New with Symphony

The Macro

Having created the data form and entered all necessary COMM **S**ettings, Bill now creates the macro that will allow him to dial up automatically, select the CompuServe service for Magnum stock information, and organize this information into a data base in the spreadsheet.

The macro shown in figure 14.4 performs a number of functions. It enables Bill to dial the time-sharing service automatically at a time he sets. The {WAIT @TIME(22,0,0)} tells Symphony to wait until 10:00 before executing the rest of the statement—{BRANCH GET_PRICES}. If, however, Bill doesn't want the macro to wait until a set time before executing, he can use the second line of the macro (TEST_GET) to begin the macro immediately.

The GET_PRICES part of Bill's macro performs the actual login; sending, receiving, and capturing data; logoff; and **Q**uery **P**arse operations. You will notice from the first few statements how the process occurs. After phoning the CompuServe number, the macro begins a series of HANDSHAKE statements, which include entering User ID and password when the correct prompts are received. The other HANDSHAKE statements consist of making menu selections for indicating that Bill wants to connect with the stock information

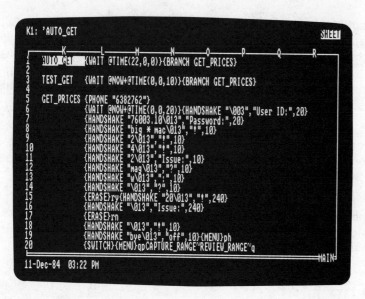

```
K1: 'AUTO_GET                                                    SHEET

        K         L         M         N         O         P         Q         R
1  AUTO_GET  {WAIT @TIME(22,0,0)}{BRANCH GET_PRICES}
2
3  TEST_GET  {WAIT @NOW+@TIME(0,0,10)}{BRANCH GET_PRICES}
4
5  GET_PRICES {PHONE "6382762"}
6            {WAIT @NOW+@TIME(0,0,20)}{HANDSHAKE "\003","User ID:",20}
7            {HANDSHAKE "76003.10\013","Password:",20}
8            {HANDSHAKE "big * mac\013","!",10}
9            {HANDSHAKE "2\013","!",10}
10           {HANDSHAKE "4\013","!",10}
11           {HANDSHAKE "2\013","Issue:",10}
12           {HANDSHAKE "mag\013","?",10}
13           {HANDSHAKE "w\013",":",10}
14           {HANDSHAKE "\013","?",10}
15           {ERASE}rv{HANDSHAKE "20\013","!",240}
16           {HANDSHAKE "\013","Issue:",240}
17           {ERASE}rn
18           {HANDSHAKE "\013","!",10}
19           {HANDSHAKE "bye\013","off",10}{MENU}ph
20           {SWITCH}{MENU}qpCAPTURE_RANGE~REVIEW_RANGE~q
                                                                        MAIN

11-Dec-84  03:22 PM
```

Fig. 14.4.

service, that he wants information on Magnum stock ("mag"), and that he wants weekly quotations from March 31, 1984, to August 9, 1984.

The remaining statements beginning with the keyword {ERASE} are important for capturing the data that Symphony receives and for creating a data base. Note, however, that {ERASE} is one bug we found in Symphony's Command Language. Although the CAPTURE operation does occur, when Symphony displays the macro keyword for CAPTURE, {ERASE} appears instead. The first {ERASE} statement, then, is used for capturing data in the Capture range, whereas the second {ERASE} statement ends the capture operation. The last two HANDSHAKE statements complete the logoff and phone hang up. The final statement in Bill's macro is very important for taking the captured Magnum stock data shown in figures 14.5 and 14.6 and converting it to a separate data base.

Because of the two different statements for executing the macro—one for executing at a set time and one for executing immediately, Bill creates three separate range names for the parts of the macro. AUTO_GET is the range name for the first statement; TEST_GET, for the second statement; and GET_PRICES, for the main part of the macro.

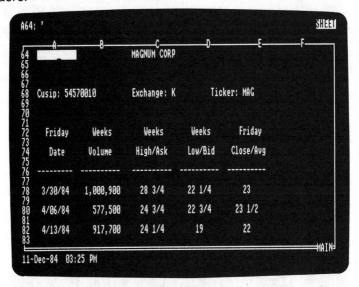

Fig. 14.5.

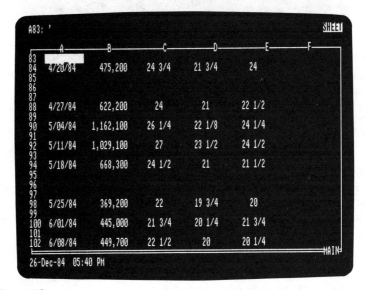

Fig. 14.6.

The only thing left for Bill to do at this point is to see whether the macro works as it should. To run the macro, Bill first makes sure that he is in a COMM window. Next, he selects the CEIS.CCF file that he created with all the necessary COMM **S**ettings for connecting with the CompuServe service. And since Bill is anxious to try out the macro immediately, he executes the macro by pressing the User key and then entering the name TEST_GET. (See figs. 14.5, 14.6, and 14.7 for the results of Bill's macro.)

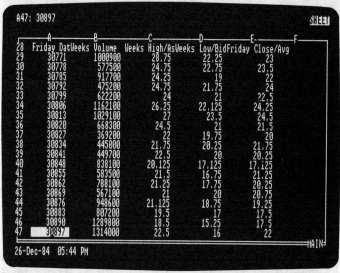

Fig. 14.7.

Graphics

The macro Bill created works well, and he is successful at receiving twenty weeks of Magnum stock information, as Uncle Al requested. After the macro has stopped, Bill has both the stock information as it was captured and a data base created through the **Query P**arse command. (See fig. 14.7.) Now Bill decides to graph the information and put the data into a text form for Uncle Al.

Bill creates two different graphs from the Magnum stock information: a Hi-Lo-Close graph shown in figure 14.8A and an XY graph shown in figure 14.9A. As indicated in the **1**st-Settings sheet for the Hi-Lo-

Close graph (fig. 14.8B), all ranges are set from the data base that Bill created using the **Q**uery **P**arse command. Important settings in the

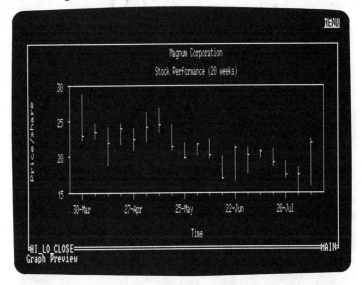

Fig. 14.8A.

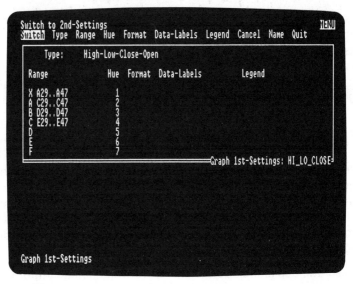

Fig. 14.8B.

2nd-Settings sheet (fig. 14.8C) include first, second, X-axis, and Y-axis titles. Notice also that Bill has set the **S**kip factor to 4; otherwise, all the dates below the X-axis will overlap.

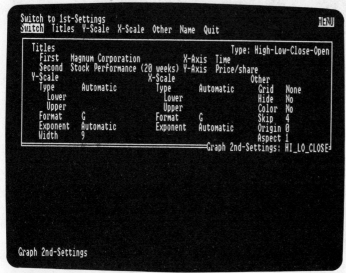

```
Switch to 1st-Settings                                            MENU
Switch  Titles  Y-Scale  X-Scale  Other  Name  Quit

 Titles                                      Type: High-Low-Close-Open
   First   Magnum Corporation       X-Axis  Time
   Second  Stock Performance (20 weeks) Y-Axis  Price/share
 Y-Scale                    X-Scale              Other
   Type      Automatic        Type    Automatic    Grid   None
     Lower                      Lower               Hide   No
     Upper                      Upper               Color  No
   Format    G                Format  G            Skip   4
   Exponent  Automatic        Exponent Automatic   Origin 0
   Width     9                                     Aspect 1
                                 Graph 2nd-Settings: HI_LO_CLOSE

 Graph 2nd-Settings
```

Fig. 14.8C.

Bill's XY graph, in figure 14.9A, shows volume and price per share at each week's closing date. As indicated in the XY graph settings sheets, this graph uses column B and column E of Bill's data base for graph range settings. As in Bill's Hi-Lo-Close graph, the XY graphs includes first, second, X-axis, and Y-axis titles. (See figs. 14.9B and 14.9C.)

Word Processing

After having created two graphs, Bill carefully analyzes the data that he now has in the SHEET and GRAPH windows. Knowing that Uncle Al was never one for taking advice from a nephew, Bill decides to print the data base of stock information and the graphs and send them off to his uncle so that Uncle Al can make his own decisions about investing in Magnum stock.

Bill also decides to include the data base within a letter, informing his uncle that all the requested information is enclosed. (See fig.

*New
with
Symphony*

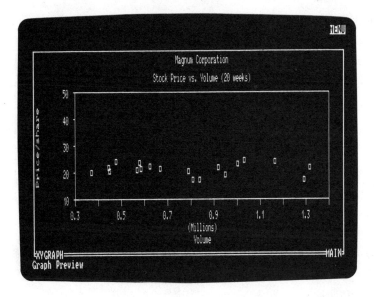

Fig. 14.9A.

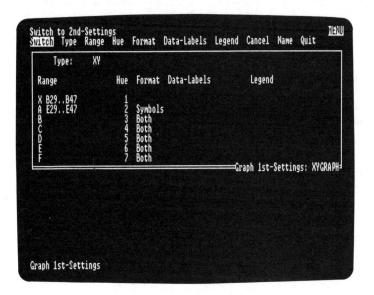

Fig. 14.9B.

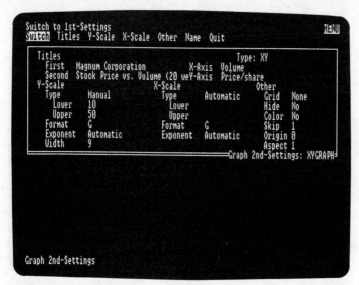

Fig. 14.9C.

14.10.) The only special requirements for the letter include setting the left margin to 1 so that the data base which he adds into the text will be aligned with the letter's text. The right margin is set to 72, and spacing for Bill's letter is set to 1. No other special format settings or format lines are required in the letter.

One special operation for creating the letter, however, involves using the SHEET **M**ove command to place the data base shown in figure 14.7 into the letter. (See fig. 14.11.) You'll recall from Chapters 6 and 8, however, that two other methods can be used to move data created in a SHEET window to a DOC window: using the SERVICES **F**ile **C**ombine **A**dd command or using the SERVICES **P**rint **S**ettings **D**estination **R**ange command. The main difference between these two methods of moving data from a SHEET window into a DOC window is that the SERVICES **P**rint **S**ettings **D**estination **R**ange command converts SHEET data so that you can use DOC commands and operations to make changes. Bill, however, uses the SHEET **M**ove command instead of either of the other two methods.

August 14, 1984

Dear Uncle Al,

You will be pleased to know that I have twenty weeks of Magnum stock
information ready for you to review. Being the wise old man that you
are, you will surely want to look closely at the information before
jumping into a decision. Of course, I know that you probably won't make
your decision hastily.

But just to help you make a good judgment, I went ahead and prepared
the stock information in a couple different forms. First, you will
notice here the listing of figures which I received when I connected
with CompuServe -- the service from which I got the Magnum stock quotes.
Here's what came in for the twenty weeks from the week ending March
30, 1984 to the week ending August 9, 1984.

Friday Date	Volume	High/Ask	Low/Bid--Fri	Close/Avg
30-Mar-84	1000900	28.75	22.25	23
06-Apr-84	577500	24.75	22.75	23.5
13-Apr-84	917700	24.25	19	22
20-Apr-84	475200	24.75	21.75	24
27-Apr-84	622200	24	21	22.5
04-May-84	1162100	26.25	22.125	24.25
11-May-84	1029100	27	23.5	24.5
18-May-84	668300	24.5	21	21.5
25-May-84	369200	22	19.75	20
01-Jun-84	445000	21.75	20.25	21.75
08-Jun-84	449700	22.5	20	20.25
15-Jun-84	838100	20.125	17.125	17.125
22-Jun-84	583500	21.5	16.75	21.25
29-Jun-84	788100	21.25	17.75	20.25
06-Jul-84	567100	21	20	20.75
13-Jul-84	948600	21.125	18.75	19.25
20-Jul-84	807200	19.5	17	17.5
27-Jul-84	1289800	18.5	15.25	17.5
03-Aug-84	1314000	22.5	16	22
09-Aug-84	1206800	22.75	21	22.75

Also, to help you analyze the data I collected, I created two graphs --
one a Hi-Lo-Close graph and the other an XY graph. Both are attached to
this letter.

Knowing that you always like to think for yourself, I won't try to tell
you what to do about investing in Magnum stock. But it could be a
terrific move for you.

If you would like any more stock information, I'll be glad to get it for
you. (I'd like to see what's happening with Ushton-Pate sometime!)
Hope to see you soon.

Your loving nephew,

Bill

P.S. If you decide you don't want to invest in Magnum stock right now
and could lend me some money for a while, I may want to do a little
investing myself.

Fig. 14.10.

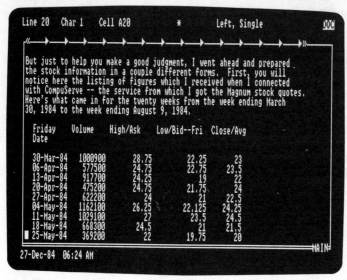

Fig. 14.11.

Printing the Graphs

To print the graphs that Bill created, he must exit from Symphony and enter the PrintGraph program by invoking DOS either through the SERVICES **A**pplication command or through the Symphony ACCESS SYSTEM. Once he has entered the PrintGraph program, he may select from among several different print options. Bill does not use any special options, but instead uses all standard defaults. He also selects both graphs at once from the list of available .PIC files and prints them one after another. See figure 14.12 for the results of running the PrintGraph program.

Conclusion

The comprehensive model in this chapter emphasizes the features that make Symphony a special program. The model draws together all the elements that make Symphony a superb integrated program providing full spreadsheet, word-processing, graphics, data management, and communications capabilities. (These applications are discussed in Chapters 3, 4, 7, 9, 11, and 12.) In addition, the model shows the power of Symphony's Command Language, which enables you to automate complex operations, such as connecting with a time-sharing service, capturing stock information, and then creating a data base from that information (Chapters 12 and 13). Finally, the model uses the main program's **P**rint commands as well as the PrintGraph program (Chapters 8 and 10).

This model completes the book's examination of the Symphony program. We hope that the overview material; the specific discussions of commands, functions, and operations; and all the examples have been both informative and useful. Your task now is to take advantage of the incredible power and multiple capabilities of the Symphony program.

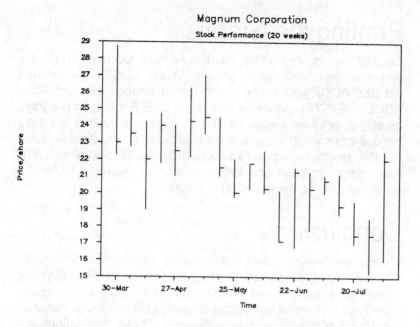

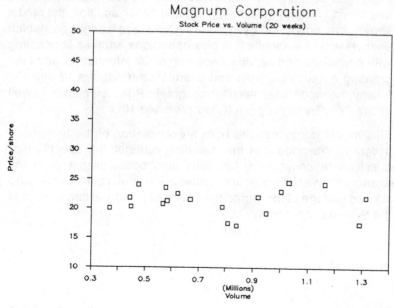

Fig. 14.12.

Appendix A

Formatting Disks (for systems with two disk drives)

To format five blank disks for copying Symphony, follow the steps outlined below.

1. Place the DOS master disk in drive A and boot DOS.

2. When you see A> on the screen, type FORMAT B: and press RETURN.

3. On the screen you will see the following:

> Insert the new diskette for drive B:
> and strike any key when ready_

Place the disk you want to format in drive B and close the drive door. Press the space bar, RETURN key, or any character key. The red light will come on again, and you will see the following message:

> Formatting . . .

After 20 to 40 seconds, you will see this message:

> Formatting . . . Format complete

> 362496 bytes total disk space
> 362496 bytes available on disk

If you see the message "bytes in bad sectors," DOS has found some parts of the disk that cannot be used to store information. The amount of available space will be reduced by the number of bytes given on this line. You can return a disk with a bad sector to your dealer for a replacement or use the disk with less storage space. Before you do either, though, try formatting the disk again. Some disks do not format properly the first time, but they may do so the second time. (See the next step for an easy way to format a second time.)

4. When you see the message

    Format another (Y/N)?_

answer **Y** for Yes if you want to format more disks or if you have a disk with a bad sector that you want to format again. But don't press RETURN. (This step is the only one in which you don't press the RETURN key.) If you're reformatting a disk with a bad sector, take the disk partially out of the drive, reinsert the disk, close the door, and tap a key. If you want to format another disk, remove the already formatted disk and place the next disk to be formatted into drive B, tap a key, and then repeat steps 3 and 4.

After you finish formatting all five disks that you'll need for copying Symphony, type **N** for No when asked if you want to format another. The A> will reappear.

Appendix B

Formatting a Disk and Adding DOS (for systems with two disk drives)

To format a disk and add DOS to the disk, complete the steps outlined below.

1. Place the DOS master disk in drive A and boot the system.

2. When you see A> on the screen, type FORMAT B: /S and press RETURN. (The /S is a switch that tells DOS to add the system to the diskette after it has been formatted.)

3. On the screen you will see

   Insert the new diskette for drive B:
   and strike any key when ready_

   Place the disk you want to format into drive B and close the drive door. Press the space bar, RETURN key, or any character key. The red light will come on again, and you will see the following message:

   Formatting . . .

   After 20 to 40 seconds, you will see this message:

   Formatting . . . Format complete

659

The disk drive will continue to spin for a few more seconds. Then you will see the following message:

System transferred

362496 bytes total disk space
 40960 taken by system
321536 bytes free

This message tells you that DOS has been transferred to the disk. It also tells you how much information the entire disk can hold, how much space is being taken by DOS, and how much free space is left.

If you see the message "bytes in bad sectors," DOS has found some parts of the disk that cannot be reduced by the number of bytes given on this line. You can return a diskette with a bad sector to your dealer for a replacement or use the disk with less storage space. Before you do either, though, try formatting the diskette again. Some diskettes do not format properly the first time, but they may do so the second time. (See the next step for an easy way to format a second time.)

4. When you will see the message

Format another (Y/N)?_

answer **Y** for Yes if you have a disk with a bad sector that you want to format again or if you want to format another disk. But don't press RETURN. (This step is the only one in which you don't press the RETURN key.) If you're reformatting a disk with a bad sector, take the disk partially out of the drive, reinsert the disk, close the door, and tap a key. If you want to format another disk, remove the already formatted disk and place the next disk to be formatted into drive B, tap a key, and then repeat steps 3 and 4.

If you do not want to format another disk, type **N** for No. Once again, you do not have to press the RETURN key. The A> will reappear.

Appendix C

1-2-3/Symphony Cross-Reference Guide

The following cross-reference guide compares 1-2-3 commands from 1-2-3's Worksheet menu with corresponding commands in Symphony. In many cases, Symphony commands operate similarly and provide the same options as 1-2-3 commands. For example, Symphony's SHEET Range Label-Alignment changes label justification in a worksheet just as 1-2-3's /Range Label-Prefix. Some Symphony commands, however, contain more options. Symphony's SHEET Query Settings Sort-Key command, for example, provides three selections for sort, whereas 1-2-3's provides two. A few Symphony commands are simply 1-2-3 commands with new names: Symphony's SHEET Settings Format Bar Graph is 1-2-3's /Worksheet Global Format +/-.

When you are comparing Symphony's commands with 1-2-3's, keep in mind the following. When we say that many 1-2-3 commands are comparable to Symphony commands, we do not mean that these commands always perform exactly the same functions as 1-2-3 commands. The differences in the Symphony program itself will cause familiar commands to function differently. For example, having different windows with different restrict ranges on one worksheet can affect the way a command functions.

This guide, though, will help you make the transition from 1-2-3 to Symphony by helping you understand quickly how the two programs are alike and how Symphony surpasses 1-2-3 in capabilities. You may also find this guide useful when you are converting 1-2-3 macros into Symphony macros, at least until a macro-conversion program from 1-2-3 to Symphony is available.

1-2-3 Commands	Symphony Commands
/Worksheet	
1. **/Worksheet**	
/Worksheet Global Format	SHEET **Settings Format**
Fixed	Fixed
Scientific	Scientific
Currency	Currency
, (comma)	Punctuated

General	General
+/-	Bar Graph
Percent	Percent
Date	Date
Text	Literal

/Worksheet Global Label-Prefix	SHEET Settings Label-Prefix
Left	Left
Right	Right
Center	Center

/Worksheet Global Column Width	SHEET Settings Width

/Worksheet Global Recalculation	SHEET Settings Recalculation
Natural	Natural
Columnwise	Column-by-Column
Rowwise	Row-by-Row
Automatic	Automatic
Manual	Manual
Iteration	Iteration

/Worksheet Global Protection	SERVICES Settings Global-Protection
Enable	No Allow changes to all cells
Disable	Yes Allow changes only to "A" cells

/Worksheet Global Default	SERVICES Configuration
Printer	Printer
Interface	Type
Auto-LF	Auto-LF
Left	Margins Left
Right	Margins Right
Top	Margins Top
Bottom	Margins Bottom
Page Length	Page-Length
Wait	Wait
Set Up	Init-String
Quit	Quit
Disk (Directory)	SERVICES Configuration File
Status	SERVICES Configuration
Update	SERVICES Configuration Update
Quit	SERVICES Configuration Quit

2.	/Worksheet Insert	SHEET Insert
	Column	Columns
	Row	Rows
3.	/Worksheet Delete	SHEET Delete
	Column	Columns
	Row	Rows

4. **/Worksheet Column Width**
    Set
    Reset
	SHEET Width
	    Set
	    Restore

5. **/Worksheet Erase**	**SERVICES New**

6. **/Worksheet Title**
    Both
    Horizontal
    Vertical
    Clear
	SHEET Settings Titles
	    Both
	    Horizontal
	    Vertical
	    Clear

7. **/Worksheet Window**
    Horizontal
    Vertical
    Sync
    Unsync
    Clear
	SERVICES Window
	    Window Create or Window Layout
	    Window Create or Window Layout

8. **/Worksheet Status**
    Recalculation
    Format
    Label-Prefix
    Column-Width
    Available Memory
    Protect
	SHEET Settings
	    Recalculation
	    Format
	    Label-Prefix
	    Width
	    SERVICES Settings
	    SERVICES Settings Global-Protection

/Range

1. **/Range Format**
    Fixed
    Scientific
    Currency
    , (comma)
    General
    + / -
    Percent
    Date
    Text
    Reset
	SHEET Format
	    Fixed
	    Scientific
	    Currency
	    Punctuated (See Chapter 4)
	    General
	    Other Bar-Graph
	    Percent
	    Date
	    Other Literal
	    Reset

2. **/Range Label Prefix**
    Left
    Right
    Center
	SHEET Range Label-Alignment
	    Left
	    Right
	    Center

3. **/Range Erase**	**SHEET Erase**

4. **/Range Name**
    Create
    Delete
    Labels
	SHEET Range Name
	    Create
	    Delete
	    Labels

Right	**R**ight
Down	**D**own
Left	**L**eft
Up	**U**p

5. **/R**ange **J**ustify   No comparable single command

6. **/R**ange **P**rotect   SHEET **R**ange **P**rotect **P**revent-Changes

7. **/R**ange **U**nprotect   SHEET **R**ange **P**rotect **A**llow-Changes

8. **/R**ange **I**nput   SERVICES **W**indow **S**ettings **R**estrict used with SHEET **R**ange **P**rotect **P**revent-Changes

/Copy   SHEET **C**opy

/Move   SHEET **M**ove

/File

1. **/F**ile **R**etrieve   SERVICES **F**ile **R**etrieve

2. **/F**ile **S**ave   SERVICES **F**ile **S**ave

3. **/F**ile **C**ombine   SERVICES **F**ile **C**ombine
   Copy   **C**opy
   Add   **A**dd
   Subtract   **S**ubtract

4. **/F**ile **X**tract   SERVICES **F**ile **X**tract
   Formulas   **F**ormulas
   Values   **V**alues

5. **/F**ile **E**rase   SERVICES **F**ile **E**rase
   Worksheet   **W**orksheet
   Print   **P**rint
   Graph   **G**raph

6. **/F**ile **L**ist   SERVICES **F**ile **L**ist
   Worksheet   **W**orksheet
   Print   **P**rint
   Graph   **G**raph

7. **/F**ile **I**mport   SERVICES **F**ile **I**mport
   Text   **T**ext
   Numbers   **S**tructured

8. **/F**ile **D**isk (Directory)   SERVICES **F**ile **D**irectory

/Print   SERVICES **P**rint

1. **/P**rint **P**rinter   SERVICES **P**rint **S**ettings **D**estination **P**rinter
   Range   SERVICES **P**rint **S**ettings **S**ource **R**ange
   Line   SERVICES **P**rint **L**ine-Advance
   Page   SERVICES **P**rint **S**ettings **P**age-Advance
   Options
     Header   SERVICES **P**rint **S**ettings **P**age **H**eader

Footer	SERVICES **P**rint **S**ettings **P**age **F**ooter
Margins	SERVICES **P**rint **S**ettings **M**argins
Borders	
Columns	SERVICES **P**rint **S**ettings **O**ther **L**eft-Labels
Rows	SERVICES **P**rint **S**ettings **O**ther **T**op-Labels
Set Up	SERVICES **P**rint **S**ettings **I**nit-String
Page Length	SERVICES **P**rint **S**ettings **P**age **L**ength
Other	
As Displayed	SERVICES **P**rint **S**ettings **O**ther **F**ormat **A**s-Displayed
Cell Formulas	SERVICES **P**rint **S**ettings **O**ther **F**ormat **C**ell **F**ormulas
Formatted	SERVICES **P**rint **S**ettings **P**age **B**reaks **Y**es
Unformatted	SERVICES **P**rint **S**ettings **P**age **B**reaks **N**o
Clear	SERVICES **P**rint **S**ettings **N**ame **R**eset
Align	SERVICES **P**rint **A**lign
Go	SERVICES **P**rint **G**o
Quit	SERVICES **P**rint **Q**uit

2. /**P**rint **F**ile   SERVICES **P**rint **S**ettings **D**estination **F**ile

/**G**raph

SHEET **G**raph

1. /**G**raph **T**ype   SHEET **G**raph 1st-Settings **T**ype
    Line **B**ar **XY** **S**tacked-**B**ar **P**ie

2. /**G**raph **X**   SHEET **G**raph 1st-Settings **R**ange **X**

3. /**G**raph **A**   SHEET **G**raph 1st-Settings **R**ange **A**

4. /**G**raph **B**   SHEET **G**raph 1st-Settings **R**ange **B**

5. /**G**raph **C**   SHEET **G**raph 1st-Settings **R**ange **C**

6. /**G**raph **D**   SHEET **G**raph 1st-Settings **R**ange **D**

7. /**G**raph **E**   SHEET **G**raph 1st-Settings **R**ange **E**

8. /**G**raph **F**   SHEET **G**raph 1st-Settings **R**ange **F**

9. /**G**raph **R**eset   SHEET **G**raph 1st-Settings **C**ancel
    Graph **X A B C D E F Q**uit

10. /**G**raph **V**iew   SHEET **G**raph **P**review

11. /**G**raph **S**ave   SHEET **G**raph **I**mage-Save

12. /**G**raph **O**ptions
    Legend   SHEET **G**raph 1st-Settings **L**egend
    Format   SHEET **G**raph 1st-Settings **F**ormat
    Titles   SHEET **G**raph 2nd-Settings **T**itle
    Grid   SHEET **G**raph 2nd-Settings **O**ther **G**rid
    Scale
      Y-Scale   SHEET **G**raph 2nd-Settings **Y**-Scale
      X-Scale   SHEET **G**raph 2nd-Settings **X**-Scale

Color	SHEET **Graph 2**nd-**Settings Other Color Yes**
B&W	SHEET **Graph 2**nd-**Settings Other Color No**
Data Labels	SHEET **Graph 1**st-**Settings Data-Labels**

13. **/Graph Name** No single command, but in Symphony replaced by GRAPH window, used with SERVICES window

14. **/Graph Quit** SHEET **Graph Quit**

/Data

1. **/Data Fill** SHEET **Range Fill**

2. **/Data Table** SHEET **Range What-If**
    1 2 Reset 1-Way **2**-Way **Reset**

3. **/Data Sort** SHEET **Query Record-Sort**
    Data Range SHEET **Query Settings Basic Database**
    Primary Key SHEET **Query Settings Sort-Keys 1**st-**Keys**
    Secondary Key SHEET **Query Settings Sort-Keys 2**nd-**Key**
    Reset SHEET **Query Settings Cancel**
    Go SHEET **Query Record-Sort**

4. **/Data Query** SHEET **Query**
    Input SHEET **Query Settings Basic Database**
    Criterion SHEET **Query Settings Basic Criterion**
    Output SHEET **Query Settings Basic Output**
    Find SHEET **Query Find**
    Extract SHEET **Query Extract**
    Unique SHEET **Query Unique**
    Delete SHEET **Query Delete**
      Cancel SHEET **Query Delete No**
      Delete SHEET **Query Delete Yes**
    Reset SHEET **Query Settings Cancel**

5. **/Data Distribution** SHEET **Range Distribution**

Index

More Computer Knowledge from Que

Que Order Line: 1-800-428-5331

LEARN MORE ABOUT LOTUS SYMPHONY
WITH THESE OUTSTANDING TOOLS FROM QUE

Symphony Tips, Tricks, and Traps

This book is a quick reference that offers shortcut procedures, help with unexpected problems, and tips on using some of Symphony's little-known capabilities. Whether you're a beginning or an experienced Symphony user, this book will help you become adept at using the program's many features.

$19.95   Available May, 1985
Order #154   0-88022-098-8

Symphony for Business

Now that you've mastered Symphony, learn how to manage your business with this powerful program. Step-by-step instructions show you how to build practical business applications, using the features of Symphony. If you use Symphony in your business, this book is a valuable resource.

$16.95   Available May, 1985
Order #168   0-88022-140-2

Using Symphony's Command Language

This excellent tutorial will help you master Symphony's Command Language. The book describes all of Symphony's macro commands and provides a library of useful command language programs. Add this book to your library and learn to take full advantage of Symphony's Command Language.

$17.95   Available May, 1985
Order #173   0-88022-146-1

Symphony: Advanced Topics

For experienced Symphony users, this book provides additional help in using Symphony's powerful capabilities effectively. Discussions cover Symphony's five environments and the concept of integration. For an in-depth study of all of Symphony's applications, this book is an essential investment.

$17.95   Available May, 1985
Order #172   0-88022-145-3

Look for these new Symphony titles coming soon from Que!

Que Corporation

7999 Knue Road
Indianapolis, IN 46250
(317) 842-7162
(800) 428-5331

Invest in

AbsoluteReference™
THE JOURNAL FOR 1-2-3™ AND SYMPHONY™ USERS

today!

Call now or use this convenient form.
1-800-428-5331

fold here
- -

Please send me 12 issues of **Absolute Reference.** I have enclosed payment of $60.00.

Name _____

Address _____

_____

City _____ State _____ ZIP _____

METHOD OF PAYMENT:

Check ☐   VISA ☐   MasterCard ☐   AMEX ☐

Cardholder Name _____

Card Number _____

Please enclose full payment of $60.00

FOLD HERE

- -

_____

_____

_____

AbsoluteReference™
THE JOURNAL FOR 1-2-3™ AND SYMPHONY™ USERS

P.O. Box 50507
Indianapolis, IN 46250